Concepts of Law Enforcement Administration

. . .

Revised First Edition

Edited by John T. Foust
University of Maryland

 cognella
San Diego, CA

Bassim Hamadeh, CEO and Publisher
Christopher Foster, General Vice President
Michael Simpson, Vice President of Acquisitions
Jessica Knott, Managing Editor
Kevin Fahey, Cognella Marketing Manager
Jess Busch, Senior Graphic Designer
Melissa Barcomb, Acquisitions Editor
Sarah Wheeler, Project Editor
Stephanie Sandler, Licensing Associate

First published in the United States of America in 2013 by Cognella, Inc.

Printed in the United States of America

ISBN: 978-1-62131-596-4 (pbk)

www.cognella.com 800.200.3908

For my wife, Janie, for her continued support while endless hours were spent on this project and for my son, Jonathan, my daughter, Melissa, and for my grandchildren, Travis and Martha.

—John T. Foust

CONCEPTS OF LAW ENFORCEMENT ADMINISTRATION

Edited by John T. Foust

CONTENTS

CONCEPT #4: ESTABLISH SOUND PRACTICES OF ACCOUNTABILITY

CONCEPT #5: MANAGE YOUR RESOURCES EFFICIENTLY

CONCEPT #6: INSTITUTE POSITIVE VALUES AND ETHICAL GUIDELINES

CONCEPT #7: HIRE AND MANAGE YOUR PERSONNEL EFFECTIVELY

CONCEPT #8: UNDERSTAND MAJOR PERSONNEL LEGAL ISSUES

CONCEPT #1: UNDERSTAND THE BASICS OF ADMINISTRATION

Before moving into some of the more focused concepts, which come in later chapters, it is important to first have an understanding of some of the basics. In this chapter you will have five major readings: Development of Police Administration, Principles of Organization, Implementing Community Policing: The Administrative Problem, The Police and Neighborhood Safety: Broken Windows, and Intelligence Led Policing.

In the development of police administration you will see how policing has grown and changed over the last one-hundred years in the United States. This history is important to understand as practices that you may want to implement may have already been tried and found to be ineffective. Also, you will learn that administrators do no operate in a vacuum, sealed off from the rest of the world. Instead, they operate and work within social, legal, and political contexts. In the principles of administration reading some additional basic concepts are presented and discussed. These include: authority, chain of command, unity of command, and span of control.

From the first reading you will have learned that we are now in what is called the community policing era of law enforcement. This era is not without problems, so you have a reading on implementing community policing. This is necessary because in some cases the implementation of the community policing philosophy has been met with resistance within some agencies. This reading addresses some of theses issues, with a focus on administrative problems relating to middle management.

An introductory chapter would not be complete without information on crime prevention and crime causation. As an administrator's existence may very well depend on crime rates, this reading should spark some interest, along with a desire for additional information on the topic. The reading on the police and neighborhood safety is a classic on the topic and it is equally important as it is directly related to the philosophy of community policing.

This chapter concludes with a reading on intelligence led policing. You will learn what intelligence is and why it is critical. You will learn the difference between tactical intelligence and strategic intelligence. You will learn that the term "intelligence led policing" developed in Great Britain and then came to the United States. In closing you will see how this method of law enforcement blends with community policing, specifically problem oriented policing.

Development of Police Administration

By Gary Codner

THE DEVELOPMENT OF POLICE ADMINISTRATION

The development of police administration had to await the development of organized policing. The year 1829 marks the origin of organized, paid, civilian policing as we currently know it. In that year, the Metropolitan Police Act became English law, culminating a long and emotional debate. Prior to that time, law enforcement in England and America had been the province of ordinary citizens, volunteers, night watchmen, private merchant police, soldiers, personal employees of justices of the peace, constables, sheriffs, and slave patrols. This informal and unorganized law enforcement approach, which had proved satisfactory for centuries, was overwhelmed by the Industrial Revolution, which spawned rapid urbanization and upwardly spiraling crime rates.

The Metropolitan Police Act of 1829 authorized Sir Robert Peel to establish a police force for the metropolitan London area, and 1,000 men were quickly hired. Where no police force at all had previously existed, there suddenly stood a large organization. The basic organizational and managerial problems faced by Peel and his police commissioners, Charles Rowan and Robert Mayne, were essentially the same as those faced by police chiefs today. How were they to let their officers know what was expected of them,

how were they to coordinate the activities of all those officers, and how were they to make sure that directions and orders were followed?

Some of Peel's answers to these questions can be found in the fundamental principles of his Peelian Reform:

1. The police should be organized along military lines.
2. Securing and training proper persons is essential.
3. Police should be hired on a probationary basis.
4. The police should be under governmental control.
5. Police strength should be deployed by time and area.
6. Police headquarters should be centrally located.
7. Police record keeping is essential.

The foundation of Peel's approach to police administration is in his first two principles. Although he believed strongly that the police and the military should be separate and distinct agencies, he turned to the military for his model of efficient organization. He also turned to many former military officers in recruiting his first police officers.

That Peel should borrow his organizational style from the military was not at all unusual. The military and the Church were actually the only large-scale organizations in existence at that time. Both were organized similarly, although their members bore different titles. Both were centralized; a few people held most of the power and made most of the decisions, whereas many people just did as they were told. In addition, both operated under a system of graded authority; for example, generals had full authority, colonels and majors had a little less, captains and lieutenants had less still, sergeants had only enough to direct their privates, and privates had none at all.

It was natural, then, that Peel should borrow the centralized organizational form of the military model. His personnel practices, though, were not copied from the military, which at that time was composed largely of debtors, criminals, and draftees, with officers drawn from the wealthy and aristocratic classes. The military was chronically in need of people and would accept anyone into its ranks. Peel, however, was highly selective in choosing his police. Only a small percentage of applicants was accepted, and a probationary period was used to weed out those whose performance was unsatisfactory. The standards of conduct were very rigid, so many officers were dismissed, especially in the early years of organizational development.

Peel's approach to police administration can thus be summed up as follows: (1) centralized organization with graded authority, and (2) selective and stringent personnel standards. He fashioned his approach in 1829 and it stands up well even today.

The Political Era

One obstacle to the adoption of Peel's approach in the United States was the enduring view of police work as essentially undemanding physical labor. This widely held belief prevented the establishment of the rigorous personnel standards advocated by Peel. As a result, the pay and status derived from police work have tended to be low, and the job, until recently, has attracted mainly those whose job prospects elsewhere were bleak.

Stringent personnel standards in the early days of American policing were also subverted by the influence of local politics (see "Politics and the New York Police," p. 6). Local politics served as the vehicle for bringing immigrant groups into the American social structure, and police jobs were part of local political patronage. Initially, police work was the domain of certain politically powerful ethnic groups rather than a profession of highly qualified people who could meet rigid standards. Consequently, police officers were likely to be dismissed by their agencies not

---

POLITICS AND THE NEW YORK POLICE

An important reason for the discrepancy between ideals and practice, in addition to public expectations of the police, was the force's involvement in partisan politics. Decentralization and political favoritism weakened discipline. Before 1853 patrolmen looked to local politicians for appointment and promotion. Consequently, they were less amenable to their superior officers' orders, and friction developed which "soon ripened into the bitterest hatred and enmity, and which were carried out of the department into the private walks of life," Policemen participated in political clubs, often resigning to work for the reelection of their aldermen, who left the positions vacant until they won the election and could reappoint the loyal patrolmen. Chief Matsell said that this politicking kept the department in "constant excitement." Discipline improved somewhat under the 1853 commission, which cut the tie to local aldermen and prohibited participation in political clubs. However, the commission had little chance to improve its effectiveness, for favoritism was rife under Mayor Fernando Wood, elected in 1854. Captains were not promoted from the ranks but "taken from the citizens, and placed over Lieutenants and Sergeants of ten years' experience, depressing the energies of the men."

Source: Wilbur R. Miller, *Cops and Bobbies: Police Authority in New York and London, 1830–1870* (Chicago: University of Chicago Press, 1977), p. 43.

because of unsatisfactory performance, but because they belonged to the wrong political party.

During the political era of American policing, decentralized organizational structures were favored over centralized ones. In big-city police departments the real power and authority belonged to precinct captains, not to chiefs or commissioners. Detectives usually reported to these precinct captains rather than to a chief of detectives at headquarters. The reason for this decentralized approach was to protect local political influence over the police. Local political leaders ("ward bosses") picked their own precinct captains and expected them to be very responsive. A strong central headquarters might have interfered with this politically based system.

The Professional Era

Although complaints about police abuses and inefficiency were common in the 1800s, widespread criticism of the political model of policing, including its decentralization and acceptance of mediocre personnel, did not emerge until the beginning of the twentieth century. Since then, however, police practitioners, academics, and investigating commissions have decried the poor quality of police personnel; pointed out the need for intelligence, honesty, and sensitivity in police officers; called for stricter organizational controls; and thus reaffirmed Peel's philosophy.

Among the individuals most vocal and noteworthy in support of both centralized organization and higher police personnel standards were August Vollmer, Bruce Smith, and O.W. Wilson. Each strongly believed police work to be a demanding and important function in a democratic society, requiring officers able to deal flexibly and creatively with a wide variety of situations. They agreed that physical power was an important attribute, but thought that good judgment, an even temperament, and other human qualities and skills were more important. They believed strongly in education, training, discipline, and the use of modern technology in policing. They and other leaders advocated a professional model of policing.

Supporting their views were the findings and recommendations of investigating commissions, most notably the Wickersham Commission in the 1930s and the President's Crime Commission in the 1960s. The Wickersham Commission found that the American police were totally substandard; the President's Commission found that insufficient progress had been made from the 1930s to the 1960s. Both found that the quality of police personnel was low in terms of carrying out the job to be done and in comparison to the rest of the population, and both called for substantial upgrading of police personnel.

Through the mid-1960s the need for better police personnel and stricter organizational controls dominated the literature and practice of police administration. Since then, however, other important issues—such as the poor state of police–community relations, the need for a more diverse police workforce, the ineffectiveness of traditional police strategies, and the need for more flexibility within police organizations—have come to the forefront. These other issues have arisen because of both the successes and the failures of the professional model of policing.

The Community Era

In most major jurisdictions today, the need for intelligent, sensitive, flexible people in policing has been accepted. More well-educated people are being hired as police officers than was the case 30 or more years ago. Over the long run, police salaries have been improving, along with occupational status. Police agencies are more selective when choosing their officers.

Quality is subjective, however. Many police departments, in their quest for higher-caliber personnel during the professional era, emphasized educational attainment, physical skills, appearance, conformity, abstinence from experimentation with drugs, and spotless police records. Use of such criteria sometimes made it more difficult for local people, women (with less upper body strength, on average, than men), and members of minority groups (who, in some jurisdictions, are less likely to have attended college and more likely to have been arrested for minor offenses) to obtain police employment. The lack of these kinds of employees in turn created police–community relations problems for more than a few police agencies.

Questions also began to arise about the more centralized structures and stricter organizational controls that characterize the professional model. The rigid, military approach no longer seems to fit the demanding, variable, discretion-laden nature of the police job. Nor does it seem appropriate for management of the better-educated, more knowledgeable police officers of today. Other kinds of organizations, in both the business and government sectors, have moved away from centralized, military forms of organization in favor of more flexible arrangements.

The professional model of policing has come under criticism on other fronts as well. The very idea of professionalism may encourage police officers to think of themselves as better than the average person. Separation of policing from politics, when taken to extremes, can result in police who are so independent of political control that they are no longer responsive or accountable to the public.

Perhaps most damaging to the professional model is the question of its effectiveness. During the model's heyday in the 1960s and 1970s, crime was not reduced, but instead increased more than in any other time in recent memory. Also, the key strategies of the professional model (preventive patrol, rapid response, and follow-up investigations) have each been found to be far less effective than originally thought (as explained in Chapter 13).

Beginning in the 1980s and especially in the 1990s, the community policing model came to dominate U.S. policing. The community-oriented model advocates, among other things, more decentralized organizational structure, closer ties to the community, a stronger focus on prevention, and a problem-solving approach to police work. This model supports the need for high-quality personnel, but emphasizes education and creativity over conformity, physical attributes, and unnecessarily rigid background characteristics.

Even the most fervent supporters of community-oriented policing (COP) see the continued necessity of some elements of the professional model, however. The need for high standards, thorough training, and sound organization and management in policing

are widely accepted. If it is to be successful, COP will have to learn from and build upon the professional model. The ideas and information presented throughout this text are equally important whether one is primarily following the professional model or community model of policing.

THE SOCIAL CONTEXT OF POLICE ADMINISTRATION

Just as current police administration can be explained in part by its past, so too can its form and substance be explained in part by the social context within which policing operates. We have already mentioned, for example, that the low status of police work in America helped to explain the unsatisfactory quality of police applicants and thus the inability of police administrators to implement stringent personnel standards.

The police seem perpetually to be the brunt of scathing criticism—this has been evident in the aftermath of such high-profile events as the Rodney King beating, the O.J. Simpson trial, the tragic conclusion of the Waco, Texas, stand-off, the assault on Abner Louima in New York, and most recently in the mishandling of Ryan Moats in Dallas on his way to pay his last respects to his gravely ill mother-in-law. One reason for the apparently constant dissatisfaction with the police in American communities is the lack of agreement in society about what the objectives or role of policing should be. General agreement does not exist in society on the most important goals of policing, not to mention the means of attaining those goals. In addition to the disagreement among people about what the police should be doing, individuals often change their opinions and priorities over time or in response to certain perceived emergencies, so that the unfathomable "will of the community" is always changing. As a result, even the police administrator who tries to provide the community with the type of police service that' it desires is unlikely to escape criticism.

Diverse communities present special challenges for police. Not only do individuals differ in their opinions and preferences, but so do segments of the community. In Chicago, where community policing was implemented and evaluated over the period 1994–2003, there were significant differences among whites, African Americans, and Latinos in the perceived seriousness of physical decay (graffiti, abandoned cars, abandoned buildings, trash and junk) and social disorder (disruption around schools, groups of people loitering, public drinking) in their neighborhoods, with Latinos reporting the most serious problems. These groups also differed in their evaluations of police performance and responsiveness, with whites giving police the highest marks.

The social implications and environment of policing have been highlighted over the last 50 years in discussions and debates about police–community relations. Mass altercations in the 1960s between minority groups and the police, as well as between students and police, dramatically demonstrated that police relations with at least these communities were less than ideal. In urban areas, the estrangement of the police and the community extended beyond civil disorder to everyday policing, as many other groups seemed also to regard the police as an army of occupation. The problem of police relations with these and other segments of the community made it clear that the police operate in a social system that they can neither take for granted nor totally control. Different community groups view the police differently and have varying notions of the priorities and objectives of law enforcement and criminal justice (see "Police Role in the Ghetto" p. 10).

POLICE ROLE IN THE GHETTO

Police work in the ghetto encompasses a series of roles and/or responsibilities. The various attributes of the job can appear, at times, to be working at cross-purposes, but under closer examination the ambiguities of the police role in the ghetto bear definite societal intentions. On the one hand, the police are expected to represent the strong arm of the law; they must do battle with the ghetto's rugged individualism. But on the other hand, they must be able to show compassion and understanding to the public being served: the mother of the lost child, the victim of a crime. As to the other side of the ledger, ghetto residents may see the police as their oppressors, but at the same time the residents cannot do without the social services the police provide. In the absence of these services, the ghetto community would be hard-pressed to maintain social equilibrium. The police may be in adversary relations with the ghetto, but they are also a necessary linchpin of the community.

Source: Basil Wilson and John L. Cooper, "Ghetto Reflections and the Role of the Police Officer," *Journal of Police Science and Administration 7*, No. 1 (March 1979): 35, with permission of the international Association of Chiefs of Police.

Most recently, police–minority relations have been brought to the forefront in discussions about "driving while black," racial profiling, and biased-based policing. The fundamental issue in these discussions is whether the police have been fair and equitable when using their authority to stop, and sometimes search, individuals and vehicles. From a civil liberties and minority group perspective, it sometimes seems that police power to stop and search is used disproportionately against people of color. In return, police officials often assert that they are simply trying to address problems of crime, drugs, and gangs, often in response to urgent requests from minority and low-income neighborhoods. Finding common ground between these opposing perspectives has not been easy.

In the United States, the belief that elected leaders care "what people like me think" has been on the decline since the 1950s ... Yet during the 1990s, Chicago bucked the trend. There were positive shifts in views of policing, and support for the police grew among all major population groups. To be sure, there remained plenty of room for improvement. After more than a half-decade of community policing, public perceptions of police job performance just hit the 50 percent mark among African Americans and Latinos, and their perceptions of police responsiveness did not rise much above that level. But a larger proportion of residents in all groups reported that police were helpful, concerned, and fair, and the trend line for other aspects of their jobs was in the right direction.

Source: Wesley G. Skogan, *Police and Community in Chicago: A Tale of Three Cities* (New York: Oxford University Press, 2006), p. 303.

The community policing model attempts to address such perplexing problems in several ways. Through closer contact with individual citizens and community groups, police are trying to stay attuned to the public's changing needs and priorities. Departments are also seeking a more representative workforce, including increasing numbers of civilians and volunteers to augment sworn officers. In addition, police are varying their enforcement strategies and programs from one neighborhood to the next, instead of applying one uniform approach throughout the entire community. Despite these new efforts, however, it remains difficult in heterogeneous communities to police in a way that satisfies all citizens (see "Community Policing in Chicago"). The same diversity that makes the United States such a vibrant and resilient country makes effective and responsive policing a major challenge. This challenge will only increase in the future as America's population becomes even more diverse.

THE POLITICAL CONTEXT OF POLICE ADMINISTRATION

Part of the environment of police administration is the governmental and political system. We have already noted that, during its development, American policing was closely tied to local politics and that this relationship had important consequences for police decision making and police personnel standards. Although this undesirable political relationship is greatly diminished today, the political environment of police administration is still an important factor to consider in understanding and explaining police behavior, practices, and organizations.

In our junior high school civics classes we all learned about the American government's system of checks and balances and separation of powers. The Founding Fathers dispersed authority among the legislative, executive, and judicial branches of government in order to prevent any one person or branch from becoming all-powerful. The legislative branch was assigned the roles of enacting laws and appropriating funds. The executive branch was given the tasks of implementing and enforcing the laws. The judicial branch was directed to review the constitutionality of legislative enactments and to adjudicate alleged violations of the laws.

The police are a part of the executive branch of government. Their role, then, is to enforce the laws enacted by the legislature and to refer alleged violations of those laws to the judiciary. In actual practice, of course, policing is considerably more complex and less mechanical than this description suggests. Police officers utilize discretion in such a way that they do not enforce all of the laws all of the time; their efforts are not universally reviewed by the courts; and many of their practices involve activities not related specifically to law enforcement. Nevertheless, it remains useful to keep in mind that the police make neither the laws nor the decision between the guilt or innocence of a suspect brought to court. These matters, though important to policing, are within the domain of other branches of the government.

Another important characteristic of our governmental system is federalism. Besides being distributed among different branches of government, power in our system is also dispersed through several levels of government. As a result, some functions are performed by the national government, some by the states, some by counties, some by local communities, and some are shared.

Policing in America is basically a local function, although the states and the national government are also involved with law enforcement and cannot be ignored. Three-quarters of our nation's one million-plus police protection employees work for local governments, and 90 percent of the 18,000 or so police agencies in this country are local police departments or sheriff's departments. One consequence of the local character of American policing is that most of the country's law enforcement agencies are small—one-half have 10 or fewer sworn employees. Therefore, police administration in the United States frequently involves organizing and managing fairly small departments, a fact that is important to keep in mind, because the natural tendency when speaking of administration is to immediately think of large, complex organizations.

With respect to objectives, priorities, and budgets, police administrators deal primarily with city councils, city managers, mayors, and other local executive and legislative units. State and national law enforcement organizations deal with state and national executive bodies, respectively. Even local police, however, have relationships with the state and national governments. The bulk of the law that most police enforce is state law enacted by state legislatures. Also, in many areas, the correctional and judicial systems, both of which are important to policing, are operated by counties and by states. Finally, since the 1960s, many local police administrators have had increased contacts with state and national government officials who control special anticrime funds, drug enforcement monies, and other federal funds used to augment local law enforcement budgets. In the 1990s, most of these federal funds were for the hiring of additional

police officers to perform community policing duties in local communities. From 2001 to 2009, federal funding available to local police shifted substantially to homeland security, and for the most part was not available to support officer or civilian positions; much of this funding was for the purchase of specialized technology and equipment. In 2009 this trend reversed, with a return to federal funding for police officer positions and other operational expenses. Part of this turnaround is because the Democrats won control of the White House and Congress, and part is because of increased federal funding aimed at spurring economic recovery.

Although the political environment of local police administration varies from agency to agency, some regional patterns can be discerned. In the Northeast, local city and town government is very strong and partisan. Police chiefs and other administrators are frequently changed after elections, and local partisan politics have a strong influence on day-to-day policing. In the West, by contrast, local politics are much more likely to be nonpartisan, with college-trained city managers who, like elected mayors in the East, exercise much of the authority. Police administrators in the West are more likely to be given authority and responsibility for everyday police operations, and "professional" police administration is more apparent. Moreover, in the West, and in the South, the county plays a larger role than elsewhere. In many rural areas, the elected county sheriff is the paramount law enforcement officer as well as one of the most prominent politicians. Some counties also have county-wide police agencies serving under an appointed chief who is responsible to a county executive or county council. In other areas, however, particularly the Northeast, the county is an insignificant level of government, and frequently the sheriff is responsible only for serving civil court papers or running a county jail.

Thus, the political and governmental environment of police administration varies widely. Whatever the local circumstances, police administration is strongly influenced by these factors. Along with the historical and social contexts, the political context of police administration has important implications for the people, processes, and organization of policing.

THE LEGAL CONTEXT OF POLICE ADMINISTRATION

Although police work involves much more than just enforcing the law, police administration is constrained and affected by the law in a number of ways. For example, the criminal law defines what acts are crimes and what actions police officers may legally take in a variety of situations. Each year legislatures define new criminal acts, such as identity theft, computer crime, stalking, hate crime, and carjacking, that fall within police jurisdiction. Legislatures also sometimes revise police authority, such as in permitting (or even mandating) warrantless arrests for misdemeanor spousal assault based solely on probable cause. In addition, the courts interpret and redefine the law continuously by their trial and appellate decisions.

One aspect of the law that is always in flux is constitutional law. At both the state and national levels, the courts interpret and reinterpret passages in constitutional law pertaining to limitations on police authority, such as search and seizure and interrogation of suspects. The courts also determine the precise meaning of individual rights that police officers must protect, such as the rights of assembly and free speech.

Police departments sometimes inherit new duties and responsibilities through legislation. Handgun waiting periods and registration laws, for example, frequently assign to police the task of checking the criminal records of handgun purchasers. Police are often required by new laws to conduct background checks on school bus drivers, day care providers, and others entrusted with the safety and well-being of children. Revised domestic violence legislation sometimes requires police officers to provide protection and transportation to spousal assault victims.

Even more common is for police administration to be constrained and regulated by law. In the personnel area, federal legislation protecting the employment rights of women, minorities, older workers, and the disabled has left most police administrators thoroughly confused about the types of hiring practices they can and cannot employ. Many traditional police practices related to roll calls, lunch breaks, on-call assignments, and special assignments have fallen afoul of the federal Fair Labor Standards Act. Police departments' internal disciplinary procedures in many jurisdictions are governed by a Police Officer's Bill of Rights enacted into state law. Laws also regulate the use of radio equipment, the maintenance of documentary records, the disposal of found and seized property, and myriad other matters.

Over the last several decades police administrators have become increasingly concerned with civil law, particularly civil liability. Many police trainers, supervisors, and managers are now so worried about being sued that they suffer from "litigiphobia." In the past, the police officer who made a false arrest, used excessive force, or failed to protect a crime victim might be sued; today, such a suit commonly includes others in the chain of command as defendants, alleging that they failed to properly train, direct, supervise, or control the officer. These kinds of civil suits are particularly effective if it can be shown that administrators encouraged or permitted a pattern of improper conduct to develop and continue.

Clearly, police administration takes place in a complex and changing legal environment. Although it is not yet the case that police administrators must be lawyers, they certainly need access to sound legal advice. And although police executives need not develop phobias about their civil liability, prudent risk management is warranted. The best protection is provided by thorough and systematic application of the modern principles of police administration presented in this text.

Principles of Organization

By Gary Codner

DELEGATION OF AUTHORITY

In a properly organized police department, the chief delegates authority for decisionmaking to people at all levels within the organization. Authority is the power to make decisions or to perform tasks. The ultimate authority in a police department lies with the chief, who must wisely and widely delegate authority to others so that decisions can be made and tasks performed.

Every person within an organization who is expected to perform a specific task should be delegated the necessary amount of authority to perform it well. In police departments in which chiefs do not understand this necessity, there will be few operational decisions made and little work accomplished. For example, when the chief of one small department was first appointed, there was only one other member of the department. Thirty years later, the department had more than 20 members. Although the chief was well-intentioned and had the best interests of the department and the town at heart, the department had grown so much that he was not able to adjust to the fact that he could no longer retain all authority and make all decisions in the department. He gave the one lieutenant and three sergeants little authority to make decisions and to assume command and supervisory responsibilities. As a result, the patrol officers' work was totally unsupervised. The sergeants were little more than patrol officers with three stripes on their sleeves and greatly resented the fact that the chief would not give them the authority to do their job. Both the town and the department suffered because of the chiefs unwillingness to delegate his authority to others who needed it to do their work and meet their responsibilities.

The failure to delegate authority is not at all uncommon in police organizations. In many instances police chiefs simply do not understand the mechanics of the delegation process. In other cases, chiefs are unwilling to delegate authority, fearing that it will be abused by subordinates and reflect negatively on both the department and themselves. Many chiefs are aware that ultimate responsibility is theirs and, accordingly, are extremely cautious about allowing others within their organizations the opportunity to make mistakes that could prove to be embarrassing. Often, though, police chiefs are the least qualified people within their organizations to make decisions, because they are generally furthest removed from the people and the situations their decisions will affect.

The ironic aspect of this unwillingness to delegate authority is that it affects administrative matters more than operational matters. Police chiefs often refuse to delegate the authority for such actions as purchasing a tire to keep a patrol car on the road, issuing flashlight batteries, switching from summer-weight to winter-weight uniforms in the autumn, or making minor work schedule alterations. Yet the authority to use force or to take away a person's freedom is delegated to the lowest-ranking members of the organization, almost without a second thought. Perhaps it is because police chiefs realize that such awesome legal authority is so widely delegated that they jealously guard the limited administrative authority they have.

In delegating authority, chiefs should make absolutely certain that everyone within their departments has a precisely defined understanding not only of the authority he or she has been delegated, but also of the circumstances under which that authority may be used. In order to be sure that the person receiving delegated authority thoroughly understands it, it should be delegated in writing. Except for emergency situations, a chief of police should never delegate authority using only the spoken word. Confusion, forgetfulness, and misunderstandings can quickly dissipate authority that is not in writing. It is imperative then that any delegation of authority be put in writing.

Just as the chief has total authority over the entire police department, officers in high-ranking positions have more authority than those in lower ranks. Captains generally would have more authority than lieutenants; lieutenants, more authority than sergeants. A captain in charge of an operations bureau, for example, should have the authority to decide what priorities will be assigned to various types of investigations. The captain exercises authority by establishing these priorities responsibly in terms of a number of factors, which might include workload, seriousness of the offense, current crime problems, and availability of personnel. The captain might reasonably choose to delegate the authority to establish the priorities to the lieutenant in charge of the investigations division or retain the authority and establish the priorities personally. As a good administrator, the captain should probably delegate the authority to the lieutenant in writing. The lieutenant, however, should not delegate this authority to Investigative sergeants. The lieutenant, with an overview of the entire investigations division, is in a much better position than the sergeants to establish investigative priorities because he or she knows the work of the entire division.

Whenever feedback within a police system indicates that authority is being abused or that officers to whom authority has been delegated are not using it responsibly, that authority must be recovered or taken back. When they delegate authority, police chiefs must be fully aware that the delegation is never permanent. This must also be understood by everyone to whom authority is delegated. When a department is reorganized, when duties are rearranged or reassigned, and when departmental objectives, policies, and programs are modified, authority will inevitably be recovered. The delegation of authority and the recovery of authority are continuing processes by which the organization is made more responsive to the interests of its clientele (citizens, in the case of a police department) and more productive in terms of its output (services).

If the concepts of authority, responsibility, and accountability are fully understood by everyone within a police department and if the chief follows some simple principles of organization in administering the agency, there should be no difficulty in using authority delegation as an organizational device to increase departmental efficiency and effectiveness.

THE AUTHORITY-LEVEL PRINCIPLE

The authority-level principle is based on the premise that authority exists within an organization at all levels and only decisions that cannot be made at a given level because of lack of authority should be referred upward for resolution. It is based on the assumption that within an organization there will be problems everywhere that must be solved continually if the organization is to meet its goals and objectives. Further, it dictates that "all decisions should be made as low as possible in an organization."[3]

In police departments in which functions have been improperly grouped, the chain of command is not in effect, and individuals at various ranks lack the authority to do their jobs, departmental personnel tend to ignore problems or rely on the chief to make most of the decisions. Ignoring the problems is the easier of the two alternatives; the chief, lacking a viable chain of command, will in all likelihood never be advised that problems exist.

The authority-level principle is perhaps the most difficult principle of organization to put into effect. Weak command-level personnel and inept supervisors can be expected to avoid their problem-solving responsibilities and allow problems to increase in number and severity. Insistence that problems that cannot be solved at lower levels be communicated upward is, therefore, essential In police departments, this insistence should be procedurally formalized, with officers and managers at all levels required to write regular reports on problems that have surfaced that they lack the authority to solve themselves. This procedure was developed as a result of the work of Hrand Saxenian, a management consultant and former Harvard Business School professor who successfully applied it in working with business and industry. By writing down their problems and passing along their reports to the person within the organization to whom they report and from whom they receive their authority through the chain of command, they are in fact referring the problems upward for solution. When superiors receive reports outlining problems from subordinates, it is incumbent on them, if they have the necessary authority, to solve the problems themselves. If they lack the authority to solve the problems, they, too, are obliged in their regular reports to their superiors to list the problems that they lack the authority to solve personally. If such a system is put into effect, and if reports are kept by the department, accountability can be placed on officers who are shirking their problem-solving responsibilities.

Most problems in a majority of departments will probably be solved more informally. For example, a patrol officer who is having mechanical difficulties with a patrol vehicle should only need to mention this to the sergeant in order to have arrangements made for the vehicle's repair. If this problem is then solved, it would not be listed among the problems the sergeant outlined in his or her regular report. On the other hand, if the sergeant refuses to make arrangements to have the vehicle repaired, thereby refusing to

make a decision on the matter, it would be the patrol officer's responsibility to list this as a problem in his or her report. By insisting that the patrol officer reduce this problem to writing, and by keeping the reports for at least a year, it will be a relatively easy matter for the lieutenant in charge of the shift, or for the captain in charge of operations, to place accountability on the sergeant for not dealing with a problem for which authority had been delegated. Both the captain and the lieutenant should, by departmental policy, be required to make periodic spot checks on reports in an effort to find problems that their subordinates may be attempting to keep from them.

Although this example may seem to be a rather inconsequential matter, it should be understood that when combined with a number of other little problems, this problem can seriously impede the effectiveness of the patrol division, in one police department studied by one of the authors, minor problems similar to the one above seriously affected the morale of police officers and stood in the way of achieving departmental goals and objectives. Almost no problems were solved at the operating level, and no systems existed for referring problems upward. Although the department consisted of almost 200 police officers, it had a very loosely knit chain of command and no organization chart, if the chief was aware of the principle of accountability or of the authority-level principle, he was certainly not applying them to the management of the department. As a result, portable radios were in varying stages of disrepair, and many were missing. Police vehicles were poorly equipped and maintained. Several would have had difficulty passing state inspection; one ear had a nonfunctioning front headlight, another had a blown muffler. A patrol vehicle was once out of service for five days because no one assumed the responsibility of cleaning vomit from its rear floor rug. Patrol cars had no fire extinguishers or first aid kits. These and other problems remained unsolved because no one had the authority to solve them and because the chief was either unaware of or chose to ignore their existence. He simply did not know how to apply the basic principles of police organization to his department. He, the officers in his department, and the citizens in his community all suffered as a result of his inability to manage.

The authority-level principle, if it is applied consistently throughout the organization, will help to solve many problems that would otherwise go unsolved. It is a device that all police chiefs should utilize to the fullest extent if they expect their departments to meet their goals and objectives.

KEY ORGANIZATIONAL PRINCIPLES

This section discusses several fundamental organizational principles: chain of command, unity of command, span of control, and grouping like functions. Along with the concepts of authority, responsibility, and accountability, these principles are used to help guide the structure of police organizations.

Chain of Command

Chain of command, also referred to as the scalar principle, is an organizational mechanism that establishes formal lines of communication within a police department. It is founded on the premise that the clearer the line of authority from the ultimate authority to every subordinate, the more effective decisionmaking and organizational communication will be. It establishes a vertical flow of information, directives, and orders downward through an organization. The chain of command establishes a direct path between every person in the department and the chief. The path may also be viewed as a two-way street whereby information may flow upward through the organization from subordinates through superiors and ultimately to the chief.

The schematic design that establishes the chain of command is the organization chart. Organization charts may be very simple or very complex, depending on department size. Regardless of their simplicity or complexity, however, they all show the relative positions of all subsystems within the police department. The organization chart in Figure 5.2, for example, shows a chain of command from chief to operations lieutenant to shift sergeant to patrol officer. In the same chart, the chain of command links the crime prevention officer and the chief directly.

Figure 5.2: Organization Chart for a 26-Member Police Department

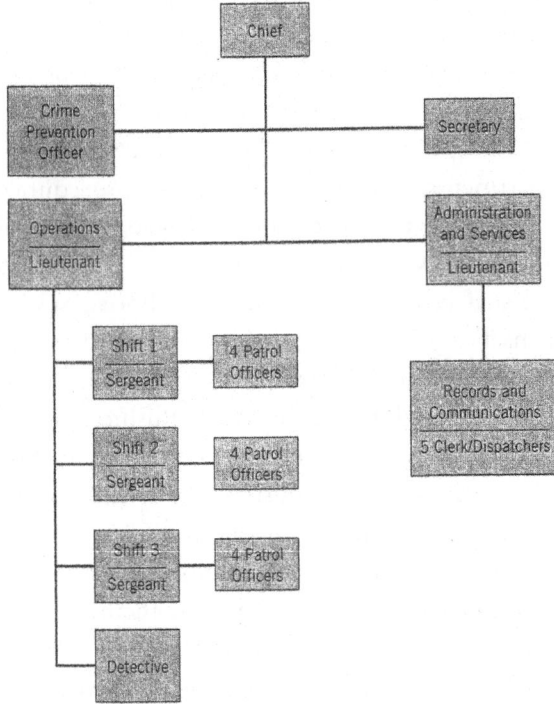

The chain of command is an invaluable organizational tool because it establishes formal communication links. If a department is to be properly organized, these communication links must be used by everyone within the organization to communicate formally. If the chain of command is not used for all formal communicating, serious organizational difficulties can be anticipated. For example, a chief of police who disregards the chain of command by issuing an order directly to a patrol officer is breaking the chain and dissipating the authority of all those within the chain who have varying degrees of authority over what the patrol officer does. If the chief makes a habit of issuing orders directly to patrol officers, they quickly learn that the chain of command is inconsequential in internal communications and that they, too, may disregard it in their efforts to communicate upward in the organization.

In applying the chain of command to the organizing of a police department, a chief should consider the fact that there are various levels of management, each with somewhat different functions. For our purposes, we can group these levels of management into three categories:

1. chief administrative level
2. command level
3. supervisory level

The chief administrative level, always the top level within the organization, consists of the chief and the chief's staff. The command level generally is comprised of all officers of the rank of lieutenant and above who have authority and overall responsibility for line, or staff functions. The supervisory level consists of ranking officers below the rank of lieutenant who are assigned to supervisory duties. Most departments have sergeants, and many have corporals who fall into this category.

Ranking officers who neither command nor supervise line or operational functions are generally referred to as staff personnel. Although they hold rank and often perform important functions, they do not have command or supervisory authority over anyone. Most often staff personnel are assigned to higher levels of management. A lieutenant, for example, who is assigned to the operations bureau as legal advisor is in a staff position, not a command-level position, even though the work is performed at the command level. Another lieutenant assigned to the operations bureau might have the overall responsibility for running a patrol shift. Because the assignment would involve command responsibilities, this lieutenant would be considered to be in a command-level position.

Unity of Command

The principle of unity of command insists that the reporting relationship between subordinate and superior be on a one-to-one basis. A subordinate should not be expected to report to more than one superior or take orders from more than one superior.[4]

If a person is expected to take orders from more than one superior, tremendous confusion can result. A young boy whose father tells him to mow the lawn and whose mother tells him to wash the dishes instead will be wrong regardless of what he does. His parents have violated the principle of unity of command. They have both given the youngster orders, and they both expect him to follow through.

The consequences of this situation in a family setting are not disastrous. However, consider the case of a patrol officer who receives three different patrol assignments from the sergeant, lieutenant, and chief, respectively. Both the sergeant and the lieutenant will be upset by the chief's action, and the patrol officer will be totally frustrated: which of the three superiors' orders should be followed?

This kind of problem must be taken into consideration when a police department is organized; departmental policy must stipulate that each officer takes orders from and reports directly to only one person: his or her immediate superior in the chain of command. If the chief wants to issue an order to a patrol officer, it must be understood by everyone that this can be done only through the chain. In this instance, the chief would tell the lieutenant how to assign the patrol officer, the lieutenant would tell the sergeant, and the sergeant, as the patrol officer's immediate superior, would issue the order to the officer.

The principle of unity of command is a simple device that helps to avoid confusion in the issuance of orders. It makes all personnel within the organization more comfortable in their roles and more secure in terms of reporting relationships.

Practical necessities sometimes complicate unity of command, however. In the 26-member police department described in Figure 5.2, for example, the five clerk/dispatchers report to the lieutenant in charge of administration and services. Because they work shifts, though, the lieutenant frequently will not be on duty when they are in this department, the on-duty clerk/dispatcher would typically be directly supervised by the on-duty patrol shift sergeant. Out of necessity, the clerk/dispatchers would be required to take orders from these patrol sergeants regarding, for example, when they could take their meal breaks. Ultimately, though, they would remain responsible to their superior in the chain of command, the lieutenant in charge of administration and services.

Standard 11.2.1 Each employee is accountable to only one supervisor at any given time.

Standard 12.1.2 A written directive establishes the command protocol for the following situations, at a minimum:

    a. in the absence of the chief executive officer;
    b. in exceptional situations;
    c. in situations involving personnel of different function engaged in a single operation; and
    d. in normal day-to-day agency operations,

Standard 12.1.3 A written directive requires employees to obey any lawful order of a superior, including any order relayed from a superior by an employee of the same or lesser rank. The directive must also include procedures to be followed by an employee who receives a conflicting or unlawful order.

Source: *Standards for Law Enforcement Agencies: The Standards Manual of the Law Enforcement Agency Accreditation Program*, Fifth Edition. Fairfax, VA: Commission on Accreditation for Law Enforcement Agencies, Inc., 2006.

In situations such as these, which often arise in police agencies because they provide 24-hour-a-day service, two adjustments to the unity of command principle are required: (1) it must be clear to employees which supervisors have the authority to command them under what circumstances; and (2) at any given time, the employee should be expected to take orders from only one superior. With these adjustments, the principle of unity of command can be made compatible with the practical realities of police work.

Span of Control

The total number of subordinates reporting to a single superior is referred to as that superior's span of control. The chief who commands three captains has a span of control of three. The patrol sergeant who supervises the activities of nine patrol officers has a span of control of nine. The operations lieutenant in Figure 5.2 has a span of control of four—the three shift sergeants and the detective.

Early theorists believed that the proper number of persons within a span of control, could be precisely established. Formulas were developed to "prove" that six or seven or some other number of people was the optimum number that could be supervised with ease. Over the years, however, it became apparent that the complexities of tasks and responsibilities, the skills

of subordinates, and the talents of supervisors make it impossible to establish an ideal span of control. Rather, determining a given span of control is based on a subjective evaluation of the number of people a given supervisor can supervise effectively. Peter E. Drucker even suggests that a supervisor's span include a few more persons than he or she can closely supervise, thus making it impossible for a supervisor to do subordinates' work.[5]

It is useful to think of a span of control as narrowing progressively toward the top of the organization. Thus, a police chief has the smallest span of control. A good rule of thumb is that the span should be devised according to the degree of responsibility and authority that exists at a particular level in the hierarchy. The greater the degree of authority and responsibility that exists, the narrower the span of control.

Depending on circumstances, however, this general guideline need not always be followed. It is possible, for example, that a chief might have a span of control consisting of four captains, whereas a lieutenant who is in charge of a patrol shift in that department has responsibility over only three sergeants. As John R. Pfiffner and R. Vance Presthus point out, "there is no constant number applicable to every situation."[6] In short, span of control is an organizational supervisory tool that, if used with care and revised through experience, can contribute significantly to organizational solidarity.

Grouping Like Functions

Police officers have many basic responsibilities and work in a variety of ways. They direct traffic, intercede in family disputes, counsel youth, make arrests, drive patrol vehicles, conduct surveillances, enforce laws, write reports, maintain records, interrogate suspects, interview complainants and victims, testify in court, enforce parking regulations, investigate accidents, supervise subordinates, prepare budgets, provide for the safety of schoolchildren, give first aid, inspect liquor establishments, book prisoners, check doors and premises at night, collect and preserve evidence, perform Breathalyzer tests, deliver babies, and engage in myriad other functions that come within the purview of their mission. Their duties are many and are often conflicting.

Because a police organization cannot have a separate unit to perform each of the tasks listed above, it becomes necessary to combine them in some systematic way. The most useful way of grouping functions is through application of the principle of functional definition, which in police circles is usually referred to as grouping like functions. This principle holds that functions that are similar should be grouped together organizationally. Functions are similar when:

1. the same level of authority is required for their execution
2. responsibility for them is executed at the same time or in the same place
3. they require the same amount of training and/ or degree of skill to be performed

It is through the grouping of similar functions that the various units within a police organization are formed. Chiefs of police should make a concerted effort to group similar tasks together logically within the organizational framework.

The chief should be guided not only by similarities in functions but also by the size of the department. In a department with one chief and four patrol officers, the chief would in all likelihood perform all administrative and auxiliary service functions as well as numerous operational tasks. The patrol officers would probably be assigned exclusively to operational responsibilities. In departments with mote personnel available to perform specialized functions, any number of possibilities exists for grouping like functions.

You should note that the organization chart for a 26-member police department depicted in Figure 5.2 does not have a box for each and every one of the 30 police organizational tasks described in Chapter 4. Still, those tasks must be performed within this department, as in any other. Many of the 20 administrative and auxiliary services tasks, for example, would probably be performed by the chief or the lieutenant in command of administration and services. With respect to these and the operational tasks, the chief should be careful in delegating authority so that it is clear which tasks are the responsibility of which personnel.

Unless a conscious effort is made to group like functions in some systematic, logical way, officers within the department will eventually become confused about how they should perform assigned tasks. In one department, a sergeant assigned to the day shift was given responsibility for the safety of children as they traveled to and from school in this position, the sergeant served as supervisor for more than 50 school crossing guards who assisted youngsters across busy city streets. That the sergeant and the crossing guards were placed organizationally in the same division was an appropriate grouping of similar functions.

The sergeant, however, was also assigned the task of inspecting the operations division's police vehicles at 8:00 A.M. Monday through Friday. These inspections usually lasted between 15 and 30 minutes. With schools opening at 8:30 A.M., the half hour between 8:00 and 8:30 was critical in terms of the sergeant's major responsibilities. His assignment to vehicle inspection at that time meant that he had to neglect his primary functions in order to perform a task very different from his major responsibilities.

In assigning the sergeant to dissimilar functions, the chief violated the principle of functional definition; it was a serious violation because it was made at the peril of youngsters walking to school. Although important, the vehicle inspection function should have been performed by someone else, logically by someone assigned to the operations division. School safety and vehicle inspections are dissimilar functions and should not, unless the department is a small one, be performed by the same person or by the same group of persons. Although, depending on circumstances, the same level of authority may be required for their execution, the two tasks are not executed in the same place and do not require the same degree of skill or training to be performed.

A good rule of thumb in organizing a department is to group all operational duties, all administrative duties, and all auxiliary service duties separately. If a department is not large enough to accommodate these groupings, a distinction should be made organizationally between line and staff duties. Line duties are departmental functions that are operational in nature; staff duties are those performed within the administrative and auxiliary service components of the organization.

Over the last few years, in conjunction with growing interest in community policing, the criterion of "place," or geography, has become more important in grouping similar functions together. Departments that once gave greater emphasis to "time" in organizing patrol units (making the shift the primary building block of patrol operations) are now emphasizing place by creating beat teams and similar geographically focused units. In addition, departments that once organized largely on the basis of function (due to skill and training requirements of different specialized jobs) are now organizing more on the basis of geography. Under this model, for example, detectives report to an area commander rather than to a chief of detectives based at headquarters. Some departments have also reduced the number of functionally specialized jobs (detectives, traffic officers, etc.), arguing that neighborhood-based patrol officers can perform many of these functions, and can perform them more effectively due to their in-depth knowledge of their geographic areas of responsibility.

Grouping like functions inevitably raises the issue of specialization. In a five-member police agency, the patrol and investigative functions must be grouped together as similar functions and performed by the same people. A 30-member department, on the other hand, might lend itself to the establishment of both a patrol division and an investigations division. In a much larger department, where the availability of personnel would suggest further specialization, the patrol division might be subdivided into a number of subsystems to include a tactical unit, an emergency unit, a family crisis intervention unit, a helicopter unit, a scuba unit, a mounted unit, a canine unit, and a bomb unit. Similarly, the investigation division in the larger department could be subdivided into a vice unit, a narcotics unit, a shoplifting unit, a hotel unit, a stolen auto unit, a fraud unit, a homicide unit, a burglary unit, a robbery unit, a cybercrime unit, and a liquor violations unit.

Care should be taken in determining the degree of specialization that should be introduced in any police department. Although traditional organization theorists tend to believe that effectiveness increases with specialization, this is not necessarily so. It was originally believed that the more concentrated the talents and energies of a worker, the greater the worker's productivity. The assembly line, the logical manifestation of this belief, revolutionized the manufacture of goods. In time, however, problems arose. Many workers became bored with the sameness of their routine. As boredom increased, so too did absenteeism and labor problems. Thus, it is necessary to find a balance between specialization and adequate assignment of personnel In other words, it is probably acceptable to have someone specialize in a certain type of crime in the investigative unit, but the amount of time that the person spends in the unit should be taken into consideration as well. While it is desirable to have individuals who have specialized areas in which they are proficient, it is also desirable to have individuals who are versatile and can work effectively in more than one area.

In police departments, specialization tends to deflect efforts away from meeting total organizational objectives and to concentrate efforts on attaining the narrower goals of the specialist's subunit. If a narcotics detective, for example, is paying an addict-informant for information, a real possibility exists that the informant may be committing burglaries to support his or her drug habit. Although the objectives of the narcotics detective may be satisfied by the information provided by the addict-informant, the overall goal of the department to decrease crime is not. The narcotics detective is, in fact, working against the overall goals and objectives of the department because the goals and objectives of the special unit seem to demand it. The tendency of subunits in an organization to pursue their own narrow objectives, regardless of the effect on overall organizational goals, is sometimes called suboptimization.

A related problem caused by specialization is that if some activity or function is assigned to a specific officer or unit, then the rest of the organization often believes that it is no longer responsible for that function. This happened in many police departments in the early stages of implementing community policing and problem-oriented policing.[7] Moreover, specialized officers and units can easily become isolated from the rest of the organization, which can impede communication, reduce effectiveness, and lead to misunderstandings and stereotyping.

Decisions about how much specialization there should be in organizing a police department are vitally important because they will directly influence the department's overall effectiveness. In departments with many specialized subunits, the chain of command becomes a less effective communication device. These units tend to work independently of one another. Information tends to be guarded on a unit-proprietary basis and not shared with the rest of the department. Detectives in some departments have been known to pocket arrest warrants in anticipation of making a major arrest themselves. Specialization tends to increase unit competition and negate departmental cohesiveness.

The problem of specialization versus generalization does not lend itself to an easy solution. Perhaps the best advice on the use of specialization in police organization came from Thomas Reddin, former chief of the Los Angeles Police Department. Reddin suggested that when specialization is considered to be absolutely necessary, personnel should be rotated frequently through specialized positions: "a good general rule to follow is to specialize if you must, generalize if you can."[8] This proposal seems to be an excellent rule to follow in organizing any size police department.

Implementing Community Policing

The Administrative Problem

By George Kelling and William Bratton

The current generation of police leadership, tuned to changes in American society, technology, and economics, is revising the strategy of municipal policing. Whether identified as community or problem-oriented policing, the current changes represent nothing less than a strategic shift in the basic "business" of policing. As dedicated as they are, as supported by research, as responsive to neighborhood demands for change, this generation of reformers finds regeneration and strategic repositioning as difficult as has any other. Why is it that innovators of every generation have so much difficulty shifting the strategies of their organizations and professions?

For police executives, three sources of resistance seem to be foremost in their minds and conversations: unions, detectives, and mid-management. This paper will deal with mid-management. We have repeatedly heard top police executives say with frustration, "If only it wasn't for mid-management," or "If only I could wipe out lieutenants, I could really change this department." The experience with team policing during the 1970's seemed to confirm this impression empirically. Sherman et al. conclude in their case studies of team policing: "Mid-management of the departments [studied], seeing team policing as a threat to their power, subverted and, in some cases, actively sabotaged the plans."[1]

Yet, there are problems with this formulation. Review of the literature on mid-management presents a more complicated picture. On the one hand, many articles, especially those in journals of a semi-popular nature, portray mid-managers as a dying breed in organizations, especially in those organizations that are being downsized or in which their services or products are information-based. Certainly, many organizations are portrayed as top-heavy, especially at mid-managerial levels. This is not just a "pop" view; Peter Drucker states it strongly.

> [M]iddle managements today tend to be overstaffed to the point of obesity. ... This slows the decision process to a crawl and makes the organization increasingly incapable of adapting to change. Far too few people, even in high positions with imposing titles, are exposed to the challenge of producing result.[2]

Mid-management ranks are bloated in many police departments: some have many captains and lieutenants without commands but serving as aides, often doing relatively menial work that could be carried out by a secretary or administrative assistant.

It does not follow from this, however, that mid-managers—captains and lieutenants—are a hindrance to innovation per se. Having too many mid-managers is a different issue from suggesting that mid-managers are inherently resistant to change. Indeed, many people who study organizations, especially in the private sector, identify the locus of innovation precisely in mid-management. Probably the work of Rosabeth Moss Kanter is most noteworthy in this regard. She argues that middle managers are essential to the process of innovation, and argues even more strongly that creativity can originate only in middle management.[3] Perhaps the experience of mid-management in organizational change in the private sector is instructive as we consider the current changes in policing. The role of mid-management in change—which for reasons that will become apparent, we call the *administrative problem*—is a generic issue in innovation and the strategic repositioning of organizations.

DEFINING THE ADMINISTRATIVE PROBLEM

Considering the circumstances within which early 20th-century police reformers like August Vollmer and O.W. Wilson found themselves, the law enforcement strategy they constructed had much to commend it. Those circumstances included extensive political corruption of police agencies, widespread financial corruption of police officers and departments, extensive police abuses of their authority, and large-scale inefficiencies. To counter these circumstances, reformers redefined the basic strategy of American policing. They narrowed police functioning to criminal law enforcement. They centralized police organizations, standardized and routinized the official functioning of police, and measured their success by arrests and clearances and the newly created Uniform Crime Reports.

Over time, this strategy became consistent, coherent, integrated, marketable, and dominated the police field. This strategy has shaped both how police are thought about and how they think about themselves. It has been so potent that for a generation, questioning it was tantamount to uttering "fighting words." To suggest that the police role was more complex was heard as tantamount to demeaning police, reinviting political meddling and financial corruption into policing, suggesting that police were social workers,

and pandering to criminals.[4] Real policing was law enforcement, crime fighting.

The business of policing in this strategy had two elements. The first element, crime fighting, was conducted through preventive patrol, interception patrol, rapid response to calls for service, and criminal investigations. The intent of preventive patrol was to create a feeling of police omnipresence in a community; the intent of interception patrol and rapid response was to intercept crimes in progress; and the intent of criminal investigation was to investigate crimes. In each of the latter two activities, the goal was to arrest offenders and feed them into the criminal justice system.

Controlling officers was the second element of the strategy. At first, this assertion seems strange—control of officers should be a means of improving police performance, not an end in itself. Yet, one has to put oneself in the position of the reformers. For them, political meddling, corruption, and abuse were so rampant in policing that it was impossible to direct effectively efforts to any desired goal; therefore, control was in the forefront of all their innovations.[5] Concern for means overshadowed ends. Control became the strategy. Thus, it is no surprise that even as recently as the 1970's in New York City, patrol officers were constrained from making low-level drug arrests because administrators feared they would be corrupted. As Herman Goldstein observes: "It is a sad commentary on the state of policing in this country that the need to control corrupt practices stands in the way of more effective policing."[6]

Much could be written about the fact that control of officers was central to the reform strategy: its wisdom, its efficacy, the extent to which it interfered with good policing activity, how the public came to judge police departments as it does, and other issues. Our purpose here, however, is simply to argue that the basic business of police organizations was twofold: law enforcement and control of officers.

Early reformers confronted three sets of problems as they attempted to shift the strategy of policing to law enforcement: entrepreneurial, tactical, and administrative. In this respect, they were similar to entrepreneurs and owners/executives in commerce. They had to define their *core services* in a changing environment, the *engineering services* required to produce their services, and the *administrative mechanisms* to ensure production. For police reformers:

1. entrepreneurial problems included redefining core police services and ensuring that an adequate market or demand for such services existed;
2. engineering problems included devising the tactics and technologies that were required to provide those services; and
3. administrative problems included creating the organizational structure and managerial processes required to develop, maintain, and monitor the organization's activities.

For each of these problems, police reformers such as Vollmer and Wilson devised solutions.

The entrepreneurial solution

The entrepreneurial solution was discussed above. The reformers emphasized crime fighting and control of officers as their core services and systematically marketed them as their core competencies. Allying themselves with progressive reformers, police leaders adroitly steered public attention towards what they perceived as a major crime wave, police corruption, and political interference. They accomplished this reorientation of the public to the new business of policing through advertising, public relations, public education, local and national commissions (e.g., Wickersham[8]), and police surveys (assessments of local police departments by recognized national experts like Vollmer and Bruce Smith).[9]

The tactical solution

The tactical solutions of the reformers initially centered on patrol and criminal investigation. At first, patrol was modified by the rather simple move of abandoning foot patrol for cars (during the 1930's and 1940's). Primary justifications for putting police into automobiles were to match the speed and mobility of criminals in cars and to increase the sense of the

prowess of the officer, equipped as the officer would be with a powerful car. Later, reformers developed the more sophisticated tactics of preventive patrol, rapid response to calls for service, and interception patrol.

Additionally, criminal investigation came into its own during the reform era. Previously, criminal investigation units and detectives had unsavory reputations. Recruited from the private sector until the early 20th century, detectives and detective units and agencies (the Bureau of Investigation—the predecessor of the FBI) were noted for corruption and unprofessional behavior. J. Edgar Hoover's strategy for eradicating corruption from the Bureau of Investigation and converting it into the highly respected and professional FBI became the model for local police chiefs and helped reshape the public view of local police department detectives as well.

Detectives began to look and act like professionals. They worked regular hours, controlled their own schedule, saw people by appointment, "took over" crime scenes, controlled esoteric information, and in other ways operated with professional prerogatives. Additionally, detectives became the "stuff" of movies, radio, and later, television. As a consequence, they became the leading edge in the law enforcement strategy. Their prestige and external and internal clout soared. The successful cop? A detective. The failed cop? An unpromoted patrol officer.

The administrative solution

The administrative problem for the reformers consisted of the need to establish the structural and administrative mechanisms required to produce the desired services. The administrative solution was large-scale adoption of the ideas of Frederick Taylor, the renowned early 20th-century organizational theorist. Known as scientific (or classical) management, Taylor's work focused on improving productivity by rationalizing both production efforts (human work) and management. His concepts and practices have become well known. They include: time and motion studies; routinization and simplification of work tasks; division of work tasks; and administrative control mechanisms, which include unity of command, layers of command, close supervision, span of control, and linking productivity to reward systems.

The undertakings of reformers to rationalize the productive work (tactics and technologies) of patrol officers are now well known: narrowing the official responsibility of patrol to law enforcement; reducing, even attempting to eliminate, patrol officer discretion; and developing routinized patrol tactics (preventive patrol and rapid response to calls).

The reformers' rationalization of administration—their attempts to solve the administrative problem—as well as the attempts by the current generation of reformers are the central concerns of this paper. Consider the situation of a chief of police during the early decades of this century. Generally a political appointee, the chief served at the pleasure of the mayor. Tenure or contracts for chiefs were unheard of. Police districts were contiguous with wards and ward leaders made most of the police appointments, administrative and operational. The links between ward leaders and police were so close during this political era of policing that historians like Fogelson have dubbed police "adjuncts" of urban political parties (machines).[10]

In these circumstances, police reformers needed to accomplish two things to gain control over their departments. The first was to sever *all levels* within police departments from undue external influences. This was accomplished largely by adopting the political agenda of progressive reformers: centralization of urban services (taking control away from ward leaders); election of council persons-at-large (weakening neighborhood-based ward politicians); strengthening mayors and creating city management forms of government; creating civil service (hiring, retaining, promoting, and terminating personnel on the basis of merit); removing control of police chiefs from politicians; and developing mechanisms to protect the tenure of police chiefs. Elements of this agenda were achieved with varying degrees of success; however, the overall results were so successful that by 1977, Herman Goldstein appropriately pointed out that many, if not most, police departments had achieved such degrees of autonomy that they were virtually unaccountable to local government.[11]

The second task for police reformers was to extend the reach of police chiefs into the department itself. That is, police executives had to implement and maintain over time their strategy by socializing and managing personnel; devising a range of specialized tactical functions; establishing new relations to the external environment; maintaining equipment, including a fleet of automobiles and later telephone, radio, and computer equipment; controlling financial functions, including recordkeeping, allocating resources, and reporting; and developing the means of reporting on the achievements of their new strategy.

In some respects, their responsibility was akin to that of late 19th-century owner-managers in industry who, confronted with the need to extend their reach into their increasingly large enterprises, "literally invented the methods and systems of administrative coordination and, in the process, gave definition to a wide range of functions such as finance, collection, service, marketing, distribution, pricing, sales, training, and labor management."[12] That is, police reformers, like owner-managers of burgeoning industrial enterprises some decades earlier, created a mid-management infrastructure, the purpose of which was to ensure the implementation and maintenance of the reform strategy. Creating functional organizations, as opposed to the geographically based organizations of early policing, chiefs delegated to a midmanagerial group specific authority over functions that included training, analyzing and planning, accounting, reporting, allocating personnel, scheduling, and other functions. Over time, the skills required to manage these functions became increasingly complex, resulting in, a management group that had many of the skills of professional managers in the corporate world: planning, fiscal and budgeting analysis, marketing, research, and education.

Police chiefs extracted from their own executive functions, authority, and skill the elements that could be rationalized. Chiefs delegated these functions to midmanagers—captains and lieutenants who oversaw administrative units and patrol operations on a day-to-day and shift-to-shift basis. Administratively, captains generally head departments and units such as planning and the police academy.

In operations, captains serve usually as district/precinct/area commanders and commanders of special units. Responsible to inspectors/assistant chiefs/majors, captains in patrol direct activities in a geographical area. Responsibilities of these captains include the establishment of district priorities; supervision of operations; relations with community and neighborhood groups; coordination with other patrol districts and police units; direction of assignments, scheduling, instructions, procedures, and communications; preparation of the district budget; and the preliminary handling of citizen complaints against officers. Generally, captains work business hours and days. In special units, captains have similar duties, but usually have citywide responsibility for a function, such as handling juveniles, rather than for a geographical area.

Lieutenants work directly under captains. Often designated as "desk officers" in patrol units, lieutenants are responsible for the shift-to-shift operation of a district or function. As such, most lieutenants work shifts. During shifts, lieutenants are responsible for equipment; proper preparation of all reports; review of field investigation; maintenance of logs; transmission of all orders; supervision of sergeants; investigation of complaints; and other administrative duties. Typically, lieutenants "sign off" on all reports and district records. As such, they are the guarantors of line performance. But under the reformers, captains and lieutenants also gained control of the *practice, knowledge, and skill base* of the occupation. This requires some explanation.

As part of the law enforcement strategy, reformers moved to simplify and routinize the work of patrol officers, the service base of the occupation. This was accomplished in policing, as it was in industry, by attempting to reduce the discretion of line personnel, those providing the service of the organization. To accomplish this, the essence or the craft of the work had to be understood and then distilled by engineers and planners (mid-managers). Once understood and distilled, the productive efforts of workers could be reduced to relatively simple and repetitive tasks. In

this way, both skill and knowledge about productivity were concentrated in the managerial domain.[13] Sparrow et al. capture this:

Police officers, for all their field's talk about professionalism, are treated not like professionals but like factory workers. The duties and methods of their jobs are presumed to have been well worked out. Someone else has already done the thinking; only their faithful adherence to procedure and their willingness to show up for work are required. Their superiors, for the most part, merely supervise and discipline.[14]

The concentration of expertise, the practice skill, was located in the leadership of line operating units (patrol and special units) and staff units like planning and the training academy. Mid-managers would thus define the problems that police would address and the methods that police would use to manage them.

The task of police officers was simply nondiscretionary law enforcement. If someone breaks the law, he or she is arrested. If laws are not broken, nobody need fear the police. Some training in procedure was required but, as Bittner has noted, all a police officer really needed in this view of police work was a little common sense and the "manly virtue" of being able to overcome resistance.[15]

Thus, the solution to the administrative problem in police departments was the establishment of a powerful mid-management group that: 1) extended the reach of chiefs throughout police departments and 2) became the locus of the practice and skill base of the occupation. As such, mid-managers became *the leading edge in the establishment of centralized control over police departments' internal environment and organizational operations.*

In the following section of this paper, we will examine the way in which mid-management's role in the establishment of centralized control over the police organization plays itself out in contemporary efforts at police reform. We will begin by reviewing three 1970's efforts funded by the Police Foundation in Dallas, Texas; Cincinnati, Ohio; and Kansas City, Missouri. Projects in these three cities consumed at least one-third of the Police Foundation's original $30 million endowment from the Ford Foundation. The work in Dallas is largely forgotten. Cincinnati is recalled as the final major test of team policing. The work in Kansas City is considered path breaking in policing. Following this, we will examine more recent attempts to strategically reposition police departments in Baltimore County, Maryland; Madison, Wisconsin; Houston, Texas; Reno, Nevada; and the New York City Transit Police Department.

THREE CASES: DALLAS, CINCINNATI, AND KANSAS CITY

Dallas. Although the Police Foundation had given a few small grants, the centerpiece of its strategy was the Major Cities Program. The central idea of this program was to identify police departments that had an unusual potential for change and to help them overhaul thoroughly and radically their organization and operations. They, then, would become national models for the profession. The Dallas Police Department (DPD) was to be the first Major City.

Given the assumptions of such an approach, no city could compare with Dallas. The vision of its chief, Frank Dyson, was revolutionary. In today's organizational language, his vision of policing and his attempts at reform would be understood as a strategic repositioning of the Dallas Police Department. The very nature of the business of the organization would change: official recognition would be given to all police activities; authority would devolve to operational levels of the department; community needs would determine operational priorities; police would be accountable to the community; management and personnel processes and physical structures would be altered to facilitate such devolution of authority and community priority-setting; and police would develop close relations with other community institutions.

The model for instituting these reforms emphasized careful planning, creating systems to support such a strategy (e.g., recruitment, preservice and inservice training), developing a management infrastructure to maintain and monitor the strategy, and changing the definitions of organizational, unit, and individual performance.

Planning for these activities was conducted by the Office of Program Administration (OPA). This office was headed by a confidante of Chief Dyson who was widely viewed in the department as a police renegade. The staff of OPA was made up mainly of newly hired civilians. The dominant view of those involved in planning for the implementation of the effort was that the plan, while worthy and innovative, threatened the vested interests of major segments of DPD. For example, detectives were to be decentralized, and the rank of lieutenant was to be eliminated. OPA responded to the anticipated resistance by developing an official policy of maximum secrecy during the planning stages. To facilitate this secrecy, OPA offices were moved out of police headquarters to a relatively inaccessible location. (Other reasons existed for moving—shortage of space, for example—but inaccessibility was a major goal of OPA.)

Mid-managers generally were described by key personnel in OPA as "perchers"—persons who merely filled organizational slots, without contributing to the organization. They, especially lieutenants, were viewed as the primary source of resistance to the effort to change.

Elements of the plan were implemented, primarily those having to do with improving the personnel processes of the DPD. But before a single operational element of the strategy was in place, Dyson was fired, the operational thrusts of the effort were abandoned, and the planning unit that was charged with designing the implementation plan was renounced and liquidated. Essentially, the overthrow resulted from a coalition among detectives, the media, and the Dallas Police Association, which at that time was dominated by detectives. The detectives opposed the plan because of decentralization. The news media, especially the print press, were exasperated by the continuing attempts to maintain the plan in virtually total secrecy. Broad-based opposition arose to minority recruitment. The DPA sided with the detectives, not surprising since detectives dominated its leadership. Fiscal improprieties within OPA were alleged. No champions arose to defend the plan. City officials began to fear for the city's image.

Cincinnati. Cincinnati was the second Major City effort of the Police Foundation. Cincinnati had a reputation both of high integrity and for being one of the more progressive police departments in the United States during the 1950's and 1960's. It also was quite militaristic; for example, officers saluted their superiors. Stanley Schrotel was considered one of the country's premier reform chiefs during his tenure in the 1960's and early 1970's. Like many departments at the time, the Cincinnati Police Department (CPD) was enjoying a period of expanding resources.

The major goal of the project was to increase the sensitivity and responsiveness of police to the communities they served. This was to be accomplished largely through the decentralization of police services. This effort, called team policing, encouraged officers to identify special needs of the community and to devise police responses to those needs. This gave sergeants and officers responsibility for determining the content and method of their work. Patrol officers were to work interactively among themselves and with their supervisors to formulate policing tactics for their neighborhoods.

The experimental phase of the effort was mounted by a task force in selected areas of the city. The planning phase for the experiment lasted for 2 years. The implementation of the experiment proceeded smoothly. The officers involved adopted the program enthusiastically, and top management provided the necessary organizational support. Over time, however, upper and mid-management began to intrude on team responsibility. Allocation of personnel to teams had to be made by mid-management. Authority for team leaders to assign officers to dress in plain clothes for surveillance or investigative work was withdrawn in the name of uniform dress standards. Management also adopted a program of management by objectives (MBO). This effort:

> ... became a means through which headquarters imposed standardized demands for increasingly rigid levels of measurable activity. [Team policing] officers found their MBO plans were continually returned until they included all CPD priorities.

Perhaps inadvertently, MBO helped to destroy the autonomy of team policing and to recentralize control of the police.[16]

Despite these difficulties, team policing was found to be more effective than traditional policing in a variety of dimensions: crime reduction, clearances, fear reduction, and citizen satisfaction. CPD was sufficiently satisfied with the results of the experiment to expand team policing department wide in 1975. The Police Foundation extended its evaluation to monitor the expansion. Convinced that CPD had learned to conduct team policing, management bypassed the careful planning that characterized the experimental phase–all that was necessary was to direct the other districts to operate as the experimental district had been operating.

By the end of 1975, the evaluation team concluded that while some of the form of team policing still existed, little of substance remained. The evaluators believed that the effort had suffered lack of support from both top and mid-management, the latter due in part to the fact that middle-level managers had never been fully drawn into the program, and they tended to view it as a threat to their traditional authority.

Kansas City. Chief Clarence Kelley, later to become director of the FBI, had wanted Kansas City to receive one of the Police Foundation's Major City grants. Somewhat jaded by the Dallas experience, the foundation's board of directors was backing away from the Major City concept. Kansas City was turned down as a Major City, but the Foundation offered assistance in the development of specific projects.

The hub of Kansas City's approach to projects was the 300 new officers that had been authorized and funded by government. Kelley wanted to allocate them in ways that maximized their impact on crime. The top command staff was convened with several consultants invited by both the Kansas City Police Department (KCPD) and the foundation to determine how to use the personnel. Two ideas surfaced: use the new officers as backup in the current allocation scheme to achieve shorter response times and add the new officer group to the total officer pool and reduce beat size.

Kelley was dissatisfied with these ideas. With advice from the lead consultant, Robert Wasserman, he decided to create task forces in each of the three districts and the special operations unit. These task forces, made up of all ranks in the units, were to determine what special problems existed in their domain and devise tactics to deal with those problems. The Police Foundation would fund the evaluations. The special operations unit, for example, decided it wanted to experiment with forms of interception patrol: location-oriented patrol (LOP) and perpetrator-oriented patrol (POP). The unit devised its plans, received approval for operations from the KCPD command staff and for evaluation funds from the Police Foundation, implemented its efforts in a quasi-experimental design, maintained the project for the required time, terminated the project, and then returned to business as usual. The Central and Northeast Districts went through similar processes.

The South Patrol District responded to the chief's mandate somewhat more literally than the other districts. Carefully analyzing its own problems, it determined that the most serious problem in the district was juvenile behavior around the schools. Two points of view developed. The first was that preventive patrol and rapid response to calls for service were so important that the new officers had to be used to patrol and respond to calls, regardless of the seriousness of the juvenile problem. The other was that officers should be sequestered to deal specifically with the identified problem.

A debate emerged about the value of preventive patrol. Influenced by Wasserman, and later by one of the authors of this paper (Kelling), the South Patrol Task Force decided to address the issue of the value of preventive patrol by conducting an experiment in preventive patrol before moving on to the problem of juveniles around the schools. Like the other KCPD units, the South Patrol District devised its plans, received approval for operations from the KCPD command staff and for evaluation funds from the Police Foundation, implemented its efforts in an experimental design, maintained the project for the required time, terminated the project, and then returned to business as usual.

What do we learn from these three cases? In Dallas, Frank Dyson had a vision of a new police strategy. Mid-management was perceived as the enemy in repositioning the department. While this need not have been a self-fulfilling prophecy, no credible internal champions developed inside the department to defend the efforts or to provide alternate interpretations of the motives or goals of the innovators. The effort was dead before it got started.

In Cincinnati, team policing was misinterpreted as a tactical innovation rather than as a strategic repositioning. Some middle-management resistance was noted during the maintenance phase of the experiment; it was not sufficient, however, to derail the effort. Despite these early warnings, no special efforts were made to capture, orient, or train mid-management before department wide implementation of team policing. Team policing waned and died.

In Kansas City, a series of projects was planned and implemented to improve the functioning of the department. Middle managers were involved in planning all of the experiments and, with some problems, successfully implemented, maintained, and terminated the projects. Lest the achievements seem modest, it should be recalled that the projects were hardly simple or easy to administer. The patrol experiment, the first successful experiment conducted in policing, was extremely complicated, and was held in place for a full year.

Simultaneously, the department fielded a quasi-experiment in special operations, a peer review project to control use of force, and several other projects. These projects were developed and maintained through working collaborations between mid-managers (most often district commanders), their key aides, working task forces, outside consultants, and representatives of the KCPD planning unit. Moreover, although it did hire some Police Foundation consulting and evaluation staff, the department went on, independent of the foundation, to conduct with funds from the National Institute of Justice the first major research into rapid response to calls for service.

Stepping back somewhat, this capacity for project implementation in Kansas City ought not to have been surprising. Police departments have extensive experience managing projects. The President of the United States comes to town? The police department sets in motion a massive project to insure his protection, reroute traffic, and manage large masses of citizens, some of whom may be demonstrating, while simultaneously maintaining business as usual. Business robberies increase before Christmas? The police department sets in place a special holiday anti-robbery effort. Drug dealing becomes an aggravated problem in a neighborhood? A drug unit conducts a targeted effort.

In other words, managing special projects is a core competency of the current police strategy. And whether the competency is at the service of traditional police issues, such as controlling drug dealing in a neighborhood, or at the service of creative experimentation, mid-management has shown remarkable ability to implement and manage projects.

These experiences suggest that attempts to strategically reposition an organization without bringing mid-management along, in fact defining mid-management as the enemy as was done in Dallas, is done at great risk. No champions develop. It follows that CEO's alone do not reposition an organization. Even when involved, mid-management has the potential to mildly subvert a project, as occurred in Cincinnati.

This does not mean, however, that mid-management is inherently anti-innovation. As the experience in Kansas City suggests, when innovative projects are conducted that are congruent with the then-current strategy of the organization, and when mid-managers are brought into the planning and implementation efforts, they can perform successfully, if motivated to do so. Indeed, mid-managers demonstrate considerable creativity and resourcefulness in *project* or *tactical* innovations. The critical issue is whether mid-management can play an equally positive role in *strategic* innovation.

COMMUNITY POLICING, MID-MANAGEMENT, AND THE ADMINISTRATIVE PROBLEM

Repositioning through problem solving: Baltimore County. Captain Fred Kestler was responsible for taking the Baltimore County Police Department's successful experimentation with problem solving and implementing it departmentwide. BCPD's successful experimentation is detailed elsewhere,[17] but under the leadership of Chief Neil Behan, the county police pioneered in problem—solving methodology.

Chief Behan has summarized his management philosophy: "My management style is to direct people toward an idea and let them develop the how-to. One, they can do it better than I can do it, and two, then they have ownership. The ownership's got to happen, and if they're just following orders it's not going to happen, or only with great difficulty."[18]

Under this philosophy, Chief Behan used the resources created by 45 new positions to create three special 15-person COPE units (Citizen-Oriented Police Enforcement), one for each of the department's three districts. Headed by lieutenants and freed from many administrative and operational restrictions—they could establish their own schedules and did not have to respond to calls for service—their task was to fight fear. The units' early results were mixed: a few success stories, a lot of time spent surveying, and a nettlesome tendency to return to traditional tactics.

With encouragement from Gary Hayes, then director of the Police Executive Research Forum, and Herman Goldstein, a professor at the University of Wisconsin Law School, COPE adopted, with Chief Behan's blessing, a problem-solving methodology. The units produced a respectable number of successful interventions to reduce fear and crime in neighborhoods, although with some unsuccessful experiences. Generally, however, the efforts were well thought of in both the department and the community.

One of the major problems was the deteriorating relationship with regular patrol units. From the patrol units' point of view, the COPE units had all the "perks" without being responsible for the press of constant calls for service. For Chief Behan, already nervous about the idea of special units, the answer was to adopt the COPE methodology departmentwide. Captain Fred Kestler, formerly one of the lieutenants in charge of a COPE unit, was given the responsibility of implementing "precinct problem solving" throughout patrol in one of Baltimore County's three districts. The experiences there would frame the implementation of the COPE methodology throughout the county. These efforts are now underway.

Repositioning through experimental decentralization: Madison and Houston. W. Edward Deming's approach to attaining quality in the production of goods and services is central to Chief David Couper's approach to repositioning the strategy of the Madison Police Department.[19] Chief Couper depends on quality leadership, organizational decentralization, creation of a work environment that encourages creativity and that ensures high levels of job satisfaction, a "customer" orientation, developing close linkages to neighborhoods and communities, and use of problem solving as defined by Herman Goldstein.[20]

After a multirank task force planned details of quality policing, the Experimental Police District (EPD) was created under command of Captain Ted Balistrieri and Lieutenant Mike Masterson. Each allowed himself to be nominated for his position and was then selected by the officers who volunteered to work in EPD.

The chief provided the guiding vision of EPD. The planning task force initially shaped the policies and practices of EPD; however, within those loose guidelines, EPD was free to innovate. The innovations were wide-ranging and included the extensive use of problem solving; encouragement of more collegial relations between officers and ranks; modified rollcalls (rollcalls became district conferences about problems and tactics); and modified reporting procedures (while the rest of the department retained the former procedures).

While EPD experimented with quality policing, the rest of the organization performed, for the most part, as usual. At times, business as usual conflicted with quality policing. Non-EPD police saw EPD as draining resources away from the total organization and providing special privileges to organizational favorites. Some non-EPD lieutenants were bothered by what they perceived as inconsistency in handling calls for service, complaints, disciplinary procedures, and other procedural matters. Opponents of decentralization, especially lieutenants, rallied around these complaints. The strongest opposition to the EPD came from detectives, who claimed that investigations done by decentralized investigators were simply not up to the caliber of those conducted by centralized detectives.

Nonetheless, EPD is now institutionalized. Although plans for additional police stations have been curbed because of Madison's financial circumstances, plans for administrative and operational decentralization of the rest of the department are now proceeding.

In Houston, former Chief Lee Brown had been a strong advocate of what he termed the "philosophy" of community policing. Building on formal experiments in fear reduction and the planning activities of multirank "executive sessions" (meetings oriented around substantive and administrative issues associated with community policing), Houston's approach was similar to Madison's: innovate in one district, learn from successes and failures, and then go citywide. Operationalization of community policing in Houston's target area, Westside, was left to mid-managers.

Then-Deputy Chief Elizabeth Watson and Captain William Young were the second management team to head Westside. The first team either could not or would not move the district in the directions Chief Brown wanted. Watson and Young inherited what they believed to be a highly resistant group of sergeants and lieutenants who would not come on board with the plans-the major obstacle to innovation. Closer analysis by Watson and Young revealed that most sergeants and lieutenants simply did not know what was expected of them. They knew what had been expected in their old roles, but had little idea of their new roles and responsibilities. The field operations commander, Tom Koby (now chief in Boulder, Colorado), designed a cascading training program. Each rank would be charged with defining the responsibilities of, and a training program for, the rank immediately below its own. Captains would define the role of lieutenants and prepare training for them; in turn, lieutenants would do the same for sergeants. Note that defining the problem and devising solutions were not pushed up to higher level command or aside to staff units, but rather were pushed *down* to the ranks involved for identification and solution.

The Westside district continued to implement the community policing philosophy. Elizabeth Watson was promoted to Houston's chief of police when Lee Brown became commissioner of the New York City Police Department. Captain Young was reassigned to the second district to be decentralized under the long-range plan. Political and financial uncertainties threatened the move to community policing in Houston, however. When a new mayor was elected in 1992, Chief Watson was replaced by Sam Nuchia. Watson then became chief of police in Austin, Texas.

Repositioning in response to crisis: Reno, Nevada, and the New York City Transit Police Department. Frustrated with the performance of the Reno Police Department (RPD), citizens of the Nevada city twice rejected attempts to override a statewide tax cap. From the point of view of the RPD, the situation was acute: by 1987, the police department had shrunk from 305 to 225 officers, while the city's population had increased from 103,000 to 123,000. Calls were up substantially. Surveys indicated that citizens believed the police were efficient, nonetheless held them in relatively low esteem.

Believing that repositioning the department to community policing was essential if RPD was to thrive, Chief Robert Bradshaw planned and implemented citywide Community-Oriented Policing Plus (COP+), a community/problem-oriented approach to policing. While involving many levels of personnel in planning for the effort and providing extensive training, the most dramatic change was organizational. From its previous functional organization, Chief Bradshaw reorganized the department geographically, dividing the city into three areas, each with three subdivisions. After a week's retreat, during which broad discussions were held about the nature of community policing and the plans for organizational change, these captains were given complete responsibility for their areas, including the option of calling in a tactical unit if required, and reported directly to Chief Bradshaw rather than through a chain of command.

To ensure that activities were coordinated among the three areas and that RPD did not Balkanize into three departments, the chief, the three area captains, and the remaining command staff had daily meetings. Each captain would present major problems in his or her area to the group, and the group would consult about possible solutions in light of the department's new strategy.

The three area captains, although they worked much harder than they had previously, became champions of the changes. Not only did surveys indicate that Reno's citizens noted positive changes in RPD, the voters also overrode the State's tax restraints to increase their financial support of RPD. Although Chief Bradshaw resigned in 1991, the department continues to operate out of this new strategy and structure.

In New York, the Transit Police Department (TPD) polices the city's subway system. When TPD required a new chief in April of 1990, the department was moribund. The reasons for this are complicated. Primarily, however, the condition sprang from political indecision about whether TPD should be merged with the New York City Police Department (NYPD). This debate had gone on for years without resolution.

The consequence of the indecision was a department in limbo, without champions. Radios were inadequate. Officers in the subways, even when patrolling alone, were regularly out of radio contact. Vehicles were decrepit and available in insufficient numbers to respond to emergencies or to back up officers who worked alone. The physical facilities, district stations, were woefully inadequate—an insult to officers. Morale was low. The department had lost its pride, lack of which showed in the demeanor and dress of officers. Sector team policing, a major attempt to decentralize authority that was modeled on team policing, lagged and, with a few exceptions, existed in name only.

These were the chronic problems of TPD. In 1989, however, the department had entered a crisis. Surveys of citizens and subway users pointed to an acute problem for citizens and subway users: ridership was dropping as a consequence of passenger fear of disorderly behavior associated with both farebeating and use by the homeless of the subway stations as surrogate shelters. Estimates of revenues lost from farebeating ranged from $60 million to $120 million a year.

Despite these problems, police remained fixed on robbery as their priority: officers preferred it, the union insisted on it, and management oriented its tactics around it. To be sure, special units were assigned to deal with the disorder created by the homeless and farebeating, and at times these special units were quite large. Nonetheless, the basic strategy of TPD remained oriented around robbery.

In some respects, this was not hard to understand: leaders and staff of TPD longed to be "crime fighters" like their aboveground colleagues (or at least to the extent they believed their NYPD colleagues were). For transit police, concentrating on farebeating and disorderly behavior was demeaning. Nonetheless, the leadership of the Metropolitan Transit Authority (MTA) and the New York City Transit Authority (NYCTA) persisted. When TPD's chief retired, they sought a chief who would refocus TPD strategy.

After his appointment in April 1990, William Bratton (coauthor of this paper) initiated a series of changes. Cognizant of the need to refocus the department, his first concern nevertheless was to redress the consequences of years of neglect. The fleet of cars was replaced and additional cars added. New personal radios were purchased as a "quick fix" to the communications problem, and financial support was sought, with the full support of MTA and NYCTA, to install a state-of-the-art radio communications capacity. Uniforms were redesigned with the special needs of transit police in mind, and the changeover was initiated. A long-range plan was developed to revamp or reconstruct district stations. Departmental values were reviewed and revised with input from all levels of the department. Use-of-force policies were reviewed and strengthened. Certification was accomplished in 1991.

As part of this process, the department set out a plan of action to establish long-range goals. The main goal was to "take back the subway" for passengers by reducing disorder, farebeating, and robbery. Strengthened district command was supported by problem-solving teams composed of personnel from all levels. District captains were charged with identifying the most critical problems in their districts and adopting tactics that both targeted those problems and enriched the work of line patrol officers.

Within this general definition of the business of TPD, and within its values, district commanders were free to innovate. In District 4, Captain Francis M. O'Hare instituted 4—ACES (the Anti-Crime Enforcement Squad). With officers rotating through this district unit, 4—ACES concentrates on apprehending serious offenders by enforcing laws against fare beaters.[21] Captain Mike Ansbro, in District 30, developed "Operation Glazier" to fix "broken windows." As one method of increasing the sense of police presence in the subway in this district, trains stop briefly in stations, the sound system announces that officers are checking the trains, and they do. In District 34, Captain Gerald Donovan introduced the TCOP (Transit Community-Oriented Policing) program (a takeoff on the NYPD's CPOP—Community Patrol Officer Program), which encourages officers to familiarize themselves with the employees, passengers, and ordinary problems found within the officers' "own" areas. Officers are expected to identify problems and propose solutions.

Direct communication channels between district captains and the chief help ensure that departmental priorities are maintained in each district. Promotions above the rank of captain are now linked to performance as a district commander rather than to a staff assignment. All indicators of police activity, save one—felony arrests-are up by substantial amounts. Robberies have declined every month since the new strategy began.

Not only can mid-managers (as earlier shown) demonstrate considerable creativity and resourcefulness in *project* or *tactical* innovations, these experiences in Madison, Houston, Baltimore County, Reno, and the New York City Transit Police Department suggest that mid-managers also are at the heart of *strategic* innovations.

CONCLUSION:
THE ADMINISTRATIVE SOLUTION

This paper began by examining the role of mid-management, especially captains and lieutenants, in policing during the past 50 years. Largely that role has been to extend the reach of management into the day-to-day operations of police departments by standardizing and controlling both organizational procedures and officer performance. As such, captains and lieutenants have been the leading edge of the control functions of police departments. They, especially lieutenants, are the guarantors of quality-the buck stops with them. They sign off on shift reports.

Discussion of the role of middle management in strategic innovation of police departments, at least at a casual level, has tended to focus on its resistance to change. We have seen, however, that whether one considers project or strategic innovation, abundant examples of mid-management creativity exist. Abundant examples of mid-management resistance to change exist as well, whether one thinks of the Police Foundation efforts of the 1970's or of current examples.

Perhaps such resistance to change should not be surprising if we recall that in the past, one of the basic functions of captains and lieutenants—their raison d'être—has been to forestall creativity and innovation.

Consider the situation of lieutenants. They are responsible for the activities of patrol officers during a shift. Departmental procedures are in place for responding to calls for service, filing forms, receiving complaints. In the name of new models of policing (formerly called team policing, now called community or problem-oriented policing), officers respond differently to calls, modify reporting procedures, alter practices, and establish new priorities. Officers are encouraged to innovate, to be risk-takers, to be creative.

Yet, lieutenants still perceive themselves as accountable to captains for the maintenance of patrol priorities; to detectives and ultimately to the prosecuting attorney for offense reports; and to communications for the proper response of officers to calls for service. Lieutenants, in the past, were on the leading edge of

a prime mid-management responsibility: maintaining control and ensuring that operations functioned according to the book. Now lieutenants, attempting to maintain the standards that have been their reason for being, find themselves cast as the *lagging edge:* a major source of resistance to innovation. Such a characterization of mid-managers in policing is not surprising, given their basic function.

This conflict is not of their own making; mid-managers are victims more than culprits in a process that catches them between conflicting role demands (control your officers so that all former expectations can be met *versus* encourage your officers to be creative and self-initiating). Focusing on mid-managers as a source of resistance may be exactly the wrong approach.

As Drucker points out:

> [T]o focus on resistance to change is to misdefine the problem in a way that makes it less, rather than more, tractable. The right way to define the problem so as to make it capable of resolution is as a challenge to create, build, and maintain the innovative organization, the organization for which change is norm rather than exception, and opportunity rather than threat.[22]

This conceptualization appropriately shifts the focus from the resistance of mid-managers to the responsibilities of top management—CEO's, chiefs. The question becomes: how should top management behave to ensure that those in the organization who have been the organization's champions for standardization and control—captains and lieutenants–become its leading edge for creativity and innovation? We believe some principles emerge from police experience in innovation to date.

First, the experiences in Kansas City, Cincinnati, Madison, Reno, and Houston suggest that when mid-managers are involved in the process of planning innovations, they are capable of providing instrumental leadership regardless of whether the innovations are programmatic or strategic. Alternatively, whenever mid-managers are kept out of planning or perceived as a source of resistance, they *are* a potentially strong source of resistance. Mid-managers must be included in the planning process.

Second, chiefs have to acknowledge that mid-managers have legitimate vested self-interests that must be served if commitment to change is to be secured. Middle managers have legitimate professional goals. When innovations threaten mid-managers' achievement records and performance indicators, it should be expected that they will be less than enthusiastic about change. If goals have been predicated on successful control, they must be replaced with goals predicated on creativity. Experiences in all the examples noted above make this abundantly clear. It is the function of the CEO to shape the new goals and to tie professional rewards to them.

Third, when CEO's (chiefs) create a strong vision of the business of the organization, mid-managers (captains and lieutenants) are prepared to pick up the mantle and provide leadership in innovation. The experiences in Madison, Baltimore County, Houston, Reno, and the Transit Police attest to mid-management leadership when a relatively clear mandate is given by the chief, preparatory experiments or efforts are conducted, clear authority to implement is granted, and rewards are linked to performance. All the cases above provide examples of the innovativeness of mid-managers when values and strategy are articulated clearly and when mid-managers are given the space and freedom to innovate within their context. Rosabeth Moss Kanter's work gives similar examples from the private sector.[23]

Fourth, mid-managers must believe that they can succeed.[24] The vision or new direction of the CEO must be clearly articulated, bolstered unwaveringly, tied to organizational "winners," and supported through resource allocation, administrative action, and emergent policies and procedures. Early milestones of success must be clearly identified, and management must provide feedback about successes and failures.

Fifth, organizations must develop tolerance for failure. This is difficult in the public sector, in which rewards for success are rare but penalties for failure are potentially severe.[25] Nevertheless, if managers

are to be risk-takers, they must be buoyed by their sense of mission and their commitment to improve service Respect and rewards should be given for acknowledging failure and backtracking; covering up or perpetuating failures must be perceived as a serious breach of responsibility. Finishes, whether efforts are successful or not, must be as valued as starts.

Finally, given the importance of attempting to develop a system in which innovation and renewal are to be valued, mid-managers will need to add skills not necessarily in their current repertoire, dominated as police organizations have been by the need to control. We will mention just two here.

First, managers must develop team-building skills. Building coalitions, managing task forces, establishing linkages between departments and other units of the organization, and building relationships with consumers of police services will require extraordinary team-building skills. Such skills must be basic in mid-managers.

Second, mid-managers must be real managers, not overseers. The focus of overseers is control. Overseers know best and their purpose is to ensure that their instructions are followed. Managers view their responsibilities differently. Their task is, or ought to be, to develop personnel who will be free to innovate and adapt-break the rules if necessary on behalf of the values of the organization. Thus, the core competency of managers is to make long-term investments in people, their staff. They teach and create an organizational climate in which persons can experiment; but primarily they present themselves as models for persons in their charge. That is, they coach, lead, protect, inspire, understand mistakes, and tolerate failure.

The idea that mid-managers are spoilers, that they thwart project or strategic innovation, has some basis in fact. Mid-managers improperly directed can significantly impede innovation. Yet, ample evidence exists that when a clear vision of the business of the organization-its purpose or objective-is put forward, when mid-managers are included in planning, when their legitimate self-interests are acknowledged, and when they are properly trained, mid-managers can be the leading edge of innovation and creativity.

NOTES

1. Lawrence W. Sherman, *Team Policing: Seven Case Studies,* Washington, D.C., Police Foundation, 1973: 107.

2. Peter Drucker, *The Frontiers of Management,* New York, Truman Talley Books, 1986: 200.

3. Rosabeth Moss Kanter, "The middle manager as innovator," *Harvard Business Review,* July–August 1982: 95–105.

4. For a detailed discussion of these issues, see George L. Kelling and Mark H. Moore, "The evolving strategy of policing," *Perspectives on Policing* 4, Washington, D.C., National Institute of Justice and Harvard University, November 1988.

5. See, for example, George L. Kelling and James K. Stewart, "The evolution of contemporary policing," in *Local Government Police Management,* ed. William A. Geller, Washington, D.C., International City Management Association, 1991: 5–6.

6. Herman Goldstein. "Toward community-oriented policing: Potential, basic requirements, and threshold questions," *Crime & Delinquency* 33: 1 (January 1987): 21.

7. This categorization is based on Raymond E. Miles and Charles C. Snow, *Organizational Strategy, Structure, and Process,* New York, McGraw-Hill, 1978.

8. The National Commission on Law Observance and Enforcement, established by President Hoover in 1929, was usually called "the Wickersham Commission" after its chairman, former Attorney General George W. Wickersham.

9. See Kelling and Stewart, note 5 above, at p. 8 for a discussion of reformers' use of these techniques.

10. Robert M. Fogelson, *Big-City Police,* Cambridge, Harvard University Press, 1977.

11. Herman Goldstein, *Policing a Free Society,* Cambridge, Massachusetts, Ballinger, 1977: 134–1 36.

12. Shoshana Zuboff, *In the Age of the Smart Machine: The Future of Work and Power,* New York, Basic Books, 1988: 108.

13. Zuboff, n. 12, p. 69.

14. Malcolm K. Sparrow, Mark H. Moore, and David M. Kennedy, *Beyond 911: A New Era for Policing,* New York, Basic Books, 1990: 120.

15. Egon Bittner, "Introduction," *Aspects of Police Work,* Boston, Northeastern University Press, 1990: 6.

16. Alfred I. Schwartz and Sumner M. Claren, *The Cincinnati Team Policing Experiment: A Summary Report,* Washington, D.C., Police Foundation, 1977: 46.

17. "Fighting fear in Baltimore County," Case No. C16-90–938.0, Case Program, John F. Kennedy School of Government, Harvard University, Cambridge, 1990.

18. "Fighting fear, …"n. 17, p. 3.

19. W. Edwards Deming, *Out of the Crisis,* Cambridge, MIT Press, 1986.

20. David C. Couper and Sabine H. Lobitz, *Quality Policing: The Madison Experience,* Washington, D.C., Police Executive Research Forum, 199 1.

21. Captain O'Hare, in a delicious parody of MTA advertisements that focused on Chief Bratton and his videotaped "Chief's Messages," created his own videos.

22. Peter Drucker, *Management: Tasks, Responsibilities, Practices,* New York, Harper & Row, 1974: 797.

23. Kanter, "Middle manager, …"n. 3 above.

24. William D. Guth and Ian C. MacMillan, "Strategy implementation versus middle management self-interest," *Strategic Management Journal* 7 (1986): 3 13–327.

25. Alan Altshuler and Marc Zegans, "Innovation and creativity: Comparisons between public management and private enterprise," *Cities,* February 1990: 16–24.

The Police and Neighborhood Safety

Broken Windows

By James Q. Wilson

James Q. Wilson is Shattuck Professor of Government at Harvard and author of Thinking About Crime. *George L. Kelling, formerly director of the evaluation field staff of the Police foundation, is currently a research fellow at the John F Kennedy School of Government, Harvard.*

In the mid-1970s, the state of New Jersey announced a "Safe and Clean Neighborhoods Program," designed to improve the quality of community life in twenty-eight cities. As part of that program, the state provided money to help cities take police officers out of their patrol cars and assign them to walking beats. The governor and other state officials were enthusiastic about using foot patrol as a way of cutting crime, but many police chiefs were skeptical. Foot patrol, in their eyes, had been pretty much discredited. It reduced the mobility of the police, who thus had difficulty responding to citizen calls for service, and it weakened headquarters control over patrol Officers.

Many police officers also disliked foot patrol, but for different reasons: it was hard work, it kept them outside on cold, rainy nights, and it reduced their chances for making a "good pinch." In some departments, assigning officers to foot patrol had been used as a form of punishment. And academic experts on policing doubted that foot patrol would have any impact on crime rates; it was, in the opinion of most, little more than a sop to public opinion. But since the state was paying for it, the local authorities were willing to go along.

Five years after the program started, the Police Foundation, in Washington, D. C., published an evaluation of the foot-patrol project. Based on its analysis of a carefully controlled experiment carried out chiefly in Newark, the foundation concluded, to the surprise of hardly anyone, that foot patrol had not reduced crime rates. But residents of the foot-patrolled neighborhoods seemed to feel more secure than persons in other areas, tended to believe that crime had been reduced, and seemed to take fewer steps to protect themselves from crime (staying at home with the doors locked, for example). Moreover, citizens in the foot patrol areas had a more favorable opinion of the police than did those living elsewhere. And officers walking beats had higher morale, greater job satisfaction, and a more favorable attitude toward citizens in their neighborhoods than did officers assigned to patrol cars.

These findings may be taken as evidence that the skeptics were right-foot patrol has no effect on crime; it merely fools the citizens into thinking that they are safer. But in our view, and in the view of the authors of the Police Foundation study (of whom Kelling was one), the citizens of Newark were not fooled at all. They knew what the foot patrol officers were doing, they knew it was different from what motorized officers do, and they knew that having officers walk beats did in fact make their neighborhoods safer.

But how can a neighborhood be "safer" when the crime rate has not gone down—in fact, may have gone up? Finding the answer requires first that we understand what most often frightens people in public places. Many citizens, of course, are primarily frightened by crime, especially crime involving a sudden, violent attack by a stranger. This risk is very real, in Newark as in many large cities. But we tend to overlook or forget another source of fear—the fear of being bothered by disorderly people. Not violent people, nor, necessarily, criminals, but disreputable or obstreperous or unpredictable people: panhandlers, drunks, addicts, rowdy teenagers, prostitutes, loiterers, the mentally disturbed.

What foot-patrol officers did was to elevate, to the extent they could, the level of public order in these neighborhoods. Though the neighborhoods were predominantly black and the foot patrolmen were mostly white, this "order-maintenance" function of the police was performed to the general satisfaction of both parties.

One of us (Kelling) spent many hours walking with Newark foot-patrol officers to see how they defined "order" and what they did to maintain it. One beat was typical: a busy but dilapidated area in the heart of Newark, with many abandoned buildings, marginal shops (several of which prominently displayed knives and straight-edged razors in their windows), one large department store, and, most important, a train station and several major bus stops. Though the area was run-down, its streets were filled with people, because it was a major transportation center. The good order of this area was important not only to those who lived and worked there but also to many others, who had to move through it on their way home, to supermarkets, or to factories,

The people on the street were primarily black; the officer who walked the street was white. The people were made up of "regulars" and "strangers." Regulars included both "decent folk" and some drunks and derelicts who were always there but who "knew their place." Strangers were, well, strangers,

and viewed suspiciously, sometimes apprehensively. The officer—call him Kelly—knew who the regulars were, and they knew him. As he saw his job, he was to keep an eye on strangers, and make certain that the disreputable regulars observed some informal but widely understood rules. Drunks and addicts could sit on the stoops, but could not lie down. People could drink on side streets, but not at the main intersection. Bottles had to be in paper bags. Talking to, bothering, or begging from people waiting at the bus stop was strictly forbidden. If a dispute erupted between a businessman and a customer, the businessman was assumed to be right, especially if the customer was a stranger. If a stranger loitered, Kelly would ask him if he had any means of support and what his business was; if he gave unsatisfactory answers, he was sent on his way. Persons who broke the informal rules, especially those who bothered people waiting at bus stops, were arrested for vagrancy. Noisy teenagers were told to keep quiet.

These rules were defined and enforced in collaboration with the "regulars" on the street. Another neighborhood might have different rules, but these, everybody understood, were the rules for *this* neighborhood. If someone violated them the regulars not only turned to Kelly for help but also ridiculed the violator. Sometimes what Kelly did could be described as "enforcing the law," but just as often it involved taking informal or extralegal steps to help protect what the neighborhood had decided was the appropriate level of public order. Some of the things he did probably would not withstand a legal challenge.

A determined skeptic might acknowledge that a skilled foot-patrol officer can maintain order but still insist that this sort of "order" has little to do with the real sources of community fear—that is, with violent crime. To a degree, that is true. But two things must be borne in mind. First, outside observers should not assume that they know how much of the anxiety now endemic in many big-city neighborhoods stems from a fear of "real" crime and how much from a sense that the street is disorderly, a source of distasteful worrisome encounters. The people of Newark, to judge from their behavior and their remarks to interviewers, apparently assign a high value to public order, and feel relieved and reassured when the police help them maintain that order.

Second, at the community level, disorder and crime are usually inextricably linked, in a kind of developmental sequence. Social psychologists and police officers tend to agree that if a window in a building is broken *and is left unrepaired,* all the rest of the windows will soon be broken. This is as true in nice neighborhoods as in run-down ones. Window-breaking does not necessarily occur on a large scale because some areas are inhabited by determined window-breakers whereas others are populated by window-lovers; rather, one unrepaired broken window is a signal that no one cares, and so breaking more windows costs nothing. (It has always been fun.)

Philip Zimbardo, a Stanford psychologist, reported in 1969 on some experiments testing the broken-window theory. He arranged to have an automobile without license plates parked with its hood up on a street in the Bronx and a comparable automobile on a street in Palo Alto, California. The car in the Bronx was attacked by "vandals" within ten minutes of its "abandonment." The first to arrive were a family—father, mother, and young son—who removed the radiator and battery. Within twenty-four hours, virtually everything of value had been removed. Then random destruction began—windows were smashed, parts torn off, upholstery ripped. Children began to use the car as a playground. Most of the adult "vandals" were well dressed, apparently clean-cut whites. The car in Palo Alto sat untouched for more than a week. Then Zimbardo smashed part of it with a sledgehammer. Soon, passersby were joining in. Within a few hours, the car had been turned upside down and utterly destroyed. Again, the 'vandals" appeared to be primarily respectable whites.

Untended property becomes fair game for people out for fun or plunder, and even for people who ordinarily would not dream of doing such things and who probably consider themselves law-abiding. Because of the nature of community life in the Bronx—its anonymity, the frequency with which cars are abandoned and things are stolen or broken, the past experience of "no one caring"—vandalism begins much more quickly than it does in staid Palo Alto, where people

have come to believe that private possessions are cared for, and that mischievous behavior is costly. But vandalism can occur anywhere once communal barriers—the sense of mutual regard and the obligations of civility—are lowered by actions that seem to signal that "no one cares."

We suggest that "untended" behavior also leads to the breakdown of community controls. A stable neighborhood of families who care for their homes, mind each other's children, and confidently frown on unwanted intruders can change, in a few years or even a few months, to an inhospitable and frightening jungle. A piece of property is abandoned, weeds grow up, a window is smashed. Adults stop scolding rowdy children; the children, emboldened, become more rowdy. Families move out, unattached adults move in. Teenagers gather in front of the corner store. The merchant asks them to move; they refuse. Fights occur. Litter accumulates. People start drinking in front of the grocery; in time, an inebriate slumps to the sidewalk and is allowed to sleep it off. Pedestrians are approached by panhandlers.

At this point it is not inevitable that serious crime will flourish or violent attacks on strangers will occur. But many residents will think that crime, especially violent crime, is on the rise, and they will modify their behavior accordingly. They will use the streets less often, and when on the streets will stay apart from their fellows, moving with averted eyes, silent lips, and hurried steps. "Don't get involved." For some residents, this growing atomization will matter little, because the neighborhood is not their "home" but "the place where they live." Their interests are elsewhere; they are cosmopolitans. But it will matter greatly to other people, whose lives derive meaning and satisfaction from local attachments rather than worldly involvement; for them, the neighborhood will cease to exist except for a few reliable friends whom they arrange to meet.

Such an area is vulnerable to criminal invasion. Though it is not inevitable, it is more likely that here, rather than in places where people are confident they can regulate public behavior by informal controls, drugs will change hands, prostitutes will solicit, and cars will be stripped. That the drunks will be robbed by boys who do it as a lark and the prostitutes' customers will be robbed by men who do it purposefully and perhaps violently. That muggings will occur.

Among those who often find it difficult to move away from this are the elderly. Surveys of citizens suggest that the elderly are much less likely to be the victims of crime than younger persons, and some have inferred from this that the well-known fear of crime voiced by the elderly an exaggeration: perhaps we ought not to design special programs to protect older persons; perhaps we should even try to talk them out of their mistaken fears. This argument misses the point. The prospect of a confrontation with an obstreperous teenager or a drunken panhandler can be as fear-inducing for defenseless persons as the prospect of meeting an actual robber; indeed, to a defenseless person, the two kinds of confrontation are often indistinguishable. Moreover, the lower rate at which the elderly are victimized is a measure of the steps they have already taken—chiefly, staying behind locked doors—to minimize the risks they face. Young men are more frequently attacked than older women, not because they are easier or more lucrative targets but because they are on the streets more.

Nor is the connection between disorderliness and fear made only by the elderly. Susan Estrich, of the Harvard Law School, has recently gathered together a number of surveys on the sources of public fear. One, done in Portland, Oregon, indicated that three fourths of the adults interviewed cross to the other side of a street when they see a gang of teenagers; another survey, in Baltimore, discovered that nearly half would cross the street to avoid even a single strange youth. When an interviewer asked people in a housing project where the most dangerous spot was, they mentioned a place where young persons gathered to drink and play music, despite the fact that not a single crime had occurred there. In Boston public housing projects, the greatest fear was expressed by persons living in the buildings where disorderliness and incivility, not crime, were the greatest. Knowing this helps one understand the significance of such otherwise harmless displays, as subway graffiti. As Nathan Glazer has written, the proliferation of graffiti, even when not obscene, confronts the subway rider with the "inescapable knowledge that the environment he must endure for an hour or more a day is uncontrolled and uncontrollable, and that anyone can invade it to do whatever damage and mischief the mind suggests."

In response to fear, people avoid one another, weakening controls. Sometimes they call the police. Patrol cars arrive, an occasional arrest occurs, but crime continues and disorder is not abated. Citizens complain to the police chief, but he explains that his department is low on personnel and that the courts do not punish petty or first-time offenders. To the residents, the police who arrive in squad cars are either ineffective or uncaring; to the police, the residents are animals who deserve each other. The citizens may soon stop calling the police, because "they can't do anything."

The process we call urban decay has occurred for centuries in every city. But what is happening today is different in at least two important respects. First, in the period before, say, World War II, city dwellers—because of money costs, transportation difficulties, familial and church connections—could rarely move away from neighborhood problems. When movement did occur, it tended to be along public-transit routes. Now mobility has become exceptionally easy for all but the poorest or those who are blocked by racial prejudice. Earlier crime waves had a kind of built-in self-correcting mechanism: the determination of a neighborhood or community to reassert control over its turf. Areas in Chicago, New York, and Boston would experience crime and gang wars, and then normalcy would return, as the families for whom no alternative residences were possible reclaimed their authority over the streets.

Second, the police in this earlier period assisted in that reassertion of authority by acting, sometimes violently, on behalf of the community. Young toughs were roughed up, people were arrested "on suspicion" or for vagrancy, and prostitutes and petty thieves were routed. "Rights" were something enjoyed by decent folk, and perhaps also by the serious professional criminal, who avoided violence and could afford a lawyer.

This pattern of policing was not an aberration or the result of occasional excess. From the earliest days of the nation, the police function was seen primarily as that of a night watchman: to maintain order against the chief threats to order—fire, wild animals, and disreputable behavior. Solving crimes was viewed not as a police responsibility but as a private one. In the March, 1969, Atlantic, one of us (Wilson) wrote a brief account of how the police role had slowly changed from maintaining order to fighting crimes. The change began with the creation of private detectives (often ex-criminals), who worked on a contingency-fee basis for individuals who had suffered losses. In time, the detectives were absorbed into municipal police agencies and paid a regular salary; simultaneously, the responsibility for prosecuting thieves was shifted from the aggrieved private citizen to the professional prosecutor. This process was not complete in most places until the twentieth century.

In the 1960s, when urban riots were a major problem, social scientists began to explore carefully the order-maintenance function of the police, and to suggest ways of improving it—not to make streets safer (its original function) but to reduce the incidence of mass violence. Order-maintenance became, to a degree, coterminous with "community relations." But, as the crime wave that began in the early 1960s continued without abatement throughout the decade and into the 1970s, attention shifted to the role of the police as crime-fighters. Studies of police behavior ceased, by and large, to be accounts of the order-maintenance function and became, instead, efforts to propose and test ways whereby the police could solve more crimes, make more arrests, and gather better evidence. If these things could be done, social scientists assumed, citizens would be less fearful.

A great deal was accomplished during this transition, as both police chiefs and outside experts emphasized the crime-fighting function in their plans, in the allocation of resources, and in deployment of personnel. The police may well have become better crime-fighters as a result. And doubtless they remained aware of their responsibility for order. But the link between order-maintenance and crime-prevention, so obvious to earlier generations, was forgotten.

That link is similar to the process whereby one broken window becomes many. The citizen who fears the ill-smelling drunk, the rowdy teenager, or the importuning beggar is not merely expressing his distaste for unseemly behavior; he is also giving voice to a bit of folk wisdom that happens to be a correct generalization—namely, that serious street crime flourishes in areas in which disorderly behavior goes unchecked. The unchecked panhandler is, in effect, the first broken window. Muggers and robbers, whether opportunistic or professional, believe they reduce their chances of being caught or even identified if they operate on streets where potential victims are already intimidated by prevailing conditions. If the neighborhood cannot keep a bothersome panhandler from annoying passersby, the thief may reason, it is even less likely to call the police to identify a potential mugger or to interfere if the mugging actually takes place.

Some police administrators concede that this process occurs, but argue that motorized-patrol officers can deal with it as effectively as foot-patrol officers. We are not so sure. In theory, an officer in a squad car can observe as much as an officer on foot; in theory, the former can talk to as many people as the latter. But the reality of police-citizen encounters is powerfully altered by the automobile. An officer on foot cannot separate himself from the street people; if he is approached, only his uniform and his personality can help him manage whatever is about to happen. And he can never be certain what that will be—a request for directions, a plea for help, an angry denunciation, a teasing remark, a confused babble, a threatening gesture.

In a car, an officer is more likely to deal with street people by rolling down the window and looking at them. The door and the window exclude the approaching citizen; they are a barrier. Some officers take advantage of this barrier, perhaps unconsciously, by acting differently if in the car than they would on foot. We have seen this countless times. The police car pulls up to a corner where teenagers are gathered. The window is rolled down. The officer stares at the youths. They stare back. The officer says to one, "C'mere." He saunters over, conveying to his friends by his elaborately casual style the idea that he is not intimidated by authority. "What's your name?"

"Chuck." "Chuck who?" "Chuck Jones." "What'ya doing, Chuck?" "Nothin'." "Got a P.O. [parole officer?" "Nah." "Sure?" "Yeah." "Stay out of trouble, Chuckie." Meanwhile, the other boys laugh and exchange comments among themselves, probably at the officers expense. The officer stares harder. He cannot be certain what is being said, nor can he join in and, by displaying his own skill at street banter prove that he cannot be "put down." In the process, the officer has learned almost nothing, and the boys have decided the officer is an alien force who can safely be disregarded even mocked.

Our experience is that most citizens like to talk to a police officer. Such exchanges give them a sense of importance, provide them with the basis for gossip, and allow them to explain to the authorities what is worrying them (whereby they gain a modest but significant sense of having "done something" about the problem). You approach a person on foot more easily, and talk to him more readily than you do a person in a car. Moreover, you can more easily retain some anonymity if you draw an officer aside for a private chat. Suppose you want to pass on a tip about who is stealing handbags, or who offered to sell you a stolen TV. In the inner city, the culprit, in all likelihood, lives nearby. To walk up to a marked patrol car and lean in the window is to convey a visible signal that you are a "fink."

The essence of the police role in maintaining order is to reinforce the informal control mechanisms of the community itself. The police cannot, without committing extraordinary resources, provide a substitute for that informal control. On the other hand, to reinforce those natural forces the police must accommodate them. And therein lies the problem.

Should police activity on the street be shaped in important ways, by the standards of the neighborhood rather than by the rules of the state? Over the past two decades, the shift of police from order-maintenance to law-enforcement has brought them increasingly under the influence of legal restrictions, provoked by media complaints and enforced by court decisions and departmental orders. As a consequence, the order-maintenance functions of the police are now governed by rules developed to control police

relations with suspected criminals. This is, we think, an entirely new development. For centuries, the role of the police as watchmen was judged primarily not in terms of its compliance with appropriate procedures but rather in terms of its attaining a desired objective. The objective was order, an inherently ambiguous term but a condition that people in a given community recognized when they saw it. The means were the same as those the community itself would employ, if its members were sufficiently determined, courageous, and authoritative. Detecting and apprehending criminals, by contrast, was a means to an end, not an end in itself; a judicial determination of guilt or innocence was the hoped-for result of the law-enforcement mode. From the first, the police were expected to follow rules defining that process, though states differed in how stringent the rules should be. The criminal-apprehension process was always understood to involve individual rights, the violation of which was unacceptable because it meant that the violating officer would be acting as a judge and jury—and that was not his job. Guilt or innocence was to be determined by universal standards under special procedures.

Ordinarily, no judge or jury ever sees the persons caught up in a dispute over the appropriate level of neighborhood order. That is true not only because most cases are handled informally on the street but also because no universal standards are available to settle arguments over disorder, and thus a judge may not be any wiser or more effective than a police officer. Until quite recently in many states, and even today in some places, the police make arrests on such charges as "suspicious person" or "vagrancy" or "public drunkenness"—charges with scarcely any legal meaning. These charges exist not because society wants judges to punish vagrants or drunks but because it wants an officer to have the legal tools to remove undesirable persons from a neighborhood when informal efforts to preserve order in the streets have failed.

Once we begin to think of all aspects of police work as involving the application of universal rules under special procedures, we inevitably ask what constitutes an "undesirable person" and why we should "criminalize" vagrancy or drunkenness. A strong and commendable desire to see that people are treated fairly makes us worry about allowing the police to rout persons who are undesirable by some vague or parochial standard. A growing and not-so-commendable utilitarianism leads us to doubt that any behavior that does not "hurt" another person should be made illegal. And thus many of us who watch over the police are reluctant to allow them to perform, in the only way they can, a function that every neighborhood desperately wants them to perform.

This wish to "decriminalize" disreputable behavior that "harms no one"—and thus remove the ultimate sanction the police can employ to maintain neighborhood order—is, we think, a mistake. Arresting a single drunk or a single vagrant who has harmed no identifiable person seems unjust, and in a sense it is. But failing to do anything about a score of drunks or a hundred vagrants may destroy an entire community. A particular rule that seems to make sense in the individual case makes no sense when it is made a universal rule and applied to all cases. It makes no sense because it fails to take into account the connection between one broken window left untended and a thousand broken windows. Of course, agencies other than the police could attend to the problems posed by drunks or the mentally ill, but in most communities—especially where the 'deinstitutionalization" movement has been strong—they do not.

The concern about equity is more serious. We might agree that certain behavior makes one person more undesirable than another, but how do we ensure that age or skin color or national origin or harmless mannerisms will not also become the basis for distinguishing the undesirable from the desirable? How do we ensure, in short, that the police do not become the agents of neighborhood bigotry?

We can offer no wholly satisfactory answer to this important question. We are not confident that there is a satisfactory answer, except to hope that by their selection, training, and supervision, the police will be inculcated with a clear sense of the outer limit of their discretionary authority. That limit, roughly, is this—the police exist to help regulate behavior, not to maintain the racial or ethnic purity of a neighborhood.

Consider the case of the Robert Taylor Homes in Chicago, one of the largest public -housing projects in the country. It is home for nearly 20,000 people, all black, and extends over ninety-two acres along South State Street. It was named after a distinguished black who had been, during the 1940s, chairman of the Chicago Housing Authority. Not long after it opened, in 1962, relations between project residents and the police deteriorated badly. The citizens felt that the police were insensitive or brutal; the police, in turn, complained of unprovoked attacks on them. Some Chicago officers tell of times when they were afraid to enter the Homes. Crime rates soared.

Today, the atmosphere has changed. Police-citizen relations have improved—apparently, both sides learned something from the earlier experience. Recently, a boy stole a purse and ran off. Several young persons who saw the theft voluntarily passed along to the police information on the identity and residence of the thief, and they did this publicly, with friends and neighbors looking on. But problems persist, chief among them the presence of youth gangs that terrorize residents and recruit members in the project. The people expect the police to "do something" about this, and the police are determined to do just that.

But do what? Though the police can obviously make arrests whenever a gang member breaks the law, a gang can form, recruit, and congregate without breaking the law. And only a tiny fraction of gang-related crimes can be solved by an arrest; thus, if an arrest is the only recourse for the police, the residents' fears will go unassuaged. The police will soon feel helpless, and the residents will again believe that the police "do nothing." What the police in fact do is to chase known gang members out of the project. In the words of one officer, "We kick ass." Project residents both know and approve of this. The tacit police-citizen alliance in the project is reinforced by the police view that the cops and the gangs are the two rival sources of power in the area, and that the gangs are not going to win.

None of this is easily reconciled with any conception of due process or fair treatment. Since both residents and gang members are black, race is not a factor. But it could be. Suppose a white project confronted a black gang, or vice versa. We would be apprehensive about the police taking sides. But the substantive problem remains the same: how can the police strengthen the informal social-control mechanisms of natural communities in order to minimize fear in public places? Law enforcement, per se, is no answer. A gang can weaken or destroy a community by standing about in a menacing fashion and speaking rudely to passersby without breaking the law.

We have difficulty thinking about such matters, not simply because the ethical and legal issues are so complex but because we have become accustomed to thinking of the law in essentially individualistic terms. The law defines *my* rights, punishes *his* behavior, and is applied by *that* officer because of *this* harm. We assume, in thinking this way, that what is good for the individual will be good for the community, and what doesn't matter when it happens to one person won't matter if it happens to many. Ordinarily, those are plausible assumptions. But in cases where behavior that is tolerable to one person is intolerable to many others, the reactions of the others—fear, withdrawal, flight—may ultimately make matters worse for everyone, including the individual who first professed his indifference.

It may be their greater sensitivity to communal as opposed to individual needs that helps explain why the residents of small communities are more satisfied with their police than are the residents of similar neighborhoods in big cities. Elinor Ostrom and her co-workers at Indiana University compared the perception of police services in two poor, all-black Illinois towns—Phoenix and East Chicago Heights—with those of three comparable all-black neighborhoods in Chicago. The level of criminal victimization and the quality of police-community relations appeared to be about the same in the towns and the Chicago neighborhoods. But the citizens living in their own villages were much more likely than those living in the Chicago neighborhoods to say that they do not stay at home for fear of crime, to agree that the local police have "the right to take any action necessary" to deal with problems, and to agree that the police "look out for the needs of the average citizen." It is possible that the residents and the police of the small

towns saw themselves as engaged in a collaborative effort to maintain a certain standard of communal life, whereas those of the big city felt themselves to be simply requesting and supplying particular services on an individual basis.

If this is true, how should a wise police chief deploy his meager forces? The first answer is that nobody knows for certain, and the most prudent course of action would be to try further variations on the Newark experiment, to see more precisely what works in what kinds of neighborhoods. The second answer is also a hedge—many aspects of order-maintenance in neighborhoods can probably best be handled in ways that involve the police minimally, if at all. A busy, bustling shopping center and a quiet, well-tended suburb may need almost no visible police presence. In both cases, the ratio of respectable to disreputable people is ordinarily so high as to make informal social control effective.

Even in areas that are in jeopardy from disorderly elements, citizen action without substantial police involvement may be sufficient. Meetings between teenagers who like to hang out on a particular corner and adults who want to use that corner might well lead to an amicable agreement on a set of rules about how many people can be allowed to congregate, where, and when.

Where no understanding is possible—or if possible, not observed—citizen patrols may be a sufficient response. There are two traditions of communal involvement in maintaining order. One, that of the "community watchmen," is as old as the first settlement of the New World. Until well into the nineteenth century, volunteer watchmen, not policemen, patrolled their communities to keep order. They did so, by and large, without taking the law into their own hands—without, that is, punishing persons or using force. Their presence deterred disorder or alerted the community to disorder that could not be deterred. There are hundreds of such efforts today in communities all across the nation. Perhaps the best known is that of the Guardian Angels, a group of unarmed young persons in distinctive berets and T-shirts, who first came to public attention when they began patrolling the New York City subways but who claim now to have chapters in more than thirty American cities. Unfortunately, we have little information about the effect of these groups on crime. It is possible however, that whatever their effect on crime, citizens find their presence reassuring, and that they thus contribute to maintaining a sense of order and civility

The second tradition is that of the "vigilante." Rarely a feature of the settled communities of the East, it was primarily to be found in those frontier towns that grew up in advance of the reach of government. More than 350 vigilante groups are known to have existed; their distinctive feature was that their members did take the law into their own hands, by acting as judge, jury, and often executioner as well as policeman. Today, the vigilante movement is conspicuous by its rarity, despite the great fear expressed by citizens that the older cities are becoming "urban frontiers." But some community-watchmen groups have skirted the line, and others may cross it in the future. An ambiguous case, reported in *The Wall Street Journal,* involved a citizens' patrol in the Silver Lake area of Belleville, New Jersey. A leader told the reporter, "We look for outsiders." If a few teenagers from outside the neighbors hood enter it, "we ask them their business," he said. "If they say they're going down the street to see Mrs. Jones, fine, we let them pass. But then we follow them down the block to make sure they're really going to see Mrs. Jones."

Though citizens can do a great deal, the police are plainly the key to order-maintenance. For one thing, many communities, such as the Robert Taylor Homes, cannot do the job by themselves. For another, no citizen in a neighborhood, even an organized one, is likely to feel the sense of responsibility that wearing a badge confers. Psychologists have done many studies on why people fail to go to the aid of persons being attacked or seeking help, and they have learned that the cause is not "apathy" or "selfishness" but the absence of some plausible grounds for feeling that one must personally accept responsibility. Ironically, avoiding responsibility is easier when a lot of people are standing about. On streets and in public places, where order is so important, many people are likely to be "around," a fact that reduces the chance of any one person acting as the agent of the community. The

police officer's uniform singles him out as a person who must accept responsibility if asked. In addition, officers, more easily than their fellow citizens, can be expected to distinguish between what is necessary to protect the safety of the street and what merely protects its ethnic purity.

But the police forces of America are losing, not gaining, members. Some cities have suffered substantial cuts in the number of officers available for duty. These cuts are not likely to be reversed in the near future. Therefore, each department must assign its existing officers with great care. Some neighborhoods are so demoralized and crime-ridden as to make foot patrol useless; the best the police can do with limited resources is respond to the enormous number of calls for service. Other neighborhoods are so stable and serene as to make foot patrol unnecessary. The key is to identify neighborhoods at the tipping point—where the public order is deteriorating but not unreclaimable, where the streets are used frequently but by apprehensive people, where a window is likely to be broken at any time, and must quickly be fixed if all are not to be shattered.

Most police departments do not have ways of systematically identifying such areas and assigning officers to them. Officers are assigned on the basis of crime rates (meaning that marginally threatened areas are often stripped so that police can investigate crimes in areas where the situation is hopeless) or on the basis of calls for service (despite the fact that most citizens do not call the police when they are merely frightened or annoyed). To allocate patrol wisely, the department must look at the neighborhoods and decide, from first-hand evidence, where an additional officer will make the greatest difference in promoting a sense of safety.

One way to stretch limited police resources is being tried in some public-housing projects. Tenant organizations hire off-duty police officers for patrol work in their buildings. The costs are not high (at least not per resident), the officer likes the additional income, and the residents feel safer. Such arrangements are probably more success than hiring private watchmen, and the Newark experiment helps us understand why. A private security guard may deter crime or misconduct by his presence, and he may go to the aid of persons needing help, but he may well not intervene—that is, control or drive away—someone challenging community standards. Being a sworn office—a "real cop"—seems to give one the confidence, the sense of duty, and the aura of authority necessary to perform this difficult task.

Patrol officers might be encouraged to go to and from duty stations on public transportation and, while on the bus or subway car, enforce rules about smoking, drinking disorderly conduct, and the like. The enforcement need involve nothing more than ejecting the offender (the offense, after all, is not one with which a booking officer or a judge wishes to be bothered). Perhaps the random but relentless maintenance of standards on buses would lead to conditions on buses that approximate the level of civility we now take for granted on airplanes.

But the most important requirement is to think that to maintain order in precarious situations is a vital job. The police know this is one of their functions, and they also believe, correctly, that it cannot be done to the exclusion of criminal investigation and responding to calls. We may have encouraged them to suppose, however, on the basis of our oft-repeated concerns about serious, violent crime, that they will be judged exclusively on their capacity as crime-fighters. To the extent that this is the case, police administrators will continue to concentrate police personnel in the highest-crime areas (though not necessarily in the areas most vulnerable to criminal invasion), emphasize their training in the law and criminal apprehension (and not their training in managing street life), and join too quickly in campaigns to decriminalize "harmless" behavior (though public drunkenness, street prostitution, and pornographic displays can destroy a community more quickly than any team of professional burglars).

Above all, we must return to our long-abandoned view that the police ought to protect communities as well as individuals. Our crime statistics and victimization surveys measure individual losses, but they do not measure communal losses. Just as physicians now recognize the importance of fostering health rather than simply treating illness, so the police—and the rest of us—ought to recognize the importance of maintaining, intact, communities without broken windows.

Intelligence Led Policing

By Marilyn Peterson

INTRODUCTION

A critical lesson taken from the tragedy of September 11, 2001, is that intelligence is everyone's job. A culture of intelligence and collaboration is necessary to protect the United States from crimes of all types. Likewise, for intelligence to be effective, it should support an agency's entire operation. Crime prevention and deterrence must be based on all-source information gathering and analysis.

However, not all agencies have the resources to mount full-scale intelligence operations. The average city police department in the United States had 41 sworn personnel in 2001 and would not be expected to have intelligence analysts on staff. How then can an intelligence model be established that will provide support for all agencies?

The needs of agencies—from the very small to the very large—must be considered if intelligence-led policing is to be established in the United States. This document examines how law enforcement agencies can enhance their intelligence operations for homeland security and traditional enforcement and crime prevention, regardless of how sophisticated their intelligence operations are. It explores the meaning and uses of intelligence, provides examples of intelligence practices, and explores how to establish and maintain an intelligence capability.

INTELLIGENCE ISSUES

Introducing intelligence-led policing into U.S. law enforcement agencies is problematic for several reasons. First, many agencies do not understand what intelligence is or how to manage it. Second, agencies must work to prevent and respond to day-to-day crime at the same time they are working to prevent terrorism. Third, the realities of funding and personnel resources are often obstacles to intelligence-led policing. Although the current intelligence operations of most law enforcement agencies prevent them from becoming active participants in the intelligence infrastructure, this problem is not insurmountable.

What Is Intelligence?

Because of misuse, the word "intelligence" means different things to different people. The most common mistake is to consider "intelligence" as synonymous with "information." Information is not intelligence. Misuse also has led to the phrase "collecting intelligence" instead of "collecting information." Although intelligence may be collected by and shared with intelligence agencies and bureaus, field operations generally collect information (or data).

Despite the many definitions of "intelligence" that have been promulgated over the years, the simplest and clearest of these is "information plus analysis equals intelligence."

The formula above clarifies the distinction between collected information and produced intelligence. It notes that without analysis, there is no intelligence. Intelligence is not what is collected; it is what is produced after collected data is evaluated and analyzed.

If intelligence is analyzed information, what is analysis? Some agencies contend that computer software can perform analysis for them; thus, they invest in technology rather than in trained analysts.

However, analysis requires thoughtful contemplation that results in conclusions and recommendations. Thus, computers may assist with analysis by compiling large amounts of data into an easily accessible format, but this is only collated data; it is not analyzed data or information, and it falls far short of intelligence. For information to be useful, it must be analyzed by a trained intelligence professional. In other words, intelligence tells officials everything they need to know before they knowledgeably choose a course of action. For example, intelligence provides law enforcement executives with facts and alternatives that can inform critical decisions.

Tactical Intelligence Versus Strategic Intelligence

The distinction between tactical and strategic intelligence is often misconstrued. Tactical intelligence contributes directly to the success of specific investigations. Strategic intelligence deals with "big-picture" issues, such as planning and manpower allocation.[3] Tactical intelligence directs immediate action, whereas strategic intelligence evolves over time and explores long-term, large-scope solutions.

Some professionals refer to "evidential intelligence," in which certain pieces of evidence indicate where other evidence may be found.[4] Evidential intelligence can help prove a criminal violation or provide leads for investigators to follow.[5]

The term "operational intelligence" is sometimes used to refer to intelligence that supports long-term investigations into multiple, similar targets. Operational intelligence is concerned primarily with

identifying, targeting, detecting, and intervening in criminal activity[6]

Why Intelligence Is Critical

Intelligence is critical for decision making, planning, strategic targeting, and crime prevention. Law enforcement agencies depend on intelligence operations on all levels; they cannot function effectively without collecting, processing, and using intelligence.

Decisionmaking

Gathering information and deciding what to do with it are common occurrences in law enforcement operations. Law enforcement officers and managers are beset by large quantities of information, yet decisions are often based on information that may be incomplete, inaccurate, or misdirected. The move from information gathering to informed decision-making depends on the intelligence/analytic process, and results in a best estimate of what has happened or will happen.

Questions have been asked about the extent to which substantive analysis was performed prior to September 11 to test hypotheses of attacks by foreign terrorist groups against the United States, and whether domestic agencies were told to assess these threats or to develop a plan of action and present it to decisionmakers. It appears that decisionmakers relied on raw intelligence reports that may have raised concerns but did not guide informed decisions.

Experience shows that intelligence and analysis must be strengthened to meet the threat of terrorism against the United States. Law enforcement personnel have a key role to play in making this happen.

Planning

Intelligence is critical to effective planning and subsequent action. In many law enforcement agencies, planning is performed without an understanding of the crime problems facing the jurisdiction and without sufficient operational input. In these instances, strategic planning bears no resemblance to strategic analysis or strategic intelligence. Instead, it relates only to funding issues and operational constraints. Essentially a budget exercise, this type of planning suffers from a disconnect between the major issues facing a community and the manner in which funds are spent to address those needs.

Law enforcement executives are being encouraged to view policing as a business. The United Kingdom's *National Intelligence Model* notes that:

> *The law enforcement business is about the successful management and reduction of crime and other law enforcement problems. ... The vital central ingredient in successful planning is identification and understanding*
>
> - *an accurate picture of the business,*
> - *what is actually happening on the ground,*
> - *the nature and extent of the problem,*
> - *the trends, and*
> - *where the main threats lie.* [7]

By adhering to these principles, commanders can create responsive enforcement plans that meet the needs of the community. This cannot be done through sheer managerial vision. It must be embedded in critical thinking based on intelligence and analysis.

Strategic Targeting

Strategic targeting and prioritization are other critical roles of intelligence. Law enforcement agencies with tight budgets and personnel reductions or shortages must use their available resources carefully, targeting individuals, locations, and operations that promise the greatest results and the best chances for success. Case or lead overloads can reduce investigators' efficiency unless they know how to identify the most fruitful leads. Intelligence enables officers to work more efficiently.

For example, to help fight terrorism and domestic extremism, the California Department of Justice examines group characteristics, criminal predicates, target analyses, and intervention consequences to determine which groups pose the greatest threat to

the state.[8] By reviewing and comparing this information, the agency can prioritize which groups require the earliest intervention. In addition, response strategies can be selected based on an understanding of the group's activities and an awareness of what resources are available.

Crime Prevention

The final area in which intelligence is critical is crime prevention. Using intelligence from previous crimes in local and other jurisdictions, indicators can be created and shared among law enforcement agencies. Comparing the indicators from local neighborhoods, analysts can anticipate crime trends and agencies can take preventive measures to intervene or mitigate the impact of those crimes.

HOW WE GOT WHERE WE ARE TODAY: AN OVERVIEW OF INTELLIGENCE HISTORY

Law enforcement intelligence is an outgrowth of military and national security intelligence. Military intelligence dates back to ancient times; references to it can be found in Chinese writings (Sun Tzu) and the Bible (Numbers 13). Security intelligence was adapted for use in law enforcement operations after World War II. Today, communications intelligence methods used by the military influence how law enforcement analyzes telephone records, and techniques used to manage human intelligence sources inform the management of confidential informants.

The original blueprint for intelligence work was published by the Law Enforcement Assistance Administration of the U.S. Department of Justice in 1971. In 1973, the National Advisory Commission on Criminal Justice Standards and Goals made a strong statement about intelligence. It called on every law enforcement agency and every state to immediately establish and maintain the capability to gather and evaluate information and to disseminate intelligence in a manner that protects every individual's right to privacy while it curtails organized crime and public disorder.[9]

The standards went on to note that every state should establish a "central gathering, analysis and storage capability, and intelligence dissemination system" in which law enforcement agencies participate by providing information and receiving intelligence from the system. It further stated that every agency with more than 75 personnel should have a full-time intelligence capability.[10]

When first instituted, intelligence units within law enforcement departments were not governed by policies that protected civil liberties and prevented intelligence excesses. During the 1970s, a number of intelligence units ran afoul of good practices, and, as a result, some agencies shut down their intelligence functions voluntarily, by court order, or from political pressure. In 1976, in response to the problem of intelligence abuses, standards were developed that required a criminal predicate for subjects to be entered in criminal intelligence files. During this time, the Law Enforcement Intelligence Unit (LEIU) *File Guidelines* were developed, along with those of the California Department of Justice and the New Jersey State Police.

Between the late 1970s and the turn of the century, major intelligence initiatives were underway. Some of these initiatives, such as the Regional Information Sharing Systems (RISS) centers, did not even use the term "intelligence." The primary basis for intelligence sharing in the 1980s and 1990s was the *Criminal Intelligence System Operating Policies* (28 C.F.R. Part 23), which was written to apply to the RISS centers. By 2004, more than 7,100 agencies or agency branches were members of the nationwide RISS network.

When the RISS centers were being developed in 1980, the International Association of Law Enforcement Intelligence Analysts (IALEIA) was formed. Its annual meetings were held in conjunction with those of the International Association of Chiefs of Police (IACP). The 1990s saw the creation of several federal centers to support intelligence and information sharing. The National Drug Intelligence Center (NDIC) was established in Johnstown, Pennsylvania, and the Financial Crimes Enforcement Network (FinCEN) was formed in northern Virginia.

Both had tactical and strategic intelligence responsibilities. Concurrently, the High Intensity Drug Trafficking Areas (HIDTAs) system was formed as a model of federal, state, and local cooperative efforts and information sharing.

A month after September 11, 2001, the Investigative Operations Committee of IACP recommended to its leadership that an Intelligence Sharing Summit be held in March 2002. The summit was attended by more than 100 intelligence experts representing federal, state, local, and tribal law enforcement from the United States and Europe. Summit attendees examined the General Criminal Intelligence Plan and the United Kingdom's National Intelligence Model (NCIS 2000) as potential blueprints for intelligence-led policing in the United States.

Key recommendations from the IACP summit were as follows:

- Promote intelligence-led policing.
- Provide the critical counterbalance of civil rights.
- Increase opportunities for building trust.
- Remedy analytic and information deficits.
- Address training and technology issues.

The primary outgrowth of the summit was the creation of the Global Intelligence Working Group (GIWG), which comprises approximately 30 intelligence professionals. GIWG met quarterly during 2003 and developed the *National Criminal Intelligence Sharing Plan (NCISP),* which was released and approved by the U.S. Attorney General in October 2003. *NCISP* contained 28 recommendations for major changes in how policing is approached. Where appropriate, those recommendations appear in this document.

Understanding the Intelligence Process

NCISP categorizes the intelligence process according to six steps: planning and direction, collection, processing/collation, analysis, dissemination, and reevaluation (see figure 1).

Planning and Direction

Planning how data will be collected is key to the intelligence process. Effective planning assesses existing data and ensures that additional data collected will fill any gaps in the information already on file. As one federal manager put it, "Don't tell me what I know; tell me what I don't know."

To be effective, intelligence collection must be planned and focused; its methods must be coordinated, and its guidelines must prohibit illegal methods of obtaining information.[11] Inaccurate collection efforts can result in a flawed result, regardless of the analytical skills employed.

Planning and collection are a joint effort that requires a close working relationship between analysts, who understand how to manage, compile, and analyze information, and intelligence officers, who know the best ways to obtain information.

Planning requires an agency to identify the outcomes it wants to achieve from its collection efforts. This identification directs the scope of the officers' and agents' investigations—for example, a straightforward inquiry to identify crime groups operating in a jurisdiction or a more complex inquiry to determine the likelihood that criminal extremists will attack a visiting dignitary.

Collection

Intelligence analysis requires collecting and processing large amounts of information.[12] Data collection is the most labor-intensive aspect of the intelligence process. Traditionally, it has been the most emphasized segment of the process, with law enforcement agencies and prosecutors dedicating significant resources to gathering data. New technology and new or updated laws have supported this emphasis.

Historically, the following have been the most common forms of data collection used in intelligence units:

- Physical surveillance (either in person or by videotape).
- Electronic surveillance (trap and trace or wiretap).
- Confidential informants.
- Undercover operators.
- Newspaper reports (now also Internet sources).
- Public records (e.g., deeds, property tax records).

Today many other overt and covert sources are available. Contact information for some organizations and commercial databases are available in the appendixes.

Processing/Collation

Processing/collation involves sifting through available data to eliminate useless, irrelevant, or incorrect information and to put the data into a logical order. This organization makes it easier to identify relationships among entities and uncover relevant information.[13] Today, collation is performed using sophisticated databases with text-mining capabilities.

Database design is critical for retrieving and comparing data. Many computer software companies offer database products, but most require fine-tuning to tailor them to law enforcement agencies' needs. Smaller agencies often use "off-the-shelf" software to reduce costs. Fortunately, technology now allows different databases to interact through text-mining features.

Processing and collation also involve evaluating the data being entered. Information placed into an intelligence file is evaluated for the validity of the information and the reliability of its source.

Information placed into an intelligence system must meet a standard of relevance—i.e., it must be relevant to criminal activity associated with the informant (28 C.F.R. Part 23.20.a.).

Analysis

Analysis converts information into intelligence. As one authority on the subject notes, "Without the explicit performance of this function [analysis], the intelligence unit is nothing but a file unit."[14]

Analysis is quite simply a process of deriving meaning from data. The analytic process tells what information is present or missing from the facts or evidence. In law enforcement intelligence operations, data are analyzed to provide further leads in investigations, to present hypotheses about who committed a crime or how it was committed, to predict future crime patterns, and to assess threats facing a jurisdiction. Thus, analysis includes synthesizing data, developing inferences or conclusions, and making recommendations for action based on the data and inferences. These inferences constitute the finished intelligence product.

The process, along with investigative experience, also points out what has been done and what operational steps need to be taken. Thus, potential areas for further investigation may be recommended.[15] It is important to remember that the analyst *recommends* but does not direct or decide on policy alternatives to minimize crime problems.[16]

In 2004, a broad range of analytic techniques and methods were available to support law enforcement:

- **Crime analysis:** Crime pattern analysis, geographic analysis, time-series analysis, frequency-distribution analysis, behavioral analysis, and statistical analysis.
- **Investigative (evidential) analysis:** Network analysis; telephone record analysis; event, commodity, and activity-flow analysis; timeline analysis; visual investigative analysis; bank record analysis; net worth analysis; business record analysis; content analysis; postseizure analysis; case analysis; and conversation analysis.
- **Strategic analysis:** Threat assessments, premonitories, vulnerability assessments, risk assessments, estimates, general assessments, warnings, problem profiles, target profiles, and strategic targeting.

Dissemination

Dissemination requires getting intelligence to those who have the need and the right to use it in whatever form is deemed most appropriate. Intelligence reports kept within the intelligence unit fail to fulfill their mission. Those who need the information are most often outside the intelligence unit; therefore, the current dissemination protocol is to share by rule and withhold by exception.

Reevaluation

Reevaluation is the task of examining intelligence products to determine their effectiveness. Part of this assessment comes from the consumers of intelligence; that is, the managers, investigators, and officers to whom the intelligence is directed.

One way to reevaluate intelligence is to include a feedback form with each product that is disseminated. To make sure the comments are valuable, the feedback form should ask specific questions relating to the usefulness of the intelligence.

WHERE WE STAND TODAY

Several current strategies and philosophies in law enforcement have a direct bearing on intelligence-led policing.

Intelligence-Led Policing

The term "intelligence-led policing" originated in Great Britain. The Kent Constabulary developed the concept in response to sharp increases in property-related offenses (e.g., burglary and automobile theft) at a time when police budgets were being cut. Officials believed that a relatively small number of people were responsible for a comparatively large percentage of crimes. They believed that police officers would have the best effect on crime by focusing on the most prevalent offenses occurring in their jurisdiction.[19]

The Kent Policing Model, as it was originally called, de-emphasized responses to service calls by prioritizing calls and referring less serious calls for general nonpolice services to other agencies. Thus, more police time was available to create intelligence units to focus, initially, on property-related offenses in each of the jurisdiction's nine service areas. The result was a 24-percent drop in crime over 3 years.[20]

Intelligence-led policing focuses on key criminal activities. Once crime problems are identified and quantified through intelligence assessments, key criminals can be targeted for investigation and prosecution. Because the groups and individuals targeted in Kent were those responsible for significant criminal activity, the ultimate reduction in crime was considerable. The constabulary noted that "It has given the Kent Constabulary the ability to confront crime in an active, rational fashion and to build continually on each success."[21]

Intelligence-led policing in the United States has benefited from the recent development of "fusion centers," which serve multiagency policing needs. These fusion centers—derived from the watch centers of old—provide information to patrol officers, detectives, management, and other participating personnel and agencies on specific criminals, crime groups, and criminal activities. For example, they may support anti-terrorism and other crime-specific objectives. The centers may search numerous public and private databases to gather and analyze information. They may also generate intelligence products of their own, providing overviews of terrorist or other crime groups, analysis of trends, and other items of information for dissemination to participating agencies.

Since 2003, fusion centers have been established in many states. Currently, there are fusion centers in at least 25 states with more under development or being planned. The Iowa Fusion Center is part of that state's Law Enforcement Terrorism Prevention Program and a product of its State Homeland Security Strategy. The center serves as a clearinghouse for all potentially relevant, domestically generated homeland security data and information, leading to proper interpretation, assessment, and preventive actions.[22] It has several objectives, including providing a center for statewide strategic intelligence, centralized information management systems, regional operations support, and a 24-hour, 7-day-a-week watch center. It also supports multiagency information exchange and assigns an intelligence officer to each region.[23]

Funding for fusion centers is available through federal and state sources. As such, a center's mission can be limited to anti-terrorism, but many times includes all significant crimes, or targets different types of crime, such as identity theft, insurance fraud, money laundering, cigarette smuggling, armed robbery, and document fraud. The "all crimes" approach has recently been endorsed and recommended by many criminal intelligence advisory and policy groups.

Good policing is good terrorism prevention. In other words, professional policing of any kind is instrumental in uncovering intelligence associated with both terrorist activities and conventional crimes. Encouraging this perspective enables local police departments to involve line officers more actively and to reinforce the fact that enforcement, crime prevention, and terrorism prevention are interrelated. This approach helps to balance the current emphasis on anti-terrorism activities with traditional anticrime efforts. Many line officers want to define their role in the fight against terrorism. Intelligence-led policing can help clarify their contributions in this regard.

National Intelligence Model— United Kingdom

The United Kingdom's National Intelligence Model function to be community safety, crime reduction, criminal control, and disorder control.[24] To achieve these results, the model outlines the following objectives:

- Establish a task and coordination process.
- Develop core intelligence products to drive the operation.
- Develop rules for best training practices at all levels of policing.
- Develop systems and protocols to facilitate intelligence.[25]

Regular meetings keep participants focused on the stated goals and sustain the intelligence cycle.

Following are a few examples of how this model concept might function when adapted to U.S. circumstances:

- A county sheriff's office identifies narcotics control as its top priority and develops strategies accordingly. The office targets known offenders and groups, shuts down open-air drug markets and crack houses, and participates in school-based drug awareness programs to help prevent drug use.

- A statewide agency identifies vehicle insurance fraud as a top area for enforcement. The agency targets those involved in staged accidents, identifies communities in which insurance fraud is prevalent, looks for similar methods of operation that may indicate ongoing fraudulent activity, and mounts a public education campaign.

- A police agency in a small city makes safe streets a priority. The agency focuses on directed enforcement in identified hotspots. It also targets career criminals whose apprehension will significantly reduce the number of crimes being committed. Preventive measures include enhanced patrols, improved street lighting, and crime watch programs.[26]

Each of these examples shows how prioritizing a particular criminal activity helps identify appropriate response strategies. Some of these responses are enforcement solutions, while others are environmental, educational, or community-oriented solutions.

Problem-Oriented Policing

Problem-oriented policing (POP) is a policing philosophy developed by Herman Goldstein.[27] As originally conceived, problem-oriented policing views crime control as a study of problems that leads to successful enforcement and corrective strategies. The model contends that "analysis, study, and evaluation are at the core of problem-oriented policing."[28]

POP requires assessing each new problem and developing a tailored response. This approach requires ongoing creativity, not simply finding one good idea and applying it unilaterally.

The SARA (Scanning, Analyzing, Responding, and Assessing) model is sometimes considered to be synonymous with problem-oriented policing, but it is a broader analytic model used in many fields. Nonetheless, the SARA model can be applied to collecting and applying intelligence. Scanning may be viewed as part of the collection process. Analysis and

assessment are part of the intelligence process, and response is the outcome of the intelligence process.

Blending Intelligence and Problem-Oriented Policing

As noted earlier, intelligence operations are compatible with problem-oriented policing. Although the problem-oriented policing and SARA models align with intelligence processes, the intelligence aspects associated with problem-oriented policing often have been ignored.

Both community-oriented policing (COP) and problem-oriented policing have been used for crime analysis, which is statistical and incident-based, rather than strategic intelligence analysis, which looks at large-scope problems or models. Intelligence is a formal process of taking information and turning it into knowledge while ensuring that the information is collected, stored, and disseminated appropriately. Crime analysis data, usually collected for investigative purposes, typically does not meet the same standards as intelligence data—even though inferences may be drawn and recommendations may be made based on crime data. Confusion about the distinction between crime analysis data and intelligence data interferes with proper analysis and data handling in the police environment.

However, intelligence efforts do not always apply the first step in SARA (i.e., "Scan") and may benefit from developing more robust scanning mechanisms. At this point in the process, intelligence meets with standard patrolling and community-oriented policing because scanning occurs on the street. Research suggests that problem-solving analysts should "embrace both SARA and NIM" in the United Kingdom and show how the two merge.[29] Incorporating POP and SARA into intelligence-led policing is an excellent recommendation for U.S. agencies as well.

The U.S. model for intelligence-led policing incorporates the intelligence capabilities of all agencies. Traditionally, municipal agencies have relied on crime analysts, whereas agencies at the regional, state, and federal levels have used intelligence analysts. However, keeping crime analysis and intelligence analysis separate is not necessary. Agencies that can afford only one or two analysts must use professionals who can perform all types of analyses, not just statistical, network, or financial analyses.

Now is the time to eradicate the artificial barriers between local and regional-state-federal analysts. Analysts need to become familiar with a range of sources and techniques, rather than specializing in niche areas such as burglaries, gangs, or organized crime. Although some agencies may assign analysts to particular tasks, agencies will be best served by analysts who can perform all intelligence tasks regarding past, current, and potential crimes. This flexibility is made possible by a model that blends intelligence-led and problem-oriented policing.

This kind of intelligence blending also needs to take place at the beat level. Patrol officers are the eyes and ears of the police effort, and they must be encouraged and trained to look and listen intelligently. Information from field interviews, interactions with business people, and other activities and observations must be captured and forwarded to intelligence staff members who can analyze the data, arrive at appropriate courses of action, and send information back to the beat officers. The common practice of hoarding information or sharing it only with patrol officers should not continue; everyone with a need to know should receive intelligence results. For example, when intelligence officers are made aware of suspicious activities, they can analyze the information and provide officers on the street with pertinent guidance regarding officer safety and crime trends.

Police-Community Partnerships

COP has been an accepted policing strategy in the United States for the past decade. The tenets of COP include the following:

- Community policing partnerships.
- Crime prevention.
- Problem solving.

The fight against terrorism calls for locating and measuring terrorist risks to prevent terrorist actions, and local police have been enlisted in these efforts. How do local police determine potential threats in a given jurisdiction? They must know the community— i.e., its makeup, its ties to other countries or particular belief structures, and its potential for containing extremist or terrorist group members. Police officers are particularly familiar with a community and its norms. For example, while on patrol, officers get to know who among community members associates with whom; they have firsthand knowledge of people's work and leisure habits. Goldstein recognized the need to make greater use of rank-and-file police officers. He believed that rank-and-file officers should be given greater latitude to think and be creative in their daily work and that management should tap their accumulated knowledge and expertise, enabling officers to be more satisfied with their jobs and providing the citizenry with a higher return on their police investment.[32]

Empowering local officers with decision making authority and making them aware of terrorist indicators may be key in preventing a terrorist attack.[33] Community- and problem-oriented policing support local awareness and involvement in solving crime problems. This involvement extends to anti-terrorism efforts. However, in the wake of the September 11 terrorist attacks, some agencies shifted officers from community policing to anti-terrorism efforts,[34] which may be counterproductive in helping to deter a terrorist attack.

Local law enforcement has been brought into the anti-terrorism fight and recognized for the role it plays. Alerts and information are being shared with local police more broadly than ever before. Methods for reporting suspicious activity to federal agencies have been created through regional and state links. Private citizens also have been included in the intelligence matrix through suspicious-activity tip lines, working groups with critical infrastructure managers, and other mechanisms to encourage reporting of unusual behavior that may be related to terrorism or other criminal activities.

These models illustrate that community- and problem-oriented policing are not at odds with policing against terrorism; instead, they are collaborative and complementary approaches.

Levels of Intelligence

For intelligence to work effectively, it must be a function that every department, regardless of size, can use. In general, law enforcement agencies can be categorized according to four levels of intelligence operations. The following categories are examples, not precise descriptors of any one agency's capabilities. Many variations in intelligence capabilities exist, and looking at an agency's size and resource capability is only one way of explaining those differences. For purposes of discussion, however, the following categories are used to identify a plan of action.

Level 1 intelligence is the highest level, the ideal intelligence-led policing scenario wherein agencies produce tactical and strategic intelligence products that benefit their own department as well as other law enforcement agencies. The law enforcement agency at this level employs an intelligence manager, intelligence officers, and professional intelligence analysts. Examples of level 1 intelligence agencies include the High Intensity Drug Trafficking Area (HIDTA) Intelligence Support Centers, the Financial Crimes Enforcement Network, and some state agencies that provide intelligence products, by request, to local law enforcement, such as the California Department of Justice, the Florida Department of Law Enforcement, the Arizona Department of Public Safety, and the Illinois State Police. Probably fewer than 300 agencies in the United States operate at level 1. These agencies may have hundreds or even thousands of sworn personnel.

The National Drug Intelligence Center is another example of a level 1 intelligence operation. NDIC, which has a higher ratio of analysts to sworn personnel than perhaps any U.S. agency, provides both tactical and strategic products in support of other agencies. It produces individual drug threat assessments for each state and a national drug threat assessment. It also uses "flying teams" of analysts who provide exploitation and postseizure analysis of documentation collected during investigations by other agencies. It does not, however, have an investigative mission of its own, as state and federal police agencies do.

Level 2 intelligence includes police agencies that produce tactical and strategic intelligence for internal consumption. In other words, these agencies generally use intelligence to support investigations rather than to direct operations. Such agencies may have a computerized database that is accessible to other departments, but they typically do not assign personnel to provide significant intelligence products to other agencies. These departments may have intelligence units and intelligence officers, analysts, and an intelligence manager. Some examples of level 2 intelligence agencies are state police agencies, large city police departments, and some investigating commissions. Agencies at this level may have hundreds to thousands of sworn personnel. Probably fewer than 500 agencies in the United States operate at this level.

An example of this type of agency might be a state-level law enforcement agency with police and/or prosecutorial powers. Such agencies use intelligence analysis to support investigations into complex crimes such as organized crime, insurance fraud, and environmental crime. From time to time, this type of agency might produce a threat assessment or other strategic product to help guide its efforts. Most of its investigations are conducted independently, although the agency may sometimes join task force operations.

Level 3 intelligence is the most common level of intelligence function in the United States. It includes law enforcement agencies with anywhere from dozens to hundreds of sworn employees. These agencies may be capable of developing intelligence products internally, but they are more likely to rely on products developed by partner agencies, such as RISS centers, HIDTAs, federal intelligence centers, and state agencies. Some level 3 agencies may hire private intelligence analysts for complex cases. These types of departments do not normally employ analysts or intelligence managers, but they may have named one or more sworn individuals as their "intelligence officers" and may have sent them to intelligence and/or analytic training. Thousands of agencies nationwide are in this category. One authority notes that *while smaller agencies may not be able to devote a full-time position to the criminal intelligence function ... [they] need to understand the proactive concept of criminal intelligence and recognize that most law enforcement agencies, regardless of size, are susceptible to organized criminal activity that may extend beyond jurisdictional boundaries. Their personnel should be trained to recognize and report indications of organized crime, gang activity, and criminal extremist and terrorist activity. The information should then be shared with intelligence-trained personnel from neighboring agencies. ...*[35]

The same authority notes that "A viable option for ... a medium-sized agency is to enter into a networking or mutual aid criminal intelligence agreement ... with any number of surrounding law enforcement jurisdictions."[36]

Level 4 intelligence is the category that comprises most agencies in the United States. These agencies, often with a few dozen employees or less, do not employ intelligence personnel. If they assign someone to intelligence operations, that person generally has officer, gang officer, or counter-terrorism officer members; most are involved in a limited information-sharing network made up of county or regional databases. Some departments have received intelligence awareness training and may be able to interpret analytic products. Agencies that currently have no knowledge of or use for intelligence analysis should strive to achieve this basic intelligence capability. Such agencies can enhance their knowledge through online and other free training services. When properly trained, these agencies will be able to use any intelligence materials provided to them and to apply basic intelligence techniques to enhance their daily police operations.

A number of agencies may not fit strictly into one of these four categories. Some agencies may fall somewhere between level 3 and level 4, with a centralized database providing data support to numerous agencies but with no direct analytic support. Others may have analysts who support the mission of a specific bureau or section but who have no agency wide responsibility to provide products and direction. The key to intelligence-led policing is that sufficient interest and training should exist to create a culture of knowledge and intelligence in agencies nationwide.

CONCEPT #2: BE AN EFFECTIVE LEADER AND MANAGER

Leadership is not magnetic personality/that can just as well be a glib tongue. It is not making friends and influencing people /that is flattery. Leadership is lifting a person's vision to higher sights, the raising of a person's performance to a higher standard, the building of a personality beyond its normal limitations.

—Peter F. Drucker

In this section you will learn some of the basic ideas about leadership and management. How you behave and act is instrumental to the success or failure of your agency. As an administrator your employees will look to you to lead them through difficult times. They will look to you to ensure that their job needs are met.

What is a leader and what are the traits of a leader? This question has existed for centuries and there may be no absolute answer. However, we do know that there are certain traits that effective leaders possess. This chapter begins with a reading that addresses leadership traits and the relevance and importance of certain traits. As you work through leadership roles you may realize that there are additional traits that leaders possess. Also, you may realize that some traits are more predominant or important than others. Often this is dictated by the environment in which you work and the employees you have working for you.

The second reading in this section, although short, addresses leadership issues too, but now from a law enforcement perspective. This reading offers a practical approach to leadership. In other words, many of the traits previously discussed are now put into action. Continuing on with this concept of leadership and management is an article on supervisory styles. You will see how certain styles influence or elicit police officer behaviors, either in a positive or negative way.

The final reading in this section deals with micromanagement. You have heard the term before but exactly what does it mean and what are the consequences of micromanagement. You will learn that this is a style of management is where the manager becomes too involved in the details of the work of employees. The results of this can hinder the progress of workers and it actually takes away the self-confidence and drive of employees. Managers would be best served if they remember what Theodore Roosevelt once said, "The best executive is the one who has sense enough to pick good men to do what he wants done, and self-restraint to keep from meddling with them while they do it."

Leadership:

Do Traits Matter?

By Shelley Kirkpatrick

EXECUTIVE OVERVIEW

The study of leader traits has a long and controversial history. While research shows that the possession of certain traits alone does not guarantee leadership success, there is evidence that effective leaders are different from other people in certain key respects. Key leader traits include: drive (a broad term which includes achievement, motivation, ambition, energy, tenacity, and initiative): leadership motivation (the desire of lead but not to seek power as an end in itself): honesty and integrity: self-confidence (which is associated with emotional stability): cognitive ability: and knowledge of the business. There is less clear evidence for traits such as charisma, creativity and flexibility. We believe that the key leader traits help the leader acquire necessary skills; formulate an organizational vision and an effective plan for pursuing it: and take the necessary steps to implement the vision in reality.

ARTICLE

Few issues have a more controversial history than leadership traits and characteristics. In the 19th and early 20th centuries, "great man" leadership theories were highly popular. These theories asserted that leadership qualities were inherited, especially by people from the upper class. Great men were born, not made (in those days, virtually all business leaders were men). Today, great man theories are a popular foil for so-called superior models. To make the new models plausible, the "great men" are endowed with negative as well as positive traits. In a recent issue of the *Harvard Business Review,* for example, Slater and Bennis write,

> *"The passing years have … given the coup de grace to another force that has retarded democratization—the 'great man' who with brilliance and farsightedness could preside wth dictatorial powers as the head of a growing organization."¹*

Such great men, argue Slater and Bennis, become "outmoded" and dead hands on "the flexibility and growth of the organization." Under the new democratic model, they argue, "the individual is of relatively little significance."

Early in the 20th century, the great man theories evolved into trait theories. ("Trait"is used broadly here to refer to people's general characteristics, including capacities, motives, or patterns of behavior.) Trait theories did not make assumptions about whether leadership traits were inherited or acquired. They simply asserted that leaders' characteristics are different from non-leaders. Traits such as height, weight, and physique are heavily dependent on heredity,

Shelley Kirkpatrick, "Leadership: Do Traits Matter?" *Academy of Management Executive,* vol. 5, no. 2, pp. 48–60.

whereas others such as knowledge of the industry are dependent on experience and learning.

The trait view was brought into question during the mid-century when a prominent theorist, Ralph Stogdill, after a thorough review of the literature concluded that "A person does not become a leader by virtue of the possession ofsome combination of traits."[2] Stogdill believed this because the research showed that no traits were universally associated with effective leadership and that situational factors were also influential. For example, military leaders do not have traits identical to those of business leaders.

Since Stogdill's early review, trait theory has made a come back, though in altered form. Recent research, using a variety of methods, has made it clear that successful leaders are not like other people. The evidence indicates that there are certain core traits which significantly contribute to business leaders' success.

Traits *alone,* however, are not sufficient for successful business leadership—they are only a precondition. Leaders who possess the requisite traits must take certain *actions* to be successful (e.g. formulating a vision, role modeling, setting goals). Possessing the appropriate traits only makes it more likely that such actions will be taken and be successful. After summarizing the core leadership traits, we will discuss these important actions and the managerial implications.

THE EVIDENCE: TRAITS DO MATTER

The evidence shows that traits do matter. Six traits on which leaders differ from non-leaders include: drive, the desire to lead, honesty/integrity, self-confidence, cognitive ability, and knowledge of the business.[3] These traits are shown in Exhibit 1.

Drive

The first trait is labeled "drive" which is not to be confused with physical need deprivation. We use the term to refer to a constellation of traits and motives reflecting a high effort level. Five aspects of drive include achievement motivation, ambition, energy, tenacity, and initiative.

Achievement. Leaders have a relatively high desire for achievement. The need for achievement is an important motive among effective leaders and even more important among successful entrepreneurs. High achievers obtain satisfaction from successfully completing challenging tasks, attaining standards of excellence, and developing better ways of doing things. To work their way up to the top of the organization, leaders must have a desire to complete challenging assignments and projects. This also allows the leader to gain technical expertise, both through education and work experience, and to initiate and follow through with organizational changes.

The constant striving for improvement is illustrated by the following manager who took charge of a $260 million industrial and office-products division:[4]

After twenty-seven months on the job, Tom saw his efforts pay off: the division had its best first quarter ever. By his thirty-first month, Tom felt he had finally mastered the situation. … [Tom] finally felt he had the structure and management group in place to grow the division's revenues to $400 million and he now turned his attention to divesting a product group which no longer fit in with the growth objectives of the division.

Managers perform a large amount of work at an unrelenting pace. To perform well, a leader needs to constantly work toward success and improvement. Superior managers and executives are concerned with doing something better than they or other shave ever done it. For example, at PepsiCo only "aggressive achievers" survive. Similarly, Thomas Watson of IBM has been described as "driven throughout by a personal determination to create a company larger than NCR."[5] This brings us to a second related motive: ambition.

Ambition. Leaders are very ambitious about their work and careers and have a desire to get ahead. To advance, leaders actively take steps to demonstrate their drive and determination. Ambition impels leaders to set hard, challenging goals for themselves and their organizations. Walt Disney, founder of Walt Disney Productions, had a "dogged determination to succeed" and CE. Woolman of Delta Air Lines had "inexhaustible ambition."

Effective leaders are more ambitious than nonleaders. In their 20-year study, psychologists Ann Howard and Douglas Bray found that among a sample of managers at AT&T, ambition, specifically the desire for advancement, was the strongest predictor of success twenty years later. The following character sketches of two managers who successfully progressed illustrate the desire for advancement:[6]

I want to be able to demonstrate the things I learned in college and get to the top," said Al, *"maybe even be president. I expect to work hard and be at the third level within 5 years, and to rise to much higher levels in the years beyond that. I am specifically working on my MBA to aid in my advancement. If I'm thwarted on advancement, or find the challenge is lacking, I'll leave the company.*

[He] had been promoted to the district level [after 8 years] and certainly expected to go further. Although he still wouldn't pinpoint wanting to be president (his wife's dream for him), he certainly had a vice presidency (sixth level) in mind as early as year 2 in the study, after his first promotion.

The following sketches characterize two less ambitious individuals:

Even though Chet had the benefits of a college degree, his below-average scholastic performance did not fill him with confidence in his capabilities. He hedged a bit with his interviewer when asked about his specific aspirations, saying he wasn't sure what the management levels were. When pressed further, he replied, "I'd like to feel no job is out of my reach, but I'm not really possessed of a lot of ambition. There are times when I just want to say, 'To hell with everything.' "

After [his] promotion to the second level, he looked more favorably upon middle management, but he still indicated he would not be dissatisfied to stay at the second level. [He] just seemed to take each position as it came; if he ever looked ahead, he didn't appear to look up.

Energy. To sustain a high achievement drive and get ahead, leaders must have a lot of energy. Working long, intense work weeks (and many weekends) for many years, requires an individual to have physical, mental, and emotional vitality.

Leaders are more likely than nonleaders to have a high level of energy and stamina and to be generally active, lively, and often restless. Leaders have been characterized as "electric, vigorous, active, full of life" as well as possessing the "physical vitality to maintain a steadily productive work pace."[7] Even at age 70, Sam Walton, founder of Wal-Mart discount stores, still attended Wal-Mart's Saturday morning meeting, a whoop-it-up 7:30 a.m. sales pep rally for 300 managers.

The need for energy is even greater today than in the past, because more companies are expecting all employees, including executives, to spend more time on the road visiting the organization's other locations, customers, and suppliers.

Tenacity. Leaders are better at overcoming obstacles than nonleaders. They have the "capacity to work with distant objects in view" and have a "degree of strength of will or perseverance."[8] Leaders must be tirelessly persistent in their activities and follow through with their programs. Most organizational change programs take several months to establish and can take many years before the benefits are seen. Leaders must have the drive to stick with these programs, and persistence is needed to ensure that changes are institutionalized.

An example of heroic perseverance in the face of obstacles, from American history, is the tale of John Paul Jones, a captain in the newly formed American Navy. On September 25, 1779, John Paul Jones, aboard the Bonhomme Richard, engaged in battle with the English ship, Serapis off the cost of England. After being bombarded with cannon fire by the Serapis, having two old cannons explode causing a fire, and being fired at by their supposed ally, the Alliance, Jones appeared to have lost the battle. When asked to surrender in the face of almost certain defeat, Jones made his immortal reply: "I have not yet begun to fight."

Determined to sink the Serapis, Jones spotted an open hatch on the Serapis' deck and ordered a young sailor to climb into the rigging and toss grenades into the hatch, knowing the English had stored their ammunitions there. After missing with the first two grenades, the third grenade disappeared into the hatchway and was followed by a thunderous explosion aboard the Serapis. Engulfed in flames, the English captain surrendered to Jones. Even though the entire battle had gone against him, John Paul Jones was determined not to give up, and it was this persistence that caused him to finally emerge victorious.

It is not just the direction of action that counts, but sticking to the direction chosen. Effective leaders must keep pushing themselves and others toward the goal. David Glass, CEO of Wal-Mart, says that Sam Walton "has an overriding something in him that causes him to improve every day. ... As long as I have known him, he has never gotten to the point where he's comfortable with who he is or how we're doing." Walt Disney was described as expecting the best and not relenting until he got it. Ray Kroc, of McDonald's Corporation, was described as a "dynamo who drove the company relentlessly."[9] Kroc posted this inspirational message on his wall:

Nothing in the world can take the place of persistence. Talent will not; nothing is more common than unsuccessful men with great talent. Genius will not; unrewarded genius is almost a proverb. Education will not; the world is full of educated derelicts. Persistence, determination alone are omnipotent.

Persistence, of course, must be used intelligently. Dogged pursuit of an inappropriate strategy can ruin an organization. It is important to persist in the right things. But what are the right things? In today's business climate, they may include the following: satisfying the customer, growth, cost control, innovation, fast response time, and quality. Or, in Tom Peters' terms, a constant striving to improve just about everything.

Initiative. Effective leaders are proactive. They make choices and take action that leads to change instead of just reacting to events or waiting for things to happen; that is, they show a high level of initiative. The following two examples from consultant Richard Boyatzis of McBer and Company illustrate proactivity:[10]

I called the chief, and he said he couldn't commit the resources, so I called the budget and finance people, who gave me a negative response. But then I called a guy in another work group who said he was willing to make a trade for the parts I needed. I got the parts and my group was able to complete the repairs.

One of our competitors was making a short, half-inch component and probably making $30,000–$40,000 a year on it. I looked at our line: we have the same product and can probably make it better and cheaper. I told our marketing manager: "Let's go after that business." I made the decision that we would look at it as a marketplace rather than looking at it as individual customers wanting individual quantities. I said, here's a market that has 30,000 pieces of these things, and we don't give a damn where we get the orders. Let's just go out and get them. We decided we were going to charge a specific price and get the business. Right now we make $30,000–440,000 on these things and our competitor makes zero.

Instead of sitting "idly by or [waiting] for fate to smile upon them," leaders need to "challenge the process."

Leaders are achievement-oriented, ambitious, energetic, tenacious, and proactive. These same qualities, however, may result in a manager who tries to accomplish everything alone, thereby failing to develop subordinate commitment and responsibility. Effective leaders must not only be full of drive and ambition, they must *want to lead others.*

Leadership Motivation

Studies show that leaders have a strong desire to lead. Leadership motivation involves the desire to influence and lead others and is often equated with the need for power. People with high leadership motivation think a lot about influencing other people, winning an argument, or being the greater authority. They prefer to be in a leadership rather than subordinate role. The willingness to assume responsibility, which seems to coincide with leadership motivation, is frequently found in leaders.

Sears psychologist Jon Bentz describes successful Sears executives as those who have a "powerful competitive drive for a position of ... authority ... [and] the need to be recognized as men of influence."[11] Astronauts John Glenn and Frank Borman built political and business careers out of their early feats as space explorers, while other astronauts did not. Clearly, all astronauts possessed the same opportunities, but is was their personal makeup that caused Glenn and Borman to pursue their ambitions and take on leadership roles.

Psychologist Warren Bennis and colleague Burt Nanus state that power is a leader's currency, or the primary means through whcih the leader gets things done in the organization. A leader must want to gain the power to exercise influence over others. Also, power is an "expandable pie," not a fixed sum; effective leaders give power to others as a means of increasing their own power. Effective leaders do not see power as something that is competed for but rather as something that can be created and distributed to followers without detracting from their own power.

Successful managers at AT&T completed sentence fragments in the following manner:[12]

"When I am in charge of others I find my greatest satisfactions."

"The job I am best fit for is one which requires leadership ability."

"I depend on others to carry out my plans and directions."

A manager who was not as successful completed the sentence fragment "Taking orders …" with the ending "is easy for it removes the danger of a bad decision."

Successful leaders must be willing to exercise power over subordinates, tell them what to do, and make appropriate use of positive and negative sanctions. Previous studies have shown inconsistent results regarding dominance as a leadership trait. According to Harvard psychologist David McClelland, this may be because there are two different types of dominance: a personalized power motive, or power lust, and a socialized power motive, or the desire to lead.[13]

Personalized Power Motive. Although a need for power is desirable, the leader's effectiveness depends on what is behind it. A leader with a personalized power motive seeks power as an end in itself. These individuals have little self-control, are often impulsive, and focus on collecting symbols of personal prestige. Acquiring power solely for the sake of dominating others may be based on profound self-doubt. The personalized power motive is concerned with domination of others and leads to dependent, submissive followers.

Socialized Power Motive. In contrast, a leader with a socialized power motive uses power as a means to achieve desired goals, or a vision. Its use is expressed as the ability to develop networks and coalitions, gain cooperation from others, resolve conflicts in a constructive manner, and use role modeling to influence others.

Individuals with a socialized power motive are more emotionally mature than those with a personalized power motive. They exercise power more for the benefit of the whole organization and are less likely to use it for manipulation. These leaders are also less defensive, more willing to take advice from experts, and have a longer-range view. They use their power to build up their organization and make it successful. The socialized power motive takes account of followers' needs and results in empowered, independent followers.

Honesty and Integrity

Honesty and integrity are virtues in all individuals, but have special significance for leaders. Without these qualities, leadership is undermined. Integrity is the correspondence between word and deed and honesty refers to being truthful or non-deceitful. The two form the foundation of a trusting relationship between leader and followers.

In his comprehensive review of leadership, psychologist Bernard Bass found that student leaders were rated as more trustworthy and reliable in carrying out responsibilites than followers. Similarly, British organizational psychologists Charles Cox and Cary Cooper's "high flying" (successful) managers preferred to have an open style of management, where they truthfully informed workers about happenings in the company. Morgan McCall and Michael Lombardo of the Center for Creative Leadership found that managers who reached the top were more likely to follow the following formula: "I will do exactly what I say I will do when I say I will do it. If I change my mind, I will tell you well in advance so you will not be harmed by my actions."[14]

Successful leaders are open with their followers, but also discreet and do not violate confidences or carelessly divulge potentially harmful information. One subordinate in a study by Harvard's John Gabarro made the following remark about his new president: "He was so consistent in what he said and did, it was easy to trust him." Another subordinate remarked about an unsuccessful leader, "How can I rely on him if I can't count on him consistently?"[15]

Professors James Kouzes, Barry Posner, and W.H. Schmidt asked 1500 managers "What values do you look for and admire in your superiors?" Integrity (being truthful and trustworthy, and having character and conviction) was the most frequently mentioned characteristic. Kouzes and Posner conclude:

Honesty is absolutely essential to leadership. After all, if we are willing to follow someone, whether it be into battle or into the boardroom, we first want to assure ourselves that the person is worthy of our trust. We want to know that he or she is being truthful, ethical, and principled. We want to be fully confident in the integrity of our leaders.

Effective leaders are credible, with excellent reputations, and high levels of integrity. The following description (from Gabarro's study) by one subordinate of his boss exemplifies the concept of integrity: "By integrity, I don't mean whether he'll rob a bank, or steal from the till. You don't work with people like that. It's whether you sense a person has some basic principles and is willing to stand by them."

Bennis and Nanus warn that today credibility is at a premium, especially since people are better informed, more cautious, and wary of authority and power. Leaders can gain trust by being predictable, consistent, and persistent and by making competent decisions. An honest leader may even be able to overcome lack of expertise, as a subordinate in Gabarro's study illustrates in the following description of his superior: "I don't like a lot of the things he does, but he's basically honest. He's a genuine article and you'll forgive a lot of things because of that. That goes a long way in how much I trust him."

Self-Confidence

There are many reasons why a leader needs self-confidence. Being a leader is a very difficult job. A great deal of information must be gathered and processed. A constant series of problems must be solved and decisions made. Followers have to be convinced to pursue specific courses of action. Setbacks have to be overcome. Competing interests have to be satisfied. Risks have to be taken in the face of uncertainty. A person riddled with self-doubt would never be able to take the necessary actions nor command the respect of others.

Self-confidence plays an important role in decision-making and in gaining others' trust. Obviously, if the leader is not sure of what decision to make, or expresses a high degree of doubt, then the followers are less likely to trust the leader and be committed to the vision.

Not only is the leader's self-confidence important, but so is others' perception of it. Often, leaders engage in impression management to bolster their image of competence; by projecting self-confidence they arouse followers' self-confidence. Self-confident leaders are also more likely to be assertive and decisive, which gains others' confidence in the decision. This is crucial for effective implementation of the decision. Even when the decision turns out to be a poor one, the self-confident leader admits the mistake and uses it as a learning opportunity, often building trust in the process. Manor Care, Inc., for example, lost over $21 million in 1988 when it was caught holding a large portion of Beverly Enterprise's stock. Chairman and CEO Stewart Bainum, Jr. stated, "I take full and complete responsibility for making the acquisition."[16] Considered to be the "best managed company in the [nursing home] industry," Manor Care's stock has rebounded, and it seems to be making a comeback. Less successful managers are more defensive about failure and try to cover up mistakes.

Emotional Stability. Self confidence helps effective leaders remain even-tempered. They do get excited, such as when delivering an emotionally-charged pep talk, but generally do not become angry or enraged. For the most part, as long as the employee did his/her homework leaders remain composed upon hearing that an employee made a costly mistake. For example, at PepsiCo, an employee who makes a mistake is "safe … as long as it's a calculated risk."

Emotional stability is especially important when resolving interpersonal conflicts and when representing the organization. A top executive who impulsively flies off the handle will not foster as much trust and teamwork as an executive who retains emotional control. Describing a superior, one employee in Gabarro's study stated, "he's impulsive and I'm never sure when he'll change signals on me."

Researchers at the Center for Creative Leadership found that leaders are more likely to "derail" if they lack emotional stability and composure. Leaders who derail are less able to handle pressure and more prone to moodiness, angry outbursts, and inconsistent behavior, which undermines their interpersonal relationships with subordinates, peers, and superiors. In contrast, they found the successful leaders to be calm, confident, and predictable during crisis.

Psychologically hardy, self-confident individuals consider stressful events interesting, as opportunities for development, and believe that they can influence the outcome. K. Labich in *Fortune* magazine argued that "By demonstrating grace under pressure, the best leaders inspire those around them to stay calm and act intelligently."[17]

Cognitive Ability

Leaders must gather, integrate, and interpret enormous amounts of information. These demands are greater than ever today because of rapid technological change. Thus, it is not surprising that leaders need to be intelligent enough to formulate suitable strategies, solve problems, and make correct decisions.

Leaders have often been characterized as being intelligent, but not necessarily brilliant and as being conceptually skilled. Kotter states that a "keen mind" (i.e., strong analytical ability, good judgement, and the capacity to think strategically and multidimensionally) is necessary for effective leadership, and that leadership effectiveness requires "above average intelligence," rather than genius.

An individual's intelligence and the perception of his or her intelligence are two highly related factors. Professors Lord, DeVader, and Alliger concluded that "intelligence is a key characteristic in predicting leadership perceptions."[18] Howard and Bray found that cognitive ability predicted managerial success twenty years later in their AT&T study. Effective managers have been shown to display greater ability to reason both inductively and deductively than ineffective managers.

Intelligence may be a trait that followers look for in a leader. If someone is going to lead, followers want that person to be more capable in *some* respects than they are. Therefore, the follower's perception of cognitive ability in a leader is a source of authority in the leadership relationship.

Knowledge of the Business

Effective leaders have a high degree of knowledge about the company, industry, and technical matters. For example, Jack Welch, president of GE has a PhD in engineering; Geroge Hatsopolous of Thermo Electron Corporation, in the years preceding the OPEC boycott, had both the business knowledge of the impending need for energy-efficient appliances and the technical knowledge of thermodynamics to create more efficient gas furnaces. Technical expertise enables the leader to understand the concerns of subordinates regarding technical issues. Harvard Professor John Kotter argues that expertise is more important than formal education.

Effective leaders gather extensive information about the company and the industry. Most of the successful general managers studied by Harvard's Kotter spent their careers in the same industry, while less successful managers lacked industry-specific experiences. Although cognitive ability is needed to gain a through understanding of the business, formal education is not a requirement. Only forty percent of the business leaders studied by Bennis and Nanus had business degrees. In-depth knowledge of the organization and industry allows effective leaders to make well-informed decisions and to understand the implications of those decisions.

Other Traits

Charisma, creativity/originality, and flexibility are three traits with less clear-cut evidence of their importance to leadership.[19] Effective leaders may have charisma, however, this trait may only be important for political leaders. Effective leaders also may be more creative than nonleaders, but there is no consistent research demonstrating this. Flexibility or adaptiveness may be important traits for a leader in today's turbulent environment. Leaders must be able to make decisions and solve problems quickly and initiate and foster change.

There may be other important traits needed for effective leadership, however, we believe that the first six that we discussed are the core traits.

THE REST OF THE STORY

A complete theory of leadership involves more than specifiying leader traits. Traits only endow people with the potential for leadership. To actualize this potential, additional factors are necessary which are discussed in our forthcoming book 'The Essence of Leadership' (written with additional authors).

Three categories of factors are discussed here: skills, vision, and implementing the vision. *Skills* are narrower in meaning than traits and involve specific capacities for action such as decision making, problem solving, and performance appraisal.

The core job of a leader, however, is to create a *vision*—a concept of what the organization should be. To quote Bennis and Nanus, "a vision articulates a view of a realistic, credible, attractive future for the organization, a condition that is better in some important ways than what now exists. A vision is a target that beckons."[20] Next the leader must *communicate* this vision to followers through inspirational speeches, written messages, appeals to shared values and above all through acting as a role model and personally acting in a way that is consistent with the vision. Third, the leader must develop or at least help to develop a general *strategy* for achieving the vision (i.e. a strategic vision).

Implementing the vision requires at least six activities:

1. *Structuring.* Today's effective organizations have minimal bureaucracy: small corporate staffs, few layers of management and large spans of control. The leader must insure that the organization's structure facilitates the flow of information (downward, upward, and diagonally). Information from customers regarding product quality and services is especially crucial.

2. *Selecting and Training.* Leaders must make sure that people are hired who have the traits needed to accept and implement the vision. Maintaining and upgrading skills is assured by constant training, as is commitment to the organization's vision.

3. *Motivating.* Leaders cannot achieve the vision alone; they must stimulate others to work for it too. They must generate enthusiasm, commitment, and compliance. Besides communicating the vision, effective leaders use at least six procedures to motivate followers.

Formal authority. The leader is the "boss" and must use his or her legitimate power constructively. The leader must start by asking directly for what he or she wants. *Thriving on Chaos* author Tom Peters said that if one wants something, then "Just ask for it."

Role Models. Leaders must behave the way they wish their followers would behave. For example, if they want subordinates to be customer-oriented, they should spend time themselves talking to customers. This has far more influence on employees than just telling them that customers are important.

Build subordinate self-confidence. If employees have been carefully selected and trained, such confidence will be justified. Jay Conger calls the process of strengthening subordinates' belief in their capabilities "empowerment."[21]

Delegation of authority. Giving autonomy and responsibility to employees also creates empowerment. In their book *Superleadership*, Charles Manz and Henry Sims[22] argue that delegating authority actually enhances the power of leaders by helping their subordinates become capable of attaining organizational goals. Effective delegation, of course, pre-supposes that subordinates are capable of holding the responsibilities they are given (as a result of extensive training and experience).

Specific and challenging goals.[23] Ensuring that subordinates have specific and challenging goals lead to higher performance than ambiguous goals. Challenging goals are empowering, because they demonstrate the leader has confidence in the follower. Goals must be accompanied by regular feedback indicating progress in relation to the goals. Feedback, in turn, requires adequate performance measurement.

For goals to be effective employees must be committed to them. Inspiration, modeling, training, and delegation all facilitate commitment.

Rewards and punishments. Effective leaders are not tolerant of those who reject the vision or repeatedly fail to attain reasonable goals. Rewards (and punishments) send messages not only to the employee in question but also to others; followers often direct their own actions by looking at what happens to their peers. People may learn as much or more by observing models than from the consequences of their own actions.[24] Rewards may include pay raises, promotions and awards, as well as recognition and praise. Effective leaders do not just reward achievement, they celebrate it.

4. *Managing Information.* Leaders have a profound influence on how information is managed within the organization. Effective leaders are effective information gatherers because they are good listeners and encourage subordinates to express their opinions. They stay in contact with the rest of the organization by, in Tom Peters' terms, "wandering around." Leaders actively seek information from outside the organization. Good leaders also disseminate information widely so that followers will understand the reasons for decisions that are made and how their work fits into the organization's goals. At the same time, effective leaders try not to overwhelm subordinates with too much information.

5. *Team Building.* Achieving goals requires collaboration among many (in some cases, hundreds of thousands) individuals. Leaders need to help build effective teams, starting with the top management team.[25] While an effective leader cannot do everything, he or she can insure that everything gets done by hiring, training, and motivating skilled people who work together effectively. And they, in turn, can build effective teams of their own.

6. *Promoting Change and Innovation.* Finally, effective leaders must promote change and innovation. The vision, since it pertains to a desired future state, is the starting point of change. This must be reinforced by constant restructuring, continual retraining to develop new skills, setting specific goals for innovation and improvement, rewarding innovation, encouraging a constant information flow in all directions and emphasizing responsiveness to customer demands.

It is clear that leadership is a very demanding activity and that leaders who have the requisite traits—drive, desire to lead, self-confidence, honesty (and integrity), cognitive ability, and industry knowledge—have a considerable advantage over those who lack these traits. Without drive, for example, it is unlikely that an individual would be able to gain the expertise required to lead an organization effectively, let alone implement and work toward long-term goals. Without the desire to lead, individuals are not motivated to persuade others to work toward a common goal; such an individual would avoid or be indifferent to leadership tasks. Self-confidence is needed to withstand setbacks, persevere through hard times, and lead others in new directions. Confidence gives effective leaders the ability to make hard decisions and to stand by them. A leader's honesty and integrity form the foundation on which the leader gains followers' trust and confidence; without honesty and integrity, the leader would not be able to attract and retain followers. At least a moderate degree of cognitive ability is needed to gain and understand technical issues as well as the nature of the industry.

Cognitive ability permits leaders to accurately analyze situations and make effective decisions. Finally, knowledge of the business is needed to develop suitable strategic visions and business plans.

MANAGEMENT IMPLICATIONS

Individuals can be *selected* either from outside the organization or from within non- or lower-managerial ranks based on their possession of traits that are less changeable or trainable. Cognitive ability (not to be confused with knowledge) is probably the least trainable of the six traits. Drive is fairly constant over time although it can change; it is observable in employees assuming they are given enough autonomy and responsibility to show what they can do. The desire to lead is more difficult to judge in new hires who may have had little opportunity for leadership early in life. It can be observed at lower levels of management and by observing people in assessment center exercises.

Two other traits can be developed through experience and *training*. Knowledge of the industry and technical knowledge come from formal training, job experience, and a mentally active approach toward new opportunities for learning. Planned job rotation can facilitate such growth. Self-confidence is both general and task specific. People differ in their general confidence in mastering life's challenges but task-specific self-confidence comes from mastering the various skills that leadership requires as well as the technical and strategic challenges of the industry. Such confidence parallels the individual's growth in knowledge.

Honesty does not require skill building; it is a virtue one achieves or rejects by choice. Organizations should look with extreme skepticism at any employee who behaves dishonestly or lacks integrity, and should certainly not reward dishonesty in any form, especially not with a promotion. The key role models for honest behavior are those at the top. On this issue, organizations get what they model, not what they preach.

CONCLUSIONS

Regardless of whether leaders are born or made or some combination of both, it is unequivocally clear that *leaders are not like other people.* Leaders do not have to be great men or women by being intellectual geniuses or omniscient prophets to succeed, but they do need to have the "right stuff" and this stuff is not equally present in all people. Leadership is a demanding, unrelenting job with enormous pressures and grave responsibilities. It would be a profound disservice to leaders to suggest that they are ordinary people who happened to be in the right place at the right time. Maybe the place matters, but it takes a special kind of person to master the challenges of opportunity. Let us not only give credit, but also use the knowledge we have to select and train our future leaders effectively. We believe that in the realm of leadership (and in every other realm), the individual does matter.

NOTES

This article is based on a chapter of a forthcoming book by Edwin A. Locke, Shelley A. Kirkpatrick, Jill K. Wheeler, Jodi Schneider, Kathryn Niles, Harold Goldstein, Kurt Welsh, & Dong-OK Chah, entitled The Essence of Leadership. We would like to thank Dr. Kathryn Bartol for her helpful comments on this manuscript.

1. P. Slater and W.G. Bennis, "Democracy is Inevitable." *Harvard Business Review,* Sept-Oct, 1990, 170 and 171. For a summary of trait theories, see R.M. Stogdill's *Handbook of Leadership,* New York: Free Press, 1974). For reviews and studies of leadership traits, see R.E. Boyatzis, *The Competent Manager* (New York: Wiley & Sons, 1982); C.J. Cox and C.L. Cooper, *High Flyers:*

An Anatomy of Managerial Success (Oxford: Basil Blackwell): G.A. Yukl, Leadership in Organizafions (Englewood Cliffs, NJ: Prentice Hall, 1989), Chapter 9.

2. R.M. Stogdill, "Personal Factors Associated with Leadership: A Survey of the Literature," *Journal of Psychology,* 1948, 25, 64.

3. See the following sources for evidence and further information concerning each trait: 1) drive: B.M. Bass's Handbook *of Leadership* (New York: The Free Press, 1990); K.G. Smith and J.K. Harrison, "In Search of Excellent Leaders" (in W.D.Guth's *The Handbook of Strategy,* New York: Warren. Gorham, & Lamont, 1986). 2) desire to lead: V.J. Bentz, "The Sears Experience in the Investigation, Description, and Prediction of Executive Behavior," (In F.R. Wickert and D.E. McFarland's *Measuring Executive Effectiveness,* (New York: Appleton-Century-Crofts, 1967); J.B. Miner, "Twenty Years of Research on Role-Motivation Theory of Managerial Effectiveness," *Personnel Psychology,* 1978, *31,* 739–760. 3) honesty/integrity: Bass, op. cit; W.G. Bennis and B. Nanus, *Leaders: The Strategies* for Taking Charge (New York: Harper & Row, 1985); J.M. Kouzes and B.Z. Posner, *The Leadership Challenge: How to Get Things Done in Organizations* (San Francisco: Jossey-Bass); T. Peters, Thriving on Chaos (New York: Harper & Row, 1987); A. Rand, for (he *New Intellectual* (New York: Signet, 1961). 4) self-confidence: Bass, op. cit and A. Bandura, *Social Foundations of Thought and Action: A Social Cognitive Theory,* (Englewood Cliffs, NJ: business: Bennis and Nanus, op. cit.; J.P. Prentice-Hall). Psychological hardiness is discussed by S.R. Maddi and S.C. Kobasa, The *Hardy Executive: Health Under Stress* (Chicago: Dorsey Professional Books, 1984); M.W. McCall Jr. and M.M. Lombardo, *Off the Track: Why and How Successful Executives get Derailed* (Technical Report No. 21, Greensboro, NC: Center for Creative Leadership, 1983). 5) cognitive ability: R.G. Lord, C.L. DeVader, and G.M. AUiger, "A Meta-analysis of the Relation Between Personality Traits and Leadership Perceptions: An Application of Validity Generalization Procedures," *Journal of Applied Psychology,* 1986; 61, 402–410; A. Howard and D.W. Bray, *Managerial Lives* in Transifion: Advancing *Age and Changing Times* (New York: Guilford Press, 1988). 6) knowledge of the business: Bennis and Nanus, op. cit.; J.P.Kotter, *The General Managers* (New York: MacMillan); Smith and Harrison, op. cit.

4. From J.J. Gabarro, *The Dynamics of Taking Charge* (Boston: Harvard Business School Press, 1987).

5. All PepsiCo references are from B. Dumaine, "Those high flying managers at PepsiCo," Forfune, April 10, 1989, 78–86. The Watson quote is from Smith and Harrison, op. cit., as are the Disney and Woolman quotes in the following paragraph.

6. The four quotes are from Howard and Bray, op. cit.

7. From Kouzes and Posner, op. cit., pp. 122 and V.J. Bentz, op. cit The Sam Walton quote is from J. Huey, "Wal-Mart: Will it take over the world?," Fortune, January 30, 1989, 52–59.

8. From Bass, op. cit.

9. The Walton quote is from Huey, op. cit., and the Kroc quote is from Smith and Harrison, op. cit. The quote on Kroc's wall is taken from Bennis and Nanus, op. cit.

10. From Boyatzis, op. cit. Also, Kouzes and Posner, op. cit. stress the importance of leader initiative.

11. From Bentz, op. cit.

12. From Howard and Bray, op. cit.

13. The distinction between a personalized and a socialized power motive is made by D.C. McClelland, "N-achievement and entrepreneurship: A longitudinal study," journal of Personality and Social Psychology, 1965, *1,* 389–392. These two power motives are discussed further by Kouzes and Posner, op. cit. '

14. From McCall and Lombardo, op. cit

15. From Gabarro, op. cit.

16. K.F. Girard examines Manor Care in "To the Manor Born," *Waifield's,* March, 1989, 68–75.

17. From K. Labich, "The Seven Keys to Business Leadership," *Fortune,* October 24, 1988, 58–66.

18. From Lord, DeVader, and Alliger, op. cit

19. For research on charisma, see Bass, op. cit. and R.J. House, W.D. Spangler, and J. Woycke, "Personality and charisma in the U.S. presidency: A psychological theory of leadership effectiveness (Wharton School, University of Pennsylvania, 1989, unpublished manuscript), on creativity/originality, see Howard and Bray, op. cit. and A. Zaleznik, *The Managerial Mystique* (New York: Harper and Row, 1989); on flexibility, see Smith and Harrison, op. cit.

20. From Bennis and Nanus, op. cit.

21. From J.A. Conger, Charismatic *Leadership: The Elusive Factor in Organizational Effectiveness* (San Francisco: Jossey-Bass, 1988).

22. C. Manz and H.P. Sims, Superieadership; *Leading Others to Lead Themselves* (New York: Prentice Hall, 1989).

23. See E.A. Locke and G.P. Latham, *A Theory of Goal* SeHing & *Task Performance* (Englewood Cliffs, NJ: Prentice Hall, 1990).

24. *See* Bandura, op. cit.

25. See D.C. Hambrick, "The top management team: Keys to strategic success," *California Management Review*, 1987, *30*, 1–20.

ABOUT THE AUTHORS

Shelley A. Kirkpatrick is a doctoral student in the organizational behavior program at the University of Maryland, College Park. She holds a BS in industrial/organizational psychology from Bowling Green State University. Her research interests include leadership and motivation. She is co-author of theforthcoming book *The Essence of Leadership.*

Edwin A. Locke is chair of the Management and Organization faculty at the University of Maryland, College Park. He is an internationally known behavioral scientist with over 135 articles and five books to his credit. He is most well known for his work on goal setting, most recently summarized in his book with Gary Latham entitled *A Theory of Goal Setting and Task Performance* (Prentice Hall, 1990). He is also a co-author of the forthcoming book *The Essence of Leadership.* Dr. Locke is a fellow of the American Psychological Association, the American Psychological Society, and the Academy of Management.

Be an Effective Leader

By Donald Patterson

As in any organization, leaders of law enforcement agencies want to see results. At the core of their success is the ability to motivate employees to act. While some people may think of such influence in terms of strength, force, dominance, and control, it also can be subtle. Of course, any leader can use their official position within a department or group to get action from personnel. However, the most successful ones use their personal qualities to motivate their staff.

POSITIONAL AUTHORITY

Positional influence comes from a leader's assignment within an agency. It does not extend upward or horizontally, only downward, and includes formal authority and the ability to reward and discipline.

Formal authority, or legitimate power, grows in scope and magnitude as someone's rank increases. It is based on the organization's rules and policies, which usually describe responsibilities or authorization to make decisions in terms of an individual's position. For example, lieutenants may approve crime prevention programs, deployment strategies, and schedule rotations, as well as give orders to lower-ranking officers.

Examples of rewarding others for performance and behavior can include granting merit raises, promotions, assignments, vacations, awards, and flexible schedules. The rank of leaders and, often, the specific assignment, help determine the type of reward power they possess. For instance, the sergeant of a patrol shift may approve vacations or choice assignments, and the captain in charge of the motor pool may determine who gets new units first.

Disciplining employees for ineffectiveness or rule violations includes, perhaps, transfers, demotions, or suspensions. The amount and type of disciplinary authority also depends on a leader's assignment and rank. For example, a sergeant may have authorization to counsel an employee but not to issue a letter of discipline. A lieutenant may be able to approve a letter of discipline but not to order days off as punishment.

Leaders who rely on their formal power as a control mechanism can lessen the chance of their employees' success.[1] Some such individuals use demands and threats to achieve outcomes, striving not to understand the process of how their staff members achieve final results but only to issue commands and have them carried out without question or comment. Often, they view the organization as a machine and leadership as a science.[2] Police agency leaders who use such tactics may do so out of the belief that it is necessary to maintain control of officers during emergencies.

PERSONAL QUALITIES

Most law enforcement executives do not address crises every day. Instead, they primarily focus on their interactions with others. With their schedules revolving around meetings, projects, and committees, successful leaders recognize the importance of quality interpersonal skills. They realize that they operate in an environment in which they must influence even those beyond the scope of their authority, such as peers, superiors, and people outside the agency.[3] To help create, forge, and maintain necessary relationships, they use their personal qualities, which include charisma, expertise, and knowledge.

Employees identify with and admire charismatic leaders who use their personality, excitement, and motivation to influence staff members. Many people lacking other leadership qualities can lead successfully because they have strong charisma.

Expertise refers to leaders' mastery of a specific topic or skill. It includes their ability not only to perform the task themselves but also to facilitate others' work in that area.[4] People respect such leaders and find them credible.

Leaders obtain some knowledge because of their position, but they also gain a lot of it by seeking it out. And, they can influence the organization effectively by sharing that knowledge with others. Staff members prefer to be led that way.[5] One of employees' main complaints is the lack of communication between ranks and divisions.

People must communicate and share information for successful interactions.[6]

Leadership as an Art

Effective leaders who use their personal strengths to influence others and achieve outcomes remain consistent, even when they move from one assignment to another. Personnel follow and respond to them. While many employees attempt excellence at work by nature, most excel because the organization's leaders create a favorable environment, which includes quality interactions with peers, subordinates, and superiors.

Getting things done depends on relationships, which leaders enhance by exercising their personal influence factors.[7] Today, many officers do not perform particular duties merely because someone tells

them to—they want reasons for tasks or why certain policies and procedures exist. In short, they want communication and interaction with their superiors.

Leaders who use their own personal qualities to influence employees tend to view the organization as a living organism and an open, fluid system that, unlike a machine, changes, grows, and adapts. They see leadership as an art that they must practice, hone, and modify to maintain their effectiveness When viewed this way, leadership is based not on a place in the organization but on an interactive process of honest, clear communication. Such a leadership style results in increased employee motivation, productivity, and job satisfaction.[9]

Practicing an art is a process. Effective leaders take the time and effort necessary to build relationships with their subordinates, peers, and superiors. Each interaction promotes, maintains, or inhibits a leader's effectiveness. While the end goal may be known, the actual path is subject to influence. Successful leaders modify their leadership style based on these relationships. This is one of the characteristics of leaders who constantly practice the art of leadership—making decisions, adjusting, improving, listening, learning, and going forward.

Practical Approach

The author offers a practical model for leaders striving to successfully motivate their employees. It can be summarized by the acronym RACURP, which stands for rationality, acceptance, communication, understanding, reliability, and persuasion.[10]

- *Rationality*: Leaders should try to balance emotions and objectivity. While too little emotion impairs motivation and creativity, too much clouds judgment. Officers have physically survived based on concrete information. After spending most of their careers insulating themselves from their feelings, they do not want to hear emotional arguments or rationale. Leaders should concentrate on presenting facts.
- *Acceptance*: Law enforcement personnel tend to view disagreements as win–lose situations. And,

barriers in relationships can occur in these instances. How ever, disagreements can be healthy; a diversity of opinions creates synergism. Successful leaders welcome differing viewpoints and input from others. Doing so allows conversation about and exploration of the topic. Otherwise, people do not know what they do not know. Honest disagreement usually results in better products and decisions.

- *Communication*: Leaders have a vested interest in maintaining working relationships with everyone they encounter. Communication makes this possible. To this end, successful leaders understand the importance of actively listening to others. While most people listen only briefly before they start formulating a response, leaders should put the effort and energy into truly understanding what their staff members say. And, they must take the time to craft their own message and make it clear.

- *Understanding*: Effective leaders seek to understand situations, as well as the opinions and positions of others. This allows them to resolve problems better. When interacting, they assume a need to learn more and delay making decisions until they grasp available and relevant information. Leaders realize that without concrete data about a situation, their minds will fill in the missing information based on, perhaps, inaccurate or limited perceptions, leading to faulty conclusions. By striving to understand, leaders can grasp and explain behavior or positions that may not make sense at first. Conversely, jumping to conclusions can hinder the opportunity to explore solutions successfully. Proper communication alleviates misunderstanding.

- *Reliability*: Successful leaders are reliable and consistent. They do not base their decisions and responses to situations on their feelings but on who they are and what they believe in. They only do things that better their interpersonal relationships and the organization, whether or not they reciprocate. Consistency breeds trust. For example, leaders who truly have an open-door policy will stop and listen to someone who walks into their office. If they simply do not have time, they should explain why and meet with that person as soon as possible. One instance of not having time for an employee could ruin a leader's reputation for reliability. A single inconsistency can negatively impact communication and impair a leader's flow of accurate and timely information. To maintain trust, leaders must provide support and encouragement and show true interest at all times.

- *Persuasion*: As a true act of leadership, persuasive leaders will use their personal influence, not coercive means, to help motivate employees. While honestly persuading others, truly effective leaders will try to minimize their use of positional power. High-performing leaders stand their ground on principle and let their personal strengths influence personnel.

CONCLUSION

Successful leaders help others around them succeed and see forward progress and completed projects. They empower others and get them committed to the goals and mission of the organization. Effective leaders help develop their employees, encouraging and enabling them to grow both professionally and personally. The success of these leaders stems from their personal qualities and support of others' endeavors toward the accomplishment of the organization's mission and goals. Truly successful leaders get things done through the artful application of personal influence.

NOTES

1. James Kouzes and Barry Posner, *Leadership Challenge* (San Franciso, CA: Jossey-Bass, 2003).
2. Terry Mangan, personal conversation with author, FBI Academy, Executive Leadership Course, November 2004.
3. Daniel Katz and Robert Kahn, *The Social Psychology of Organizations* (New York, NY: John Wiley and Sons, 1966).

4. John French and Bertram Raven, "The Bases of Social Power," in *Studies in Social Power*, ed. Dorwin Cartwright (Ann Arbor, MI: Institute for Social Research, The University of Michigan, 1959).

5. Donald Patterson, "Power in Law Enforcement: Subordinate Preference and Actual Use of Power in Special Weapons Teams (SWT)" (PhD diss., The Fielding Institute, Santa Barbara, CA, 1990).

6. Kerry Patterson, Joseph Grenny, Ron McMillan, and Al Switzler, *Crucial Conversations* (Highstown, NJ: McGraw-Hill, 2002).

7. Robin Sharma, *The Greatest Guide* (New York, NY: Harper Collins, 2006).

8. Terry Mangan, personal conversation with author, FBI Academy, Executive Leadership Course, November 2004.

9. Philip Podsakoff and Chester Schriesheim, "Field Studies of French and Raven's Bases of Power: Critique, Reanalysis, and Suggestions for Future Research," *Psychological Bulletin* 97, no. 3 (1985).

10. The author developed the acronym RACURP as a summary of the main interaction and conflict resolution strategies presented in a series of books that include Roger Fisher, Bruce Patton, and William Ury, *Getting to Yes: Negotiating Agreement Without Giving In* (New York, NY: Houghton Mifflin, 1991); Roger Fisher and Scott Brown, *Getting Together: Building Relationships As We Negotiate* (New York, NY: Penguin Group, 1989); and Roger Fisher, Elizabeth Kopelman, and Andrea Schneider, *Beyond Machiavelli: Tools for Coping with Conflict* (New York, NY: Penguin Group, 1996).

How Police Supervisory Styles Influence Patrol Officer Behavior

By Robin Engel

Does field supervision of patrol officers matter? Chances are that personal experience, common sense, and intuition would elicit a quick "yes" from most police administrators and managers. But does street-level evidence justify that viewpoint?

The answer is a qualified yes, according to recent field research. Research findings not only confirm that view but also shed light on how frontline supervisory styles can influence such patrol officer behavior as making arrests, issuing citations, using force, and engaging in community policing.

The study involved field observations of and interviews with sergeants and lieutenants who directly supervised patrol officers in the Indianapolis, Indiana, Police Department and the St. Petersburg, Florida, Police Department. The research is based on data from the Project on Policing Neighborhoods (POPN), a 2-year research project sponsored by the National Institute of Justice that broadly examined policing issues, especially the effects of community policing initiatives on police and the public (see "The Project on Policing Neighborhoods").

The most important finding was that style or quality of field supervision can significantly influence patrol officer behavior, quite apart from quantity of supervision.[1] Frontline supervision by sergeants and lieutenants can influence some patrol officer behavior, but the study found that this influence varies according to the style of supervision. An "active" supervisory style— involving leading by example—seems to be most influential despite potential drawbacks. Indeed, active supervisors appear to be crucial to the implementation of organizational goals.

This report in NIJ's Research for Practice series addresses three principal questions:

- What are the four supervisory styles identified by the research?
- How do those styles influence patrol officer behavior?
- What are the implications for departmental policy and practice?

FRONTLINE SUPERVISORY STYLES

The study's field observations and interviews identified four main supervisory styles: traditional, innovative, supportive, and active. Supervisor characteristics include personal features such as age as well as level of training and experience (see exhibit 1). Each of the four styles encompasses about 25 percent of the 81 field supervisors (see exhibit 2). In general, none of the four supervisory styles was found to be ideal. Each style has benefits and drawbacks. (See "Study Methodology.")

The active style of supervision emerged as having the most influence over patrol officers' behaviors.

Exhibit 1. Characteristics of 81 supervisors

Characteristics	Minimum	Maximum	Mean
Supervisor age (years)	31	70	44
Years of experience as a supervisor	1	33	10
Percentage of supervisors who were female			15
Percentage of supervisors who were nonwhite			15
Percentage of supervisors who held a 4-year college degree			51
Amount of training* in community policing	1	5	4
Amount of knowledge† about community policing	1	3	2
Amount of training in supervision, management, leadership	1	5	4
Amount of knowledge about supervision, management, leadership	1	3	1

Note: 17 lieutenants and 64 sergeants.

*Amount of training: 1 = none, 2 = less than 1 day, 3 = 1–2 days, 4 = 3–5 days, 5 = more than 5 days.

†Amount of knowledge: 1 = very knowledgeable, 2 = fairly knowledgeable, 3 = not very knowledgeable.

Exhibit 2. Distribution of supervisory styles, in percent

	Traditional	Innovative	Supportive	Active
Gender				
Male ($n = 69$)	22	30	25	23
Female ($n = 12$)	50	8	17	25
Race				
White ($n = 69$)	26	26	25	23
Nonwhite ($n = 12$)	25	33	17	25
Location				
Indianapolis lieutenants ($n = 17$)	12	35	24	29
Indianapolis sergeants ($n = 39$)	18	28	26	28
St. Petersburg sergeants ($n = 25$)	48	20	20	12
Total ($N = 81$)	26	27	23	23

Note: Each percentage is the proportion of field supervisors associated with the style noted in the far left column. Thus, traditional supervisors constituted 26 percent of all 81 supervisors, 22 percent of 69 male supervisors, etc.

Officers with active supervisors were more likely than those with other types of supervisors to use force and spent more time on self-initiated activities, community policing activities, and problem solving.

Traditional supervisors.

Traditional supervisors expect aggressive enforcement from subordinates rather than engagement in community-oriented activities or policing of minor disorders. They are more likely than other types of supervisors to make decisions because they tend to take over encounters with citizens or tell officers how to handle those incidents.

Traditional sergeants and lieutenants are highly task oriented and expect subordinates to produce measurable outcomes—particularly arrests and citations—along with paperwork and documentation.

Less inclined toward developing relationships, traditional supervisors give more instruction to subordinates and are less likely to reward and more likely to punish patrol officers. The traditional supervisor's ultimate concern is to control subordinate behavior.

Traditional supervisors are more likely to support new policing initiatives if they are consistent with aggressive law enforcement. More than 60 percent of these supervisors "agree strongly" that "enforcing the law is by far a patrol officer's most important responsibility," compared with 14 percent of innovative supervisors, 11 percent of supportive supervisors, and 11 percent of active supervisors. Along with their no-nonsense approach to policing, traditional supervisors strictly enforce rules and regulations and adhere to the chain of command.

Innovative supervisors.

Innovative supervisors are characterized by a tendency to form relationships (i.e., they consider more officers to be friends), a low level of task orientation, and more positive views of subordinates. These supervisors are considered innovative because they generally encourage their officers to embrace new philosophies and methods of policing.

Innovative supervisors are defined by their expectations for community policing and problem-solving efforts by subordinates. For example, 96 percent of

The Project On Policing Neighborhoods

NIJ is committed to providing relevant research that helps practitioners in the field. This Research for Practice is one in a series of reports from the Project on Policing Neighborhoods (POPN) conducted in 1996–1997. POPN researchers examined police and citizen interaction, attitudes, and behaviors in 12 neighborhoods in Indianapolis, Indiana, and 12 similar neighborhoods in St. Petersburg, Florida. They directly observed patrol officers on duty, interviewed patrol officers and their supervisors, and conducted telephone surveys of individuals randomly selected in each neighborhood.

NIJ is publishing several reports that summarize scholarly reports and articles written by POPN researchers. The summaries present key information that police managers need to know about problem solving and community policing. Additional topics will include encounters with juvenile suspects, gender differences in officer attitudes and behavior, police attitudes toward the public and the public's attitudes toward police, how officers spend their time with the community, and race and everyday policing.

Knowledge about how officers interact with neighborhood residents and other officers can help law enforcement administrators improve policies and practices and lead to better community relations. With this goal in mind, NIJ invites comments and suggestions concerning this research. To comment, write to Steve Edwards, National Institute of Justice, 810 Seventh Street, N.W., Washington, DC 20531; e-mail edwardss@ojp.usdoj.gov; or call 202–307–0500.

these supervisors reported that they "agree strongly" that "a good patrol officer will try to find out what residents think the neighborhood problems are," compared to 48 percent of traditional supervisors, 68 percent of supportive supervisors, and 68 percent of active supervisors.

One goal of innovative supervisors is to help subordinates implement community policing and problem-solving strategies by coaching, mentoring, and facilitating. They are less concerned with enforcing rules and regulations, report writing, or other task-oriented activities than traditional supervisors.

Unlike traditional supervisors, innovative supervisors generally do not tell subordinates how to handle situations and do not take over the situations themselves. They are more likely to delegate decision making. They spend significantly more time per shift dealing with the public or other officers than other supervisors do (15 percent compared with 9 percent).

Supportive supervisors.

These supervisors support subordinates by protecting them from discipline or punishment perceived as "unfair" and by providing inspirational motivation. They often serve as a buffer between officers and management to protect officers from criticism and discipline. They believe this gives their officers space to perform duties without constant worry of disciplinary action for honest mistakes.

In some cases, supportive supervisors do not have strong ties to or positive relations with management. They may attempt to shield patrol officers from the police administration. Thus, some supervisors classified as supportive may function more as "protectors" than "supporters."

Of supportive supervisors, 68 percent reported that "protecting their officers from unfair criticism and punishment" is one of their most important functions, compared with 10 percent of traditional supervisors, 5 percent of innovative supervisors, and no active supervisors.

The protective role adopted by some supportive supervisors can be a problem, however. Other research has found that shielding officers from accountability mechanisms within the department can lead to police misconduct.[2]

Supportive supervisors are less concerned with enforcing rules and regulations, dealing with paperwork, or ensuring that officers do their work. They may encourage officers through praise and recognition, act as counselors, or display concern for subordinates' personal and professional well-being. The study found that supportive supervisors praise or reward subordinate officers significantly more often during an average shift (3 times per shift) than do other supervisors (2 times per shift).

Active supervisors. Active supervisors embrace a philosophy of leading by example. Their goal is to be heavily involved in the field alongside subordinates while controlling patrol officer behavior, thus performing the dual function of street officer and supervisor.

Almost all active supervisors (95 percent) report that they often go on their own initiative to incidents that their officers are handling, compared to 24 percent of traditional supervisors, 55 percent of innovative supervisors, and 68 percent of supportive supervisors.

Active supervisors also give importance to engaging in patrol work themselves. They spend significantly more time per shift than other supervisors on general motor patrol (33 percent compared with 26 percent) and traffic encounters (4 percent compared with 2 percent). These supervisors attempt to strike a balance between being active in the field and controlling subordinate behavior through constant, direct supervision. Supervisors with an active style are characterized by directive decision making, a strong sense of supervisory power, and a relatively positive view of subordinates.

Although active supervisors believe they have considerable influence over subordinates' decisions, they are less likely to encourage team building, coaching, or mentoring. One possible explanation for this is that they are reluctant to become so involved that they alienate subordinate officers. A fine line separates an active supervisor from being seen as over controlling or micromanaging.

IMPACT OF SUPERVISORY STYLE ON PATROL OFFICERS

What impact does supervisory style have on patrol officer activities? The study examined the influence of 64 sergeants' supervisory styles on the behavior of 239 patrol officers, having identified the sergeant-supervisor of each officer. The study's findings focus on how likely officers were to make arrests, issue citations, and use force as well as how much time per shift they allocated to community policing activities, administrative duties, and personal business.

Arrests and citations.

Supervisory style did not affect the likelihood that patrol officers would make arrests or issue citations in either traffic or nontraffic situations. In nontraffic encounters, however, the mere presence of a field supervisor, regardless of style, significantly influenced officer behavior; the longer a supervisor was present, the more likely patrol officers were to make an arrest.

Use of force. Patrol officers with active supervisors were twice as likely to use force[3] against suspects as officers whose supervisors employ other styles. In addition, active supervisors themselves used force against

---

Community Policing in Field Training and Supervision

Although not part of POPN research, a study conducted by Robin N. Haarr, Ph.D., under NIJ grant 96–IJ–CX–0060, also looked at influences on patrol officer behavior, particularly new recruits. This research also found that field supervisors have crucial influence, although in a different context.[a]

A separate study of how police recruits are taught community policing principles provides some guidance for police managers on how field training and actual policing experience may supersede academy training in influencing the attitudes and beliefs of new officers.

The 3-year study surveyed police recruits at four intervals[b] during their training and first year on the job. It focused on academy "reform training"[c] designed to change recruits' attitudes positively toward community–oriented policing and problem-solving policing.

The research found that academy reform training often proved ineffective because it was not followed up during field training, and factors contradicting academy training[d] dominated recruits' actual policing experiences. The study also found that recruits' beliefs about the nature of policing were firmly established before training even begins:

> *The best predictors of attitude change were by far the attitudes that recruits brought with them to the academy. In other words, police recruits are not empty vessels to be filled with new attitudes and values related to policing.*[e]

Nonetheless, academy reform training did influence recruits' beliefs about police work before field training. But the study found "little evidence of a formal and/or systematic approach to incorporating community policing and/or problem-solving training into the field training process."[f] Thus, community policing principles—already on shaky ground because of recruits' previously held beliefs—often appeared to be academic:

> *It seems unreasonable to expect police recruits to continue their commitment to community policing and problem-solving policing principles and practices if they leave the training academy and return to a police agency that does not require its officers to engage in community policing or problem-solving activities.*[g]

It falls to police leadership, the study concluded, to set the tone for community policing. When supervisors and the organization practice community-oriented and problem-solving policing, recruits will too. The study recommends that academy-taught principles be coupled more closely with field training and actual police practices.

Notes

a. Haarr, R.N., *The Impact of Community Policing Training and Program Implementation on Police Personnel,* final report for the National Institute of Justice, grant number 96–IJ–CX–0060, Washington, DC; National Institute of Justice, 2000, NCJ 190680.

b. Surveys were administered on the first day at the academy, near the last day at the academy, 12 weeks later (near the end of field training), and at the end of 1 year on the job.

c. "Reform training" is defined as "training designed to alter an officer's perception of the world and/or police work. ... In the case of community policing training, the goal is to replace outdated attitudes and beliefs about policing with new attitudes and beliefs that are consistent with community policing and problem-solving policing philosophies and strategies." (Haarr, *The Impact of Community Policing Training and Program Implementation on Police Personnel,* pp. 3–4.)

d. Such as shift, coworkers' attitudes, and precinct location.

e. Haarr, p. v.

f. Ibid., p. 176.

g. Ibid., p. 175.

suspects more often than other types of supervisors. The mere presence of a supervisor at the scene, however, did not have a significant influence on police use of force.

Self-initiated activities.

Patrol officers with active supervisors spent more time per shift engaging in proactive (self-initiated) activities than officers with other supervisors. The former spent 15 percent of their time per shift being proactive, in contrast to 14 percent, 13 percent, and 11 percent for officers under supportive, traditional, and innovative supervisors, respectively. Proactivity excludes time spent on dispatched or supervisordirected activities, general patrol, traveling to a location, personal business, and administrative activities.

Community policing and problem solving. Officers with active supervisors spent more time per shift engaging in problem solving and other community-policing activities than officers with other types of supervisors. Officers under active supervision spent 11.3 percent of their time per shift on problem solving, compared with 10.7 percent for officers with supportive supervisors, 9.4 percent for those with traditional supervisors, and 8.0 percent for officers with innovative supervisors. Although differences between these percentages seem small, they can produce substantial differences in the amount of time spent on community policing by an entire patrol force over the course of a year.

At first glance it appears contradictory that officers with innovative supervisors spent the least amount of time on community policing and problem solving. This finding suggests that simply having an innovative supervisory style does not necessarily translate into more innovative activities from subordinates. Possibly, innovative supervisors may be more inclined to encourage community building tactics, while active supervisors may encourage more aggressive enforcement, which may lead active supervisors and their subordinates to be more engaged with problem solving and other citizen interactions.

Administrative activities.

Patrol officers with active supervisors spend significantly less time per shift on administrative tasks. Officers under active supervision spent 13 percent of their time dealing with administrative matters, compared with 19 percent for patrol officers with traditional supervisors and 17 percent for those with innovative or supportive supervisors.

Personal business. Supervisory style has little effect on the time patrol officers spend conducting personal business (nonwork-related encounters and activities,

including meal and restroom breaks). Overall, officers spent 16 percent of their time on personal business.

IMPLICATIONS FOR POLICY AND PRACTICE

Collectively, the research findings indicate that supervisory styles affect some types of subordinate behavior. Police administrators are encouraged to consider supervisory style in setting department goals and training.

Compared with other styles, an active supervisory approach appears to wield the most influence over

---

Study Methodology

This study used data collected for the POPN multimethod study of police patrol in the Indianapolis, Indiana, and St. Petersburg, Florida, police departments, which were implementing community policing at the time of the study.

The core methodology was systematic social observation of patrol officers in the field. Trained observers accompanied officers on their work shifts and took field notes. Officers assigned to each of the 24 study beats were observed for approximately 240 hours. Researchers observed more than 5,700 hours of patrol work during the summer of 1996 in Indianapolis and the summer of 1997 in St. Petersburg. From their field notes, observers prepared narratives and coded data items about officer activities.

Researchers also interviewed patrol officers and frontline supervisors about their personal characteristics, training and education, work experience, perceptions of their beats, attitudes toward the police role, and perceptions of their department's implementation of community policing and problem solving. Participation was voluntary and confidential. To encourage candid responses to potentially sensitive questions about the quality of supervision, officers were not asked for their supervisors' names. Officers were matched with sergeants through other information.

Review of prior research identified 10 attitudinal dimensions that potentially shape supervisors' styles:

- How they make decisions.
- How they distribute power.
- The extent to which they attempt or avoid exerting leadership.
- The priority they place on aggressive enforcement.
- The priority they attach to community policing and problem solving.
- How they view subordinates.
- Whether they engage in inspirational motivation.
- How task oriented they are.
- Whether they focus on building friendships and mutual trust with subordinates.
- Whether they focus on protecting subordinates from unfair criticism and punishment.

Factor analysis of these dimensions revealed the four individual supervisory styles: traditional, innovative, supportive, and active.

---

patrol officer actions. The findings suggest that to best influence their patrol officers' behavior, field supervisors must lead by example—the hallmark of an active style.

One clear implication of the research is that police administrators and managers would be well-advised to direct and train field supervisors to become more involved and set an example of the behavior they expect from subordinates.

(For discussion of a different study that examined supervisory practices and officer training, see "Community Policing in Field Training and Supervision.")

An active supervisory style, however, has potential problems. Leading by example can be positive or negative, depending on the example set. As noted previously, for instance, active supervisors and their subordinates are more likely to use force against suspects.

One reason why active supervisors might promote greater use of force and proactivity (which could expose the officer to greater risk if things go wrong) is that by taking precisely the risks that he/she wants the officer to take, the active supervisor demonstrates that "if it's safe for Sarge, then it's safe for me, too."

Supervisory styles influenced only those officer behaviors that are hardest to monitor and measure, such as use of force, problem solving, and proactivity. Conversely, supervisory styles did not significantly affect officer behaviors that are relatively easy to monitor and measure, such as making arrests and issuing citations. One reason may be that supervisors have more influence in situations where patrol officers have the most discretion. Perhaps the less certain the task and the less visible its performance, the more opportunity a sergeant may have to define the duties of subordinates, who may appreciate such clarification of their roles.

Another possible explanation is that such easily measured officer activities as arrests and citations may be most influenced by policy guidelines from higher ranking officials. This effect is likely to be relatively uniform regardless of field supervisors' styles. Thus, the place to look for supervisory influence over these activities may be at the district or departmental level, not the field supervisory level.

Leading by example is an effective frontline supervisory tool only if the example supports departmental goals. For instance, many officers at both sites had received relatively little training in community policing and were skeptical about its worth. Sergeants who practiced an active supervisory style supplemented training deficiencies while building the self-confidence of subordinate officers.

These findings strongly suggest that police administrators are more likely to achieve departmental goals if they align them with supervisory practice and encourage field supervisors to "get in the game."

NOTES

1. "Quantity" is used here in the sense of amount of supervision, i.e., the number of supervisors, the amount of interaction between supervisors and subordinates, and time spent on supervised encounters between patrol officers and citizens. This study is unique in its focus on the quality and style—as well as quantity—of patrol officer supervision.

2. For example, see Christopher Commission, Report of the Independent Commission on the Los Angeles Police Department, Los Angeles Independent Commission on the Los Angeles Police Department, 1991; Mollen Commission to Investigate Allegations of Police Corruption, Commission Report, New York: The Mollen Commission, 1994; Skolnik, J.H., and J.J. Fyfe, Above the Law: Police and the Excessive Use of Force, New York: Free Press, 1993; and Kappeler, V.E., R.D. Sluder, and G.P. Alpert, Forces of Deviance: Understanding the Dark Side of Policing, 2nd edition, Prospective Heights, IL: Waveland Press, 1998.

3. Use of force includes firm grip or nonpain restraint, pain compliance (hammerlock, wristlock, finger grip, carotid control, bar arm lock), impact or incapacitation (striking with body or weapon, mace, taser), or drawing or discharging a firearm.

RECOMMENDED READING

This report was based on the following articles:

Engel, R., "Patrol Officer Supervision in the Community Policing Era," *Journal of Criminal Justice* 30(1) (January/February 2002): 51–64.

Engel, R., "Supervisory Styles of Patrol Sergeants and Lieutenants," *Journal of Criminal Justice* 29(4) (July/August 2001): 341–355.

Engel, R., "The Effects of Supervisory Styles on Patrol Officer Behavior," *Police Quarterly* 3(3) (September 2000): 262–293.

Other related articles and reports. Bergner, L., "Building Teamwork Among Officers," *Law Enforcement Trainer* 12(6) (November/ December 1997): 10–12.

Haarr, R., "Making of a Community Policing Officer: The Impact of Basic Training and Occupational Socialization on Police Recruits," *Police Quarterly* 4(4) (December 2001): 402–433.

Mastrofski, S., R. Parks, A. Reiss, Jr., and R. Worden, *Policing Neighborhoods: A Report from St. Petersburg*, Research Preview, Washington, DC: U.S. Department of Justice, National Institute of Justice, July 1999, NCJ 184370.

Mastrofski, S., R. Parks, A. Reiss, Jr., and R. Worden, *Policing Neighborhoods: A Report from Indianapolis*, Research Preview, Washington, DC: U.S. Department of Justice, National Institute of Justice, July 1998, NCJ 184207.

Mastrofski, S., R. Parks, and R. Worden, *Community Policing in Action: Lessons from an Observational Study*, Final Report to the National Institute of Justice, 1998.

Weisburd, D., and R. Greenspan, et al., *Police Attitudes Toward Abuse of Authority: Findings From a National Study*, Research in Brief, Washington, DC: U.S. Department of Justice, National Institute of Justice, May 2000, NCJ 181312.

Community policing. For more information on community policing, visit the Office of Community Oriented Policing Services Web site at *www.usdoj.gov/cops/* or write to U.S. Department of Justice, Office of Community Oriented Policing Services, 1100 Vermont Avenue, N.W., Washington, DC 20530.

Micromanagement
Dealing with Red Pen Supervisors

By Tracey Gove

Many well-intentioned, hard-working law enforcement supervisors and managers have been condemned as "micromanagers." So culturally taboo is the label within the workplace that many supervisors will go to any length to avoid the accusation and reputation. Although it is an apt title for some, there are misconceptions about what it means to be a true micromanager.

The term is often mentioned in private-sector management literature; however, the criminal justice field remains conspicuously silent about the definition of the term, what can spark the accusation, root causes, when it is appropriate, how to avoid the behavior, and how best to handle micromanagers. Most police personnel believe they have been micromanaged to some extent in their careers; uncovering the hidden truths about this management style will better enable organizations to recognize true micromanagement and will help supervisors cultivate ways of avoiding this behavior.

WHAT IS MICROMANAGEMENT?

The most common meaning associated with micromanagement is to provide supervisory oversight with excessive control and attention to details that are best left to the operational personnel. A micromanager is typically one who is obsessed with control and is overly concerned with all aspects of employee work. Micromanagers tend to dictate every detail of the work for which their subordinates are responsible, and they truly believe that their way is not only the best but also the only way to accomplish a goal. Rather than help, true micromanagers impede work progress and risk stifling the growth of subordinate officers as well as the police agency as a whole.

Studies have shown, however, that micromanagement is effective over the short term.[1] Simply by virtue of their position, supervisors are best suited to select an immediate course of action, provide direction, and oversee results ensuring that vital tasks are completed on time and without error. But if such stringent management is left unabated for a longer period, it will have several destructive effects.

EFFECTS OF MICROMANAGEMENT

Micromanaged employees become disengaged from their work, leading to lower productivity, a behavior that spreads to colleagues.[2] Consequently, motivation is lost, quality drops, and esprit de corps can be irreparably damaged. Officers, the agency, and ultimately the community suffer.

Employment professionals have found micromanagement to be one of the top three "misery factors" that lead to employee resignation.[3] In the current era of staffing shortages and the attendant difficulty in filling open vacancies, this should be of utmost concern to law enforcement leaders.

The micromanagement approach, executed over the long term, is generally seen as ineffective, in that time better spent on assigned work is lost in overattention to detail. In addition, spending an inordinate amount of time on tasks that should be delegated can cause burnout and leave little time for managers to build a vision and focus on the future. Studies have shown that such negative behavior can lead to career derailment.[4]

IS MICROMANAGING EVER APPROPRIATE?

As key players in the success of their agencies, it is the responsibility for law enforcement managers to monitor progress, control quality, evaluate performance, make decisions, provide instruction, and offer advice and guidance.[5] To this end, there are times when supervisors might need to provide more intensive oversight and intervention. In other words, in police work, there are certain situations that require micromanagement.

High-Profile Cases: When subordinate officers or supervisors are working on a sensitive or high-profile investigation, managers will need to know explicit details to ensure a thorough and proper investigation, to implement an immediate change in direction when necessary, and to report to the agency's administration on the case's progress.

Time Constraints: When time constraints dictate the quick completion of an investigation or other project, managers will need all of the explicit details. Managers hold the key position in gathering all facts, making rapid decisions, acquiring the necessary personnel and resources, and reporting to stakeholders.

Inability to Perform: When subordinate officers or supervisors are not able to perform at the basic level of competency, managers must involve themselves to develop their subordinates' competency.[6] For example, a new officer might not yet have acquired the necessary skills to complete tasks, or a veteran officer is building new skills in a new position. In both scenarios, the subordinates will require a great deal of direction and coaching from their supervisors.

Unwillingness to Perform: Subordinate officers or supervisors who are unwilling to perform the work required of them also need micromanagement.[7] For example, employees who are disgruntled, apathetic, or burned out from years of stress might need close monitoring or discipline, when appropriate, to get them on track.[8]

Marginal Workers: Subordinate officers or supervisors whose work quality is marginal or who face performance issues need special attention and guidance. This type of oversight, usually formal in nature, is often only temporary, until the marginal employees elevate their performance to at least a satisfactory level.

FALSE ACCUSATIONS OF MICROMANAGEMENT

A claim of micromanagement is often a false accusation. Law enforcement supervisors must remain aware of instances when proper oversight may be misconstrued as micromanagement. The following scenarios provide examples of times when this is likely to happen.

Some supervisors monitor and evaluate the work of their officers more than other supervisors. This, by itself, does not indicate a clear-cut case of micromanagement; rather, these supervisors might have a management style that takes a more interactive approach than does that of their peers.

Other supervisors monitor and evaluate the same as their colleagues but come across as more controlling. This may be due to personality, style, or a lack of what has been termed "process fairness." Simply put, process fairness is taking the time to communicate with employees, explaining actions and decisions, making time to answer questions, and treating workers justly.[9]

New or less experienced officers might be more accepting of their supervisors' input. However, conversely, a squad of seasoned officers with many years of experience are more apt to reject, and might even resent, the same amount of supervision. Furthermore, it bears mentioning that police officers typically possess so-called type A personalities, which serve them well on the street. This same temperament, however, can cause them to find even reasonable levels of oversight troublesome. It also makes them more likely to speak up.

Employees have been known to use the accusation of micromanagement as a "smokescreen" or an attempt to undermine authority.[10] Nobody likes being called a micromanager, since the term carries a negative stigma that conjures up images of a meddlesome boss bereft of any concern for employee independence or competence. Some workers are aware of this and will use the term inappropriately as a means to deflect attention from their own performance issues or to stave off discipline.[11] Legitimate supervisory oversight becomes maligned into something more sinister. When an officer says, "My supervisor is a micromanager," many times what they really mean is, "I want to be left alone" or "No one should question what I'm doing." New supervisors should be keenly aware of this tendency, as their authority will likely be challenged at some point.

Inconsistent decision making by supervisors faced with similar situations can also be to blame for an accusation of micromanagement. Some supervisors become less concerned with doing things right and more concerned with making friends and building personal camaraderie. Supervisors with this style refuse to hold officers accountable for their actions even in the face of obvious issues. They subscribe to the philosophy of "going along to get along" rather than doing their jobs properly. Unfortunately, this makes the jobs of more conscientious supervisors much more difficult, as they are perceived to be micromanagers compared with the more lenient supervisor.

The agency's overall management culture might run contrary to the supervisor's particular style. When top executives demonstrate a laissez-faire style, this top-down management culture pervades the agency. A supervisor who strays from this culture will likely be seen as a micromanager. Lastly, there might be a lack of support from middle or upper-level managers

at times when a supervisor holds officers accountable. This too will skew perceptions. If an individual supervisor is not provided with the proper support, the supervisor might appear to be overly concerned with developing issues and might cast the shadow of micromanagement.

TRUE MICROMANAGEMENT

Not all supervisors who micromanage do so intentionally or even knowingly. Most are acting on what they perceive to be the best interest of their agencies and are unaware that their workers are discontent. In this regard, there are circumstances and other factors that may unwittingly cause supervisors to engage in micromanagement.

Pressure from the agency's administration for better performance can often lead to supervisors taking excessive control. These supervisors believe that a failure to increase productivity, quality, or quantity will reflect poorly on their ability and will therefore have a negative impact. Too often in organizations, supervisors are rewarded for results rather than the process.[12] Ideally, consideration and evaluation would be given to both. In addition, administrators who micromanage tend to develop and promote those most like them, thereby sending a message that to be promoted or gain influence, supervisors should micromanage.[13]

Newly promoted supervisors might have problems adjusting to their new responsibilities. The attention to detail, control, and autonomy that was important as an officer before promotion follows into the new position. The new supervisor fails to see the "big picture" of the responsibilities attendant with promotion. As such, there can be problems with delegation and teamwork. Many will return to what is comfortable and familiar, performing tasks themselves to ensure that the work is done properly.

There may be a lack of trust in subordinate officers. This can result from previous performance issues or simply from unfamiliarity with the work histories and ethics of officers under a supervisor's command. It may also stem from the supervisor's own insecurity.

Similar to a lack of trust, some supervisors believe in their self-perceived "superior" ability compared with that of their subordinates. In this situation, there is a failure to empower subordinate officers, thereby stifling creativity, job knowledge, and professional development.

Finally, some well-intentioned supervisors erroneously mistake micromanagement for mentoring. Rather than utilizing mentorship strategies (such as setting goals, building a vision, offering counsel and support, and modeling appropriate behavior) these supervisors strictly direct, control, and assume subordinates' work under the flawed belief that officers will benefit from a more hands-on, direct approach.

SYMPTOMS OF MICROMANAGEMENT

A supervisor who strictly adheres to the philosophy, "If you want something done right, you have to do it yourself," runs the risk of micromanagement. It is important for supervisors and managers to take an honest look at themselves to determine if they engage in this behavior. The following are telltale characteristics of micromanagers:

- They are overly critical of subordinates; when reviewing work, they tend to find something wrong every time—suffering from what is called the "red pen" syndrome.
- They are easily irritated if decisions are made without their input.
- They spend an inordinate amount of time overseeing simple tasks.
- They seldom praise and never seek out opportunities to provide praise.
- They pride themselves as being "on top of" their officers' work.
- Subordinates appear frustrated, depressed, and/or unmotivated.
- Subordinates never take initiative, instead seeking permission from their supervisors before doing anything.[14]

The first step away from micromanagement is for supervisors to admit being micromanagers. Only

then can a conscious effort be made to work toward a more inspired management style. Awareness and commitment are crucial to successful change.[15] A rapid transformation is unlikely; committed supervisors are best served by focusing improvement efforts on one or two specific characteristics that are causing the micromanaging tendency and then building momentum from incremental successes.[16]

When delegating responsibility, upfront communication becomes essential. Time should be spent detailing tasks and expectations at the outset rather than saying nothing and critiquing at the end.[17] As with most remedies to micromanaging, communicating at appropriate times and in the proper manner is crucial.

Open-ended questions that spark problem solving should be used when employees are uncertain on how to proceed or when mistakes are made. For example, rather than stating, "This was not handled properly—here is how it should be done," the supervisor should ask, "What are some ways this situation could be handled differently in the future?" The phrasing of the question evokes discovery, action, and creative problem solving as the subordinate looks forward in time.[18] Conversely, supervisors should avoid the use of the word *why* when phrasing such questions. This style of questioning (for example, "Why was this done?") is typically perceived as an attack on a decision. Subordinates do not have the opportunity to explore other options, as they think to the past and immediately attempt to defend their behavior or motivation.[19]

Progress reports should be requested at predetermined intervals for more complicated tasks. This way, subordinates do not have to guess about when to provide updates, and supervisors do not have to badger employees for information. Regular updates not only allow for better communication; they also allow for early adjustments when problems are found.

Praise is a necessary part of supervisory feedback, as micromanagement is often mistaken for a simple lack of social support. Too often, supervisors look to correct behavior rather than to provide praise.[20] New supervisors are especially prone to this trap. When an evaluation is given only after mistakes are made, the shadow of micromanagement is cast. Seeking out praiseworthy actions will change the perspectives of both supervisors and subordinates, each seeing the other in a more positive light.

Coaching ability should be developed, and supervisory style should be consistent across situations and among officers. Special attention should be given to avoid what is termed the "halo effect," in which supervisors base their opinion of an officer on only one aspect of the officer's performance. For example, an officer who has been a poor performer in the past is expected to continue making mistakes. The officer's supervisor then notices only negative factors about the officer's work and overlooks or minimizes any successes.

Supervisors need to maintain an open mind, be flexible in thought, and engage in participative management, whereby officers are allowed to provide input. In this manner employees are most likely to buy into their supervisors' management style and feel empowered to make sound decisions themselves. There also needs to be an allowance for and an acceptance of mistakes (to the extent possible in law enforcement work). Errors will happen, and when they do, an appropriate response is critical.

ADVICE FOR SUBORDINATES

The advice from career consultants on dealing with micromanagers is mixed. Some recommend that subordinates use assertive communication, whereby they confront their managers, point out the specific micromanaging behaviors, and ask for the opportunity to gain their managers' trust.[21] Others say that this approach will not work and that it could make things worse, as micromanagement is a "personality aberration of insecure individuals."[22]

One common thread, however, is that subordinates cannot change micromanagers. The focus of subordinates when dealing with this type of behavior should be on adapting their own style to meet managers' expectations. Effective strategies should not involve trying to "fix" micromanagers.[23] Some practical strategies follow:

- First, false accusations of micromanagement, as previously discussed, should be ruled out. If a supervisor is not a true micromanager, other strategies might be more successful in improving the supervisor-subordinate relationship.
- "Battles" should be chosen carefully, as micromanagers feel a need to "win" all the time.
- The source of managers' controlling behaviors should be identified.
- Heavy preemptive communication, involving frequent updates and activity reports, should be utilized to ensure that managers are fully aware of progress on assignments or projects. Micromanagers crave information.
- Hypothetical questions and options should be used when discussing alternative solutions to a problem, as this allows for a nonthreatening approach to collaborative decision making.
- A clear understanding of the priority and importance of each task should be ascertained and occasionally confirmed in case of unknown or unexpected changes.
- The "best practices" of others should be considered. Micromanagers tend to back off with some more than others, and astute subordinates will watch closely to learn the secrets of those who are given more slack.[24]

Others recommend that subordinates perform the following actions:

- Carefully document their own daily performance to prove success as an effective independent worker in an attempt to gain trust and in case of a dispute.
- Keep a record of managers' requests in case they say one thing and do another; this can be pointed out.
- Seek help from the department head or human resources to resolve serious issues. Outside sources, such as the agency's employee assistance program or a career counselor, can also be consulted if employees are feeling particularly frustrated.[25]

Law enforcement officers hold the community's trust, something that must be earned every day. No other job has the potential to spark a conflict or cause public outcry as does police work. Although it would be easier to take a hands-off approach to supervision, law enforcement supervisors have a broad range of accountability, including officers, the administration, the police organization, the municipality or government served, and the community. Media headlines are awash with examples of police misconduct and civil litigation. Often, these issues are the result not of too much oversight but rather of too little. The courage to do what is right and hold officers accountable without micromanaging is a delicate but necessary balance that law enforcement supervisors must strike. Armed with the knowledge of what specifically constitutes micromanagement and strategies for avoiding the behavior will help supervisors and managers ensure healthy productivity without overstepping the bounds of good leadership.

NOTES

1. Florence Stone, "Micromanagement: How to Think More Strategically and Less Operationally," *Performance and Profits* (American Management Association) 1, no. 4 (April 2006), http://www.amanet.org/performance-profits/editorial.cfm?Ed=251 (accessed June 11, 2008).

2. Christina Bielaszka-DuVernay, "Essentials: Micromanage at Your Peril," *Harvard Management Update* 12, no. 2 (February 2007): 3.

3. Susan K. O'Brien, "Managing Your Micromanager," cited in Richard L. Porterfield, "The Perils of Micromanagement," *Contract Management* 43, no. 2 (February 2003): 21, http://www.ncmahq.org/files/Articles/5531D_micromanage.pdf (accessed June 11, 2008).

4. Craig Chappelow, "Is George Guilty of Micromanagement?" in Bronwyn Fryer, "The Micromanager," *Harvard Business Review* 82, no. 9 (September 2004): 9, http://dorawood.com/viewFileNavBean.pdf (accessed June 11, 2008).

5. Steve Lemmex, "What Is Micromanagement? And What You Can Do to Avoid It," Global Knowledge Training, 2007, http://images.globalknowledge.com/wwwimages/whitepaperpdf/WP_Micromanage_Lemmex.pdf (accessed June 11, 2008).

6. Ibid.

7. Ibid.

8. Ibid.

9. Joel Brockner, "Why It's So Hard to Be Fair," *Harvard Business Review* 84, no. 3 (March 2006): 122–129, http://www.hbsp.harvard.edu/hbsp/hbr/articles/article.jsp?articleID=R0603H&ml_action=get-article&print=true (accessed June 11, 2008).

10. Adam Hanft, "Grist: Micromanagers, Unite!" *Inc.com*, December 2004, 128, http://www.inc.com/magazine/20041201/ahanft.html (accessed June 11, 2008).

11. Ibid.

12. Wally Adamchik, "Supervising Employees: When Your Supervisors Micromanage," The Sideroad, http://www.sideroad.com/Leadership/supervising-employees.htm (accessed June 11, 2008).

13. Josephine Rossi, "Micromanagement: Necessary Evil, Evil Incarnate, or Something In-Between?" *T+D*, July 2005, 18, http://findarticles.com/p/articles/mi_qa5366/is_200507/ai_n21375269 (accessed June 11, 2008).

14. Lemmex, "What Is Micromanagement?"

15. Mike Toten, "What If You Are the Micromanager?" WorkplaceInfo, August 16, 2005, http://www.workplaceinfo.com.au/nocookie/alert/2005/050816530.htm (accessed June 11, 2008).

16. Ibid.

17. Joan Lloyd, "Are You a Micromanager?" Joan Lloyd at Work, August 22, 2007, http://www.joanlloyd.com/articles/open.asp?art=/articles/1227.htm (accessed June 11, 2008).

18. Laura Whitworth, Henry Kimsey-House, and Phil Sandahl, *Co-Active Coaching: New Skills for Coaching People toward Success in Work and Life*

(Palo Alto, California: Davies-Black Publishing, 1998).

19. Ibid.

20. For additional information, see Tracey G. Gove, "Praise and Recognition: The Importance of Social Support in Law Enforcement," *FBI Law Enforcement Bulletin* 74, no. 10 (October 2005): 14–19, http://www.fbi.gov/publications/leb/2005/oct05leb.pdf (accessed June 11, 2008).

21. Jeff Davis, "Tips for Coping with a Micromanager," TechRepublic, July 9, 2002, http://articles.techrepublic.com.com/5100-1035_11-1043727.html (accessed June 11, 2008).

22. Ibid.

23. Harry E. Chambers, "How to Succeed with a 'My Way' Boss," Career-Intelligence.com, 2004, http://www.career-intelligence.com/management/Micromanager.asp (accessed June 11, 2008).

24. Ibid.

25. Beverly West, "Manage Your Micromanager," Monster Career Advice, 2007, http://career-advice.monster.com/conflict-management/Manage-Your-Micromanager/home.aspx (accessed June 11, 2008).

CONCEPT #3: BUILD RELATIONS: BOTH INTERNALLY AND EXTERNALLY

The police are the public and the public are the police; the police being only members of the public who are paid to give full time attention to duties which are incumbent on every citizen in the interests of community welfare and existence.

—Sir Robert Peel

As you have seen from chapter one, law enforcement administrators must work within social, legal and political contexts. To be effective in all of these areas one must build relations, both within the agency and outside of the agency. The world of private business is full of advice and techniques for success and many of these ideas work effectively of law enforcement. Some of the basics include treating people with courtesy and respect, knowing your customers and always striving for quality service. These basic ideas will help lay the foundation to building relations, but who should you be concerned about?

Internally, you should build relations with your employees, your employees' families, and collective bargaining units. Internal relations should involve both sworn and civilian staff. Externally, there are a limitless number of relations that you may build. It would be helpful to build relations with utility companies, hospitals, other law enforcement agencies, public works departments, transportations agencies, special interest groups, minority groups, senior citizens, and the list goes on and on. In the political arena it is important to remember that you must work with elected officials and you must have good rapport with them. This is especially important in regard to your budget and other action that may require political approval. As the possibilities of relationship building may be limitless a good approach would be to ask yourself one question weekly. Who can I build a new relationship with this week?

This chapter could be a book unto itself, but as other topics are equally important we are limited to selected readings. Five readings have been selected for this chapter, with the first two being related to effective use of the media. There is a long standing distrust by law enforcement of the media and this readings explain this distrust, but more importantly they help to explain how to overcome this distrust, so that you can make effective use of the tool.

The third reading is related to the psychological influence of the uniform. Policing in the United States has gone through not only eras of policing, but also changes in uniform style. For example, traditional caps have been an integral part of uniforms, but now there has been widespread departure form this. Also, now we see many officers dressed in Para-military uniforms with combat boots, tactical vests and leg holsters. What does this do to community relations? What does this do for officer safety? There is no doubt that appearance does have an effect on people, so the administrator must ask these and other questions to determine the most effective uniform for the law enforcement function at hand.

The fourth reading in this chapter discusses building trust and confidence in the community. Then, one more reading is presented with a focus on a particular group of people. Information is presented on police discretion and mentally ill persons. This is an important topic as research indicates that over twenty-five percent of Americans ages 18 and older suffer from a diagnosable mental disorder in a given year.

Surviving the Circus

How Effective Leaders Work Well with the Media

BY GERALD GARNER

At is no secret that many police officers who would not pause before entering a darkened building to pursue an armed offender blanch at the approach of a twenty something news reporter armed with a pad and pencil. The men and women who lead law enforcement agencies cannot afford to be so shy. For police leaders, the ability to communicate clearly is a necessity; communicating effectively with the public is an *absolute* necessity. The news media represent police leaders' most valuable tools for reaching that public.

The truth is that law enforcement executives' lives are better if they enjoy a good working relationship with the local media. That does not require that they "kiss up" to anyone. It also does not mean that they must like every reporter they encounter. It does require that they make an earnest effort to work constructively with the media and ensure that the other members of their agencies do the same.

An effective working relationship with the media starts with establishing credibility. Police leaders' reputations for integrity are their most precious assets. Personal integrity includes the responsibility for telling the truth—that includes being truthful with reporters. Police leaders really can survive the media circus—even when they find themselves in the center ring.

FINDING COMMON GROUND FOR MUTUAL BENEFIT

Contrary to the opinions of some, law enforcement leaders and journalists actually can work together effectively. But police leaders and journalists looking to nourish mutually beneficial working relationships first have some baggage to overcome. In the "bad old days," many reporters tended to see cops as often brutal, frequently lazy, and not very bright. Police bosses were seen as evasive, if not outright liars. They were viewed as cynical and secretive.

For their part, police viewed journalists as bleeding hearts who were predisposed to believe a crook over a cop. Reporters were seen as self-appointed police experts who knew nothing about real police work or the dangers cops faced. Some law enforcement officers saw reporters as hating all authority figures. In that atmosphere, it is hardly surprising that law enforcement leaders and reporters viewed each other as enemies. In that environment, misbehavior on both sides was hardly a rarity.

In reality, police and reporters have a lot in common. Both law enforcement agencies and the media are highly visible, powerful institutions. Both professions attract ambitious, strong-minded employees who possess a strong sense of justice and a desire to help others. Both professions are frequently criticized by the public they serve and are highly sensitive to that criticism. The professionals of both can be highly defensive and feel that they are poorly understood by their critics. Both professions are sometimes secretive about their operations and their methods for gathering information. Professionals in both endeavors see themselves as vital to the public welfare.

As successful leaders in both law enforcement and journalism can relate, both sides can win in the police–media relationship. Getting along is much more rewarding than fighting. Each field of work has a lot to offer the other. Reporters often view law enforcement agencies as their best sources for the type of news in which the public is interested. Peace officers are great sources of interesting information. The law enforcement community has the exciting, attention-grabbing visuals that electronic media require. Simply put, maintaining a good relationship with local agencies can make reporters' jobs much easier.

Nurturing a positive working relationship with the media can prove equally beneficial to law enforcement leaders. Through the press, they can tell the public of the good work done by their personnel. With a positive police–press relationship in place, agencies can educate their communities' residents to protect themselves and can warn them of imminent danger. On the other hand, hostile media can make the police leaders' jobs much harder. Although ethical law enforcement leaders would never curry favor with the press solely for selfish purposes, the fact remains that supportive media can make it a lot easier for chiefs to do—and keep—their jobs.

INTERVIEW GUIDELINES

Law enforcement leaders can take several measures to encourage a favorable state of affairs with the media that cover their agencies. Perhaps the foremost of these measures is to ensure that the agency's message is delivered accurately to an interested public; the most effective means of disseminating these messages is through media interviews. Giving an interview while remaining in complete control should be the goal of every police leader. This can be accomplished by following some basic guidelines.

Potential interviewees should keep in mind that they have something interviewers want: information. Interviewees should have their own objectives in mind and produce the sought-after information when the opportunity presents itself. In that way, they can be sure to put the information *they* want in front of the public.

Next, leaders should determine if they are the appropriate individuals to answer reporters' questions. If, for example, the questions are anticipated to be of a highly technical nature, leaders may be better served by having a staff member with the appropriate specialized knowledge standing by to assist in answering questions.

Police leaders should attempt to see themselves in their interviewers' shoes. What would they want to know if the roles were reversed? It is also acceptable to ask interviewers what questions are going to be posed. This way, police leaders can then gather the facts they need and prepare themselves to answer the queries. Nevertheless, an interviewee should always expect surprise questions. This does not mean the interviewer is being devious; it may simply mean that the interviewee's responses have created additional questions in the mind of the reporter.

If there is any time at all to do so, police leaders should practice out loud answering the questions they are expecting. If there is not enough time for a full-scale rehearsal, interviewed subjects can at least practice their answers mentally.

Wise and ethical police leaders will always tell the truth, and nothing but the truth, during a media interview. They will remain mindful that their credibility is a precious asset not to be wasted. If they do not know the answer to their interviewers' questions, they will say so and offer to get the necessary information, if available, as soon as possible.

Interviewees should strive for a professional yet relaxed demeanor. If the interview is conducted on camera, they should avoid looking careless or sloppy but should also avoid a ramrod-straight posture that makes them look like robots. They likewise should avoid distracting mannerisms such as cramming their hands in their pockets or rattling their keys or pocket change. They should also make eye contact with interviewers throughout, rather than stare into the camera.

Media-savvy law enforcement officials will keep their voices at a normal, conversational level during a taped or live interview. There is no need to shout or otherwise speak abnormally. They will also keep their comments direct, concise, and brief, realizing that their words likely will merit no more than 15 seconds on the broadcast news. They will have very little time to get their point across, so it is vital that they choose their words well.

Police leaders should not hesitate to correct themselves, either during or immediately after the interview, if they realize they have answered a question incorrectly or provided inaccurate information. Accuracy is vital.

DEALING WITH DIFFICULT QUESTIONERS

Although most newspersons are honest, hard-working people who are simply trying to do a difficult job well, occasionally some will be less than above-board with their tactics. As a result, smart law enforcement leaders should be on the lookout for the tricks of less-than-straightforward interviewers.

Convoluted questioners will pose queries that are so long, multifaceted, and outright confusing that law enforcement leaders may have no idea what they are answering. The solution for interviewees is simply to ask questioners good-naturedly to slow down and repeat questions one part at a time. In this way, interviewees can complete their answers to one question before moving on to the next.

The wise leader also will remain on the lookout for *interrupters*. These reporters have the nasty habit of injecting their own opinions or comments before interviewees can finish answering a question. The best response interview subjects can give in this situation is to continue to talk, over the interviewer, if necessary, until they have finished answering. It may sound rude, but it may also be necessary for the speakers to get their important points across without interference.

Misinterpreters may also pose a problem for law enforcement executives. These individuals may lead off an interview by presenting false information or may later sum up comments incorrectly. Interviewees' response should be to correct misinterpreters immediately, even if the interview is live. The danger of leaving bad information in front of the public is too great to do anything less.

The *dead air ploy* can also take in the unaware. Reporters trying this stunt will silently and expectantly stare at their subjects when the latter have finished responding to a question. The hope is that the interviewees will become uncomfortable with the silence and talk some more, perhaps in the process revealing something they had not planned to say. The solution is as simple as it is effective: when finished with a reply, interviewees merely stop talking and stare back at their questioners. After a couple of rounds of this contest, interviewers often get the message and allow the session to proceed in an up-front fashion.

Finally, *ambush interviewers* present a special challenge. These characters may jump their prey in the station house parking lot or just about anywhere else where their quarry does not expect them. Their goal is to obtain an unrehearsed, emotional, and perhaps controversial response from their victims. If law enforcement professionals respond in an unprofessional manner, the ambushers have gotten what they want. Wise leaders refuse to be provoked into responses that will almost certainly guarantee them a spot on the evening news. Instead, they remain calm, courteous, and in control. Interviewees should respond just as they would in any other interview; that is, as professionals. Doing so will make them look good even as it disappoints their tormentors.

A final piece of interview advice is in order for police leaders. Many public figures have seen their careers unravel after an inappropriate comment was picked up by a camera and/or a microphone they thought was turned off. Intelligent leaders will eliminate inappropriate and off-color remarks from their vocabulary. They also will treat every microphone and camera in the area as perpetually live and act accordingly.

HANDLING BAD NEWS

As any law enforcement executive will admit, media duty is a lot more fun when the news being reported bathes the organization and its leader in a favorable light. The reality is, however, that sooner or later bad news visits every law enforcement organization. Whether emanating from a "bad" shooting, a pursuit gone sour, or some other episode of police misconduct, bad news will happen eventually. How law enforcement leaders handle it will go a long way in determining how well they and their agencies survive the crisis. Following some commonsense guidelines for handling bad news will help take some of the sting out of the disaster as well as help it pass more quickly. Survival steps include the following.

Tell the Truth: This is not the time for police leaders to lose their reputation for credibility. Wise leaders will say nothing at all rather than lie. A reputation for truthfulness, once lost, is difficult to reestablish.

Never Say "No Comment": Responding to a question with "no comment" makes law enforcement leaders sound like gangsters in front of a congressional committee. There are better ways of saying essentially the same thing. "I can't answer that just yet because the investigation is still in progress" is one alternative.

Keep Consistent Media Rules during an Incident: When organizations that are normally open and accessible to the media suddenly alter policies to allow no one to speak, they send a signal that they have something to hide. Indeed, a recent experience may convince law enforcement managers that media policies need revision. But rules should be revised only after the current incident is well in the past.

Do Not Hide: When normally accessible police leaders shove others out front during a crisis, they earn the mistrust of the news media and, very likely, the hostility of their own people. Leaders should remain highly visible both inside and outside their organizations during difficult times. They should be the individuals speaking for their organizations.

Convey a Sense of Normalcy: To maintain confidence in a law enforcement agency, both the media and the larger public must see the agency and its leaders carrying on "business as usual," even during difficult times. For one thing, that means continuing to convey the story of the good work that the organization's members are doing. Leaders must scrupulously avoid portraying their agencies as going into a "sandbagging" mode.

Do No Harm: Police leaders should follow the same advice that guides medical professionals: "first, do no harm." One way they can make it worse is by lying. Another is by dribbling out the bad news and making the media "work" to get it. A third is by making the negative event a bigger story than it really is by overresponding to it, "hunkering down" for a siege, or launching a verbal attack on the news organization reporting the story. Media-savvy leaders keep things in perspective and recognize that Monday's "big deal" is often largely forgotten by Friday.

Stay Calm and in Control: Law enforcement executives who lose their self-control and melt down in front of media reps have practically guaranteed themselves time on television channels 2 through 12. Such a performance will benefit neither them nor their agencies. It is vital that leaders maintain their professionalism and self-control even in the face of extreme provocation. It is worth remembering that bad news will pass, and sunnier days are ahead.

FOSTERING POSITIVE MEDIA RELATIONSHIPS

Law enforcement leaders well-versed in using the media as a means to praise and protect their agencies follow some commonsense guidelines for governing their personal relationships with the press. They will, for instance, maintain good relations with their primary media contacts whenever given a reasonable chance to do so. That means they may have a social cup of coffee with reporters even when there is no pressing news. They are willing to trust their media contacts—up to a point. But they will never forget that even their friends in the media will "burn" them, on occasion.

Likewise, intelligent leaders are cautious about going "off the record" with even their closest media confidantes. They realize that once they say something, the reporter is under no legal obligation not to use it. Media-wise leaders follow a simple rule of thumb: "If you do not want to reveal it to the whole world, do not provide it to the media."

Experienced law enforcement professionals know that it is generally better to get along than battle unnecessarily. That simple advice also applies to their personal relationships with the media. Recall the old saw that it does not pay to pick a fight with someone who buys ink by the barrel. At the same time, police leaders should not hesitate to complain loudly but professionally when they have evidence that they or their agencies have been skewered by unfair media treatment. But shrewd leaders pick their battles well. They know not to air a grievance just because they do not like the news that a media organization is reporting. They reserve their criticism for inaccuracies, editorializing, or other examples of poor journalism disguised as legitimate news stories. When they do complain, they offer specifics rather than just an emotional tirade. They know that a calm, reasoned objection is more likely to get results than one that can be dismissed as the emotional response of a justly stung "offender."

Police leaders should also realize that it is not all about them. They should maintain a sense of modesty when dealing with reporters. They should know that their media contacts are seeking the insight and information they possess; the media are not out to make them famous. They should understand that when they are gone, the media will lavish equal attention on their replacements.

Finally, wise law enforcement executives use the full services of the media when they have good news to spread. They do not wait to be contacted by reporters about the exceptional work done by their employees. They instead take a proactive approach with radio, television, and print media by contacting media sources via news release, press conference, an offer of a personal interview, or all of these methods of disseminating information. They do not overlook the growing value of the Internet for getting out the good word, either. They are quick to go to the media when they need the public's help with a case or to spread important information, such as crime prevention advice, both quickly and widely. They know that maintaining a positive working relationship with the media will make it possible to count on the media's good offices when the chips are down and they need quick access to the public.

CONCLUSION

Working with the media is not complicated. Collaborating positively is a lot more rewarding than fighting with each other. Police leaders and reporters have a lot to offer each other. Each can help the other succeed. Together, they can really achieve that rarest of scenarios: a win-win situation. But best of all, the taxpayers benefit, from learning about the threats to public safety and what their law enforcement officers are doing about those threats. The ensuing free flow of information benefits all involved.

Gerald W. Garner, a veteran of 40 years in the law enforcement profession, is chief of the Greeley, Colorado, Police Department and a former police public information officer. Holding degrees in the administration of justice as well as journalism, he has authored two books on police–media relations and has instructed on the topic for the IACP and the U.S. Federal Bureau of Investigation's National Academy.

The Media, the Public and the Law Enforcement Community

Correcting Misperceptions

BY MICHAEL TOOLEY, HEFFREY LINKENBACH, BRIAN LANDE, AND GARY LANDE

The law enforcement profession has always been a tough business. Over the course of a career, law enforcement officers see the best and the worst in humanity. They may be thanked for what they do and then be spit upon not an hour later. Sometimes this leaves officers confused as to how the public they serve feels about them—and consequently, how they feel about the public.

Law enforcement officers often wear Kevlar vests to protect themselves from lawbreakers' bullets. Over the years, officers also tend to develop an emotional "Kevlar exterior" to protect themselves from the negative things they see and feel.

In spite of well-developed emotional armor, it is sometimes impossible not to let some of this negativity slip inside and bring an officer down. But there are ways to cope. In Montana, for example, a partnership has been established between university-based researchers and the Montana Highway Patrol to help those who pledge a life of continuously *positive* service through the badge.

The formation of this partnership followed a legislative session in 2005, in which a task force was established to bring about change in Montana's impaired-driving statutes. As the work of the group progressed, both law enforcement personnel and academics who were participating realized that they had much to contribute through the shared aspects of their respective disciplines.

One important revelation resulting from the work of the task force was that laws and those who enforce them enjoy enormous support from the public. This countered the perceptions of some participants, who had seen the worst in people over many years—people who did not support the mission and the actions of modern law enforcement agencies. The partnership formed when officers and researchers decided to take a closer look at this discrepancy.

Research conducted by Montana State University in the summer of 2006 points out numerous misperceptions on the part of the law enforcement community. What the mainstream media report and what the public as a whole believes are not the same. The research revealed overwhelming support for police officers and their efforts to reduce crime and keep neighborhoods safe. On the street, however, it is easy for officers to believe that the opposite is true, because they generally do not come into contact with the supportive segment of the population. The same research indicates that many police officers do in fact feel distrusted and unappreciated by the public.

POLICE PERCEPTION STUDY

The Montana Highway Patrol, in conjunction with researchers from Montana State University, conducted a study of how law enforcement officers across the United States believe they are perceived by the public—how officers see themselves in a "social mirror" of sorts. An additional survey was conducted to see how the public really feels about the law enforcement community.[1] Initially, the study was restricted to measuring the support the public had for the enforcement of impaired-driving laws, but as the study design phase continued, it became obvious that the underlying issue of trust in police officers to do their jobs also needed to be measured to determine if the perceptions of the public and those of the police were in agreement.

What the study found in the survey of law enforcement officers was as surprising as it was troubling. Regardless of where researchers looked, no matter the differences in agencies and communities, there appeared to be a nationwide consensus opinion among law enforcement officers that they are distrusted by the public. For example, a state trooper in Boston, Massachusetts, stated, "People don't like us much," while a police officer in Portland, Oregon, said that he was angry because people form a negative opinion of him without even knowing him. Boston and Portland are 3,092 highway miles apart. It is unlikely that these officers have ever met, yet they have the same negative opinion of how the public views them. Researchers asked why they feel the way they do; both said it was because of the negative press coverage they routinely saw on television.

Time and time again, despite vast differences in communities, the study found that law enforcement officers firmly believed that the populations they serve had primarily negative perceptions of them. This pervasive feeling is not new. Consider this excerpt from a study of police behavior by William Westley, a social scientist:

> The policeman finds his most pressing problems in his relationships to the public. His is a service occupation but of an incongruous kind, since he must discipline those whom he serves. He is regarded as corrupt and inefficient by, and meets with hostility and criticism from, the public. He regards the public as his enemy, feels his occupational [responsibilities] to be in conflict with the community, and regards himself to be a pariah. The experience and feeling give rise to a collective emphasis on secrecy, an attempt to coerce respect from the public, and a belief that almost any means are legitimate in completing an important arrest. These are for the policeman basic occupational values. They arise from his experience, take precedence over his legal responsibilities, [and] are central to an understanding of his conduct.[2]

Although this was written by someone familiar with the profession only from a research perspective, parts of it could have been written by the state trooper from Massachusetts or the police officer from Oregon. The negative perception is as real today as it was when Westley wrote about it in 1953.

PUBLIC SUPPORT OF POLICE

It is very unfortunate that officers see themselves as distrusted and underappreciated, but the good news is that the Montana State research also points out that the law enforcement community holds numerous misperceptions about the way it is viewed. What the mainstream media report and what the public as a whole believes are not the same. The innovative research conducted in the summer of 2006 shows that there is overwhelming support for police officers and their efforts to reduce crime and keep neighborhoods safe.

Specifically, 85.3 percent of persons responding to the national survey Montana State conducted stated that they were supportive of the law enforcement community, whereas only 10 percent stated that they were not. On the street, it is easy for an officer to believe that the opposite is true, because they generally do not come into contact with one of the 85.3 percent. Officers are judging the people that make up their day-to-day work world not based on an objective view of reality but rather based on powerful misperceptions that bias their attitudes and behavior.

Interestingly, the study found that two important groups do feel that law enforcement officers are not generally trustworthy. First, African Americans were much more likely to report negative feelings; this is not surprising, according to the sociologist Loâ°c Wacquant, and is likely related to disproportionately high incarceration rates and withdrawal of governmental resources at all levels from poor black communities since the urban riots of the late 1960s.[3] As a result, the most visible daily representation of the government is now the police. With greater opportunity for contact comes greater opportunity for conflict—and greater opportunity for police officers to make mistakes or either intentionally or unintentionally create negative perceptions. None of these issues foster much support for the police.

Another group that has less than a favorable opinion of law enforcement officers in general comprises victims of such crimes as impaired driving. Although the overall numbers of support are high, the survey's results indicate at least two areas of opportunity to improve perceptions of the profession.

Even though some of the survey's results were not ideal, these results are a great starting point for launching a positive community norms campaign to improve morale and public service in law enforcement agencies. The general public supports what the profession does in the community regardless of negative perceptions of some members of society and especially negative press coverage. But officers themselves are not immune to the effects of media reports on their actions.

MEDIA INFLUENCE ON PUBLIC PERCEPTION

Police officers take seriously news representations of what they do. They believe that the way the profession is represented in the media both reflects and creates a real public sentiment.

Highlighting this predicament in 2006, a 23-year-old black male was killed by three police officers—an incident that was especially emotional because it occurred just hours before the man was to be married. Most police departments have an internal review policy, and the city police department that was involved has a very well-developed review protocol. In an effort to avoid causing interference, or the perception of interference, in other processes (such as internal and external investigations), the department does not release the results of its reviews until those other processes have run their course. For this reason, very little is said on behalf of the police department during this lengthy period of time.

Meanwhile, the media has a limited amount of information with which to generate a story. Invariably much of that information comes from the angry and grieving relatives of the deceased. So the story that is told for many months, as the department's legal and internal review processes continue, is very much one-sided, almost always casting the police in a negative light. In the present case, the state criminal charges against the officers were dismissed. However, the officers still potentially face federal civil rights charges as well as internal sanctions from their department.

It is easy to put oneself in the place of an inexperienced 23-year-old police officer watching the evening news. She watches the story unfold and sees days and weeks of follow-up stories that send the same message: the public believes that the police are violent, corrupt, and untrustworthy. This is not the picture of appreciated and valued public service that the young officer had in mind when she raised her hand and took the oath of office perhaps only one year earlier.

However, the data obtained from the Montana studies indicate that, frankly, police officers and administrators have not given the public enough credit. As mentioned earlier, the national survey information states that more than 80 percent of individuals across the United States describe themselves as supportive or very supportive of the law enforcement community. Approximately the same number feel safer when they see a law enforcement officer nearby, compared to only 11 percent who do not feel safer in an officer's presence.

The national survey results show that people typically disregard media reports when it comes to forming their own opinion of law enforcement officers.

In reality, people's opinions are formed by their own experiences with law enforcement agencies. How people are treated by officers and the behavior they actually observe in a police–citizen encounter are the two major factors in determining their opinions. This is an important fact that savvy police administrators have driven home for years.

Good police officers are always aware of their physical surroundings. However, the same officers are often unaware that perception issues may be media driven. Officers across the United States have greatly overestimated the ability of the media to influence public opinion of policing.

In fact, data from the Montana State University public survey show that 77 percent of respondents stated that media coverage of law enforcement agencies did not change their opinion of police officers one way or another. Of the remainder, more people gained a more positive view of the profession through the media than a negative view. These numbers run totally counter to the perceptions of many law enforcement officers.

INTERNAL INFLUENCE ON LAW ENFORCEMENT ATTITUDES

This negative way the law enforcement community believes the public perceives it is reinforced not only by the public and the media but often by senior officers as well: at police academies, at the station, in training, and in the lunch room. Biased media coverage only confirms what they already "knew" from years of police work and shared stories in the squad room.

Are there consequences to police officers believing that the public distrusts them? What happens if police administrators come to take for granted a culture of negativity? Can negative attitudes about, and expectations of, groups turn misperceptions into reality? The risk to police and sheriff's departments is that prolonged negative feelings can become self-fulfilling; an untrusted, unappreciated department can come to find itself at odds with a public it perceives as ungrateful, self-entitled, uncooperative, or worse—"stupid." This potentially dangerous situation not only can give

rise to demeanor complaints against officers but can raise the stakes to the possibility of violence between officers and the public.

The potential for disaster begs the following question: what can police chiefs and sheriffs do to ameliorate the negative sentiments that their "troops" take home from their day-to-day encounters, their viewing of the news, and the culture of the squad room?

> You never change things by fighting the existing reality. … To change something, build a new model that makes the existing model obsolete.
>
> R. Buckminster Fuller

USING SOCIAL NORMS THEORY TO TRANSFORM THE CULTURE OF A DEPARTMENT

Social norms theory, a sociological theory that attempts to explain how the perceptions of a group can shape the group's behavior, suggests that when police officers come to believe that their peers have negative beliefs about the populations they serve, they are likely to take on those attitudes themselves.[4]

Social science research, including interviews, surveys, and observations of the public's attitudes toward the law enforcement community, can shed light on the reality of public support for law enforcement agencies. Such data reveal that police officers significantly misperceive the public's support for them. Chiefs, by sharing this information, then have the power to bring their employees' perceptions into agreement with reality.

Studies such as those conducted by Montana State University can be used to assist chiefs in transforming the culture of their agencies from negative to positive. In short, if chiefs want to change their agencies' culture, they need to encourage their officers to stop telling antagonistic stories about their relationship with the public. Data gathered on what the public thinks of its agencies as well as what it considers to be serious problems allow agencies to have an objective sense of where they stand and how well they are doing in meeting public expectations. Officers will think and function differently when they are given an accurate sense of how their communities perceive and support them.

Why might changing police officers' perceptions of how the public views them transform their behavior? Social norms theory states that, to a large extent, people's behavior and attitudes are influenced by their perception of normal behaviors and beliefs within their social group. According to social norms theory, people tend to misperceive (that is, exaggerate) the negative behaviors and attitudes of their peers. If people think that negative behavior is typical, they are more likely to engage in that type of behavior.

But such perceptions are often incorrect. If negative behaviors or attitudes are perceived to be the standard in a social group, the social urge to conform will negatively affect overall behavior and attitudes of the group members. Alternatively, by educating a group about the sort of positive behavior that is in fact the usual and expected practice among their peers, behaviors and attitudes can be affected in a positive manner.

INTEGRATING THE "THIN BLUE LINE" INTO GENERAL SOCIETY

The law enforce ment community has been described in countless ways, but arguably the most famous is its representation as the "thin blue line" that protects the law-abiding side of society from the criminal side.

It should come as no surprise, then, that the individuals who make up the thin blue line—which is actually not just blue but also brown, green, beige, and white should think of themselves as set apart from normal society. Since they form a boundary, they cannot truly belong to either side; for this reason, they usually belong only to each other. They are their own social group.

In most parts of the United States, law enforcement officers tend to associate only with other law enforcement officers and their immediate families. Even their families associate mainly with other law enforcement families. The result is a unique societal group with its own norms and practices—one that is susceptible to the phenomenon described by social norms theory.

Knowing this fact gives police administrators the opportunity to take advantage of social science to improve morale within their departments, which in turn positively affects their service to the public.

Police chiefs and other ranking officers need to understand for themselves that their departments are overwhelmingly supported. One particular area that the public supports is the enforcement of the motor vehicle code. The surveys performed by Montana State University in 2006 indicated that the public believes that impaired-driving violations are a major threat to their personal safety and the safety of their friends and relatives. Moreover, they wanted to see police officers, district attorneys, and judges take an active and strong stand on offenses related to impaired driving.

The study also found that police officers typically thought there was minimal support for their activities related to impaired driving. Officers reported that this belief influenced their interest and willingness to enforce what in fact were popular laws because they believed that the public thought exactly the opposite. Officers need to be disabused of these impressions if they are to enforce impaired-driving laws—and indeed to perform any of their duties—with maximum effectiveness.

Knowing that a nationwide misperception exists is the first step toward eliminating it and boosting morale within law enforcement agencies. One concept that can help this cause is called the "science of the positive," the aim of which is to promote authentic community transformation through the adoption of a portfolio of applied strategies. This concept offers a new twist on social norms theory that may be appropriate for use in law enforcement agencies.

TURNING THE TIDE OF MISPERCEPTION

Addressing social norms is a new and sometimes controversial approach to changing behaviors. A social norms campaign challenges people's commonly held perceptions about the environments in which they live and the behavior of their peers, as well as their beliefs about how problems should be confronted. A campaign of this sort informs line officers, supervisors, and administrators of the realities of their respective positions within their communities. Agencies can improve the reception of such a campaign and reduce the inevitable criticisms of it if they educate key stakeholders and community members about social norms theory and win stakeholder and community support before the campaign begins.

To help people better understand and accept social norms, it can be helpful to frame it within the larger context of the science of the positive. The Positive Community Norms Model (PCN) is a process of promoting health and safety norms within a community based on the theory of the science of the positive. PCN incorporates multiple social change theories through a unifying community development process. Consistent with both the spirit of community policing and other law enforcement strategies, this model is a way to approach issues from a positive rather than a negative perspective. It is a move away from the media-driven "if it bleeds, it leads" sensationalizing mentality. PCN and the science of the positive hold that people's behavior can be shaped through positive modeling and reinforcement rather than through threats and punishment.

It is worth bearing in mind that many members of the media decided to enter their profession for the same reason that law enforcement officers enter theirs: to make a positive difference in their world.

The positive aspects of the law enforcement profession are well known to those who serve in it. However, officers can be affected when public perceptions and conversations are skewed in the media. It is critical to understand that to promote positive community norms, agencies must work proactively with the media and use the tools of social science. It is time for agencies to allow their perceptions to be buoyed by the reality of public support for their actions; through that positive affirmation, the law enforcement community can change the perceptions and the reporting of the media.

Framing this mission in this way calls to mind the words of a great visionary, R. Buckminster Fuller: "You never change things by fighting the existing reality. ... To change something, build a new model that makes the existing model obsolete."

Notes:

1. MOST of Us Institute for Social Norms, "Americans' Attitudes toward Drinking, Driving, and Law Enforcement: The Results of a Telephone Survey" (unpublished, Montana State University, 2006).

2. William A. Westley, "Violence and the Police," *American Journal of Sociology* 59 (July 1953): 35.

3. Loïc Wacquant, "Deadly Symbiosis: Rethinking Race and Imprisonment in Twenty-first-Century America," Boston Review 27, no. 2 (April—May 2002), http://bostonreview.net/BR27.2/wacquant.html (accessed April 9, 2009).

4. See, for example, H. Wesley Perkins and Alan D. Berkowitz, "Perceiving the Community Norms of Alcohol Use among Students: Some Research Implications for Campus Alcohol Education Programming," *International Journal of the Addictions* 21 (1986): 961–976.

The Psychological Influence of the Police Uniform

By Richard Johnson

Most people can identify law enforcement officers by their official police uniform. When citizens on a busy street need help, they scan the crowd of pedestrians looking for the distinctive uniform of a police officer. Normally, drivers who arrive at an intersection and find a person in a police uniform directing traffic willingly submit to that person's hand directions. Criminals usually curb their unlawful behavior when they spot a uniformed police officer. Many parents teach their children to respect and trust a person in police attire. Police academy recruits relish the day when they finally wear their official uniforms.

The crisp uniform of the police officer conveys power and authority. When officers put on their uniforms, citizens believe that they embody stereotypes about all police officers. Research has suggested that clothing has a powerful impact on how people perceive each other. The police officer's uniform has a profound psychological impact on others, and even slight alterations to the style of the uniform may change how citizens perceive them.

The police uniform represents a tradition as old as the field of law enforcement. In 1829, the London Metropolitan Police, the first modern police force, developed standard police apparel. These first police officers, the famous "Bobbies" of London, wore a dark blue, paramilitary-style uniform. The color blue helped to distinguish the police from the British military, who wore red and white uniforms. In 1845, the city of New York established the first official police force in the United States. Based on the London police, the New York City Police Department adopted the dark blue uniform in 1853. Other cities, such as Philadelphia, Boston, Cincinnati, Cleveland, Buffalo, and Detroit, quickly followed by establishing police departments based on the London model and included the adoption of the dark blue, paramilitary-style uniform.[1]

Today, most U.S. law enforcement agencies continue to select police uniforms generally dark in color with a paramilitary appearance. Agencies may prefer dark colors for their ease in cleaning and their ability to help conceal the wearer in tactical situations. Dark colors help hide stains and keep officers hidden from criminals, especially at night.[2] However, why do most agencies insist that patrol officers dress in uniforms? Perhaps, the uniform actually psychologically influences the public's perception of officers.

THE SOCIAL SIGNIFICANCE OF CLOTHING

Individuals seek clues about others from their appearance. Clothing provides one powerful clue to an individual's background[3] and serves as a mental shortcut to identify a person's sex, status, group membership, legitimacy, authority, and occupation. Clothing and physical appearance are important in the initial development of social relationships.[4] Studies have revealed that physical appearance, including clothing, remains the factor used most often in developing a first impression of someone[5] and has an even greater effect than personality.[6]

In early social interactions, clothing has a significant psychological influence on people's perceptions. In one study, personnel administrators rated the competency of similar female job applicants. They consistently rated the women in conservative, slightly masculine attire as the most competent.[7] In another experiment, both high school students and teachers rated pictures of female athletes dressed either in uniforms or casual clothes. Participants perceived all of the athletes in uniform as being more professional, possessing higher ability, and having more team spirit.[8] Similarly, other research revealed that both students and teachers rated photos of students dressed in private school-type uniforms as having higher scholastic ability.[9]

Additionally, the uniform worn by a police officer elicits stereotypes about that person's status, authority, attitudes, and motivations. The police uniform identifies a person with powers to arrest and use force and establishes order and conformity within the ranks of those who wear it by suppressing individuality.[10] The police uniform can have extraordinary psychological and physical impact. Depending on the background of the citizen, the police uniform can elicit emotions ranging from pride and respect, to fear and anger.

THE POWER OF THE POLICE UNIFORM

Research has supported suggestions about the police uniform's power and authority. In one study, individuals ranked 25 different occupational uniforms by several categories of feelings. The test subjects consistently ranked the police uniform as the one most likely to induce feelings of safety.[11] In another experiment, participants consistently rated models as more competent, reliable, intelligent, and helpful when pictured in a police uniform, rather than in casual clothes.[12] When an individual wearing a police-style uniform stood on a sidewalk near a corner, drivers committed fewer turn violations at that intersection. This occurred even though the uniform did not

represent a real police department in the area, and the individual did not display a badge or weapon.[13]

In one experiment to test the power of the police uniform, a research assistant randomly approached pedestrians on a city street and ordered them to either pick up a paper bag, give a dime to another person, or step back from a bus stop.[14] The research assistant alternately wore casual clothes, a milk delivery uniform, or a grey, police-style uniform bearing a badge but lacking weapons. Only the police-style uniform resulted in a high rate of cooperation from citizens. More-over, obedience to the police-style uniform usually continued even after the research assistant quickly walked away and did not watch to ensure compliance.[15]

CHANGES IN THE UNIFORM STYLE

Although the police uniform in general suggests the authority of the wearer, details about a police officer's uniform, such as the style of hat or the tailoring, can influence the level of authority emanating from the officer. Study participants in one experiment evaluated photographs of uniformed male and female police officers wearing nine different styles of head gear, including no hat at all. Even though psychological tests showed that participants perceived the officers to have authority under all of the circumstances, the type of hat varied the level of authority attributed to the officer. The traditional "bus driver" garrison cap and the "smoky bear" campaign hat conveyed more authority than the baseball cap or no hat at all.[16]

Many studies have addressed the influence of eliminating the paramilitary style of the police uniform. In one experiment, students viewed black and white drawings of three styles of police uniforms. Two of the uniforms represented a traditional paramilitary style, but lacked a duty belt or weapons. The third, nontraditional uniform consisted of a sport coat, or blazer, over slacks and a shirt with a tie. Although students ranked all three uniforms similarly for objectivity and trustworthiness, the blazer-style uniform ranked slightly higher for professionalism.[17] However, a similar experiment using color photos found the traditional, paramilitary style uniforms ranked as more honest, good, helpful, and competent than the blazer uniform.[18]

In 1969, the Menlo Park, California, Police Department discontinued their traditional navy blue, paramilitary-style uniforms and adopted a nontraditional uniform hoping to improve police-community relations. The new, nontraditional uniform consisted of a forest green blazer worn over black slacks, a white shirt, and a black tie. Officers displayed their badges on the blazer and concealed their weapons under the coat.[19] When other agencies heard about Menlo Park's attempt, over 400 other police departments in the United States also experimented with a blazer-style uniform.[20]

After wearing the new uniforms for 18 months, the Menlo Park police officers displayed fewer authoritarian characteristics on psychological tests when compared to officers in the surrounding jurisdictions.[21] Also, after wearing the uniforms for over a year, assaults on the Menlo Park police decreased by 30 percent and injuries to civilians by the police dropped 50 percent. Originally, the department thought the uniform changes resulted in these decreased rates, but other variables factored in at the same time. The number of college-educated officers in the department increased dramatically and the agency abolished its traditional autocratic management style during this same time period.[22]

In 1977, after using the blazer-style uniform for 8 years, the Menlo Park Police Department determined that it did not command respect; therefore, they returned to a traditional, paramilitary-style uniform. A final evaluation showed that, although assaults on officers had dropped during the first 18 months of the new uniform implementation, the number of assaults steadily began to rise again until it doubled the amount of the year before the uniform change occurred. During the 4 years after the Menlo Park police returned to a traditional uniform, the number of assaults on their officers dropped steadily.[23]

Experiments with hats and the style of the police uniform suggest that changes in the design of a police uniform can have an effect on the perceived authority, power, and ability to control. Does the color of the uniform psychologically influence the people who view it and have an effect on the officer wearing the uniform as well?

THE INFLUENCES OF COLOR

Many police departments in the United States use darker colors for their uniforms, such as black, blue, brown, green, or grey. Just as with the style of the police uniform, the color of the uniform also has meaning. Psychological tests have found that individuals associate colors with specific moods. For example, people generally associate red with excitement and stimulation, which explains why agencies often use it for flashing emergency vehicle lights. These tests also have found that individuals associate the color blue with feelings of security and comfort and the color black with power and strength.[24]

Studies of both U.S. high school and college students have found that students perceived light colors, such as white and yellow, as weak, but also as good and active. The same students perceived dark colors, such as black and brown, as strong and passive, but also as bad. Cultural influences did not affect these results, which did not vary with the race of the students.[25]

People in Europe, Western Asia, Central Africa, and the Middle East had similar perceptions of colors. Across all cultures studied, people consistently associated light colors with goodness and weakness and dark colors as strong, but evil.[26] On psychological inventories, test subjects rated lighter colors as more pleasant and less dominant. Dark colors, on the other hand, elicited emotions of anger, hostility, dominance, and aggression.[27]

Color has a considerable impact on clothing and perceptions of the wearer. When people rated pictures of models for attractiveness, clothing color appeared the most common determinant.[28] Individuals perceived job applicants wearing dark business suits as more powerful and competent than those who wore lighter colored suits.[29] Another interesting study found that referees who viewed several videotaped plays of a football game more likely assessed stiffer penalties against a football team wearing a black uniform than against a team wearing a brightly colored uniform. The referees consistently perceived the team in black as more aggressive. An analysis of all professional football and hockey teams in the United States, which found that teams in darker uniforms received far more penalties for roughness than teams in lighter uniforms, supported this experiment. Again, these results suggest that referees negatively perceive teams in darker uniforms.[30]

"The police uniform also may influence the safety level of the officer who wears it."

Moreover, experiments have suggested that athletes act more aggressively when dressed in dark colors. One researcher asked college students dressed in black jerseys and grouped into teams of five to rank which sports they would most like to play. The students consistently ranked the most aggressive sports, such as football and rugby, at the top of the list. A new group of students dressed in white jerseys repeated the experiment. This time, the students selected less aggressive sports, such as baseball or basketball.[31]

Applying the results of these studies in color to the police uniform suggests that darker police uniforms may send negative subconscious signals to citizens. A dark police uniform may subconsciously encourage citizens to perceive officers as aggressive, evil, or corrupt and send a negative message to the community. The experiment with the colored jerseys also suggests that police officers in dark uniforms subconsciously may act more aggressively; therefore, departments should consider modifying police uniform colors.

In one experiment, researchers presented subjects with color photos of two traditional paramilitary-style uniforms. One of the uniforms consisted of the dark navy blue shirt and pants commonly worn by municipal police agencies today. The other traditional uniform resembled that of California sheriff's deputies, consisting of a khaki shirt and dark green pants. Although subjects ranked both uniforms similarly as good, honest, helpful, and competent, the lighter colored sheriff's uniform rated noticeably higher for warmth and friendliness. Because the sheriff's uniform only has a light colored shirt, with the pants still very dark,[32] a half dark uniform sends a better message than the all dark blue or black uniform.

With today's focus on community-oriented policing and efforts to present a friendlier image to the public, the color of the police officer's uniform might make the task more difficult than necessary. Because of citizens' negative psychological perception of dark colors, they may perceive a police officer in a negative manner partly because of the officer's uniform color. If referees believe athletes wearing black exhibit more aggressive behavior, citizens might perceive officers in black uniforms as more aggressive than those wearing lighter colored uniforms.

OFFICER SAFETY CONCERNS

The police uniform also may influence the safety level of the officer who wears it. Dark colored uniforms may elicit subconscious negative feelings from citizens, who may perceive the officer as aggressive, and subsequently, encourage them to consider violent action when confronted by the police.

In addition to the color, the condition of a police officer's uniform and equipment also can have an impact on the officer's safety. Interviews with prison inmates who have murdered police officers indicate that the killers often visually "sized up" the officer before deciding to use violence. If the officer looked or acted "unprofessional" in the assailant's eyes, then the assailant felt capable of successfully resisting the officer. A dirty or wrinkled uniform or a badly worn duty belt may convey to suspects that officers have complacent attitudes about their job. This complacency can invite violence[3]

In many situations involving the use of force, the fact that a police officer has a distinguishable uniform can help prevent the officer's injury or death. An officer in plainclothes risks harm by citizens and other officers as a result of misidentification. In certain scenarios, almost all police officers immediately would draw their weapon on people wearing jeans and a T-shirt and carrying a gun in their hand. A plainclothes officer chasing a burglary suspect through backyards at night risks being shot by a home owner who believes the officer is a criminal. The uniform helps both citizens and fellow police officers identify the wearer as having a legitimate purpose for trespassing, using force, or carrying a weapon.[34]

CONCLUSION

The uniform of a police officer conveys the power and authority of the person wearing it. Research has shown that clothing, including the police uniform, has a powerful psychological impact. When individuals come into contact with each other, they subconsciously search for clues about the other person to understand the context of the encounter. The police uniform represents a powerful clue to the wearer's authority, capability, and status.

Additionally, research has revealed that the uniform has a subconscious psychological influence on people, based on the person's preconceived feelings about police officers. Citizens in the presence of a person in a police uniform cooperate more and curb their illegal or deviant behaviors.

Alterations to the traditional, paramilitary police uniform can result in changes in public perceptions. The style of the clothes, the type of hat worn, the color of the material, and even the condition of the clothes and equipment have an influence on how citizens perceive officers. For these reasons, police administrators seriously should consider their uniform policies. Selecting a uniform style, following regulations on properly wearing the uniform, maintaining uniforms, and designing policies to address when officers may wear plainclothes should command serious attention from department managers. After all, the uniform stands as one of the most important visual representations of the law enforcement profession.

NOTES

1. L. M. Friedman, *Crime and Punishment in American History* (New York, NY: Harper Collins, 1993); and C. D. Uchida "The Development of the American Police: An Historical Overview," in *Critical Issues in Policing,* 2d ed., eds. R. Dunham and G. Alpert (Prospect Heights, IL: Waveland, 1993).

2. E. W. Grosskopf, "The Role of Police Uniforms," *Law and Order,* August 1982, 27–29.

3. D. G. Myers, *Social Psychology,* 4ᵗʰ Edition (New York, NY: McGraw-Hill, 1993), 186–217.

4. N. Joseph and N. Alex, "The Uniform: A Sociological Perspective," *American Journal of Sociology* 77 (1972): 719–730; S. B. Kaiser *The Social Psychology of Clothing* (New York, NY: Macmillan, 1985); L. Shaw, "The Role of Clothing in the Criminal Justice System," *Journal of Police Science and Administration* 1 (1973): 414–420.

5. S. J. Lennon and L. L. Davis, "Categorization in First Impressions," *The Journal of Psychology* 123 (1989): 439–446.

6. B. Connor, K. Peters, and R. Nagasawa, "Person and Costume: Effects on the Formation of First Impressions," *Home Economics Research Journal* 4 (1975): 32–41.

7. S. Forsythe, M. Drake, and C. Cox, "Influence of Applicant's Dress onbInterviewer's Selection Decisions," *Journal of Applied Psychology* 70 (1985): 374–378.

8. M. Harris, S. Ramsey, D. Sims, and M. Stevenson, "Effects of Uniforms on Perceptions of Pictures of Athletes," *Perceptual and Motor Skills* 39 (1974): 59–62.

9. D. Behling, "School Uniforms and Personal Perception," *Perceptual and Motor Skills* 79 (1994): 723–729.

10. Supra notes 2 and 4 (Joseph and Alex; Shaw).

11. S. Balkin and P. Houlden, "Reducing Fearbof Crime Through Occupational Presence," *Criminal Justice and Behavior* 10 (1983): 13–33.

12. M. Singer and A. Singer, "The Effect of Police Uniforms on Interpersonal Perception," *The Journal of Psychology* 119 (1985): 157–161.

13. C. Sigelman and L. Sigelman, "Authority and Conformity: Violation of a Traffic Regulation," *Journal of Social Psychology* 100 (1976): 35–43.

14. This experiment was conducted by psychologist Dr. Leonard Bickman.

15. L. Bickman, "The Social Power of the Uniform," *Journal of Applied Social Psychology* 4 (1974): 47–61.

16. J. Volpp and S. Lennon, "Perceived Police Authority as a Function of Uniform Hatband Sex," *Perceptual and Motor Skills* 67 (1988): 815–824.

17. D. F. Gundersen, "Credibility and the Police Uniform," *Journal of Police Science and Administration* 15 (1987): 192–195.

18. R. Mauro, "The Constable's New Clothes: Effects of Uniforms on Perceptions and Problems of Police Officers," *Journal of Applied Psychology* 14 (1984): 42–56.

19. J. Tenzel and V. Cizanckas, "The Uniform Experiment," *Journal of Police Science and Administration* 1 (1973): 421–424.

20. J. Tenzel, L. Storms, and H. Sweetwood, "Symbols and Behavior: An Experiment in Altering the Police Role," *Journal of Police Science and Administration* 4 (1976): 21–27.

21. Supra note 19.

22. Supra notes 18, 19, and 20.

23. Supra note 18.

24. M. Luscher and I. Scott, *The Luscher Color Test* (New York, NY: Washington Square Press, 1969); L. B. Wexner, "The Degrees to Which Colors Are Associated with Mood-tones," *Journal of Applied Psychology* 38 (1954): 432–435.

25. J. Williams, "Connotations of Color Names Among Negroes and Caucasians," *Perceptual and Motor Skills* 18 (1964): 721–731; J. Williams and C. McMurty, "Color Connotations among Caucasian Seventh Graders and College Students," *Perceptual and Motor Skills* 30 (1970): 707–713.

26. Supra note 24 (Luscher and Scott); F. Adams and C. Osgood, "A Cross-cultural Study of the Affective Meanings of Color," *Journal of Cross-cultural Psychology* 4 (1973): 135–156; J. Williams, J. Moreland, and W. Underwood, "Connotations of Color Names in the U.S., Europe, and Asia," *Journal of Social Psychology* 82 (1970): 3–14.

27. P. Valdez and A. Mehrabian, "Effects of Color on Emotion," *Journal of Experimental Psychology: General* 123 (1994): 394–409.

28. D. J. Radeloff, "Role of Color in Perception of Attractiveness," *Perceptual and Motor Skills* 70 (1990): 151–160.

29. M. Damhorst and J. Reed, "Clothing Color Value and Facial Expression: Effects on Evaluations of Female Job Applicants," *Social Behavior and Personality* 14 (1986): 89–98.

30. M. Frank and T. Gilovich, "The Darker Side of Self- and Social Perception: Black Uniforms and Aggression in Professional Sports," *Journal of Personality and Social Psychology* 54 (1988): 74–85.

31. Ibid.

32. Supra note 18.

33. R. Adams, T. McTernan, and C. Remsberg, *Street Survival: Tactics for Armed Encounters* (Northbrook, IL: Calibre Press, 1980); A. Pinizzotto & E. Davis, "Cop Killers and Their Victims." *FBI Law Enforcement Bulletin* (December, 1992): 9–11; C. Remsberg, *The Tactical Edge: Surviving High-Risk Patrol* (Northbrook, IL: Calibre Press, 1986).

34. Ibid.

Making Every Encounter Count

Building Trust and Confidence in the Police

By Jake Horowitz

Several years ago in the Flatbush neighborhood of Brooklyn, New York, police officers responded to a report of youths stealing from a street vendor. When the uniformed officers arrived on the scene, the youths reacted confrontationally: "Why are you harassing me? I'm just on my way home from school. How dare you! You're just doing this 'cause I'm black."[1]

A large group of onlookers formed. One of the officers said that he sensed the youths were hoping to "get the crowd working against us … [so we would] … just back off." While the officer was explaining to the crowd why they were there, a woman in the crowd spoke up. "I remember this guy," she told the others. "I got my purse robbed 2 months ago and he was really good; he treated me well. I think he's a good cop and I trust him."

The woman's unsolicited comments quelled the crowd, which quickly dispersed without incident. The officer later reflected on the encounter. "I never forgot that lesson," he noted. "You never know when treating people well will pay off—not just in satisfying what you owe to citizens—but in this larger communal sense of gaining allies."

WHAT FACTORS AFFECT PUBLIC SATISFACTION WITH THE POLICE?

Satisfaction with the police, while generally high, is unevenly distributed. Understanding why some

people harbor negative views about police officers is the first and most important step in building a positive relationship with the community.

NIJ recently funded five studies exploring factors that influence satisfaction with the police. The research suggests that satisfaction is shaped by demographic variables, neighborhood crime conditions, and experiences with the police—whether first hand or indirect. Race was not found to directly determine level of satisfaction. Instead, researchers concluded that race, due to its correlation with other demographic variables, neighborhood crime rates, and experiences with police, was an indirect influence on the level of satisfaction with the police.

Although community members' views about the police may be stubbornly resistant to change, police officers and policymakers should appreciate that treating individuals respectfully and professionally during each encounter can establish, build, and maintain crucial support for the police within the community.

THE IMPORTANCE OF QUALITY TREATMENT

When people form opinions of the police based on their interactions, they tend to focus on the process more than the outcome. Impressions of police encounters are influenced by the demeanor as well as the actions of the officer. People pay close attention to the "neutrality of decision making, respectful and polite interpersonal treatment, and ... opportunities for input into decisions," noted Tom Tyler of New York University.[2] Researchers often refer to this as a person's sense of "procedural justice."

People base their impressions of the police on their own personal experiences and on secondhand reports of police encounters. However, because most Americans do not directly interact with the police in any given year, they are forming their opinions on the basis of word-of-mouth accounts from others.

Early studies of satisfaction with police showed that a person's unpleasant experiences had a greater impact than pleasant experiences.[3] Newer studies, however, have found that pleasant experiences have a greater influence than researchers originally thought.[4] As illustrated by the Flatbush officer's experience described at the beginning of this article, positive experiences with the police can have a ripple effect throughout the community.

> *Every encounter—both pleasant and unpleasant—with the public can greatly affect the community's level of satisfaction with the police.*

The implication: Every encounter—both pleasant and unpleasant—with the public can greatly affect the community's level of satisfaction with the police.

It also appears that people bring different expectations to their encounters with the police, depending upon whether those encounters are police- or citizen-initiated. In the past, it was widely assumed that police-initiated encounters had the greatest impact on citizen attitudes.[5] But NIJ-funded research at the University of Illinois at Chicago contradicts that belief. Instead, researchers found that negative encounters have a greater tendency to erode satisfaction with the police when they are citizen-initiated.[6] This finding raises the possibility that individuals' unmet expectations of how the police could or should have assisted them during an encounter may be as influential in forming opinions as the experience itself, regardless of whether citizens or police initiate the contact.

RACE AND THE CONTEXT OF NEIGHBORHOODS

Trust and confidence in the police, however, are built on more than police encounters. Recent NIJ studies also explored the role of race in the formation of opinions about the police.

Although the data show that Caucasians hold the police in higher regard than African Americans or Hispanics, race was not found to directly influence how people form opinions about police. In fact, when researchers controlled for factors such as the level of neighborhood crime, the reported quality of police-citizen encounters, and other demographic variables, such as age, income, and education, the effects of race disappeared entirely or were substantially reduced. Researchers concluded that race affects satisfaction with the police indirectly and in conjunction with other factors, including the level of crime within one's neighborhood.[7]

> *The challenge for law enforcement officers is to treat each encounter—whether with a suspect, witness, or complainant—as if it is that person's first contact with police.*

People in low-crime neighborhoods tend to credit police officers with securing and maintaining low crime rates. As a result, perceptions of the police in those neighborhoods are mostly positive. In neighborhoods with higher crime rates—where racial and ethnic minorities are disproportionately represented—the level of community satisfaction with police is substantially lower. These findings illustrate that, in addition to unpleasant police encounters, individuals' dissatisfaction with crime rates in their community can negatively affect their view of police.[8]

THE IMPACT OF ATTITUDES ON PERCEPTIONS OF POLICE

Some would argue that satisfaction with law enforcement is a dynamic concept, evolving with each citizen's interaction with the police. But recent research challenges that contention. Attitudes toward the police appear to be relatively stable, and people's preexisting views shape their perceptions of future encounters. Researchers at the University of Illinois—Chicago found that residents' initial attitudes toward the police played a critical role in determining their judgments of subsequent experiences and in the formation of future attitudes toward police.[9]

The challenge for law enforcement officers is to treat each encounter—whether with a suspect, witness, or complainant—as if it is that person's first contact with police. If he or she believes that the officer was fair and professional, then that person is more likely to have positive impressions of future encounters with police. Making this effort with each and every interaction is an important investment in building goodwill within the community.

STEPS TO ENHANCING A POSITIVE PUBLIC IMAGE

Public consent and support of law enforcement are two of the most critical tools on a police officer's "belt." People who believe that the police are performing their duties with professionalism and integrity are more likely to obey laws and support the system by acting as witnesses, for example.[10]

NIJ's continuing research into the determinants of satisfaction, trust, and confidence in the police reveals that attitudes toward the police are shaped by a combination of demographic variables, neighborhood conditions, direct and vicarious police citizen encounters, and prior attitudes. The police cannot control some of these factors; others, however, are a direct consequence of an individual officer's actions and demeanor. Therefore, officers should focus their efforts where they can have the most direct impact: in each day-to-day interaction with the public.

The first step in building good relations with the community is to understand and respond to the expectations of people across a range of possible police encounters. Departments might also consider tracking the level of satisfaction through community surveys. This feedback could be used to design police training and intervention programs. In the end, NIJ's research illustrates that it behooves our Nation's police officers to pay close attention to developing what might be called their "bedside manner."[11]

NCJ 216524

For More Information

This article is primarily based on several studies funded by NIJ. The principal investigators published their findings in *Police Quarterly* 8 (3) (September 2005), available at http://pqx.sagepub.com/content/vol8/issue3. The articles are:

- Miller, J., R.C. Davis, N.J. Henderson, J. Markovic, and C. Ortiz, "Measuring Influences on Public Opinion of the Police Using Time-Series Data: Results of a Pilot Study."
- Rosenbaum, D.P., A.M. Schuck, S.K. Costello, D.F. Hawkins, and M.K. Ring, "Attitudes Toward the Police: The Effects of Direct and Vicarious Experience."
- Skogan, W.G., "Citizen Satisfaction With Police Encounters."
- Tyler, T.R., "Policing in Black and White: Ethnic Group Differences in Trust and Confidence in the Police."
- Weitzer, R. and S.A. Tuch, "Determinants of Public Satisfaction With the Police."

NOTES

1. Conversation between the author and a New York City police officer assigned to the Flatbush neighborhood, April 2004.
2. Tyler, T.R., "Policing in Black and White: Ethnic Group Differences in Trust and Confidence in the Police," *Police Quarterly* 8 (3) (September 2005): 339, available at http://pqx.sagepub.com/content/vol8/issue3.
3. Skogan, W.G., "Asymmetry in the Impact of Encounters With Police," *Policing & Society* 16 (2) (2006): 99.
4. Rosenbaum, D.P., A.M. Schuck, S.K. Costello, D.F. Hawkins, and M.K. Ring, "Attitudes Toward the Police: The Effects of Direct and Vicarious Experience," *Police Quarterly* 8 (3) (September

2005): 360, available at http://pqx.sagepub.com/content/vol8/issue3.

5. Ibid., 359.

6. Ibid.

7. Weitzer, R., and S.A. Tuch, "Determinants of Public Satisfaction With the Police," *Police Quarterly* 8 (3) (September 2005): 292; and Skogan, W.G.,"Citizen Satisfaction With Police Encounters," *Police Quarterly* 8 (3) (September

2005): 316. Both articles available at http://pqx.sagepub.com/content/vol8/issue3.

8. Weitzer and Tuch, "Determinants of Public Satisfaction," 292.

9. Rosenbaum et al., "Attitudes Toward the Police," 343.

10. Tyler, "Policing in Black and White," 333.

11. Skogan, "Citizen Satisfaction," 310.

Keeping the Peace

Police Discretion and Mentally Ill Persons

By Linda Teplin

In many urban centers, responding to mentally ill people has become a large part of the police peacekeeping function. Several factors have increased the likelihood of police encounters: deinstitutionalization in the 1960's, cutbacks in Federal mental health funding, and changes in the legal code governing patient rights and affirming the right of a mentally ill person to live in the community without psychiatric treatment.[1]

At the same time, society's tolerance of mentally ill persons in the community is limited. Given the stereotype of mentally disordered people as dangerous,[2] citizens often call upon the police to "do something" in situations involving mentally ill individuals, particularly when they exhibit the more frightening and disturbing signs of mental disorder.[3]

THE POLICE ROLE IN HANDLING MENTALLY ILL PERSONS

Police involvement with mentally ill persons is grounded in two common law principles: (1) The power and responsibility of the police to protect the safety and welfare of the public, and (2) *parens patriae*, which dictates protection for disabled citizens such as mentally ill persons.

Most mental health codes specify the parameters of police involvement with mentally ill persons and instruct police to initiate a psychiatric emergency apprehension whenever the person is either dangerous to self or others or is unable to provide for basic physical needs so as to protect him/herself from serious harm.

Although the law legitimizes the police officer's power to intervene, it does not—and cannot—dictate the officer's response in any given situation. As with all law enforcement decisions, the police must exercise discretion in choosing the most appropriate disposition.

Officers who encounter an irrational person creating a disturbance have three choices: transport that person to a mental hospital, arrest the person, or resolve the matter informally. In making these judgments and in trying to calm situations on their own, the police are called upon to act as "street-corner psychiatrists."

But their options are, in practice, limited. Initiating an emergency hospitalization often is fraught with bureaucratic obstacles and the legal difficulties of obtaining commitment or treatment. In addition, many psychiatric programs will not accept everyone, particularly those considered dangerous, those who also have substance abuse disorders, or those with numerous previous hospitalizations.[4] (See "Law Enforcement Options for Handling Mentally Ill Persons," page 10.)

OFFICER DECISION MAKING REGARDING MENTALLY ILL PERSONS

The seminal study of police officer decision making regarding encounters with mentally ill citizens was

Egon Bittner's in 1967.[5] Bittner found that the police reluctantly made psychiatric referrals and initiated hospitalization only when the individual was causing or might cause serious trouble. Even so, officers resorted to a mental hospital only in the absence of other alternatives.

Almost 15 years later, a study by the author of this article found that little had changed. In 1980, researchers began recording firsthand observations about how police officers handled mentally disordered persons in a large northern city and how these interactions differed from interactions with people who were not mentally disordered.[6]

They found that police resolved situations informally in 72 percent of the cases, made an arrest in 16 percent of the cases, and initiated emergency hospitalization in 12 percent of the cases.

Since the study in the early 1980's, the author has conducted two subsequent studies to determine the prevalence rates of mental disorder in male and female adult jail detainees.[7] In the subsequent studies, nearly 9 percent of male detainees and more than 18 percent of female detainees met the criteria for a lifetime severe mental disorder (schizophrenia or major affective disorder).

A number of mental health professionals have commented on what some observers believe is the

---

Law Enforcement Options for Handling Mentally Ill Persons

Law enforcement officers have two basic ways to respond in situations involving mentally ill people who are causing a disturbance: formally (either hospitalization or arrest) or informally.

Officers' decisions to hospitalize, arrest, or deal with a mentally ill person informally are based less on the degree of symptomatology than on the demands and constraints of the situation. Officers' first choice is usually informal disposition.

Formal Options

Hospitalization. Police use of hospitals is limited by the number of psychiatric beds in the community and by the criteria for admission. Virtually every officer in the study was aware of the stringent requirements for admission into the local psychiatric hospital: Individuals had to be seriously ill—for example, be actively delusional or suicidal. Police knew that persons who were mentally retarded, alcoholic, or categorized by hospital staff as "dangerous" often were not welcome at the hospital, nor were persons with criminal charges pending, no matter how minor.

Furthermore, handling mentally ill persons was not regarded by officers as a "good pinch" and was largely unrewarded by the department, further deterring psychiatric referrals. In addition, officers perceived the rapid deinstitutionalization of mentally ill persons as a personal slight on their judgment and a sign of the hospital's unwillingness to "do something."

Still, occasionally the police did take someone to the hospital, as shown in the following scenario:

We were on the scene in less than a minute. The citizen in question was a black male, about 45 years old, standing on the sidewalk with his arms outstretched, spinning around in circles. ... The officer and the sergeant got the man to stop spinning. They attempted to question him, but the man was completely out of it. He gave no indication that he understood what was going on. He didn't talk at all during the encounter. The officer called for a wagon to take the man to the hospital.

Arrest. While arrest was not a frequent disposition, the arrest rate for persons exhibiting signs of mental illness was greater than that of other citizens involved in similar types of incidents. Arrest often was the only step available to the officer in situations where individuals were not sufficiently disturbed to be accepted by the hospital, but were too public in their deviance to be ignored.

It was common for an officer to obtain a signed complaint in situations where he or she thought an individual required hospitalization. The aim was to ensure the ready availability of an alternative disposition—arrest—in the event that the hospital found the individual unacceptable for admission. The officers' apparent ingenuity was borne out of necessity since hospital admission criteria were so stringent. A typical example:

> The officer said this man had been on the street calling women names, calling them whores, and shouting at black people, calling them names and chasing them. … A woman had signed a complaint for his arrest because he was bothering her. The man sounded like a paranoid schizophrenic. … He was very vague about himself and who he was and felt that people were out to get him. … When he was taken to his cell, he began shouting to be let out and he kept shouting. … He was charged with disorderly conduct. The officer said there wasn't enough to take him into the mental health center because his behavior wasn't that severe for the hospital to accept him.

Likewise, when an individual was defined as "too dangerous" by the hospital, arrest was the only alternative available to the officer:

> A young man was banging on his mother's door with a meat cleaver. … He was threatening to kill someone else and wanted to get into his mother's home for a gun. She wouldn't let him in and had called the police to get rid of him and/or to calm him down. When the police got there, officer II decided the man needed to be hospitalized as he was dangerous to himself and others. So they called for a wagon to take the man to the mental health facility … but they also wanted a complaint signed by the mother for disorderly in case [the hospital wouldn't take him]. It turned out that the hospital would indeed not take the man, so he ended up being locked up for disorderly.

Ironically, it was precisely the requirements for emergency psychiatric detention set forth in most mental health codes—"dangerous to self and others"—that rendered mentally disordered citizens undesirable to hospitals and resulted in their arrest.

Persons whose symptoms crossed the boundaries of the caretaking systems met a similar fate. Mental health programs found persons with alcohol problems disruptive to the patient environment and often would not accept them for treatment. Conversely, detoxification facilities felt they were not equipped to deal with persons exhibiting signs of mental disorder and would turn away persons with such mixed symptoms. In general, jail became the place of last resort. Because mental health … and substance abuse systems tended to design their programs as though clients were "pure types," a number of people were unacceptable for treatment in any health care facility.

The seriousness of an incident also helped to determine the disposition. This did not always mean the seriousness of the offense. For example, situations in which the citizen was disrespectful of the officer were nearly always thought to be "serious." So were situations that were public, offended "decent" people, and had a willing complainant. For example, an elderly woman told police that a man sleeping in a car behind her apartment building had acted crazy the night before and had thrown rocks at the building. It looked as though the man had cut off all his hair, injuring his head in the process, and he was disoriented and filthy. The police told him he would be booked for property damage and probably disorderly conduct.

In sum, the police resorted to arrest in three types of situations:

- When an individual was thought to be either unacceptable to the hospital or when his or her symptoms made him fall through the cracks of various caretaking systems.
- When public encounters exceeded the community's tolerance for deviant behavior.
- When the police felt it was likely that the person would continue to cause a problem if something were not done.

In general, police made a formal disposition—hospitalization or arrest—when the situation, if unchecked, would escalate and require further police assistance. The large grey area between behavior that is mentally disordered and that which is merely disorderly allows officers a great deal of discretion in choosing the disposition. The seriousness of psychiatric symptoms is only one of the determining factors.

Informal Options

Informal dispositions require neither paperwork nor unwanted "downtime"—hours off the street. Emotionally disturbed people who were likely to be handled by informal means were categorized as neighborhood characters, troublemakers, and quiet, unobtrusive "mentals."

Neighborhood Characters. Neighborhood characters were persons whose idiosyncrasies were well known to police in their precinct. Virtually any officer could talk about "Crazy Harry," "Batman," or "Mailbox Molly." These were neighborhood characters who were defined by police as "mentals" but who were never hospitalized because they were known quantities. Police had certain expectations regarding the parameters of their behavior. As a consequence, the police tolerated a greater degree of deviance from them. More important, officers' familiarity with each citizen's particular symptoms enabled them to "cool them out," making an informal disposition that much easier. The following is a rather common encounter of this type:

> There's a lady in the area who claims she has neighbors who are beaming rays up into her apartment. The officer said he usually handles the situation by telling her, "We'll go downstairs and tell the people to stop beaming the rays," and she's happy. The officer seemed quite happy about this method of handling the problem. He could do something for the lady, and even though it's not the same kind of assistance he might give another type of situation, he could allay the lady's fears by just talking to her.

Troublemakers. If an emotionally disturbed citizen has been labeled a "troublemaker," hospitalization or arrest is very unlikely. Intervention in such cases is considered not worth the trouble. An example was a woman rejected by the mental hospital, who, "whenever she came into the station, caused an absolute disruption. She would take off her clothes, run around the station nude, and urinate on the sergeant's desk. Officers felt it was such a hassle to have her in the station and in lockup that they simply stopped arresting her."

Quiet, Unobtrusive "Mentals." Persons whose symptoms of mental disorder are relatively unobtrusive are likely to be handled informally. They offend neither the populace nor the police with obvious manifestations of their illness, and their symptoms are not considered serious enough to warrant hospitalization. Moreover, quiet "mentals" are considered more disordered than disorderly and so are unlikely to provoke arrest.

Through officers' experiences with neighborhood characters, they know just how to soothe the emotionally disturbed person, to act as a "street-corner psychiatrist." In this way, they help to maintain many mentally ill people within the community and make deinstitutionalization a more viable public policy.

Sources:

- Teplin, L.A., "Psychiatric and Substance Abuse Disorders Among Male Urban Jail Detainees," *American Journal of Public Health*, 84 (1994):290–293.
- Teplin, L.A., *Keeping the Peace: The Parameters of Police Discretion in Relation to the Mentally Disordered*, Research Report, Washington, D.C.: U.S. Department of Justice, National Institute of Justice, April 1986 (NCJ 101046).
- Teplin, L.A., K.M. Abram, and G.M. McClelland, "Prevalence of Psychiatric Disorders Among Incarcerated Women I: Pretrial Jail Detainees," *Archives of General Psychiatry* 53 (1996):505–512.

"criminalization of mentally disordered behavior"[8] and have speculated that persons who previously were treated within the mental health system increasingly are being shunted into the criminal justice system.[9] Perhaps in response to this outcry, a number of professional organizations—the American Bar Association and the National Coalition for Jail Reform, for example—sought to develop innovative policy guidelines and/or alternatives to handle mentally ill persons within the criminal justice system.

It is plausible to imagine that criminalization of mentally ill persons may be occurring. Given all the bureaucratic and legal roadblocks to making mental health referrals, the police might see arrest as a simpler and more reliable way of removing an individual from the community. Those rejected as inappropriate by the mental health system must be accepted by the criminal justice system, which does not have the luxury of turning away clients.

Consequently, jails and prisons may have become the long-term repository for people with mental disorders. (See "Many Arrestees in Lockups Are Mentally Ill," page 14.)

However, the criminalization hypothesis has been based largely on intuition and casual observation. Research is not definitive. Of the 1,798 citizens involved in the observational study of police-citizen encounters discussed above, 506 (28 percent) were considered by the police to be suspects in a crime, and of these, 148 were arrested.

The probability of being arrested was 67 percent greater for suspects exhibiting signs of mental disorder than for those who apparently were not mentally

Table 1: Relationship Between the Presence of Mental Disorder and Arrest

| | Percent of Mental Disorder | | |
	No	Yes	Total
Arrest			
No	343 (72%)	16 (53%)	359 (71%)
Yes	133 (28%)	14 (47%)	147 (29%)
Total	476 (94%)	30 (6%)	506 (100%)

Chi-Square = 4.801 with 1 degree of freedom p < .05

Chi-Square (corrected for continuity) = 3.936 with 1 degree of freedom p < .05

ill. Fourteen of the 30 mentally disordered suspects, or 47 percent, were arrested, compared to 133 of the 476 other suspects, or 28 percent. (See table 1.) Clearly, mentally ill citizens in the study were being treated as criminals.[10]

EXPLANATIONS FOR A HIGHER ARREST RATE

Several explanations are possible for the higher arrest rate among persons who exhibited signs of serious mental illness, including, in part, that officers lacked knowledge of the symptoms of severe mental disorder. Many mental disorders are associated with a number of disconcerting symptoms. Although some symptoms, such as verbal abuse, belligerence, and disrespect, are not themselves against the law, such behaviors may provoke an officer to respond more punitively.

Also, as a result of the severe reductions in mental health services— both inpatient and outpatient— the criminal justice system may have become the default option for dealing with individuals who cannot or will not be treated by the mental health system.

That the criminal justice system is the default option is borne out of the common police practice of obtaining a signed complaint against an individual thought to need psychiatric hospitalization so that officers can arrest him if the hospital finds him unacceptable for admission. It also is evident in the arrest of persons with mixed symptoms. Police officers often make the rounds of service agencies—from the halfway house to the hospital to the detox center—before resorting to arrest.

IMPLICATIONS OF CRIMINALIZING MENTAL ILLNESS

The evidence that mentally ill persons are being criminalized is of concern because the criminal justice system is not designed to be a major point of entry into the mental health system. An arrest labels a mentally ill person as "criminal" and may doom that person to be arrested in cases of future disorderliness. And once incarcerated, jail hardly is an ideal treatment center for mentally ill persons. The cacophony of the jail setting works against even the recognition of mental disorder.

If the criminal justice system has indeed become the point of entry for psychiatric treatment, budget cuts in the mental health area simply shifted the financial burden to jails and prisons.

POLICY RECOMMENDATIONS

The findings that mentally ill people are being criminalized suggest the need for several changes in both the criminal justice and mental health systems:

- The public mental health system must evolve to meet the challenges of deinstitutionalization. Policymakers must recognize the need for significant increases in funding for mental health services in the community. The public mental health system and the criminal justice system must collaborate so that police officers have several alternatives, not just arrest or hospitalization, when handling mentally ill persons in the community.
- A more integrated system of caregiving must be designed to reduce the number of persons who fall through the cracks into the criminal justice "net" and to provide effective community services to persons who are arrested and released.
- The least restrictive alternative should be used, and whenever possible, mentally ill persons with misdemeanor charges pending should be treated in a mental health facility. The latter recommendation is consistent with that of the American Bar Association guidelines.[11] In this way, mentally ill individuals would not become victims of their own disorder unless they commit serious crimes.
- Police officers must receive adequate training in recognizing and handling mentally ill citizens so that individuals who are more disordered than disorderly are referred to the appropriate system. The police also must have a clear set of procedures to handle such persons, including negotiated "no-decline" agreements with hospitals. Such agreements would give police a designated place to take apparently mentally ill citizens. These agreements also are vital for establishing a successful liaison

between the police department and the mental health system and ending the refusal of hospitals to treat some people.

Although these recommendations require an increase in levels of funding, such a plan is likely to be financially prudent in the long term. Certainly, deinstitutionalizing the mentally ill with only the barest of community-based support did not decrease the need for treatment.[12] We may simply have shifted the burden (and the costs) from the mental hospital to the jail.

Despite this trend, policies have reduced both funding levels and Federal involvement in providing funds for mental health treatment. This has had serious consequences for the deinstitutionalized person.

It is likely that supporting mental health programs at current levels will increase the probability that mentally ill persons publicly exhibiting their disorder will be processed through the criminal justice system.

Some jurisdictions, however, are attempting to develop innovative strategies to reduce criminalization of mentally ill persons and improve services for offenders in the community. Some initiatives are designed to prevent arrest. Others address the mentally ill person's need for referral and treatment later on in criminal justice system processing—at a pretrial hearing, during detention, or after release.

People with mental disorders must not be criminalized as a result of inadequate funding for the mental health system. A long-term commitment to funding mental health care is required so that the

---

Many Arrestees in Lockups Are Mentally Ill

According to the Bureau of Justice Statistics, in mid-1998 an estimated 16 percent, or 283,800, of inmates in the Nation's prisons and jails were mentally ill. Another 16 percent, or 547,000, probationers also were considered mentally ill.

The analysis may actually undercount the number of incarcerated mentally ill people since it relied on inmates acknowledging to an interviewer that they either had a mental or emotional condition or had ever been admitted overnight to a mental hospital.

State prisons hold

Mentally Ill Inmates and Probationers

Percent who reported ...	State prison	Federal prison	Jail	Probation
Mental or emotional condition	10%	5%	11%	14%
Overnight stay in a mental hospital	11%	5%	10%	8%
Percent estimated to be mentally ill*	16%	7%	16%	16%

* Persons who reported a mental or emotional condition or an overnight stay in a mental hospital.

Source: Ditton, Paula M., "Mental Health and Treatment of Inmates and Probationers," Washington, D.C.: U.S. Department of Justice, Bureau of Justice Statistics, 1999 (NCJ 174463).

most inmates, and mentally ill people in State prisons were more than twice as likely as other inmates to have been homeless in the 12 months prior to their arrest (20 percent versus 9 percent). They also reported far higher rates of physical and sexual abuse; almost one-third of men and more than three-quarters of women said they had been abused in the past.

Although prison and jail are not the best places to receive treatment, a large share of emotionally disturbed inmates secured psychological treatment there. Since admission, 61 percent of these inmates in State and Federal prison and 41 percent of the mentally ill in local jails reported that they had received treatment for a mental condition— either counseling, medication, or other services.

most appropriate and effective treatment programs may be provided within the least restrictive setting possible.

Many deinstitutionalized adults, for example, can be productive members of the community if they live in structured settings where they are encouraged to take their medications regularly. Policies must be modified and resources allocated to see that the civil rights of mentally ill persons are protected, while providing the most humane and effective treatment available.

NOTES

1. Cf. *O'Connor v. Donaldson*, 422 U.S. 563 (1976); *Rennie v. Klein*, 653 F.2d 836 (3d Cir. 1981); *Rogers v. Okin*, 634 F.2d 650 (1st Cir. 1980).

2. Shah, S., "Dangerousness and Civil Commitment of the Mentally Ill: Some Public Policy Considerations," *American Journal of Psychiatry* 132 (1975):501–505; Fracchia, J., D. Canale, E. Cambria, E. Ruest, and C. Sheppard, "Public Views of Ex-Mental Patients: A Note on Perceived Dangerousness and Unpredictability," *Psychiatric Reports* 38 (1976):495–498.

3. Bittner, E., "Police Discretion in Emergency Apprehension of Mentally Ill Persons," *Social Problems* 14 (1967):278–292.

4. See, for example, Matthews, A., "Observations on Police Policy and Procedures for Emergency Detention of the Mentally Ill," *Journal of Criminal Law, Criminology, and Police Science* 61 (1970):283–295; Bowden, P., "Men Remanded into Custody for Medical Reports: The Outcome of the Treatment Recommendation," *British Journal of Psychiatry* 136 (1978):1045–1048; Kirk, S., and M. Therrein, "Community Mental Health Myths and the Fate of Former Hospitalized Patients," *Psychiatry* 38 (1975):209–217.

5. Bittner, "Police Discretion in Emergency Apprehension of Mentally Ill Persons."

6. Researchers observed 283 randomly selected police officers in the large northern city for 2,200 hours over a 14-month period during 1980–81. Excluding traffic stops, the data included 1,072 police-citizen encounters involving 2,122 citizens. Of the citizens involved in these encounters, 85 in 79 encounters were defined by the researchers as mentally disordered. The field researchers ascertained the presence of mental disorder with a symptom checklist that listed the major characteristics of severe mental illness—for example, confusion/disorientation, withdrawal, unresponsivity, paranoia, inappropriate or bizarre speech and/or behavior, and self-destructive behaviors. The field observers defined a person as being mentally disordered if he or she possessed at least one of these traits and met a common-sense standard for mental illness. For example, a street person who was found by the police to be shouting and running down the street naked on a cold night in January would have been coded as being mentally disordered. However, similar behaviors exhibited on a warm June evening by a group of drunken college students would be recognized as bizarre, but not indicative of mental disorder. See Teplin, L.A., *Keeping the Peace: The Parameters of Police Discretion in Relation to the Mentally Disordered*, Research Report, Washington, D.C.: U.S. Department of Justice, National Institute of Justice, April 1986 (NCJ 101046).

7. Teplin, L.A., Karen M. Abram, and Gary M.McClelland, "Prevalence of Psychiatric Disorders Among Incarcerated Women: I. Pretrial Jail Detainees," *Archives of General Psychiatry* 53 (1996): 505–512; and Teplin, L.A., "Psychiatric and Substance Abuse Disorders Among Male Urban Jail Detainees," *American Journal of Public Health* 84 (1994): 290–293.

8. Abramson, M., "The Criminalization of Mentally Disordered Behavior: Possible Side Effects of a New Mental Health Law," *Hospital and Community Psychiatry* 23 (1972):101–105.

9. Rachlin, S., A. Pam, and J.Milton, "Civil Liberties Versus Involuntary Hospitalization," *American Journal of Psychiatry* 132 (1975):189–191; Swank, G., and D.Winer, "Occurrence of Psychiatric Disorder in a County Jail Population," *American Journal of Psychiatry* 133 (1976):1331–1333;Whitmer, G., "From

For More Information

- For information about officers' alternatives to arrest, see Deane, M.W., H.J. Steadman, R. Borum, B.M. Veysey, and J.P. Morrissey, "Emerging Partnerships Between Mental Health and Law Enforcement," *Psychiatric Services* 50 (1999):99–101.

- For information about innovations in providing services to mentally ill offenders, see Steadman, H.J., S.M. Morris, and D.L. Dennis, "The Diversion of Mentally Ill Persons From Jails to Community-Based Services: A Profile of Programs," *American Journal of Public Health* 85 (1995):1630–1635; and Catherine Conly, *Coordinating Community Services for Mentally Ill Offenders: Maryland's Community Criminal Justice Treatment Program*, Washington, D.C.: U.S. Department of Justice, National Institute of Justice, April 1999 (NCJ 175046).

- For information about innovative police procedures for encounters with mentally ill citizens, see Wellborn, J., "Responding to Individuals With Mental Illness," *The FBI Law Enforcement Bulletin* 68 (1999):6–10; and Zealberg, J.J., S.D. Christie, J.A. Puckett, D. McAlhany, and M. Durban, "A Mobile Crisis Program: Collaboration Between Emergency Psychiatric Services and Police," *Hospital and Community Psychiatry* 43 (1992):612–615.

- For more information on deinstitutionalization, police handling of mentally ill citizens, and services provided to offenders, both in jails and in the community, see:

  - Baker, D., "Special Treatment: A One-of-a-Kind Court May Offer the Best Hope for Steering Nonviolent Mentally Ill Defendants into Care Instead of Jail," *ABA Journal* 84 (1998):20–22.
  - Patch, P.C., and B.A. Arrigo, "Police Officer Attitudes and Use of Discretion in Situations Involving the Mentally Ill: The Need to Narrow the Focus," *International Journal of Law and Psychiatry* 22(1) (1999):23–35.
  - Wachholz, S., and R. Mullaly, "Policing the Deinstitutionalized Mentally Ill: Toward an Understanding of Its Function," *Crime, Law and Social Change* 19(3) (1993):281–300.
  - Borum, R., M. Williams, M.W. Deans, H.J. Steadman, and J. Morrissey, "Police Perspectives on Responding to Mentally Ill People in Crisis: Perceptions of Program Effectiveness," *Behavioral Sciences and the Law* 16(4) (1998):393–405.
  - Lamb, H.R., "Deinstitutionalization at the Beginning of the New Millennium," *Harvard Review of Psychiatry* 6(1) (1998):1–10.
  - Lamb, H.R., L.E. Weinberger, and B.H. Gross, "Community Treatment of Severely Mentally Ill Offenders Under the Jurisdiction of the Criminal Justice System: A Review," *Psychiatric Services* 50(7) (1999):907–913.
  - Steadman, H.J., S.M. Morris, and D.L. Dennis, "The Diversion of Mentally Ill Persons From Jails to Community-Based Services: A Profile of Programs," *American Journal of Public Health* 85 (1995):1630–1635.
  - Steadman, H.J., M.W. Deane, J.P. Morrissey, M.L. Westcott, S. Salasin, and S. Shapiro, "A SAMHSA Research Initiative Assessing the Effectiveness of Jail Diversion Programs for Mentally Ill Persons," *Psychiatric Services* 50(12) (1999):1620–1623.
  - Steadman, H.J., J.J. Cocozza, and B.M. Veysey, "Comparing Outcomes for Diverted and Nondiverted Jail Detainees With Mental Illnesses," *Law and Human Behavior* 23(6) (1999):615–627.

Hospitals to Jails: The Fate of California's Deinstitutionalized Mentally Ill," *American Journal of Orthopsychiatry* 50(1) (1980); Morgan, C., "Developing Mental Health Services for Local Jails," *Criminal Justice and Behavior* 8 (1981):259–273; and Lamb, H., and R. Grant, "The Mentally Ill in an Urban County Jail," *Archives of General Psychiatry* 39 (1982):17–22.

10. Teplin, L.A., "Criminalizing Mental Disorder: The Comparative Arrest Rate of the Mentally Ill," *American Psychologist* 39(7) (1984):794–803.

Copyright 1984 by the American Psychological Association. Reprinted by permission of the publisher and author.

11. "Criminal Justice Mental Health Standards," Washington, D.C.: American Bar Association, Criminal Justice Standards Committee, 1986.

12. Bachrach, L.L., *Deinstitutionalization: An Analytical Review and Sociological Perspective*, Washington, D.C.: U.S. Government Printing Office, Mental Health Statistics Series D, No. 4; DHEW No. ADM 79–351.

CONCEPT #4: ESTABLISH SOUND PRACTICES OF ACCOUNTABILITY

No police department should hire more quickly than they can assimilate the people that they bring in, and we did. I take responsibility for it. It was the first opportunity I had to hire, and I wanted to do it, and I take responsibility.

—Chief Daryl Gates

Accountability is a word that resembles a concept rather than a word with a concrete definition. In part, it means the obligation to bear the consequences for the failure to perform as expected or required. Accountability means that you are responsible for someone or some activity. This chapter contains five readings which will help to answer some of the important questions on this topic. These questions include: What are administrators accountable for? Who else is accountable? Who is accountable to whom? What are the consequences?

The first reading on professional policing deals with the consequences of improper action and it illustrates some of the legal rulings that have occurred throughout the years. Unfortunately, in law enforcement there is sometimes resistance to change. At other times, change does occur but sometimes too slowly. When this happens, the courts end up with rulings which

set precedents for your future actions and behaviors. When this occurs, your flexibility ability becomes restricted and your ability to manage is directed by those outside of your agency. The goal of this first reading is to let you realize that it is much more beneficial to take the initiative and do what is right, rather than wait until the courts rule against you.

The second reading focuses on police accountability and community policing. The focal point of this reading is on accountability to the community. Mechanisms of control are discussed, which include supervision, training and audit mechanisms. Also discussed are methods of discipline, rewards and peer control.

The third reading in this chapter describes an event that occurred in 2005 where the Los Angeles Sheriff's Department (LASD) fired over 100 shots at a motor vehicle they believed contained an armed criminal suspect. The incident created widespread criticism of the law enforcement actions. However, through quick actions on the part of the LASD and their taking accountability for their behavior, the negative consequences of this event were minimized.

The fourth reading in this chapter, Failure in Criminal Investigations, describes what can go wrong when accountability mechanisms are not in place in a particular unit. This reading describes "traps" that detectives and managers can fall into, which ultimately lead to failures in investigations. Although this reading focuses on one unit, it should be realized that accountability issues exist at all levels of the agency.

To overcome the possibility of failure and to help implement practices of accountability, it is imperative that policies exist and for that reason your fourth reading discusses developing a police department policy manual. Many agencies, to this day, do not have policy manuals. Although somewhat understandable, because of the time and effort that must be put into the development of manuals, this is an unacceptable practice. Both officers and managers need guidance, direction and often limitations; all of which are addressed in policy manuals. Also, you will find that a good manual may protect the agency from liability claims as they arise.

This chapter concludes with a reading on use of force investigations. Perhaps no other topic on accountability, in the eyes of the public, is more important that this one. Use of force investigations can either alienate your agency from the public or they can solidify the integrity of your agency. As you will learn, it is often not the use of force that outrages the community, but rather how the agency responds to that use of force.

Professional Policing

By David Thomas

Policing from the 1880s to today can be chronicled in many different ways. Germann Day, and Galatti (1976) describe three hundred years of policing prior to 1978 as "operations that have ranged from the most sordid to the most splendid, and with practitioners whose capacity and character have spanned a continuum from the most incompetent and corrupt to the most brilliant and edifying" (p. 74).

The observations of Germann et al. (1976) and Vollmer (1971) in regard to professionalism help us to understand that policing does not happen in a vacuum independent of society. In fact, it is just the opposite: what has happened in America culturally has had a direct impact on the profession of policing. The history of modern policing can best be examined by looking at a host of commissions that have demanded change. The other form of oversight that needs to be examined in relationship to the history of policing is the landmark court cases that have mandated change and provided guidance.

WICKERSHAM COMMISSION, 1930

The Wickersham Commission was formed after a decade of criminal influence in policing that was directly related to the enactment of the Volstead Act of 1919 (Prohibition), followed by the Great Depression of 1929. It was during this time that organized crime rose to power, with tentacles that reached politicians, judges, and police in the form of payoffs and threats.

The **Wickersham Commission**, formally known as the *National Commission on Law Observance and Enforcement,* was appointed by President Herbert Hoover on May 20, 1929. The commission, which completed its work in 1930, published fourteen reports on subjects such as prohibition laws; criminal statistics; prosecution; enforcement of deportation laws; child offenders in the federal system; criminal procedure; penal institutions, probation, and parole; crime and the foreign born; costs and causes of crime; and the police. Another report on the controversial Mooney-Billings case was submitted to the commission but not officially published. Most of the commissions' reports had little impact except for one entitled "Report on Lawlessness in Law Enforcement According to Walker and Boehm (1997), that report detailed police misconduct in the forms of protracted questioning, threats and methods of intimidation, physical brutality, illegal detention, and refusal to allow suspects access to counsel (p. 9).

KERNER COMMISSION, 1967

The 1960s in the United States was a time of social change on all fronts. The generation we now know as *baby boomers* was on college campuses opposing the Vietnam War; then they were known as the hippie generation, draft dodgers, and the counterculture. Some were members of groups like the *Students for a Democratic Society (SDS),* which initially promoted civil rights, voting rights, and urban reform, although they were most noted for their opposition to the Vietnam War. Students marched on college campuses, burned their draft cards, and participated in peaceful protests such as sit-ins; in some cases, groups such as the *Weather Underground* participated in acts of terrorism. Finally, illegal drugs such as marijuana, LSD, and heroin were introduced into college campuses. The theme of the day was "Make Love Not War!" (Barber, 2008; Leen, 1999).

The antiwar protests of the 1960s were marked by years of civil disobedience and many clashes with the police. One of the most violent clashes with police was during the 1968 Democratic Convention in Chicago. There were five days of riots with protesters attempting to march to the convention. Rioters and innocent bystanders were beaten by the police, The police action was televised around the world (Kush, 2004; Walker, 1968). The most haunting conflict of the time was the *Kent State shootings* in 1970. College students were protesting the Vietnam War, more specifically the U.S. bombing of Cambodia. Ohio National Guardsmen opened fire on the protesters, killing four unarmed students (Hensley, 1981; Rosinsky, 2008).

In the south, the civil rights movement was beginning. The movement officially began with the landmark decision in *Brown v. Board of Education of Topeka, Kansas,* in 1954, and a number of significant events during the years that followed forced the issue of equality: 1955, Rosa Parks refused to move to the back of the bus; 1957, Central High School in Little Rock, Arkansas, was integrated; 1960, in Greensborough, North Carolina, four black students peacefully staged a sit-in at the local Woolworth's lunch counter; 1963, in Birmingham, Alabama, police turned fire hoses and police dogs loose on peaceful protesters; 1963, at the March on Washington, Martin Luther King delivered his "I Have a Dream" speech; the Civil Rights Act was signed by President Lyndon Johnson; the Voting Rights Act was passed by Congress; 1965, the Watts race riots took place in Los Angeles, California; and

in 1965, President Johnson signed Executive Order 1146, "which was the beginning of affirmative action (Bullard & Bond, 1994; Dierenfield, 2008).

It is Interesting that each of the movements in the United States moved in parallel ways and often supported one another. The media played a significant role in bringing these events to our living rooms. The Vietnam War was the lead story at 6:00 p.m., offering daily body counts of both the enemy and Americans. The civil rights movement also played out in the media. Although the protesters and leaders usually were peaceful and had taken a vow of nonviolence, their oppressors used violence as a tactic of fear to maintain control. There were bombings, assassinations, murders, and hangings—all of which were played out in the media for all the world to see.

The 1960s is often described as a time of turmoil in the United States. The protectors of the day, as they are today, were the police. America viewed police action that included beating students with batons, the use of tear gas to disperse protesters, and the use of police dogs and fire hoses on civil rights protesters. The bottom line is that the police action was less than professional, and often the police used excessive force. It is because of this that the police were seen as oppressors and not protectors of all in American society.

The **Kerner Commission** was established by President Lyndon B. Johnson in 1967 to examine the causes of the inner city riots, the two most violent of which were in Detroit and Newark. The commission was to answer the questions: What happened? Why did the riots happen? and What could be done to prevent them in the future? The commission created a hierarchy of common complaints. There were a total of twelve complaints, with each complaint being assigned to one of the three different levels of intensity. Police practices were the number one complaint assigned to the first level of intensity.

The commission noted: "The abrasive relationship between the police and the minority communities has been a major—and explosive—source of grievance, tension and disorder. The blame must be shared by the total society" (Kerner Commission, 1968, p. 14). The real cause of the tension was the demands on police service as a result of a higher crime rate, aggressive patrol practices, and no effective mechanism for grievances to be heard because of poor police practices.

A summary of the commissions findings included a review of police operations and recommendations to eliminate a sense of insecurity within the community, provide a mechanism for complaints, develop policies to assist in decision making, recruit more Negro officers and promote them accordingly, and develop a "Community Service Officer Program" to attract Negroes to the profession of policing (Kerner Commission, 1968, p. 15). The commission's recommendations are important because these same issues, as well as others, seem to be central to the lack of professionalism that dates back to the beginning of the profession.

FBI COUNTERINTELLIGENCE PROGRAM (COINTELPRO), 1956–1971

The FBI's COINTELPRO was charged with targeting foreign intelligence agencies operating in the United States during the Cold War. However, the mission changed in the 1960s and it became the political police in the United States. The FBI mounted counterintelligence programs to disrupt, misdirect, discredit, or otherwise neutralize the civil rights, black liberation, Puerto Rican independence, antiwar, and student movements of the 1960s (Churchill and Vander Wall, p. x). Churchill and Vander Wall (2002) show the actual letter sent by the FBI in 1964 in an attempt to get Martin Luther King to commit suicide (p. 99), other forged letters to activists and their supporters in an attempt to destroy their credibility and sway their followers, FBI-authored articles that were published in friendly media as if they were their own, and cartoon leaflets pitting one group against another (p. xi).

Many may wonder why some Americans are leery of the Patriot Act, which gives law enforcement unfettered access to personal records, allows wire tapping without warrants, and gives police the ability to declare individuals an *enemy combatant of the state* and place them in jail without due process. It is because of the aforementioned acts. The FBI has

been a strong organization with a reputation of being professional and above reproach, but conduct such as this has made the average American question the professionalism of the organization.

LAW ENFORCEMENT ASSISTANCE ADMINISTRATION (LEAA), 1968

In response to the Kerner Commission's findings, the **Law Enforcement Assistance Administration (LEAA)** was formed. The LEAA was funded due to the passage of the Omnibus Crime Control Act of 1968. The goal of the LEAA was to professionalize policing by offering monies for education, training of local officers, bomb squads, pilot programs studying alternatives to incarceration, drug treatment programs, and state court organization. The LEAA was disbanded in 1981 and was the forerunner to the National Institute of justice,

KNAPP COMMISSION REPORT ON POLICE CORRUPTION (KNAPP COMMISSION), 1970

The **Knapp Commission** was established by Mayor John Lindsay to investigate corruption within the New York City Police Department (NYPB). The commission was established in response to a 1970s *New York Times* article that detailed widespread corruption within the NYPD. The article, entitled "Graft Paid to Police Here Said to Run into the Millions" presented a survey in which officers spoke to the *Times* with complete anonymity and provided chilling accounts of the corrupt practices. Burnham (1970) states the officers discussed how they paid to work good patrol zones on Sunday and how businesspeople and criminals alike paid police to operate. Those who had paid the police included builders, numbers operators, and liquor dealers; the pay totaled in the millions (pp. 1,18).

Upon completion of a two and one-half year investigation, the commission determined that corruption within the agency was widespread. They noted that there were two types of officers: *meat-eaters* and *grass-eaters.* The meat-eaters were officers who took large sums of money without hesitation and pushed for the big dollars. The grass-eaters, who were more prevalent and were considered a scourge of the department, were officers who would take small amounts of money all the time. The commission noted that the grass-eaters made corruption "respectable" (Knapp Commission, 1972, p. 4). Such conduct destroys both public confidence and morale within the organization.

Another concept discussed by the commission was the **rotten apple theory.** Simply put, if the department acknowledged that an officer was corrupt, then that officer would have to be removed from fellow officers and categorized, which would cause the organization to look at all the other officers who associated with the "rotten apple." The commission noted that the NYPD ignored the existence of corruption in the department because there was no way to determine how many of a rotten apple's associates had become tainted, and trying to do so would destroy or tarnish the agency's public image (Knapp Commission, 1972, pp. 6–7).

FAILURE OF THE FBI CRIME LAB, 1989

The FBI Crime Lab was known for its excellent work. In fact, many agencies sent their evidence to the FBI Crime Lab for processing because of the quality of work. However, in 1989, the Crime Lab was given notice that there were problems with its lead bullet, DNA, and explosives analyses (Bergman & Berman-Barrett, 2008; Pyrek, 2007). Beecher-Monas (2007) notes that an investigation into the FBI Crime Lab revealed substandard work, inadequate training of lab technicians, rendered opinions that exceeded the findings, testimony tailored to meet the needs of cases, and a lack of objectivity in report preparation (p. 102). This type of behavior is far from professional.

O'Hara (2005) argues that such findings must be classified as an institutional failure and that such organizations draw a curtain around themselves, refusing to allow outsiders to view or challenge their conduct Ultimately this behavior is supported by professional privilege and political power (p. 149). However, this privilege is far from professional and should be considered destructive entitlement.

Thomas (2008) describes destructive entitlement as a belief that we as individuals should be treated fairly and with a sense of justice. This expectation is understood in a host of relationships, including husband–wife, employer–employee, government–citizen, teacher–student, and doctor–patient relationships, to name a few (p. 177). Because of the FBI's reputation, the organization was entitled to respect, and it was assumed they would be fair and just; however, because they failed to meet the professional standards, they have lost their credibility.

INDEPENDENT COMMISSION ON THE LOS ANGELES POLICE DEPARTMENT (CHRISTOPHER COMMISSION), 1991

The **Christopher Commission** was established in 1991 after the beating of Rodney King by the Los Angeles Police Department and the Los Angeles riots. The commission was charged, with investigating the agency's failure to supervise in regard to complaints of excessive force, the culture and officer attitudes toward the minority community, the inability of the community to redress complaints against officers, and the lack of leadership, both sworn and civilian.

The commission completed a survey regarding ethnic bias and excessive force that included 960 officers. The results were as follows:

- 24.5% of the 650 officers who responded agreed that racial bias (prejudice) on the part of officers toward minority citizens contributes to a negative interaction between police and the community; 55.4% disagreed; and 20.1% had no opinion.
- 27.6% of the respondents agreed that an officer's prejudice toward a suspect's race may lead to excessive force; 57.3% disagreed; and 15% had no opinion (City of Los Angeles, p. 69).
- The commission also noted that this issue dates back some twenty-five years to the 1965 Los Angeles riots. The McCone Commission in 1965 observed that there were many reasons for the riots; however, police brutality in the African American community was a recurring theme and one of the causes. In 1965, the McCone

Commission recommended open communication between the African American community and the police.

COMMISSION TO INVESTIGATE ALLEGATIONS OF POLICE CORRUPTION AND ANTI-CORRUPTION PROCEDURES OF THE POLICE DEPARTMENT (MOLLEN COMMISSION), 1992

The Mollen Commission was established in 1992 by Mayor David Dinkins to investigate corruption in the New York City Police Department. Mayor Dinkins authorized the commission with three mandates: to investigate the extent and nature of corruption within the NYPB; to evaluate the department's ability to detect and prevent corruption; and to recommend changes to enhance the department's effectiveness. The commissions' investigation, which lasted twenty-two months, stated that corruption extended far beyond the corrupt cop. The commission discovered that corruption was allowed to exist because of officers' fears of being labeled a rat and of the potential consequences for being honest, and because supervisors were willfully blind, fearing scandal more than the acts of corruption (City of New York, 1994, p. 14).

The commission also noted that there had been a change in the type of corruption within the ranks of the NYPD. The new generation of corrupt officer was influenced by the drug trade and the explosion of crack cocaine. Those who participated were no longer grass-eaters but had become the meat-eaters and were involved in brutality, sale and distribution of narcotics, and robbery of their competition. The commission described the officers as working in crews ranging from five to ten members each, These **crews** participated in acts of violence that were used to earn respect, extort profit, relieve frustration, and administer street justice (City of New York, 1994, p. 34).

The commissions' investigation of violence was quite interesting because the commission opted to address this subject, whereas other commissions such as the Knapp Commission had focused solely on corruption. The Mollen Commission found that brutality was common, although difficult to quantify, in large drug-infested minority communities. Even honest officers were reluctant to report or discuss brutality; officers were more open when it came to the issue of corruption (City of New York, 1994, p. 58).

The issues presented in the Mollen Commission's report mirror those in the 1972 Knapp Commission report, with one distinct difference: the type of corruption in the NYPD had changed to include crews who were now the major players/meat-eaters, as opposed to grass-eaters. This change meant that the NYPD had become an agency of good cops with a few bad apples. In response to the Mollen Commission findings, it was recommended that the city of New York establish a permanent independent commission to oversee corruption in the NYPD. On February 27, 1995, Mayor Rudolph Giuliani established the Commission to Combat Police Corruption.

RAMPART SCANDAL (LAPD), 2000

The Rampart Scandal was investigated by the Rampart Independent Review Committee. This committee was sanctioned by the Los Angeles Board of Police Commissioners to investigate the operations, policies, and procedures of the Los Angeles Police Department as a result of the Rampart Scandal. The investigation was an examination of an antigang unit known as the Community Resources Against Street Hoodlums (CRASH). CRASH was very successful in reducing violent crime. The officers were given great latitude in order to accomplish this goal, but doing so cost the LAPD due to a host of scandals that shook not only the law enforcement community but also the citizens they served. The bottom line is that there was no trust because of the unit's actions.

The behaviors of the officers in CRASH were exactly the same as those investigated by the Mollen Commission in New York City five years earlier. After the Christopher Commissions' report, the LAPD had set out to change from what they described as the professional police model to the community policing model. The **professional police model** is defined by the LAPD as being focused on crime fighting with minimal contact with the public (Rampart

Independent Review Panel, 2000, p. 7). The transition to community policing, however, never took place. The administration was never sold on the concept and never made it an agency priority. As a result, it was business as usual, with the community advising that the LAPD had never utilized community resources to create partnerships. The most notable observation regarding management was that they managed the department from the top down, rather than promoting collaborative partnerships and problem solving (p. 7).

Because the LAPD's style of policing had never changed and CRASH was given great latitude, a particular type of officer and culture had been bred. Three separate incidents brought CRASH officers to the forefront: a bank robbery committed by Officer David Mack; the theft of narcotics from an evidence locker by Officer Rafael Perez; and allegations of excessive force by Officer Brian Hewitt, as well as other members of the unit (Rampart Independent Review Panel, 2000, p. 44).

The Rampart Independent Review Panel had a host of findings, but the one that stands out most is number three, which focused on the agency's relationship with the community. in fact, the committee noted: "LAPD's failure to treat communities as full partners In law enforcement is related to its failure to treat its officers as partners" (Rampart Independent Review Panel, 2000, p. 99).

MOVEMENT TOWARD PROFESSIONAL POLICING

Vollmer (1971) argued that policing needed to become professional. Today the standards are higher and more stringent than even The selection process is arduous, with many steps—each of which can lead to elimination from the process if a candidate does not meet the standard. Then there is the academy, which has a minimum of a 20% attrition rate, and finally the field training program. Yet the profession still has a host of issues (Ervin, Flores-Macias, Lee, & Taylor, 2002,. p. 6). Each of the commissions discussed has examined the actions of officers in either the LAPD or NYPD, but the problems found are not limited to those departments; they are problems that are associated with the profession as a whole.

Educational standards, administrative oversight, policy manuals, and codes of ethics all contribute to the professional conduct of law enforcement officers. Policing conduct has another form of oversight as well. The courts have handed down a number of decisions that limit the power of the police officer and ensure that citizens receive due process. Law enforcement has faced a number of challenges since its inception in 1066 (see Figure 1-1).

Police Accountability and Community Policing

By George Kelling

The accountability of individual police officers is a fundamental issue for police executives. This is fitting: police officers are the public officials society has authorized, even obliged, to use force. Ensuring that police officers use that warrant equitably, legally, and economically on behalf of citizens is at the core of police administration. The enduring concern of police executives to ensure accountability in American policing is a reflection of their professional commitment.

Not only is it fitting that a police executive give high priority to ensuring the accountability of police officers, it is essential to surviving as the leader of a police department. Police chiefs continually worry about abuse of authority: brutality; misuse of force, especially deadly force; over-enforcement of the law; bribery; manufacture of evidence in the name of efficiency or success; failure to apply the law because of personal interests; and discrimination against particular individuals or groups. These issues are grist for the mill of persistent and influential watchdog groups concerned about impartial enforcement under the law-the media, civil rights groups, and lawyers. Rising crime or fear of crime may be problematic for police administrators, but rarely does either threaten their survival. Scandals associated with abuse of authority, however, do jeopardize organizational stability and continuity of leadership.

As a consequence, it is not surprising that police leaders have developed organizational mechanisms of control that seek to ensure police accountability to both the law and the policies and procedures of police departments. This paper reviews the ways police administrators try to control the accountability of individual police officers and examines the relationship between accountability procedures and community policing.

The paper's focus on accountability and community policing results from the concerns of many police executives and policymakers that certain characteristics of community policing threaten police officer accountability. These characteristics of community policing include organizational decentralization; increased intimacy between police officers and citizens and neighborhoods; receipt and interpretation of citizen demand for service by individual patrol officers; and development of patrol and policing tactics (problem solving, for example) by patrol officers at a neighborhood or community level. All of these characteristics require increased officer use of discretion and empowerment of patrol officers. Advocates of community policing who call for empowerment of officers should be extraordinarily scrupulous about ensuring that officers are held accountable for their actions.

Police organizations, like all organizations, rely on distinctive structural forms and management processes to maintain accountability. Characteristically, their structures are centralized with functionally defined bureaus, and their management processes emphasize preservice training and elaborate command and control mechanisms. In many respects, police organizations have typified the classical command and control organization that emphasizes top-level decisionmaking: flow of orders from executives down to line personnel, flow of information up from line personnel to executives, layers of dense supervision, unity of command, elaborate rules and regulations, elimination of discretion, and simplification of work tasks.

Command and control management has met two sets of needs in American policing. First, command and control systems have strengthened the ability of police to respond to civil disturbances, riots, labor disputes, and other problems for which coordinating large numbers of police was required.

Second, command and control systems have resolved many of the inherent tensions of policing—tensions, for example, between constraints imposed on police by law and the opportunities for effectiveness provided by their warrant to use force. There are other tensions as well—tensions between efficient processing of offenders and protection of their constitutional guarantees; between conflicting definitions of morality in communities and neighborhoods; between competing political interests.

Command and control systems have appeared to resolve these tensions by (1) instituting rules that prescribe the behavior of officers; (2) creating dense patterns of command and supervision to enforce these rules; (3) establishing the principle of unity of command to eliminate ambiguity in the chain of authority; and (4) routinizing the job of police officers by defining it as law enforcement.

This strategy has its successes. These successes include reduced political control of officers; reduced corruption; improvement in qualifications and training of police officers; constraints on police officer use of force, especially deadly force; production of more equitable police service; and arguably, enhancement of the tenure of police chiefs. Additionally, command and control management has improved the capacity of police to respond to riots and other disturbances that require coordinated group responses.

But there are strains in this strategy as well. As logically appealing as the command and control organization seems, many aspects of police work are not compatible with classical command and control organizations. First, patrol work is not amenable to attempts to simplify or routinize it. The types and multiplicity of problems with which police deal preclude the simplification or routinization of patrol work.[1] The metaphor of the assembly line, basic to classical management theories, has proved to be inapplicable to the realities of patrol. Second, police officers, unlike assembly-line workers or military troops, do not work under the direct scrutiny of supervisors. Even when sergeants are in the field, the unpredictable timing and location of police activities thwart ordinary supervision of performance. Consequently, although serious attempts have been made to eliminate or structure discretion, it has remained an integral and pervasive feature of police work,[2] especially at the level of patrol officer.

This strain between the realities of police work and the command and control systems of departments creates problems for administrators. First, the mechanisms of command and control are elaborate and expensive to maintain; layers of command, extensive training, and the maintenance of multitudinous rules and procedures obligate time, personnel, and money. Second, the discontinuities between organizational prescriptions and work realities are not lost on police officers. The results? At least two: (1) considerable role strain on officers who are portrayed as professionals on one hand but treated as recalcitrant semi-skilled workers on the other and (2) the rise of the union movement, which, at times, fosters acrid labor-management relationships.

Further, there are additional, more subtle costs to police departments. First, use of individual discretion has been driven underground; creativity and productive adaptations go unrecognized and unrewarded. Second, police departments often fail to tap the potential abilities of their officers. An ethos of "stay out of trouble," which has developed in many departments, stifles officers who are otherwise resourceful and abets officers who "perch" in their positions. Finally, a police culture has developed that maintains values that are alien to both police departments and communities. This police culture is characterized by suspiciousness, perceptions of great danger, isolation from citizens, and internal solidarity (the "blue curtain").

MANAGING POLICE CULTURE

Are there alternatives to command and control for managing police culture and improving accountability?

It is generally acknowledged that a primary determinant of police officer behavior is the culture within which officers find themselves. This is true not only in policing, but also in most other types of organizations. Good management is often described as the management of organizational culture[3]

The tendency in policing, however, is to emphasize the importance of the formal elements of the organization and ignore the informal elements (organizational myths, heroes and villains, informal patterns of communication, the norms and mores of the organization, etc.). The point, however, is not whether culture is influenced, but who influences it. To the extent that management has not worked to shape police culture, other forces have.

Often, management's attempt to manage culture through command and control merely fosters suspicion, isolation, insularity, demeaning perception of citizens, grumpiness, the "blue curtain," and cynicism[4] The result is an attitude on the part of police officers that says: "Management, leave me alone—let me do my work." In the worst of circumstances, police culture implies: "I am being paid for being a police officer. Beyond staying out of trouble, if you want me to do anything, bring me in on overtime."

The traditional approach has been to work against culture through the use of command and control. That workers do not like work and have little to contribute to its substance or conduct are basic tenets of classical organizational theory. Alternate managerial approaches recognize the importance of informal leadership and peer influences, assume that workers do care about the substance of their work, and strive to use informal leadership and peer influences on

behalf of the mission of the organization. We believe that successful management of culture is achieved in three ways:

- Leadership through values.
- Accountability to the community.
- Administrative mechanisms of control.

LEADERSHIP THROUGH VALUES

All organizations have values. They are implicit in every action of organizational incumbents. When explicit, statements of values attempt to set forth the beliefs of an organization, the standards that are to be maintained by its members, and the broader mission expected to be achieved through their activities. Most often, values operate at several levels of individual and organizational awareness. At times, workers make decisions by considering and selecting from alternatives—well aware of their value implications. At other times, workers make decisions without conscious recourse to their value dimensions. Often the values that undergird routine decisions and practices are so deeply ingrained as to make them automatic.[5]

Values, even those we consider positive, can conflict. For example, loyalty to peers can conflict with the maintenance of high standards of professional practice. When police officers decide to close their eyes to the incompetence or corruption of colleagues and draw the "blue curtain" around them, they choose the value of loyalty to peers over other values, such as quality service to the community. In many police departments, other values, some explicit and others implicit, can be identified that shape and drive police performance: "stay out of trouble," "we are the finest," "machismo," "serve and protect," and many others.

The responsibility of police managers is to (1) identify values that flow from the law and the Constitution, that represent the highest norms of the profession, and that are consistent with the ideals of communities and neighborhoods, and (2) enunciate them persuasively and unambiguously.

How are a department's values properly enunciated? First, many departments make their values explicit through the development of concise value statements. Such practices are not new in policing: O.W. Wilson developed visionary value statements both in Wichita and Chicago; the Los Angeles Police Department's statement of values had its origins in the administration of Chief Ed Davis. More recently, such statements have been developed in departments in Houston, Texas; Madison, Wisconsin; Dayton, Ohio; and many others.

Second, statements of policy, on issues such as use of deadly force for example, are derived from departmental values and inform and guide police officers and citizens—whether the department maintains a clear-cut value statement or not—about values of the department. Equally important, the absence of policy statements in crucial areas such as use of deadly force expresses values and creates policy as well through administrative inaction.[6] In turn, procedures (methods of performance that direct action in distinct situations) and rules (specific prohibitions or requirements stated to prevent deviance) are derived from value-based policies.[7]

Without rejecting all procedures and rules, the primary focus in value-based administration and leadership is not on prohibitions constraining officers but rather on encouraging police officers to weigh their actions constantly in light of departmental values. This switch in emphasis from rule conformity alone to quality action and outcome empowers officers to select appropriate courses of action from within a range of options rather than in the rote fashion too often prescribed by advocates of command and control. Leadership by values addresses the issue of accountability by attempting to link the nature of police work (application of discretionary judgments to a wide range of problems) with mechanisms of control that emphasize professional self-regulation rather than mere obligatory accommodation to rules.

ACCOUNTABILITY TO THE COMMUNITY

Two familiar forms of police accountability to communities are community relations units and civilian review boards. Community relations units are supposed to carry the message of police departments to communities but have proven to be insufficiently responsive to community definitions of problems and solutions. In the few places where they exist, civilian review boards focus primarily on the performance of individual police officers, particularly on mistakes and incompetence.

The difference between the role of citizens in community policing and in civilian review boards is that civilian review boards concentrate on perceived or real abuses while community policing focuses on the substantive issues of problems, crime, and quality of life in neighborhoods. Citizens bring to the relationship their sense of community, knowledge about the problems in their neighborhoods, their own capacities to solve problems, and the potential to support or authorize police action. Police bring to communities concerns not only for their welfare but for the constitutional rights and the welfare of all individuals and the community-at-large-thus countervailing the tendencies of neighborhood residents to be overly parochial or opposed to the legitimate interests of strangers or particular subgroups.

To us, accountability to the community means something different. It implies a new relationship to the community in which police departments establish an understanding with communities. This can take several forms. One form is for the community to be brought into policy-setting procedures-a practice pioneered during the 1960's by Chief Robert Igleburger of Dayton, Ohio. A second form of new relationship to the community, but not necessarily exclusive of the first, is for both police and citizens to nominate the problems with which police and citizens will deal, the tactics that each will use to address those problems, and the outcomes that are desired.

The understanding between police and community, more or less explicit, establishes a mutual accountability. It provides measures against which each can evaluate the other. This understanding does not abrogate police officers' responsibility for their professional knowledge, skills, or values. Likewise, it does not free citizens from their responsibility for their own safety. To use a medical analogy, it makes physician and patient accountable to each other.

ADMINISTRATIVE MECHANISMS OF CONTROL

The list of administrative mechanisms of control that are available to managers is conventional: education, training, rewards, discipline, peer influence, direction, supervision, recognition, and career opportunities. Use of, and emphases on, these mechanisms varies across occupations. Police in the past, using classical organizational principles, have emphasized direction, supervision, discipline, and preservice training. (This does not mean that other mechanisms were not used as well. The primary mechanisms, however, were those we identified.) These mechanisms can be adapted by police to improve accountability, just as they have been adapted by many other professional and private sector organizations. In the section that follows we shall briefly discuss the adaptation of control mechanisms to contemporary policing: supervision, training, program auditing, discipline, reward, and peer control.

SUPERVISION

Supervision of police is essential to improving the quality of police services. Typically, police administration portrays supervisors as directors who oversee workers who perform specific activities laid out in advance by management. Given the conditions of police activity, however—officers work alone, events occur in locations and at times that make them unavailable for direct oversight, the problems citizens present to police require novel solutions-different forms of supervision are required. These forms of supervision are more akin to coaching than directing. They include teaching, reviewing, considering alternatives, training, and other similar techniques.

A special function of supervisors is to empower officers. By empower we mean providing officers with the authority to use their knowledge, skill, and values to identify problems and work toward their solution. Empowerment of officers is the opposite of encouraging them to "stay out of trouble" or "not bother" their sergeants. Confronted with ambiguous problems not responsive to standard solutions, police officers can be empowered by sergeants to search for creative solutions to problems rather than respond in some rote fashion. Organizational policies should be sufficiently pliable to accommodate the breadth of discretion that officers will be expected to exercise under this arrangement.

It is our contention that as departments shift away from the authoritarian model of policing to a more flexible community-oriented approach, a reexamination of the structure of the bureaucracy will be essential to the efficient performance of the officer on the beat as well as the effectiveness of the department's operations.

We recognize that the complexity of this issue mandates far more thought and consideration than can be given in this paper. Departments cannot expect to eliminate an entire structure one day and begin with a new one the next. But they must begin to address the question of whether or not the existing rank structure and its functioning lend themselves to the type of police performance required to meet the needs and expectations of the communities served by the department.

This is particularly true in cities with a diverse ethnic and cultural mix. In these jurisdictions, the varying interests and demands of neighborhoods necessitate flexibility at the point of contact through which the department provides the services. This means that patrol officers need greater discretion and flexibility and less rigid adherence to monolithic rules and procedures. Thus, it might be possible to eliminate some of the tiers of authority within the bureaucracy while at the same time being more cost effective.

We should begin with the establishment of a career track for patrol officers that would provide incentives for meeting specialized goals. Many of these goals could be the result of an accord between neighborhoods and department representatives in which the line officer is an active participant, provided with sufficient authority to draw upon required departmental resources to achieve objectives.

This requires more functional supervision than direct line authority over the officer. Therefore, it would be possible under this configuration to reduce the number of sergeants and increase the opportunities for advancement within the patrol officers' line. Thus, promotions based upon abstract examinations could be replaced by a more practical system of performance measures that link community needs with departmental objectives.

TRAINING

Police recruit training is organizationally based, preservice training that emphasizes law, rules and procedures, and officer discipline.[8] This is consistent with the thrust of earlier reform to enhance the lawfulness and eliminate the discretion of police officers. It can be argued that this training serves its purpose very well, at least as far as it goes. It does emphasize important values: adherence to law and discipline.

The difficulty with training that concentrates primarily on law and discipline is that it fails to take into account the workaday circumstances of police officer activity: dealing with unpredictable events, most often when alone and without available supervision. Knowledge of law in such circumstances is important, but insufficient. More often than not it tells officers what they cannot do rather than what they can or should do. Military discipline is almost irrelevant under conditions in which a police officer confronts a situation alone, diagnoses it, selects one set of responses from a range of alternatives, and develops followup plans.

For routine circumstances, officers require basic knowledge about the kinds of events they encounter, skills that are applicable in such encounters, and values that inspire and constrain officers in their practice.[9] Moreover, the knowledge, skills, and values that are required to shape officer discretion in the handling of events must be internalized into the professional self of each officer. This can come about only through prolonged socialization that emphasizes discretionary application of a range of skills to a variety of real-world circumstances. Yet, academy training is notoriously deficient in the provision of such training.

There are models from other disciplines for the acquisition of such knowledge, skills, and values:

engineering, education, and others. They offer possibilities for police leaders for the future.

AUDIT MECHANISMS

No matter how good the training, how instrumental management has been in shaping the culture, and how positive supervision has been, the circumstances of police work will continue to allow for corruption, malfeasance, and incompetence. Policing is not unique in this respect, but stakes are higher when lethal governmental power is involved. There are reasons to believe that skillful administration will reduce such problems. Even so, managers will have to be ever vigilant.

One form of vigilance is auditing. An analogy is found in a financial audit of a business. It is conceded that a financial audit cannot be universal; indeed, attempts to audit everything may result in auditing nothing. Audits, instead, sample a representative number of transactions (events) from the relevant universe. There is nothing to prevent police from adopting similar schemes. An example: undercover decoy squads are often valuable anticrime units. They can be problematic, however. It is not uncommon for enthusiasm to become zealotry. Auditing a given sample of arrests by interviewing witnesses, defendants, and other interested parties is one way of maintaining control of such units. Another example is found in departments that routinely send postcards to a sample of "customers" to determine how satisfied they were with police service. Other departments routinely monitor samples of citizen complaints to determine whether they are being properly handled.

Three additional points should be made about audits. Typically, audits tend to become inspections of production quantity rather than quality. We are concerned about quality over quantity. It is well known that the number of arrests is a measure subject to enormous manipulation if not carefully monitored to ensure that the arrests are legitimate, properly conducted, appropriate, and fair. If arrests are to be a measure of individual or unit effectiveness, the only systematic means of ensuring their quality is through careful auditing of each step of the process that led to the arrest.

Second, audits are a form of after-the-fact accountability. They are no substitute for other mechanisms of administrative control, like leadership, education, and training, that attempt to ensure quality performance in advance rather than discover mistakes after they occur.

Finally, audits can be administered in a variety of ways. They can be carried out by high-level inspectors as well as by sergeants who are responsible for units. In some circumstances, they can be carried out by specially charged task forces comprised of officers of varying ranks, including patrol.

DISCIPLINE

Discipline will always be an important mechanism to ensure officer accountability: every organization, no matter how well managed, will have a small number of officers who perform irresponsibly or incompetently. Because the stakes are so high in policing, strong messages must be given to officers at all levels that incompetent performance—brutality and corruption, for example—is intolerable. We believe that if supervision and audits are well performed and documented, discipline can be exercised in ways that are both fair and perceived as fair.

One caveat, however. Line officers are understandably sensitive about how discipline is exercised in many departments. In a world in which staying out of trouble is a primary measure of officer adequacy, it should be no wonder that discipline is seen as arbitrary and unjust. Too often discipline follows the commission of mistakes, rather than officer incompetence or irresponsibility. Mistakes, incompetence, and irresponsibility are different issues. Mistakes, which are bound to occur in all work, should routinely evoke coaching, consideration of options, training, and other such control options. Incompetence and irresponsibility should result in discipline. Managers cannot have it both ways. They cannot ask officers to be risk-takers and then discipline them when occasional mistakes occur. Those who take risks on behalf of an organization—if they use methods and have goals that are within the values of that organiza-

tion—and then make mistakes, need support and assistance, not discipline.

REWARDS

Rewards continue to be powerful motivators for workers. Rewards can take the form of increased pay, job perks, promotion, special assignments, recognition, and other forms. Police agencies have used every conceivable form. The questions that arise in policing about rewards are not whether they are used fairly and appropriately. Questions about the fairness and propriety of police reward systems are based on the concern that only a small range of police officer activities is reflected in current measures of police performance. A good many areas—dispute resolution, crime prevention, problem solving, and order maintenance, for example—are rarely reflected in the data collected about officer performance. Given the importance of these activities in community policing, ways of evaluating the quality with which officers perform these functions and then linking these evaluative measures to rewards will have to be developed. A research project funded by the National Institute of Justice now underway in Houston will attempt to develop performance measurement criteria consistent with the priorities of community policing.

Two innovative ways of recognizing and rewarding officers, methods compatible with other elements of community policing, would be peer review of performance and performance contracts. Peer review of performance is discussed below. Performance contracts, a method of supervision in which a supervisor or colleagues negotiate a set of performance goals over a distinct period of time, are now being experimented with in Madison, Wisconsin. There, in an experiment in community policing and organizational decentralization, officers and their supervisors are negotiating personal performance contracts for the purpose of evaluating the performance of patrol officers.

PEER CONTROL

Peer control is an important means of achieving accountability. Although heavy reliance on peer control has been traditional in the professions of medicine, law, and science, it has not always ensured the desired quality of performance. However, when combined with other mechanisms of control, it will continue to be an important means of maintaining the standards of professional performance for police.

Despite the potential of peer review, police administrators have been reluctant to use methods of control that exploit opportunities for collegial or peer review. There have been exceptions to this generalization: the Peer Review Project in Kansas City during the mid-1970's (which focused on excessive use of force) and stress and alcohol-abuse programs in other departments. Other exceptions that come to mind are the Home Beat Officer program in the London Metropolitan Police, the Senior Lead Officer program in the Los Angeles Police Department, and the current experiment in decentralization in Madison where officers have elected their own lieutenants. For the most part, however, collegial review of basic police practice has been extremely limited.

CONCLUSION

The concern of this paper is not the reduction of police accountability but rather its increase and strengthening. In a sense, there is a paradox. Those mechanisms that have seemed most certain to ensure control (command and control systems) have created the illusion of control, but often little more than that. Other mechanisms of control recognize and promote the use of discretion by police officers. These mechanisms, such as auditing, rewards, and peer control, offer significant opportunities for increasing officer accountability.

From this brief discussion of managing police culture and accountability, it is clear that we do not believe that community policing threatens police accountability. Rather, the proper management of community policing adds additional opportunities for the maintenance of accountability in police organizations.

NOTES

1. Mary Ann Wycoff, The *Role of Municipal Police: Research as Prelude to Changing It,* Washington, D.C., Police Foundation, 1982.

2. Herman Goldstein, *Policing a Free Society,* Cambridge, Massachusetts, Ballinger, 1977.

3. See, for example, Edgar H. Schein, *Organizational Culture and Leadership,* San Francisco, Jossey-Bass, 1985.

4. For a discussion of police culture see, for example, Peter K. Manning, *Police Work,* Cambridge, MIT Press, 1979.

5. For an extended discussion of values in police departments, see "Values in Policing" by Robert Wasserman in this same series.

6. See, for example, *City of Canton, Ohio* v. *Geraldine Harris, Willie G. Harris, Bernadette Harris,* Amicus Curiae Brief of the American Civil Liberties Union and ACLU of Ohio in Support of Respondents in the Supreme Court of the United States, October term, 1987.

7. The authors thank Los Angeles Chief of Police Daryl Gates for helping us think through the relationship between values, policies, procedures, and rules, although he is in no way responsible for our conclusions.

8. For a discussion of recruit training and socialization, see John Van Maanen, "Observations on the making of policemen," *Human Organization* 32,4 (Winter 1973): 407–418.

9. An extreme example of the role of values is found in police use of deadly force. As important as rules and procedures may be, no set of rules about its use will ever be able to take into account all of the exigencies that occur in real-world situations. As a consequence, even in life-threatening circumstances, use of deadly force will always be discretionary, guided, at best, by values expressed through departmental policies.

What Real Police Accountability Looks Like

The "120" Shots Incident

BY SAMUEL WALKER

THE INCIDENT

On May 9th, 2005, Los Angeles Sheriff's Department Deputies (LASD) fired 120 shots at a motor vehicle driven by a man they believed to be a criminal suspect. The deputies believed the man may have been armed a potential threat their lives.

The public reaction to the shooting was swift and negative. A video tape recording of part of the incident was broadcast internationally and many media accounts referred to it as a "debacle." Residents of the Compton community of Los Angeles where the incident occurred denounced the LASD. Compton is an extremely poor community, where the population is about 55% Latino and 40% African American. Both local and national civil rights leaders called for a federal investigation of the incident.

The suspect's vehicle matched the description of one involved in a previous shooting, although he was eventually found to be unarmed and probably not involved in the previous incident. Struck by two bullets and hospitalized for about two weeks, he was subsequently arrested and charged with driving under the influence of drugs and evading the police.

By the morning of May 10th, the "120 shots" incident appeared to be simply the latest in a long history of police shooting incidents. The basic elements are now familiar: an apparent over-reaction by police officers to an African American suspect and an unnecessary use of deadly force.

The subsequent response of the LASD, however, was very different from the standard police shooting incident scenario. This report describes that response and comments on its larger significance for police accountability.

THE RESPONSE

The response of the LASD to the "120 shots" incident included three steps that serve as a model for real police accountability.

** Through their attorney, LASD Deputies apologized to the community for the incident.[1]

** In less than a month, Sheriff Lee Baca instituted a new use of deadly force policy specifically addressing shooting at moving vehicles.[2]

** Within one month, Sheriff Lee Baca disciplined 13 deputies for their role in the incident.[3]

THE SIGNIFICANCE OF THE RESPONSE

The response of the LASD is extremely significant in several respects.

** No one can recall rank and file officers ever apologizing to the community for a shooting or use of physical force incident.

** The speedy revision of the LASD shooting policy represents an effort by the organization to learn from controversial incidents and to revise policy to prevent similar incidents from occurring in the future.[4]

** The disciplinary actions against the involved deputies was both speedy and transparent.

** The LASD response reflects the impact of citizen oversight on the department. The LASD has two oversight agencies, the Office of Independent Review and the Special Counsel.[5]

BACKGROUND AND CONTEXT

The response of the LASD to the "120 shots" incident needs to be seen in the larger context of the history of police accountability.

Shootings and alleged use of excessive force have been a major controversy in this country for over 50 years. That controversy has been primarily one of race and ethnic relations. People of color have been the primary victims of police misconduct.[6]

The allegations of discrimination voiced by people of color consists of two components. First, that they are the victims of unjustified shootings and excessive use of force; and second that the police have failed to respond to their concerns and have neither investigated controversial incidents thoroughly or disciplined officers guilty of misconduct.

APOLOGIZING TO THE COMMUNITY

The apology to the community by the officers involved in the incident represents an unprecedented step in terms of acknowledging the impact of police actions on affected communities.

To be sure, the officers did not acknowledge any wrongdoing. They also spoke through their attorney and not individually. Nonetheless, the gesture of apologizing for the impact of their actions was genuine. Even though the officers did not themselves speak, they appeared at the press conference and did not hide behind an impersonal press release.

The idea of apologizing to the community, moreover, came from one of the deputies and not from their attorney or the LASD.

Additionally, Sheriff Lee Baca promptly appeared on local and national television and candidly discussed the incident. He also went to several community meetings, walked the street where the incident occurred accompanied by the Rev. Al Sharpton, and talked with neighborhood residents.

One of the major sources of tensions between the police and communities of color has been the very strong sense among community residents that the police never admit that anything bad happened. Over the decades this has created a sense that the police are insensitive, do not listen, and do not care about community concerns.

The so-called "code of silence," under which individual police officers not only refuse to acknowledge any mistake but in many cases refuse to cooperate with investigators has long been recognized as one of the greatest obstacles to police accountability.[7] By acknowledging that a mistake occurred the LASD deputies involved in ths incident should be commended for taking a courageous and important step forward into a new era of police-community relations.

LEARNING FROM CONTROVERSIES

By swiftly revising its use of force policy, the LASD embraced one of the most important new developments in police accountability.

Traditionally, controversial force incidents were investigated in a narrow criminal law/disciplinary framework. Investigators asked only whether the officer(s) involved violated the criminal law and/or violated department policy. The answer was either yes or no. If yes, the officer(s) should be prosecuted or disciplined. If the answer was no, the case ended.

Law enforcement agencies with a strong commitment of accountability today recognize that they can —and should—learn from controversial incidents. A force incident can and should be studied to see if the department can make any changes that would help to prevent similar incidents in the future.[8]

These changes might include revision of department policy (or even the development of a policy where none exists) to provide officers with better guidance in handling incidents of this sort, changes in training for officers, or new procedures to ensure better supervision on the street. An investigation might determine, for example, that the department has a policy on these kinds of situations but does not offer sufficient training over it. Or, an investigation might find that officers need retraining over the policy and the kind of incidents involved.

In fact, the Office of Independent Review (OIR) within the LASD had been developing a revised policy to address the issue of vehicle-related shootings for almost a year. The 120 shots incident provided momentum and a bit of urgency to a process that was already underway. In this process representatives of the OIR met with the Sheriff and departmental executives about the issue and received strong support to proceed with the revised policy. Once a proposed revision was finalized, LASD held "meet and confer" meetings with two unions representing peace officers and then swiftly implemented the changes.[9]

The role of the OIR in this process is explained in more detail later in the section on citizen oversight.

A third response focuses on the officers involved. A sophisticated Early Intervention System (EIS) is capable of determining whether any officer has a record of incidents reflecting questionable judgment in critical incidents.[10] Following the 120 shots incident, LASD commanders accessed the department EIS to determine whether any of the officers involved had histories of involvement in similar situations or disciplinary records that indicated a need for special intervention.

The new LASD policy was criticized by at least one group in the news media, although those comments were apparently based on a reporter's second hand account of the policy and there was a more "Wheels of Discipline" in the two studied.[11] The important point is that there is room for debate over this and every policy covering critical incidents. Law enforcement agencies should continually reexamine their policies. It is naive to think that potential problems will be solved by a one-time "fix." The ongoing debate

should take several forms. First, law enforcement agencies themselves should continually reexamine their policies. And as recommended above, any and every controversial incident should be studied to see if some change in policy, training or supervision is needed. Second, the community should be a part of this reexamination process.

PROMPT AND OPEN DISCIPLINE

Almost as surprising as the apology by the LASD deputies was the promptness and openness of the discipline they received. Just one month after the original incident, eleven deputies were suspended for between 2 to 7 days. Another deputy was suspended for 15 days.

Comparing this case with a videotaped beating by Los Angeles Police Department (LAPD) officers a year earlier, the Los Angeles Times headlined a story on the "Different Speeds for Wheels of Discipline" in the two departments.[12]

Not only was discipline speedy but it was open. In many communities, law enforcement agencies do not release information about disciplinary actions. In some agencies, the union contract forbids public release of such information.

The lack of prompt and open discipline has long been a source of discontent in people of color communities. The long delays create the impression that the department is dragging its feet, and by implication is not serious about discipline. The lack of openness creates the impression that the department is covering up its refusal to discipline officers.

It should be noted that prompt discipline was possible because the deputies involved agreed to cooperate with the investigation. Under an existing settlement agreement, they could have asserted a right to delay cooperation until possible criminal charges were settled. And in most jurisdictions, internal administrative discipline is postponed until possible criminal charges have been resolved. Most of the deputies in this incident, in fact, allowed OIR representatives to sit in on their interviews with internal investigators[13]

The willingness of the deputies to cooperate says something important about the culture of LASD. Evidently, the deputies—who were represented by their union attorney—concluded that it was best to cooperate in this matter rather than aggressively assert every legal right they were entitled to. Across the country, the typical scenario involves officers under investigation using every possible means to thwart or delay investigations. These actions reflect often bitterly hostile relations between management and the rank and file. They also have a damaging effect on community perceptions of the department in question. The cooperation of the LASD deputies in this matter clearly suggests a different attitude, a sense that cooperation is in the best interests of the department, the community, and the officers themselves. This is a development of major significance.

THE ROLE OF CITIZEN OVERSIGHT

The response of the LASD to the 120 shots incident, which was so different from the traditional response of law enforcement agencies to shooting incidents, reflects the impact of citizen oversight on the department.

While many law enforcement agencies bitterly oppose *any* form of oversight, the LASD is closely monitored by *two* oversight agencies: the Special Counsel and the Office of Independent Review.[14]

The Special Counsel was created in 1993 as an outgrowth of the 1992 Kolts Report on the LASD. Under a contract with the Los Angeles County Board of Supervisors and directed by Merrick Bobb, the Special Counsel has examined a wide range of administrative and policy issues within the LASD and issued 19 reports since 1993. Originally created to help reduce the cost of civil litigation against the LASD, Bobb and his staff have examined anything and everything that might impact the department. The Special Counsel's reports are readily available on the web(www.parc.info) and create a new degree of openness and transparency. In several instances, these reports have brought to light problems and data that were embarrassing to the department. The open-

ness and candor, however, create a climate in which organizational change can occur.

In 2001 Sheriff Lee Baca established the Office of Independent Review (OIR). Staffed by six attorneys and directed by Mike Gennaco, a former Assistant U. S. Attorney, the OIR also investigates incidents and issues that involve potential misconduct by deputies. It also publishes periodic reports and posts them on the web (www.laoir.org).

The existence of two oversight agencies has contributed to developing a climate of accountability in the LASD in several different ways.

First, there is a direct effect as both the Special Counsel and the OIR recommend specific policies or revisions of existing policies to address problems that have been identified. The Special Counsel, for example, has closely examined the canine unit and recommended a number of administrative changes. The result has been a precipitous drop in the number of citizens bitten by LASD canines.

As mentioned earlier, the OIR had begun to review the issue of shootings at vehicles about a year before the 120 shots incident. Reviewing shooting incident files, one OIR staff member noticed a disturbing pattern of vehicle shootings. This lead to a deeper review of incidents, discussions among OIR staff, consultation with the LASD training unit, research on policies of other law enforcement agencies, and the drafting of a revised policy. The 120 shots incident provided momentum for this process and, at the direction of Sheriff Baca, brought it to a speedy completion.

Additionally, OIR staff members attended all of the community town hall meetings held in response to the incident where they were able to explain the LASD investigative process. It is possible that this independent perspective on shooting investigations helped to reduce tensions in the Compton community. Finally, OIR staff met with the media to discuss in detail the results of the internal investigation of the incident.

Second, the existence of two oversight units has, in ways that are difficult to measure, created a climate of accountability within the LASD. Over the years, LASD commanders and deputies have grown accustomed to close scrutiny by non-sworn investigators and to having the results of their investigations released in public reports. Traditional police culture has embodied secrecy, resistance to outside inquiry and hostility to criticisms by outsiders. The existence of the Special Counsel and the OIR builds a very different culture, one of responsiveness and openness.

Third, the publicly available reports of both the Special Counsel and the OIR create a climate of openness and transparency in the eyes of the community. Ordinary citizens, elected officials and media personnel can read about what is going on inside the LASD. It's all there: problems that have been identified, changes that are recommended, the implementation of those changes, and the results in terms of officer performance. This represents a radical departure from the traditional closed culture of American policing.

CONCLUSION

The response of the Los Angeles Sheriff's Department to the 120 shots incident of May 9, 2005 was very different from the traditional police shooting incident scenario. The LASD acted promptly and openly to address community concerns, revise its policies to prevent similar incidents, and to discipline the officers involved.

Several factors contributed to this response. Most important was the leadership of Sheriff Lee Baca who addressed community concerns personally, brought the policy review to completion, and disciplined the officers involved.

Institutionally, the LASD had in place an accountability mechanism, the Office of Independent Review, that was already working on a revised policy that directly related to this incident. And it should be noted that the OIR was created at the initiative of Sheriff Baca.

It is also extremely noteworthy that by publicly apologizing to the community the deputies involved took an unprecedented step and set a new standard for officer accountability.

The response reflects a general culture of openness and responsiveness in the LASD, one that is quite different from the traditional "circle the wagons" and deny any wrongdoing response. In the end, this is what real police accountability looks like: acknowledging mistakes, promptly and openly imposing appropriate discipline, taking immediate preventive steps, having in place a process for identifying problems and initiating corrective measures. This is a style of accountability that other law enforcement agencies can and should emulate.

NOTES

1. Jeremiah Marquez, "Apology in L.A. Shooting Rare From Police," *Los Angeles Times*, May 31, 2005.
2. Andrew Blankenstein, "Sheriff Alters Vehicle Shooting Policy," *Los Angeles Times*, June 9, 2005.
3. Associated Press, "13 Los Angeles Deputies to be Punished for 120 Shots Fired at Car," June 10, 2005.
4. This process is described in Samuel Walker, *The New World of Police Accountability* (Thousand Oaks: Sage, 2005).
5. Walker, *The New World of Police Accountability*. Samuel Walker, *Police Accountability: The Role of Citizen Oversight* (Belmont: Wadsworth, 2001).
6. The long history of the controversy can be traced from the Kerner Commission report, National Advisory Commission on Civil Disorders, *Report* (New York: Bantam Books, 1968), to the more recent Jerome H. Skolnick and James J. Fyfe, *Above the Law* (New York: The Free Press, 1993) written in the wake of the Rodney King incident.
7. "Code of Silence," in Human Rights Watch, *Shielded from Justice: Police Brutality and Accountability in the United States* (New York: Human Rights Watch, 1998), pp. 68–71.
8. This point is forcefully made in the PARC report on use of force in the Portland, OR, Police Bureau: Police Assessment Resource Center, *The Portland Police Bureau: Officer-Involved Shootings and In-Custody Deaths* (Los Angeles: PARC, 2003). Available at www.parc.info.
9. Interviews with OIR staff.
10. Samuel Walker, *Early Intervention Systems for Law Enforcement Agencies: A Planning and Management*

Guide (Washington, DC: Department of Justice, 2003. Available at www.ncjrs.org and www.cops. usdoj.gov.

11. Blankenstein, "Sheriff Alters Vehicle Shooting Policy."

12. Amanda Covarrubias and Andrew Blankenstein, "Different Speeds for Wheels of Discipline," *Los Angeles Times*, June 11, 2005.

13. Despite the enormous importance of police unions and collective bargaining agreements in policing, there are no detailed studies of their impact on policing and disciplinary practices.

14. Oversight agencies are discussed in detail in Walker, *The New World of Police Accountability*.

Failure in Criminal Investigations

By Kim Rossmor

It seems most unlikely that, with all the checks and balances of the criminal justice system, someone today could be convicted of a crime he or she did not commit. The unfortunate reality, however, is that it does happen.

Developments in DNA analysis have resulted in the discovery of 240 such cases in the United States, some more egregious than others. How is this possible?

The Innocence Project,[1] dedicated to exonerating wrongfully convicted people through DNA testing, has identified a number of contributing causes, including eyewitness misidentification, improper forensic science, false confessions, police/prosecutorial misconduct, lying informants, and bad lawyering (see figure 1).

However, there is an important causal factor missing in this list developed by the Innocence Project: faulty investigative thinking. During the investigation of a case, even the best and most ethical detectives can fall prey to several traps. Organizational awareness of these subtle hazards and appropriate investigative procedures and supervision can reduce the risk of detectives falling prey to these hazards.

While the imprisonment of an innocent person is a travesty of justice, a criminal investigative failure more commonly results in the offender escaping justice (a wrongful conviction also allows the real offender to go free). The damage resulting from criminal investigative failures, whether to victims, innocent people, or the public, is significant. Consider homicide alone—there have been approximately 16,000 homicides annually in the United States between 2000 and 2009, with a clearance rate of 63 percent.[2] In other words, on average, every day, 16 murders occur that might never be solved and their perpetrators never arrested.

The key failings in investigative thinking can be grouped into three areas: cognitive biases, organizational traps, and probability errors. Like cascading failures in airplane crashes, an investigative failure often has more than one contributing factor.

COGNITIVE BIASES

Perception and Memory Limitations. A witness to a crime must observe, interpret, remember, recall, and then communicate information to a police investigator who, in turn, must understand and record it. Each stage has the potential for error. People are influenced by experiences and expectations, and different people view the world through different lenses. What witnesses think they see is a function of what they expected to see, what they wanted to see, and what they actually saw; the more ambiguous the last, the greater the influence of the first two factors.

Similarly, what people remember depends upon what they believe. The human brain does not objectively record data, and memories are subjective interpretations that are seldom reinterpreted, even when information changes. People tend to remember those facts consistent with their theories, and forget those that are not. More weight is placed on evidence that supports a hypotheses ;this phenomenon is called belief perseverance.

Belief perseverance is illustrated in the case of David Milgaard, convicted as a teenager in the 1969 rape and murder of nursing assistant Gail Miller in Saskatoon, Saskatchewan, Canada. After 23 years in prison, he was exonerated when DNA testing determined the semen stains on the victim's clothing came from Larry Fisher, a serial rapist who caught the bus at the same stop as Miller did every morning. However, even after Fisher's conviction, there are still people who cannot accept Milgaard's innocence, "explaining" the DNA evidence by suggesting Milgaard had first murdered Miller, and then Fisher happened to come along, find her body, and have sex with it.

At some point, belief perseverance conflicts with Occam's razor, or the principle of parsimony. When more than one explanation for an event is possible, the best choice is the simplest (the one with the fewest assumptions). Do not make things more complicated than necessary.

Intuition. Humans use two types of decision-making processes: the intuitive and the rational. Intuition falls between the automatic operations of perception and the deliberate operations of reasoning. This is what is meant by the misnomer "gut instinct." Intuition, however, is often misunderstood. It is not a paranormal ability or a form of extrasensory perception; while it operates at a below-consciousness level, intuition is still based on normal sensory input.

Intuition is automatic and effortless, fast and powerful. It is learned slowly. Because of its nature, intuition is difficult to control or modify. It can be influenced by emotion and is often prone to error. Typically, intuition involves the use of heuristics (cognitive shortcuts).

In contrast, reasoning is slow and effortful, vulnerable to interference and easily disrupted. However, it is flexible and controllable. Reasoning can overrule intuition.

Different situations require different types of judgment. When data are unreliable and incomplete or quick decisions under chaotic and uncertain conditions are necessary, intuitive decision making is preferable. Such situations can occur on the street or on a battlefield

However, when we have reliable and adequate data, and time for proper analysis, reasoning produces the most accurate results. Complex and rule-bound tasks, such as major crime investigations or courtroom prosecutions, require careful analysis and sound logic.

Heuristics and Biases. Clear and rational thinking is not easy. People sometimes exhibit limited rationality in the face of life's complexities because human brains are not wired to deal effectively with uncertainty. People therefore employ heuristics—intuitive rules of thumb—to make judgments under such conditions. A heuristic does not have to be correct most of the time, as long as it promotes survival. While a street police officer's intuition may sometimes be wrong, it is still an unwise thing to ignore.

While these mental shortcuts work well most of the time, under certain conditions they can lead to cognitive biases. Cognitive biases are mental errors caused by this simplified information-processing technique. They can result in distorted judgments and faulty analyses. Like optical illusions, cognitive biases are consistent and predictable.

Psychologists have identified many heuristics and biases, some of which are particularly problematic for criminal investigators. The anchoring heuristic results from the strong influence of the starting point on the final estimate. The available information determines first approximations, so if we have limited or incorrect information, our starting point will be wrong. There have been many murder cases in which detectives were led astray because the crime appeared to be something other than what it was.

Tunnel vision—one of the leading causes of wrongful convictions—results from a narrow focus on a limited range of possibilities. Consequently, alternative theories to the crime are not considered and potential suspects are eliminated from the investigation. This heuristic is particularly ill-suited to solving complex, dynamic investigations. Focusing on the first likely suspect, then closing the investigation off to alternative theories is a recipe for disaster.

One example of tunnel vision is the case of Rachel Nickell, an attractive 23-year-old woman murdered on London's Wimbledon Common in July 1992. Her throat was cut, and she was stabbed 49 times. The only witness to the attack was her two-year-old son. In September, New Scotland Yard detectives received a tip regarding an odd man named Colin Stagg. For the next year, he was their investigative focus. In August 1993, after a covert operation involving an undercover policewoman who "befriended" Stagg to obtain (unsuccessfully) further incriminating information, he was finally arrested.

The case went to trial in September 1994. The judge quickly threw out most of the prosecution's evidence. Calling the covert operation misconceived, he stated, "I am afraid this behavior betrays not merely an excessive zeal, but a substantial attempt to incriminate a suspect by positive and deceptive conduct of the grossest kind."[3] The prosecution withdrew the charges, and Stagg was released.

Several years later, enhanced DNA from Nickell's clothing was linked to Robert Napper, a psychopath now detained indefinitely in Broadmoor, a secure hospital, for murder and rape.

Confirmation bias is a form of selective thinking in which an individual is more likely to notice or search for evidence that confirms his or her theory, while ignoring or refusing to search for contradicting evidence. Confirming evidence is given more weight, while contradicting evidence is given less weight. The components of confirmation bias include failure to seek evidence that would disprove the theory, not utilizing such evidence if found, refusing to consider alternative hypotheses, and not evaluating evidence diagnosticity.

ORGANIZATIONAL TRAPS

A criminal investigator operates within an organizational structure with its own unique dynamics. The powerful police subculture has long been recognized as possessing both positive and negative characteristics,

some of which can influence the dynamics of a major crime investigation.

Inertia and Momentum. Law enforcement agencies are conservative, often suffering from bureaucratic inertia—a lethargy or unwillingness to evolve or act. Change is disruptive, and requires effort, time, and money. This inertia can slow a police agency's response to a new crime problem. Moreover, when a response finally does occur, it is often insufficient. Organizational inertia was a problem in the Green River Killer investigation in Washington State;[4] by the time a functional task force was formed, the killer had stopped.

Organizational momentum—the inability to change direction in the midst of a major investigation—is the opposite problem. It is difficult for investigators to redirect their focus from an established theory of a crime, or a particular suspect, especially if the organization has to then publicly admit it was wrong.

Assumptions and Red Herrings. Investigators must outline their assumptions. If a particular assumption later turns out to be invalid, then everything that flowed from it must be rethought. As the human mind does not automatically reevaluate information, specific organizational procedures are necessary to address this situation. Documenting assumptions facilitates this process and protects investigations from "creeping credibility"—what happens when an idea or theory gains credence not from supporting evidence, but from the passage of time. A possibility hardens into a probability, and then crystallizes into fact.

Large investigations can also suffer from rumors. Detectives should always understand their knowledge base and be able to answer the question: "How do we know what we think we know?"

President John Kennedy's assassination has provided fertile ground for conspiracy theorists, many of whom fall victim to the traps discussed here. For example, they have questioned how the "magic bullet" could have exited Kennedy's throat and entered the right shoulder of Texas Governor John Connally Jr. seated in front of the president in the motorcade limousine.

However, conspiracy theorists have assumed the limousine seating was arranged in the same manner as a normal vehicle, with Governor Connally positioned directly in front of President Kennedy. In reality, the limousine had been specially altered and had three rows of seats, with two Secret Service agents in the front, the Connallys in the middle, and the Kennedys in the rear. President Kennedy's seat was positioned significantly higher and outboard of Governor Connally's. Furthermore, Governor Connally was turned to the right as he waved to the crowd. Consequently, the two men's torso alignment is consistent with the "single bullet theory."

Red herrings—tips that misdirect an investigation—can be particularly dangerous in high-profile major crime cases. Constant media attention brings forth a flood of public information, some of it relevant, most of it not. Witness misinformation has sent several high-profile investigations down the wrong path. Suspect vehicle sightings appear to be particularly problematic—for instance, the white box truck/van reported so often during the Washington, D.C., Sniper shootings[5] (the criminals actually drove a blue Chevrolet Caprice sedan). Once followed, red herrings can be very hard to shake. They have been responsible for great waste: millions of dollars of police resources and time, higher victim counts, and unsolved crimes.

Ego and Fatigue. Ego, both personal and organizational, can prevent investigators from adjusting to new information or seeking alternative avenues of exploration. Sometimes the most prestigious law enforcement agencies are the most reluctant to admit mistakes. But truth is more important than reputation. An investigator must have the flexibility to admit his or her original theory was incorrect, and avoid falling into the ego trap. Stubbornness, which often accompanies ego, is just as problematic.

Fatigue, overwork, and stress—endemic in high-profile crime investigations—can create problems for investigative personnel. Tiredness dulls even the sharpest minds. Critical assessment abilities drop in overworked and fatigued individuals, who start to engage in uncritical "automatic believing."

Groupthink. Groupthink is the reluctance to think critically and challenge the dominant theory. (No one wants to tell the emperor he has no clothes.) It occurs in highly cohesive groups under pressure to make important decisions. The main symptoms of groupthink include the following:

- Power overestimation—belief in the group's moral purpose, resulting in risk taking and blindness to the ethical consequences of decisions
- Close-mindedness—group rationalizations and discrediting of warnings
- Uniformity pressures—conformity demands and self-censorship

Groupthink has several negative outcomes. Group members selectively gather information and fail to seek expert opinions. They also neglect to critically assess their ideas and examine few alternatives. Groupthink can be a disaster in a major crime investigation.

PROBABILITY ERRORS

The justice system—required to make decisions based on often uncertain or incomplete information—revolves around probabilities. Important legal concepts such as "probable grounds," "balance of probabilities," and "guilt beyond a reasonable doubt" are influenced by concepts of probability. Unfortunately, the human mind is not good at understanding probability, and, as a result, humans often make irrational decisions. Probability errors in criminal investigations can misdirect investigators, prosecutors, and juries.

Uncertainty in Language. Discussing chance, likelihood, or risk involves talking about probability. However, words to describe mathematical probabilities—"unlikely," "frequent," "risky"—are not well matched to underlying numbers. They also mean different things to different people at different times. Furthermore, the real probability of an event is often unknown. Ambiguity in statements of probability can become a problem during an investigation or criminal trial, as happened during the rape and murder trial of David Milgaard discussed on page 56. Sperm recovered at the crime scene contained type A antigens. When Milgaard's saliva was tested, however, the results showed he was a non-secretor. About 80 percent of the North American population are secretors—individuals whose saliva, semen, and other bodily fluids contain ABO antigens from which their blood type can be determined; non-secretors do not possess this genetic trait.

To circumvent this problem, the prosecution advanced the possibility of blood contamination, and the pathologist supported this theory in his testimony. When asked under what conditions human blood could get into seminal fluid or spermatozoa in males, he answered: "One would be local injury to the male genitals. A second and quite common occurrence would be any inflammation, either internal or external, of the male genitals."[6]

But when the pathologist said "quite common," was he speaking from the perspective of a doctor treating such an infliction, from a lifetime risk perspective, or from the perspective of someone suffering from the problem on a given day? It is only the last perspective that was relevant for Milgaard's guilt. It turns out that such a medical condition is actually quite rare.

Coincidence. Skeptical detectives often say they do not believe in coincidences. However, when looking for patterns within a large number of items (events, suspects), coincidences are inevitable. A task force that has examined hundreds of suspects will find some of them, by sheer chance, appear circumstantially guilty. Efforts to solve a crime by "working backwards" (from the suspect to the crime, rather than from the crime to the suspect) are susceptible to errors of coincidence. These types of errors are often seen in the proffered "solutions" to such famous cases as Jack the Ripper.

Computation Mistakes. In November 1999, British solicitor Sally Clark was convicted of smothering her two infant sons, who died a year apart from sudden infant death syndrome (SIDS or crib death). At her murder trial, pediatrician Sir Roy Meadow testified that the probability of two crib deaths occurring in a single family of affluent means was "vanishingly small," approximately 1 in 73,000,000. He calculated this number by squaring 1/8,543, the probability of a single SIDS case in England.[7]

There were several problems with Dr. Meadow's analysis. First, he incorrectly assumed that crib deaths are independent within a single family, ignoring the possibility of a genetic effect. Second, he committed an ecology fallacy in treating individual-level risk as equivalent to average overall population risk. Third, because crib deaths are relatively common but nonrandom events, recurrence happens somewhere in England about once every 18 months. The Royal Statistical Society issued a press release stating there was no statistical basis for Dr. Meadow's estimation.[8] In 2003, Clark's conviction was quashed upon appeal.

Another probability error arose during the O.J. Simpson murder trial. Harvard law professor Alan Dershowitz testified for the defense regarding Simpson's previous domestic assault on Nicole Simpson. Claiming "academic expertise in this area," he concluded that extremely few domestic battery cases result in murder, that battery is not a good independent predictor of murder, and that discussing their statistical relationship might confuse the jury.[9]

They were not the only ones confused—it turns out Dershowitz answered the wrong question. At issue is not the probability that a battered woman will be murdered by her abuser, but rather the probability that a battered and murdered woman was killed by her abuser. The former probability—the evidence given at trial—is less than 0.04 percent.[10] The latter, correct probability, however, is almost 90 percent.[11] Unbelievably, the prosecution let this testimony go unchallenged.

Errors of Thinking. Two errors relate to understanding probability within the court context: the prosecutor's fallacy and the defense attorney's fallacy. The latter is the conscious result of a clever defense lawyer who is able to convince a jury or judge to consider the probability of items of evidence of guilt in isolation (to minimize their impact), rather than in totality. The prosecutor's fallacy is more insidious because it typically happens by mistake. It occurs when the probability of the evidence given guilt is equated to the probability of guilt given the evidence. If the evidence is highly probable given the hypothesis, it does not follow that the hypothesis itself must be highly probable.

The case of the Birmingham Six in England[12] is an infamous example of the prosecutor's fallacy. In 1974, horrendous bomb explosions in two Birmingham pubs killed 21 people and injured 182. The bombings were attributed to the Provisional IRA. Special Branch officers detained a group of six men traveling to a funeral in Belfast. Their hands were swabbed, and the swabs subsequently analyzed for traces of nitroglycerine. A forensic scientist testified, during what was the largest mass murder trial in Britain, that he was 99 percent certain the defendants had handled explosives, based on the results of his tests.[13]

What he should have said was the test is positive 99 percent of the time if someone has handled explosives. It was later disclosed that many other substances can produce positive test results, including nitrocellulose, which is found in paint, playing cards, soil, gasoline, cigarettes, and soap. The defendants had played a game of cards on the train shortly before their arrest. The convictions of the Birmingham Six were overturned on appeal.

WRONGFUL INNOCENCE CLAIMS

Ironically, the same factors that can lead to wrongful convictions are also found in wrongful innocence claims. Several imprisoned and truly guilty criminals have made loud and persistent cries of innocence, ensnaring well-meaning but undiscerning supporters. Such cases typically involve a coordinated campaign, with lawyers, reporters, politicians, and academics crusading for the release of the "wronged" party. Unsurprisingly, it turns out that crusaders are no more immune to psychological biases, group dynamics, and probability misunderstandings than police investigators and prosecutors.

The Benjamin LaGuer case is a typical example. In January 1984, LaGuer was charged with rape, assault, robbery, and burglary in relationship to the brutal sexual assault of a 59-year-old woman. He was convicted and given a life sentence. LaGuer has always claimed to be innocent, and his efforts for release have been supported by a number of scholars, politicians, and journalists. In 2002, DNA proved them all wrong.[14]

LaGuer continues to refuse to accept responsibility for his actions, and his supporters have only enabled him (some of whom are now arguing the DNA evidence was contaminated).

The supporters of these criminals suffered from the halo effect, a cognitive bias whereby one positive trait (intelligence, talent, charm) influences the perception of other traits (moral rehabilitation, lack of dangerousness). Charisma, intelligence, and communication skills are trademarks of criminals successful in convincing others of their "innocence." Unfortunately, these characteristics have nothing to do with actual innocence. In fact, the opposite traits—dislikeable personalities, low intelligence, and poor communication skills—are more likely to be correlated with wrongful convictions.

Well-intentioned people eager to help often do not question their mission's validity. Wrongful convictions do occur, and innocent people are imprisoned. But as DNA testing shows, most claims of prisoner innocence are false.[15] In any criminal investigation— especially a long and complicated one—mistakes and errors occur. Nevertheless, these mistakes do not automatically translate into the accused's innocence.

The best approach is to seek the truth—an objective, careful truth based on evidence, facts, logic, and skepticism—not a subjective dogmatic opinion, entangled by biases, egos, and politics.

PREVENTING INVESTIGATIVE FAILURES

A major crime "whodunit" can be challenging and difficult. Factors identified with cognitive and organizational failures (low information levels, limited resources, and pressure to obtain quick results) are all too common in such investigations. The potential benefits of advanced forensic techniques, comprehensive criminal databases, and highly skilled police personnel are undermined by the wrong mind-set and a limited organizational approach.

There are three rules of investigative failure that detectives should keep in mind:

- One mistake, one coincidence, and one piece of bad luck can produce an investigative failure.

- Once one mistake has been made, the likelihood of further mistakes increases.
- Usually the biggest problem is refusing to acknowledge the original mistake.

Police agencies should ensure that detectives and their managers are aware of these traps. Investigations should be led by the evidence, not by the suspects. Case conclusions should be deferred until sufficient information has been gathered, and tunnel vision should be avoided at all costs. Investigative managers must remain neutral and encourage open inquiries, discussion, and dissent. Assumptions, inference chains, and uncertainties need to be recognized and recorded. Outside help should be sought when necessary.

Being aware of these problems, however, is usually not enough. Police agencies need to establish organizational mechanisms to mitigate their risk.

The criminal investigation process plays an important and special role in countries governed by the rule of law. Its function is to seek the truth, without fear or favor. That task, integral to both public safety and justice concerns, must be conducted in an unbiased and professional manner. If it is not, the result is unsolved crimes, unapprehended offenders, and wrongful convictions. Understanding what can go wrong is the first step towards preventing a criminal investigative failure.

Dr. **Kim Rossmo** is the University Endowed Chair in Criminology and the Director of the Center for Geospatial Intelligence and Investigation in the Department of Criminal Justice at Texas State University. He has a Ph.D. in criminology from Simon Fraser University, and was formerly a detective inspector with the Vancouver Police Department. He is a member of the IACP Police Investigative Operations Committee. His second book, *Criminal Investigative Failures*, was recently published by Taylor & Francis (2009).

Notes:

1. The Innocence Project is a national organization whose mission is to exonerate wrongfully convicted persons through DNA testing and reform the criminal justice system to prevent future wrongful convictions; for more information, visit http://www.innocenceproject.org/.
2. D. Kim Rossmo, *Criminal Investigative Failures*, (Boca Raton, FL: Taylor and Francis, 2009).
3. Paul Britton, *The Jigsaw Man* (London: Bantam Press, 1997): 366.
4. Carlton Smith and Thomas Guillen, *The Search for the Green River Killer* (New York, NY: Penguin Books, 1991).
5. Newseum, "D.C. Sniper," http://www.newseum.org/exhibits_th/fbi_feat/index.aspx?item=sniper_index&style=c (accessed August 17, 2009).
6. *Her Majesty the Queen v. David Edgar Milgaard,* 1970 QB 1157–1158.
7. Celia Hall, "'Statistical Error' in Child Murder Trial," *Telegraph* (December 31, 1999), http://www.telegraph.co.uk/htmlContent.jhtml?html=/archive/1999/12/31/nsal31.html (accessed July 12, 2008).
8. "Royal Statistical Society Concerned by Issues Raised in Sally Clark Case," news release, October 23, 2001, http://www.rss.org.uk/PDF/RSS%20Statement%20regarding%20statistical%20issues%20in%20the%20Sally%20Clark%20case,%20October%2023rd%202001.pdf (accessed August 17, 2009).
9. Alan M. Dershowitz, *Reasonable Doubts: The Criminal Justice System and the O.J. Simpson Case* (New York: Simon and Schuster, 1996): 104.
10. Alan M. Dershowitz, *Reasonable Doubts.*
11. Ibid.
12. The Birmingham Six are Hugh Callaghan, Patrick Joseph Hill, Gerard Hunter, Richard McIlkenny, William Power, and John Walker, who were sentenced to life imprisonment in 1975.
13. Bernard Robertson and Georges A. Vignaux, *Interpreting Evidence: Evaluating Forensic Evidence in the Courtroom* (Chichester: John Wiley and Sons, 1995).

14. David Arnold, "Convict's Cause Is Tested: Supporters Shaken by DNA Findings," *The Boston Globe*, March 28, 2002, http://truthinjustice.org/laguer.htm (accessed August 17, 2009).

15. Mathew Bruun, "DNA Findings Difficult to Rebut: Doctor Rejects LaGuer Claims," *Worcester Telegram and Gazette*, March 31, 2002.

Developing a Police Department Policy-Procedure Manual

By W. Dwayne Orrick

INTRODUCTION

This guide has been designed to assist police agencies in smaller communities with the development and revision of their policy-procedure manuals. The policy and procedures manual is the foundation for all of the department's operations. When properly developed and implemented, a policy-procedure manual provides staff with the information to act decisively, consistently, and legally. It also promotes confidence and professional conduct among staff.

Service delivery by agencies in smaller communities is often more responsive than departments in larger communities due to knowledge of the community and partnerships within the community. In addition, officers working in smaller agencies must be prepared for the same challenges and situations as their colleagues in larger organizations. The only real difference between large and small is the degree of specialization in job assignments in smaller departments. Smaller agency officers are generalists, often seeing the case through from start to finish. Because of this, officers in smaller departments are provided more latitude to perform their jobs and are not locked into the same routine every day, allowing for more growth, job enhancement and satisfaction for the employees of these departments. Therefore, policies and procedures for smaller agencies must be as thorough and complete as in their larger counterparts.

The remainder of this guide will focus on the *process* of developing a manual in smaller departments. It will explore the general rules for developing policies, how to form a policy committee, sources of information, how to organize the manual, steps for writing a policy, implementing a new policy, and for compliance inspections.

DEFINITIONS

Organizations call their policy and procedures manual different names—policy and procedures, operations manual, standard operating procedures. Regardless of the name, the document provides staff with the guidance necessary to perform department operations. Before outlining the process for developing an operations manual, it is necessary to provide a baseline of terminology. Several terms will be used during the development of a manual. It is necessary to distinguish between each:

- Standard - Guidelines or performance requirements that establish benchmarks for agencies to use in developing the organizational structure and measuring its service delivery system.

- Policy - A course or line of action adopted and pursued by an agency that provides guidance on the department's philosophy on identified issues.

- Procedure - A detailed description of how a policy is to be accomplished. It describes the steps to be taken, the frequency of the task, and the persons responsible for completing the tasks.

- General Orders - Written directives related to policy, procedures, rules and regulations involving more than one organizational unit. General orders typically have a broad statement of policy as well as the procedures for implementing the policy.

- Special Orders - Directives regulating one segment of the department or a statement of policy and procedure regarding a specific circumstance or event that is temporary in nature.

- Personnel Orders - Announcements of changes in status of personnel such as transfers or promotions.

- Rules and Regulations - Procedures that apply each and every time a situation occurs with specific guidelines for staff to follow. Rules and regulations usually proscribe specific behavior that will result in employees being disciplined for failing to follow the guidelines provided.

- Employee Handbook - Manual provided by the governing authority that introduces employees to the organization, its benefits/compensation package, and an abbreviated listing of policies.

RULES FOR EFFECTIVE MANUAL DEVELOPMENT AND IMPLEMENTATION

When developing operational policy and procedures, several general principles should be remembered.

- First, the operations manual should be comprehensive, providing staff with direction and guidance for all aspects of the department's operations.

- Second, the manual should be clearly written and easy to use.

- Third, the manual should be consistent with and mirror the organizational philosophy, legal requirements and applicable standards.

- Fourth, staff should be involved in the development of the manual and kept informed of any changes.

- Fifth, staff should receive adequate training and participate in open, frank discussions about the policy and the reasons for its requirements.

- Sixth, the operations manual should be considered a living document. Routine inspections and reviews should be completed to ensure compliance with its directives so that the manual remains current.

- Seventh, The manual should reflect and incorporate accepted state and national best practices, for example, model policies like those developed by the IACP's National Law Enforcement Policy Center or other law enforcement organization's general guidelines for policy-procedure manuals as developed by CALEA (Commission on Accreditation for Law Enforcement), state law enforcement associations and others.

FORMATION OF THE POLICY COMMITTEE

Developing a policy manual is a critical undertaking. One of the first tasks to be completed is the selection of a policy project coordinator. The selection of the proper person for this position is critical to the success of the development and implementation of the operations manual. In most agencies, this appointment is not a full-time assignment. Instead, the person must complete these responsibilities in addition to their current duties. As the leader, the policy project coordinator must have the authority, knowledge, and motivation to make assignments, draft policies, coordinate meetings, and complete the process. In addition, the coordinator must have sufficient administrative or clerical support to expedite the development process.

While one person can write the manual, the final product will likely be more complete, comprehensive and accepted by staff, if the document is developed with contribution from both sworn and civilian representatives of the agency. Diverse, heterogeneous groups tend to be more effective with complex problems and assignments than a homogeneous group or an individual. Therefore, it is strongly suggested that as many staff as practical be involved in the manual's development and implementation. To accomplish this, many departments have organized policy committees to assist with development of the manual.

Involving staff in the developmental process provides a vehicle for employees' abilities and potentials to be both challenged and recognized. It is recommended that the chief post a memorandum or intra-office e-mail explaining the development/revision process of the operations manual. Supervisors should ask persons who are interested to assist with the effort. In addition to volunteers, the policy committee should involve employees who may be critical of the department's operations. Many times, these officers provide information to improve the department operations. Inclusion of those with vocal opposition provides a safe avenue for discussion and promotes resolution. Alternatively, alienation of those critics of policy and procedures only undermines agency cohesion and morale. Finally, there may also be a need to involve persons from other agencies, particularly those with special knowledge areas.

SOURCES OF INFORMATION

When preparing to develop each area of the manual, a variety of sources should be reviewed for information to be included in the policy.

The local government's charter usually outlines the department's authority. Similarly, local, state, and federal laws and applicable court decisions proscribe standards of performance for department compliance.

Collective bargaining agreements, consent orders, and court decrees often:

- List requirements for the employment process;
- Describe individual duties and responsibilities;
- Outline discipline and grievance procedures, compensation and benefits programs.

The governing authority's procedures are binding upon the department's operations in many areas, particularly employment procedures and compensation benefits. The department's procedures cannot be in conflict with policies of the governing authority or they will automatically be considered null and void.

Intergovernmental agreements and contracts for services, such as detention of inmates or dispatch operations, may include requirements that should be considered and included in the operational procedures.

Mutual aid agreements, emergency operation plans and previously agreed upon protocols (i.e. child abuse/molestation investigations) often outline binding procedures for officers to follow while working with other agencies. Because these documents are often updated on a schedule different than the review of the manual, it is good to place the latest copy of the agreements in the appendices and refer to them in the body of the policy.

Standards such as the *Standards for Law Enforcement Agencies* by the Commission on Accreditation for Law Enforcement Agencies (CALEA) or standards promulgated for state certification programs provide the benchmarks for professional conduct and are an excellent cornerstone for department operations.

Existing departmental policies, procedures, and general orders, oftentimes provide ample direction for officers and should not be arbitrarily abandoned. With a little modification to ensure consistency in structure with the new manual, these procedures can be easily included in the manual. In many cases, the informal manner in which the department is operating simply needs to be recorded.

Since police operations are similar throughout the United States, there is no need to reinvent the wheel. Policies from other departments are an excellent resource for expediting the development process. Copies of manuals may be acquired from neighboring departments that have completed state certification or national accreditation. In addition, manuals can be obtained or requested on internet sites such as IACP Net. In many cases, these policies can be downloaded in an electronic format, which simplifies the editorial process. The tendency is for departments to copy manuals from other communities verbatim. This process is completely acceptable if the manual represents the department's philosophy and procedures and is consistent with legal guidelines. However, this is usually not the case and considerable editing is usually required.

Model policies provide a basic document to use as a starting point in the development of a manual. There are a number of sources for model operating policies including the IACP National Law Enforcement Model Policy Center and the National Center for Rural Law Enforcement. In addition, some state agencies and state police chiefs' associations have developed policies to assist agencies in their area. Because of the diversity in the size of communities, state laws, and operational philosophies between agencies, it is difficult to develop a policy that is applicable in all departments. Consequently, model policies should be thought of as general guidelines to be used in the development of the department's manual.

Tips:

- Academic research journals, trade magazines, and training lesson plans are a good source for policy and procedure background information and address areas that may be overlooked in particular subjects. Examples: Journal of Criminal Justice and An International Journal of Police Strategies and Management
- Interview subject matter experts such as records clerks, evidence custodians, and narcotic agents, or persons whose contributions are critical to the manual's success, such as other chiefs, legal counsel.

ORGANIZATION OF THE MANUAL

Before beginning to write the manual, several issues relating to formatting must be discussed and decided including scope, headers, pagination, key phrases, and index.

The scope of the manual must be identified. Most smaller agencies have a comprehensive manual that regulates all of the department's administration and operations. Larger agencies have found it necessary to have more than one manual for functional areas such as administration, patrol, investigations, and detention.

The beginning of each new section of the manual should be divided with a tab that readily identifies the chapter's subject or number. Each policy must have a header that includes the Agency's Name, Chapter/Policy number, Title, Effective Date (originally implemented), Revised Date (Current Revision), Number of Pages in the section, and to whom the policy is distributed. Before the policies can be finalized, the format for the header must be designed and approved.

Because manuals tend to be rather voluminous, it is necessary to develop a pagination system. This system should identify the exact policy and page. For example, 5-1.3 indicates the location is Chapter 5.1, page 3. There are several derivations of this format, but the pagination must allow staff to easily identify and locate the policy and page number.

To ensure consistency, key phrases such as detention facility vs. jail, investigator vs. detective, must be identified, discussed, and decided upon for consistency throughout the entire manual.

As the policy manual is being developed, broad topic areas to be covered must be identified. Reviewing model manuals or other departments' policies may provide insight into developing these categories and the specific policies to be included in each area. Each policy should be organized in the sequential order they are to appear in the manual. Some policies may not be finalized until issues are addressed and resolved in other policies. Therefore, it may be necessary for the coordinator to prioritize the order in which the policies must be composed.

Finally, some departments have found it useful to provide an index in the appendices of the manual to assist in readily locating relevant policies. The index cannot be compiled until the manual is completed.

COMMITTEE REVIEW

After the topics to be included in the manual have been identified and finalized, the drafting of policies can begin. To ensure the manual is developed in a timely manner, a schedule should be developed to outline the tasks to be completed, time expected to complete the tasks, persons responsible, and deadlines for completing each task. This schedule helps the committee to prioritize their work activity and focus their attention on the manual's development. For the same reasons, an agenda should be developed and distributed at every committee meeting. Otherwise, the meetings will likely get off track and fail to accomplish anything. There are a number of ways to compose an operations manual. The process of policy development typically includes the following steps:

PROCEDURE DEVELOPMENT STEPS

Before embarking upon the procedure development, it is recommended the committee take the time to identify and articulate the department's core values, mission statement and vision statement. Of course the department's manual can be developed without these documents, but they can prove invaluable to developing the organization and its culture. Embedding the organizational values throughout the manual will encourage desired behaviors by officers and encourage a strong and consistent value system throughout the department.

Some departments have found it necessary to contract with a facilitator to assist with the development of these statements. An excellent source for developing these documents in-house can be obtained from the IACP Services, Support and Technical Assistance for Smaller Agencies Project Staff at IACP. Contact Elaine Deck at (800) THE-IACP extension 262 for more information.

When writing the procedures, the use of scenarios can be helpful tools in the development process, clarifying each component of the procedure and the supporting agency values and mission. Completing the scenario helps to identify the duties and functions that must be completed with each task.

POLICY DEVELOPMENT STEPS

1. The policy committee meets and members reach a consensus regarding what should be included in each section. Any discussion points, questions, and concerns identified during meetings should be noted by the coordinator and provided at next meeting.

2. Using the information provided by committee, the project coordinator (or the designated committee member) develops all draft policy (see "Steps for Developing an Operations Manual" below). The policy development committee should not be used to write the manual. If members were expected to compose the manual as a collective group, it would never get done.

3. Copies of the draft policy are sent to committee members for review and comment.

4. Committee members may individually return their draft copies with comments to the coordinator or meet as a group to discuss their concerns. As the manual is reviewed, committee members should be primarily concerned with the validity of the policies. That is, does the policy regulate or direct department operations and employee conduct in the manner in which it was intended. Any contradictions, gaps, or inconsistencies should be identified and corrected. This review should also ensure each policy is grammatically correct, correctly spelled, and easily understood.

5. The coordinator reviews the comments by the committee and makes the necessary changes to the drafts.

6. Copies of the second draft are sent to the committee members for review. In some cases, it may be necessary to repeat Steps 4 and 5.

7. The coordinator submits the final draft to the department's legal counsel to ensure the proposed policy is in compliance with current local, state, and federal laws. There are differing opinions about the decision to have legal counsel review each policy or restricting the review to areas of high liability and where legal questions exist. This is a decision that should be made by leaders in each community.

8. When the legal review is complete, any comments or changes may be sent to the committee for final review. In some communities, it may be necessary to send the approved policy to the City Manager for review.

9. Upon final review, the coordinator places the policy in final form and prepares it for distribution to department staff.

STEPS FOR WRITING OPERATING PROCEDURES

1. Start with the end in mind. Assuming an officer completes the scenario successfully, identify the desired outcome. (Goal)
2. Review the literature/research material for issues that should be addressed in the policy being developed. Also review the committee's notes of discussion points, questions, and concerns.
3. Outline the actions/steps to be completed to achieve the goal or complete the function successfully. (What)
4. Place the outline steps in sequential order. (When)
5. Identify the person/positions to be involved in completing the tasks in Steps 2 and 3. (Who)
6. Be sure to identify and include any special equipment, supplies and material to be used with the procedure.
7. Compose the draft directive and submit it to the policy committee for review.

It should be noted the tone of the language used in the manual subtly impacts the organizational culture. Unreasonable restrictions in operational policy have oftentimes been the source of dissension between line and supervisory staff. The purpose of the manual is to empower the staff. So it is important to recognize every possible scenario cannot be identified and officers should be allowed the latitude they need for making decisions in unusual circumstances. If a negative tone is used in the manual (e.g., shall not, will not, are not, forbidden) it can permeate the ranks and promote cynical attitudes in staff. Consequently, the text of the manual should avoid focusing on prohibited acts, but rather emphasize conduct the department expects and supports of officers. Finally, there are very few absolutes in law enforcement. The courts have ruled that terms such as should, are to, and directed to, are not absolute. Only "shall" means under all circumstances and conditions. It is difficult to identify when officers are to act in the same manner without regard to the circumstances. Therefore, the use of absolute language should be avoided whenever possible.

IMPLEMENTATION AND CONFIDENTIALITY

After the manual has received final approval, it is ready to be implemented. Each officer should be issued a copy. Before this can occur, sufficient copies must be produced. In small agencies this can be accomplished by printing copies with a high capacity laser printer or photocopy machine. Larger agencies have found it necessary to contract with an outside copy center or commercial printer. If an outside printer is used, organizational security may dictate a contract agreement with the printer to ensure extra or disregarded copies are destroyed or returned to the department. Some agencies also post their manual on the department's computer server to ensure accessibility and allow easy search and reference at all times. Check with City Hall or an attorney for assistance.

Most departments issue their manuals in a three ring binder. This allows easy modification and addition to existing policy. As each manual is issued it should be stamped with a sequential serial number that is recorded as being assigned to the officer. As with most department equipment, officers may be required to sign for the manual when it is issued to them. Many agencies inappropriately require officers to sign a form indicating they have received, read, understand and agree to follow its requirements.

Once the manuals are issued, staff should be given ample time to read it before the training program begins. Since most manuals are rather substantial, officers will need a minimum of several days and likely weeks to thoroughly read the material. This gives officers time to note legitimate questions regarding the policy requirements and expectations of their performance.

After being provided sufficient opportunity to read the policy, officers must be trained on the manual and fully understand its requirements before it can be implemented. This training should cover administrative and operational topics, with particular emphasis being placed on high-liability issues. This process usually requires several sessions and may include both classroom as well as practical exercises. To ensure officers understand the policy and its expectations, some agencies test officers after the training. If an officer fails a test or several officers miss the same question, additional training is required. In addition to introductory training, time should be designated during every in-service training class to review the department's operational procedures relating to the topic of instruction and the department's performance standards. This is a convenient way to ensure training is relevant and staff remains current on the department's standards of conduct.

Some departments issue the policies to officers as they are developed and approved. This incremental approach has the advantage of allowing staff more time to digest requirements of the policy. At the same time, tracking and maintaining records of distribution are more cumbersome.

When the training is complete, documentation should be maintained that officers have been issued their manuals, trained on the content and understand its requirements. This documentation may include a copy of the manual, lesson plan, sign-in attendance sheets, tests given to measure comprehension and officers' test scores.

INSPECTION AND REVIEW

Once the new manual has been implemented, only half of the work is completed. Department officials must ensure the policies are being followed. If the work is not done in accordance with the policy, the manual is meaningless because the custom is the policy. This situation is more problematic than not having a policy. Informal customs attack the credibility of the department's operational procedures and administration. It also increases the department's exposure to potential liability.

What gets inspected is what gets done. There are several ways to ensure compliance with the manual. One way is to form a check sheet that lists various inspections that are to be conducted, by staff and the frequency of the inspections. It is a simple process of checking off when the inspection is complete. In some cases, policy may require internal and external inspections.

In the event officers are not in compliance with the department policy, a decision must be made as to the appropriate corrective action, ranging from remedial training to counseling to punishment. In some cases, a change in policy may be required.

Finally, the entire manual should be reviewed on at least an annual basis. This review helps to ensure the manual is in compliance with current management, operational, and legal standards. Instead of trying to eat the elephant in one bite, it is best to coordinate this review with key personnel over several weeks. As the review is conducted, listen to the staff persons who are closest to the service delivery. They know the problems and often times have the best ideas for addressing them. If modifications are necessary, the same procedures outlined in this guide should be followed for updating, distributing, and training staff of the changes.

CONCLUSION

Developing, maintaining, and revising a police department's operations manual is a monumental undertaking. However, if completed properly, the community, its governing authority, chief executive, and department's staff can be assured their operations are in compliance with current standards. It will ensure staff act in a consistent, professional and legal manner. It will also ensure department staff are prepared for unusual circumstances and the correct course of action is identified.

BIBLIOGRAPHY

1. Carpenter, Michael, "Put it in Writing: The Police Policy Manual", *FBI Law Enforcement Bulletin*, October 2000.

2. Orrick, Dwayne, *Model Jail Operations Manual for Georgia Detention Facilities*, Georgia Department of Community Affairs, 1987

3. Prince, Dr. Howard, John Halstead, and Larry Hesser, *Leadership in Police Organizations*,

International Association of Chief's of Police, 2002, p.208.

4. Kinnaird, Brian A., "Policy and Procedure Manual: A Didactic Model for Law Enforcement Administrators", *Sheriff*, February 2002.

5. Martin, Mark D., *Developing and Revising Detention Facility Policies and Procedures*, National Institute of Corrections, U. S. Department of Justice, April 2002

Police Investigations of the Use of Deadly Force Can Influence Perceptions and Outcomes

By Shannon Bohrer and Robert Channey

"When a police officer kills someone in the line of duty—or is killed—it sets in motion a series of internal and external reviews and public debate that normally does not end until several years later when the civil and criminal court trials are over."[1]

Basic law enforcement training covers using force, including deadly force, and investigating crimes, even those involving assaults and shootings by police. The relationship between these two events—the use of force and the police investigation of this use of force—can have far-reaching consequences, both good and bad, for the public, the department, and the officers involved.[2]

The law enforcement profession spends considerable time and resources training officers to use firearms and other weapons and to understand the constitutional standards and agency policies concerning when they can employ such force. Society expects this effort because of the possible consequences of officers not having the skills they need if and when they become involved in a critical incident.

In addition to receiving instruction about the use of force, officers are taught investigative techniques. They must reconstruct the incident, find the facts, and gather evidence to prosecute the offenders. And, historically, they have done this extremely well. But,

is the same amount of attention paid to examining the investigative process of the use of deadly force and how this can affect what occurs after such an event? Are there any reasons why the police should approach the investigation of an officer-involved shooting differently? To help answer these questions, the authors present an overview of perceptions about these events and some elements that law enforcement agencies can incorporate into investigations of officer-involved shootings that can help ensure fair and judicious outcomes.

PERCEPTIONS OF DEADLY FORCE

All law enforcement training is based on the two elements of criticality and frequency. Skills that officers need and are required to have to perform their duties fall into both:

1) how often they use them and 2) how crucial it is to have them. Training officers to handle potentially lethal incidents, by nature, is vitally important. Investigating officer-involved shootings constitutes a critical function, but, for most departments, it does not occur that frequently. Only examining training needs from the perspective of preparation for the event does not necessarily take into account what can occur afterward. Just because the officer had the right to shoot and the evidence supports the officer's

Shannon Bohrer and Robert Channey, "Police Investigations of the Use of Deadly Force Can Influence Perceptions and Outcomes," *FBI Law Enforcement Bulletin*, vol. 79, no. 1, pp. 1–7. Copyright in the Public Domain.

actions may not guarantee a positive, or even a neutral, reception from the public.

In addition, *who* the police shoot seems to mold some perceptions. For example, a bank robber armed with a shotgun presents a different connotation than a 14-year-old thief wielding a knife.[3] Sometimes, it is who the police shoot that also can set the tone for the direction of the investigation surrounding the incident.

The Officer's Perception

Interviews conducted with officers who have been involved in shootings have revealed that while many were well trained for the event, they often were not prepared for the investigation afterward.[4] Some believed that these investigations centered on finding something that officers did wrong so they could be charged with a crime or a violation of departmental policy.[5] Others felt that the investigations were for the protection of the agency and not necessarily the officers involved.[6]

Officers can have broad perceptions that often depend upon their experiences of being involved in a critical incident or knowledge of what has happened to other officers.

A trooper with the Arizona Department of Public Safety commented, "I did not choose to take that man's life … He chose to die when he drew a gun on an officer. It was not my choice; it was his."[7]

The Public's Perception

Perceptions by the public of officer-involved shootings usually are as wide and diverse as the population, often driven by media coverage, and sometimes influenced by a long-standing bias and mistrust of government.[8] Documented cases of riots, property damage, and loss of life have occurred in communities where residents have perceived a police shooting as unjustified. Some members of the public seem to automatically assume that the officer did something wrong before any investigation into the incident begins. Conversely, others believe that if the police

shot somebody, the individual must not have given the officer any choice.

The Department's Perception

Departmental perceptions can prove diverse and difficult to express. For example, when interviewed, one chief of police advised that "it is sometimes easier to go through an officer being killed in the line of duty than a questionable police shooting."[9] The chief was referring to the public's response, including civil unrest, to what was perceived as an unjustified police shooting. At various levels, however, administrators may feel that a full and fair investigation will clear up any negative perceptions by the public. While not all-inclusive, departmental perceptions include many instances when an officer-involved shooting was viewed with clear and objective clarity before, during, and after the investigation.[10]

ELEMENTS OF THE INVESTIGATION

Few events in law enforcement attract the attention of the media, the political establishment, and the police administration more than an officer-involved shooting. In some instances, such intense interest can affect the investigation. Is this scrutiny related to the incident, the investigation, or both? Does it affect the focus and outcome of the investigation? And, conversely, can the investigative process influence this close observation of the incident?[11]

With these issues in mind, the authors offer six elements for investigating officer-involved shootings. While they are not meant to be all-inclusive or broad enough to cover every conceivable situation, they can be useful as a guide.

The Investigators

The first element involves investigators who have correct and neutral attitudes. Not all officers are suited to conducting police-shooting investigations. Examining such incidents requires open-minded, experienced investigators who have empathy toward the involved officers and members of the general public.

Starting with the right investigators will ensure that the process has a solid foundation.

If possible, at least two primary investigators should oversee the case from the beginning until the end. They should be responsible for such activities as supervising the crime scene investigation, reviewing witness statements and evidence and laboratory reports, and coordinating with the criminal justice system. They should not be heavily involved in the initial routine investigation except for handling the interaction with the involved officers, including taking statements.

The Crime Scene

The second element entails the appropriate response to and protection of the crime scene. Homicide or criminal investigators should protect the site. They need to take their time and broaden the protected area, possibly adding a safety zone beyond the immediate vicinity. They should establish a press area with a public information officer available to respond to media inquiries.

Before inspecting the crime scene, the investigators should videotape it and the surroundings and then periodically videotape the area, along with any crowds and parked vehicles, during the course of the examination. Such information may prove valuable later in locating additional witnesses. They should use up-to-date technology and evidence-gathering methods, calling on experts as needed.

Before releasing the crime scene, the investigators should consult with the criminal justice officials who will be responsible for the case. It can be easier to explain the circumstances of the incident while still in control of the location where it occurred.[12]

The Involved Officers

Removing the involved officers from the scene as soon as possible and taking them to a secure location away from other witnesses and media personnel constitute the third element. The investigators need to explain to the officers that these actions will help maintain the integrity of the case. They also should invite the

officers to stay within a protected area to participate in the follow-up investigation. When possible, they should only take statements from the involved officers once they clearly understand all of the facts and crime scene information. Moreover, in the initial and early stages of the investigation, authorities never should release the names or any personal information of the involved officers.[13]

Sometimes, it is beneficial for involved officers to revisit the crime scene later to help them recall events. If at all possible, the investigators should accompany them.

It is important to keep the involved officers informed. Someone should contact them on a regular basis. In many agencies, the officers have advocates, including peer support, union representation, and legal aid. Keeping the officers advised may require the investigators to go through the advocate.[14]

The Civilian Witnesses

The fourth element highlights the importance of investigators gaining the confidence and respect of civilian witnesses. After all, they need their assistance. In most cases, investigators should handle them the same way as involved officers.

Before interviewing the witnesses, investigators should have a full understanding of the crime scene and the facts of the shooting. If any statements conflict with the crime scene examination or information from other people who observed the incident, investigators should have the witnesses view a crime scene videotape or take them back to the site to help them recall events. They may wish to consult with the criminal justice investigating authority beforehand to ensure that the revisit does not invade the privacy or cause harm to the witnesses. And, of course, investigating authorities never should release any information concerning the witnesses.

The Criminal Justice Authorities

The fifth element, the need to have these cases vetted through the criminal justice process as soon as possible, proves critical to the involved officers, their families, and their employing agencies. Sometimes, backlogs may delay report completion but should not hinder clearance procedures.[15] Close consultation with the appropriate criminal justice authority may alleviate the need for a completed formal report if a written statement for the proper authority confirms the facts. For example, medical examiners and ballistic experts can provide their findings to investigators with formal reports to follow.

Presentations of the investigation should include all videotapes, photographs, and copies of all statements, investigative reports, and other necessary documents. Throughout the criminal justice proceedings, investigators should update the involved officers and their departments about the progress of the case.

The Media

As the final element, the department's public information officer should contact the media before their representatives approach the agency.[16] In the early stages of the investigation, the department should demonstrate that it wants to cooperate with the media. By informing the public through press releases and interviews, the agency shows that it is investigating the incident and that as information *can* be released, it *will* be. Departments should remember that the proverbial "no comment" often gives the impression that the police are hiding something.

Without a positive relationship with the media, poor communication between the public and the police can develop, creating a lack of faith in the management and operations of the department and mistrust from all parties. The time to prepare press releases for officer-involved shootings is *before* one occurs.

In addition, agencies should encourage the media to print and air stories on the responsibilities of officers and the training conducted to enhance their abilities. General information on past shootings, simulator experiences, and the perspective of the reasonable objective officer can help develop a cooperative association.[17] Such a collaborative effort between the police and the media is not a magic pill and will not alleviate all of the public misperceptions and problems.

However, it may reduce or prevent false perceptions, especially with officer-involved shootings.[18]

Finally, investigators should review all of the related printed materials and media interviews to identify further witnesses and, if needed, interview them as soon as possible. Sometimes, these individuals may not understand why the police would want to interview them after they have talked to the media, so a diplomatic approach can prove helpful. This highlights the importance of a positive working relationship that often can result in shared information between the media and the police.

CONCLUSION

Often, it is not a law enforcement shooting that generates negative consequences, but, rather, it is how the involved agency handles the incident that can foster and feed misperceptions. As a Santa Monica, California, police officer pointed out, "No one knows about the hundreds of instances when a police officer decides not to shoot. Perhaps, no one cares. After all, people say we're trained to handle such things, as if training somehow removes or dilutes our humanity."[19]

While the six elements presented in this article may not be all-inclusive, they offer an outline that may reduce the negative events that sometimes occur in these situations. Having the appropriate investigators and a positive working relationship with the media constitute the bookends of an effective process. After all, the right investigators are the foundation for a thorough investigation, and a cooperative connection with the media forms the basis of public understanding. Joining together and sharing information can help both the police and the media deal with officer-involved shootings in a fair and judicious manner.

NOTES

1. Darrel W. Stephens, foreword to *Deadly Force: What We Know*, by William A. Geller and Michael S. Scott (Washington, DC: Police Executive Research Forum, 1992).

2. For an overview of legal concerns, see Thomas D. Petrowski, "Use-of-Force Policies and Training: A Reasoned Approach," *FBI Law Enforcement Bulletin*, October 2002, 25–32 and Part Two, November 2002, 24–32.

3. Shannon Bohrer, Harry Kern, and Edward Davis, "The Deadly Dilemma: Shoot or Don't Shoot," *FBI Law Enforcement Bulletin*, March 2008, 7–12; Larry C. Brubaker, "Deadly Force: A 20-Year Study of Fatal Encounters," *FBI Law Enforcement Bulletin*, April 2002, 6–13; and George T. Williams, "Reluctance to Use Deadly Force: Causes, Consequences, and Cures," *FBI Law Enforcement Bulletin*, October 1999, 1–5.

4. Anthony J. Pinizzotto, Edward F. Davis, and Charles E. Miller III, U.S. Department of Justice, Federal Bureau of Investigation, *In the Line of Fire: Violence Against Law Enforcement* (Washington, DC, 1997); and *Violent Encounters: A Study of Felonious Assaults on Our Nation's Law Enforcement Officers* (Washington, DC, 2006).

5. Interviews with students attending the Management Issues: Law Enforcement's Use of Deadly Force course taught at the FBI's National Academy from 1995 through 1999. The FBI hosts four 10-week National Academy sessions each year during which law enforcement executives from around the world come together to attend classes in various criminal justice subjects.

6. Feedback from students attending the Instructor Training Liability Issues course taught at the Firearms Instructor Schools, Sykesville, Maryland, from 2001 through 2009.

7. American Association of State Troopers, *AAST Trooper Connection*, September 2008.

8. U.S. Department of Justice, Community Relations Service, *Police Use of Excessive Force: A Conciliation Handbook for the Police and the Community* (Washington, DC, June 1999). This publication provides options for addressing controversy surrounding the use of excessive or deadly force and offers guidelines for resolving community disputes. Readers can access *http://www.usdoj.gov/crs/pubs/pdexcess.htm* for the June 2002 updated version.

9. In 1993, Edward F. Davis was an instructor in the FBI Academy's Behavioral Science Unit when he interviewed the chief about police and the use of force. The chief's comment could be misconstrued because it was part of a larger dialogue about police use of force and community relations, although it demonstrates perceived and sometimes real concerns. Specifically, the chief was referring to the fact that the department seemed to pull together when an officer is killed and the opposite often occurs when the shooting is questioned in the media.

10. Because of Robert Chaney's (one of this article's authors) extensive experience in investigating police shootings while serving with the Washington, D.C., Metropolitan Police Department and then reviewing such incidents for final disposition when later employed by the U.S. Attorney's Office for the District of Columbia, he understands the value of the process and how this can affect public perceptions and investigative outcomes.

11. William A. Geller and Michael S. Scott, *Deadly Force: What We Know* (Washington, DC: Police Executive Research Forum, 1992).

12. Robert Chaney's (one of this article's authors) experience includes a close working relationship with the criminal justice authority (in his case, the criminal justice authority was the U.S. Attorney's Office). The close working relationship can be critical with shootings that have the potential for negative publicity.

13. U.S. Department of Justice, Community Relations Service, *Police Use of Excessive Force: A Conciliation Handbook for the Police and the Community*.

14. Laurence Miller, "Officer-Involved Shooting: Reaction Patterns, Response Protocols, and Psychological Intervention Strategies," *International Journal of Emergency Mental Health* 8, no. 4 (2006): 239–254.

15. Henry Pierson Curtis, "Deadly Force Investigations Can Take Years in Some Florida Counties," *Orlando Sentinel*, November 11, 2007; Todd Coleman, "Documenting the Use of

Force," *FBI Law Enforcement Bulletin*, November 2007, 18–23; and Geller and Scott.

16. For additional information, see Brian Parsi Boetig and Penny A. Parrish, "Proactive Media Relations: The Visual Library Initiative," *FBI Law Enforcement Bulletin*, November 2008, 7–9; James D. Sewell, "Working with the Media in Times of Crisis: Key Principles for Law Enforcement," *FBI Law Enforcement Bulletin*, March 2007, 1–6; and Dennis Staszak, "Media Trends and the Public Information Officer," *FBI Law Enforcement Bulletin*, March 2001, 10–13.

17. Brook A. Masters, "Under the Gun: I Died, I Killed, and I Saw the Nature of Deadly Force," *Washington Post*, February 13, 2000.

18. Anthony J. Pinizzotto, Edward Davis, Shannon Bohrer, and Robert Chaney, "Law Enforcement Perspective on the Use of Force: Hands-On, Experiential Training for Prosecuting Attorneys," *FBI Law Enforcement Bulletin*, April 2009, 16–21.

19. Geller and Scott, 1.

CONCEPT #5: MANAGE YOUR RESOURCES EFFICIENTLY

The pen is mightier than the sword, but no match for the accountant.

—Jonathan Glancey

Historically, the topic of resources has been of major concern to administrators in all geographic areas of the country. As crime rates rise and calls for service increase, it seems that chiefs and sheriffs have always had to learn to do more with less. Now, in this depressed economy, this topic is of even greater importance. In recent years, law enforcement officers in both large and small jurisdictions have been laid off. Furloughs have become commonplace and budgets have plummeted.

Your first reading discusses police department budgeting in general. Basic ideas and concepts are discussed, which may help in the development of future budgets. Next is a reading on the strategic management of police resources. You have your budget, but the now focus is on using it wisely. Reorganizing, flexibility, creativity and doing more successful work are the themes of this reading. Also discussed are call management and differential response strategies.

The third reading in this chapter is on activity based budgeting, a strategy for budget development that addresses the connection between workload and costs.

Although many budget styles exist, this style describes control and economy; two important issues in our current economic state. Although this style may never be fully implemented as it is impossible to identify all law enforcement tasks, it does give the administrator an option and another perspective to work with in the budget development process.

The Federal government, state governments, private foundations and other organizations often have funds available for specific law enforcement functions. Although dollar amounts may have decreased in recent years, these outside sources of funding will always be available. For this reason, your fourth reading discusses writing successful grant proposals. Major topics include funding sources, supporting data, ethical considerations and the writing process.

Next, this chapter moves into two specific areas of expenditures: vehicles and overtime. The fifth reading in this chapter discusses fleet management. With fully equipped vehicles costing well over $20,000 each, this reading is presented to generate thoughts and ideas for further inquiry. Issues discussed include the bid process, life-cycle estimates, purchase and lease options, vehicle rotations and replacement and fleet liability. The sixth reading in this chapter discusses police overtime. Major topics include analyzing overtime, recording overtime, managing overtime and supervising overtime. As you will read, there is often a breakdown in one or more of these areas, which could have detrimental effects on future funding.

The seventh and final reading in this chapter deals with corporate strategies for policing. The law enforcement resources of both money and authority are discussed in this reading. The emphasis in this reading is on how to best use these two resources. Utilization of these resources is compared to the private sector where executives develop a corporate strategy. Such a strategy is possible in law enforcement and this reading explains how administrators may borrow some of these concepts or develop their own strategies for resource management.

Police Department Budgeting

INTRODUCTION

Police departments are major participants in municipal budgeting. According to the U.S. Department of Commerce, police departments spent $20.9 billion in 1991–92. To a degree, municipal agencies in the budget process compete with each other for limited resources. In that competition, police departments have a definite advantage: the public's interest in safety. Even as crime rates fall nationwide, most police departments continue to be successful in obtaining federal, state, and local funding. Yet not all departments are equally successful.

Under a grant from the National Institute of Justice of the U.S. Department of Justice, the Police Executive Research Forum (PERF) undertook this project to discover why and how some police departments are much more successful than others in obtaining funding. The methodology was both quantitative and qualitative. In 1998, PERF sent a survey to all municipal or metropolitan police departments serving more than 50,000 persons. The response rate was 61 percent. In April 1999, PERF held a one-day focus group session with police executives from five agencies. Four criteria were used to select the participants: their departments had been highly successful in increasing their budgets during fiscal years 1997 and 1998; they represented different forms of local government; they were geo-

graphically diverse; and they were diverse with respect to the size of population served.

This report summarizes the literature on budgeting by police departments and other government agencies. It then presents the findings of the 1998 PERF survey. Finally, it offers highlights of the 1999 focus group of police executives.

REVIEW

Law enforcement agencies gauge their budgetary success in two ways: (1) whether they have maintained a harmonious working relationship with the local government chief executive and budget staff and (2) how successful they were in expanding their prior year's base budget or, in times of fiscal retrenchment, how successful they were in defending their base against cuts. Duncombe and Kinney found that state agency heads believed that keeping a good relationship was much more important than increasing appropriations (1987: 27). Still, getting budget requests funded is an important barometer of budgetary success.

Successful Budget Strategies

Research suggests that police agencies primarily employ these budget strategies:

* Use crime and workload data judiciously.

- Capitalize on sensational crime incidents (ideally not occurring locally).
- Carefully mobilize interest groups.
- Plan strategically.
- Participate carefully in the federal grant process.
- Maintain a close working relationship with the local government chief executive and governing board members.
- Involve all levels of the police department.

Use Data Judiciously. Government executives and police professionals have received considerable guidance on measuring and evaluating police performance. Numerous organizations and researchers have developed measures of patrol services, investigations, traffic services, drug control, crime prevention and control, community policing, and overall police effectiveness.

How do performance indicators relate to budgetary outcomes? Greene, Bynum, and Cordner found that increased workload was the second greatest factor contributing to an increase in positions (1986: 537).

Capitalize on Sensational Crimes. Research on the effect of sensational crimes on police funding decisions has been limited, and results are mixed. One survey indicated that critical incidents were not a significant factor in budgetary success (Greene et al., 1986: 537). However, the study also found that certain critical incidents, such as killings of police officers, were responsible for a "massive infusion of resources into the problem area despite economic conditions, public ideology, or political considerations" (Hudzik et al., 1981).

Mobilize Interest Groups. Government agencies often mobilize interest groups to build support for their budget requests. Wildavsky and Caiden note that federal agencies influence policy makers by finding a clientele, serving it, expanding it, and securing feedback from it (1997: 57–58). Federal agencies are described as forming either iron triangles or issue networks. An iron triangle is a fixed relationship between legislative committees, the agencies they oversee, and their allied interest groups. Issue networks, on the other hand, is a loose-knit, changing relationship between interest groups, involved citizens, experts, and agencies concerned with a particular issue (Heclo, 1979: 102). Police departments tend to form issue networks, not iron triangles. Hudzik found that law enforcement agencies formed relationships with particular constituents to secure funding, but that such relationships were highly transitory, rising to support an agency one year and disappearing the next (1978).

Police departments have always had a natural constituency of neighborhood groups, civic organizations, and business groups concerned about crime. Moreover, the widespread adoption of community policing has greatly expanded both the formal and informal ties that police departments have to the community. Police agencies place school resource officers in public schools and meet routinely with established neighborhood organizations, civic groups, business groups, and victims' organizations. In addition to these permanent relationships, police officers form temporary issue networks with community groups to address particular problems, often identified by the citizens themselves. Once the problems are solved, the coalitions dissolve.

Because police departments are so visible in the community and crime is so emotionally laden, police departments enjoy considerable public support, which sometimes manifests itself in the budget process. Police departments have effectively blocked funding cuts by taking their case to the public (Green et al., 1986). Interest group support can also help police departments obtain more funding.

Plan Strategically. Strategic planning explores policy alternatives, emphasizing the future implications of present decisions (Bryson, 1995: 5). It also develops a statement of long-range goals and objectives and is a sound management practice that should occur before the budget cycle. The long-range strategic plan enables decision makers to make better one-year, operating budget policy decisions. Bryson surmises, however, that most budgets are formed without strategic thought (1995: 152). The reason may be similar to that behind Rubin's finding that some mayors did not want budget performance targets published because they feared that their political opponents would unfairly dwell on missed targets (1990).

Participate Carefully in Federal Grants. Police departments access a variety of external funding sources, primarily grants from state and federal government agencies, foundations, and business groups. Often funds are spent on sophisticated technology, which may increase a police department's effectiveness or efficiency. Technology may free up officers' time, yet technology also may require expensive support. After obtaining a grant, a police executive may find it difficult to obtain additional funding from local government for support and maintenance. Therefore, police executives must take care to think through all the related costs before accepting government grants.

Maintain Close Relationships. It is important for police executives to maintain close working relationships with both government chief executives and elected board members. Those relationships may have to be tailored to the particular officeholders. For some, crime may be an overriding concern, while for others it may not be. Responding quickly and accurately to governing board members is critical.

Involve All Departmental Levels. In the 1980s and 1990s, a marked shift occurred in organization behavior in both the private and public sectors. Viewing the success of the Japanese, especially in manufacturing, American businesses and government agencies adopted such successful techniques as total quality management (TQM), quality circles, reengineering, team engineering, and strategic planning. One cornerstone of these reforms has been employee empowerment. In *Reinventing Government*, David Osborne and Ted Gaebler document the success of public agencies that have used empowerment and competition to improve performance.

SURVEY

Following two waves of pre-tests, the mail survey was administered to 490 municipal police agencies. The sample comprised all police departments serving populations of 50,000 or more. One follow-up to non-respondents was carried out by mail.

The survey yielded 297 responses (61 percent). Consistent with the survey population, responding agencies ranged in size from 100 personnel to 46,431, with a mean of 862 (including both sworn and civilian personnel). Twenty-nine percent of respondents had fewer than 200 personnel, 41 percent had 201–500, and 30 percent had more than 500. The service populations for the responding agencies ranged from 47,500 to 1.822 million, with an average of 208,037.

Key findings are presented in the following categories: personnel spending, budget size indicators, budget growth, budget growth indicators, budget processes, capital budgets, and additional resources.

Personnel Spending. Police agencies responding to the survey spent, on average, 85 percent of their budgets on personnel, ranging from 61 to 98.5 percent.

Budget Size Indicators. The study found a strong correlation between operating budgets and several other indicators: workload (Part I UCR and calls for service), population, and tax revenue. Differences in tax revenue, service population, total number of personnel, and calls for service explained about 90 percent of the variation in agency budgets.

Budget Growth. Most departments reported increases in their operating budgets from one year to the next. To identify agencies successful in the budgetary arena, PERF added the percentage budgetary increases from 1996 to 1997 with increases from 1997 to 1998. Among respondents, the average budgetary increase over that period was 12.7 percent, ranging from a decrease of 9.6 percent to an increase of 60 percent. In this study, 29 police agencies reported large gains—that is, 20 percent or more for the two-year period.

Budget Growth Indicators. Departments with large gains in operating budgets differ in some important ways from the average department in this study. The agencies reveal no distinction by tenure of the police chief, agency size, or political structure. The most significant difference appears to be population growth. Only 25 percent of departments in this study reported a major increase in population (10 percent or more) from 1992 to 1997. However, among police departments with large increases in their operating budgets, 52 percent had experienced that large amount of population growth.

The policy objectives of police departments highly successful in the budgetary arena also differ from those of the average respondent in the study. PERF's study asked respondents to indicate up to three policy objectives of the agency's chief executive. Departments with the objectives of increasing agency staffing and modernizing the department fared somewhat better in the budgetary process than other agencies. Among all agencies, the most commonly reported objective was to implement or expand community policing. Seventy-four percent of all respondents reported this as one of the chief's primary policy objectives, while only 55 percent of departments with large budget expansions reported community policing as among the top policy objectives.

Major crime events, such as killings of police officers and increases in crime, may also positively affect police funding. The PERF survey found that agencies with large budget increases were slightly more likely to have experienced such critical events.

Budget Processes. The local budgetary process is the relevant policymaking arena for police chiefs, according to Greene et al. (1986). When in danger of losing resources, those authors say, police agencies can benefit significantly by taking their case to the public because police services are a visible local function. Police in this study reported that community groups often have an active voice in the local police budgetary process: 68 percent of respondents reported that neighborhood groups took an active role, 42 percent said business groups did so, and 34 percent reported civic groups as taking such a role. These constituents were heard primarily through public hearings (reported by 62 percent of respondents), lobbying of council members or the mayor (reported by 59 percent), and letter-writing (reported by 41 percent).

The form of budget used also seems to affect police departments' strategic approach to budgeting. The line-item budget is typically considered a mechanism of control (Pursley, 1993; Rubin, 1990; Hudzik, 1978), while program or mission-oriented budgets are more likely to relate policy goals to budgets and hence are useful for police in meeting policy objectives, such as community policing. In PERF's study, 51 percent of respondents reported that line-item was the sole budget format; 10 percent reported using a program budget format; 5 percent used a performance budget, which is zero-based or target; and 2 percent named a mission-driven budget. Thirty-two percent reported using a combination of these budget formats; two-thirds of those respondents combined program and line-item budgets.

Other budgetary practices, too, may constrain the ability of police departments to engage in linking policing objectives with funding. Over half of respondents reported that budgetary limits or targets are typically set by the mayor, city manager, or finance director. In a third of agencies, budgetary targets or limits are negotiated between the city manager or mayor and department heads, while in 11 percent of agencies, targets or limits are determined by revenue projections. In 92 percent of cases, revenue projections precede or coincide with expenditure projections, providing either an explicit or implicit goal for the budgetary process.

Despite numerous controls of police objectives by the budgetary process, more than half the agencies in this survey (55 percent) have a written strategic plan, and another 13 percent have some form of strategic plan that may be incorporated in council goals or capital improvement plans. Stamper (1992:154) urges that budgetary processes be the "preeminent management function" and be linked closely with planning processes, especially long-range planning. In contrast to Hanna (1987: 34), who says that police chiefs have little control over budget decisions, "which are ultimately made outside the police department," the existence of long-range strategic plans suggests that police may have an activist role in shaping the jurisdiction's budget.

Capital Budgets. Operating budgets are not the only budgetary issue. In this study, 71 percent of respondents reported they have separate budgets for capital expenditures, 17 percent said they do not, and 13 percent reported they have a somewhat separate capital budget, often depending on the value of items purchased or varying from year to year.

Among departments with separate capital budgets, major technology items (such as dispatch systems or mobile data terminals) and major equipment purchases are the most commonly included expenditures. But capital budgets also include expenditures for buildings (75 percent of respondents), vehicles (59 percent), and property (48 percent). Despite their inclusion of large-cost items, capital budgets were typically dwarfed by operating budgets. For 1997-1998, among the 164 agencies reporting separate capital and operating budgets, capital budgets exceeded operating budgets in only one department.

Additional Funding Resources. Even operating and capital budgets together do not tell the entire story of the police budget process. Grants are relatively common among police departments, as is shown in the table below. Funds from the Bureau of Justice Assistance (BJA) and the Office of Community Oriented Policing Services (COPS) are widely tapped, as are funds from the U.S. Department of Housing and Urban Development (HUD). About 47 percent of departments reported receiving discretionary grants from the Office of National Drug Control Policy, Drug Enforcement Administration, Office for Victims of Crime, and Bureau of Alcohol, Tobacco and Firearms.

In addition, some departments routinely tap into non-government sources of funding. About 8 percent of agencies reported grants from private foundations in amounts ranging from $500 to $242,760. About 10 percent of police agencies received grants from local corporations in amounts ranging from $414 to $7,641,214. Police departments with these outside funding sources reported receiving a range of $1 to $32 per capita. Success in obtaining grants was somewhat related to having a full-time grant seeker. Overall, 28 percent of respondents reported having a full-time employee or contractor charged with seeking out grants, while 38 percent of the agencies with higher grants per capita reported having at least one full-time grant seeker.

Sources of Grants to Police Departments

Funding Source	Departments Receiving Funds (n=299)	Range
BJA	155	$1,231–$28,277,320
COPS	200	$2,622–$99,317,610
HUD	88	$3,366–$62,682,000
NHTSA	67	$1,049–$6,680,701
Foundations	24	$500–$242,760
Businesses	30	$414–$7,641,214
Discretionary Grants	139	$6,161–$21,620,099
Other Sources	130	$5–$64,892,873

The Strategic Management of Police Resources

By David Kennedy

Many American police departments feel themselves to be slowly drowning in a rising tide of serious crime and calls for service. Over the last decade, department workloads have risen steadily while their resources have stayed constant or often declined.[1] Police executives generally have responded by striving to enhance the efficiency of police operations and focus police resources on only the more serious calls. Computer-aided dispatching and other information systems have been employed to make the most of the patrol force, and many departments no longer respond at all to nuisance calls or provide services like escorts and house checks that the public once took for granted. Nonetheless, police in many cities find themselves more and more pressed, a problem recently greatly exacerbated—even in smaller communities—by unprecedented increases in drugs and violence.

It is thus understandable that many departments find calls for community policing unrealistic. As most police—and most mayors—understand the concept, community policing means taking on difficult new responsibilities, like fighting fear and solving community problems, using fresh tactics like foot patrol and community organizing. What room could there possibly be to do new jobs when the department can scarcely do the old ones?

Mayor Bud Clark of Portland, Oregon, was a community policing enthusiast when he took office in 1985, but he saw no place for the new strategy in what both he and the police agreed was a short-handed, overworked department. "Community-oriented policing means less relying on heavyhanded law enforcement and more getting at root causes," said Chuck Duffy, a Clark aide. "But we recognized the fact that you can't do it well un-less you have an adequate level of police officers, because you've got to do the community outreach stuff with police on top of your base of patrol officers, and we were having trouble with our base."

Such sentiments are often, and understandably, expressed by police and municipal officials. They are the sum of four widely held beliefs about contemporary policing (until recently, nearly universally held). One is that the public demand for police services, particularly for 911 rapid-response services, is largely out of police control. The second is that departmental resources are, in the main, already deployed to best advantage, efficiently and effectively. The third is that community policing (like other new policing strategies such as problem-oriented policing) is a discretionary add-on to the core job of policing. Because it is seen as "soft," aimed more at community and public relations than at crime control, it is often delayed and resisted when crime and workloads are on the rise. (In other words, the real job of policing is traditional enforcement, and departments should not be distracted from that mission.) The fourth belief is that police resources, meaning police department budgets, are largely static, particularly in the current climate of fiscal constraint. The largest gains a department can hope to make, on this line of thinking, are still small—an improvement in patrol deployment here, a few extra positions there. It is no surprise that the police find large increases in calls for service, or striking new challenges like the crack epidemic and waves of youth violence, very difficult to meet.

Increasingly, however, there is reason to believe that none of these four beliefs is true. The concrete experience of numerous innovative police departments—including Portland, which found ways to move into community policing despite resource constraints—is proving otherwise. The police can, in fact, manage public demand and expectations for police services. They can deploy their current resources in new and improved ways. They can use community and problem-solving policing strategies to achieve ambitious crime-control objectives. And they can find and win new resources, budgetary and otherwise, to help them do their various jobs. These are fundamental, not marginal, gains; they hold out the hope of major advances in the struggle to fight crime and improve the quality of life in troubled cities. This paper will take each of these arguments in turn, then turn to a discussion of their combined significance for the future of policing.

CALL MANAGEMENT AND DIFFERENTIAL RESPONSE

No challenge is more immediate, no job more demanding, in many police departments than the crushing burden of answering the public's calls for service. Individual officers in busy cities feel the weight on every shift. "If you drive out there and make yourself available for calls, you wouldn't be available one minute that night for anything else," says Los Angeles Police Department patrol officer Joe Ciancanelli. "There wouldn't be a dull moment, no time for anything." Patrol forces have, over the last 10 years, increasingly been restricted to answering the tolling of the 911 bell. Fewer and fewer people and less and less time are available for foot patrol, problem

solving, crime prevention, or any other important tasks a chief might want the force to perform. That concern is heightened by a growing sense that for the vast majority of calls for service, rapid response is not—contrary to several generations of police belief and expectations—an appropriate or effective crime-fighting tool. Most dispatched calls—50 to 90 percent, in most jurisdictions—are not about crime. In only a small percentage of those that are about crime—less than 5 percent of all dispatched calls, in most cities—does the officer have a chance to intervene or make an arrest.[2] Nobody doubts that for that crucial 5 percent, the response should be immediate and authoritative. But in the other 95 percent, the scene is cold and the officer can do little more than take a report and soothe the victim. "Most of the time," says Ernest Curtsinger, chief of the St. Petersburg, Florida, Police Department, "irrespective of the call, you get there and the bad guy is gone and the real emergency situation is over." The high hopes once pinned on rapid response and 911 systems have turned, in many police quarters, to a profound concern about their insatiable appetite for resources. "We have created," says one chief, "a monster."

At the same time, many police executives despair of winning public acceptance for any other way of delivering police services, even approaches like problem solving that might actually improve conditions and cut down on the volume of calls coming into departments. Rapid response, in this view, is a promise that the police have made to the public and that cannot be broken, regardless of its operational shortcomings. "People expect us to come when they call; that's an absolute," says one chief. "Believing anything else is a pipe dream."

Other executives, though, are looking for new ways both to handle calls and to reshape public expectations. Their goal is generally to preserve, and even enhance, their departments' ability to respond immediately to true emergencies while finding more efficient, and perhaps more effective, ways to respond to less urgent calls without disappointing the public in the process. Evidence is accumulating that it can be done.

Much of the work being done in this area builds on one core idea: that the public will not insist on immediate responses to non emergency calls, if it is properly prepared for what to expect instead. As long ago as 1976, research showed that public satisfaction with police handling of calls was less influenced by the speed of response than it was by the difference between anticipated and actual response times.[3] The public's expectations, in other words, seemed to be central to their sense of how well the police were performing. Could those expectations be deliberately reshaped?

In the early 1980's, the National Institute of Justice designed its Differential Police Response experiments to find out. The DPR research tested public reaction to a range of alternative response strategies for non emergency calls—walk-in and mail-in reporting, telephone report units, officer response delayed by up to half an hour, officer response by appointment, and the like—in Garden Grove, California; Greensboro, North Carolina; and Toledo, Ohio. Dispatchers were carefully trained in how to rank calls and, when appropriate, inform callers about the new responses. Administrative mechanisms were developed in each department to make sure that what dispatchers promised—for instance, to have an officer arrive to take a report at a particular time—was actually delivered.

The results were striking. More than 90 percent of callers in all three cities who received the alternative responses were satisfied with them (with the exception of the write-in option, which proved less popular).[4] Nearly half of all calls could have been so handled (not that many were, because of the experiments' designs).[5] Even with the limited proportion of alternative responses permitted in the experiments, patrol workload was reduced by as much as one-fifth.[6] Instituting and staffing the alternatives turned out to be fairly straightforward and inexpensive; in Toledo, for instance, 4 report-takers in a headquarters telephone unit were worth 10 in the field. Many of the alternatives were, and more could have been, staffed by civilians. The speed and quality of rapid response to priority calls was unaffected. Overall, the NIJ report concluded, "Police departments can achieve a sizable reduction in the number of non-emergency calls for

service handled by immediate mobile dispatch, without sacrificing citizen satisfaction."[7] Contemporary reports from the field bore them out. Some departments were able to take as much as 45 percent of their reports over the phone.[8]

While that view has gained some currency in policing in recent years, it has generally done so against the grain of police wishes and preferences. Conditions may have made it impossible to answer every call with a dispatched officer, and differential response strategies (particularly telephone reporting units) are no longer as rare as they once were, but there is often a lingering sense that they represent an unfortunate backing away from the ideals of policing. Nor, in most departments, have call management and differential response had much effect on the nature and role of the patrol force. Street officers may be less burdened as a result, but the basic job of patrol and response remains largely as before.

This is beginning to change. Police executives are increasingly undertaking call management and differential response as part of a purposeful shift to new community and problem-solving policing strategies, and with the express intent of substantially reshaping patrol (and often other) operation.[9] Chief Darrel Stephens, for instance, relied heavily on a relatively traditional telephone report-taking unit to make room in the Newport News department to do problem-solving policing, which proved successful against a wide variety of crime and order problems.[10] In St. Petersburg, Florida, call management allowed the department to shift significant resources into community policing while simultaneously cutting response times to high-priority calls by more than 20 percent.[11]

The Reno, Nevada, Police Department, a recent convert to community policing, splits its patrol force on a day-to-day basis between special projects and mobile response. Call management is handled through the headquarters dispatching center, which presents callers with a wide variety of service options for non-emergency calls. Where an officer's presence is appropriate or insisted upon, the dispatcher keeps callers apprised of when one should be available. Because mobile response is now handled by perhaps half as many officers as in the pre-community policing department, getting a car to a low-priority scene often takes several hours. But with careful departmental attention to explaining why, citizen satisfaction—tracked by formal polling—has remained high.[12]

There is reason to believe that problem solving can reduce calls for service. Addresses and areas that generate repeat calls for service are easily identified by police from departmental information, and efforts to address these repeat calls often feature in departments' problem-solving efforts. In one now-classic example, a sergeant in the Philadelphia Police Department solved a noise problem caused by a jukebox bar and cut calls for service that had been coming in at a rate of a thousand a year down to zero.[13] In Florida, Tampa's QUAD program against street drug dealing appears to have cut citywide calls for service considerably.[14] And, while they generally lack firm proof, officers and supervisors involved in problem solving are invariably convinced that their work lowers their departments' call loads. Difficult though the job may be, making room in departments for proactive, problem-solving policing appears likely to pay substantial returns.

The new strategies' overall emphasis on such things as devolution of police authority, beat integrity, and street-level problem solving is beginning to give rise to new models of call management. One of the most interesting comes from the Houston Police Department, which—as part of its neighborhood-oriented policing philosophy—has planned a high-tech decentralization of call management. Priority one and two calls would still be dispatched from headquarters. Other calls, though, would be patched through via in-car video display terminals to shift sergeants, who would be expected to manage both their officers, via radio, and the callers, via cellular phone. The sergeants' job would be to provide the best mix of police response for their areas, balancing the need to work on community and problem-solving projects against the need to respond to individual callers—and, where necessary, to explain and justify their decisions to the public.[15] The result, if the scheme works, will be call management and police services custom-tailored precinct by precinct, and even shift by shift, to Houston's varied and ever-changing needs.

Two additional important points should be made about community policing and call management. First, community policing itself seems to perform a call management function. Calls in the pioneering Flint, Michigan, foot patrol districts, for instance, dropped 43 percent over the course of that department's formal experiment. Some of the decline was attributable to problem solving, but much of it was due to residents in the districts passing minor complaints directly to the foot officers rather than making formal calls for service. The foot officers then handled them as and when they wished. This was a far more efficient scheme than dispatching officers to every such call, and a much more popular one than refusing service for calls that failed to merit a formal dispatch, or promising a rapid response that in fact took hours to materialize.

Second, community policing makes formal call management schemes easier to sell to the public. When call management is used solely to relieve the workload on traditional patrol operations, the public is asked to give up something tangible and immedi—ate—a response—in exchange for an efficiency gain that is usually perceived to benefit only the department. With community policing, the public arguably gets something—more responsive, more effective policing—for its sacrifice. As the Newport News, Reno, and other departments can attest, the public often finds this a welcome trade.

REORGANIZING TO MAKE THE MOST OF DEPARTMENTAL RESOURCES

Just as departments can reexamine their service preferences and obligations, they can reexamine their allocation and utilization of personnel. The first step is often simply to take a fresh look, with basic principles of good management in mind, at how a department does business. Police agencies, like all organizations, have a tendency to get set in their ways, and a management review, performed internally or by consultants, can often uncover significant room for improvement. For example, the Rivlin Commission on Budget and Financial Priorities of the District of Columbia examined the Washington, D.C., Police

Department in 1990. The Commission discovered that the department, though an extreme case, had the highest overtime expenses in the country, due chiefly to rigid work rules and hugely inefficient arrangements for the booking and charging of arrestees; the lowest proportion of civilian employees among 13 major departments; no capacity for crime and workload analysis, and therefore none for efficient personnel allocation; and actual assignment practices that bore little relation to formal ones (500 assignments to patrol existed only on paper, while the Youth Division had more than twice its authorized strength).[16] While few departments may be in such dire straits, many could benefit from a similar examination.

Beyond such fundamental attention to rationalization and efficiency, policing is increasingly seeing moves toward a major, sometimes radical, strategic redistribution and reprogramming of departmental resources. One of the most visible is shifting people— and authority—out of headquarters and specialist units back to field commands. When Sir Kenneth Newman took over the London Metropolitan Police Department in 1982, he both "desquadded," returning 10 percent of all headquarters squads and 1,200 additional headquarters posts to the field, and "flattened" the rank structure, entirely eliminating a senior rank that stood between Scotland Yard and its territorial commands. John Avery, commissioner in New South Wales, Australia, shifted much of his detective force to the field and put it under the authority of patrol commanders. Lee Brown put nearly 500 officers back on patrol when he took over in Houston, and began a similar but even more ambitious program in New York.[17] The Reno department effectively eliminated all supervisory ranks between chief and area captain. Such moves are in part efforts to ease the burden of call response and other field activities. More fundamentally, however, they are intended to promote decentralization, precinct- and street-level problem solving, and responsiveness to the community.

In most departments, headquarters functions have long been valued more highly than precinct functions, and the work of detectives and other specialists more highly than that of patrol. Generations of police chiefs have found creating special squads an attractive

response to new problems. It can be done fast; the new unit, consistent with traditional police concern for centralized command and control, can be easily monitored and supervised from headquarters; and the department has something concrete to point to, demonstrating it has taken the problem seriously. Unfortunately, such units, once established, are difficult to disband and tend to monopolize responsibility for the problem. In this way, they limit opportunities for police officers to learn how to handle such problems, and drain strength and creativity from geographic commands and more general functions like patrol.

Many departments now are trying to reverse that tendency by enhancing the authority and discretion of geographic commands. In New South Wales, for instance, detectives probably do not do any more detecting than they did before the shift. However, they worked before according to headquarters' interest in major cases and clearance rates, while now they are guided in part by geographic commands' assessments of the problems and community needs they face. The same is true with shifts of narcotics, juvenile, vice, and other specialists into geographic lines (though care must be taken to preserve the department's capacity to act against highly mobile crime). Not only are more personnel in the field, but the department's over-all capacity also is deployed for maximum problem-solving and community-service effectiveness.

This is, in a way, a new version of the very promising but generally short-lived team policing experiments of the 1970's.[18] Those programs often failed because the demands of rapid response and headquarters expectations ran counter to teams' interest in local problem solving. New strategies, new allocations of resources, and new lines of authority give the new teams a much better chance to succeed.

Less tangible but no less important than these changes, in many innovative departments, is a major development in the philosophy of police administration. Police departments have long been governed by a paramilitary command-and-control approach that puts a premium on close supervision and the prevention of corruption and operational error. The traditional emphasis on discipline and propriety is laudable, but many modern police executives have come to believe that the paramilitary approach won that ground at the cost of organizational flexibility, responsiveness, and innovation. They are actively seeking ways to gain those qualities without at the same time opening the door to police misbehavior.

Beginning to emerge is a managerial and organizational style that looks more toward the best in private-sector and professional organizations than toward policing's own heritage. Modem police executives, no less than the CEO's of innovative high-tech firms, directors of teaching hospitals, or senior partners in architecture firms, are coming to believe that one of their main jobs is forging departments that are tied closely to their clients and in which junior and senior officers alike have the freedom and support to contribute as fully as they are able.[19] This new environment, combined with schemes like call management, resource shifts like enhancing the strength and authority of patrol, and ideas like problem solving, can create significant new police capacities. Traditional policing, with its enforced focus on individual calls for service, gives patrol officers little choice but to handle each incident quickly and with little attention to underlying causes.

The new strategies, by letting officers look at patterns and clusters of calls and complaints, create within the department the capacity to investigate and intervene in situations that previously would have been handled far more superficially. Houston's Neighborhood Oriented Policing created institutional ground so fertile that one tactical squad sergeant was able to craft a scheme for putting a major open-air drug bazaar out of business, win community and departmental support for it, and see it through not only the elimination of the drug problem but through the area's commercial redevelopment—all by reprogramming precinct resources and putting them to new use.[20] Such individual successes, if they can be made the rule rather than the exception in policing, would represent not just more efficient, but substantially more effective, use of police resources.[21]

It increasingly appears that such stories could become policing's norm. In fact, the outlines of a very promising progression now are visible. The beginning came in the 1970's with programs like team policing, the Los Angeles Police Department's Senior Lead Officers, and Flint's foot patrol program, aimed at cultivating officers' contact with the community through innovative use of a relatively small proportion of the force.[22] These programs often showed considerable operational promise, but they also showed insightful police executives that bottom-up, community-focused policing was not easily commensurable with the claims and procedures of a predominantly response-oriented department. Over the course of the next decade came a host of attempts to shift departments wholesale into a new community-policing style, most notably in America by Lee Brown in Houston, but in different ways in a number of other departments as well. This was a time of striking, but frustratingly partial, results. Success stories like Link Valley in Houston; the Community Mobilization Project in Los Angeles; problem-solving policing in Newport News, Virginia; and many others seemed to herald the ability of police to prevent crime and solve problems in league with public and municipal allies. Generally, however, they remained isolated tales, both in the effect they had on cities and in the proportion of police effort they represented even in the most dedicated and experimental departments.[23]

A third phase now appears to be beginning, in which departments more or less familiar with community-policing ideas apply them wholesale to policing cities, or to solving major citywide problems. This is happening first, predictably enough, in smaller cities whose forces can shift more readily to the new style. In some of these places, community policing is beginning to deliver on its promise of making a dent in serious crime. In Reno, Nevada, the police credit the new style with ending overt public drug dealing in the city and driving off the Los Angeles-based gangs that were establishing a beachhead in town. In Gainesville, Florida, a problem-solving approach cut convenience-store robberies by 65 percent. Tampa police, whose city was being overrun by crack and crack-related violence, organized a citywide problem-solving and community-policing approach that eliminated street dealing almost entirely and brought overall crime levels down to pre-crack levels. Reported crime was down 12.4 percent in 1989; in some hot spots reported crime was down more than 20 percent.[24] All of these gains were made without additional resources (at least initially, a point we will return to), simply by employing smarter and more effective policing. One can hope that more cities will soon be able to tell similar stories.

If it is true that new policing strategies can make such striking improvements in police performance, then the most crucial resource management decision facing police executives is a new and extremely fundamental one: how to craft their departments in these new shapes, and how to manage the transition from here to there. Facing this task squarely is essential if the new strategies are to succeed. The new strategies are not programmatic add-ons to a police department's traditional organization and functions. Community organizing and problem solving represent a fundamentally different approach to doing the job of policing than do rapid response and retrospective investigation. They represent, in fact, an approach that is in many important ways incompatible with traditional police organization and tactics.

Making patrol officers responsible for problem solving, for example, means granting them a degree of operational discretion and giving them time to think and work that are not easily combined with a centralized dispatching operation devoted to minimizing response time to calls for service. Developing a departmental capacity to respond in a comprehensive fashion to community concerns—be they narcotics, guns, or the homeless—cannot easily be combined with a structure of detectives and other specialist squads operating largely autonomously from patrol and other geographic commands. The creativity, flexibility, and individual initiative that community policing demands cannot easily be combined with the paramilitary hierarchy and often draconian management style common to traditional departments. The list goes on and on; points of conflicts are many and severe

There is, here, both bad news and good news. The bad news is that the job of shifting a department, especially a large department, into the new strategies is a large and probably long one. The good news is that making that transition—not finding new resources—is the fundamental challenge facing a police executive interested in the strategies' potential. *How much money?* and *How many people?* while clearly still critical are no longer the central resource questions. The fundamental questions are *Money for what?* and *People for what?* As Houston, Newport News, Reno, and other departments are demonstrating, high workloads and limited resources are not necessarily insurmountable obstacles to moving successfully into community and problem-solving policing. The new ideas, to a considerable degree, open up to reconsideration all departments' traditional resource allocations. Just what can then be done with them the profession is only beginning to discover.

NEW RESOURCES

This is not to say that most police departments would not find more money and other resources very welcome, particularly as they move from traditional policing to more community-oriented, problem-solving policing. During that difficult transition, departments are in some ways in the worst of both worlds: they must invest in the reorganization, training, and technology the new strategy demands, and suffer the dislocations and inefficiencies of change without yet realizing many of the new strategy's promised gains. With most departments stretched to their limits already, additional resources would be useful. Fortunately, much is possible on this front. The experience of many departments shows that even cities in serious fiscal trouble often can find ways to offer their police significant new support.

One approach is for departments to raise, or cause to be raised, nontax revenues. A National Institute of Justice report on supplementing police budgets found the most promising avenues to be donation programs and asset forfeiture.[25] Businesses in Oakland, California, for instance, concerned that declining police budgets would threaten the planned revitalization of the city's commercial areas, raised more than $ 750,000 for the Oakland Police Department.[26] The Miami Police Department netted $5.5 million over 3 years from seizing and auctioning property used in criminal enterprises.[27] Cash assets seized through drug and money-laundering enforcement have proved important in many jurisdictions. In addition, many departments have experimented with user fees (for instance, for answering private burglar alarms), fees-for-services (for instance, for extra patrol in malls), and in-kind contributions (for instance, management training).

Such efforts can be significant, but they also raise important management and equity issues. Private funding, both of a general nature and for particular details, can create questions of improper access to and control over a public service. Aggressive asset seizure programs can create questions of public authority being deployed for narrow institutional interests. Many departments have managed to avoid any cast of impropriety, but in each instance careful attention to actual and apparent conflicts is essential.

Some special relationships with the private sector, as in programs in which police managers attend corporate training programs, are by their nature much more benign. They can also be extremely important, particularly in departments working to reshape their administrative structures and cultures. Kevin Tucker, who took over the Philadelphia Police Department after the disastrous MOVE bombing, made this kind of management training a key part of his strategy to move the department toward more flexible, community-oriented policing.[28] The alliance not only built the kind of capacity in the department that Tucker wanted, it enlisted the cachet of private-sector management ideas in the service of his controversial reforms.

The new policing strategies create fresh and important opportunities for bringing outside resources to bear on police problems. Community and problem-solving police departments have shown, over and over again, that they can draw heavily on help from outside the department to handle what traditional police departments would have considered entirely police business. This is welcome news. It seems more and more apparent that the police alone cannot solve many crime and order problems, but that in partnership with others who have resources of their own to offer—time, money, expertise, ideas, energy, equipment, and more—perhaps they can. It has become, therefore, the aim, on both theoretical and pragmatic grounds, for innovative police departments to invest a good deal of effort in enlisting the aid of others, and to tackle problems by allying police resources and strengths with those of others.

Police give up something when they enter into such partnerships: their claim that responsibility for public safety is theirs and theirs alone. But they gain more than they lose. When public safety becomes a joint police, community, and municipal responsibility, others have to chip in as well. The resulting contributions can be of major importance. When the Houston Police Department, together with a coalition of community organizations, tackled the Link Valley drug market, local people cleaned up the area (a daylong effort by hundreds of volunteers and a large number of corporations), donated technical help with deed and title searches, and made sure that city departments delivered on their obligations to bring property owners into code compliance. When Tampa's police took on the city's crack dealers, they needed—and received—the active help of citizens in identifying, monitoring, and tracking street dealers, and of city departments in cleaning up street-dealing sites, taking down abandoned buildings, and closing down businesses fronting for traffickers.

These cooperative relationships are not always easy. The police and other parties do not always have the same agenda, or agree on the merit and propriety of particular ends and means. Police should be sensitive to the possibility, or the perception, that they are demanding too much in the way of public resources, or doing so in a way that slights other departments' procedures and priorities.[29] But the proven power of partnerships between the police and the public, and the police and other government agencies, means that, with the new strategies, police effectiveness becomes not just a matter of their own resources and operational capacity, but their ability to design solutions that capture the support and active aid of others. That ability has only begun to be developed, even in the most innovative departments.

Finally, the new approaches to policing change the nature of the political dialog about police resources. With the traditional strategy, the political question was basically whether a city wanted to buy more policing: more patrol, more investigation, quicker response. In today's climate, where municipal fiscal crisis and near-crisis are the norm, more of the same can be hard to justify. The new strategies, in important contrast, foster a debate over what kind of policing cities want. Do citizens want foot patrol officers in their neighborhoods? Do they want fear reduction? Do they want a department that both answers emergency calls promptly and has time for attending to neighborhood nuisances? The public is skeptical that simply hiring more people to do traditional police work is worth doing. But hiring more people to do different things is another matter entirely.

There are numerous examples that the public is more willing to pay for a new kind of policing than it is for the old. In 1982, the citizens of financially strapped Flint, Michigan, voted a $3.5 million tax increase specifically to continue the city's innovative foot patrol program (previously grant-funded), a move it repeated twice subsequently.[30] The Reno department shifted to community policing in the explicit hope that it would lead to increased public support. A 1987 study had revealed that 6 of 10 residents thought the police were doing a bad job, and the city had twice voted down a tax override to increase the police budget. Late in 1987, the department switched to community policing, which proved so popular that less than 6 months later Reno voted for a 40 percent increase in police strength. By the first half of 1989, public satisfaction had increased to nearly 90 percent.[31] Baltimore County, Maryland, and Portland, Oregon, both experienced similar, if less dramatic, increases in tax revenues after undertaking community policing. Portland won its extra money after going through two chiefs in less than 2 years, in considerable part due to intragovernmental feuding over funds. "Their answer to everything was just 'more,'" a Portland official said of one of the fired chiefs' maneuverings.[32] When a new chief proposed a

strategy that was not just more, but different, the city proved more than willing.

CONCLUSION

Policing, then, need not feel that its ability to manage its business and explore innovative strategies is hamstrung by today's admittedly punishing workload. Departments can, experience shows, manage their call burdens; they can deploy their resources in new and more productive ways; they can pursue promising new approaches to policing; and they can, at least sometimes, win substantial new resources, both financial and otherwise. It is not yet clear which techniques, and which combinations of techniques, are most effective, though certain tendencies and directions appear to be evident. It is clear, though, that police departments can explore these areas even where call loads are heaviest; that, indeed, exploring them is probably an essential step toward addressing those calls, and the crime and disorder that lie behind them. A warning is in order here regarding expectations and criteria of success. The new strategies carry no guarantee that they will be accompanied by reductions in calls for service, reported crime, or overall police workload. They may well lead to a rise in calls and reported crime, especially in troubled and demoralized parts of cities, as residents come to believe that the police can and will help with their problems. This is no bad thing, but it does mean that departments (and elected officials and newspapers) that look for an automatic reduction in crime statistics and officers' workload can be disappointed and misled when the reduction fails to materialize. Officers' workload likewise may well rise, or at least not fall, since the community organizing, service delivery, and problem solving that the new strategies require all take time. The hope is that, in the long run, they will improve conditions sufficiently that both demands for service and overall workload will start to decline. Even that cut in workload can be swallowed up, however, if departments take on new responsibilities such as fighting fear (as with COPE in Baltimore County) or coordinating the delivery of municipal services (as community police officers in Los Angeles, Houston, and many other departments tend to do).

This basic fact—that even new strategies of policing that prove effective in traditional terms will not necessarily mean less work for the police—has a major implication for police executives. Policing success will not relieve chiefs of their responsibilities for managing department resources to best effect, and may in fact add to and complicate them. The new strategies, with their wider range of tactics, new menus of possible responsibilities, and new roles for officers and managers, will require more, not less, in the way of strategic management and hard choices about resource allocation.

David M. Kennedy is a Research Fellow in the Program in Criminal Justice Policy and Management, John F. Kennedy School of Government, Harvard University.

Editor of this series is Susan Michaelson, Assistant Director of the Program in Criminal Justice Policy and Management, John F. Kennedy School of Government, Harvard University.

Opinions or points of view expressed in this publication are, those of the author and do not necessarily reflect the official position or policies of the U.S. Department of Justice or of Harvard University.

The National Institute of Justice is a component of the Office of Justice Programs, which also includes the Bureau of Justice Assistance, Bureau of Justice Statistics, Office of Juvenile Justice and Delinquency Prevention, and the Office for Victims of Crime.

Notes

1. For an account of this pressure in one large urban department, particularly its impact on proactive and community work, see David M. Kennedy, "Neighborhood Policing in Los Angeles," John F. Kennedy School of Government Case Study C16-87-717.0, Harvard University, Cambridge, 1987.

2. For a nice summary of this research, see John E. Eck and William Spelman, *Problem Solving: Problem-Oriented Policing in Newport News.*

Washington, D.C., Police Executive Research Forum, 1987: 13–14.

3. Tony Pate et al., *Police Response Time: Its Determinants and Effects.* Washington, D.C., Police Foundation, 1986; Stephen L. Percy, "Response Time and Citizen Evaluation of Police," *Journal of Police Science and Administration* 8, 1 (March 1980): 75–86; and James M. Tien et al., *An Alternative Approach in Police Patrol: The Wilmington Split-Force Experiment,* Cambridge, Massachusetts, Public System Evaluation, Inc., 1977, all cited in J. Thomas McEwen et al., *Evaluation of the Differential Police Response Field Test.* Washington, D.C., National Institute of Justice. 1986: 42.

4. *DPR Field Test,* note above, p. 17.

5. *DPR Field Test,* p. 16.

6. *DPR Field Test,* p. 101.

7. *DPR Field Test,* p. 16.

8. Thomas J. Sweeney, "Managing Time-the Scarce Resource," *Law Enforcement News,* January 11, 1982.

9. For three recent discussions of community and problem-solving policing, see Commissioner Lee P. Brown, *Policing New York City in the 1990's: The Strategy for Community Policing.* New York, New York City Police Department, January 1991; Herman Goldstein, *Problem-Oriented Policing.* New York, McGraw-Hill, 1990; and Malcolm K. Sparrow, Mark H. Moore, and David M. Kennedy, *Beyond 91 1:A New Era for Policing.* New York, Basic Books, 1990.

10. *Problem Solving,* n. 2 above: 40.

11. Chief Ernest Curtsinger, St. Petersburg Police Department, personal communication.

12. Captain Jim Weston, Reno Police Department, personal communication.

13. *Problem-Oriented Policing,* n. 9 above: 81.

14. The exact impact is hard to figure, inasmuch as Tampa went to a 911 system for the first time late in 1988, just before QUAD was begun. Although it is impossible to ascribe the change with certainty to QUAD, after calls had been rising for years, they fell from 606,755 to 549,402 between 1989 and 1990.

Against regional and statewide trends, Tampa's crime rate, index crimes per 100,000, and drug-related homicides also fell during the same period. See David M. Kennedy, "Closing the Market: Controlling the Drug Trade in Tampa, Florida," Washington, D.C., National Institute of Justice, forthcoming (1992).

15. Chief Elizabeth Watson, Houston Police Department, personal communication.

16. James J. Fyfe and Patrick V. Murphy, "D.C. Police: Trim the Fat," *Washington Post*, November 27, 1990, p. A21. See also "Financing the Nation's Capital: The Report of the Commission on Budget and Financial Priorities of the District of Columbia," Washington, D.C., November 1990.

17. Commissioner Lee P. Brown, New York City Police Department, personal communication.

18. See, for instance, Lawrence Sherman et al., *Team Policing: Seven Case Studies.* Washington, D.C., Police Foundation, 1973.

19. See, for instance, David C. Couper and Sabine H. Lobitz, *Quality Policing: The Madison Experience.* Washington, D.C., Police Executive Research Forum, 1991, and *Policing New York City in the 1990's,*" n. 9 above: 66–72.

20. David M. Kennedy, "Fighting the Drug Trade in Link Valley," John F. Kennedy School of Government Case Study Cl6-90-935.0, Harvard University, Cambridge, 1990.

21. For more examples from probably the toughest policing environment of all, New York City, see "CPOP: Community Policing in Practice," New York, Vera Institute of Justice, October 1988. This paper is included in the excellent James E. McElroy et al., *CPOP: The Researck—An Evaluative Study of the New York City Community Patrol Officer Program.* New York, Vera Institute of Justice, 1990.

22. On team policing, see *Team Policing,* n. 18 above. On Los Angeles' senior lead officers, see "Neighborhood Policing in Los Angeles," n. 1. On the Flint foot patrol experiment, see Robert Trojanowicz, *An Evaluation of the Neighborhood Foot Patrol Program in Flint, Michigan.* East Lansing, Michigan State University, 1982.

23. On Link Valley, see *"Fighting the Drug Trade in Link Valley,"* n. 20 above. On Houston and other innovative departments, see *Beyond 911,* n. 9. On Newport News, see *Problem Solving,* n. 2.

24. See n. 14 above.

25. Lindsey D. Stellwagen and Kimberly A. Wylie, *Strategies for Supplementing the Police Budget.* Washington, D.C., National Institute of us-tice, May 1985: 2.

26. *Strategies for Police Budget,* note above.

27. *Strategies for Police Budget: 3.*

28. *Beyond 91 1,* n. 9 above: 8 1.

29. For an account of how one local government dealt with these tensions, see David M, Kennedy, "Fighting Fear in Baltimore County," John F. Kennedy School of Government Case Study Cl6-90-938.0, Harvard University, Cambridge, 1990: 16–17.

30. Edwin Meese III and Bob Carrico, "Taking Back the Streets: Police Methods That Work," *Policy Review,* Fall 1990: 24.

31. Jim Weston, "Community Oriented Policing: An Approach to Traffic Management," Unpublished paper, November 8,1990, p. 2.

32. David M. Kennedy, "Patrol Allocation in Portland, Oregon (Part B): PCAM in the City," John F. Kennedy School of Government Case Study C15-88-819.0, Harvard University, Cambridge, 1988: 5. "PCAM stands for "Patrol Car Allocation Model."

Activity Based Budgeting

Creating a Nexus Between Workload and Costs

By Jon Shane

At some point in their careers, executives will need to develop a budget. Indeed, this represents a primary responsibility. A budget is merely a plan described in financial terms. Knowing which budget plan to choose, however, depends on what a manager needs to convey. Many budget styles exist, each with a different purpose. For example, the most common government budget, the line-item style, is oriented toward control and economy and answers the question, What is to be bought? A program budget, directed at planning and effectiveness, responds to the inquiry, What is to be achieved? And, a performance budget, disposed toward management and efficiency, replies to the query, What is to be done. Each has its place depending upon the goal. However, one style, activity based budgeting, has gained popularity over the last few years because of its ability to link activities to expenses, giving executives a better understanding of the full costs of service and resource allocation.

Activity based budgeting is an outgrowth of activity based costing, similar to zero-based budgeting.[2] This budget type accounts for how staff members allocate their efforts among activities. After calculating the full cost of each task, managers can establish mechanisms that link support functions to the primary obligations of the organization-in a law enforcement environment, the main activities are the direct costs of program delivery (e.g., patrol services, investigations,

tactical operations, and traffic control).[3] By developing a comprehensive activity-based budget, executives can create a clear nexus between workload and costs. Once they develop this, executives and managers can exercise control in several ways by assigning personnel based upon a demonstrated need; expanding or contracting personnel proportionately as the need changes; uncovering waste and hidden costs; viewing which activities are most and least expensive; assessing the full efficiency of the organization; identifying places to cut spending; establishing a cost baseline that may be influenced through process or technology changes that reduce effort requirements for the activity;[4] and, perhaps most important, arguing from an informed, objective position in favor of the organization's budget. To illustrate activity based budgeting, the author presents the activities of a hypothetical police department's patrol force to determine the number of officers required to handle the workload; the cost of salaries, materials, and equipment; and the distribution of time across three primary categories of patrol work: calls for service, administrative duties, and proactive functions.

Jon M. Shane, "Activity-Based Budgeting: Creating a Nexus Between Workload and Costs," *FBI Law Enforcement Bulletin*, vol. 74, no. 6, pp. 11–23. Copyright in the Public Domain.

Accountability

Being entrusted with public monies requires the utmost integrity and responsibility. In recent years, efforts have begun to make budgets more readable and understandable. Activity-based budgeting is transparent and eliminates hidden costs. This allows a manager to see at a glance the most expensive activities and where to exercise control.

One of the keys to accountability involves the person assigned to handle the budget having real control over the resources that take the form of decision-making authority, information, and skills. After all, managers "cannot be responsible for a budget in which they have no authority to approve expenditures."[5]

Politics of Budgeting

Appropriations battles are common. In fact, an executive charged with budget implementation and control should expect them from subordinates who look to that person to exercise leadership and to argue on their behalf for what they need to carry out their functions. In preparing for battle, an executive will find it useful to know that "budgets reflect choices about what government will and will not do; budgets reflect priorities—between police and flood control, day care, and road repair; budgets reflect the relative proportion of decisions made for local and constituency purpose and for efficiency and effectiveness and broader public goals. [Most important], public budgets are not merely technical managerial documents; they also are intrinsically and irreducibly political."[6] Because their budgets are politically driven, executives should understand elected leaders' platforms, often mutually beneficial when seeking funds. The police department must compete with the other elements of city government for limited funds, making it of paramount importance for its leader to prepare a sound budget justification.

SUCCESSFUL STRATEGIES AND

Strategies

Strategies differ from justifications. A strategy is an approach, a careful plan or method, or the art of devising or employing plans toward a goal. A justification means to prove or show to be just, right, or reasonable or to show to have had a sufficient legal reason.[7] The chief executive's goal is to retain the agency's base budget and, if possible, to increase it above the current year's appropriations. Developing a logical strategy provides the means to that end.

In November 2002, the Police Executive Research Forum (PERF) posted the final draft of roundtable discussions with several police chiefs from around the country. Among the different budget strategies they considered, using crime and workload data was first on the list.[8] Earlier research revealed that "increased workload was the second greatest factor contributing to an increase in positions."[9] While not infallible, workload data is reasonable and objective. The other strategies discussed by PERF included "capitalize on sensational crime incidents (ideally, not occurring locally), carefully mobilize interest groups, plan strategically, participate fully in the federal grant process, maintain a close working relationship with the local chief executive and governing board members, and involve all levels of the police department."[10] In addition, aggregate population and population density; age, sex, race, and ethnic composition; education levels; and per capita and median household income can support a budget proposal.

Justification

Budget strategies and their attendant analysis are important, but justification remains the primary ingredient to the success of the agency's budget. A solid justification includes all of the relevant information for the legislative body, the budget office, and the city's chief executive. The department should justify the budget in three separate spending categories: mandatory, base, and discretionary.

Figure 1: Principal Modalities (Major Activities)

Service Demands	Acuity				
	Hours Per Unit	Units Per Year	Total Employee Hours Per Modality	Officers Required	Percentage Allocation
Murder	3	41	246	2	0.20%
Robbery	1.5	2,110	6,330	2	5.15%
Burglary	1	1,877	3,754	2	3.05%
Court Appearances	1.5	1,234	9,255	5	7.53%
Theft (shoplifting and all others)	0.58	6,522	7,566	2	6.15%
Arson	1	51	102	2	0.08%
Rape	1.5	88	264	2	0.21%
Fraud	0.75	211	158	1	0.13%
Prostitution	0.33	1,003	662	2	0.54%
Gambling Offense	0.42	468	197	1	0.16%
Vicious Animal	0.33	214	141	2	0.11%
Bomb Threat	1	12	24	2	0.02%
Fire (car, house, building)	1.5	123	369	2	0.30%
DWI	1	44	88	2	0.07%
Emotionally Disturbed Person	1	120	240	2	0.20%
Traffic Control	2	2,190	13,140	3	10.69%
School Crossing	2	1,080	6,480	3	5.27%
MV Pursuit	0.75	81	243	4	0.20%
Arrest (average for all types of arrests)	1.5	15,264	45,792	2	37.25%
Warrant Service	0.75	73	110	2	0.09%
Code Enforcement Violations	0.33	315	104	1	0.08%
Juvenile Condition (curfew, truancy, and all others)	0.75	457	343	1	0.28%
Street Collapse	1	14	28	2	0.02%
Wires Down	1	58	58	1	0.05%
Burglar Alarm (residential, commercial)	0.33	2,555	1,686	2	1.37%
Suicide	1.5	22	66	2	0.05%
Sick/Injured Person	0.75	720	540	1	0.44%
Train Accident	8	1	48	6	0.04%
Kidnapping	3	11	66	2	0.05%
Carjacking	1	77	154	2	0.13%
Drug Sales	0.3	5,041	3,025	2	2.46%
Assault (shooting, stabbing, blunt force)	0.75	1,000	1,500	2	1.22%
Stolen Vehicle Report	0.75	2,645	1,984	1	1.61 %
Assist Officer (back up)	0.25	152	76	2	0.06%
Directed Patrol Activities	0.33	5,475	3,614	2	2.94%
Shots Fired	0.33	730	482	2	0.39%
Domestic Violence	1.25	3,255	8,138	2	6.62%
Motor Vehicle Accident (with or without injuries)	1	1,825	3,650	2	2.97%
Disorderly Conduct (fight, loud music, noisy crowds)	0.3	2,555	1,533	2	1.25%
Man with a Gun	0.42	401	674	4	0.55%
Total		**60,115**	**122,927**		**100.00%**

Mandatory Expenditures

Federal, state, or local laws govern mandatory expenditures, such as social security, pensions, unemployment contributions, and contractually negotiated benefits. Salaries also may fall into this category, except for those considered discretionary. It is best to justify mandatory budget expenditures by citing the applicable federal, state, and local laws.

Base Expenditures

Essential for the agency's continued operation, base expenditures include utilities, equipment, supplies and materials, and other consumables. Justification in this category comes from analyzing previous budgets and projections for service delivery. The executive must be prepared to explain increases in operating expenditures, such as developing a special task force to address a spike in drug crime. Budget review members always welcome workload and performance improvement data.

Discretionary Expenditures

Discretionary expenditures enhance an existing level of service. These costs do not affect the department's operations but contribute to improved service delivery or a particular program's efficiency. A valid example is hiring. By hiring more officers, the agency expects to improve response time and reduce fear of crime, but not having the extra officers does not adversely impact the organization's ability to provide basic service. In defending discretionary spending, the executive must convince the budget review members of the necessity or worthiness of the proposal. Once again, workload and performance data are at the top of the list for developing the rationale.

THE WORKLOAD ANALYSIS

Objectivity denotes a recurring theme in budget development. The department will find an objective budget, based on empirical data, the most reasonable and the easiest to justify. A question often raised in law enforcement circles is, How many officers do we need or should we have? Typical responses cover a range of options, including as many as we can afford, as many as the mayor and council want, or as many as the people of the city will pay for. While these statements have merit, "the only logical and defensible means of determining how many persons should be assigned to patrol duty is through a careful and systematic analysis of the duties performed by patrol officers."[11] This is true of any position within the police department; therefore, the first step toward a logical budget justification starts with a workload analysis.

Data Collection

A workload analysis is "the process of collecting and analyzing data on patrol activities for the purpose of more efficient scheduling and deployment of manpower."[12] In activity-based budgeting, the process begins by collecting data on calls for service, generally captured by a computer aided dispatch system (CAD). If the department does not have a CAD system, it will have to capture the data manually. The agency must have at least 1 complete year of data to account for seasonal fluctuations or other anomalies that might occur. A better data set would encompass 2 years of information to clarify these same variables and also to illuminate personnel trends. For example, gaining or losing officers may adversely impact how the organization handles calls for service, including the amount of time required to do so. The data set must include the—

- type of call;
- average number of hours spent handling the call;[13]
- number of calls of that type for the year (or the period being examined);
- number of officers required to handle the call; and
- total employee hours per modality.[14]

Once the agency has captured the principal modalities, it should format them for a typical computer spreadsheet application. After arranging the columns, the department can easily calculate the total employee hours per modality.[15]

Figure 2:   Distribution of Time

Activity	%	Time	Daily/Minutes	Daily/Hours	Split Force	Force Allocation
Service Demands	60%	122,927	288	4.8	88	66%
Administrative	10%	20,488	48	0.8	0	0%
Proactive	30%	61,463	144	2.4	45	34%
Total	**100%**	**204,878**	**480**	**8**	**134**	**100%**
Availability		2,086	(40 hours per week, 52.14 weeks per year)			
Effective Strength		98.23	FTE Patrol Officers			
Relief Factor		1.360	FTE Patrol Officers			
Actual Strength		134	FTE Patrol Officers			

Figure 1 represent the principal modalities and the acuity.[16] The hours per unit show the average amount of time spent handling a single call for service of that type (e.g., one murder will require 3 hours). The units per year comprise the total number of calls for service for that type (e.g., 41 murders occurred for the year). The department can derive the total employee hours per modality by simply multiplying the hours per unit times the units per year times the number of officers required. For example, a call for a murder takes two officers 3 hours to handle. Over the course of 1 year, officers will handle 41 murders for a total of 246 employee hours. The agency repeats these calculations for each modality and then sums the units per years and the total employee hours per modality. The sums of these two categories provide the foundation for future calculations and for activity-based budgeting develpoment. Units per year equal 60,115 while hours per employee modality total 122,927. The department can add the percentage allocation as a last column. This will provide an excellent visual representation of which activities consume the most, as well as the least, of the budget.

Figure 3: Nonproductive FTE (Relief Factor)

Time Off	Days	Hours
Vacation	28	224
Compensatory	5	40
Sick Leave	15	120
Personal	3	24
Training	8	64
Bereavement	10	80

Total Time Off	69	552
Work Year	260.70	2,086
Personnel Availability	191.70	1,534
Relief Factor	**1.360**	**1.360**

In addition, figure 1 shows that arrests consumed 37.25 percent of the time, followed by traffic control duty with 10.69 percent. The department can order the percentages from highest to lowest, or vice versa, and contrast them against each other for comparison purposes, thereby revealing efficiency. In short, the executive sees where time is spent, thus influencing processes or technology changes that reduce effort requirements for the activity.

Distribution of Time

The next step involves one of the most important in the budget development process because what happens with the distribution of time directly affects the budget. After determining the baseline calculations, it becomes necessary to distribute the time across three primary categories: service demands (i.e., calls for service), administrative duties, and proactive functions.

The first category, service demands, proves critical because the other areas receive their allotted time based on how much time this one consumes. The sum of employee hours per modality (122,927) represents 100 percent of the workload. Obviously, police officers must service. These include administrative duties (e.g., submitting reports and attending meetings) and proactive functions (e.g., community policing and directed or self-initiated tasks). An agency cannot

Figure 4: Supervisory and Investigative Staff

By ratio:	1 Sergeant per 7 Officers	Sergeants	19.08	effective strength
	1 Lieutenant per 5 Sergeants	Lieutenants	3.82	effective strength
	1 Detective per 20 Officers	Detectives	8.82	effective strength
	Sub Total		**31.71**	FTE Support Staff
	Management Staff			
Not by ratio:	1 Captain per command	Captain	1.000	effective strength
	1 Executive Officer	Executive Lieutenant	1.000	effective strength
	Sub Total		**2.000**	FTE Command Staff (managers)
	Support Staff for Management			
By ratio: 4 support staff members per manager		Civilian Aides	8.000	effective strength
	Sub Total		**8.000**	FTE Civilian Aides
		Total	**41.71**	

realistically formulate a budget around 100 percent of the total employee hours per modality without factoring in these other responsibilities. This reveals where prudent management decisions must be made regarding how much of the officers' time the department is willing to distribute across these three categories. In other words, the lower the percentage of time allocated for service demands, the more police officers the organization will need.

After determining the total hours, the agency calculates the effective strength of its patrol force,[17] which differs from the actual strength. Based on a work year of 2,086 hours, the effective strength is 98.23 full-time equivalent (FTEs) patrol officers. Because officers do not actually work 2,086 hours per year, one additional calculation becomes necessary, the relief factor. Figure 2 depicts the distribution of time across the three primary management categories and the effective patrol force strength.

Force Strength and the Relief Factor

Actual patrol force strength is the number of officers required to handle the workload. The relief factor, also known as nonproductive FTE, accounts for officers' time off for various reasons. Hours, the more basic and preferred work unit for these calculations, are more discreet and flexible, rather than days, which the author presents only for illustrative purposes. The relief factor is derived by a two-part subtraction and division equation. For example, figure 3 begins with

a work year of 2,086 hours. By subtracting 552 hours of allotted time off (i.e., nonproductive FTE), the difference of 1,534 denotes personnel availability. Dividing the work year (2,086) by personnel availability (1,534) results in the quotient of 1.36. This means that it takes 1.36 police officers for every position to provide an acceptable level of service 365 days per year, 24 hours per day.

The final step, actual patrol strength, is determined by multiplying the effective strength by the relief factor. The effective strength is 98.23; the actual strength is 134 (134 = depicted in figure 2, 134 officers are required to carry out 204,878 hours of patrol operations over a period of 1 year.)

Management and Support Staff Positions

Because law enforcement agencies operate with command rank personnel, supervisors, and support staff, they must account for these employees to develop an accurate budget. Depending upon contractual stipulations or other managerial prerogatives, a department may or may not justify these positions by ratio. If not by ratio, then the agency only needs a fixed number. Figure 4 outlines the staff necessary to complete a department's workforce, and figure 5 shows the total personnel complement. Now that the agency has projected its workload and staffing needs, it can use the results to develop an activity-based budget.

Figure 5: FTE Subtotal

Position	Complement	Work Hours	Relief?	
Captain	1	9–5 MF	No	Actual Strength
Executive Lieutenant	1	9–5 MF	No	Actual Strength
Lieutenant	5	24/7	Yes	Actual Strength
Sergeant	26	24/7	Yes	Actual Strength
Detective	9	9–5 MF	No	Actual Strength
Patrol Officer	134	24/7	Yes	Actual Strength
Civilian Aides	8	9–5 MF	No	Actual Strength
Total FTEs	**184**			Actual Strength

Figure 6: Salary Calculations (includes relief factor)

FTE	Salary	Benefits at 20%	Salary Cost	Title
134	$71,214	$14,243	$11,451,211	**Patrol Officers**
1	$108,109	$21,622	$129,731	**Captain**
1	$92,016	$18,403	$110,419	**Executive Lieutenant**
26	$84,789	$16,958	$2,645,417	**Lieutenant**
5	$77,215	$15,443	$463,290	**Sergeant**
9	$72,214	$14,443	$779,911	**Detective**
8	$27,125	$5,425	$260,400	**Support staff**
184			**$15,840,379**	**Total Salary Cost**
		divided by	122,927	total employee hours per modality
		Rate per employee hour	**$128.86**	

BUDGET DEVELOPMENT

Salary Calculations

Calculating salaries constitutes the first element of activity-based budgeting. In many instances, personnel account for more than 90 percent of total budget expenses. The goal at this point is to establish the rate per employee hour. Establishing this figure creates a baseline from which to work and also is necessary for monitoring purposes. If the department needs to reduce expenses, it may not be able to do so from salaries because these usually are contractual. Knowing how much it costs to perform the required work can benefit managers and supervisors as they monitor individual and collective performance. The equation of salary times benefits times FTE or total employee hour.

Figure 6 outlines the FTE salary calculations, including the benefits package, and shows the rate per employee hour as $128.86.

Materials and Equipment Costs

In lean fiscal times, agencies generally reduce training and equipment budgets. Figure 7 depicts the total and unit costs for materials and equipment.

Materials usually consist of consumable supplies, such as pens, paper, flares, and crime scene tape. A simple calculation based on a fixed amount per employee can determine the unit cost for materials. In the example, materials are appropriated at $700 per employee or $128,480 total. By dividing the derive the unit cost for materials as $2.14.

Figure 7: Materials and Equipment

Materials		Equipment			
			Quantity	**Unit Cost**	**Useful Life/yrs**	**Cost**
Paper, Pencils, Reports, Forms, Crime Scene Tape, Flares and all other Consumable Supplies (@ $700 per employee) $128,480	Computers	15	$1,700	5	$5,100
Total $128,480	Shotguns	25	$700	15	$1,167
divided by units per year 60,115	Typewriters	15	$300	5	$900
Unit Cost $2.14	Marked Police Cars	36	$35,000	3	$420,000
	Prisoner Van	1	$40,000	6	$6,667
	First Aid Kit and Replacements	80	$140	3	$3,733
	Nontraditional Vehicles	5	$19,000	7	$13,571
	Night Vision Equipment	5	$7,500	7	$5,357
	Walk-through Metal Detector	1	$5,500	10	$550
	Gas Masks	200	$320	7	$9,143
	Mesh Traffic Vests	50	$30	5	$300
	Tripod Scene Lighting	5	$1,000	7	$714
	Megaphones	10	$90	7	$129
	Prisoner Legirons	25	$43	10	$108
	Snow Blower	1	$2,600	5	$520
	Laser Printers	10	$1,400	5	$2,800
	Unmarked Police Cars	6	$28,000	5	$33,600
	Traffic Cones	100	$35	10	$350
	Suites of Furniture	5	$7,500	10	$3,750
	Photocopier	1	$25,000	6	$4,167
	Fax	4	$499	3	$665
	Total $513,290				
	divided by units per year 60,115				
	= equipment per unit **$8.54**				

Figure 8: The Activity-Based Budget: Present Level of Service

	Units Per Year	Hours Per unit	Officers Required	Total Hours	Salary Per hour	Salary Per unit	Material Per unit	Equipment Per unit	Unit Cost	Total Cost	Percentage Allocated
Murder	41	3	2	246.00	$257.72	$773.16	$2.14	$8.54	$783.84	$32,137.31	0.19%
Robbery	2,110	1.5	2	6,330.00	$257.72	$386.58	$2.14	$8.54	$397.26	$838,210.65	5.09%
Burglary	1,877	1	2	3,754.00	$257.72	$257.72	$2.14	$8.54	$268.40	$503,779.40	3.06%
Court Appearances	1,234	1.5	5	9,255.00	$644.30	$966.45	$2.14	$8.54	$977.13	$1,205,774.74	7.32%
Theft (all types)	6,522	0.58	2	7,565.52	$257.72	$149.48	$2.14	$8.54	$160.15	$1,044,521.19	6.34%
Arson	51	1	2	102.00	$257.72	$257.72	$2.14	$8.54	$268.40	$13,688.20	0.08%
Rape	88	1.5	2	264.00	$257.72	$386.58	$2.14	$8.54	$397.26	$34,958.55	0.21%
Fraud	211	0.75	1	158.25	$128.86	$96.65	$2.14	$8.54	$107.32	$22,644.70	0.14%
Prostitution	1,003	0.33	2	661.98	$257.72	$85.05	$2.14	$8.54	$95.72	$96,010.59	0.58%
Gambling Offense	468	0.42	1	196.56	$128.86	$54.12	$2.14	$8.54	$64.80	$30,324.99	0.18%
Vicious Animal	214	0.33	2	141.24	$257.72	$85.05	$2.14	$8.54	$95.72	$20,484.81	0.12%
Bomb Threat	12	1	2	24.00	$257.72	$257.72	$2.14	$8.54	$268.40	$3,220.75	0.02%
Fire (all types)	123	1.5	2	369.00	$257.72	$386.58	$2.14	$8.54	$397.26	$48,862.52	0.30%
DWI	44	1	2	88.00	$257.72	$257.72	$2.14	$8.54	$268.40	$11,809.43	0.07%
Emotionally Disturbed Person	120	1	2	240.00	$257.72	$257.72	$2.14	$8.54	$268.40	$32,207.53	0.20%
Traffic Control	2,190	2	3	13,140.00	$386.58	$773.16	$2.14	$8.54	$783.84	$1,716,602.49	10.41%
School Crossing	1,080	2	3	6,480.00	$386.58	$773.16	$2.14	$8.54	$783.84	$846,543.69	5.14%
MV Pursuit	81	0.75	4	243.00	$515.44	$386.58	$2.14	$8.54	$397.26	$32,177.75	0.20%
Arrest (all types)	15,264	1.5	2	45,792.00	$257.72	$386.58	$2.14	$8.54	$397.26	$6,063,719.11	36.79%
Warrant Service Code	73	0.75	2	109.50	$257.72	$193.29	$2.14	$8.54	$203.97	$14,889.52	0.09%
Enforcement	315	0.33	1	103.95	$128.86	$42.52	$2.14	$8.54	$53.20	$16,757.86	0.10%
Juvenile Condition	457	0.75	1	342.75	$128.86	$96.65	$2.14	$8.54	$107.32	$49,045.62	0.30%
Street Collapse	14	1	2	28.00	$257.72	$257.72	$2.14	$8.54	$268.40	$3,757.54	0.02%
Wires Down	58	1	1	58.00	$128.86	$128.86	$2.14	$8.54	$139.54	$8,093.08	0.05%
Burglar Alarm (all types)	2,555	0.33	2	1,686.30	$257.72	$85.05	$2.14	$8.54	$95.72	$244,573.34	1.48%
Suicide	22	1.5	2	66.00	$257.72	$386.58	$2.14	$8.54	$397.26	$8,739.64	0.05%
Sick/Injured Person	720	0.75	1	540.00	$128.86	$96.65	$2.14	$8.54	$107.32	$77,271.00	0.47%
Train accident	1	8	6	48.00	$773.16	$6,185.29	$2.14	$8.54	$6,195.96	$6,195.96	0.04%
Kidnapping	11	3	2	66.00	$257.72	$773.16	$2.14	$8.54	$783.84	$8,622.20	0.05%
Carjacking	77	1	2	154.00	$257.72	$257.72	$2.14	$8.54	$268.40	$20,666.50	0.13%
Drug Sales	5,041	0.3	2	3,024.60	$257.72	$77.32	$2.14	$8.54	$87.99	$443,566.72	2.69%
Assault (all types)	1,000	0.75	2	1,500.00	$257.72	$193.29	$2.14	$8.54	$203.97	$203,965.97	1.24%
Stolen Vehicle	2,645	0.75	1	1,983.75	$128.86	$96.65	$2.14	$8.54	$107.32	$283,863.62	1.72%
Assist Officer	152	0.25	2	76.00	$257.72	$64.43	$2.14	$8.54	$75.11	$11,416.08	0.07%
Directed Patrol	5,475	0.33	2	3,613.50	$257.72	$85.05	$2.14	$8.54	$95.72	$524,085.74	3.18%
Shots Fired	730	0.33	2	481.80	$257.72	$85.05	$2.14	$8.54	$95.72	$69,878.10	0.42%
Domestic Violence	3,255	1.25	2	8,137.50	$257.72	$322.15	$2.14	$8.54	$332.83	$1,083,349.10	6.57%
Motor Vehicle Accident	1,825	1	2	3,650.00	$257.72	$257.72	$2.14	$8.54	$268.40	$489,822.80	2.97%
Disorderly Conduct	2,555	0.3	2	1,533.00	$257.72	$77.32	$2.14	$8.54	$87.99	$224,819.08	1.36%
Person Armed with a Weapon	401	0.42	4	673.68	$515.44	$216.49	$2.14	$8.54	$227.16	$91,091.48	0.55%
Total	60,115			122,927						$16,482,149	100.00%

The larger category of equipment consists of various items necessary to adequately carry out the functions of the patrol officer. Equipment typically has a useful life of more than 3 years; however, this is not a rule. The agency can calculate equipment expenditures by spreading the cost of individual items across their useful life spans. Incurring the full expense of the equipment will not come until the department must replace the items. Therefore, the agency can predicate the cost upon the equipment's useful life. The total cost for equipment as $513,290. The department can derive the unit cost the same way it did for materials, which reveals a unit cost for equipment of $8.54.

Present Level of Service

The final step, calculating the costs for the present level of service, involves reconciling all of the previous calculations to form the activity-based budget. First, the agency replicates figure 8, which holds the principal modalities. These serve as the foundation upon which the remainder of the budget will rest. The department must conduct a few additional calculations to arrive at the total cost. These include salary per hour and per unit costs of salary, material, and equipment, along with the unit and total costs.

Salary Per Hour

By multiplying the rate per employee ($128.86) by the total number of officers required, the department can calculate the salary per hour cost. For example, the total number of officers required to handle a murder is two; multiplying this by the rate per employee hour results in a salary per hour of $257.72.

Per Unit Costs

"Unit costs compare the volume of work anticipated to the items needed to complete the work and the funds required to purchase the items. This method [is] used to justify the need for personnel or equipment. …"[18] This reveals the most salient feature of activity-based budgeting because identifying the individual costs is what this budget plan seeks to accomplish. To determine the salary per unit cost, the department multiplies the hours per unit (3) by the salary per hour ($527.72), obtaining the salary per unit cost for the modality of murder of $773.16.

Budget Summary			
Total from Figure 6. Salary Calculations	**Salaries** $15,840,379	96.11%	
Total from Figure 7 Materials and Equipment	**Materials** $128,480	0.78%	
	Equipment $513,290	3.11%	
	Total $16,482,149	100.00%	

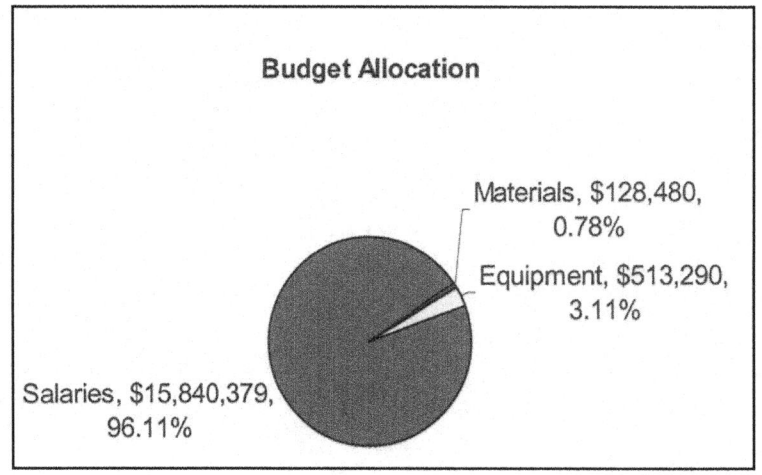

Unit Cost

The unit cost is the sum of salary per unit ($773.16), materials per unit ($2.14), and equipment per unit ($8.54) costs. The department's unit cost for murder totals $783.84.

Total Costs

Total costs, the final calculation in the budget, are derived by multiplying the units per year for each modality (41) by the unit cost ($783.84). The total cost for the murder modality is $32,173.31.

Figure 8 demonstrates the completed activity-based budget plan outlining the entire cost for salaries, materials, and equipment. It becomes readily apparent that the percentage of the budget allocated per modality in figure 8 approximates the percentage of time allocated per modality in figure 1.

Budget Summary

Once the department has prepared the activity-based budget, it will find it useful to create a small budget summary by category, which would include salaries, materials, and equipment. The budget summary will help to reconcile the individual pieces of the budget. The total cost presented in figure 8 is $16,482,149. when summing the categories (salaries, materials, and equipment) in the budget summary, the total must equal the activity-based budget total. A simple pie chart of the finished budget gives a valuable perspective of how the department will distribute its funds.

CONCLUSION

Activity-based budgeting, an objective way to link workload to costs, is easy to design. Each division of the police department can create one to examine its operational efficiency. Connecting all of the individual budgets provides the organization with a comprehensive picture of its operating posture. Supervisors can use it to make adjustments in processes or shift personnel. Administrators can employ it to create partnership programs with the police department.

In this sense, it is useful to see the proportion of the activity-based budget allocated to each partner. The department also can use it to justify hiring and promoting personnel. By using accepted industry standards of span of control, an executive can argue in favor of hiring and promoting based upon the volume of work.

Beyond its internal uses, activity-based budgeting has other merits. Many Grant programs require one so grantors can see where their money is being spent and how efficiently grantees can administer the programs. Activity-based budgeting easily can be turned into a performance-based budget by attaching performance standards. It also can be used together with benchmarking to identify best practices.[19] The basic steps in corporate benchmarking include deciding what process to benchmark, studying the process in their organization, identifying benchmarking partners, analyzing the processes of benchmarking partners to identify differences that account for superior performance, adapting and implementing best practices, and monitoring and revising.[20] In the police department example, effecting arrests consumes nearly 37 percent of the activity. Benchmarking them could determine if a more efficient way exists to process arrests, including new technology that reduces the effort.

"Activity-based budgeting (ABB) holds [some] promise as a … solution to the faults and frustrations of traditional budgeting methods:

1. Traditional budgets don't identify waste. ABB exposes nonvalue costs.
2. Traditional budgets focus on workers. ABB focuses on workload.
3. Traditional budgets focus on division cost. ABB also focuses on process cost.
4. Traditional budgets focus on fixed versus variable costs. ABB also focuses on used versus unused capacity.
5. Traditional budgets measure 'effect.' ABB measures root 'cause.'"[21]

It also provides an alternative to traditional government budgets; the line item may be required by law, but nothing prevents an organization from adopting activity-based budgeting to solve internal problems. After all, "what is the bottom line when there is no 'bottom line'? Performance!"[22]

NOTES

1. S.L. Riley and Peter W. Colby, *Practical Government Budgeting: A Workbook for Public Managers* (Albany, NY: State University of New York Press, 1991).

2. A zero-based budget begins by preparing an operating plan or budget that starts with no authorized funds. For this type of budget, an organization must justify each activity every time it prepares a new budget.

3. D. Maddox, *Budgeting for Not-for-Profit Organizations* (New York, NY: John Wiley and Sons, 1999).

4. Ibid., 228.

5. Ibid., 20.

6. I.S. Rubin, *The Politics of Public Budgeting: Getting and Spending, Borrowing and Balancing,* 4th ed. (New York, NY: Chatham House, 2000).

7. Both definitions retrieved on August 31, 2004, from *http://m-w.com*.

8. Police Executive Research Forum, Police *Department Budgeting: A Guide for Law Enforcement Chief Executives* (Washington, DC, 2002).

9. J.R. Greene, Tim S. Bynum, and Gary W. Cordner, "Planning and the Play of Power: *Resource Acquisition Among Criminal Justice Agencies,*" *Journal of Criminal Justice* 14 (1986): 529–544.

10. Supra note 8, 2; and Aaron Wildavsky, The *Politics of the Budgetary Process*, 3rd ed. (Boston, MA: Little Brown and Company, 1979), 63–126.

11. C.D. Hale, *Police Patrol: Operations and Management* (New York, NY: John Wiley and Sons, 1981).

12. Ibid., 163.

13. Any portion of an hour is calculated as such. For example, 20 minutes is captured as .33 hours and 47 minutes as .783 hours.

14. In budgeting, modalities are the attributes (i.e., major activities) being examined. In this case, they are the types of calls for service.

15. In budgeting, acuity is the distinct detail, the calculations that comprise the budget.

16. Due to rounding, some numbers may not add to totals shown in the figures or referred to in the text of this article.

17. The effective strength of the patrol force is how many officers are on duty at a given time. Supra note 11, 167.

18. Supra note 1, 54.

19. In public sector application, the term benchmarking "features the identification of a point of reference for comparison or measurement purposes. With a benchmark, public officials can measure the performance gap between where they are and where they want to be and can track their progress in closing the gap." D.N. Ammons, "A Proper Mentality for *Benchmarking*" in Gerald J. Miller, W. Bartley Hildreth, and Jack Rabin, *Performance-Based Budgeting* (Boulder, CO: Westview Press, 2001), 419–429.

20. Ibid., 423.

21. T. Pryor, Integrated Cost Management Systems, Inc., *What Happened to ABB?* (2004); retrieved on December 23, 2004, from http://www.icms.net/newsJ8.htm.

22. P.F. Drucker, *Managing the Nonprofit Organization: Principles and Practices* (New York, NY: Harper Perennial, 1990).

Writing a Winning Grant Proposal

By Jon Shane

At a time when many communities, through their elected officials, are asking law enforcement agencies to do more with less, using grant funds to supplement departmental budgets provides a perfect route toward achieving their goals. Policing is an expensive endeavor, sometimes accounting for as much as 20 to 30 percent of a city's entire budget, with the police department often dedicating 90 to 97 percent of its budget to salaries and benefits. That leaves very few dollars for equipment or overtime to embark upon new initiatives. Grant programs, however, can provide a source of relief for fiscally strapped cities and towns. Whether their law enforcement agencies are large or small, all communities can benefit from using grants.[1]

During the 1970s, the Law Enforcement Assistance Administration (LEAA) began establishing grant programs. The LEAA program sought to improve the infrastructure and to bring about change within law enforcement agencies. Purchasing equipment, sharing technology, hiring personnel, and increasing training were the themes. Although much has changed since the 1970s, much has not. These same themes continue to dominate most program strategies.

Improvement and change represent the key considerations of most grants. Whether a department's current methods and operations need improvement or its practices need to change to conform to contemporary standards, grants serve to bridge the gap between imagination and practice.

Receiving grant funds can prove advantageous. A combination of hiring initiatives and equipment purchases will improve service delivery while bolstering a department's image and reputation. Moreover, the public is the indirect recipient of the grant award. A department's grantsmanship can have a profound effect on crime, the fear of crime, correctional measures and alternatives, juvenile delinquency, and the overall quality of life for every citizen the agency serves.

Conversely, disadvantages also can occur when applying for funding. The process can be labor intensive and involve conducting research, designing charts, obtaining letters of support, gathering endorsements, and forming partnerships. Then, should funding be awarded, the department must adhere to special conditions set by the funding source. Finally, the funding source monitors and tracks the grant. Did the department meet its intended goals? Did the department supplant?[2] Is the department at risk for an audit? The funding source also requires a myriad of different forms and reports—usually on a monthly, quarterly, and annual basis—all due amid the department's regular work, of course.

All too frequently, criminal justice agencies find themselves separated from the grant process because of inexperience. Where do we find the funds? How do we apply? What's expected of us? These questions come from *all* agency executives seeking grant funds for the first few times. The assumption is that when the chief says to the deputy chief, "I want you to apply for this grant. Just write it up and get it done," miraculously, the funding source will select *that* proposal over the 2,000 other proposals it receives. Not so, grants are both competitive and often discretionary. To the uninitiated, writing competitive discretionary grants is intimidating. The entire research and writing process often appears to require a creative genius *and* may not result in an award. However, if departments follow some basic principles, they can learn not only *where* to seek funding but *how* to write a winning grant proposal and improve their prospects for obtaining some much-needed funds.

FUNDING SOURCES

Departments can contact a variety of funding sources, from federal and state agencies to private corporations. The most overlooked source is the private sector. Many companies have a philanthropic extension willing to fund projects and programs that represent their company's interests.[3] Another source is the National Criminal Justice Reference Service (NCJRS), a federally sponsored information clearinghouse for people around the country and the world involved with research, policy, and practice related to criminal and juvenile justice and drug control.[4]

When contacting the funding source, the department should ask for an RFP (request for proposal), the official announcement from the source indicating the availability of grant funds. The funding source may have many RFPs available. If so, a department should specify which RFPs it needs, such as ones for hiring personnel, purchasing equipment, or creating a special initiative for a target population. If the funding source states that it does not have an RFP that fits a specific program, then the department should request all available RFPs. Sometimes, the person receiving the call may not have sufficient training to interpret the request, possess a criminal justice background, or fully understand what the caller actually means. Once the department receives the RFPs, it can digest the individual programs and determine whether funding is applicable.

LIFE OF A GRANT

The life of a grant begins with the decision to apply for funding. Usually, a member of the command staff or the chief executive first creates the interest (e.g., the desire to form a new anticrime task force, to enhance services for domestic violence victims, or to implement an overtime program for DWI). Once officials determine that their current operating budget is insufficient to harness the idea, the grant process begins.

Because the funding process can prove labor intensive and intimidating and depending on the jurisdiction's form of government and the level of bureaucracy, the grant development team may face a very cumbersome application process or, instead, one that flows rather easily. The typical grant application process involves about 15 steps that represent approximately 4 to 6 months of effort. In most situations, a department spends approximately 30 to 50 percent of the time waiting for the funding source to review the proposal. Departments must remember that if the funding source is a government entity, it receives hundreds, possibly thousands, of applications from agencies around the country. The source must account for each proposal, assign each one to a reviewer, and ensure that each proposal completes the review process (i.e., gets accepted or rejected for funding) before, finally, making the award announcement.

Whatever the process, the grant development team should not become discouraged. The rewards, both personal and organizational, are tremendous. A great sense of accomplishment occurs when the team submits the final draft request and receives the award letter congratulating the department.

INFORMATION COLLECTION

Before beginning the writing process, the department should gather sources of information and conduct a literature review on the topic. An excellent starting place is the grant writer's own knowledge and experience. Life experience (particularly within a person's profession) provides riches from which to draw information. The various assignments grant writers may

Sample Goals and Objectives

Goals

- To reduce narcotics complaints by 25 percent within the first 6 months
- To secure guilty pleas or convictions in 80 percent of all cases

Objectives

- To deploy the Tactical Narcotics Team, which will use covert surveillance techniques within the target area, for the first 8 weeks
- To deploy the Special Investigation Unit, which will conduct undercover (UC) and confidential informant (CI) narcotics "buy" operations within the target area, for the first 12 weeks
- To deploy the Special Investigation Unit, which will apply for search warrants at locations within the target area in response to the UC and CI intelligence, throughout the duration of the program
- To employ the Emergency Response Team, which will execute all search and arrest warrants within the target area, throughout the duration of the program
- To assign a special narcotics prosecutor, who will investigate and prosecute all individual cases as part of a RICO scheme when the case involves a firearm or the weight of the contraband seized equals or exceeds 1 U.S. pound, throughout the duration of the program
- To assign uniformed patrol officers, who will conduct situational crime prevention operations for those locations within the target area that are responsible for 10 or more calls for service, during the last 15 weeks of the program

have held throughout their careers, along with their educational pursuits or other jobs, all contribute to their personal libraries of information.

In addition, a natural corollary flows from using personal experiences to using the knowledge of others. Therefore, grant writers should consider conducting interviews. First, they should define the purpose of the interview. After preliminarily researching the topic, they should select potential interviewees, targeting those at the top (e.g., executives, administrators, division heads, section chiefs, and directors). Such individuals likely will have a broad understanding of the policies, issues, and procedures on the topic in question. Often, they can provide grant writers with specific information necessary to the proposal, and, if not, they at least can identify the correct person to contact.

Probably, the most convenient and extensive way to gather materials is via the Internet, using meta search engines[5] to reduce the amount of time spent

researching the topic. Moreover, every accredited college or university has a Web site. Also, NCJRS and the National Council on Crime and Delinquency (NCCD) collection, along with local libraries' reference sections, provide other places to assemble materials. Finally, research groups dedicated to improving policing can offer indispensable information to grant writers.[6]

SUPPORTING DATA

After gathering resource materials and beginning the writing process, it then becomes necessary to garner support for the idea. Support for the program can come from a variety of origins, such as authorities (subject-matter experts), concrete examples, or statistical illustrations.

Authoritative Support

For nearly every program that a department can conceive, an authoritative documented source exists that will support the concept.[7] Grant writers use authoritative support when they cite respected authors or publications on the topic under consideration. This demonstrates that the department is not just espousing a theory or advancing a supposition but showing that recognized authorities have studied the topic scientifically or proven the theory. Most people are influenced by the testimony of others when dealing with unfamiliar topics. The reader (in this case, the review team) will tend to respect the direct quotations or paraphrased statements of authorities because of the special knowledge or experience that these individuals possess about the topic in question.

Concrete Examples

"Research has shown that vivid, concrete examples have more impact on [readers'] beliefs and actions than any other kind of supporting material."[8] With examples, ideas become specific, personal, and lively.[9] Grant writers can use two types of examples, factual and hypothetical. A factual example describes a true incident as it relates to the proposal. A hypothetical example, on the other hand, depicts an imaginary situation (often, fiction based on fact) that relates to the general principle of the proposal. By using a hypothetical example, the grant writer creates a realistic scenario related directly to the proposal and captivates the reader (again, the review team). Then, by incorporating real statistics into the example, the writer gives the perception that this undoubtedly could happen in real life. Indeed, the grant writer *should* use statistics to support a hypothetical example so that it does not seem too far-fetched.

Statistical Illustrations

Because this is an age of statistics, expressing what actually is meant numerically often gives others a sense of security in their own knowledge. It also affords the reader the opportunity to visualize the intensity of what is being said or to feel the impact of a particular problem. A widely shared belief infers that when used properly, statistics offer an effective way to clarify and support ideas. To avoid falling victim to unreliable statistics, grant writers should ask two questions: 1) Are the statistics from a reliable source? and 2) Are the statistics representative? If the answer to either of these questions is no, then the writers risk misrepresenting what they wish to portray.

Primarily, grant writers should use statistics to quantify ideas and give them numerical precision. Whenever possible, the writers should include visual aids to clarify statistical trends. A simple pie chart, time line, or bar graph will show the relationship between a time period and the particular social condition.

ETHICAL CONSIDERATIONS

The goal of grant writing is to receive funding—but not at any cost. Writing, a form of power, carries a heavy ethical burden. People will be influenced and persuaded by presentation. This is how one department's proposal receives funding over the others. The question of ethics in grant writing usually centers around the writer's goals and methods.

Grant writers must make sure that their goals are ethically correct. As criminal justice professionals and (probably) government representatives, grant writers who laud worthless or wasteful programs place their departments on shaky ethical ground. Similar caution extends to the writer's methods as well. Even if the goals are ethically correct, grant writers are not being ethical if they employ cheap and careless methods. Basically, this signifies that the "ends do not justify the means." Writers should review five recognized considerations for ethical grant writing.

1. Subject awareness: Grant writers have an obligation to themselves, the granting agency, and the public they serve. They must understand the program for which the department is applying and how it relates to the city, the department, and its mission or vision statement. *Service* is the credo, not self-service.

2. Honesty: Writers must remain cognizant of the temptation to distort facts and figures for their own purposes. Responsible writers do not falsify facts, present few facts as representative of the whole picture, or use tentative findings as conclusive evidence.

3. Valid reasoning: Responsible grant writers take affirmative steps to avoid making hasty generalizations, asserting casual connections where none really exist, using invalid or absurd analogies/examples, and yielding to prejudices.

4. Sound evidence: A grant that is awarded is not full of "fluff." It contains real circumstances supported by qualified, objective sources and avoids plagiarizing.

5. Plagiarizing: Generally, grant proposals are a collaboration between the writers and their sources. To be fair and ethical, the writer must acknowledge borrowing another person's ideas and words by documenting the source. To borrow without proper documentation constitutes a form of dishonesty known as plagiarism. Plagiarism occurs in two forms: 1) borrowing someone else's ideas, information, or language without documenting the source and 2) documenting the source but paraphrasing the source's language too closely, without using quotation marks to indicate that the writer borrowed the words and phrases.[10] Writers should consult a reputable writing handbook and give credit where credit is due. In short, if they use another person's material, they must cite it.

WRITING PROCESS

Needless to say, the process of actually writing the grant will test the writer's determination and creativity, but can coalesce into a comprehensible, meaningful, and persuasive document that brings money into the department. Grant writers are selling something—a concept, a belief in their cities and departments. They must convince people to invest in them because they have a worthwhile service to offer. Therefore, grant writers should draft their proposals with the two basic principles of presentation and content at the forefront.

Presentation

Presentation probably represents the single most salient feature of grant packages because no second chances exist in first impressions. Therefore, the grant writer should—

- create the document on a quality word processing program, *never* handwrite the proposal;
- put headers and footers in the document and number each page;
- use letterhead with original signatures and never fold or crease the paper;
- print in color, but do not make the document gaudy with too many different colors;
- include charts and graphs to depict data;
- organize the document logically and according to RFP requirements;
- grammar check and spell check the document and have it proofread by another person;
- bind the document in quality material; and, most of all,
- follow the instructions offered by the funding source.

Content

Content includes the language, grammar, and punctuation that the writer employs. Words are the tools of the writing craft. Writers must choose the right words for the task they want to accomplish. They should not use words unless they know their meanings. If uncertain, writers should check the dictionary. They also should vary their words, but not use complicated ones, except when explaining or clarifying difficult subjects (e.g., DNA testing procedures, forensic science materials, or computer equipment). Writers always should use bias-free language. They should not refer to all members of an occupational group with a masculine pronoun. Instead, they should say *he* or *she* or change the noun to plural and use the pronoun *they*. Writers should work with the eight parts of speech—nouns, pronouns, verbs, adjectives, adverbs, prepositions, conjunctions, and interjections— recognized as the traditional parts of English grammar. Finally, writers should ensure that they correctly employ all of the common punctuation marks, including the period, comma, exclamation point, question mark, semicolon, and colon.

PROPER ORGANIZATION

The funding source sets the substantive provisions of the grant. These will vary among sources, but all have the basic requirements of the problem statement, goals and objectives, program strategy, and budget narrative. Other substantive requirements that funding sources may desire include management structure, organizational capability, an abstract, a curriculum vitae of each participant, matching funds requirement (local match sources), projected milestones or accomplishments, geographic location, a statement of the program's anticipated contribution to criminal justice policy and practice, the program's continuation and retention, additional resource commitments, and a statement of the program's contribution to the state's strategy (Byrne formula).[11]

Because many departments seeking grant funds do not follow a predefined format, their applications may not flow logically. By following some simple steps, however, grant writers can ensure that their proposals have a smooth continuity, thereby increasing their chances of obtaining an award.

Cover

Grant writers should design a bold and attractive cover that includes the name of the grant, a subtitle if necessary, the names of both the grant program and the funding source, the date of submission, the city and state, and the department's name. They should use graphics and color to heighten the appearance of the cover.

Table of Contents

Grant writers always should include a table of contents so reviewers can refer easily to a specific provision without fumbling through each page. They should use an outline format and indent the subsections for clarity.

Abstract

Some funding sources require an abstract, a one-page description of what the program proposes to do and the expected results. It summarizes the important points of the program and highlights the key aspects of the problem statement, the program description, and the goals and objectives.

Problem Statement

The problem statement is the bedrock upon which all else rests. If no problem exists, the department needs no funding. Grant writers should set a historical perspective that leads from the beginning of the problem, through different time periods, and up to the current condition. If it is a crime problem, insofar as possible, they should make a correlation between the crime problem and an underlying criminological theory (e.g., rational choice, routine activities, social disorganization, or conflict). Also, writers should identify the antecedents that preexisted or currently coexist with the crime problem. They should use statistics and a variety of charts to bolster their claims and extract percentages, show rates, and add trend lines.

Goals and Objectives

Often used interchangeably, goals and objectives, in fact, are two distinct criteria that must be met. A goal is a broad general statement explaining what the grant program is expected to accomplish. Goal statements often start with an action indicator, such as *to* or *will* (e.g., to reduce inmate population, to decrease fear of crime, will strengthen community partnerships, will minimize the temptation to join a gang). By contrast, objectives are specific, precise, and exact statements that lead step by step to the achievement of the goals.

Four elements of an objective— subject, assignment, condition, and standard—must be met for it to be measurable.

1. The subject represents *who* is tasked with doing something (e.g., the tactical narcotics team, the patrol division, the municipal court system). The subject is the element or person that will be responsible for accomplishing what the program is designed to do.

2. The assignment depicts *what* the subject is to do (e.g., to effect arrests for curfew violations, to expedite incoming prisoners, to conduct a workload analysis). The assignment, an action, explains the specific task (or responsibility) required of the subject in question.

3. The condition denotes the given *circumstances* under which the task must be performed. Conditions, either environmental or situational (e.g., in the field, at the domestic violence advocacy center, in the county jail), explain

Funding Sources

Federal

Bureau of Justice Assistance (BJA)
1-800-421-6770
http://www.ojp.usdoj.gov/BJA/

Office of Juvenile Justice and Delinquency Prevention (OJJDP)
202-307-5911
http://ojjdp.ncjrs.org/

National Institute of Corrections (NIC)
1-800 995-6423
http://www.nicic.org/

The Office of Community Oriented Policing Services (COPS Office)
1-800-421-6770 or 202-616-3031
http://www.usdoj.gov/

Office for Victims of Crime (OVC)
1-800-627-6872
http://www.ojp.usdoj.gov/ovc/

National Institute of Justice (NIJ)
1-800-851-3420
http://www.ojp.usdoj.gov/nij/

State

Contact the state's "administrative agency for assistance." For example, in New Jersey, it is the State Division of Criminal Justice, and, in California, it is the Office of Criminal Justice Planning.

The state's administrative agency is responsible for passing through federal funds to local jurisdictions.Often, the federal government does not make funds directly available to the local jurisdiction. Instead, the federal government passes the money to the administrative agency, which then disseminates it to the local jurisdictions.

A significant source of funding for programs on a state level is the Edward Byrne Memorial State and Local Law Enforcement Assistance Formula Grant Program (Byrne Formula Grant). Contact the state's administrative agency to obtain a copy of this program.

Private

There are thousands of private foundations that fund hundreds of program areas each year. Besides the Internet or the library as a research mechanism, companies, such as Research Grant Guides (P.O. Box 1214, Loxahatchee, FL 33470, 561-795-6129), publish resource guides to assist agencies in targeting only those foundations awarding programs in a particular geographical area.

Such guides are extremely useful. First, they are categorized so agencies only need to review the guide for the category for which they are interested (e.g., equipment grants, building grants, social service grants). Then, they are arranged by state, further organizing each guide into a comprehensible format.

how, where, and with what the assignment is to be done. Because the condition represents the "given" circumstances under which the assignment will be performed, the objective often contains that word (e.g., Given a cellular telephone, the neighborhood patrol officer will. ...).

4. The standard specifies *how well* the task must be accomplished. The standard defines what the expected or anticipated results will be (e.g., without error, with 90 percent accuracy, according to approved agency policy and procedure, within the first month).

Program Strategy

The program strategy is the specific method or activities that the department will employ for the duration of the grant program. In this section, the grant writer must provide a clear statement of how the department is going to organize and administer the project to meet the intended goals and objectives. The writers should confer with the various departmental elements involved in carrying out the plan and identify what each is prepared to commit (e.g., 15 police officers from the drug squad, 1 municipal prosecutor dedicated to the program, 5 street sweepers from the sanitation department for neighborhood clean up, and 3 drug and alcohol counselors from social services). If required by the RFP, the grant writer must identify specific individuals who, by virtue of training and experience, will carry out portions of the program and attach their resumes. In short, this section requires that the writer states the means that the department will use to achieve the ends.

Budget Narrative

The budget narrative details a comprehensive itemization and explanation of the costs incurred from the administration and implementation of the program. Budgeted expenses must be reasonable, allowable, and cost-effective for the activities proposed in the program strategy. The budget narrative also must describe and explain how each particular item was calculated. Typical budget categories include personnel, fringe benefits, travel, equipment, supplies, contracts, utilities, construction, indirect costs, and consultants. When creating the budget, the department must not overlook one important issue— the budget must be in proportion to the goals and objectives. Often, the goals of the project far exceed the funds being requested, thus making the goals unattainable. This is known as the *reasonableness* requirement of the budget.

Appendix

Often, a grant application has a page restriction limiting the narrative portion. If this is the case, writers should include an appendix that contains all of the charts, tables, and supporting documents. They should not waste valuable space in the actual narrative section, but append all supporting materials and use an in-text citation (e.g., see chart 1 in appendix). In this way, writers can include organizational charts setting forth specific elements, flowcharts depicting a particular process, Gantt charts[12] denoting a sequence of events and milestones, and additional statistical data. A variety of off-the-shelf, user-friendly software applications exist for creating charts and diagrams. These programs can illustrate complex processes and strategies and can present ideas and information with greater impact through the power of clear visual communication.

CONCLUSION

Whenever criminal justice agencies are tasked with addressing a problem, they should consider the grant process as a viable solution. They can use grants to start new initiatives or supplement existing ones. Funding sources disperse millions of federal, state, and private funds every year, but agencies have to enter the process to win the award.

If grant writers apply the basic principles of researching, writing, and organizing to the process, they will add strength and credibility to their applications. And, once the award letter comes congratulating the agency on winning the grant, they can proclaim proudly that their efforts directly contributed to successfully gaining some much-needed funds for their agency to create or maintain quality programs to safeguard their community.

NOTES

1. Since 1993, the author has sought and received nearly $40 million in federal and state funding for his agency and community.

2. Grant funds always must supplement the city's budget, not supplant the previously authorized budget. Supplanting can occur in several ways, most commonly when the agency uses grant funds *in place of* previously appropriated funds. For example, a city has appropriated $3 million for vehicles. Its police department then receives a grant for $3 million and purchases vehicles from grant funds and does not buy any vehicles from the previously budgeted funds. The department just *supplanted* the original funds with the grant funds. This always is impermissible and may result in the city having to return that portion of the funds that was supplanted. Other more subtle ways of supplanting also can occur. If cities are not certain about whether they are supplanting, they should contact the funding sources and pose their scenarios to them.

3. A project, usually short in duration, has a narrow purpose (e.g., to computerize the department or to replace the department's fleet). Normally long in duration, a program is a system of opportunities designed to meet a social need (e.g., a quality-of-life issue or an auto-theft-suppression effort). Private companies enjoy associating their names with projects and programs that reflect their business (e.g., insurance companies often donate vehicles, while computer firms provide hardware and software).

4. For more information, contact NCJRS at *http:// www.ncjrs.org* or at 800-851-3420.

5. A meta search engine, an Internet "search engine of search engines," accesses several other Internet search engines at the same time for the information requested. This covers more territory with one request as opposed to having to go through each individual search engine.

6. For example, the Police Foundation, an independent and unique resource for policing, acts as a catalyst for change and advocate for new ideas and has a Web site at *http:// www.policefoundation.org*. Also, the Police Executive Research Forum (PERF), a national membership organization of progressive police executives from the largest city, county, and state law enforcement agencies, is dedicated to improving policing and advancing professionalism through research and involvement in public policy debate. Its Web site is *http:// www.policeforum.org*. Both organizations have conducted studies, such as *The Newark Foot Patrol Experiment*, *The Kansas City Preventive Patrol Experiment*, *Racially Biased Policing: A Principled Response*, and *The Police Response to Gangs: Case Studies of Five Cities*, and have compiled publications on preparing grant proposals.

7. For example, if the program is a patrol augmentation program, grant writers could consider authors, such as Charles D. Hale or Tony Pate; for a community policing program, they might try authors Robert Trojanowicz, James Q. Wilson, and George L. Kelling; for a problem-solving or situational crime prevention program, they could review works by Ronald V. Clarke, Marcus Felson, or Herman Goldstein; for a juvenile justice program, they might consider authors John T. Whitehead and Steven P. Lab; and for a supervision program, they could look at works by Nathan F. Iannone. These individuals represent some of the most influential academics and practitioners who have used scientific methods to lend credibility to the social sciences, particularly policing.

8. Thomas R. Kobella, Jr., "Persuading Teachers to Reexamine the Innovative Elementary Science Programs of Yesterday: The Effect of Anecdotal Versus Data Summary," *Journal of Research in Science Teaching* 23 (1986): 437–449.

9. For example, the Bible is an extraordinary source of examples where stories, parables, and anecdotes make abstract principles clear and compelling.

10. Diana Hacker, *The Bedford Handbook for Writers* (New York, NY: St. Martin's Press, 1991).

11. Edward Byrne Memorial State and Local Law Enforcement Assistance Formula Grants, Office of Justice Programs, Bureau of Justice Assistance, U.S. Department of Justice, Washington, DC 20531; contact the State and Local Assistance Division at 202-305-2088 or access *http://www.usdoj.gov*.

12. In 1917, Henry L. Gantt, an American engineer and social scientist, developed a horizontal bar chart as a production control tool to provide a graphical illustration of a schedule that helps to plan, coordinate, and track specific tasks in a project.

Fleet Management

Vehicle Rotation Criteria

By Curtis W. Exley

If one common denominator exists that links law enforcement agencies across America, it is the ever-present patrol vehicle. From small-town police departments to large state agencies, the need for economical, high-performance, and comfortable patrol vehicles remains absolute.

While the demand for police vehicles is universal, each agency has its own specific needs. Those needs should focus on agency objectives, financial and operating capabilities, replacement specification, and overall efficiency. With each specific category in mind, the requirement for improved fleet management should become clear.

Transportation equipment costs rank second as the greatest expenditure that a law enforcement agency faces, just below personnel salaries and benefits. Considering cost and frequency of fleet vehicle replacement, law enforcement agencies must consider improved strategies for developing budget estimates and priorities. These estimates should include the bidding process, life-cycle estimates (i.e., vehicle operation and maintenance), purchase and lease options, vehicle rotation or replacement, and fleet liability.[1]

PROCUREMENT OF LAW ENFORCEMENT VEHICLES

Throughout the United States, law enforcement agencies of all sizes annually purchase a varied number of vehicles to replace outdated or worn-out equipment and, when possible, to increase the size of existing fleets. Procurement is a small word given to a large and extremely detailed process. Once an agency begins the procurement process, it must examine a wide range of considerations, then prioritize and evaluate them. Agencies should weigh specifics on equipment, such as size, dynamics, acceleration, top speed, braking, ergonomics, communications, and fuel economy, according to their relative importance.[2]

However, one of the major areas of concern over procurement speaks directly to budget constraints and the number of vehicles necessarily targeted for replacement. "The posture of the company operationally and financially needs to be explored and the fleet's strategies should compliment the company's strategies short and long term."[3]

A law enforcement agency continually evaluates its budget according to specific needs and potential for growth, coupled with its ability to match increasing costs of equipment and calls for service. External factors, such as politics, hiring standards, and downsizing, ultimately take precedent over equipment prior to the bidding process. Once an agency has established the budget and given a dollar amount to the area of equipment, the bid process can begin.

Curtis W. Exley, "Fleet Management: Vehicle Rotation Criteria," *FBI Law Enforcement Bulletin*, vol. 71, no. 8, pp. 1–10.

Bid Process

All agencies, large or small, have mandatory guidelines that they follow. However, new data and specified requirements on vehicle equipment pose additional responsibilities on the individuals or groups responsible for outlining criteria involved with the bidding process. Typically, agencies base selection of option packages on input from other departments and line personnel, word-of-mouth, or what they learn at law enforcement conferences.

After this, agencies review performance tests. Two agencies, the Michigan State Police and the California Highway Patrol, represent trend setters in performance testing.[4] Each year, the two agencies perform a series of predetermined tests that rate police vehicles on their capabilities and performance qualities. These tests ultimately give light to a specific vehicle that has placed highest in all categories and will predominantly depict what most agencies will strive to attain with their bidding process. "Every year since 1978, the Michigan State Police has conducted performance tests on a wide variety of police and special service vehicles. The results of these tests are plugged into a unique competitive bidding formula. One percent of the lowest bid is used as a bid adjustment figure. Better vehicle performance, in six weighted categories from top speed to fuel economy, is rewarded with a dollar and cents advantage."[5]

Once the agency has reviewed all of the data provided by budget analysts and performance standard testing, it can begin the bidding process. "The purchasing process of police cars typically begins with a law enforcement agency drawing up a wish list for what it wants in a vehicle. This list, called a specification, is then submitted to area auto dealers (in some cases, corporate representatives) for bids. The dealers calculate how much the vehicle will cost them, equipped as requested, from the manufacturer and then tack on their overhead costs along with a profit."[6]

For years, the perception has existed that most agencies opted for the lowest bid on their fleet vehicles. Often, the manufacturer or dealer with the sharpest pencil merits the award of the bid. This, in itself, can translate into the ideology of the lowest bid.

In actuality, however, it usually is the auto dealer's sales team that steps outside the traditional paradigms of pricing. When that occurs, agencies can get the vehicles they want.

In line with the bid process, a procedure called "piggybacking" gives smaller agencies the ability to acquire vehicles under the umbrella of a larger agency's bid. In this approach, smaller agencies will attach themselves and their number of required fleet vehicles to a larger agency's bid. This proves advantageous to all who participate as each entity can profit from the cost reduction acquired by ordering a larger number of vehicles. However, the one drawback is that smaller agencies have to accept the standards that the larger agency has endorsed.

As the bidding process nears completion, including requests for specialty, high-performance vehicles, each agency waits its turn for the manufacturers to work through the hundreds of orders. This way, each agency can project a target date as it waits for the acquisition of next year's fleet. The fleet manager must project target dates with acute accuracy so that appropriate priorities can materialize and aging equipment still will fall within the serviceable requirements of the agency. Failure to accurately project equipment life-cycle estimates can have a tremendous effect on maintenance budgets, causing major complications for any agency, large or small.

Life-Cycle Estimates

Considering the cost and frequency of vehicle rotation or replacement, law enforcement agencies must find better strategies for developing life-cycle estimates, including vehicle replacement, operation, and maintenance. The development of strategies can improve vehicle operating efficiency, reduce unnecessary equipment costs, and improve overall agency efficiency.

Because the needs, objectives, and financial and operating capabilities of agencies differ, each agency must analyze the advantages and disadvantages of its methods of maintaining equipment to determine which method will best contribute to the overall objectives of the agency in a cost-effective manner.[7]

"Most of all, economic life is of critical importance to equipment managers. It relates to the total stream of costs associated with the specific unit over a period of time. Therefore, it has impact upon both capital and operating budgets. The economic life of a unit refers to the length of time the average total vehicle cost is at a minimum. Total unit expense encompass all costs associated with the ownership of the vehicle."[8]

The initial purchase price of a vehicle does not always accurately or completely indicate the cost of the vehicle. While the price of a new vehicle represents the expenditure to acquire the automobile, several component factors determine the cost. The identification and analysis of these components of cost form the basis of life-cycle costing.

Agencies should apply life-cycle costing (a method for projecting and evaluating the costs of one particular vehicle with another similar, yet alternative, vehicle) to determine when they should rotate or replace a vehicle. The optimum time to replace a vehicle is when its total costs, averaged over the vehicle's lifetime, are at a minimum. This concept, referred to as the economic life expectancy of the vehicle,[9] includes such costs as depreciation, operating expenses, maintenance, and downtime. Agencies can reasonably expect that some cost components will rise during the economic life of a vehicle, whereas others can decline.[10]

While optimum replacement of a vehicle represents an annual economic dilemma, the key factors in evaluating an efficient replacement program have specific data collection requirements that constitute major concerns in any life-cycle costing. These include initial acquisition costs, purchase price of the vehicle, cost of specifications preparation, preparation for use, operating expenses, insurance, preventive maintenance and repair costs, downtime, and costs related to the disposal of the vehicle.

With this data, a trade-off in costs occurs between young and old fleets. However, the younger the fleet, the lower the fuel, maintenance, and repair costs, but the higher the capital outlay. Because a younger fleet is less prone to breakdowns, these increased capital costs are reduced somewhat by a decreased need for backup or spare vehicles.[11]

An agency must set priorities to determine which vehicles it needs to replace with its available funding. If an automobile is due to be replaced, an agency should project the total costs of that unit for the following year and compare that cost to the proposed replacement price. An agency should use the price difference, in itself, as the basis for not holding the current vehicle beyond its economic point of replacement. "In order to maintain the lowest cost and maximum vehicle availability for top utilization, replace older vehicles when the cost to operate and maintain them is higher than a new vehicle or when technical obsolescence occurs. This is the basic concept of life-cycle costing and good business common sense."[12]

Once an agency has determined its basis for life-cycle costing, it has the responsibility to place its funding within the most appropriate areas when replacing its fleet. This has brought to light the consideration of a new and recently developed option. Dollar for dollar, which is best—leasing or buying?[13]

Purchase and Lease Options

When should an agency purchase a vehicle? When it has money. Should an agency lease or own? That depends on the amount of money available and the number of vehicles needed. If agencies have cash, they own. If a poor cash flow exists, they have the option to choose the action of using someone else's money by leasing.

Leasing, a recent development, allows agencies to acquire new, updated vehicles with the latest engineering changes. It also allows them to take advantage of increased efficiencies and productivity demands on operations. Agencies also can lower annual operating and maintenance costs due to the new technology. Vehicle maintenance costs of older vehicles change, based on use, proper or improper application, fleet mix, density, and operational or ergonomic modifications.[14]

Over the past few years, many organizations and fleet managers have pondered the issue of fleet leasing. In today's market, leasing represents a viable option that has sustained merit and is increasing in popularity, especially for smaller agencies. With leasing, agencies look to step outside the traditional paradigms of buying vehicles. All agencies need to focus on what makes the most common business sense when they tie the bidding process, life-cycle costing, and specific-use requirements of patrol vehicles together.

In private industry today, fleet-vehicle leasing is a common practice, with cost as the reason most often cited. As always, a multitude of financial options exists when considering cost and programs available, money management, and budget constraints.[15] "A national account agreement offers fleet managers a variety of branded products and services from multiple vendors nationwide at uniform, predetermined, and usually discounted prices."[16]

Many lease options or packages exist and vary from company to company. However, a consensus of fleet managers nationwide revealed four basic sources for national lease programs.

1. Direct from the manufacturer/vender: The end-user (fleet) can negotiate a national account agreement directly with the manufacturer or service provider. However, agencies must obtain individual agreements for each category of service or product, as well as for each brand name. This method results in multiple billings and is subject to fleet-size requirements. This would constitute a viable option through specific vendors for smaller fleets operated locally.

2. Through an independent service company: These companies negotiate agreements with multiple vendors for a variety of services, products, and brand names of vehicles within each category. They often will perform as a vendor by generating their own programs, including statistical reporting. Some positive features include the agency obtaining complete coverage, benefitting from single-source central billing, and maximizing all available discounts in light of the service company's huge volume.

3. Through a leasing company: Working with a leasing company proves essentially the same as dealing with an independent service company. However, the use of only national account program coverage, if and when it is available, may be subject to maximum fleet-size requirements. For those fleet managers that use a purchase/disposal program, this method carries the added advantage of combining both programs together for a total package.

4. In-house programs: Larger fleets, operating thousands of vehicles, can develop their own national account program. They can negotiate agreements with manufacturers/vendors for desired services and brand name vehicles when desired. With this approach, multiple billings still would occur, but would enable a company-owned fleet to maximize its available discounts. The advantages in taking this approach would depend on the anticipated lower cost of services and products as opposed to the cost of setting up and maintaining the program.[17]

Regardless of the type of lease program, agencies need to pay particular attention to the detailed requirements listed within any lease agreement. Law enforcement is noted for its 24-hour service and the maximized operations of fleets during strenuous use periods and in all variables pertaining to weather conditions. They also commonly alter the vehicles to accommodate the installation of radios, light bars, video cameras, screens, shotgun racks, and other necessary equipment. When looking at lease options, open-ended leases stand as the most practical for law enforcement. "Fleet administrators should be looking at open-ended leases where it doesn't matter whether holes are drilled into the vehicles or how many miles they've been driven or how old the cars are."[18]

An open-ended lease gives equity participation, the same as owning the vehicle. At the end of the use cycle, the vehicle will sell for whatever the sale value is at that time. Then, the lessee and the lessor mutually agree on the differential between the sale price and the remaining book balance. If the sale price is higher than the book balance, the agency obtains credit. If the sale of the vehicle is less than the book balance, the agency owes the lessor additional depreciation money. "The state of Michigan put financial models through several different versions and scenarios and each time the models showed that leasing saved the state money.

One reason was that the state deferred capital cash expenditures, paying instead only the lease costs incurred in each individual year. We flattened the state's budget in that lease payments are consistent year after year and there are no varying years where we need to go ask for increased appropriations. We are constantly replacing vehicles based on replacement criteria."[19]

For some smaller agencies or municipalities, another option— tax-exempt, lease-purchase financing—exists. This type of lease provides the best of both ownership and leasing: no major capital outlay for acquisition of vehicles and payment spread out over 2 to 5 years. With this option, the agency acquires ownership at the conclusion of the lease term. In that regard, it resembles a conditional sale or an installment purchase transaction. "… Municipal leases are specially designed contracts that do not create general obligation debt. The lease payment is generally an operating expense in the municipality budget even though the agreement may cover many years."[20]

The tax-exempt, lease-purchase agreement allows a governmental entity to acquire essential vehicles immediately. An agency finances the costs at tax-exempt rates and pays no federal income tax on the interest. This type of program is very advantageous if coupled with the open-ended lease.

It affords the agency the ability to acquire the vehicles it needs without major cash outlays, long-term debt obligations, or, in most cases, voter approval.[21]

However, when a lot of fleet managers take their own fleet and compare it against a lease, they typically leave out money costs because these do not appear on their budget line. Most fleet managers factor in depreciation, but they fail to consider other costs.[22]

Replacement Criteria Polling

The author polled several law enforcement agencies to obtain the established guidelines that they follow regarding mileage restrictions and vehicle rotation. The figures received gave merit to the informal survey conducted by the Michigan State Police as the numbers prescribed with rotation fell well within the survey's established parameters. The mean average for fleet vehicle rotation of these 15 agencies was 70,800 miles.

Agency Polled	Mileage Restriction
Ada County, Idaho, Sheriff's Office	80,000 miles
Boise, Idaho, Police Department	80,000 miles
California Highway Patrol	75,000 miles
Idaho State Police	85,000 miles
Kansas Highway Patrol	45,000–50,000 miles
Kent, Washington, Police Department	45,000 miles
Las Vegas, Nevada, Metro Police Department	45,000 miles
Michigan State Police	60,000–70,000 miles
Missouri Highway Patrol	45,000–50,000 miles
Montana Highway Patrol	87,000 miles
Nevada Highway Patrol	80,000 miles
Oregon State Police	90,000 miles
South Dakota Highway Patrol	80,000 miles
Washington State Patrol	75,000 miles
Wyoming Highway Patrol	100,000 miles

Therfore, while leasing represents a very versatile option, the majority of administrators responsible for police is the only sensible path to take. They believe that considering all factors involving mileage restrictions, life-cycle costing, used-vehicle disposal, and money costs, purchasing the fleet remains the best alternative. "Any time money is involved, whether you use it in an owned environment or a leased environment, there is a cost of using money. When administrators don't identify that money cost, they come up with the conclusion: When comparing to lease costs which do include interest, ownership is less costly."[23]

In the end, only individual fleet managers can determine which is more advantageous for them. They have to weigh all of the advantages and disadvantages of leasing versus buying. As money gets tighter, all governmental entities must seek more creative ways to spread costs. Once an agency determines the direction fleet acquisition will take, it must establish parameters for vehicle replacement.

Vehicle Rotation or Replacement

Establishing fleet vehicle replacement criteria proves a delicate and time-consuming task. Fleet managers continually seek new and innovative ways to aid them in their timely decisions.[24] Typically, they base their evaluation of existing fleet equipment and ideal replacement decisions on criteria in several major areas. Because replacement criteria is not always detectable from the outward appearance or operation of the vehicle, agencies must establish such guidelines at the time of purchase.

Today, it is commonplace for all governmental entities to follow the requests of the public and stretch existing tax dollars. City councils, police commissions, and state legislatures continue to ask law enforcement agencies of all sizes to reduce their budgets. This results in agencies buying less, stretching supplies, and making things last longer, including patrol vehicles.

If an agency must make its vehicles last longer, it has to ask what its needs are and how it can work smarter to calculate how long a vehicle will last. That is a difficult, if not impossible, question to answer.

"When asked how long a car will last, automobile manufacturers respond, 'That is like asking, how high is up?' They're not dodging the question; the fact is no one has done research on the subject. Even two of Michigan's major universities, Wayne State and the University of Michigan, have no idea of how long an automobile will last, despite the fact that they have large engineering schools that supply engineers to all the major automobile companies."[25]

An informal survey by the Michigan State Police shows that most police agencies take their patrol cars out of service between 60,000 and 100,000 miles. At the extreme ends of the mileage spectrum, some departments run cars only 45,000 miles and others up to 150,000 miles. Some agencies, bound by state law, must take their vehicles out of service at a specific mileage. Others use their vehicles for primary service until 50,000 miles and then place them into backup service, low-mileage service, or take them out of service completely and sell them at auction.[26]

Overall, with the cumulation of independent studies, benchmarking standards, technical data, and cost analysis surveys, fleet managers are aided in their decision-making process when they set their rotation or replacement standards. However, elected officials, who see budget constraints and want to make the dollars stretch even farther, continually challenge these standards. Therefore, fleet managers must look at one of the most important issues when deciding how long their agencies can afford to keep their vehicles safe, especially when trying to cut corners to appease citizens concerned with government spending. "When I'm chasing someone at 100+ mph in a car with over 100,000 miles on it, how safe am I? Even with the best of care and detailed safety inspections, potential problems can be undiscovered. While many parts failures are irritating at low speeds, at high speeds they can be disastrous, even deadly."[27]

Agencies should base replacement criteria for a fleet vehicle on elements surrounding the age of the vehicle, operating costs, mileage, vehicle fatigue, and current usefulness. These individual areas have their own importance and may seem insignificant; however, when considering the criteria in combinations, they provide a whole new perspective.[28]

With high-mileage vehicles, the most common reaction concerns the engine, transmission, and differential. While those objects represent the heart of the automobile and the highest cost items, they are the ones least likely affected overall by high mileage. In fact, the drivetrain of a police car with 100,000 miles on it may well be in better condition than the proverbial "little old lady's 25,000-mile sedan only driven to church and the supermarket."

More than 75 percent of engine wear occurs on startup and shutdown. During those times, bearings are not lubricated and literally run dry for a short period of time. Short trips, where the engine and other components never get a chance to fully warm up, also are hard on a vehicle because moisture does not evaporate and can mix with the normal products of fuel combustion to form acids that attack bearings and other engine parts. As long as the prescribed maintenance intervals are followed, drivetrain components usually incur the more minor problems a high-mileage vehicle will suffer.

The ancillary parts of the vehicle are the ones that will break down. Suspension components wear out or weaken and break. Parts, such as bushings, deteriorate. Brake and fuel lines and wiring harnesses wear through at body attachment points or where they pass through frame members. Interior components, such as seats, controls, and interior upholstery, show signs of wear thousands of miles before a mechanical component. "Look at a 2-year-old patrol car; it will still look good on the outside while the interior shows wear on the seats, arm rests, pedals, and other areas. The passenger seat may look new, but the driver's seat, well sprung, showing the effects of thousands of hours of patrol."[29]

Engineers agree that two factors determine the life expectancy of a vehicle: environment and maintenance. Maintenance is seldom a problem for police agencies; common sense dictates that they take care of their equipment. As long as agencies follow the manufacturer's recommended maintenance schedules during the life-cycling process, their cars should hold up reasonably well.[30]

However, even regular maintenance does not guarantee that a vehicle will stay in good condition forever. Automobiles are made of plastic, steel, rubber, and aluminum, which will weaken over time. There has to be a point when those materials are not strong enough to take the wear and tear police give them.

Because no definitive information exists on how long various parts last in a vehicle, the question of when safety-related parts become dangerous constitutes an arguable point. Safe-operating procedures should dictate that parts be replaced at an arbitrary point before they show excess wear and certainly before any potential weakness and failure can occur. Arbitrary or scheduled replacement of parts leads to another problem—expense. Higher maintenance downtime increases costs. Mechanics and replacement components create expenses; moreover, cars off the road do not produce results, they produce bills.[31]

The other factor that determines the life expectancy of a vehicle is the conditions it operates under. Not just the use aspect, such as law enforcement or civilian, but the actual environment. The ideal environment for anything composed primarily of steel is a warm, dry climate such as the American Southwest. Because the area is warm and dry, steel is less likely to rust. In areas where there is more moisture or corrosive elements, such as salt, metal life expectancy is much shorter. States where salt or chemicals are used on the highways in winter or the coastal states where salt is always in the atmosphere provide the ideal recipe for short vehicle life.

Overall, a newer car may cost more money, but it can save the agency money in reduced fuel and maintenance costs. Also, an agency's image can suffer if all it uses are older cars. How safe will citizens feel when they see a 10 year-old patrol car on the streets? They may applaud the agency's fiscal responsibility, but they also may ask why the cars are not safer and more up-to-date.

Fleet Liability

A final point rests with litigation. What are the legal consequences of keeping a car too long? All in all, the concept of saving money by repairing cars or keeping them too long can be expensive. If an older car causes a crash,[32] is the officer, agency, or fleet manager open to litigation that could cost several times the replacement of the entire fleet? Agencies should not take lawsuits or litigation lightly. There are cases on file providing data where agencies have lost lawsuits because of poorly maintained equipment, which was the main cause in automobile crashes. A jury may hesitate to find fault with a case involving a new patrol vehicle, but has less of a problem finding guilt with an agency operating poorly maintained or out-of-date equipment.

In the private sector, the National Association of Fleet Administrators (NAFA) presents factual information that identifies the personal liability that fleet managers and their employers face when insufficient or improper maintenance causes traffic-related fatalities. They contend that this liability has surfaced specifically in the area of poorly maintained trucks or commercial carriers. NAFA has identified the area of commercial carrier/big-rig liability because of the tremendous amount of money attached to the suits. Facts state that when a tractor trailer is wrecked, the money figures run well over $150,000. Trucking companies that have large fleets of trucks are thought to have easy access to cash pools through insurance carriers. Therefore, they are projected as easy targets for litigation. Once the suit is filed, those individuals who manage the fleet are identified in the suit. Although NAFA has addressed this issue specifically concerning commercial/big-rig fleets, they want fleet managers who oversee fleets of all sizes to become aware of this increasing risk, as government also is sometimes viewed as having "deep pockets." "The cost associated with good maintenance pales in comparison to the price that you and your employer will pay if a poorly maintained truck in your fleet kills an innocent person. In New Jersey, for example, fleet managers and company owners have been convicted of manslaughter and jailed when their poorly maintained trucks caused traffic fatalities. Even when criminal prosecution is not called for, an investigation may expose a company to civil liability which can cripple or even destroy it. Strict adherence to some very basic principles will drastically reduce your liability as a fleet administrator and prevent you and your company from falling prey to risk."[33] While legal standards often are different for commercial and public enterprises and liability for state and municipal agencies often is limited by law, the issue of liability still is a major concern for law enforcement agencies.

With these types of issues becoming more prevalent with time, it becomes absolutely necessary to assess the risks and reevaluate the old ways of doing business. By making safety one of the top priorities and continually evaluating the life-cycling process, law enforcement agencies can replace older equipment with newer equipment, which will save lives and protect them from issues surrounding liability.

RECOMMENDATIONS

Research on fleet management points to a fleet remaining as new as possible. Most information states that the optimum mileage for rotation stands anywhere between 50,000 and 70,000 miles. Mechanical repairs go up quite substantially after a vehicle reaches an average of 70,000 to 75,000 miles.

Increase in the speed limits on state and federal highways is taking place nationwide. With the increase in the speed limits, additional stress occurs on each police vehicle that patrols the highways. This is because of the higher and longer sustained speeds that officers must use to overtake violators. Once the police vehicle has reached the higher speeds, it will incur additional wear and tear on an already taxed brake system as the driver must apply the brakes longer to slow down the vehicle.

With these areas of concern in mind, all agencies should take a long, hard look at their rotation policies. Law enforcement agencies should give specific consideration to not exceeding a 70,000- to 75,000-mile vehicle rotation policy. Agencies should place the safety of the men and women operating the vehicles above any other considerations.

CONCLUSION

The patrol vehicle represents a major expenditure for law enforcement agencies. Those elected officials who want to tighten government spending have begun to challenge the current methodology used for determining vehicle replacement. More and more law enforcement agencies are being forced into keeping fleet vehicles longer. Therefore, the equipment sustains more mileage and wear and tear before being rotated out of fleets.

When looking at an appropriate time to rotate a vehicle out of service, agencies need to consider several items. First, they must take a candid look at the bidding process. If agencies address the proper specifications, they should have little problem in picking the best vehicle from the published performance testing. Second, when they decide which fleet vehicles are appropriate for their needs, they must look at their financial options. Some agencies have the capabilities to purchase their fleets and others have opted to lease. Third, once agencies receive their fleet of new vehicles, they must evaluate and project the economic life expectancy of the equipment. This happens during the vehicle life-cycling process and includes maintenance, operating expense, downtime, and depreciation. Fuel savings represent a big factor as a younger vehicle gets better fuel economy. Fourth, agencies must look at the established requirements surrounding mileage restrictions and extended warranties. Some agencies have rigid guidelines that require mandatory rotation at given intervals. Finally, agencies must give proper consideration to litigation surrounding the vehicles that comprise their fleets. If vehicles are causing crashes, it is imperative that agencies make adjustments in their replacement policies.

All and all, fleet rotation is not a simple process. Administrators must consider many factors and reevaluate them annually. The safety of their officers and the public they serve, the image their agencies project, and the efficiency and effectiveness of their operations depend on their decisions regarding how they manage their vehicle fleets.

NOTES

1. The author based this article on research that he conducted for his agency in 1996. The purpose of the project was to provide factual data and alternative measures that agencies should consider when establishing fleet vehicle rotation criteria. For more recent references on this topic, see Tom Yates, "Time and Money Saved: Illinois State Police Bring Fleet Management Close to State-of-the-Art," *Law and Order*, March 1997, 84–86; "Extended Replacement Cycles Can Bring Positive Results," *NAFA Fleet Executive*, November 1997; "Resolving the Lease vs. Ownership vs. Reimbursement Question," *NAFA Fleet Executive*, October 1998; "Depreciation: For Many, *the* Key to Controlling Fleet Costs," *NAFA Fleet Executive*, January 1999; "Demystifying the Science of Ergonomics and How It Applies to Fleet" and "Fleet Managers Share Productivity Tips," *NAFA Fleet Executive*, February 1999; "Refurbishment: A Less Costly Alternative to Vehicle Replacement," *NAFA Fleet Executive*, March 1999; "Taking the Sting Out of the Lease vs. Buy vs. Reimburse Question," *NAFA Fleet Executive*, June 1999; and the National Association of Fleet Administrators (NAFA) Web site *http:// www.nafa.org*.

2. Mark Levine and Dierdre Martin, "The Procurement of Police Cars," *Law Enforcement Technology*, September 1989, 22–23 and 39–43.

3. John E. Dolce, *Analytical Fleet Maintenance Management* (PA: Society of Automobile Engineers, Inc., 1994).

4. Supra note 2.

5. Ed Sanow, "1996 Michigan State Police Vehicle Tests," *Law Enforcement Technology*, November 1995, 23–28.

6. Supra note 2.

7. Bob Duran, "The Price Is Right," *Police Technology and Management*, September 1990, 28–31.

8. Supra note 3.

9. "Saving Dollars with Preventive Maintenance," *Business Vehicle Management*, First Quarter 1996, 22–24.

10. Supra note 7.

11. David Griffith and Associates, LTD, "Benchmarking for Quality in Public Service Fleets," *National Association of Fleet Administrators* (1993): 14–26.

12. Supra note 3.

13. "How National Account Programs Can Control Fleet Expenses," *Automotive Fleet*, February 1996, 18–22.

14. Supra note 3.

15. "Police Fleets Question the Benefits of Buying vs. Leasing," *NAFA Fleet Executive*, October 1995, 10–16.

16. Supra note 13.

17. Supra note 13.

18. Supra note 15.

19. Supra note 15.

20. Supra note 15.

21. Supra note 3.

22. Supra note 15.

23. Supra note 15.

24. Supra note 3.

25. Tom Yates, "It Ain't the Years, It's the Miles," *Law and Order*, August 1992, 69–72.

26. Supra note 5.

27. Supra note 25.

28. Supra note 7.

29. Supra note 25.

30. Supra note 3.

31. Supra note 25.

32. Crash is the current term used in the industry because it more clearly defines an incident that may be caused by certain elements or actions as opposed to a strictly "accidental" occurrence.

33. Supra note 15.

Police Overtime

An Examination of Key Issues

BY DAVID BAYLEY AND ROBERT WORDEN

There is a sense both inside and outside the law enforcement community that overtime is overused, misused, and only halfheartedly controlled. Federal officials want to be sure that the funds they award to local police agencies for overtime payments are well spent. Local police agencies are equally concerned. For this reason, the National Institute of Justice commissioned a study of the use of Federal funds provided to local law enforcement agencies for overtime. (See "Methodology" and "Federal Funding of Police Overtime.") This Research in Brief reports what we have learned about improving the management of overtime in American police departments.

The study discovered enormous differences among local police departments in the attention given to the issue, the capacity to produce information about it, and the policies and procedures for managing it. Clearly, some departments do an excellent job of managing overtime. This Research in Brief also shares information about some of these practices as a way to help agencies grappling with the issue and attempts to answer the following questions: Can overtime be responsibly managed? If so, how?

Very little has been written about the management of overtime, except to report that overtime management is viewed as a recurring problem by both private- and public-sector managers.[1] Regarding overtime in policing, almost no information exists in the public domain. For this study, researchers canvassed the major professional organizations specializing in police research, as well as prominent police scholars, and could not find any studies of the use of overtime in policing. Management consultants write private reports to individual police agencies that sometimes address the overtime issue, but this is unpublished literature that is generally not available.

Police departments themselves have vast experience in managing overtime, but they have not yet shared that knowledge. Professionals contacted often chuckled when told of the topic being studied, urging that the research proceed but indicating that there were good reasons why no studies had been performed previously. The universal opinion was that the inquiry was long overdue but that the subject matter might prove too sensitive to study successfully. Readers should understand, therefore, that what the authors present here by way of suggestions for managing overtime very much represents a first cut at a difficult subject.

How does one control overtime in policing? The answer: by recording, analyzing, managing, and supervising. This Research in Brief will examine each of these activities, so that police managers may better understand what they can do in a practical way to improve overtime performance.

The four activities listed would appear to suggest a temporal order of tasks for police departments:

build databases, analyze them for patterns, make appropriate managerial decisions, and supervise the resulting policies. Nothing could be more mistaken. The key element that precedes all others is management. Useful records systems cannot be constructed unless managers anticipate what they need to know. Management is also essential for analysis, and analysis needs to be specified before responsive data systems can be designed. In other words, although it is certainly true that analysis cannot be done without records, records cannot be sensibly constructed without prefiguring analysis. Recording, analyzing, managing, and supervising are interactive, not sequential. The key is managing. One of the problems besetting contemporary policing, as managers everywhere ruefully recognize, is that the new computer-based information systems pour out data that are not used. Unmanaged information systems are like the legendary sorcerer's apprentice—madly producing data that bury consumers.

In short, the management of overtime comes in two forms: creating an infrastructure for recording and analyzing the use of overtime and making policies about overtime based on an understanding of what is happening. The first sort of management precedes all other activities. The second sort can only take place if the first sort has been done well.

Recognizing that managerial decisions about the kinds of analysis and, consequently, of records that are needed must be made at the very beginning of any attempt to control overtime, the topics will be presented in the following order: analysis, recording, managing, and supervising.

ANALYZING OVERTIME

What should managers know to ensure that overtime is used responsibly? What are the major questions they must continually ask about overtime in their departments?

Are overtime expenditures justified in terms of the work being done? Because overtime represents police work performed at premium rates—time and a half—managers need the ability to determine whether the same work could be performed at less cost on straight time. Thus, they need to know how much of their agency's work is being performed on overtime, what sort of work it is, and the circumstances of its use.

When analyzing the cost-effectiveness of overtime, it is critical to distinguish work done on paid overtime from work done on unpaid, or compensatory, overtime. Work done on paid overtime generally increases policing activity, even though paid at time and a half. The cost is borne by city councils as an addition to the police budget. Compensatory time, on the other hand, represents less policing because every hour worked must be repaid by the department at time and a half. Compensatory time comes out of existing capacity. Therefore, managers need to be able to determine whether the work performed on compensatory time is more important than work being "scrimped" through the compensatory time payback.

The implication for recordkeeping is that not only must records on paid time and compensatory time be kept, but also information on their respective uses, including the nature of the work forfeited to pay for compensatory time. These are called opportunity costs—the costs of taking one action at the expense of another.

Do the police and the local government have the capacity to pay for overtime? Answering this question requires police managers to know whether they are "on budget" throughout the year, so as to avoid cost overruns and consequent political exposure. This means managers need to know how much has been spent throughout the current fiscal year and how the rate of expenditure compares with previous years. They should also examine current expenditures against likely future contingencies; planning requires forecasting overtime needs based on analyses of past patterns. Although some overtime expenditures cannot be predicted, repeated surprises indicate a lack of analysis. As the philosopher George Santayana said, "People who do not know the past are doomed to repeat it."

Because compensatory time does not come out of existing budgetary allocations, some police departments do not monitor its use as systematically as

Methodology

Findings from this study are based primarily on information collected from three sources:

- An inventory of U.S. Department of Justice programs administered through the Bureau of Justice Assistance, Federal Bureau of Investigation, Drug Enforcement Administration, and Executive Office for Weed and Seed.
- A seven-page questionnaire on overtime expenditures and practices. This survey was mailed to 2,183 State and local police agencies—a representative sample of police departments that had responded to the 1990 Bureau of Justice Statistics Law Enforcement Management and Administrative Statistics Survey (LEMAS).[a] Followup calls were conducted with 100 of the largest police agencies, which in the aggregate account for most of the police overtime worked in the United States.
- Case studies of overtime practices in 11 police departments of various sizes nationwide.

[a] Conducted by the Bureau of Justice Statistics, the LEMAS survey included all U.S. police agencies, except for half of those with five or fewer full-time personnel, which LEMAS data show generated little overtime.

they do paid overtime. Compensatory time is not costless. Unless police departments keep close track of the amount of compensatory time earned and paid back, cities may suddenly face large unfunded liabilities—financial payouts they have not anticipated. In some departments officers who do not use their compensatory time can claim it as money at retirement. Police departments also need to track accumulations of compensatory time by individual officers, because departments cannot require officers (under the Fair Labor Standards Act or their own labor agreements) to work more than specified maximums of compensatory time without being paid.[2] Overtime beyond this amount must be paid as money. Police departments need to know where they stand with respect to this obligation.

Is overtime being abused? "Abused" here is defined as being used in ways that cannot be justified and may cause embarrassment to the organization. Generally, overtime abuses take the form of large, undetected overtime earnings by individuals or units within a police department. Such abuses represent a failure of supervision, which in turn reflects the inability of an organization to know, in a timely manner, what is happening. To avoid embarrassment, police departments need to analyze patterns of overtime expenditure—both as time and as money—by individuals,

by units, and by the nature of the work performed. Unusual payouts to individuals or units may indicate problems of organizational management.

In sum, if a police department is to manage overtime, it must be able to justify expenditures in terms of the work performed, to anticipate the rate and amount of payouts, and to explain why overtime had to be paid to particular individuals and units at particular times.

RECORDING OVERTIME

To analyze the issues described above, the following records must be current:

- **A police department's total obligations and payments for overtime,** both paid overtime and compensatory time.
- **Obligations and expenditures of overtime** by individual officers and commands or budgetary units—for example, investigations, traffic, patrol, and SWAT. Computer programs can automatically notify managers whenever overtime obligations exceed specified thresholds—for example, when a police officer earns more than 10 percent of monthly salary or at a projected yearly rate over $25,000, or when a unit's overtime budget

Federal Funding of Police Overtime

A number of observations on how Federal funds are used within local law enforcement agencies for overtime emerged from the study, including the following:

- Total Federal support for policing by State and local governments has been growing in the 1990s. Federal support for overtime has also been growing, but is difficult to estimate because expenditures are scattered among so many agencies (Department of Justice, Department of Housing and Urban Development, Department of Transportation, Department of the Treasury) and programs (Executive Office for Weed and Seed, Edward Byrne Memorial State and Local Law Enforcement Assistance Grant Program, Office of Community Oriented Policing Services).

- According to the study, the Department of Justice now accounts for approximately 60 percent of the Federal Government's expenditures on overtime by State and local law enforcement agencies.

- Federal expenditures by the Department of Justice invested in overtime by State and local law enforcement agencies do not supplant local spending on police overtime.

- By and large, overtime money is provided and used to supplement traditional programs, rather than to sponsor programmatic innovations. Federal expenditures shift enforcement priorities somewhat, but they do not bring about substantial organizational change.

- Although overtime expenditures by the Department of Justice provide a genuine increment in policing, analysis is needed to determine whether the increment is valuable enough to be paid for at premium wages.

- Police departments in the United States vary enormously in the attention they pay to overtime, their management of it, and their ability to produce information about it.

- Overtime should be viewed, within limits, as an unavoidable cost of policing. Overtime charges cannot be eliminated altogether, regardless of the number of police officers employed, because of inevitable shift extensions, court appearances, emergency situations, and contract requirements.

- Reimbursing overtime in money is preferable to reimbursing in compensatory time. Paid overtime increases policing activities, while compensatory time results in less policing because every hour worked must be repaid by the department at time and a half—time taken away from other activities.

- Reliance on overtime in American policing may have harmful consequences that are not sufficiently considered by police managers, such as exhaustion on the part of officers, unwillingness to provide any service without a tangible reward, increased antagonism between supervisors and line officers, and the undermining of professionalism.

- Overtime practices represent substantial possibilities for cost savings. Though overtime can never be eliminated, it can be more successfully controlled.

- Publicizing the practices of police departments found to excel in regulating overtime can contribute to improving overtime management nationally.

- The key to improving overtime management is foresight on the part of senior officers, which requires attention to analysis, recordkeeping, and supervision.

is running 10 percent ahead of the previous year's expenditures.

- **The uses of overtime.** Setting up a system that adequately captures the uses of overtime requires forethought because relevant categories can vary with local conditions. The most common categories are holdovers or shift extensions; backfilling or buybacks (that is, paying people on leave to fill temporary vacancies); holidays; briefings and roll calls; court appearances; callbacks to duty; emergencies such as homicides and snowstorms; planned events beyond normal duty, for example, traffic control at venues; and meetings or training outside of working hours.

Monitoring the opportunity costs associated with compensatory overtime involves identifying those tasks that were not carried out because officers were granted time and a half off. This tracking is key to determining the true public safety cost-effectiveness of claiming overtime as time, rather than as money.

- **Circumstances of overtime use.** Knowing where, when, and under what circumstances overtime was incurred is necessary if managers are to anticipate overtime, to justify its payment, and perhaps to find ways to reduce the need for overtime expenditures. For example, if overtime occurs chronically in particular units, then hiring

additional officers or reallocating existing personnel may solve the problem. On the other hand, if overtime is concentrated at particular times of the year, hiring additional staff would probably not be the solution.

- **Sources of overtime payments.** Records of such sources of overtime funding as city councils, State government, Federal Government, or private consumers should be kept. When tracking city expenditures, it would be useful to separate overtime accounts from the general fund, the police budget, and charges against the budgets of other municipal agencies.

Not surprisingly, it appears that police departments invest resources in collecting information primarily when it has clear fiscal significance. Of the police departments responding to the overtime survey, the majority

---

Dollars and Recordkeeping

In the one department surveyed in which *all* overtime is compensated with dollars, rather than compensatory time, we found one of the most complete and sophisticated information systems for monitoring overtime use.[a] In that department, hours worked and dollars paid were tracked by organizational unit and by function, and this information was updated and disseminated to department managers every 2 weeks.

By contrast, another department, in which much of the overtime was compensated with time off rather than money, had a much more limited capacity to monitor overtime. Numbers of hours worked by individuals were tracked carefully within each division over the course of each 28-day work cycle, so that steps could be taken to minimize the likelihood that patrol officers would accrue hours for which they must be compensated monetarily and at a higher (time and a half) rate. But the aggregate patterns of overtime work were not monitored, and the only information that could easily be retrieved (from payroll records) for analysis was information on expenditures. Overtime could be analyzed in terms of the activities that were performed only by manually reviewing the paper forms that officers completed.

In another department, overtime was typically compensated monetarily. However, little overtime was incurred, partly because it had to be preauthorized by supervisors, and supervisors took steps to avoid overtime work. Given that overtime was not considered a significant budgetary issue, little information was computerized for analysis. Records of overtime were available, and particularly detailed records of overtime incurred under the auspices of Federal grant programs were kept, but they were not routinely compiled and analyzed; the latter records were available in the event of a Federal audit.

[a] An equally complete and sophisticated information system was found in a department that uses both compensatory time and paid compensation. This department is widely regarded as one of the most progressively managed in the country. Furthermore, it is very concerned about the prospect of unfunded liabilities.

(69 percent) were able to provide all 5 years of expenditure information (1990–94); a much smaller percentage (38 percent) was able to provide the number of overtime hours worked.

Respondents provided limited information about overtime's functional uses. Among respondents who reported the total number of overtime hours, about 40 percent accounted for all (or virtually all) of those hours by functional category, while another 40 percent could account for about half. The limited ability to monitor and report information about overtime appeared in police agencies of all types (though sheriffs' departments in this study were somewhat less likely to be able to report overtime information, and State police agencies somewhat more likely) and occurred in all regions of the country.

Developing informative record systems need not be a particularly daunting or costly activity. Commitment seems to be the critical ingredient. Record systems can be put in place within a year or so, with the largest cost probably being incurred for staff to input data. Departments can also make the transition more easily by adapting systems already developed by other departments. Every region of the country has exemplary departments that have developed protocols for recording and analyzing data, programs that automatically provide managers with perspective on overtime. (See "Dollars and Recordkeeping.")

MANAGING OVERTIME

Again, it is important to note that managing is not a separate activity from recording, analyzing, and supervising. Recording, analysis, and supervision are required for successful overtime management, but they must be managed so that useful knowledge is available to the managers who set overtime policies. Responsible overtime management requires leadership from the top.

If the chief is indifferent about overtime, the support systems—both human and technical—necessary to manage overtime will be neglected. A chief's indifference will also leave middle managers exposed—reluctant to go where the chief prefers not to tread, but at risk if overtime problems occur.

It is also important to be realistic about what management can achieve in controlling overtime. For example, some shift extensions are inevitable because police officers generally work 8-hour shifts, and time-consuming problems can occur at any time. Sensational crimes or natural disasters are impossible to predict and require extraordinary outlays of effort. Police work also inevitably generates court appearances, roll calls, meetings, and holidays. This sort of overtime can be viewed as a fixed cost of normal policing and will occur regardless of the number of officers employed. Overtime is not a discretionary category that can simply be managed out of existence. Policymakers and the public should be wary about judging the police according to unrealistic expectations.

Overtime is also critically affected by labor rules—the "contract"—that mandate uses and rates. Visits to police departments revealed the following examples of contract stipulations with respect to overtime:

- Any court appearance by an officer, no matter how short, earned a fixed minimum amount of overtime, as much as 3 to 4 hours.
- Officers called back to work were guaranteed a minimum of 2 hours of overtime, no matter how long they actually worked.
- Supervisors who were on standby in the event of an emergency earned a minimum of 3 hours overtime.
- Patrol officers were given between 15 and 30 minutes of overtime each shift for attending roll calls.
- An officer waiting at home to be called to court was allowed a fixed amount of overtime, on the premise that the officer was forfeiting an opportunity to work at another job.
- All meetings outside the department were charged to overtime.

In the survey, 45 percent of police departments reported that overtime was governed by collective bargaining agreements; 39 percent said that such agreements applied specifically to patrol personnel, which is the largest specialty among police officers.

Some departments have tried to divide overtime expenses according to whether they are controllable—probably a fruitless exercise. The issue generally is not whether a particular form of overtime is controllable, but rather by whom and at what cost. Contract stipulations, for instance, are frequently treated as uncontrollable. This may be true from line supervisors' point of view, but not from the view of senior managers who are responsible for contract negotiations. Contract provisions are controllable in principle, even though the likelihood of doing so, given the political power of unions, is small. Even in the case of shift extensions, the option exists for police to pass work to later shifts. All overtime is potentially manageable by someone, but the costs of doing so in some cases are greater than the benefits. So, when departments say that some proportion of overtime is not controllable, they are making a judgment about options they are willing to try. Their willingness may be based on entirely correct assessments of what is likely to be achieved.

Interviews with police officers nationwide yielded several suggestions for policies to control overtime more tightly.

Court appearances. Agreements between police and court personnel could improve overtime usage. For example, policies could call for court appearances to coincide with usual working hours, rather than with time off. While officers are waiting to appear, they can be given indoor work, such as staffing property rooms, interviewing complainants, preparing shift rosters, or answering questions on the telephone. In addition, district attorneys can be asked to subpoena only those officers listed on arrest reports whose testimony might be important. There is no reason for supervisory personnel to appear in courts, since their testimony would be hearsay. Police can be asked not to list supervisory personnel on incident reports and arrest warrants.

Shift extensions. Responsibility for approving shift extensions rests with immediate supervisors.

Managers can assist immediate supervisors by providing them with updated and revised guidelines for approving shift extensions, as well as by reviewing their performances periodically. Survey results show that immediate supervisors were authorized to approve overtime in 91 percent of the responding police departments, and 73 percent had guidelines that specified the purposes for which overtime could be used.

A more general solution, well beyond the capacity of any police force to enact, is to abolish the 40-hour week as the basis for overtime, aggregating hour-maximums by months or years.[3] This would allow departments to require longer hours of work for short periods without incurring overtime costs, compensating officers by less work during slack periods. In 1995, a U.S. Representative proposed hearings on the idea.[4]

Staff size. Persistent backfilling, or employing off-duty officers to fill necessary positions, indicates a chronic shortage of personnel in relation to work needing to be completed. Since local governments determine the strength of police forces, this imbalance is generally beyond the ability of departments to fix unless hiring is allowed. Departments may, however, be able to reduce the period of the imbalance, and hence overtime, by shortening the time needed to recruit and train new police officers. Departments may even consider using civilians, volunteers, or police academy students in nonenforcement lines of police work, thereby freeing experienced personnel for tasks requiring powers of arrest or those where minimum staffing levels must be maintained.

Emergency mobilizations. By carefully studying all unplanned emergency mobilizations, departments can determine how best to use existing capacity and thereby minimize callbacks or extensions. Emergencies require overtime, but they do not justify unlimited overtime. To some degree, overtime can be minimized in emergency situations by fine-tuning responses and making them more efficient, as well as by building the capacity to handle contingencies that singly are unpredictable but in the aggregate are not. These possibilities are probably more likely for large departments, which can often develop such procedures more easily than small departments, because unpredictable events occur in greater numbers in their jurisdictions and therefore can be "averaged" on a yearly basis. In a small department, on the other hand, events such as a sensational murder may occur once every 20 years.

Special events. Departments often pay officers overtime for handling special events, such as crowd control at festivals or traffic at sporting events. Because these are episodic, it is not cost effective to maintain capacity to handle them. If these events are privately sponsored, departments might consider requiring sponsors to pay the costs of policing as a condition for granting a permit. Many large cities now require event sponsors to complete official statements regarding the effect of special events on police duties. The Madison, Wisconsin, police department, for example, requires that a police impact statement be filed as part of the permit process. In addition, cities and police departments should develop policies about when the costs of policing special events are to be publicly or privately borne. This may be a touchy political matter. For example, some local ordinances (strongly supported by police unions) require police, rather than private security, to work such events. Finally, work schedules of police could be adjusted, if permitted by contract regulations, so that officers can accumulate slack time that can later be allocated for policing predictable manpower-intensive events.

We determined from site visits that police departments throughout the country are experimenting with ways to minimize the burden of overtime. Frustrated by the rigidities of current practice and fearful of embarrassing public revelations, concerned managers are learning valuable lessons about managing overtime. Unfortunately, this knowledge is not being systematically collected and shared within the profession, which does not generally know which departments are the benchmarks for overtime management. Hence, a national canvas of techniques for managing overtime could be worthwhile to practitioners.

SUPERVISING OVERTIME

Supervision of overtime is often seen as the first line of defense against overtime abuses. Middle-rank commanders everywhere complained that one of their major responsibilities is controlling overtime. They believe it is critical to how they are judged as commanders. In fact, front-line supervision of overtime is the last line of defense, and supervisors are often made the scapegoats for more general failures of management. Most of the factors that determine overtime are beyond the control of any middle-rank manager, such as contract regulations, calls for service, crime emergencies, vacations, injuries, retirements, and approval for special events.

Although first-line supervisors formally approve overtime, in some departments their ability to refuse is restricted. Moreover, in many departments first-line supervisors are frequently not given the information needed to anticipate demands and adjust work schedules. With inadequate recordkeeping and analysis, supervisors cannot control overtime, they can only audit it. The control of overtime looks to be decentralized, but in reality it is not; it is structured by policies set at more senior levels or from outside the police force altogether.

Overtime can also be supervised by the officers themselves through peer pressure if amounts of overtime worked by individual officers are posted publicly at regular intervals. We visited several departments using this method. Knowing that overtime will be scrutinized by their peers, officers will be careful that extra hours claimed are justifiable in operational terms.

Successful management of police overtime requires assistance outside police departments. At present, police managers often fear that providing outsiders, such as city councils and the media, with information about overtime practices will expose the department to unfair criticism. This is one reason why some departments are reluctant to implement computer-based monitoring and online analysis of overtime. Police managers should realize, however, that factual information about overtime, if it is properly explained, can strengthen their position in advocating needed reforms both inside and outside their organization. Managers have more to fear from lack of information than from too much. Gradually, information in the public domain about overtime will expand. Some cities now regularly report all forms of overtime to city councils and even encourage the media to publish their departmental pattern analyses.

City councils and other outside auditors should also understand that overtime cannot be effectively controlled by frontline supervisors. They should not allow senior officers to pass the responsibility for managing overtime to junior officers. Councils and the media could be educated, most likely by police themselves, about the elements of an effective overtime management system. Analytic reports of overtime could provide police managers with information to explain to others the limits on their ability to control overtime and to construct a fact-based division of responsibilities between themselves and city councils. Police managers have more to gain from making overtime information available and visible than from keeping it hidden.

ADDITIONAL REFERENCES

Balles, Joe, et al. May 17, 1989. "City of Madison Police Department Overtime Project." Madison, WI: Police Department.

Bureau of Justice Statistics. September 1995. *Law Enforcement Management and Administrative Statistics, 1993: Data for Individual State and Local Agencies with 100 or More Officers.* Washington, DC: Bureau of Justice Statistics.

Dilulio, John, Jr., Steven K. Smith, and Aaron J. Saiger. 1995. "The Federal Role in Crime Control." In *Crime,* ed. James Q. Wilson and Joan Petersilia. San Francisco, CA: ICS Press.

Elliot, John, Timothy J. Fisher, Kay Hutchison, and Neil Turner. December 18, 1988. "City of Madison Police Over-time Final Report." Madison, WI: Police Department.

Executive Office for Weed and Seed. 1992. *Operation Weed and Seed Implementation Manual.* Washington, DC: U.S. Department of Justice.

Goldstein, Herman. 1990. *Problem-Oriented Policing.* New York: McGraw-Hill.

Kelling, George L., and Mark H. Moore. 1988. *The Evolving Strategy of Policing.* Washington, DC: National Institute of Justice.

Madison Police Department. June 1993. "Report of the Police Department Overtime Study Committee." Madison, WI: Police Department.

Nathan, Richard P. 1983. "State and Local Governments Under Federal Grants: Toward a Predictive Theory." *Political Science Quarterly* 98 (Spring): 47–57.

Nathan, Richard P. 1982. "The Methodology of Field Network Evaluation Studies." In *Studying Implementation: Methodological and Implementation Issues,* ed. Walter Williams. Chatham, NJ: Chatham House Publishers, Inc.

United States General Accounting Office. April 1993. *War on Drugs: Federal Assistance to State and Local Drug Enforcement.* Washington, DC: GAO/ GGD–93–86.

This study was conducted by David H. Bayley, Ph.D., and Robert E. Worden, Ph.D., from the School of Criminal Justice, The University at Albany, State University of New York. This research was supported by the National Institute of Justice, U.S. Department of Justice, through grant number 95–IJ–CX–0020.

Copies of the full report of the study, *Federal Funding of Police Overtime: A Utilization Study,* are available from the National Criminal Justice Reference Service (NCJRS) on a cost-recovery basis. To order, call NCJRS at 800–851–3420 and ask for NCJ 170614.

NOTES

1. The authors would like to thank Professor Hal Gueual, School of Business, The University at Albany, State University of New York, and his graduate students for searching the economic and business literature.

2. Under the Fair Labor Standards Act, an officer who agrees to work compensatory time in lieu of cash cannot accumulate more than 480 hours during a lifetime. Many union contracts stipulate more restrictive maximums.

3. Mazur, Laura, "Coming: The Annual Workweek," *Across the Board* (April 1995): 42–45.

4. Laabs, Jennifer, "The Changing Workplace Stirs Up Overtime Pay Debate," *Personnel Journal* (April 1995): 12.

Findings and conclusions of the research reported here are those of the authors and do not necessarily reflect the official position or policies of the U.S. Department of Justice.

Corporate Strategies for Policing

By Mark Moore and Robert Trojanowicz

Police departments embody a substantial public investment. Each year, the nation spends more than $20 billion to keep police departments on the street and vigilant.[1] More important, each year society puts its freedoms in the hands of the police by empowering them to use force to compel obedience to the nation's laws. That, too, is an investment, for the grant of legitimate authority is a resource granted to police by the citizens. As the Philadelphia Study Task Force explained:

> The police are entrusted with important public resources. The most obvious is money; $230 million a year flows through the police department. Far more important, the public grants the police another resource—the use of force and authority. These are deployed when a citizen is arrested or handcuffed, when an officer fires his weapon at a citizen, or even when an officer claims exclusive use of the streets with his siren.[2]

These resources—money and authority—potentially have great value to society. If wisely deployed, they can substantially reduce the level of criminal victimization. They can restore a sense of security to the nation's neighborhoods. They can guarantee civility and tolerance in ordinary social interactions. They can

provide a first-line response to various medical and social emergencies such as traffic accidents, drunkenness, domestic disputes, and runaway youths.

Stewardship over these resources is entrusted to the nation's police executives. They largely decide how best to use these assets. They make such decisions every time they beef up a narcotics unit, or establish priorities for the dispatching of calls, or write new policies governing the use of deadly force or the proper use of high-speed auto chases. At such moments, the police executives redeploy the money and authority entrusted to them in hopes that their organizations will produce greater value for society.

Judging how best to use the assets and capabilities of a police department is the principal task of police executives. As Professor Kenneth Andrews of the Harvard Business School says:

> The highest function of the executive is … leading the continuous process of determining the nature of the enterprise, and setting, revising, and achieving its goals.[3]

Performing this function well is no trivial task. It requires vision, judgment, and imagination, as well as disciplined analytical capabilities.

In the private sector, executives seek to perform this function through the development of a "corporate strategy." A "corporate strategy" defines the principal

Mark Moore and Robert Trojanowicz, "Corporate Strategies for Policing," *Perspectives on Policing*, no. 6, pp. 1–15. Copyright in the Public Domain.

financial and social goals the organization will pursue, and the principal products, technologies, and production processes on which it will rely to achieve its goals. It also defines how the organization will relate to its employees and to its other constituencies such as shareholders, creditors, suppliers, and customers. In short, a corporate strategy seeks to define for the organization how the organization will pursue value and what sort of organization it will be.[4]

A corporate strategy is developed through an iterative process that examines how the organization's capabilities fit the current and future environment. The executive surveys the environment to see what customers want to buy, what competitors are likely to sell, and what investors are willing to stake money on. He analyzes what his own organization is able to do, what new technologies and products are becoming available, and what investments could be made to widen current capabilities. A strategy is defined when the executive discovers the best way to use his organization to meet the challenges or exploit the opportunities in the environment.

In the public sector, executives often consider the question of how best to use their assets much more narrowly. They tend to assume that basic purposes and operating objectives of the organization were set long ago and now remain fixed. Their job is to optimize performance with respect to these objectives, not to consider new challenges, threats or opportunities, nor to discover new capabilities within their own organizations. They also often assume that in conducting their organization's business, they are restricted to orthodox policies and programs. While public sector executives might field a few innovative programs to deal with special problems, the innovative programs are rarely seen as part of a sustained, staged effort to change the organization's basic strategy.

Recently, some police executives have begun considering different corporate strategies of policing. While these executives see enormous value in the knowledge and skill that have accumulated within police departments over the last 50 years, they are increasingly aware of the limitations of the past conceptions. They are reaching out for new ideas about how police departments should define their basic goals,

deploy their assets, and garner support and legitimacy in the communities they now police.

The purpose of this paper is to facilitate the search for a corporate strategy of policing that can deal with the principal problems now besetting urban communities: crime, fear, drugs, and urban decay. The paper first explores the strengths and limitations of the corporate strategy that has guided policing for the last 50 years—a strategy that has been characterized (perhaps caricatured) as "professional crime fighting."[5] It then contrasts this concept with three other concepts that have been discussed, and to some degree developed, within Harvard's Executive Session on Policing. The other concepts are "strategic policing," "problemsolving policing," and "community policing."

THE CONCEPT OF CORPORATE STRATEGY

Defining a corporate strategy helps an organization, its employees, and its executives. An explicit corporate strategy tells outsiders who invest in the organization what the organization proposes to do and how it proposes to do it.

It explains to employees what counts as important contributions to the organization. It helps managers maintain a consistent focus in sifting the material that comes through their in-boxes. It directs their attention to the few activities, programs, and investments that are critical to the implementation of the proposed strategy.

For any organization, many possible strategies exist. Three criteria are useful for evaluating and choosing among them. The first is the value of the strategy if successfully implemented. The second test is feasibility—whether the strategy is internally consistent in terms of the products, programs, and administrative arrangements emphasized, and whether it is based upon solid information and proven technologies. Feasibility is related to distance from current operating practice; greater distance makes the proposed changes more costly and difficult. The final criterion involves the degree of risk associated with a given strategy. Those strategies that lie close to existing expectations and capabilities involve little risk for the manager to pursue. Those that stretch expectations and capabilities, that are founded on experiments and hunches, involve much greater risk and often depend on substantial investments for their success.

The development of a corporate strategy is a complex matter. Often, however, complex corporate strategies can be captured in relatively simple phrases or slogans. William Ruckelshaus defined the mission of the United States Environmental Protection Agency (EPA) as "pollution abatement."[6] Michael Pertschuk declared that his goal for the Federal Trade Commission (FTC) was to make it "the largest public interest law firm in the U.S."[7] These apparently simple slogans embodied complex judgments that important changes in the operations of these organizations were both valuable and feasible. "Pollution abatement" focused EPA's efforts on finding sources of pollution and restricting them, not on monitoring levels of pollution or estimating damages. Challenging the FTC to become the "largest public interest law firm" not only raised professional standards in the organization, but also redefined the principal clients of the FTC to be consumers who needed protection from businesses rather than businesses that wanted protection from other businesses.

Simplicity in defining corporate strategies is a virtue for several reasons. First, a simple concept is easy to remember and repeat and therefore more likely to guide discretionary decisions throughout a large organization. Second, a simple concept helps to focus an organization's attention by what it explicitly emphasizes, or implicitly excludes, or the way in which it contrasts with previous strategic concepts. Third, a simple phrase has the virtue of openness. Its very lack of detail allows improvisation, innovation, and evolution in the operations of the organization. Because there is no detailed plan, only general guidance, employees with new ideas can find sanction for their efforts. And because the corporate strategy sets out purposes in broad language, many outside the organization can find reasons to support the organization's efforts.

LABELS AND CORPORATE STRATEGIES OF POLICING

The simple phrases that came to stand for complex ideas about corporate strategies of policing within the discussions of Harvard's Executive Session on Policing included "professional crime fighting," "strategic policing," "problem-solving policing," and "community policing."[8] At the outset, the discussion treated these concepts as nothing more than labels to be attached to the same elements of a future strategy of policing.

Indeed, many participants thought that the elements emphasized by these new concepts had already been incorporated in contemporary versions of the professional crime-fighting model. Others saw little difference between the concepts of problem-solving policing and community policing. Since there was little substantive difference among these concepts, the only issue in choosing among them appeared to be a marketing question: how powerful were the labels in attracting support from the public, in dignifying the work of the police, and in mobilizing them to action?

In later discussions the words seemed to acquire important substantive significance, reflecting real differences in judgments about such crucial matters as:

- The fundamental purposes of the police.
- The scope of their responsibilities.
- The range of contributions they could make to society.
- The distinctive competences they had to deploy.
- The most effective programmatic and technical means for achieving their purposes.
- The most suitable administrative arrangements for directing and controlling the activities of a police department.
- The proper or most useful way to manage the relationship between the police and the communities for whom they worked.

For example, while all the concepts make crime control a central purpose of policing, the concepts of problem-solving policing and community policing accord greater significance to the order-maintenance and fear-reducing functions of the police than they hold in the concept of professional crime fighting.

Similarly, while professional crime fighting encourages the police to maintain their distance from the community to ensure the fair and impartial enforcement of the laws, community policing emphasizes a close embrace with the community to achieve more effective crime control and to ensure that the police respond to the issues that concern the community. Such differences seemed large enough for some participants to advocate adopting one concept and dismissing the others.

Still later, it seemed that the concepts were valuable because each highlighted a different challenge or defined a different frontier for police executives to explore in managing their departments for increased value and effectiveness in deploying the police against the principal problems of the cities. Many departments, for example, are still working at the frontiers defined by professional crime fighting, such as enhanced technical capacities to respond to serious street crimes, greater discipline and skill in the use of force and authority, and greater independence from inappropriate political influence.[9]

Other departments have already realized the value associated with the strategy of professional crime fighting and now face the new challenges defined by these other strategic concepts.[10] Strategic policing highlights the technical challenges of dealing with the most difficult sorts of crimes and offenders: for example, terrorism, narcotics trafficking, political corruption, and sophisticated white collar crimes.[11] Problem-solving policing emphasizes the value of being able to diagnose the continuing problems that lie behind the repeated incidents that are reported to police dispatchers and to design and implement solutions to those problems.[12] Community policing stresses the key role that a working partnership between the police and the community can play in solving crimes, reducing fear, and resolving situations that lead to crimes.[13] According to our Executive Session discussions, these are the challenges that define the frontiers of policing in the next generation.

It is possible that these challenges can all be met simultaneously by a new, integrated corporate strategy of policing. In that case, police executives would not have to choose among competing strategic conceptions. They could meet all the diverse challenges.

Alternatively, it might prove impossible to pursue all the different conceptions simultaneously. The challenges might be sufficiently diverse that, at least in the short run, managerial attention, the public's willingness to invest, and the officers' tolerance for experimentation are too limited to allow simultaneous advances on all fronts. In that case, police executives would have to decide which path to pursue first.

Or, it could be that the different strategies are somehow fundamentally incompatible—that the pursuit of one strategy makes it virtually impossible for the police agency to pursue another. This could occur if the different strategies require fundamentally different value orientations or cultures within the organization, too many different kinds of personnel and capabilities, or inconsistent administrative arrangements. In that case, police executives might have to make difficult choices among corporate strategies.

Whether executives must choose among these strategies, or whether some synthesis is possible, remains an important question. This paper seeks to help police executives answer that question. These different conceptions will be developed first as relatively complete, competing corporate strategies of policing. Then, in a concluding section, the paper will consider how, and to what degree, the apparently competing conceptions may be synthesized in an overall corporate strategy of policing.

PROFESSIONAL CRIME FIGHTING

The corporate strategy that guided policing during the last half-century is captured by the phrase professional crime fighting. This strategy achieved a great deal for the police. It carried them from a world of amateurism, lawlessness, and political vulnerability to a world of professionalism, integrity, and political independence.[14] The principal engines of this transformation include:

1. a sharpened focus on crime control as the central mission of the police;

2. a shift in organizational structure from decentralized, geographically defined units to a centralized structure with subordinate units defined by function rather than by geography; and

3. substantial investments in modern technology and training of officers.

The aim of the professional crime-fighting strategy was to create a disciplined, technically sophisticated, quasi-military crime-fighting force. Crime control and crime solving became the dominant goals in policing. Those goals, as well as the common views about the best way to achieve them, are embedded in the current standards of accreditation and form the basic assumptions underlying both the majority of police training and the deployment of police resources throughout the country.

The principal operating technologies of this strategy include (1) patrol forces equipped with cars and radios to create an impression of omnipresence and to respond rapidly to incidents of crime; and (2) investigative units trained in sophisticated methods of criminal investigation, such as automated fingerprint identification and the use of criminal histories.

In addition, this strategy emphasizes accountability to the law by seeking to eliminate police discretion through increased centralization, written policies and procedures, dense supervision, and separation of the police from the corrupting influence of local politicians.

This conception of professional crime-fighting policing embodies powerful values: crime control as an important objective, investment in police training, enhanced status and autonomy for the police, and the elimination of corruption and brutality. With the close connection to all these important values, it is no wonder that the concept of professional crime-fighting policing has been popular and endures as a corporate strategy of policing. There is much that citizens and police can rally around and great value to be claimed in pursuing this ideal.

Still, there are some obvious (and not so obvious) weaknesses of this strategy. The most significant is the limitations of professional policing in controlling crime.[15] Initially, it seemed that patrolling officers and skilled detectives would constitute an effective crime-fighting force. Several decades of operating experience with these basic crime-fighting tactics have revealed some unexpected weaknesses.

One is that the tactics are essentially reactive. They depend on someone noticing a crime and calling the police. That leaves many crimes—those "invisible others" that do not produce victims or witnesses who are willing to mobilize—beyond the reach of the police.[16] Such crimes include consensual crimes (such as drug dealing and bribery, in which the participants do not perceive themselves as victimized), extortionate crimes (such as organized criminal extortion, often rape, and child and spouse abuse, in which the victims are too afraid to come forward), dispersed crimes (such as embezzlement and fraud, in which victimization is diffused so broadly that people do not know that they have been victimized), and inchoate crimes (such as conspiracies, which do not have victims because the crimes have not yet occurred). Note that this list includes offenses which are committed by sophisticated, determined, and powerful criminal offenders. Thus, there is a gap in police capacities to deal with certain kinds of offenses and certain kinds of offenders.

A second problem with these tactics is that they fail to prevent crimes, except through the mechanisms of deterrence and incapacitation. In the professional strategy of policing, crime prevention is de-emphasized in favor of reacting after the fact. Little emphasis is given to mobilizing citizens to defend themselves. Indeed, the help of amateurs is discouraged as inconsistent with the image of a disciplined professional force that can deal with all the problems. Nor is any emphasis placed on analyzing and eliminating the proximate causes of crime. That is viewed as social work rather than crime fighting.

A less obvious weakness of this strategy lies in its discouragement of a close working relationship with the community. The concept of professional policing encourages distance between the police and the community in the interests of ensuring impartiality and avoiding corruption. That distance, useful as it is in pursuing these values, comes at a price. The police lose their intimate link to the communities. This hurts their crime-fighting capability because it cuts them off from valuable information about the people and conditions that are causing crimes.[17]

Another effect of maintaining professional distance from the community is that the police appear less accessible. Consequently the police become a less frequent recourse, even for fearful or crime-ridden communities. It is not that the police become unpopular; they remain extremely important to the community.[18] It is just that they seem less present, and therefore less able to meet the pressing needs and particular worries of citizens.

In some big cities, professional distance became particularly problematic, for just as police departments were seeking to insulate themselves from the communities and set higher professional standards, the cities began to change. In the 1960's, cities absorbed new migrant populations from the rural South, the Caribbean, Mexico, and Asia. Few police came from these immigrant populations and had little knowledge of these cultures. The result was that while the police thought of themselves as professionally distanced, the communities began to think of them as unresponsive and indifferent to their concerns. In extreme cases, communities saw the police as an alien, occupying army.[19] The political legitimacy of the police began to erode along with their operational value.

Newer conceptions of policing have developed in response to these weaknesses in professional crime fighting, just as professional crime fighting arose in response to the weaknesses of the older political conception of policing. The new conceptions differ from one another in that they respond to different weaknesses and offer different ways to eliminate the weaknesses of professional crime fighting.

STRATEGIC POLICING

The concept of strategic policing seeks to improve on professional crime-fighting policing by adding thoughtfulness and toughness to the basic mission of crime fighting and crime control.[20] In strategic policing the basic goal remains the effective control of crime. The administrative style remains centralized. And the police retain the initiative in defining and acting on the crime problems of the community. In fact their initiative is enhanced as enforcement capabilities are improved—capabilities that allow them not only to deal more effectively with ordinary street crime but also to confront sophisticated offenders who lie behind the invisible offenses described above.

With respect to ordinary street crime, strategic policing seeks improvements through directed patrol,[21] decoy operations to catch street robbers, and sting operations to disrupt burglary and fencing operations. Strategic policing recognizes that the community can be an important instrument aiding the police. Hence, block watch associations are emphasized, citizens are urged to mark their property, and the police are available to offer advice on security to businesses and private homeowner.[22] Such programs embody a strategic rather than a reactive approach to street crime.

In addition, strategic policing emphasizes an increased capacity to deal with crimes that are not well controlled by traditional methods. Two kinds of crimes are particularly salient. First are crimes committed by sophisticated, individual offenders, such as career criminals or serial murderers, who operate beyond local boundaries. Second are offenses committed by criminal associations, organized crime families, drug distribution networks, gangs, sophisticated white-collar offenders engaged in computer and credit card frauds, and even corrupt politicians—the so-called superstructure of crime.[23]

To attack the first kind of crime, more sophisticated investigative capabilities are necessary. To attack the second, the police have to employ more intrusive investigative procedures, such as informants, undercover operations, electronic surveillance, and sophisticated intelligence analysis. It is also important that the police gain some independence from their local political base. They need to widen their jurisdiction to attack the sophisticated, multi-jurisdictional criminal offender. They need to separate themselves from the influence of the local political community to be able to attack the superstructure of crime. Unless they can do this, they find themselves subject to its control, and thus occasionally hamstrung.

These points have important implications for the administrative arrangements and organizational alignments of police departments. For strategic policing in big-city departments, the need for sophisticated skills and wide jurisdictions necessitates the establishment of specialized, central investigative units. Such units are necessary to develop and sustain the appropriate skills, files, and equipment to carry out complex investigations. Centralized control of these units is also often considered essential to ensure an appropriate degree of supervision over the use of relatively controversial investigative methods. Strategic policing in suburban and rural areas requires these smaller departments to band together in regional associations. Otherwise, they cannot afford the investments in the required specialized capabilities. Nor do they have a wide enough jurisdiction to deal with offenders operating across community boundaries.

To get out from under the influence of powerful criminal elements, local police departments in both metropolitan and suburban areas form alliances with and establish operational ties to Federal enforcement agencies and the judiciary, rather than with local politicians. Such alliances enhance investigative sophistication, effectively widen jurisdictions, and ensure that powerful allies are available when locally powerful offenders are the focus of investigation.

In sum, in strategic policing the police response to crime becomes broader, more proactive, and more sophisticated. The range of investigative and patrol methods is expanded to include intelligence operations, undercover stings, electronic surveillance, and sophisticated forensic methods. The range of targets is enlarged to include sophisticated offenders and inchoate crimes. The key new investments involve the creation of specialized investigative capabilities and improved criminal intelligence functions. Patrol operations are generally reduced as a share of police operations to make room for the specialized investigative units. The community is seen as an important auxiliary to the police in dealing with crime, but the police retain the initiative in defining and acting upon crime problems. The principal value claimed by strategic policing is improved crime control. The old values of political independence, lawfulness, and technical sophistication are also protected—even promoted—as police departments form alliances with Federal law enforcement agencies rather than with local politicians. In an important sense, strategic policing represents the next step along the path marked out by professional crime fighting.

PROBLEM-SOLVING POLICING

Like strategic policing, the concept of problem-solving policing seeks to improve upon the older, professional strategy of policing by adding proactiveness and thoughtfulness. It differs from strategic policing in the focus of the analytic effort.

In professional and strategic policing, the underlying assumption is that crime is successfully controlled by discovering offenses and prosecuting the offenders. Such efforts control crime directly by incapacitating offenders. They also prevent crime by increasing the probability of arrest and successful prosecution (i.e., through general and specific deterrence). Thus, they prescribe tactics that position the police to see offenses and respond to them.

Problem-solving policing takes a different view of crime and its effective control. In problem-solving policing, one does not naturally assume that crimes are caused by predatory offenders. True, in all crimes there will be an offender vulnerable to prosecution under the law. But problem-solving policing makes the assumption that crimes could be caused by particular, continuing problems in a community, such as frustrating relationships or a disorderly milieu.[24] It follows, then, that crimes might be controlled, or even prevented, by actions other than the arrest of particular individuals. For example, the police might be able to resolve a chronic dispute or restore order to a disorderly street. Arrest and prosecution remain crucially important tools of policing. But ideas about the causes of crime and methods for controlling it are substantially widened.

This basic change in perspective requires police departments to widen their repertoire of responses to crime far beyond patrol, investigation, and arrests. For example, the police can use negotiating and conflict-resolving skills to sort out disputes before they become crime problems.[25] Disputes (between parents and children, landlords and tenants, merchants and customers, and between neighbors) might be mediated without waiting for a fight to occur and without immediate recourse to the criminal law, arrests, and prosecutions. Moreover, the police, with a heightened awareness of such underlying problems, might take such corrective action the 2d time they are called to the scene rather than the 6th or 10th time, thus making substantial savings in the use of police resources.

The police can make use of the civil powers vested in their licensing authority and other municipal ordinances to enhance neighborhood security. Bars can be cautioned on excessive noise,[26] merchants urged to comply with traffic regulations, and children cautioned on curfew violations to reduce occasions in which fear and disputes arise.

Community residents may be mobilized to deal with specific problems. They can replace lights in hallways, clean up playgrounds so that parents and young children no longer feel excluded from the park by teenagers,[27] and accompany the elderly and the vulnerable on errands.

Finally, other government organizations may be mobilized to deal with situations leading to crimes. The Public Housing Authority can be asked to repair fences to prevent incursions by predatory offenders and to seal vacant apartments to eliminate shooting galleries for drug addicts and club houses for juvenile gangs. The Public Works Department can be encouraged to haul away abandoned cars and other debris.

This change in tactics has ramifications for the organizational structure of the police department. To the extent that problem solving depends on the initiative and skill of officers in defining problems and devising solutions, the administrative style of the organization must change. Since much more depends on individual initiative, the department must become more decentralized. Otherwise, the advantages of local knowledge and adaptiveness are lost. A further implication is that generalist patrol officers, knowledgeable about the communities they serve, become the new heroes of the organization (traditionally, the heroes have been the specialist investigators).

The focus of police action is widened in a different way from that of strategic policing. Strategic policing challenges the police to deal with sophisticated crimes and powerful offenders in addition to the street crimes such as robbery, rape, and burglary that are the main focus of professional crime fighting. Problem-solving policing challenges the police to deal with the disputes and conditions that make life feel disorderly and frightening to citizens and therefore breed crime and underlie later demands on the police department.

In sum, like strategic policing, problem-solving policing seeks enhanced crime control. The means, however, are quite different. They include diagnosing underlying problems which give rise to crime (rather than identifying offenders) and mobilizing the community and governmental agencies to act on the problems (rather than arresting and prosecuting offenders). Reliance on these means naturally encourages geographic decentralization and dependence on resourceful generalist patrol officers, rather than on the centralized functional specialist units. The problem-solving approach also draws the police into a different relationship with the communities—one in which the communities and other government agencies help the police work on underlying problems. Because many of those problems are not, strictly speaking, problems of crime and criminal victimization, a police department pursuing a strategy of problem solving will end up pursuing a broader set of objectives than the effective control of street crime. It will pursue order maintenance and fear reduction objectives as well as crime control.

COMMUNITY POLICING

The third new concept, community policing, goes even further in its efforts to improve the crime control capacities of the police. To achieve that goal, it emphasizes the creation of an effective working partnership between the community and the police.

Many of the participants in the Executive Session see little difference between the strategy of problem-solving policing and community policing. They think of problem solving as a technique to be used in community policing rather than a different corporate strategy for policing. If there is a difference between the strategy of problem solving and the strategy of community policing, however, it lies in a different view of the status and role of the community institutions, and in the organizational arrangements constructed to enhance community involvement.

In community policing, community institutions such as families, schools, neighborhood associations, and merchant groups are seen as key partners to the police in the creation of safe, secure communities. The success of the police depends not only on the development of their own skills and capabilities, but also on the creation of competent communities. Community policing acknowledges that police cannot succeed in achieving their basic goals without both the operational assistance and political support of the community. Conversely, the community cannot succeed in constructing decent, open, and orderly communities without a professional and responsive police force.

To construct the working partnership and build competent communities, a police agency must view the community institutions as more than useful political allies and operational partners in the pursuit of police-defined objectives. They must see the development and protection of the institutions as partly an end as well as a means. Moreover, the police must recognize that they work for the community, as well as for the law and their professional development.

Partly to recognize the status of the community institutions and partly to develop the working partnership, police agencies pursuing the strategy of community policing must become more open to community definitions and priorities of problems to be solved. In problem-solving policing, the police retain much of the initiative in identifying problems and proposing solutions to the community. They are the experts. They know what crimes are being committed. They know what citizens have been calling to complain about. They know how police resources can be deployed to deal with the problem. In community policing, the community's views have a greater status. Their views about what constitutes a serious problem count. So do their views about what would be an appropriate police response. In short, the police seek a wider consultation and more information from the community.

Consistent with that philosophy, a police agency pursuing a strategy of community policing relies on many different organizational devices to open the department to the community. Police executives direct their officers to make face-to-face contact with citizens in their areas of responsibility.[28]

Where feasible, police executives establish foot patrols to enhance the citizens' sense of access to the department.[29] The executives restructure the organization in decentralized, geographic commands, symbolized by neighborhood police stations.[30] Community consultative groups are established and their views about police priorities are taken seriously. Community surveys, as well as crime statistics, are incorporated in evaluating the overall effectiveness of the police.

Opening police departments to community concerns inevitably changes their operational focus, at least to some degree. As in problem-solving policing, the focus widens beyond incidents of criminal victimization to include lesser disorders that stimulate fears and conditions that suggest a general deterioration of community standards; for it is these things that are often of greatest concern to citizens. The inevitable police involvement in social and medical emergencies is also viewed differently in community policing. While the police role in handling domestic disputes, runaway children, and traffic accidents is viewed as a dangerous distraction in professional crime fighting, these activities are viewed more positively in the strategy of community policing, since they provide a basis for developing the working relationship with the community. With community policing, a police executive might see value in deploying police resources for such activities as school-based drug education programs, programs to punish and educate drunk drivers, or a joint program with schools and the juvenile justice system to stop school violence and reduce truancy.[31]

The close relationship with the community also raises important questions about political interference that must be resolved with new understandings of police accountability.[32] From one perspective, creating close links with local communities increases the risk that the police will be unduly influenced by illegitimate political demands. The police might be used by powerful local interests to undermine the interests and rights of less powerful citizen groups.

From another perspective, however, the relationship enhances police accountability by making the police more responsive to community concerns as expressed in meetings, surveys, and face-to-face and telephone contacts. The issue here is whether the police are accountable to the law and its impartial enforcement, or to the community and its representatives who pass the laws and consent to be policed in a particular way.

This tension, between legal impartiality and political responsiveness as the basis of police legitimacy, can be theoretically resolved by saying that the police are strictly accountable to the law except where discretion exists. In those areas for discretion, the police may properly be guided by the desire to be responsive to legitimate expressions of neighborhood concerns. What this theoretical perspective leaves unacknowledged is that many of the most important questions facing police executives remain unanswered by the law. The criminal law simply distributes a set of liabilities through the society which the police are duty bound to act on if requested by a citizen. It does not tell police executives how they ought to deploy their resources in response to citizen complaints, nor what offenses they should emphasize as enforcement targets, nor the extent to which the police should feel responsible for preventing crime, reducing fears, or offering emergency services as well as enforcing the law.

As a practical matter, what the police must take from their legal foundation is the obligation to say no to the community when the community asks them to do something that is unfair, discriminatory, or illegal. In the end, although it is valuable for the police to seek a close working relationship with the community by being responsive to community concerns, the police must also stand for the values of fairness, lawfulness, and the protection of constitutional rights. Indeed, they must defend those interests from the interests of the politically powerful. That crucial lesson is the hard-won legacy of the strategy of professional crime fighting.

Overall, under the community policing concept, the ends, means, administrative style, and relationship with the community all change. The ends expand beyond crime fighting to include fear reduction, order maintenance, and some kinds of emergency social and medical services. The means incorporate all of the wisdom developed in problem-solving approaches to situations that stimulate calls to the police. The administrative style shifts from centralized and specialized to decentralized and generalized. The role of the community is not merely to alert the police to crimes and other problems, but to help control crime and keep communities secure. While the department remains confident in its professional expertise and committed to the fair application of the law, it is more open to discussions with local communities about its priorities, its operating procedures, and its past performances.

EXCELLENCE IN POLICING: A SYNTHESIS

The frontiers marked out for development by these different strategies of policing add up to a major challenge for police executives. If pursued simultaneously and aggressively, the different strategies would require significant changes in the mission, primary programs and technologies, and basic administrative arrangements of police departments. They would also require important changes in the relationship with the community. In some cases, the cumulative challenges merely stretch the organization to incorporate new capabilities. In other cases, however, the different challenges seem to twist the organization in opposite directions.

With respect to the mission of policing, the cumulative impact of these corporate strategies is to broaden more than to twist. The mission is no longer limited to the effective control of street crime. It also includes: (1) a strengthened attack on dangerous offenders, organized criminal groups, and white collar offenders; (2) a more determined effort to resolve the problems that underlie incidents reported to police dispatchers; and (3) a heightened concern for fear, disorder, and other problems that communities designate as high priority issues, or that the police choose to handle as the basis for forming a more effective partnership with the community. The mission might even widen to include police action on community problems such as drugs in schools, drunk driving, public drunkenness, unsupervised children, and other medical and social crises. While it is by no means easy for an executive to create an organization that can accommodate these diverse purposes, there does not seem to be any fundamental tension among these missions. Indeed, most police departments are already pursuing these diverse missions with reasonable degrees of success.

With respect to the principal programs and technologies, the cumulative impact of the challenges is once again primarily to stretch and widen, not to twist. To deal with the broader mission, new functions and programs must be created. Strategic policing demands much more effective intelligence and investigative techniques than are commonly used in professional crime fighting. Problem-solving policing demands greater diagnostic skills and a far broader repertoire of responses to problems than arrest and prosecution. Community policing demands a more varied set of interactions with individuals and groups within the community, as well as the development of new capacities to deal with community-designated problems such as teenage drug use, violence in schools, or public drunkenness.

With respect to the administrative organization of the police department, the combined set of challenges twists police organizations in opposite directions. Strategic policing requires (1) centralization (to ensure tight administrative control over sensitive intelligence and investigative functions); (2) the establishment of specialized functional units (to ensure the development and maintenance of expertise in key areas); and (3) independence from local communities (to ensure a platform from which to attack powerful local interests if they are committing crimes). Problem-solving and community policing, however, require (1) decentralization (to encourage officer initiative and the effective use of local knowledge); (2) geographically defined rather than functionally defined subordinate units (to encourage the development of local knowledge); and (3) close interactions with local communities (to facilitate responsiveness to and cooperation with the community).

Perhaps the greatest torque created by the cumulative weight of these challenges exists in the domain of community relations. It is a deep philosophical divide as well as an administrative issue. In strategic policing, the community is seen as a potential threat insofar as it conceals, even nourishes, the superstructure of crime. In community policing, the community is seen as a crucial aid in dealing with crime and fear. In strategic policing, the community is to be held at arm's length and worked on by the police department. In community policing, the community is to be embraced and worked with.

These contradictions may be more apparent than real: a product of the stylized way in which the alternative strategies are presented. But as police executives contemplate the demanding challenges envisioned in these strategies, two important conclusions emerge.

First, if police departments are to stake out the frontiers marked for exploration by these different corporate strategies, they will have to become more capacious, flexible, and innovative than they now commonly are. They will have to contain within the organization a wider and more complicated set of functional capabilities than now exists. For example, they will need:

- Sophisticated answering and call-screening capabilities to preserve time for activities other than responding to calls for service.
- Generalist patrol officers who are as comfortable outside their cars as in, and as capable of organizing meetings and mediating disputes as of making arrests.

- Analytical and intelligence capabilities that can discern both nagging community problems and activities of dangerous, sophisticated offenders.
- Sufficient flexibility in deployment and capability to deal with different sizes and kinds of problems.

Indeed, police departments might well have to shift from a relatively inflexible organizational structure based on stable, fixed chains of command to a structure based on projects and programs of different sizes and duration, led by people of many different ranks. That will cut deeply into traditional organizational structures and command relationships.

Second, if police organizations of the future are to respond to the various challenges posed by the different strategic concepts, police executives must face up to the apparent contradictions and be able to resolve them. In some cases, this will not be hard. It seems relatively simple, for example, to resolve the question of whether the police will seek to deal with street crime, sophisticated crimes, problems giving rise to incidents that trigger calls, or community-designated priorities. They have to deal with all of them. None can safely be neglected. The only thing necessary to incorporate all of these within the mission of policing is to keep reminding the officers and others that the mission properly includes all these features. No single front represents "real police work."

It also seems relatively easy to resolve the question of whether the police are responsible for managing fear and disorder as well as serious criminal victimization. The answer is clearly yes; certainly no other government agency regards itself as specifically responsible for it. Without doubt, the police are responsible for these matters not only as an important approach to crime prevention, but also as important value-creating activities in their own right.

It is a bit more difficult to resolve the apparent tension between the further development of sophisticated investigative techniques to deal with complex offenses and powerful offenders on the one hand, and, on the other, the development of the diagnostic capabilities and working community partnerships that can solve nagging community problems. There seems to be a cultural stumbling block in confronting

these challenges. The crucial difference seems to be that professional crime fighting and strategic policing focus on "serious crime," view the cause of such crimes as the bad motivations of offenders, and seek to deal with the problem by arresting and prosecuting offenders. Problem-solving policing and community policing, on the other hand, focus on anything that is named as a community problem and seek to handle the problem with any means available—not simply arrest and prosecution.

Part of the reason that these distinctions strike a sensitive nerve in police departments is that the differences are enshrined in an organizational distinction between detectives and investigative units on the one hand, and patrol officers and community relations units on the other. The long ignored reality, however, is that these apparently diverse functions have a great deal in common. Both depend on being able to see behind the surface manifestations of a problem. The attack on sophisticated crimes and dangerous offenders requires an ability to discern a common mechanism behind apparently unrelated incidents. The attack on community problems similarly requires the officers to see behind sets of incident-driven calls, widespread community fears, or persistent crime problems, and to understand and deal with the deeper causes.

Both also require a great deal of imagination and initiative on the part of the officer in devising and executing a solution to the operational problems they encounter. In both countering sophisticated crimes and problem solving in the community, the investigative approaches must be invented and tailored to individual cases.

In short, the investigative-detective style of operating needs to be applied to a wider range of problems than investigators now handle. It is therefore important that the investigative style (without the narrow focus on crimes and offenders) seep into the rest of the organization. The manager has to be aware that the same imagination and resourcefulness, which is invoked in combatting high-tech crime, can also be profitably spent on more common and more nagging problems facing the community.

Perhaps the most difficult contradictions to resolve are those related to organizational structure and to the relationship between the department and the community. These are firmly linked because the structure of the organization has strong implications for whether and how community institutions can have access to the police. Centralized structures tend to make midlevel managers responsive to the administrative demands of headquarters, rather than to the interests of local communities. Decentralized structures do the opposite. A functional organization (in which the subordinate units are based on technical specialties) tends to be unresponsive to local demands; a geographic organization (in which technical specialties are lumped together in units that are coterminous with organized communities) is much more responsive to local concerns.

Initially, the tension between the centralized, functional structures suited to professional crime-fighting policing and strategic policing, and the decentralized, geographic structures suited to problem-solving and community policing seems irreconcilable. Professional crime-fighting policing needs the tight discipline and control that centralization seems to promise. Strategic policing requires the development of specialized skills that can be produced only by committing a portion of the force to the development of those skills, and by protecting it from ordinary demands. Problem-solving and community policing, on the other hand, need decentralization to encourage the initiative of the officers. They require geographically based units to encourage the creation of working partnerships. And they need generalists to ensure that diverse skills can be combined to produce solutions to community problems.

One possible resolution of this conflict is to create specialist units, but to keep them small, and use them as consultants to the generalist units rather than rely on them for all operations within their sphere of competence. For example, one could create a narcotics squad to develop specialists who would be knowledgeable about drug problems and the complex investigative techniques they require. But they would not be responsible for all narcotics operations. Their principal assignment would be to equip and assist the generalist units as narcotics problems arose. They might also function as program managers for narcotics enforcement throughout the department as a whole.

The program would not be executed by the narcotics unit alone, but instead by many officers outside the unit's command.

An alternative would be to organize primarily around geographic commands, which would include officers qualified by training and experience in specialized functions. Assignments of officers would be created from projects and programs that varied in terms of scale and longevity. When a problem arises that requires the services of an officer skilled in, say, juvenile matters, officers would be drawn from the geographic commands to resolve the problem. When a citywide program in narcotics enforcement is needed, officers skilled in narcotics enforcement would be called on to work on the problem.

In short, instead of organizing by relatively large, durable commands, police departments would organize (and frequently reorganize) on the basis of specific problems and programs that are identified as being important. These would vary in terms of scale and longevity. This would require the police to shift from managing through specialized operational commands to managing through a combination of program managers and general geographical commands a change that challenges traditional conceptions of responsible police management.

Even harder than creating flexible responses to specific problems is the issue of how to properly structure community relations. In professional crime fighting, the community is operationally important as an aid to solving crimes. Calls from individual citizens alert the police to crimes being committed. Victims and witnesses supply the evidence necessary to convict offenders. Thus, the community is a key operational component of professional crime fighting. But a key imperative of professional crime fighting is separation from community demands lest law enforcement integrity be compromised.

Strategic policing goes even further in seeking police independence as it tries to find a secure platform from which to launch attacks on powerful offenders. Problem-solving and community policing, on the other hand, seek a closer embrace with the community. In the interests of building effective working partnerships, both problem-solving policing and community policing reach out for a close relationship and respond to community concerns.

The resolution of this paradox is conceptually simple, but exceedingly difficult to implement and to explain to outsiders. The police must remain loyal to the values that they have pursued for so long in professional policing: a commitment to the fair and impartial enforcement of the law; a capacity to use force and authority economically and fairly; a determination to defend constitutional rights, particularly those of minorities; a kind of discipline that allows them to resist both the desires of powerful people to use them for their purposes and their own impulse to use the powers of their office for expressing their own angers, fears, and prejudices; etc. At the same time, they must recognize that while these values might be tested in seeking a close connection with the community, they need not be compromised.

Indeed, to assume that the only way these values can be protected is by separating the police from the community is to give too little credit to the achievements that have been made in professionalizing the police. A true professional is one who can hold to his values (and exercise his skills) when they are tested in use. In practical terms, this means constant affirmation of these professional values throughout the organization, especially as members of the force at all levels are urged to do more to respond to the public's concerns.

These conclusions suggest the shape of a future corporate strategy of policing. It might be called "professional, strategic, community, problem-solving policing." It is a challenging task for police executives to realize such a vision. They must overcome the powerful claims of tradition in articulating the mission and organizing their departments. They must override the desires and expectations of many of their employees who have different visions of policing. They must cope with powerful external pressures to produce the illusion of accountability through rigid, centralized management. And, most important, they must cope with their own uncertainties about the best way to use the assets of their organization to produce decent, civil, tolerant communities. It is up to today's police executives to find the solution.

NOTES

1. Katherine M. Jamieson and Timothy J. Flanagan, eds., Sourcebook of Criminal Justice Statistics—1986, Washington, D.C., Bureau of Justice Statistics, 1987: 2.

2. Philadelphia and Its Police: Toward a New Partnership, A Report by the Philadelphia Police Study Task Force, March 1987: 129.

3. Kenneth R. Andrews, The Concept of Corporate Strategy, Homewood, Illinois, Richard D. Irwin, 1980: iii.

4. Ibid.: 18.

5. Mark H. Moore and George L. Kelling, "To Serve and Protect: Learning from Police History," The Public Interest 7 (Winter 1983).

6. "William Ruckelshaus and the Environmental Protection Agency," John F. Kennedy School of Government Case Program #C16–74–027, 1974.

7. "Mike Pertschuk and the Federal Trade Commission," John F. Kennedy School of Government Case Program #C16–81–387.0, 1981: 5.

8. The Executive Session on Policing at Harvard University's John F. Kennedy School of Government, Program in Criminal Justice Policy and Management, 1985–88.

9. *Philadelphia and Its Police: Toward A New Partnership.*

10. David Kennedy, "Neighborhood Policing: The London Metropolitan Police Force," John F. Kennedy School of Government Case Program #15-87-770,1987. David Kennedy, "Neighborhood Policing in Los Angeles," John F. Kennedy School of Government Case Program #C 15–86–717,1986.

11. This idea was most thoughtfully articulated in the Executive Session on Policing by Edwin Meese III, former Attorney General of the United States; Sir Kenneth Newman, former Commissioner of

Scotland Yard; and James K. Stewart, Director, National Institute of Justice.

12. John E. Eck and William Spelman, "Solving Problems: Problem-Oriented Policing in Newport News," Washington, D.C., Police Executive Research Forum, January 1987; Herman Goldstein, "Improving Policing: A Problem-Oriented Approach," Crime and Delinquency, April 1979: 236–58.

13. Susan Michaelson, George L. Kelling, and Robert Wasserman, "Toward a Working Definition of Community Policing," Working Paper No. 88–08–09, Project in Criminal Justice Policy and Management, John F. Kennedy School of Government, Harvard University, January 1988.

14. George L. Kelling and Mark H. Moore, "The Evolving Strategy of Policing," Perspectives on Policing No. 4, Washington, D.C., National Institute of Justice and Harvard University, November 1988.

15. Mark H. Moore, Robert C. Trojanowicz, and George L. Kelling, "Crime and Policing," Perspectives on Policing No. 2, Washington, D.C., National Institute of Justice and Harvard University, June 1988.

16. Mark H. Moore, "Invisible Offenses: A Challenge to Minimally Intrusive Law Enforcement," in Abscam Ethics, ed. Gerald M. Caplan, Washington, D.C., Police Foundation, 1983.

17. Wesley G. Skogan and George E. Antunes, "Information, Apprehension, and Deterrence: Exploring the Limits of Police Productivity," Journal of Criminal Justice 7, 1979: 217–42.

18. Edmund F. McGarrel and Timothy J. Flanagan, eds., Sourcebook of Criminal Justice Statistics—1984, Washington, D.C., Bureau of Justice Statistics, 1985: 215.

19. United States Kerner Commission Supplemental Studies for the National Advisory Commission on Civil Disorders, New York, Praeger, 1968.

20. This idea emerged from the Executive Session on Policing at Harvard University's Kennedy School of Government, 1985–88.

21. Integrated Criminal Apprehension Program Review of Patrol Operations Analysis: Selected Readings from ICAP Cities, Washington, D.C., Law Enforcement Assistance Administration, 1978.

22. Robert Trojanowicz et al., Community Policing Programs: A Twenty-Year View, East Lansing, Michigan State University, The National Neighborhood Foot Patrol Center, 1986: 36.

23. This idea was presented by Sir Kenneth Newman, former Commissioner of Scotland Yard, at the Executive Session on Policing.

24. Eck and Spelman, "Solving Problems: Problem-Oriented Policing in Newport News"; Goldstein, "Improving Policing: A Problem-Oriented Approach."

25. Daniel McGillis, "Community Dispute Resolution Programs and Public Policy," Washington, D.C., U.S. Department of Justice, December 1986.

26. *Philadelphia and Its Police: Toward A New Partnership.*

27. Eck and Spelman, "Solving Problems: Problem-Oriented Policing in Newport News"; Goldstein, "Improving Policing: A Problem-Oriented Approach."

28. Antony Pate et al., *Reducing Fear of Crime in Houston and Newark: A Summary Report,* Washington, D.C., Police Foundation, 1986.

29. Ibid.

30. Ibid.

31. William DeJong, "Arresting the Demand for Drugs: Police and School Partnerships to Prevent Drug Abuse," Washington, D.C., U.S. Department of Justice, November 1987.

32. George L. Kelling and Mark H. Moore, "Observations on the Police Industry,"" Working Paper #85–05–03, Program in Criminal Justice Policy and Management, John F. Kennedy School of Government, Harvard University, Cambridge, 1987.

CONCEPT #6: INSTITUTE POSITIVE VALUES AND ETHICAL GUIDELINES

*It's not hard to make decisions when you know
what your values are.*

—Roy Disney

Five readings are presented in this chapter. First is a reading on lies and deception in law enforcement. A definition of lying is provided, along with a deception continuum. In this continuum we see that there are acceptable and unacceptable lies in law enforcement. On the acceptable end are those lies which are excusable and justifiable. On the unacceptable end, there are the lies which are malicious and involve abuse of discretion. In the conclusion of these reading, recommendations are presented which include an organizational values statement that must be development by the chief executive.

Your second reading deals with noble cause corruption, or corruption that is committed in the name of good ends. This corruption involves planting evidence, falsifying testimony and lying on reports, all so that charges stick. Although noble in nature, this misconduct can have serious consequences for the enforcement agency. These consequences may range from tarnished images to multi-million dollar lawsuits.

The third reading in this chapter is a summary of a research project on the topic of police integrity. Police officers in thirty agencies were surveyed with four dimensions used to assess integrity: organizational rules, prevention and control mechanisms, the code (of silence) and public expectations. In the sampling several key findings were discovered regarding officer beliefs regarding integrity. As the survey results were obtained from officers, the findings have direct implications for administrators.

Next, is a reading on police attitudes regarding abuse of authority. In this research project nearly one thousand officers from over one hundred departments were surveyed. The officers were asked key questions regarding use of police authority, abuse of authority and whistle blowing. It was discovered that most officers do not condone abusive practices and it was discovered that a department's chief and first-line supervisors play important roles in preventing abuse.

The fifth and final reading in this chapter addresses the concept of values in policing. Values are those things that matter to us. In the world of law enforcement these things may be truth, honesty, fairness, courage or a host of numerous other key words and concepts. This reading discusses how police departments are influenced by their values, either in a positive or negative manner. You will learn how values are articulated or expressed. Also, you will learn how values can be used as a management tool. You will learn specific values in policing and then even more specific, the values of community policing. In conclusion, you will learn techniques for implementing values through written value statements.

Lies, True Lies, and Conscious Deception

Police Officers and the Truth

By Goeffrey P. Alpert and Jeffrey J. Noble, Esq.

Police officers often tell lies; they act in ways that are deceptive, they manipulative people and situations, they coerce citizens, and are dishonest. They are taught, encouraged, and often rewarded for their deceptive practices. Officers often lie to suspects about witnesses and evidence, and they are deceitful when attempting to learn about criminal activity. Most of these actions are sanctioned, legal, and expected. Although they are allowed to be dishonest in certain circumstances, they are also required to be trustworthy, honest, and maintain the highest level of integrity. The purpose of this article is to explore situations when officers can be dishonest, some reasons that help us understand the dishonesty, and circumstances where lies may lead to unintended consequences such as false confessions. The authors conclude with a discussion of how police agencies can manage the lies that officers tell and the consequences for the officers, organizations, and the criminal justice system.

Keywords: police deception; lies; investigations; ethics

To perform their job effectively, police officers lie. They use deception, manipulation, and coercion to obtain important information from suspects. Police officers often tell those suspected of committing crimes that they possess physical evidence implicating the suspect when no such evidence exists. Officers tell suspects that they have witnesses who have identified or implicated the suspect when the witness either does not exist or when the witness never made any such statement. Officers will tell suspects that some type of lie-detecting technology such as a polygraph or voice stress analyzer has conclusively shown that the suspect was lying when the officer knows that the technology does not exist, does not work, did not indicate deception, or was inconclusive. Police officers will deceive by omission, conceal their identity, and even deny that they are police officers while attempting to gain evidence of the criminal actions of another. They will work to create a perception of safety in their communities knowing full well that dangerous crime exists. Indeed, officers engage in a wide range of deception limited only by their imaginations. Although some of these deceptive practices may be excusable or justifiable, others may create ethical concerns and some are beyond the bounds of the law or ethical policing.

The police are allowed to be deceptive in certain circumstances, but they are also required to be trustworthy, honest, and maintain the highest level of integrity. Police officers are held to a higher standard than non-police as they represent the government as agents of the law and the criminal justice system. Often, their word and their "honesty" is taken over that of a civilian in legal proceedings, and judges will most frequently award a "tie," a "he said, she said," or a "swearing contest" to the officer. For example, when an officer gives a speeding ticket to an individual who protests the speed or driving, it is rare that a judge will rule that the civilian is telling the truth and the officer is telling a lie. Although officers are expected to tell the truth, and our system of criminal justice demands, and relies on it; there are transgressions, and officers have been caught stretching the truth without incident, and courts have ruled that some lies are appropriate but others are not. The purpose of this article is to explore situations when officers can lie, some reasons that help us understand the explanations given for the appropriateness and justification of the lies, and areas where lies may be lawful but may lead to unintended consequences such as false confessions. Our focus is on lies told during interrogations as well as administrative lies. We conclude with a discussion of how police agencies can manage the lies that officers tell and the consequences for the officers, organizations, and the criminal justice system.

In 1991, Hunt and Manning wrote, "Police, like many people in official capacities lie" (p. 51). Their insightful article informed us that lying is a valuable way for the police to manipulate people and situations, and officers are rewarded for their dishonesty: "Lying is a sanctioned practice" (p. 52). Beyond the police, it has been argued that deception in the workplace is functional and normal (Shulman, 2006), and that our criminal justice system is based on lies and untruths, and officials, including judges, looking the other way when the truth is inconvenient (Dershowitz, 1996, 1998). In his testimony to Congress, and his analysis of the O. J. Simpson trial, Dershowitz (1996, 1998) examined the work of police officers, defense attorneys, and prosecutors and concluded that all parties encourage or tolerate lying throughout the criminal process. His comments about the civil justice process are just as condemning. Although his "proof" may not be perfect, his arguments are compelling, and his comments about the lack of truthfulness and veracity ring true and raise enough issues and questions that they must be taken seriously. Although Deshowitz (1996, 1998) attacks our systems of justice, our focus in this article is on one aspect of justice: the police. In a law enforcement profession where officer credibility is critical, and agencies need to include some policy statement prohibiting lying (see Noble, 2003; Noble & Alpert, 2009), it is amazing that the practice not only continues but also flourishes.

As necessary and straightforward as the prohibition seems, there are underlying complexities that make it difficult if not impossible to manage and enforce. Lies are not a fixed target. Deception exists on a continuum, from what is commonly called social lies or little white lies, where no consequences follow, to egregious misconduct that warrants dismissal or prosecution. Police administrators are faced with concerns at almost all points of the continuum. Lies during the interrogation process, although lawful, may present ethical challenges. Malicious lies require the fortitude to remove the officer from the organization. But the true challenge is deciding how to deal with deceptive conduct that falls in the middle of the continuum—not so egregious that termination is the only solution yet not far enough toward justifiable or excusable that the behavior can be ignored.

What Is Lying?

A *lie* is any intentionally deceptive message communicated either verbally or in writing. Lying is a subset of the larger category of deception. Deception consists of any intention to trick others by communicating messages meant to mislead and to make the recipients believe what the agent (the person performing or committing the act) either knows or believes to be untrue. Deception involves more than spoken or written statements. It includes any intentional conduct that conveys a message to the listener—including omissions. For example, physical expressions such as a shoulder shrug, eye movement, or silence can be deceptive (Bok, 1999). Lies can be made by an individual officer, which is the focus of this article, or encouraged by organizations. Police departments encourage lying by permitting it to exist or promoting it. For example, if a call comes out at the end of an officer's shift and an officer informs dispatch that he or she is busy because he or she does not want to handle the call that will continue way past the shift change, the officer's lie is a burden on other officers and inappropriate. However, the managers may condone the behavior as they do not want to have to pay overtime to the officer.

More troubling than looking the other way at deceptive conduct that helps the organization maintain its budget, yet creates no harm to the community, are organizational tolerances and implicit support of individual officer lies that promote the organization. Consider officers who fail to take crime reports. After determining no insurance claim will be filed, these officers may convince a victim not to formally report a crime, suggesting that there is little likelihood that the offender will be identified or that the property will be recovered. Other officers may create the impression that they are documenting the crime but have no intention of actually completing the report. In both instances, the officers are motivated by laziness or incompetence. The actions of the officer who looks as if he or she is documenting the incident may appease the victim, but the result is the same. First, the lower numbers allow the organization to create an impression of addressing crime effectively. Second, these same numbers harm the community by creating a false picture of the nature and extent of crime.

Officers who lie as individuals often influence the organizational customs and culture, which include distrust and suspiciousness of citizens, and a strong loyalty to fellow officers. Thus, police culture can best be illustrated by the linkages among values, traditions, and corporate strategy. Each of these components can explain the importance of deception and lying by police officers—to protect themselves and band together against the criminals. As the organization learns to accept the behavior, the culture of the department becomes accustomed to lying, and the longer it continues, the harder it is to end (see Crank, 2004). The issues of organizational meekness or encouragement are important and can influence the culture of the agency and individual officer deception. These types of deception come in many forms, and their range can be best understood on a continuum of intent.

Deception Continuum

Deceptive conduct by the police is easier to assess when it is illustrated on a continuum. At one end of the continuum are the types of lies that may be considered acceptable. That end of the continuum contains excusable lies (lies made in jest or socially acceptable lies) and justifiable lies (lies that may be defendable based on the circumstances). The other end of the continuum contains intentional, malicious, and deceptive conduct that will take one of three forms:

- Deceptive action in a formal setting, such as testifying in court or during an investigation;
- Failure to bring forward information involving criminal action by other officers, also known as observing the so-called code of silence; and
- Creation of false evidence that tends to implicate another in a criminal act.

Intentional, malicious, and deceptive conduct in any of these three areas will permanently destroy an officer's credibility. If an officer violates these standards, there should be no alternative in an employment context other than termination or permanent removal from any possible activity that requires a reliable truthful person.

Conduct that reveals an abuse of an officer's discretion is similarly placed at the unacceptable end of the continuum. Police officers have a wide range of discretionary decision-making power that is necessary to maintaining an effective and efficient police force. The concern is not that officers are entrusted with various powers; indeed, we entrust officers with an incredible amount of power to detain, search, and arrest, all without the approval of a magistrate. But the alarm sounds when officers abuse their powers in a capricious, arbitrary, and unfair manner. When officers inappropriately use deception to target a person or group, it is an abuse of power that requires serious attention from administrators.

The center of the continuum contains a wide range of lies and deceptive practices that may be acceptable or unacceptable depending on the circumstances. These middle continuum deceptive practices are more difficult to assess. Frequently, these middle continuum deceptions involve what may be termed "administrative lies." *Administrative lies* are intentional acts of deception aimed to prevent some type of employment action rather than acts related to the officer's power as a police officer. For example, an officer may lie about completing a report or performing a minor task. Although such a transgression is not appropriate, it may or may not warrant the termination of the officer. Other examples become apparent when officers complete a variety of reports, including "use-of-force" or "response to suspect resistance" forms. Although it is well known that some officers use unnecessary and excessive force, it is unlikely that officers report that level of force on an official form (Alpert & Dunham, 2004). Furthermore, officers are not likely to admit they have been drinking on duty or fail to wear seatbelts (Kim, 1999). These omissions, incomplete reports, untruths, or lies are likely more prevalent than one would like to believe and may involve a wide variety of activities.

ACCEPTABLE CONDUCT

Excusable Lies

Excusable lies are acts of deception where there is no intent of harm and little likelihood that harm will actually occur. These acts encompass jokes, "white" lies, minor embellishments, and exaggerations. These acts are such common practice in human communication that deceptive conduct would be impossible to prevent entirely by any rule, law, policy, or manner of enforcement (Nyberg, 1993). From the social kindness of white lies to embellishments, exaggerations, and boastful behavior, the truth is concealed for a variety of reasons. The fact that we condone these activities is evident in the fact that we teach our children the art of deception at an early age (Bronson, 2008). Children learn from their parents, friends, television, books, and other sources how to deceive. They learn how to maintain a poker face, so they do not reveal information that could help observers. Young athletes learn skills necessary to survive, including a bluff, a

deceptive move, a fake throw, or a way to disguise a change in direction with a head or body fake.

Deception concerning trivial matters, often told to spare another's feelings, may also be excusable. These white lies are meant not for any personal gain but rather for social courtesy. Not every social situation calls for the whole truth. How do I look? What do you think? and What a cute baby? Sometimes benign statements or tactful silence are the most appropriate responses to some situations.

Lies made in jest, although sometimes callous and hurtful, do not affect an officer's credibility unless they are in such bad taste that they call into question the person's judgment in general. Officers frequently embellish and exaggerate the misfortunes of others in conversations with each other. A sense of humor, even where some deception is involved, helps responsible people cope with stress and grim circumstances (see Davis, 1995). Although deceptive humor is sometimes an acceptable practice, it is not a shield to the disciplinary process. When jokes become malicious lies that intentionally harm others, they must be investigated and if found harmful, discipline must be imposed. Police managers should not strive to create such a sterile workplace that humor is forbidden; they would succeed only in making themselves objects of derision and ridicule. Police leaders should seek to establish and enforce reasonable standards.

Justifiable Lies

Police officers frequently engage in deceptive conduct to perform their duties. Officers perform secretly in undercover operations seeking to gain evidence on the targets of their investigations. While undercover, they may lie about their identity, their past acts, or their plans of criminal activity. Police officers use unmarked cars and some police agencies have even created fake silhouettes of police cars to deceive motorists into decreasing their speed. Police departments around the country have embraced the *Broken Windows* theory that by addressing quality of life crimes, they can create a perception of safety and thereby actually decrease crime (Kelling & Coles, 1996). Although an effective deterrent that many studies have shown may actually reduce more serious crime, it is nonetheless deceptive in that community members may believe that certain areas are safe based on their individualized perception, created deceptively by the police, only to be victimized by the area's reality.

But perhaps most interesting, and ethically difficult, is that officers routinely lie to those suspected of committing crimes during interrogations in an attempt to elicit the truth. These acts of manipulation and deception are not only taught and encouraged but also they are lawful and permitted by the courts. Inasmuch as these acts of deception are lawful, they fall on the acceptable side of the continuum. There is, however, a legitimate concern that certain types of deceptive practices may cause an innocent person to falsely confess, that by accepting some types of deceptive practices as legitimate that the police may fashion a belief that all deception is acceptable, and a public perception that police officers are not trustworthy (Crank, 2004).

The courts have held that trickery and deceit may be used by the police to elicit a confession as long as their actions do not "shock the conscience" of the court, or be the type of action that would induce an innocent person to confess (Inbau, Reid, Buckley, & Jayne, 2004). Such a holding is reasonable in that it is counterintuitive that anyone other than someone who had been physically tortured or who is mentally ill would confess to a crime that they did not commit (Leo, 2008). After all, why else would someone confess to a crime and subject themselves to a criminal record, fine, imprisonment, or even the death penalty? Yet with the advent of DNA testing in the mid-1990s, there have been more than 50 documented cases of wrongful conviction based on the confession of an innocent person who was neither tortured nor mentally ill (Innocence Project, 2008).

The use of torture or deprivation has given way to modern interrogation techniques that rely on psychological coercive methods. The modern officer will isolate the suspect and attempt to persuade him that there is no alternative other than to confess, that the officer wants to help, and that the suspect would be better off by confessing—none of which is true (Leo, 2008). These techniques are thought to be a necessary part of policing to overcome a suspect's will not to incriminate himself or herself. These techniques are very effective, but they have also led to at least some false confessions by persuasion of a person who has no memory of the crime, or coercion by the use of promises or threats. This type of psychological coercion appears to have its greatest impact on the highly suggestible or compliant individuals, such as the mentally retarded or cognitively impaired, juveniles, or the mentally ill (Leo, 2008).

The key to determining if the confession was voluntary and valid lies in the words of the interrogator and the words of the suspect. By reviewing the actual statements, one can determine if the interrogator was overly suggestive, whether the suspect or the interrogator actually voiced the corroborating information, and whether any promises or threats were made.

UNACCEPTABLE CONDUCT

Malicious Lies

Although lies justified by necessity, lies told in jest, and white lies may be acceptable forms of deception in law enforcement, malicious lies are not. Malice on the part of the communicator includes both lies told for personal gain and lies that exceed the limits of legitimacy. The problem of police falsification was so common that that the Mollen commission (Mollen, 1994) created a new word, "testilying," to explain the problem (see Capers, 2008). For example, a police officer may be tempted to testify falsely to imprison a criminal. The public might approve of the officers' intention to remove a criminal from society, and the officer may validate his or her behavior by believing that he or she is engaging in a greater good. In this case, the ends are justified by the means. Carl Klockars (1980) referred to this dilemma as the Dirty Harry problem, and asked rhetorically "when and to what extent does the morally good end warrant or justify an ethically, politically, or legally dangerous means to its achievement?" (p. 34).

Similarly, presenting false evidence intended to harm a suspect or engaging in the so-called "code of silence" where an officer fails to come forward with information on the serious misconduct of another officer is intentional malicious misconduct. Not only is this conduct an affront to the values of policing but also under the *Brady v. Maryland* (1963) decision, that requires the police department to disclose these dishonest acts of officers, the officer would be rendered useless as a witness. In these instances, there is no alternative other than to terminate an officer who has breached his or her trust to the organization and to the community.

It is important to understand that motive or intentions can be mixed, so that a person may deceive to pursue some worthwhile utilitarian goal (such as public safety) and at the same time have a malicious disregard for the rights of the suspect and for the laws, policies, and limits that apply to policing. This willingness to betray basic principles of honesty attacks the very public safety that the person believes himself or herself to be pursuing. A police officer who by malicious disregard goes beyond the limits of legitimacy is a threat to the public safety. He or she could be capable of violating anybody's rights—poisoning the idea of public safety.

Abuse of Discretion

Police officers abuse their power when they engage in certain types of deception. Officers similarly abuse their power when they inappropriately abuse their discretion. The nature of police work demands that a significant level of discretionary decision making be placed in the hands of what are most often the least trained and the least seasoned officers in the organization. These officers, unlike professionals in other fields, typically work by themselves in a field environment where access to a supervisor is limited and seldom immediately available. Yet these officers routinely make decisions that have a tremendous impact on an individual's personal liberties. The officer has the discretion to decide to detain, arrest, and/or use force to gain compliance.

Discretionary decision making is an inherent part of police work. There is simply no reasonable alternative to granting significant discretionary abilities to police officers. It would be neither practical nor prudent to attempt to establish a policy or procedure to address every possible situation that an officer may face. Police officers are expected to properly assess situations and to exercise judgment as to when and how they should use their power. The ability to make responsible choices based on training and experience is the distinguishing feature that makes a police officer a professional.

Every day hundreds of thousands of police officers make decisions that affect a vast number of people. For the most part, these decisions are made with care and are appropriate for the situation facing the officer. Police managers are also aware that some officers will make mistakes and others will intentionally abuse their authority. Furthermore, some officers believe that if there is no rule specifying acceptable behavior for a particular situation, that they cannot be questioned on the decision-making process or the actions they take. However, this belief is simply not true. The idea of discretion is that you have choices—not that they cannot be reviewed. Discretionary decision making is indeed subject to review, and abuses of discretion may have both legal and disciplinary consequences.

When discussing discretionary decision making, there is a significant difference between mistakes and abuse of power. Mistakes in the decision-making process lead to poor conclusions. Although such decisions are improper, they can be remedied by taking action to reverse the consequences of the decision and by providing training to an officer to increase the likelihood of more reasonable decisions and conclusions in the future. The key to determining if an officer mistakenly applied discretion is whether an officer acted in good faith and relied on reasonable criteria.

In 2004, the Baltimore Police Department engaged in a practice that illustrates the hazards of police discretion when the decision-making process is based on improper criteria. The practice, which was unofficially condoned by department leaders, encouraged officers to negotiate the release of individuals arrested for drug crimes or petty offenses if the arrestee could recover and turn in a gun to the officer (Ludwig and Cook, 2003; National Research Council, 2005). When questioned about arrestees trading guns for freedom, a department commander stated that the program's goals were a worthwhile and beneficial effort to take crime guns off the streets.

Taking guns off the streets in an attempt to reduce violent crime is certainly a worthwhile goal. But the tactics employed by the Baltimore Police Department effectively subverted the justice system by not filing criminal complaints on arrestees in cases where the arrestee was able to buy his or her freedom by producing a handgun and delivering it to the police. This type of ends-justify-the-means decision making is more than merely problematic; it undermines the ability of the community to feel that they are being treated fairly. Klockars might well think that Harry Callahan were chief of a department making those decisions!

Michael Josephson (2005) of the Josephson Institute of Ethics developed an outline of criteria to determine if an officer abused his or her authority. These criteria are useful in the analysis of abuse of discretion allegations.

Proper Criteria

- officer believes that a warning will be an effective deterrent;
- the offender is apologetic or remorseful;
- seriousness of the conduct;
- mental health status;
- use of weapons, violence, or threat of violence;
- repeat offender; and
- high probability that the conduct will continue if affirmative action is not taken.

Improper Criteria

- race, ethnicity, or gender;
- appearance (enforcing laws broken by unkempt individuals while ignoring similar behavior by attractive offenders);
- wealth;
- type of vehicle;
- political reasons;
- officer laziness (to avoid work, visibility, overtime, or court);
- ends-justify-the-means thinking;

- employment of offender (police officer, firefighter, judge, or city council member).

Officers who abuse their discretion by relying on improper criteria are doing so in a malicious intentional way or as a form of noble cause corruption. These officers know that their decision making is improper and their abuse of discretion and deceit is as powerful and improper as a malicious lie. The use of appropriate criteria and the avoidance of improper criteria are critical components of an officer's discretionary decision-making model. This foundation may not prevent good-faith mistakes, but good-faith efforts to make decisions on reasonable criteria will likely earn the trust of the community.

MIDDLE OF THE CONTINUUM CONDUCT

As noted earlier, the problem for administrators is not the conduct at the ends of the continuum. Acceptable conduct requires no action and unacceptable conduct requires immediate intervention. But when conduct falls between the two extremes, decisions about discipline become more difficult. Consider the following example:

> A supervisor asks an officer whether a particular report has been completed. The report itself is of very little consequence, and the question was prompted by a routine administrative action rather than any specific employee concern. The officer has not submitted the report but quickly replies that the report was submitted. The officer then immediately completes the report and turns it in before the supervisor can discover the lie.

In this example, the officer was dishonest. He was asked a direct question by a supervisor and he lied. This misconduct is neither justifiable nor excusable. The question was not posed as part of a formal process, the officer was not engaging in an action to protect another officer, and the conduct in question did not place a community member at risk.

Is the conduct sufficiently deceptive to be punished by termination? There is a strong argument for termination in this case. After all, the officer was asked a direct question by a supervisor about a work-related subject, and the officer responded untruthfully. The difficulty for managers is balancing the necessity to have officers who are beyond reproach against the fact that all officers are human beings who sometimes make mistakes. The officer's response may best be described as a spontaneous unthinking reaction to avoid a minor reprimand from a superior. Several factors should be considered in making a final determination. Is the officer remorseful? Does the officer recognize the error? Does the officer have an otherwise acceptable record with the department? and Was the underlying issue important enough to indicate potential serious consequences from the officer's behavior?

> Consider this example:
> A dispatcher asks an officer if he is available for a call. The officer radios that he is out of service and unavailable, when in fact he does not want to receive a call because it is near the end of his shift. Based on the officer's statement, the dispatcher assigns the calls to another officer.

As in the last scenario, the officer's conduct is neither justifiable nor excusable. Once again, a determination must be made about whether the conduct is serious enough to warrant termination. This type of intentional deceptive misconduct, which can be termed "administrative deception," creates dilemmas for police management.

UNDERSTANDING LIES

Perhaps the number one lie in police work is "I don't recall." This is a classic case of deception by omission that can take several forms. First, officers can forget that an incident took place. Second, they can forget parts of the incident. Because of radio broadcasts, computer records, and testimony of other officers and witnesses, it is not likely that an officer will be able to forget an incident totally. However, if an officer is going to hide something, it is more likely that he or she will "strategically" lie to justify an action or to "win" a controversy. In this situation, officers may tell the truth about the incident but conveniently forget one issue that happens to be the critical part. For example, an officer who witnesses another officer use force on a resisting suspect may recall the specific events leading up to the final frame, but may not recall how the suspect received a serious injury. On one hand, the involved officer may explain in his or her report or to an internal affairs investigator that the suspect was fighting and when he or she was tackled, his or her head hit the pavement, causing serious injuries. The suspect, on the other hand, may claim that the officer slammed his or her head on the concrete by pulling his or her hair after he or she had quit resisting. Clearly, one of the parties is lying and independent witness statements will go a long way in convincing the investigators which version is likely to have happened (see Alpert & Dunham, 2004). Although it is obvious that these discrepancies exist, and we know that suspects lie to avoid responsibility and punishment, it is not as easy to figure out why officers lie, beyond the same reasons given for the suspects.

Using a theoretical approach designed to explain individual police officer's biased responses to minority citizens, we offer reasons why officers may become accustom to deceiving citizens and lying. Our approach is based on social psychological research on social conditioning that results in the internal justification for deceit and lies (see Smith & Alpert, 2007).

Unconscious Approval

Social psychologists have long sought to measure how and why people respond to stimuli. Specifically, cognitive theorists recognize that learning includes acquiring or reorganizing information or observations. Furthermore, the relative power of learning varies according to the degree of familiarity, success, and approval one receives from patterned responses (Brehm, Kassin, & Fein, 2002; Good & Brophy, 1990). In other words, experiences, scripts, or cognitive schema develop as shorthand for entering events into categories of memory. This process may start as simple and loosely organized experiences but can evolve into systematic and complex relationships. For example, children learn to lie from their parents and learn from the authority figures to accept lies (Bronson, 2008). Other research findings provide evidence that these schemas developed by children and adults form a mental model that plays a key role in predicting a person's responses to other individuals, places, and things in future encounters or events (Brehm et al., 2002; Bower, Black, & Turner, 1979). Once formed, persons, places, or situations that have familiar characteristics or properties will activate these cognitive schemas and result in familiar responses (Vrij, 2000). For example, it is likely that familiar behaviors or responses will be triggered when one is involved in a situation that has been successful in the past when a given response has been successful. A learned pattern of behavior is an expected response to a stressful or ambiguous situation. Once a person has identified a specific response that has been successful or "victorious," future behavioral patterns will be predicted on the previously developed schema. In other words, unless police officers who have told lies in the past with no negative consequences can "learn" to be truthful, and acquire and accumulate antideceptive attitudes and beliefs, it is likely that the deception and lies will continue and possibly grow in frequency and seriousness (DePaulo et al., 2003).

The role of stored information in decision making has been the subject of research on social cognition. The accessibility of information, its history, or the ease with which it can be recalled is a strong predictor of how people act toward others (Sherman, Judd, & Park, 1989; Tversky & Kahneman, 1973). The body of literature on social cognition suggests that responses to situations are learned behaviors that develop after repetitive activities. This learned behavior can act as organizational scripts for social memory and thus guide actions in future encounters (Noseworthy & Lott, 1984). For example, if police officers use deceptive practices and "lie" repetitively with nonnegative results, they will likely develop cognitive scripts that link deception and success. If officers are taught to be deceptive in one aspect of their work, it makes sense that when possible, the success will be transferred to other aspects of work (DePaulo et al., 2003). Over a period of time, it is likely that the police will process new situations through the filter of existing schemas and successes that become easier to recall because of the large number of times the use of deception and lying is successful and easy to do. On a more practical level, many recruits who enter police work wanting to be honest learn to lie in the academy, observe their training officers make changes in reports, reduce the seriousness of crime statistics in certain areas, and augment the information of warrants (Hunt & Manning, 1991). Finally, many of these same young officers begin to mirror the experiences of their mentors. In other words, they learn to lie, are not sanctioned for it, and come to believe it makes their work easier and less complicated. After a while, it becomes a learned behavior and one of the common tools of the job.

Specifying a Reason for Lying

Our approach begins with the notion that police officers view themselves as crime fighters—soldiers in a "war" on crime. Beyond the "winning the war" mentality, police work provides a rich environment for the ends-justify-the-means mentality. Because the police maintain social control, officers must routinely be in contact with those who break the law. Through learned and reinforced behavior, police officers are at high risk for developing a pattern and practice of deception and lying that goes beyond what is "normal" and acceptable. There exists a growing and persuasive body of literature suggests that such behavior is likely an unconscious reaction (Graham & Lowery, 2004; Greenwald & Banaji, 1995).

We propose that such *unconscious* behavior is the most plausible explanation for the widespread lying that occurs among police officers. Skolnick (1982) has informed us:

I cannot here reconcile such inconsistencies, nor am I writing to lobby the Supreme Court. But I would like to conclude by suggesting that apparent inconsistency makes law look more like a game than a rational system for enforcing justice. Because of this appearance of inconsistency, police are not likely to take the stated rules of the game seriously and are encouraged to operate by their own codes, including those which affirm the necessity for lying wherever it seems justified by the ends. (p. 54)

CONCLUSIONS/RECOMMENDATIONS

Most deceptive police practices are unlikely to stop and indeed, there is no legitimate cause that would support discontinuing undercover operations, operatives lying about their true identity, using unmarked cars, or even creating the perception of safety in absence of a safe and secure environment. Similarly, it is unlikely that the police or the courts will change their views on the use of deception to seek the truth during an interrogation. But there are steps that should be taken to ensure that officers do not slip from acceptable deception into intentional malicious deceptive misconduct. First, officers should be trained as to the possible consequences of deceptive interrogation practices, how to avoid these practices, and how to elicit a truthful confession. Second, the police should receive training on the understanding and recognition of lies and particularly of officers' unconscious approval of deceptive conduct. Finally, chief executives need to take a strong role to communicate, demonstrate, and uphold the values of professional law enforcement and be willing to separate employees from the organization who behave in a manner contrary to these high-ethical standards.

Interrogations

The advent of DNA analysis has conclusively shown that at least some individuals falsely confess to crimes and that deceptive psychologically coercive interrogation techniques particularly as they are imposed on vulnerable groups are a factor in the false confession. Because interrogations of suspects by officers intentionally occur in isolation and because

the determination of inappropriate interrogation practices such as promises, threats, or the intentional or unintentional conveyance of corroborating information to the suspect, stem to stern recordings of all interrogations of serious crimes should be mandated.

The benefits of videotaping include the following:

- provides transparency to the interview process,
- allows the detective to have greater focus on the suspect rather than on note taking,
- provides evidence that the detectives did not coerce the suspect to make admissions or to confess, and
- allows the jury to make a credibility assessment of the suspect as they were being interrogated (Cronin et al., 2007).

The recording of interrogations allows police supervisors and management along with others in the criminal justice system to evaluate the reliability of the confession. The context of any confession or statements made that can be observed in a video tape provides the best method to understand how the information was obtained or "volunteered." This evaluation would consider (a) whether the confession contains nonpublic information that can be independently verified, would be known only by the true perpetrator or an accomplice, and cannot likely be guessed by chance; (b) whether the confession led the police to new evidence about the crime; and (c) whether the suspect's postadmission narrative fits the crime facts and other objective evidence (Leo, 2008).

Some police officials have voiced concerns that include the following:

- reluctance to reveal investigative tactics (such as lying),
- a belief that recording will inhibit the suspect's cooperation,
- questions of legality,
- concerns of costs, and
- a belief that recordings might make detectives overly reliant on technology (Cronin et al, 2007; Leo, 2008).

There is no evidence that a recording will have a chilling effect on the willingness of a suspect to submit to interrogation by refusing to talk, becoming silent during the interrogation, or to not make admissions (Leo, 2008). Indeed, there are several jurisdictions that now mandate recordings for serious crimes (e.g., Alaska, Minnesota, Illinois, District of Columbia, Maine, New Mexico, Wisconsin, and North Carolina), and there is no evidence that would suggest that these jurisdictions or the many other agencies in other jurisdictions that record interrogations have had a decrease in confessions because of recording. Interestingly, a similar "chilling effect" argument was posited after the *Miranda* decision was announced. Where a tape recorder may possibly be viewed as a warning not to talk, the *Miranda* decision was specifically designed to be a red flag encouraging those suspected of crimes to seek advice of counsel. Yet *Miranda* warnings have generally been ineffective, and it is doubtful that the presence of a tape recorder could somehow convey a stronger message than the direct statements mandated by *Miranda*.

Training

Police training is generally pragmatic—rules are explained and procedures are outlined. Philosophical discussion of the rules or procedures seldom plays a meaningful role in police training. Police officers should be taught not to lie, or at least if they do, to do so in a manner that is legal, ethical, and not harmful. It is easy to imagine that an officer who is taught to deceive for a worthy purpose might extend their knowledge beyond what is permitted. Therefore, police training should contain discussion and a thorough overview of the concerns of deceptive practices and their limits.

All officers should receive training in police-induced false confessions. Interrogators should be able to recognize groups of people who may be susceptible to suggestive interrogation techniques, what causes an innocent person to confess falsely, and through this improved training, how to be more effective at eliciting truthful confessions (Leo, 2008).

Another important step for all police officers is ongoing ethics and ethical decision-making training. Many police academies have incorporated ethics training into their curriculum. These introductory courses provide the student with basic concepts that one would hope all police officers would inculcate as they enter a career in law enforcement. But as these students attend one course on how to be an ethical officer, they attend subsequent courses teaching them how to deceive to achieve the noble means of removing criminals from the streets. These deceptive techniques are further expanded as the new officers enter their field-training program where they work one-on-one with a training officer. Under this intense and isolated training environment that occurs away from supervision, young officers may be indoctrinated to types of deceptive conduct never imagined by police management. It is for these reasons that character training based on commonly held values, such as respect, responsibility, fairness, honesty, and justice be mandated as ongoing professional training for all officers (Callahan, 2004). Finally, this training must be more than merely asking officers to do the right thing. The training must be supported by an organizational culture that views character and values as the cornerstone of professionalism.

Discipline

Our final recommendation requires that chief administrators make the tough decisions that are commensurate with their position. There is simply no alternative to terminating an employee who has engaged in intentional, malicious, and deceptive conduct. As we have discussed, if an employee perjures herself or himself in court, during an internal affairs investigation, or if they fail to bring forward information involving criminal activity of other officers (code of silence) or if they create false evidence that tends to implicate another in a criminal act, including an affidavit for a warrant, that officer's employment must immediately cease.

It is the responsibility of all chief executives to develop an organizational values statement and organizational culture that is consistent with the police officers' code of ethics. These guiding documents, supported by the words and actions of the command staff, form the foundation for all discipline meted out by the organization. Additionally, an employee should not only be directed to a specific policy section identifying their misconduct but also their actions should be identified as a violation of the department's stated values.

Police officers are sufficiently sophisticated and educated to know, understand, and recognize the difference between accepted deception and deception that is neither socially nor lawfully acceptable. Organizations cannot either implicitly or explicitly allow intentional deceptive misconduct by developing or allowing internal standards, at any level in the organization, which condones such behavior. On one hand, organizations must recognize the likelihood that officers will learn how to lie and be comfortable telling lies. They must plan to train and educate officers to avoid improper behavior. One the other hand, officers must learn the consequence of telling lies; that they are held to a high standard, and that their acceptance in the community is based on honesty and integrity. If an officer believes he or she can operate by his or her own rules, get away without recalling all of the facts, and believe that the ends justify the means, then criminal justice becomes more of a game than a system or even a method.

As Hunt and Manning (1991) warned us more than a decade ago, as officers become accustomed to lying and the organization allows and encourages the behavior, both the officers and the organization will begin to believe their lies and policing becomes more isolated, loses public trust and credibility. This direction must change if policing is to gain back the respect it needs and deserves.

Alpert, G., & Dunham, R. (2004). *Understanding police use of force: Officers, suspects, and reciprocity.* New York: Cambridge University Press.

Bok, S. (1999). *Lying: Moral choices in public and private life.* New York: Vintage.

Brady v. Maryland, 373 U.S. 83 (1963).

Brehm, S., Kassin, S., & Fein, S. (2002). *Social psychology* (5th ed.). Boston: Houghton Mifflin.

Bronson, P. (2008, February 18). Learning to lie. *New York Magazine.* Retrieved on October 27, 2008, from http://nymag.com/news/features/43893/

Callahan, D. (2004). *The cheating culture.* Orlando, FL: Harcourt Books.

Capers, B. (2008). Crime, legitimacy, and testilying. *Indiana Law Journal, 83,* 835-880.

Crank, J. P. (2004). *Understanding police culture* (2nd ed.). Cincinnati, OH: Anderson.

Cronin, J. M., Murphy, G. R., Spahr, L. L., Toliver, J. I., & Weger, R. E. (2006). *Promoting effective homicide investigations.* Washington, DC: Police Executive Research Forum.

Davis, M. (1995). The sociology of humor: A stillborn field? *Sociological Forum, 10,* 327–339.

DePaulo, B. M., Lindsay, J. J., Malone, B. E., Muhlenbruck, L., Charlton, K., & Cooper, H. (2003). Cues to deception. *Psychological Bulletin, 129,* 74–118.

Dershowitz, A. (1998). *Testimony in front of the house of representatives judiciary committee.* USGPO: Washington, DC.

Dershowitz, A. M. (1996). *Reasonable doubts: The criminal justice system and the O. J. Simpson case.* New York: Simon & Schuster.

Good, T., & Brophy, J. (1990). *Educational psychology: A realistic approach.* White Plains, NY: Longman.

Greenwald, A. G., & Banaji, M. R. (1995). Implicit social cognition: Attitudes, self-steem, and stereo types. *Psychological Review, 102,* 4–27.

Graham, S. & Lowery, B. S. (2004). Priming unconscious racial stereotypes about adolescent offenders. *Law and Human Behavior, 28*(5), 483–504.

Hunt, J., & Manning, P. K. (1991). The social context of police lying. *Symbolic Interaction, 14,* 51–70.

Inbau, F. E., Reid, J. E., Buckley, J. P., & Jayne, B. C. (2004). *Criminal interrogation and confessions* (4th ed.). Sudbury, MA: Jones and Bartlett.

Innocence Project. (2008). *False confessions.* Retrieved on October 27, 2008, from http://www.innocenceproject. org/understand/False-Confessions.php

Josephson, M. (2005). *Preserving the public trust.* Los Angeles, CA: Josephson Institute of Ethics.

Kelling, G. L., & Coles, C. M. (1996). *Fixing broken windows: Restoring order and reducing crime in our communities.* New York: Simon & Schuster.

Kim, K. (1999). Lie factor in traffic safety: Comparison of police and hospital reporting of seat belt and alcohol use in Hawaii. *Journal Transportation Research Record, 1665,* 141–146.

Klockars, C. 1980. The Dirty Harry Problem. The ANNALS of the American Academy of Political and Social Science 452: 33–47.

Leo, R. A. (2008). *Police interrogation and American justice.* Cambridge, MA: Harvard University Press. Ludwig, J. & P. Cook. 2003. Evaluating Gun Policy: Effects on Crime and Violence. Washington, DC: Brookings Institution Press, 2003.

Mollen, M. (1994). *Commission to investigate allegations of police corruption and the anti-corruption practices of the police department* (Commission Report 36). City of New York.

National Research Council. Committee on Law and Justice, Division of Behavioral and Social Sciences and Education. Firearms and violence: a critical review, Washington, DC: The National Academies Press, 2005.

Noble, J. 2003. Police Officer Truthfulness and the Brady decision. The Police Chief 70: 92–101.

Noble, J. and G. Alpert. (2009). Managing Accountability Systems for Police Conduct: Internal Affairs and External Oversight. Long Grove, IL: Waveland Press.

Noseworthy, C. M., & Lott, A. J. (1984). The cognitive organization of gender-stereotypiccategories. *Personality and Social Psychology Bulletin, 10,* 474–81.

Nyberg, D. (1993). *The varnished truth, truth telling and deceiving in ordinary life.* Chicago, IL: University of Chicago Press.

Sherman, S., Judd, C. M., & Park, B. (1989). Social cognition. *Annual Review of Psychology* 40: 281-326. Shulman, D. (2006). *From hire to liar: The role of deception workplace.* Ithica, NY: Cornell University Press.

Skolnick, J. (1982). Deception by police. *Criminal Justice Ethics, 1,* 40–54.

Smith, M. R., & Alpert, G. P. (2007). Explaining police bias: A theory of social conditioning and illusory correlation. *Criminal Justice and Behavior, 34,* 1262-1283.

Tversky, A. & Kahneman, D. (1973). Availability: A heuristic for judging frequency and probability. *Cognitive Psychology 5*: 207–32

Vrij, A. (2000). *Detecting lies and deceit: The psychology of lying and the implications for professional practice.* London: John Wiley.

Geoffrey P. Alpert is a professor of criminology and criminal justice at the University of South Carolina. He has been studying high-risk police activities for more than 25 years. He has published widely in professional and academic journals, and has written more than 15 books on criminal justice issues.

Jeffrey J. Noble, Esq. is a commander with the Irvine Police Department located in southern California. He was in charge of Internal Affairs for more than 4 years. He currently manages the police resources for the area of Irvine that includes the following: University of California at Irvine, Concordia University, and the business community adjacent to John Wayne airport.

Unconstitutional Policing

The Ethical Challenges in Dealing with Noble Cause Corruption

By Thomas Martinelli

Then uncovered as a pattern or practice, the police crimes defined as noble cause corruption can result in constitutional rights litigation that can financially cripple agencies. In promoting police integrity, the U.S. Department of Justice repeatedly emphasizes the duty of law enforcement agents to respect the value and dignity of every person, including criminal citizens.[1] The Department of Justice has recently emphasized this message, and has entered into consent decrees with cities stemming from allegations of patterns of police abuse of authority.

Rogue officers are tempted to engage in noble cause corruption in situations where they perceive no administrative accountability and decide to push the constitutional envelope, even though police must know and respect the constitutional laws upon which their very authority is derived. Departmental leaders must address noble cause corruption by defining what it is, what fosters it, and how to eliminate it.

WHAT IS NOBLE CAUSE CORRUPTION?

Noble cause corruption in policing is defined as "corruption committed in the name of good ends, corruption that happens when police officers care too much about their work. It is corruption committed in order to get the bad guys off the streets the corruption of police power, when officers do bad things because they believe that the outcomes will be good."[2] Examples of noble cause corruption are, planting or fabricating evidence, lying on reports or in court, and generally abusing police authority to make a charge stick.

The policing profession attracts, among others, a certain type of individual: authoritative and responsible, one with leadership skills, who acts on behalf of others, with a high disregard for his or her own well being. Some academics suggest police applicants have a preconception of the profession-the noble cause-that makes them stand out as promising prospects. This preconceived notion is a profound moral commitment to make the world safer.[3]

Police corruption, traditionally, has been defined as the following:

- "a misuse of authority by a police officer for personal gain,"[4]
- "accepting money or money's worth to provide a service they are duty bound to provide,"[5] or
- "physical, psychological or legal abuse used by police."[6]

A recent survey demonstrated that officers felt corruption for personal gain was a much more serious charge than engaging in corrupt behavior that appears "to benefit society at large."[7] This sub cultural value system rationalizes constitutional rights violations.

Officers do not normally define "a bending of the rules for a greater good" as misconduct or as corruption; rather, they rationalize that such behavior is part of the job description, in a utilitarian sense, to get the criminals off the streets, regardless of the means.[8]

When this passion for a safer society goes unchecked, it often leads to police crime and civil rights violation. This passion-laudable in itself-can cause good officers to overzealously execute their duties, ignore the basic constitutional guidelines their profession legally demands, and expose their agency to legal liability.

Officers rationalize this misconduct because cynicism has built up, the department lacks morale and leadership, and the individual lacks faith in the criminal justice system. In their attempts to make charges stick, officers may resort to "massaging" facts in order to get a felony warrant. For example, a department's sub cultural values may dictate always arresting "the driver" in a possession of stolen motor vehicle case, with anything less considered poor police work.

This example shows how overzealous officers rationalize: Several teens are driving around in a stolen motor vehicle, and the officers stop them. The young men jump out and run away, the officers chase them, and arrest only two passengers. Unfortunately, for the officers, neither of them was driving the vehicle. The officers file a report identifying one of the teens as driving and the other as possessing contraband found on the floorboard. The officers chalk up felony arrests and call it a productive night.

As written, supervisors would have no reason to question the officers' veracity and, indeed, would applaud the arrests. Ostensibly, this appears to be good police work: a recovered stolen auto, drug dealers or users off the street, and society better off for it. However, the lies in the police report, and subsequent perjured testimony in court, are both felonies and, as such, are crimes unique to the police. When uncovered, these lies will taint previous and valid legal arrests made by the same officers or

any assisting officers involved in the foot chase and apprehension.

THE RATIONALIZATION DEFENSE

Shortcuts taken in police procedures and investigations in everyday misdemeanor arrests are a large part of noble cause corruption. Rationalizations, such as the "citizen is so drunk he won't remember what happened," may lead to officers' skipping the field sobriety tests or the breath tests, while reporting that they were performed. Before performing a breath alcohol test, officers must read specific constitutional rights to the citizen informing him or her of his or her right to refuse the test and informing the citizen that this refusal, alone, may result in a suspended driver's license. Testimony affirming that specific police procedures were followed, when they were not, is a police crime, especially when confronted with probable cause issues in pretrial motions.

Additionally, the "contempt of cop" or "it's my word against his" attitude opens the door for further shortcuts and constitutional violations. An officer may perform a valid traffic stop, but if the citizen is belligerent or disrespectful, chances are that person is going to jail. In this same vein, officers may issue "sewer tickets"-that is, write a ticket but instead of giving it to the citizen throw it in the sewer-causing a failure to appear in court, a warrant to be issued, and several future problems for the citizen.

Intentionally tainting a police photograph array for identification is another form of noble cause corruption. For example, when a community suffers a rash of armed robberies, detectives often have an idea who might be the perpetrator. Detectives provide a recent booking photograph of this person for patrol officers to carry as they attempt to locate the suspect. When the next robbery occurs, the patrol officer shows the single photograph of the suspect to the victims, who state they believe that the photo appears to be the assailant. A warrant is obtained based on this eyewitness identification, and an arrest made.

This could be good police work, except that the identification photograph array was not properly presented. The victim's independent recollection of the assailant's description is forever tainted by the officer's actions. This identification process is never documented in writing. But during the witness's testimony at trial, explaining this process at the scene opens the door for defense attorneys to argue due-process violations and obstruction of justice, and seek dismissal of all charges, and free a dangerous felon. This breach of trust, though meant in good faith to protect society, actually endangers the community and jeopardizes the public's perceptions of its police agency, when all charges are dismissed and the accused then retains legal counsel and sues the agency.

Whatever the officer's motivation to cut corners- whether citizen disrespect for authority, improving arrest numbers, or simple laziness-it is a crime, and, when discovered, it tarnishes the image of the agency and the profession.

These are just a few examples of the breaches of trust officers commit in their efforts to protect and serve, and make a society safer. The trust they breach, though, is based solely on the good faith of the citizenry policed.

SYSTEMIC ARROGANCE CONTRIBUTES TO CORRUPTION

Arrogance has no place in policing, and agencies that have a culture of arrogance will only foster allegations of organizational tolerance for noble cause corruption and betrayal of the public service philosophy. When officers and administrators believe that the ends justify their means, such as illegal searches, "articulation" in report writing, illegal arrests and "testilying," they corrupt their own system.[9]

Noble cause corruption is rooted in this sense of arrogance, in which officers will rationalize constitutional violations for their own perceived greater good: a safer community. Middle managers, then, engage in a supervisory logic of good faith based on the belief that subordinates always tell the truth and follow the law as their training dictates.[10]

When internal red flags surface-such as multiple citizen complaints for one officer, or subordinates who ask not to have to work with that officer for no specified reason-supervisors must look deeper into the reasons for this sudden turn of events. It may be personal in nature, but it is the duty of the supervisor to make reasonable inquiries into the cause.

Sometimes, supervisors may even refuse to acknowledge subordinate misconduct when reported.[11] Frequently, top police administrators become aware of police misconduct only when the media has reported such patterns and practices. The immediate but reactive promise of transparency, training reforms, and internal investigations by this time is too late- the damage has been done, the lawsuits filed, and the agency's image tarnished. Law enforcement executives must establish early warning systems and ensure proper internal accountability measures are in place to avoid developing illegal patterns and practices.

SUPERVISORY COWARDICE CONTRIBUTES TO CORRUPTION

Along with arrogance, police supervisory cowardice reinforces organizational tolerance of noble cause corruption. Cowardice in this sense is the inability of supervisors to make the difficult administrative decisions that relate to subordinate misconduct.[12] Police administrators must struggle with misconduct cases and weigh the pros and cons of the appropriate disciplinary actions. Chiefs must openly investigate allegations of scandal or politically motivated police actions and disregard their own occupational survival in this role.

Favoritism, nepotism, political concerns, or image preservation must not prevent the chief from thoroughly investigating and disciplining officers for policy violations. Impossible conflicts of interest arise in policing every day, and professional police administrators must adhere to a predetermined set of guidelines and decision-making processes to best serve their community and their agencies. Allegations of departmental cover-ups are immediately followed with calls for external investigations, removal of the chief, and massive reform.

A supervisory philosophy of discipline based on due process, fairness, and equity, combined with intelligent, informed, and comprehensive decision making, is best for the department, employees, and community. It is difficult to challenge this philosophy in a court of law by plaintiff's lawyers arguing a lack of professional integrity. Such a supervisory philosophy demonstrates the moral commitment employees look for in their leaders as well as establishes the high standard of professionalism expected in police service. It also demonstrates to the citizenry that even though officers make mistakes in executing their duties, these mistakes are acknowledged and are appropriately addressed. Policing the police reinforces the public's trust in an agency.

MEASURING PRODUCTIVITY

Traditional policing is often seen as a numbers game that places undue pressure on officers to produce high numbers of arrest and citations. This pressure may lead to situations where officers feel they must engage in acts of noble cause corruption in order to produce the arrests and clearance rates that are the tools politicians use to measure police productivity. Historically, too much emphasis has traditionally been placed on such statistics, and not enough focus has been placed on the professional aspects of service-oriented policing.

Community policing has made significant strides in the profession's ability to serve the citizenry, but it does not provide the numbers politicians need for support and reelection. Citizen surveys, however, do provide the data that police agencies can use to evaluate their effectiveness and ought to be given as much consideration as arrest rates.

As police chiefs are pressured to produce crime-reducing numbers and provide the public with a feeling of safety, the constant pressure to maintain a positive departmental image challenges a chief's own professional ethics.

Can police chiefs manage their departments' public image without sacrificing their own professional ethics? A chief who opts to cover up allegations of misconduct, or fails to adequately investigate such allegations in order to preserve the department's image, corrupts himself or herself and the department as well, and jeopardizes the community's perceptions of that chief's professional integrity.

Self-preservation may cloud a chief's decision-making processes. The chiefs who lead by example, who engage in difficult decision-making, and who habitually do what is in the best interest of the communities they serve will gain the respect of their subordinates and colleagues, as well as their citizenry.

TRANSPARENCY AND ACCOUNTABILITY

Police transparency and accountability require administrators to establish internal procedures so that allegations of misconduct and cover-up will not occur. This transparency preserves the department's public image. Failing to implement a thorough and professional internal investigative system of accountability becomes very costly in litigation. Police administrators must be fair, but vigilant, in their efforts to combat noble cause corruption in order to defend their agencies against allegations of organizational tolerance for misconduct in court.

SHARED VALUES

The key to professional policing and avoiding allegations of corruption is adhering to the profession's values. Research suggests training that continually emphasizes an agency's mission statement and articulates the chief executive's values results in a professional socialization process that rookies, officers, and middle managers can rely on throughout their careers.[13] Departmental values shape professional norms and lay the foundation for the discretionary judgments necessary for effective policing. Officers, as well as police supervisors, often lose their perspectives on constitutional policing when these values are not reinforced.

Values such as listening, communicating, impartiality, accountability at every level, humility, and honesty all make up the profile of a professional police administrator. The challenge for police chiefs today is to exhibit these values day in and day out, in every decision-making process, in order to demonstrate a habit of commitment to professionalism and to maintain their subordinates' trust.

TRAINING TO REDUCE NOBLE CAUSE CORRUPTION

How does police ethics training translate into reducing civil and criminal litigation? Noble cause corruption, when uncovered, can give rise to allegations of organizational tolerance or the civil cause of action for deliberate indifference.[14] Plaintiffs' attorneys will suggest that police chiefs had a duty to know or should have known about the patterns or practices of noble cause corruption within their ranks. Failing to adequately train, supervise, and/or discipline offending officers results in large jury awards and settlements. Clearly, the complexities of policing society are numerous, and it is impossible to draft comprehensive rules that apply to every discretionary police situation. However, police, through experience, vigilant training, supervision, individual accountability, and discipline, can root out the weeds of noble cause corruption and at the same time not destroy an individual officer's freedom to exercise individual police discretion.[15]

The law constantly balances interests, and policing is no different. Such a balancing incorporates protecting the rights of law-abiding citizens on one hand, and respecting the constitutional rights of alleged criminal citizens on the other. Without strictly adhering to policing's constitutional guidelines, departments fail to protect and serve all citizens-even the criminal citizens- and lay the foundations for noble cause corruption to fester.

A departmental values system reinforced daily through both word and deed will provide the ethical work environment a chief needs to fend off charges of noble cause corruption and the litigation associated with it.

Police chiefs must commit to annual ethics training to define noble cause corruption, reduce the potential for police criminality, and avoid the costly lawsuits and citizen distrust that are all directly related to this subtle police abuse of authority. Regular ethics and liability training provides the tools necessary to reinforce democratic policing philosophies and to properly defend against lawsuits alleging constitutional rights violations and deliberate indifference.

A comprehensive ethics-training curriculum that addresses the nuances of noble cause corruption in policing is mandatory in police administration today.

The duty to train begins at the top and a mission statement committed to constitutional policing sends a message to sworn personnel, and the public, that corrupt police acts will not be tolerated. Identifying risks and minimizing the costs of litigation have become part of professional policing.[16]

NOTES

1. U.S. Department of Justice, Principles For Promoting Police Integrity, Examples of Promising Police Practice (Washington, D.C.: U.S. Department of Justice, 2001).

2. John P. Crank and Michael A. Caldero, Police Ethics, The Corruption of Noble Cause (Cincinnati: Anderson Publishing Company, 2000).

3. Ibid.

4. H. Goldstein, Policing a Free Society (Cambridge, Massachusetts: Ballinger, 1977).

5. V. E. Kappeler, R. D. Sluder, and G. P. Alpert, Forces of Deviance, Understanding the Dark Side of Policing (Prospect Heights, Illinois: Waveland Press, 1994).

6. D. L. Carter, "Police Brutality: A Model for Definition, Perspective, and Control," in A.S. Blumberg & E. Neiderhoffer (Eds.), The Ambivalent Force (New York: Holt, Rinehart and Winston, 1985).

7. Ivkovic, Sanja, Kutnjak, "Police (Mis)Behavior: A Cross-Cultural Study of Corruption Seriousness," Policing: An International Journal of Police Strategies & Management, 28 (2005) 3: 546–566.

8. Joycelyn M. Pollock, Ethics in Crime and Justice (West/Wadsworth, 2004).

9. Kleinig, John, "Rethinking Noble Cause Corruption," International Journal of Police Science & Management. 4 (2002).

10. John P. Crank, and Dr. Michael A. Caldero, Police Ethics: The Corruption of Noble Cause

(Cincinnati: Anderson Publishing Company, 2000).

11. Kevin M. Gilmartin and J. Harris, , "Law Enforcement Ethics: The Continuum of Compromise," The Police Chief 65 (January, 1998) 1: 25–28.

12. John Kelining, "Rethinking Noble Cause Corruption," International Journal of Police Science & Management 4 (2002).

13. A.M. Jacocks, Jr., and M.D. Bowman, "Developing and Sustaining a Culture of Integrity," The Police Chief 73 (April, 2006) 4: 16–22.

14. T.J. Martinelli and Joycelyn M. Pollock, "Law Enforcement Ethics, Lawsuits, and Liability: Defusing Deliberate Indifference," The Police Chief 67 (October, 2000) 10: 52–57

15. John Kleinig, "Rethinking Noble Cause Corruption," International Journal of Police Science & Management 4 (2002).

16. Carol A. Archbold, "Managing the Bottom Line: Risk Management in Policing," International Journal of Police Strategies & Management, 28 (2005): 30–48.

The Measurement of Police Integrity

By Carl Klockars

As the history of virtually every police agency attests, policing is an occupation that is rife with opportunities for misconduct. Policing is a highly discretionary, coercive activity that routinely takes place in private settings, out of the sight of supervisors, and in the presence of witnesses who are often regarded as unreliable. Corruption—the abuse of police authority *for gain*—is one type of misconduct that has been particularly problematic. The difficulties of controlling corruption can be traced to several factors: the reluctance of police officers to report corrupt activities by their fellow officers (also known as "The Code," "The Code of Silence," or "The Blue Curtain"), the reluctance of police administrators to acknowledge the existence of corruption in their agencies, the benefits of the typical corrupt transaction to the parties involved, and the lack of immediate victims willing to report corruption.

Until recently, police administrators viewed corruption primarily as a reflection of the moral defects of individual police officers. They fought corruption by carefully screening applicants for police positions and aggressively pursuing morally defective officers in an attempt to remove them from their positions before their corrupt behavior had spread through the agency. This administrative/individual approach, sometimes called the "bad apple" theory of police corruption, has been subject to severe criticism in recent years.

This Research in Brief summarizes a study that measured police integrity in 30 police agencies across the United States. The study was based on an organizational/occupational approach to police corruption. Researchers asked officers for their opinions about 11 hypothetical cases of police misconduct and measured how seriously officers regarded police corruption, how willing they were to support its punishment, and how willing they were to report it. The survey found substantial differences in the environments of integrity among the agencies studied. The more serious the officers considered a behavior to be, the more likely they were to believe that more severe discipline was appropriate, and the more willing they were to report a colleague for engaging in that behavior.

CONTEMPORARY APPROACHES TO CORRUPTION

Pioneered by Herman Goldstein,[1] contemporary theories of police corruption are based on four *organizational* and *occupational* dimensions. Each is described below.

Organizational rules. The first dimension concerns how the organizational rules that govern corruption are established, communicated, and understood. In the United States, where police agencies are highly decentralized, police organizations differ markedly in the types of activities they officially prohibit as corrupt behavior. This is particularly true of marginally corrupt or *mala prohibita* behavior, such as off-duty employment and acceptance of favors, small gifts, free meals, and discounts. Further complicating the problem, the official policy of many agencies formally prohibits such activities while their unofficial policy, supported firmly but silently by supervisors and administrators, is to permit and ignore such behavior so long as it is limited in scope and conducted discreetly.

Prevention and control mechanisms. The second dimension of corruption emphasized in contemporary approaches is the wide range of mechanisms that police agencies employ to prevent and control corruption. Examples include education in ethics, proactive and reactive investigation of corruption, integrity testing, and corruption deterrence through the discipline of offenders. The extent to which agencies use such organizational anticorruption techniques varies greatly.

The Code. The third dimension of corruption, inherent in the occupational culture of policing, is The Code or The Blue Curtain that informally prohibits or discourages police officers from reporting the misconduct of their colleagues. The parameters of The Code—precisely what behavior it covers and to whom its benefits are extended—vary among police agencies. For example, The Code may apply to only low-level corruption in some agencies and to the most serious corruption in others. Furthermore, whom and what The Code covers can vary substantially not only *among* police agencies but also *within* police agencies. Particularly in large police agencies, the occupational culture of integrity may differ substantially among precincts, service areas, task forces, and work groups.

Public expectations. The fourth dimension of police corruption that contemporary police theory emphasizes is the influence of the social, economic, and political environments in which police institutions, systems, and agencies operate. For example, some jurisdictions in the United States have long, virtually uninterrupted traditions of police corruption. Other jurisdictions have equally long traditions of minimal corruption, while still others have experienced repeated cycles of scandal and reform. Such histories indicate that public expectations about police integrity exert vastly different pressures on police agencies in different jurisdictions. These experiences also suggest that public pressures to confront and combat corruption may be successfully resisted.

METHODOLOGICAL CHALLENGES TO THE STUDY OF POLICE CORRUPTION

Although many theories can be applied to the study of police corruption, the contemporary organizational/occupational culture theory has an important advantage over the traditional administrative/individual bad-apple theory: The organizational/occupational approach is much more amenable to systematic, quantitative research.

Corruption is extremely difficult to study in a direct, quantitative, and empirical manner. Because most incidents of corruption are never reported or recorded, official data on corruption are best regarded as measures of a police agency's anticorruption activity, not the actual level of corruption. Even with assurances of confidentiality, police officers are unlikely to be willing to report their own or another officer's corrupt activities.

Unlike the administrative/individual approach, an organizational/occupational culture approach to the study of police integrity involves questions of *fact* and *opinion* that can be explored directly, without arousing the resistance that direct inquiries about corrupt *behavior* are likely to provoke. Using this approach, it is possible to ask nonthreatening questions about officers' *knowledge* of agency rules and their *opinions* about the seriousness of particular violations, the punishment that such violations would warrant or actually receive, and their estimates of how willing officers would be to report such misconduct.

Moreover, sharply different goals and visions of police integrity characterize these two approaches to understanding corruption. The administrative/individual theory of corruption envisions the police agency of integrity as one from which all morally defective individual officers have been removed and in which vigilance is maintained to prevent their entry or emergence. By contrast, the organizational/occupational culture theory envisions the police agency of integrity as one whose culture is highly intolerant of corruption.

Methodologically, the consequences of these two visions are critical. For example, although it may be possible to use an administrative/individual approach to measure the level of corrupt behavior, the number of morally defective police officers, and an agency's vigilance in discovering misconduct, the obstacles to doing so are enormous. Using an organizational/occupational culture approach, by contrast, modern social science can easily measure how seriously officers regard misconduct, how amenable they are to supporting punishment, and how willing they are to tolerate misconduct in silence.

In an effort to measure the occupational culture of police integrity, a systematic, standardized, and quantitative survey questionnaire was designed and pretested. The survey sought information in key areas that constitute the foundation of an occupational/organizational culture theory of police integrity. At the same time, the survey responses could be used to satisfy certain basic informational needs of practical police administration. The survey attempted to answer the following questions:

- Do officers in this agency know the rules governing police misconduct?
- How strongly do they support those rules?
- Do officers know what disciplinary threat they face if they violate those rules?
- Do they think the discipline is fair?
- How willing are they to report misconduct?

For a more detailed description of the survey methodology and samples, see Survey Design and Methodology. The actions taken to enhance the legitimacy of the survey results are discussed in Validity of Survey Responses.

SURVEY RESULTS

The results of the survey, reported in exhibit 1, show that the more serious a particular behavior was considered by police officers, the more severely they thought it should and would be punished, and the more willing they were to report it. The extraordinarily high rank-order correlation among the responses to the survey questions suggests that all six integrity-related questions measured the same phenomenon—the degree of police intolerance for corrupt behavior.

Offense seriousness. The 11 case scenarios fall into 3 categories of perceived seriousness. Four cases were not considered very serious by police respondents: Case 1, off-duty operation of a security system business; Case 2, receipt of free meals; Case 4, receipt of holiday gifts; and Case 8, coverup of a police accident that involved driving under the influence of alcohol (DUI). The majority of police respondents, in fact, reported that the operation of an off-duty security system business (Case 1) was not a violation of agency policy. Respondents considered four other cases of misconduct to be at an intermediate level of seriousness: Case 10, the use of excessive force on a car thief following a foot pursuit; Case 7, a supervisor who offers a subordinate time off during holidays in exchange for tuning up his personal car; Case 9, acceptance of free drinks in exchange for ignoring a late bar closing; and Case 6, receipt of a kickback. Respondents regarded the remaining three cases—those that involved stealing from a found wallet (Case 11), accepting a money bribe (Case 3), and stealing a watch at a crime scene (Case 5)—as very serious offenses.

Discipline. In general, police officers thought that the four cases they regarded as not very serious warranted little or no discipline. Officers thought that the four cases involving an intermediate level of seriousness merited a written reprimand or a period of suspension, and that the three very serious cases merited dismissal.

To measure how officers perceived the fairness of discipline, the scores on the "discipline *would* receive" scale were subtracted from the scores on the "discipline *should* receive" scale. A difference of zero was interpreted to mean that the respondent thought the discipline was fair. If the difference was greater than

Case scenarios. The survey questionnaire presented officers with 11 hypothetical case scenarios. Displayed in exhibit A, the scenarios cover a range of activities, from those that merely give an appearance of conflict of interest (Case 1) to incidents of bribery (Case 3) and theft (Cases 5 and 11). One scenario (Case 10) described the use of excessive force on a car thief.

Respondents were asked to evaluate each scenario by answering seven questions (see exhibit B). Six of these questions were designed to assess the normative inclination of police to resist temptations to abuse the rights and privileges of their occupation. To measure this dimension of police integrity, the six questions were paired as follows:

- Two questions pertained to the seriousness of each case—one addressed the respondent's own view and the other concerned the respondent's perception of the views of other officers.
- Two related to severity of discipline— one addressed the discipline the respondent felt the behavior should receive and the other addressed the discipline the officer felt it would receive.
- Two concerned willingness to report the misconduct—one addressed the respondent's own willingness to report it, and the other concerned the respondent's perception of other officers' willingness to report it.

The remaining question asked respondents whether the behavior described in the scenario was a violation of the agency's official policy.

The incidents described in the scenarios were not only plausible and common forms of police misconduct, but ones that were uncomplicated by details that might introduce ambiguity into either the interpretation of the behavior or the motive of the officer depicted in the scenario. Some scenarios were based on published studies that had employed a case scenario approach. Others drew on the experience of the authors. Respondents were asked to assume that the officer depicted in each scenario had been a police officer for 5 years and had a satisfactory work record with no history of disciplinary problems.

Survey sample. The sample consisted of 3,235 officers from 30 U.S. police agencies. Although these agencies were drawn from across the Nation and the sample was quite large, it was nonetheless a convenience sample, not a representative sample. The characteristics of the officers in this sample are summarized in exhibit C. The majority of the police officers surveyed were employed in patrol or traffic units (63.1 percent). The overwhelming majority of respondents were line officers; only one of five police officers was a supervisor. The mean length of service for the entire sample was 10.3 years.

The sample has some biases, including overrepresentation of particular types of police agencies and particular regions of the country. Because it includes no State police agencies, only one sheriff's agency, and only one county police agency, the sample overrepresents municipal police agencies. The sample also overrepresents police agencies from the Northeast. Although the sample does include agencies from the South, Southeast, and Southwest, it does not include agencies from the West, Northwest, or Midwest.

The sample likely has another bias because not all agencies that were asked to participate in the study accepted the invitation. The reason for an agency's refusal to participate could include a fear of revealing something untoward. Agencies declined to participate despite assurances that their participation in the survey would be kept confidential; that all individual respondents would remain anonymous; and that respondents would be asked about only their opinions, not any actual misconduct. Nevertheless, the sample includes some seriously troubled police agencies. Key contacts in a number of such agencies, including senior officers and high-ranking union officials, exercised sufficient influence to arrange the participation of these agencies in the survey.

a. A number of studies of police corruption have employed a research strategy that asked police officers to evaluate hypothetical corruption scenarios. These include Fishman, Janet E., Measuring Police Corruption, New York: John Jay College of Criminal Justice, 1978; Martin, Christine, Illinois Municipal Officers' Perceptions of Police Ethics, Chicago: Illinois Criminal Justice Information Authority, 1994; Huon, Gail F., Beryl L. Hesketh, Mark G. Frank, Kevin M. McConkey, and G.M. McGrath, Perceptions of Ethical Dilemmas, Payneham, Australia: National Police Research Unit, 1995; and Miller, Larry S., and Michael C. Braswell, "Police Perceptions of Ethical Decision- Making: The Ideal vs. The Real," American Journal of Police 27 (1992): 27–45.

Exhibit A. *Case scenarios*

Case 1.	A police officer runs his own private business in which he sells and installs security devices, such as alarms, special locks, etc. He does this work during his off-duty hours.
Case 2.	A police officer routinely accepts free meals, cigarettes, and other items of small value from merchants on his beat. He does not solicit these gifts and is careful not to abuse the generosity of those who give gifts to him.
Case 3.	A police officer stops a motorist for speeding. The officer agrees to accept a personal gift of half of the amount of the fine in exchange for not issuing a citation.
Case 4.	A police officer is widely liked in the community, and on holidays local merchants and restaurant and bar owners show their appreciation for his attention by giving him gifts of food and liquor.
Case 5.	A police officer discovers a burglary of a jewelry shop. The display cases are smashed, and it is obvious that many items have been taken. While searching the shop, he takes a watch, worth about 2 days' pay for that officer. He reports that the watch had been stolen during the burglary.
Case 6.	A police officer has a private arrangement with a local auto body shop to refer the owners of cars damaged in accidents to the shop. In exchange for each referral, he receives payment of 5 percent of the repair bill from the shop owner.
Case 7.	A police officer, who happens to be a very good auto mechanic, is scheduled to work during coming holidays. A supervisor offers to give him these days off, if he agrees to tune up his supervisor's personal car. Evaluate the *supervisor's* behavior.
Case 8.	At 2:00 a.m., a police officer, who is on duty, is driving his patrol car on a deserted road. He sees a vehicle that has been driven off the road and is stuck in a ditch. He approaches the vehicle and observes that the driver is not hurt but is obviously intoxicated. He also finds that the driver is a police officer. Instead of reporting this accident and offense, he transports the driver to his home.
Case 9.	A police officer finds a bar on his beat that is still serving drinks a half-hour past its legal closing time. Instead of reporting this violation, the police officer agrees to accept a couple of free drinks from the owner.
Case 10.	Two police officers on foot patrol surprise a man who is attempting to break into an automobile. The man flees. They chase him for about two blocks before apprehending him by tackling him and wrestling him to the ground. After he is under control, both officers punch him a couple of times in the stomach as punishment for fleeing and resisting.
Case 11.	A police officer finds a wallet in a parking lot. It contains an amount of money equivalent to a full day's pay for that officer. He reports the wallet as lost property but keeps the money for himself.

Exhibit B. *Case scenario assessment options*

1. How serious do YOU consider this behavior to be?

Not at all serious   Very serious

       1   2   3   4   5

2. How serious do MOST POLICE OFFICERS IN YOUR AGENCY consider this behavior to be?

Not at all serious   Very serious

       1   2   3   4   5

3. Would this behavior be regarded as a violation of official policy in your agency?

Definitely not   Definitely yes

       1   2   3   4   5

4. If an officer in your agency engaged in this behavior and was discovered doing so, what if any discipline do YOU think SHOULD follow?

1. NONE   4. PERIOD OF SUSPENSION WITHOUT PAY

2. VERBAL REPRIMAND   5. DEMOTION IN RANK

3. WRITTEN REPRIMAND   6. DISMISSAL

5. If an officer in your agency engaged in this behavior and was discovered doing so, what if any discipline do YOU think WOULD follow?

1. NONE   4. PERIOD OF SUSPENSION WITHOUT PAY

2. VERBAL REPRIMAND   5. DEMOTION IN RANK

3. WRITTEN REPRIMAND   6. DISMISSAL

6. Do you think YOU would report a fellow police officer who engaged in this behavior?

Definitely not   Definitely yes

       1   2   3   4   5

7. Do you think MOST POLICE OFFICERS IN YOUR AGENCY would report a fellow police officer who engaged in this behavior?

Definitely not   Definitely yes

       1   2   3   4   5

Exhibit C. *Characteristics of the police agency sample*

Agency Size (number sworn officers)	Percentage of National Sample	Sample Size	Supervisory Percentage	Percentage Patrol/Traffic	Mean Length of Service (in years)
Very Large (500+)	59.9	1,937	14.8	64.2	9.18
Large (201–500)	19.7	638	23.2	60.3	12.05
Medium (76–200)	9.0	292	29.9	59.0	12.29
Small (25–75)	8.5	275	30.8	66.1	11.70
Very Small (<25)	2.9	93	35.9	64.8	11.29
Total/Average	100.0	3,235	19.8	63.1	10.30

Validity of Survey Responses

The validity of the survey's results hinges on the honesty of police officers when responding to the survey questions. Several steps were taken to enhance the legitimacy of the survey results. First, officers were asked only about their attitudes, not about their actual behavior or the actual behavior of other police officers. They also were assured that their responses would remain confidential, although police respondents are naturally suspicious of such promises.

To further allay officers' fears that their identities might be discovered, they were asked only minimal background questions: their rank, length of service, and assignment and whether they held a supervisory position. They were not asked standard questions about age, race, gender, or ethnicity in an effort to assuage fears that disclosing such information, in combination with their rank, assignment, and length of service, would make it possible to identify them.

In addition, at the end of the survey, each police respondent was asked two questions about the validity of the responses. The first was "Do you think *most police officers* would give their honest opinion in filling out this questionnaire?" The second was "Did you?" In answer to the first question, 84.4 percent of police respondents reported that they thought most officers would answer the questions honestly, and 97.8 percent reported that they themselves had done so. The responses of the 2.2 percent of police officers who reported that they had not answered the questions honestly were discarded when the survey results were analyzed.

The survey questions also were designed to minimize any temptation for officers to manipulate responses to create a favorable impression on the public or on their supervisors. Some officers, for example, might have been inclined to report that certain types of misconduct were more serious than they actually thought them to be. At the same time, however, these officers would be unlikely to report that misconduct should be punished more severely than they thought appropriate because of the possibility that they might one day be subject to such discipline, if administrators believed that they were recommending it.

Furthermore, if any substantial manipulation of answers had occurred, it would have been evident in differences in correlation coefficients among the questions about seriousness, discipline, and willingness to report. In fact, the rank order correlation between all six questions is extraordinarily high. Indeed, one could predict with great accuracy the ranking of a scenario on any one of the six questions by knowing the ranking for any other.

zero (positive), the respondent thought that the discipline was too lenient. Conversely, if the difference was less than zero (negative), the respondent thought that the discipline was too harsh.[2] In 7 of the 11 cases, the overwhelming majority of police officers in the sample thought that the discipline that would be imposed was in the "fair" range. But in the remaining four cases, including three that officers considered not serious—Case 2 (accepting free meals and discounts on the beat), Case 4 (accepting holiday gifts), Case 8 (coverup of police DUI), and Case 10 (excessive force on car thief)—more than 20 percent of police officers believed that the discipline administered by their agencies would be too harsh.

Parameters of The Code. An examination of the parameters of The Code of Silence, as revealed in the responses of police officers in the sample, indicated that the majority would not report a police colleague who had engaged in behavior described in the four

scenarios considered the least serious. At the same time, a majority indicated that they would report[3] a fellow police officer who had engaged in behavior they deemed to be at an intermediate or high level of seriousness.

AGENCY CONTRASTS IN THE CULTURE OF INTEGRITY

Measurements of the inclination of U.S. police to resist temptations to abuse the rights and privileges of their occupation are likely to prove useful for academic, historical, and cross-cultural studies of police.[4] For police administrators, however, measurements of the culture of integrity of individual police agencies are more relevant than national averages, which often mask significant differences among agencies.

To uncover these differences and allow comparisons to be made, a system was devised for ranking the responses of officers in each agency. To determine an

Case Scenario	Seriousness				Discipline						Willingness to Report			
	Own View		Other Officers		Should Receive			Would Receive			Own View		Other Officers	
	Score	Rank	Score	Rank	Score	Rank	Mode	Score	Rank	Mode	Score	Rank	Score	Rank
Case 1. Off-Duty Security System Business	1.46	1	1.48	1	1.34	1	None	1.51	1	None	1.37	1	1.46	1
Case 2. Free Meals, Discounts on Beat	2.60	2	2.31	2	2.13	2	Verbal reprimand	2.37	2	Verbal reprimand	1.94	2	1.82	2
Case 4. Holiday Gifts From Merchants	2.84	3	2.64	3	2.53	3	Verbal reprimand	2.82	3	Written reprimand	2.36	4	2.28	3.5
Case 8. Coverup of Police DUI Accident	3.03	4	2.86	4	2.81	4	Suspend without pay	3.21	4	Suspend without pay	2.34	3	2.28	3.5
Case 10. Excessive Force on Car Thief	4.05	5	3.70	5	3.76	6	Suspend without pay	4.00	6	Suspend without pay	3.39	5	3.07	5
Case 7. Supervisor: Holiday for Tuneup	4.18	6	3.96	6	3.59	5	Written reprimand	3.43	5	Written reprimand	3.45	6	3.29	6
Case 6. Auto Repair Shop 5% Kickback	4.50	7	4.26	7	4.40	8	Suspend without pay	4.46	8	Suspend without pay	3.95	8	3.71	8
Case 9. Drinks to Ignore Late Bar Closing	4.54	8	4.28	8	4.02	7	Suspend without pay	4.08	7	Suspend without pay	3.73	7	3.47	7
Case 11. Theft From Found Wallet	4.85	9	4.69	9	5.09	10	Dismissal	5.03	10	Dismissal	4.23	10	3.96	10
Case 3. Bribe From Speeding Motorist	4.92	10	4.81	10	4.92	9	Dismissal	4.86	9	Dismissal	4.19	9	3.92	9
Case 5. Crime Scene Theft of Watch	4.95	11	4.88	11	5.66	11	Dismissal	5.57	11	Dismissal	4.54	11	4.34	11

* Scores are based on officers' responses to the integrity-related survey questions.

agency's overall ranking on how its officers perceived the seriousness of a particular offense, the mean score of all responses by officers in that agency to each of the 11 case scenarios was compared to the mean scores of the remaining 29 agencies. The agency was then awarded 3 points if its mean score placed it among the top 10 agencies on any question, 2 points if it scored in the middle 10, and 1 point if it scored among the lowest 10. These scores were then totaled for all 11 case scenarios. Using this scaling system, an agency's score on its officers' perceptions of the seriousness of the offenses could range from 11 (if it ranked in the lowest third of agencies on all 11 cases) to 33 (if it ranked among the highest third of agencies on all 11 cases).[5]

These summary scores formed the basis for placing agencies in rank order from 1 to 30 (with 1 being the highest integrity rating), making it possible to say that an agency ranked "*n* out of 30" in its officers' perceptions of offense seriousness. This procedure was used to calculate a summary score and an integrity ranking for each agency's responses to each of the six questions about offense seriousness, discipline that should and would be received, and willingness to report the offense. Exhibit 2 summarizes those rankings.

The environment of integrity in two agencies. To illustrate how environments of integrity differ across U.S. police agencies, it is useful to contrast the responses of officers from two of the agencies in the sample. Agency 2, which ranked 8th in integrity of the 30 agencies surveyed, and Agency 23, which ranked in a 5-way tie for 24th place, are both large municipal police agencies. Agency 2 has a national reputation for integrity, is extremely receptive to research, and is often promoted as a model of innovation. Agency 23 has a long history of scandal, and its reputation as an agency with corruption problems persists despite numerous reform efforts. Although a local newspaper once dubbed Agency 23 "the most corrupt police department in the country," six other agencies in the sample appear to have integrity environments that are as poor or worse.

In both agencies, the correlation of the scores' rank ordering among the categories was very high, as it was for all 30 agencies surveyed. For every agency,

the mean rank order of officers' responses to the six integrity-related questions was nearly identical. Furthermore, the rank ordering of the scenarios differed little among the agencies.

Although differences in the rank ordering of the scenarios were minimal, both within and between the two agencies, discrepancies in the agencies' absolute scores reflected significant differences (see exhibits 3 and 4). Estimates of offense seriousness were consistently higher for Agency 2 than for Agency 23. The differences were especially large (between 0.5 and 1.0 on a 5-point scale) for three scenarios: Case 6 (auto repair shop kickback), Case 9 (drinks to ignore late bar closing), and Case 10 (excessive force on car thief). Police officers from Agency 2 evaluated each of these cases as substantially more serious than did officers from Agency 23.

The mean scores for discipline indicate that, in almost every case, police officers in Agency 2 not only expected more severe discipline than did officers in Agency 23, but they also thought that more severe discipline was appropriate. The differences in perceptions of discipline were especially great for the most serious types of corruption, such as the scenarios described in Case 3 (bribe from speeding motorist), Case 5 (crime scene theft of watch), and Case 11 (theft from found wallet), as well as for Case 10 (use of excessive force). While officers in Agency 2 thought that dismissal would result from the four most serious cases, officers in Agency 23 expected that dismissal would follow only one scenario, Case 5 (theft from a crime scene).

The most systematic and dramatic difference between Agencies 2 and 23, however, is evident in their attitudes toward The Code of Silence. In both agencies, few officers said that they or their police colleagues would report any of the least serious types of corrupt behavior (Cases 1, 2, 4, and 8). Officers from Agency 2 reported that they and their colleagues would report the behavior described in the seven other cases. In Agency 23, however, there was *no* case that the majority of officers indicated they would report. In sum, while The Code is under control in Agency 2, it remains a powerful influence in Agency 23, providing an environment in which corrupt behavior can flourish.

Agency Number	Own Opinion of Seriousness	Other Officers' Opinions of Seriousness	Discipline *Should* Receive	Discipline *Would* Receive	Own Willingness to Report	Other Officers' Willingness to Report	Summary Score/ Integrity Ranking
1	3	3	3	3	3	3	18/1
3	3	3	3	3	3	3	18/1
4	3	3	3	3	3	3	18/1
6	3	3	3	3	3	3	18/1
10	3	3	3	3	3	3	18/1
17	3	3	3	3	3	3	18/1
30	3	3	3	3	3	3	18/1
2	3	2	3	3	3	3	17/8
18	2	2	3	3	3	3	16/9
7	3	2	2	2	3	3	15/10
11	3	3	2	2	2	2	14/11
12	3	3	3	1	2	2	14/11
5	2	2	2	3	2	2	13/13
19	3	2	2	2	2	2	13/13
20	3	2	2	2	2	2	13/13
29	2	3	2	1	2	2	12/16
26	3	2	2	2	1	1	11/17
27	2	2	2	1	2	2	11/17
24	2	2	1	1	2	2	10/19
21	1	1	2	3	1	1	9/20
22	1	1	2	2	1	2	9/20
9	2	1	2	1	1	1	8/22
16	1	1	1	1	2	2	8/22
13	1	2	1	1	1	1	7/24
14	1	1	1	2	1	1	7/24
15	1	1	1	1	2	1	7/24
23	1	1	1	2	1	1	7/24
25	1	1	1	2	1	1	7/24
8	1	1	1	1	1	1	6/29
28	1	1	1	1	1	1	6/29

Exhibit 2. Composite scores on seriousness of offense, discipline, and willingness to report, rank-ordered by agency

CONCLUSIONS AND IMPLICATIONS

Redefining the problem of police corruption (i.e., the abuse of police authority for gain) as a problem of police integrity—the normative inclination among police to resist temptations to abuse their authority—enables the direct measurement of the major propositions of an organizational/occupational theory of police integrity. The research reported in this Research in Brief demonstrates that police attitudes toward the

Exhibit 3. Agency 2 vs. Agency 23: Officers' own perceptions of seriousness of misconduct, discipline warranted, and willingness to report offense

Case Scenario	Agency 2 (A2) vs. Agency 23 (A23) Perception of Seriousness				Agency 2 (A2) vs. Agency 23 (A23) Discipline *Should* Receive				Agency 2 (A2) vs. Agency 23 (A23) Willingness To Report			
	A2	A23	Difference	t test	A2	A23	Difference	t test	A2	A23	Difference	t test
Case 1. Off-Duty Security System Business	1.57	1.36	0.21	-2.82 p<.05	1.47	1.24	0.23	-3.60 p<.001	1.57	1.22	0.35	-4.78 p<.001
Case 2. Free Meals, Discounts on Beat	3.04	2.85	0.19	-1.80 p<.01	2.50	2.31	0.19	-2.48 p<.01	2.42	1.75	0.67	-6.67 p<.001
Case 3. Bribe From Speeding Motorist	4.94	4.78	0.16	-3.72 p<.001	5.02	4.44	0.58	-6.28 p<.001	4.67	3.02	1.65	-16.09 p<.001
Case 4. Holiday Gifts From Merchants	3.07	2.79	0.28	-2.47 p<.01	2.73	2.59	0.14	-1.35 NS*	2.74	2.05	0.69	-6.24 p<.001
Case 5. Crime Scene Theft of Watch	4.97	4.79	0.18	-4.21 p<.001	5.85	4.90	0.95	-12.64 p<.001	4.92	3.36	1.56	-15.97 p<.001
Case 6. Auto Repair Shop 5% Kickback	4.58	4.02	0.56	-6.74 p<.001	4.41	3.74	0.67	-6.47 p<.001	4.38	2.71	1.67	-15.63 p<.001
Case 7. Supervisor: Holiday for Tuneup	4.16	4.05	0.11	-1.24 NS*	3.58	3.51	0.07	-0.72 NS*	3.68	2.66	1.02	-8.68 p<.001
Case 8. Coverup of Police DUI Accident	3.16	2.68	0.48	-4.32 p<.001	2.85	2.57	0.28	-2.69 p<.05	2.67	2.03	0.64	-5.66 p<.001
Case 9. Drinks to Ignore Late Bar Closing	4.68	3.77	0.91	-9.96 p<.001	4.10	3.17	0.93	-10.45 p<.001	4.21	2.48	1.73	-16.02 p<.001
Case 10. Excessive Force on Car Thief	4.45	3.49	0.96	-10.12 p<.001	3.97	3.15	0.82	-8.30 p<.001	4.02	2.53	1.49	-13.42 p<.001
Case 11. Theft From Found Wallet	4.94	4.55	0.39	-6.85 p<.001	5.42	4.13	1.29	-14.17 p<.001	4.74	2.95	1.79	-17.41 p<.001

*Not signigicant

Exhibit 4. Agency 2 vs. Agency 23: Officers' perceptions of how most police would assess offense seriousness, discipline that offense would receive, and whether most police would be willing to report offense

Case Scenario	Agency 2 (A2) vs. Agency 23 (A23) How Most Police Regard Seriousness				Agency 2 (A2) vs. Agency 23 (A23) Discipline Would Receive				Agency 2 (A2) vs. Agency 23 (A23) Whether Most Police Would Be Willing To Report			
	A2	A23	Difference	t test	A2	A23	Difference	t test	A2	A23	Difference	t test
Case 1. Off-Duty Security System Business	1.52	1.31	0.21	-1.61 NS*	1.70	1.33	0.37	-5.08 p<.001	1.52	1.31	0.21	-3.12 p<.05
Case 2. Free Meals, Discounts on Beat	2.53	2.57	-0.04	0.41 NS*	2.77	2.51	0.26	-3.27 p<.05	2.07	1.74	0.33	-3.83 p<.001
Case 3. Bribe From Speeding Motorist	4.82	4.60	0.22	-4.25 p<.001	4.90	4.45	0.45	-5.06 p<.001	4.23	2.90	1.33	-13.89 p<.001
Case 4. Holiday Gifts From Merchants	2.73	2.61	0.12	-1.10 NS*	3.07	2.88	0.19	-1.94 p<.01	2.49	2.03	0.46	-4.65 p<.001
Case 5. Crime Scene Theft of Watch	4.93	4.62	0.31	-6.16 p<.001	5.73	4.93	0.80	-10.33 p<.001	4.63	3.25	1.38	-14.99 p<.001
Case 6. Auto Repair Shop 5% Kickback	4.31	3.75	0.56	-6.28 p<.001	4.45	3.91	0.54	-5.35 p<.001	3.92	2.64	1.28	-12.51 p<.001
Case 7. Supervisor: Holiday for Tuneup	3.85	3.85	0	0.04 NS*	3.24	3.52	-0.28	2.78 p<.05	3.34	2.60	0.74	-6.80 p<.001
Case 8. Coverup of Police DUI Accident	2.80	2.54	0.26	-2.61 p<.05	3.33	2.83	0.50	-4.92 p<.001	2.40	1.95	0.45	-4.55 p<.001
Case 9. Drinks to Ignore Late Bar Closing	4.32	3.44	0.88	-9.13 p<.001	4.11	3.29	0.82	-8.92 p<.001	3.79	2.35	1.44	-13.89 p<.001
Case 10. Excessive Force on Car Thief	4.01	3.22	0.79	-8.00 p<.001	4.11	3.46	0.65	-6.86 p<.001	3.44	2.38	1.06	-9.98 p<.001
Case 11. Theft From Found Wallet	4.83	4.24	0.59	-8.53 p<.001	5.24	4.25	0.99	-10.79 p<.001	4.38	2.74	1.64	-16.20 p<.001

* Not significant.

seriousness of misconduct, the discipline that should and would result, and the willingness of officers to tolerate misconduct in silence can be measured. Moreover, the measurements reported in this national sample are relatively easy to collect. At the same time, they demonstrate substantial differences in the environments of integrity in U.S. police agencies.

The ability to measure environments of integrity in police agencies holds great potential for academic studies of police and for practical police administration. For researchers, quantitative cross-cultural, historical, and national comparisons that were previously unthinkable have now become feasible.

Equally important, such measurements have direct implications for practical police administration because each of the propositions of an organizational/occupational theory of integrity implies a specific administrative response. If officers do not know whether certain conduct violates agency policy or what disciplinary threats the agency makes, administrators have a clear responsibility to communicate this information to officers. If officers do not regard certain misconduct as sufficiently serious, if they regard discipline as too severe or too lenient, or if they are willing to tolerate the misconduct of their police peers in silence, administrators have an obvious obligation to find out why. A police administrator can take specific actions to deal with each of these problems.

The survey instrument used in this study was designed to assess only one aspect of police integrity. In all case scenarios but one—the use of excessive force—the misconduct described was motivated by personal gain. In discussing environments of integrity, therefore, this survey makes no observation about abuses of discretion in arrests, order maintenance, discourtesy to citizens, or other police misconduct not usually motivated by temptations of gain. A second generation of this survey will explore those problems.[6]

A FINAL NOTE

This survey does not measure the extent of corruption in any police agency or institution. Rather, it measures the culture of police integrity—the normative inclination of police officers to resist the temptations to abuse the rights and privileges of their office. The survey does not identify either corrupt or honest police officers; nor does it provide any evidence of abusive or dishonest practices—past, present, or future. The survey findings do describe, in a fairly precise way, the characteristics of a police agency's culture that encourage its employees to resist or tolerate certain types of misconduct.

NOTES

1. Goldstein, Herman, *Police Corruption: Perspective on Its Nature and Control*, Washington, DC: Police Foundation, 1975; and Goldstein, H., *Policing a Free Society*, Cambridge, MA: Ballinger, 1977. See also Sherman, Lawrence W., *Scandal and Reform*, Berkeley: University of California Press, 1978; Marx, Gary, *Surveillance*, Cambridge, MA: Harvard University Press, 1991; Punch, Maurice, *Conduct Unbecoming: The Social Construction of Police Deviance and Control*, London: Tavistock, 1986; and Manning, Peter K., and Lawrence Redlinger, "The Invitational Edges of Police Corruption," in *Thinking About Police*, edited by Carl Klockars and Stephen Mastrofski, New York: McGraw-Hill, 1993: 398–412.

2. Note that the notions of "greater than zero (positive)" and "less than zero (negative)" are merely shorthand for discipline perceived as too lenient and too harsh, respectively. In other words, because the data are ordinal, positive or negative differences will not be used in any algebraic context. Rather, these differences will be used solely as indicators to classify respondents into three groups—those who perceive discipline to be fair, too lenient, or too harsh.

3. The frequency distribution of responses to the question about officers' own willingness to report a particular offense was analyzed. The five-point scale of offered answers ranged from 1="definitely not" to 5="definitely yes." A cumulative frequency above 50 percent for 1 and 2 was interpreted to indicate that police officers would

not report the offense. A cumulative frequency above 50 percent for 4 and 5, on the other hand, was interpreted to indicate that the police officers *would* report the offense.

4. See, for example, Haberfeld, Maria, Carl Klockars, Sanja Kutnjak Ivkovich, and Milan Pagon, "Disciplinary Consequences of Police Corruption in Croatia, Poland, Slovenia, and the United States," *Police Practice and Research, An International Journal* 1 (1) (2000): 41–72.

5. An alternative summary ranking system could, of course, be based on the full range of 30-point rankings for each of the 11 scenarios. This type of system would create a scale that could range from 330 (for an agency that scored the lowest of the 30 agencies on all 6 questions for all 11 scenarios) to 1,980 (for an agency that scored the highest of all 30 agencies on all 6 questions for all 11 scenarios). Such a scoring system would, however, magnify small and primarily meaningless differences in mean scores, creating a false sense of precision. The ranking system developed for and employed in this research intentionally seeks to blunt any false sense of precision by allowing agencies to score, in a sense, only "high," "middle," or "low" on any given question.

6. A summary of the status of progress with this next generation of measures of police integrity can be found on the videotape of the Research in Progress seminar "Measuring Police Integrity," presented by Carl Klockars at the National Institute of Justice in January 1999. Copies are available through the National Criminal Justice Reference Service at 800–851–3420. Please refer to NCJ 174459.

Carl B. Klockars, Ph.D., is professor in the Department of Sociology and Criminal Justice at the University of Delaware. Sanja Kutnjak Ivkovich, Ph.D., is a doctoral student at Harvard Law School. William E. Harver, Ph.D., is assistant professor of social science in the College of Arts and Sciences at Widener University. Maria R. Haberfeld, Ph.D., is assistant professor in the Department of Law, Police Science, and Criminal Justice Administration at the John Jay College of Criminal Justice, City University of New York.

Police administrators interested in applying the approach used in this study to measure the environment of integrity in their own agencies are advised to contact Professor Carl B. Klockars, Principal Investigator, Enhancing Police Integrity Project, Criminal Justice, University of Delaware, Newark, DE 19716.

Findings and conclusions of the research reported here are those of the authors and do not necessarily reflect the official position or policies of the U.S. Department of Justice.

The National Institute of Justice is a component of the Office of Justice Programs, which also includes the Bureau of Justice Assistance, the Bureau of Justice Statistics, the Office of Juvenile Justice and Delinquency Prevention, and the Office for Victims of Crime.

This and other NIJ publications can be found at and downloaded from the NIJ Web site (http://www. ojp.usdoj.gov/nij).

NCJ 181465

Quick Access to NIJ Publication News

For news about NIJ's most recent publications, including solicitations for grant applications, subscribe to JUSTINFO, the bimonthly newsletter sent to you via e-mail. Here's how:

- Send an e-mail to listproc@ncjrs.org
- Leave the subject line blank
- Type subscribe justinfo your name (e.g., subscribe justinfo Jane Doe) in the body of the message

Or check out the "Publications and Products" section at the NIJ home page: http://www.ojp.usdoj.gov/nij

or the "New This Week" section at the Justice Information Center home page:
http://www.ncjrs.org

Police Attitudes Toward Abuse of Authority

By David Weisburd

Serious cases of abuse of police authority often stimulate intense public debate. For example, a videotape of Rodney King being beaten by Los Angeles police officers or reports of the torture of Abner Louima by New York City police capture the public's attention and raise troubling questions regarding the limits of legitimate police authority in a democratic society. Are such events isolated occurrences in particular police departments or extreme examples of a more general problem plaguing police departments across the United States? Does the fact that such abuses often involve minority victims reveal important disparities in the way that law enforcement officers treat members of certain racial, socioeconomic, or cultural groups? In turn, what measures can be taken to constrain police abuse, and which are likely to be most effective? Although such questions have been raised and debated in the media, by politicians, and by police scholars and administrators, little is known about how police officers themselves view these critical issues.

With the support of the Office of Community Oriented Policing Services, U.S. Department of Justice, the Police Foundation—a nonprofit organization in Washington, D.C., that seeks to improve policing in America through research— surveyed a representative national sample of American police officers to explore their attitudes on the abuse of authority by police (see "Study Methodology"). The survey sought to determine whether officers view abuse of authority as an inevitable byproduct of increased efforts to control crime and disorder. It also asked what forms of abuse exist, how common abuse of authority is, and what strategies and tactics would be most effective in preventing police from abusing authority. The survey also considered how community-oriented policing has affected officers' attitudes on abuse of authority and the rule of law. In particular, it explored whether community policing has led police to show greater respect for the rights of citizens or, conversely, has increased the potential for police abuse and encouraged police officers to expand the boundaries of acceptable use of police authority.

Relatively few surveys of police attitudes toward abuse of authority have been conducted, and these have focused primarily on specific police agencies or local or State jurisdictions.[1] Some of these studies yield important insights regarding the problem of police abuse of authority. Studies conducted across two midwestern States (one in Illinois and one in Ohio), for example, suggest that a significant minority of police officers have observed police using "considerably" more force than necessary when apprehending a suspect. In the Illinois study, more than 20 percent of the officers surveyed reported having observed this type of abuse[2]; in the Ohio study, 13 percent of respondents had seen such abuse.[3] Moreover, both studies suggest that police harassment of minorities is not an isolated occurrence. More than 25 percent of officers surveyed in the Illinois study and 15 percent of those in the Ohio study stated that they had observed an officer harassing a citizen "most likely" because of his or her race.

Prior studies such as these provide suggestive findings on police officers' attitudes toward the abuse of authority. Nonetheless, the conclusions that may be drawn from them are limited by the fact that they were conducted in specific departments or regions of the country. Results of the Police Foundation's study, by contrast, are based on a telephone survey of a representative national sample of more than 900 American police officers. Their responses provide the first national portrait of police attitudes toward the abuse of authority.

GENERAL FINDINGS

Overview of findings. The use of force is a relatively rare occurrence in American policing,[4] but previous studies suggest that when it does occur, it may often escalate to the level of excessive force. For example, a 1996 reexamination of 5,688 cases in the 1977 Police Services Study data found that reasonable force was used in 37 cases (0.65 percent) and that improper force was used in 23 cases (0.40 percent).[5] Therefore, improper force was used in 38 percent of encounters that involved force. As the author of that study, Robert Worden, stated, "[I]ncidents in which improper force was used represent a substantial proportion of the incidents in which any force (reasonable or improper) was used."[6] In his 1980 reanalysis of 1,565 cases in Albert Reiss' 1967 data, Robert Friedrich similarly found that reasonable force had been used in 52 cases (3.3 percent) and that excessive force was used in 28 cases (1.8 percent).[7] Excessive force was thus used in 35 percent of encounters that involved force. Nevertheless, it is unclear whether the same results would be found today, because police policies and training regarding use of force have changed since these data were collected. Moreover, given the difficulties of defining excessive force in studies based on systematic social observations, a general caveat regarding these reported statistics is in order.

In trying to understand why incidents involving force escalate to the level of excessive force, the authors asked officers in the sample a series of questions about their attitudes toward the use of force and the behavior of fellow officers. Responses show that most police officers in the United States disapprove of the use of excessive force. Nonetheless, a substantial minority believed that officers should be permitted to use more force than the law currently permits and found it acceptable to sometimes use more force than permitted by the laws that govern them.[8] The officers revealed these beliefs in responses to several questions (see exhibit 1). More than 30 percent of the sample agreed or strongly agreed that police officers are not permitted to use as much force as is often necessary when making arrests. Almost 25 percent agreed or strongly agreed that, to control a person who is physically assaulting an officer, it is sometimes acceptable for the officer to use more force than legally allowable. Moreover, more than 40 percent agreed or strongly agreed that always following the rules is incompatible with getting their job done.

Although a substantial minority of officers in the sample expressed the view that the police should be permitted to use more force, the overwhelming majority did not believe that officers regularly engaged in the excessive use of force. A mere 4.1 percent thought that police officers regularly used more physical force than necessary when making arrests, and almost all of the officers (97.1 percent) agreed that serious cases of misconduct (like the Rodney King case in Los Angeles and the Abner Louima case in New York) were "extremely rare" in their departments.

Still, respondents did not give their fellow officers a completely clean report. Almost 22 percent agreed or strongly agreed that officers in their departments sometimes (or often or always) use more force than necessary, and only 16 percent reported that their fellow officers never do so (see exhibit 2). Although more than 90 percent found it inappropriate for officers to respond to verbal abuse with physical force, almost 15 percent indicated

Exhibit 1. *General attitudes toward the use of force (in percent)*

	Strongly Agree	Agree	Disagree	Strongly Disagree
Police are not permitted to use as much force as is often necessary in making arrests. (*n*=912)[a]	6.2[b]	24.9	60.5	8.4
It is sometimes acceptable to use more force than is legally allowable to control someone who physically assaults an officer. (*n*=912)	3.3	21.2	55.2	20.3
Always following the rules is not compatible with getting the job done. (*n*=919)	3.8	39.1	49.6	7.6

a. Numbers in parentheses represent valid responses.
b. The frequencies are weighted to reflect the population parameters. The 95-percent confidence intervals for responses in this exhibit range between plus or minus 1.0 percent and 4.0 percent for the frequencies reported. Such confidence intervals are commonly noted as the margin of error or sampling error of the survey findings.
Note: Totals may not equal 100 percent due to rounding.

Exhibit 2. *Use of force behavior in officers' departments (in percent)*

	Never	Seldom	Sometimes, Often, or Always
Police officers in [your department] use more force than is necessary to make an arrest. (*n*=922)[a]	16.0[b]	62.4	21.7
Police officers in your department respond to verbal abuse with physical force. (*n*=922)	31.8	53.5	14.7

a. Numbers in parentheses represent valid responses.
b. The frequencies are weighted to reflect the population parameters. The 95-percent confidence intervals for responses in this exhibit range between plus or minus 1.0 percent and 4.0 percent for the frequencies reported. Such confidence intervals are commonly noted as the margin of error or sampling error of the survey findings.
Note: Totals may not equal 100 percent due to rounding.

that officers in their departments engaged in such behavior at least sometimes.

The code of silence. Some of the strongest and most varied opinions expressed by respondents concerned the difficult question of whether officers should report other officers' misconduct. Responses on this subject suggest the possibility of a large gap between attitudes and behavior. That is, even though officers do not believe in protecting wrongdoers, they often do not turn them in.

More than 80 percent of police surveyed reported that they do not accept the "code of silence" (i.e., keeping quiet in the face of misconduct by others) as an essential part of the mutual trust necessary to good policing (see exhibit 3). However, about one-quarter (24.9 percent) of the sample agreed or strongly agreed

that whistle blowing is not worth it, more than two-thirds (67.4 percent) reported that police officers who report incidents of misconduct are likely to be given a "cold shoulder" by fellow officers, and a majority (52.4 percent) agreed or strongly agreed that it is not unusual for police officers to "turn a blind eye" to other officers' improper conduct (exhibit 3). A surprising 6 in 10 (61 percent) indicated that police officers do not always report even serious criminal violations that involve the abuse of authority by fellow officers.[9]

The role of race, class, and demeanor. The role of societal and other extralegal factors in law enforcement has long been a concern of criminologists.[10] Examining how demeanor affects police behavior, scholars have generally found that a citizen's disrespectful or hostile manner increases the likelihood

Exhibit 3. *Code of silence (in percent)*	Strongly Agree	Agree	Disagree	Strongly Disagree
The code of silence is an essential part of the mutual trust necessary to good policing. (*n*=905)[a]	1.2[b]	15.7	65.6	17.5
Whistle blowing is not worth it. (*n*=904)	3.1	21.8	63.5	11.7
An officer who reports another officer's misconduct is likely to be given the cold shoulder by his or her fellow officers. (*n*=908)	11.0	56.4	30.9	1.8
It is not unusual for a police officer to turn a blind eye to improper conduct by other officers. (*n*=908)	1.8	50.6	43.3	4.4
Police officers always report serious criminal violations involving abuse of authority by fellow officers. (*n*=899)	2.8	36.2	58.5	2.5

a. Numbers in parentheses represent valid responses.

b. The frequencies are weighted to reflect the population parameters. The 95-percent confidence intervals for responses in this exhibit range between plus or minus 0.5 percent and 4.0 percent for the frequencies reported. Such confidence intervals are commonly noted as the margin of error or sampling error of the survey findings.

Note: Totals may not equal 100 percent due to rounding.

of his or her arrest.[11] The Police Foundation's survey shows American police almost evenly divided on the issue of whether a police officer is more likely to arrest a person who displays what the officer considers to be a bad attitude. Almost half (48.8 percent) of the officers in the sample agreed or strongly agreed that a bad attitude would increase the likelihood of arrest, and just more than half (51.2 percent) disagreed or strongly disagreed with the statement (see exhibit 4).

Do other extralegal factors, such as whether a citizen is black or white, poor or middle class, make a difference in the type of treatment he or she is likely to receive from the police? The criminological literature is split on the extent to which race affects everyday policing,[12] the likelihood of being arrested,[13] and the use of excessive force.[14] Of the sample, about one in six (17 percent) believed that whites are treated better by police than blacks and other minorities, and about one in 10 (11.1 percent) believed that more police violence occurs against blacks than against whites (see exhibit 4). Fourteen percent of the sample believed that police officers use physical force against poor people more often than they do against middle-class people in similar situations. These responses suggest that most American police do not believe that race and class are important in understanding police abuse

of authority. However, findings presented later in this Research in Brief suggest that black officers and nonblack (white and other minority) police officers strongly disagree about the salience of race.

Methods of controlling abuse of authority. Officers in the sample were asked how their departments handle cases of abuse of authority. Officers overwhelmingly (92.6 percent) reported that their departments take a very tough stance on improper behavior by police and overwhelmingly (94.4 percent) disagreed with the suggestion that investigations of police misconduct are usually biased in favor of the police (see exhibit 5).

Can leadership within a department make a difference in preventing police officers from abusing authority? Policing scholars have often recognized the importance of a police chief's role. Jerome Skolnick and James Fyfe, for example, have argued that "[The chief is the main architect of police officers' street behavior. This is so because the strength and direction of street-level police peer pressures ultimately are determined by administrative definitions of good and bad policing and by the general tone that comes down from the top."[15] Almost 85 percent of the sample agreed or strongly agreed that a police chief's strong position against the abuse of authority can make a

	Strongly Agree	Agree	Disagree	Strongly Disagree
Exhibit 4. The impact of demeanor, race, and socioeconomic status on police behavior (in percent)				
A police officer is more likely to arrest a person who displays what he or she considers to be a bad attitude. (*n*=917)[a]	2.1[b]	46.7	45.1	6.1
Police officers often treat whites better than they do blacks and other minorities. (*n*=914)	1.2	15.8	57.8	25.2
Police officers are more likely to use physical force against blacks and other minorities than against whites in similar situations. (*n*=916)	1.7	9.4	55.6	33.3
Police officers are more likely to use physical force against poor people than against middle-class people in similar situations. (*n*=918)	1.9	12.3	57.9	27.9

a. Numbers in parentheses represent valid responses.

b. The frequencies are weighted to reflect the population parameters. The 95-percent confidence intervals for responses in this exhibit range between plus or minus 0.5 percent and 4.0 percent for the frequencies reported. Such confidence intervals are commonly noted as the margin of error or sampling error of the survey findings. Note: Totals may not equal 100 percent due to rounding.

big difference in deterring officers from abusing their authority (see exhibit 5).

As important as the officers in the sample viewed the role of the chief in preventing abuse, an even greater majority (almost 90 percent) believed that good first-line supervisors were effective in preventing police officers from abusing their authority (see exhibit 5). In focus-group sessions, police supervisors indicated that supervisors serving as role models was a critical aspect in good first-line leadership.[16] Although 90 percent of the survey sample stressed the importance of good supervisors in preventing abuse, only 55 percent agreed or strongly agreed that most abuse could be stopped with more effective methods of supervision (see exhibit 5).

The survey also examined the extent to which specialized training helps control the abuse of authority. Contrary to the traditional view that most important policing lessons are obtained through experience in the field rather than in the academy,[17] police scholars and professionals have recently emphasized the importance of changing models of police training, renewing departments' commitments to training, and exploring vastly different training curriculums.[18] As reflected in exhibit 5, the majority of police officers in the sample who had

received training in ethics, interpersonal skills, or cultural sensitivity believed that such training could play a role in controlling abuse of police authority. A substantial majority

(82.2 percent) of officers who had received training in law enforcement ethics (in the academy or after becoming an officer) agreed that such training was effective in preventing the abuse of authority. A similar majority (80.3 percent) of those who had received police training in interpersonal skills or relations believed that the training prevented the abuse of authority, and almost 75 percent of officers who had received training in human diversity, cultural differences, cultural awareness, or ethnic sensitivity reported that the training prevented the abuse of authority.

When asked about the effectiveness of different institutional procedures for addressing abuses of authority, most considered internal affairs units effective (78.6 percent). A much smaller percentage (37.8 percent) considered citizen review boards an effective way to prevent police misconduct.

Effects of community-oriented policing. Some scholars have suggested that community-oriented policing decreases the likelihood that officers will engage in gross forms of corruption (such as extortion) but

Exhibit 5. *Controlling abuses of authority (in percent)*

	Strongly Agree	Agree	Disagree	Strongly Disagree
Your police department takes a very tough stance on improper behavior by police. (*n*=921)[a]	35.2[b]	57.4	6.6	0.9
Investigations of police misconduct are usually biased in favor of the police. (*n*=914)	0.4	5.1	72.4	22.0
If a police chief takes a strong position against abuses of authority, he or she can make a big difference in preventing officers from abusing their authority. (*n*=920)	24.5	60.3	13.8	1.4
Good first-line supervisors can help prevent police officers from abusing their authority. (*n*=921)	22.9	66.9	9.3	0.9
Most police abuse of force could be stopped by more effective methods of supervision. (*n*=913)	7.3	48.0	39.5	5.2
(Questions below are applicable only to officers who have received training in the area specified)			**Yes**	**No**
Do you think training in ethics is effective at preventing abuse of authority? (*n*=576)			82.2	17.8
Do you think training in interpersonal skills or relations is effective at preventing abuse of authority? (*n*=674)			80.3	19.7
Do you think training in human diversity or cultural awareness is effective at preventing abuse of authority? (*n*=807)			74.9	25.1

a. Numbers in parentheses represent valid responses.
b. The frequencies are weighted to reflect the population parameters. The 95-percent confidence intervals for responses in this exhibit range between plus or minus 0.5 percent and 4.0 percent for the frequencies reported. Such confidence intervals are commonly noted as the margin of error or sampling error of the survey findings.
Note: Totals may not equal 100 percent due to rounding.

increases the chance that they will engage in softer or less serious forms of corruption (such as accepting a free lunch, professional discount, or gift of appreciation).[19] Others maintain that community policing has no discernible impact on corrupt behavior.[20] As discussed below, officers surveyed in the study generally believed that a close relationship with the community, such as that resulting from community-oriented policing, did not increase the risk of police corruption.

The study examined officers' attitudes toward police corruption in two ways. First, researchers asked officers whether they agreed with the following statement (which includes no reference to community policing): "Frequent friendly contact with local residents and merchants increases the likelihood that police officers will accept free lunches, discounts, or gifts of appreciation for effective service." Although approximately 20 percent of the officers agreed or strongly agreed with the statement, almost 80 percent disagreed or strongly disagreed with it. Second, because almost all the officers in the sample (98.4 percent) claimed to be familiar with the concept of community-oriented policing, the survey asked whether officers thought that community policing increased, decreased, or had no impact on the risk of corrupt behavior. Only 7.1 percent thought that community policing increased the risk of corruption (see exhibit 6). More than one-third (35.8 percent) of the officers thought it decreased the risk of corruption, and more than one-half (57.1 percent) believed that it had no impact (see exhibit 6).

Do officers see any relationship between community policing and excessive force? Almost none believed that community policing increased the number (2.0 percent) or seriousness (3.4 percent) of incidents involving excessive force (see exhibit 6). One-half of the

Exhibit 6. *The role of community policing (in percent)*			
	Increases	**Decreases**	**Has No Impact**
Do you think that community policing increases, decreases, or has no impact on the risk of corrupt behavior? (*n*=883)[a]	7.1[b]	35.8	57.1
Do you think that community policing increases, decreases, or has no impact on the number of incidents involving excessive force? (*n*=885)	2.0	50.9	47.1
Do you think that community policing increases, decreases, or has no impact on the seriousness of incidents involving excessive force? (*n*=884)	3.4	42.2	54.4

a. Numbers in parentheses represent valid responses.

b. The frequencies are weighted to reflect the population parameters. The 95-percent confidence intervals for responses in this exhibit range between plus or minus 0.5 percent and 4.0 percent for the frequencies reported. Such confidence intervals are commonly noted as the margin of error or sampling error of the survey findings.

officers surveyed (50.9 percent) said that community policing reduced the number of incidents involving excessive force, and 42.2 percent thought that it decreased the seriousness of incidents. Approximately one-half of the officers reported that community policing had no impact on either the number of incidents of excessive force (47.1 percent) or the seriousness of those incidents (54.4 percent) (see exhibit 6).

The community policing partnership is often a complicated one. Almost all officers in the sample (96.9 percent) indicated that police officers sometimes have to explain to individuals and groups of citizens that the police are prohibited by law from using certain tactics that citizens may encourage them to use. Approximately 2 out of 10 officers (21.4 percent), however, felt that they could use more aggressive tactics than they otherwise would if the community asked them to do so. The question of whether requests from the community sometimes lead officers to "cross the line" and use tactics prohibited by law remains unanswered.

ADDITIONAL FINDINGS BY RACE, RANK, AND SEX

The general findings described above reflect how officers in the sample (as a group) view a number of issues relating to the abuse of authority. But the data also reveal important findings regarding how different subgroups in the sample view these issues.

To identify and explore these differences, this section breaks down the officers' responses to selected questions according to the responding officers' race, rank, and sex.

Impact of race: White, black, and other minority officers. By far, the most striking differences among subgroups of officers in the sample were among police officers of different races. The sample was originally divided into two racial categories: white and nonwhite. (Officers were grouped in this manner to ensure that a sufficiently large number of officers would be included in each category.) However, after detecting strong differences in the responses of white and nonwhite officers, the authors divided the nonwhite category into two subcategories (black officers and other minority officers) and reexamined the data. The reexamination revealed that black officers' opinions on abuse of authority differed significantly from those of white and other minority officers.

The survey revealed that the attitudes of "other minority" officers were more similar to those of white police officers than to those of black officers. Although the survey may not be generalizable beyond police officers, its findings seem to corroborate the view that there is a racial divide between whites and blacks in American society—a divide so pronounced that even the apparently strong culture of policing does not transcend it.

Differences among black, white, and other minority officers did not emerge on every issue addressed by the

Exhibit 7. **Impact of officers' race on attitudes toward treatment of minority and poor citizens (in percent)**

Police officers often treat whites better than blacks and other minorities.

	Strongly Agree	Agree	Disagree	Strongly Disagree
White officers	0.7	11.2	60.5	27.7
Black officers	4.6	46.7	39.8	8.9
Other minority officers	2.4	21.0	53.8	22.9

Chi-square=41.78, *df*=6, and *p*<0.001

Police officers are more likely to use physical force against blacks and other minorities than against whites in similar situations.

	Strongly Agree	Agree	Disagree	Strongly Disagree
White officers	0.6	4.5	58.0	37.0
Black officers	9.4	47.7	42.1	0.9
Other minority officers	2.4	10.0	50.7	36.9

Chi-square=86.80, *df*=6, and *p*<0.001

Police officers are more likely to use physical force against poor people than against middle-class people in similar situations.

	Strongly Agree	Agree	Disagree	Strongly Disagree
White officers	0.8	8.0	60.1	31.1
Black officers	9.1	45.3	43.6	2.0
Other minority officers	4.2	13.0	52.9	30.0

Chi-square=85.42, *df*=6, and *p*<0.001

Note: Totals may not equal 100 percent due to rounding.

survey. When different opinions (based on race) did occur, however, the disparity was strong, and the types of questions that officers answered differently (based on their race) could be grouped into meaningful configurations. As reported earlier, 17 percent of all officers in the weighted sample agreed or strongly agreed that police officers often treat whites better than they treat blacks and other minorities. Yet more than half (51.3 percent) of the black officers agreed or strongly agreed that whites receive better treatment. By contrast, less than one-fourth of the other minority officers (23.4 percent) and less than one-eighth of white officers (11.9 percent) agreed or strongly agreed with the statement (see exhibit 7).

The divergence between the views of black officers and those of other officers was even more pronounced on the question of whether police officers are more likely to use physical force against blacks and other minorities than against whites in similar situations. Although only 1 in 20 (5.1 percent) white officers in the sample believed that blacks and other minorities received such unequal treatment, well over half of the black officers surveyed (57.1

percent) thought that police officers were more likely to use physical force against blacks and other minorities than against whites in similar situations. The opinion of other minority officers (12.4 percent of whom agreed or strongly agreed with the statement) was much closer to that of the white officers (see exhibit 7).

Black officers were also more likely than whites and other minorities to report unequal treatment by police on the basis of socioeconomic status. Although less than one-tenth of white officers in the sample (8.8 percent) agreed or strongly agreed that police officers were more likely to use physical force against poor people than against middle-class people in similar situations, more than one-half of the black officers (54.4 percent) felt that way. Again, the position of other minority officers (17.2 percent of whom agreed or strongly agreed with the statement) fell between that of the white and the black officers but closer to that of the white officers (see exhibit 7).

Exhibit 8. Impact of officers' race on attitudes toward community policing and citizen review boards (in percent)

Community-oriented policing increases, decreases, or has no impact on the number of incidents involving excessive force.

	Increases	Decreases	Has No Impact
White officers	1.2	49.2	49.6
Black officers	6.6	65.4	28.1
Other minority officers	3.9	50.1	46.0

Chi-square=20.92, *df*=4, and *p*<0.001

Community-oriented policing increases, decreases, or has no impact on the seriousness of incidents involving excessive force.

	Increases	Decreases	Has No Impact
White officers	3.2	39.0	57.9
Black officers	7.2	63.4	29.3
Other minority officers	1.0	46.8	52.3

Chi-square=27.13, *df*=4, and *p*<0.001

Citizen review boards are an effective means of preventing police misconduct.

	Strongly Agree	Agree	Disagree	Strongly Disagree
White officers	2.5	30.8	52.2	14.6
Black officers	8.4	61.4	22.3	7.9
Other minority officers	2.4	38.9	43.6	15.1

Chi-square=32.04, *df*=6, and *p*<0.001

Note: Totals may not equal 100 percent due to rounding.

Although the survey suggests that black officers are more likely than other officers to believe that minority and poor citizens are treated unfairly by police, it also indicates that black officers have greater faith in the communities they serve.[21] Approximately 65 percent of black officers (compared with 49.2 percent of white officers) believed that community-oriented policing was capable of reducing the number of incidents involving excessive force, and 63 percent of black officers (compared with 39 percent of white officers) believed that community policing could decrease the seriousness of incidents involving excessive force. Black officers' responses regarding citizen review boards further demonstrate their faith in the community—with slightly less than 70 percent of black officers in the sample agreeing or strongly agreeing that citizen review boards are effective at preventing police misconduct, compared with one-third (33.3 percent) of white officers who found the boards effective (exhibit 8).

Impact of rank: Supervisors versus nonsupervisors. Although the majority of officers in the sample—supervisors and nonsupervisors alike—agreed that supervision plays an important role in controlling abuse of authority (see exhibit 5), this belief is particularly strong among supervisors themselves. For instance, 87 percent of nonsupervisors (primarily patrol officers) and 97 percent of supervisors indicated that good first-line supervisors could help prevent police officers from abusing their authority (see exhibit 9). Similarly, 50 percent of nonsupervisors and 68 percent of supervisors believed that most police abuse of force could be stopped by developing more effective methods of supervision.

Still in keeping with their role as supervisors, but less predictable, were supervisors' responses to a series of questions about the reporting of misbehavior. More than 80 percent of supervisors believed in the value of reporting or "blowing the whistle" on fellow officers who engaged

Exhibit 9. **Comparing supervisors with nonsupervisors (in percent)**

Good first-line supervision can help prevent police officers from abusing their authority.

	Strongly Agree	Agree	Disagree	Strongly Disagree
Nonsupervisors	16.5	70.2	12.4	0.9
Supervisors	38.5	58.8	1.9	0.8

Chi-square=76.12, *df*=3, and *p*<0.001

Most police abuse could be stopped by developing more effective methods of supervision.

	Strongly Agree	Agree	Disagree	Strongly Disagree
Nonsupervisors	6.3	43.7	44.7	5.4
Supervisors	9.9	58.5	26.7	4.9

Chi-square=33.01, *df*=3, and *p*<0.001

Whistle blowing is not worth it.

	Strongly Agree	Agree	Disagree	Strongly Disagree
Nonsupervisors	3.9	24.4	61.4	10.3
Supervisors	1.1	15.6	68.4	15.0

Chi-square=24.99, *df*=3, and *p*<0.001

The code of silence is an essential part of the mutual trust necessary to good policing.

	Strongly Agree	Agree	Disagree	Strongly Disagree
Nonsupervisors	1.5	19.2	64.2	15.1
Supervisors	0.3	7.3	68.8	23.5

Chi-square=28.46, *df*=3, and *p*<0.001

It is sometimes acceptable to use more force than legally allowable to control someone who physically assaults an officer.

	Strongly Agree	Agree	Disagree	Strongly Disagree
Nonsupervisors	3.9	23.9	54.5	17.7
Supervisors	1.8	14.6	56.8	26.9

Chi-square=21.09, *df*=3, and *p*<0.001

Police department rules about the use of force should not be any stricter than required by law.

	Strongly Agree	Agree	Disagree	Strongly Disagree
Nonsupervisors	7.4	62.8	28.6	1.2
Supervisors	4.9	49.6	41.4	4.1

Chi-square=24.90, *df*=3, and *p*<0.001

Note: Totals may not equal 100 percent due to rounding.

in misbehavior, compared with slightly more than 70 percent of nonsupervisors. Similarly, supervising officers in the sample were less likely to subscribe to the code of silence, with only 7.6 percent of supervisors agreeing that the code of silence is an essential part of the mutual trust necessary to good policing (compared with 20.7 percent of nonsupervising officers). Supervisors also agreed to a lesser extent than nonsupervisors that it is sometimes acceptable to use more force than legally allowable to control someone who physically assaults an officer (16.4 percent of supervisors and 27.8 percent of nonsupervisors agreed or strongly agreed that such conduct was acceptable). Supervisors were also less likely to agree that departmental rules about the use of force should not be any stricter than those required by law (54.5 percent versus 70.2 percent) (see exhibit 9).

Impact of officers' sex. The survey revealed no meaningful differences based on the sex of the responding officers. Differences observed (between responses of male and female officers) were small in size, and no consistent theory or idea link them or suggest that they are meaningful.

The lack of meaningful difference based on sex arguably suggests that female officers have adapted to the predominantly male culture of policing, or that women who decide or "self-select" to enter policing are more likely to adapt to the culture of policing from the outset. The authors, however, feel that these would be premature conclusions. As the National Center for Women and Policing reports, women police outperform their male counterparts at defusing potentially violent situations and become involved in the use of excessive force less often than male officers.[22] The survey may not have included questions that would reveal female officers' strength in handling potentially explosive situations through strong verbal skills.

DISCUSSION

Results of the survey suggest that police officers have complex and sometimes contradictory attitudes toward the abuse of authority. On the one hand, the survey reveals positive evidence of American police officers' integrity. The majority of officers in the sample, for example, disagreed that it is acceptable to use more force than legally necessary—even to control someone who physically assaults an officer. In addition, the vast majority of responding officers described serious incidents of police abuse (such as the Rodney King and Abner Louima cases) as isolated and very rare occurrences and indicated that their departments take a tough stand on police abuse.

Notwithstanding its positive findings, the survey suggests that police abuse remains a problem that needs to be addressed by policymakers and police professionals. Even though most police officers disapprove of the use of excessive force, a substantial minority consider it acceptable to sometimes use more force than permitted by the laws that govern them. The code of silence also remains a troubling issue for American police, with approximately one-quarter of police officers surveyed stating that whistle blowing is not worth it, two-thirds reporting that police officers who report misconduct are likely to receive a "cold shoulder" from fellow officers, and more than one-half reporting that it is not unusual for police officers to turn a "blind eye" to improper conduct by other officers. These findings suggest that the culture of silence that has continually plagued the reform of American policing continues.

The survey also provides surprising and important lessons about police officers' views on ways to control the abuse of authority. Consistent with the suggestions of certain scholars and police professionals,[23] most officers believed that training and education are effective methods for reducing police abuse. A substantial majority of officers who had received training in interpersonal skills or taken courses in ethics or diversity believed that the education or training was effective in preventing misbehavior. These responses may not establish the effectiveness of such programs, but they do show that American police find them important and useful.

Officers in the sample also emphasized the importance of police management in preventing violence and other forms of police abuse. A substantial majority believed that when a chief of police takes a strong stand against police violence, rank and file officers will follow his or her lead. Similarly, officers identified strong first-line supervision as an effective way to prevent abuse and violence by police. These findings reinforce scholars' and police professionals' long-held view that developing effective methods of supervision and strong supervisors should be a first priority for police departments as they attempt to control and prevent abuse of authority.

Over the past three decades, American policing has undergone dramatic changes in organization, tactics, and philosophy. At the forefront of these changes has been a transition from traditional military and professional models of policing to innovative models of community policing. The surveyed officers believed that community policing reduces the potential for a wide range of police abuse—from petty corruption to acts of violence. The survey does not address whether community policing has, in fact, lowered the level of abuse in American policing, but it shows police officers' belief that it has.

The effect of an officer's race on his or her attitudes was particularly striking in the study. Comparing black officers' views about police abuse with those of white and other minority officers, the authors found significant and substantial differences. As discussed in detail earlier in this Research in Brief, a small minority of white officers in the sample believed that police treat white citizens better than they treat black or other minority citizens in similar situations, while a majority of black police officers held this view. Similar differences existed between black and other officers' views on the likelihood of police using force against minorities and poor citizens. In addition, the survey found that black officers had a more positive view of community policing's ability to control the abuse of police authority. The magnitude of these race-based differences in opinion suggests a large gap between black police officers and other officers in the sample. Such a deep divide was not predicted at the outset of the study and may reflect the salience of race as a central divide not only among American police officers but in American society more generally.

Notes

1. Indeed, the authors were able to identify only one national survey of police, and that survey focused on police officers' attitudes concerning rape. LeDoux, John C., and Robert R. Hazelwood, "Police Attitudes and Beliefs Toward Rape," *Journal of Police Science and Administration* 13(1985): 306–353.

2. Martin, Christine, *Illinois Municipal Officers' Perceptions of Police Ethics,* Chicago, IL: Illinois Criminal Justice Information Authority, 1994.

3. Knowles, Jeffrey J., *The Ohio Police Behavior Study,* Columbus, OH: Office of Criminal Justice Services, 1996.

4. Worden, Robert E., and Robin L. Shephard, "Demeanor, Crime, and Police Behavior: A Reexamination of the Police Services Study Data," *Criminology* 34(1996): 83–105.

5. Worden, Robert E., "The 'Causes' of Police Brutality: Theory and Evidence on Police Use of Force," in *Police Violence: Understanding and Controlling Police Abuse of Force,* ed. William A. Geller and Hans Toch, New Haven, CT: Yale University Press, 1996.

6. Ibid., 36.

7. Friedrich, Robert J., "Police Use of Force: Individuals, Situations, and Organizations," *The Annals of the American Academy of Political and Social Science* 452(1980): 82–97.

8. Questions were worded to encompass the varying laws and departmental policies that govern police officers in different jurisdictions.

9. Interpreting responses to this item is difficult, however, because respondents' disagreement with the statement, "Police officers **always** report serious criminal violations involving abuse of authority by fellow officers," does not indicate how often they believe such nonreporting occurs.

10. See, e.g., Westley, William A., "Violence and the Police," *American Journal of Sociology* 59(1953): 34–41.

11. Klinger, David A., "More on Demeanor and Arrest in Dade County," *Criminology* 34(1996): 61–82; Lundman, Richard J., "Demeanor and Arrest: Additional Evidence from Previously Unpublished Data," *Journal of Research in Crime and Delinquency* 33(1996): 306–353; Worden, "The 'Causes' of Police Brutality: Theory and Evidence on Police Use of Force" (see note 5).

12. Moreover, Stephen Mastrofski and colleagues argue that, "Despite the obvious salience of race as an issue in policing over the last 30 years, there has been remarkably little rigorous research in this area." Mastrofski, Stephen D., Roger B. Parks,

Christina DeJong, and Robert E. Worden, "Race and Every-Day Policing: A Research Perspective," paper delivered at the Twelfth International Congress on Criminology, Seoul, Korea, August 24–28, 1998: 14.

13. Michael Tonry, for example, argues that "few or no reliable, systematic data are available that demonstrate systematic [racial] discrimination" in arrest practices. Tonry, Michael, *Malign Neglect—Race, Crime, and Punishment in America*, New York, NY: Oxford University Press, 1995, 71. Although studies have found racial disparities in arrest practices, some attribute such disparities to causes other than race itself (see, e.g., Black, Donald, and Albert J. Reiss, Jr., "Police Control of Juveniles," *American Sociological Review* 35[1970]: 63–77; Lundman, Richard, Richard E. Sykes, and John P. Clark, "Police Control of Juveniles: A Replication," *Journal of Research in Crime and Delinquency* 33[1978]: 306–353). Others find an independent race effect (see, e.g., Smith, Douglas A. and Christy A. Visher. 1981. "Street-Level Justice: Situational Determinants of Police Arrest Decisions." *Social Problems* 29[2]: 167–177; Smith, Douglas A., Christy A. Visher, and Laura A. Davidson. "Equity and Discretionary Justice: The Influence of Race on Police Arrest Decisions." *Journal of Criminal Law and Criminology* 75[1]: 234–249; Worden, "The 'Causes' of Police Brutality: Theory and Evidence on Police Use of Force" [see note 5]; and Lundman, "Demeanor and Arrest: Additional Evidence from Previously Unpublished Data" [see note 11]).

14. Researchers are divided on whether racial differences in the excessive use of force exist and on whether such disparities are attributable to race itself. In his 1996 review, Kenneth Adams concludes that, "the available research on the question of whether the rate of excessive force is higher among minorities is far from determinative" (Adams, Kenneth, "Measuring the Prevalence of Police Abuse of Force," in *Police Violence: Understanding and Controlling Police Abuse of Force*, ed. William A. Geller and Hans Toch, New Haven, CT: Yale University Press, 1996: 59). Worden (see note 5), for example, finds an independent race effect, while Albert Reiss does not (Reiss, Albert J., *The Police and the Public*, New Haven, CT: Yale University Press, 1971). Others point out that "the use of physical force has special significance for racial minority communities" (Walker, Samuel, Cassia Spohn, and Miriam DeLone, *The Color of Justice: Race, Ethnicity, and Crime in America*, Belmont, CA: Wadsworth, 1996, 97. See also Ogletree, Charles, Jr., Mary Prosser, Abbe Smith, and William Talley, Jr., *Beyond the Rodney King Story: An Investigation of Police Misconduct in Minority Communities*, Boston, MA: Northeastern University Press, 1995).

15. Skolnick, Jerome H., and James J. Fyfe, *Above the Law: Police and the Excessive Use of Force*, New York, NY: The Free Press, 1993: 136; see also Skolnick, Jerome H., and David H. Bayley, *The New Blue Line: Police Innovation in Six American Cities*, New York, NY: The Free Press, 1986.

16. Weisburd, David, Rosann Greenspan, Kellie Bryant, Edwin E. Hamilton, Hubert Williams, and David Olson, *Abuse of Authority in the Age of Community Policing: A Preliminary Study of Issues and Attitudes*, Final Report to the U.S. Department of Justice, Office of Community Oriented Policing Services, Washington, DC: Police Foundation, 1998, appendix D.

17. Bayley, David H., and Egon Bittner, "Learning the Skills of Policing," *Law & Society Review* 30(3)(1984): 586–606.

18. See, e.g., Goldstein, Herman, "Improving Policing: A Problem-Oriented Approach," *Crime and Delinquency* 25(1979): 236–258; see also Trojanowicz, Robert, and Bonnie Bucqueroux, *Community Policing: How to Get Started*, Cincinnati, OH: Anderson Publishing, 1994.

19. Weisburd, David, Jerome McElroy, and Patricia Hardyman, "Maintaining Order in Community-Oriented Policing," in *Police and Policing*, ed. Dennis J. Kenney, New York, NY: Praeger, 1989.

20. McElroy, Jerome, Colleen A. Cosgrove, and Susan Sadd, *CPOP: The Research, An Evaluative Study of the New York City Community Patrol Officer Program*. New York, NY: The Vera Institute of Justice, 1990.

21. Findings regarding black officers' more optimistic view of community-oriented policing, and other minorities being closer in attitudes to whites than to blacks, are consistent with the 1997 finding of Wesley Skogan and Susan Hartnett. Skogan, Wesley G., and Susan M. Hartnett, *Community Policing: Chicago Style*, New York, NY: Oxford University Press, 1997.

22. National Center for Women and Policing, retrieved April 13, 1998, from National Center for Women and Policing, on the World Wide Web: www.feminist.org/police/ncwpAbout.html.

23. Grant, J. Douglas, and Joan Grant, "Officer Selection and the Prevention of Abuse of Force," in *Police Violence: Understanding and Controlling Police Abuse of Force*, ed. William A. Geller and Hans Toch, New Haven, CT: Yale University Press, 1996; Scrivner, Ellen M., *The Role of Police Psychology in Controlling Excessive Force*, Washington, DC: U.S. Department of Justice, Office of Justice Programs, National Institute of Justice.

David Weisburd, Ph.D., is Senior Research Scientist at the Police Foundation and Director of the Institute of Criminology at Hebrew University Law School in Jerusalem, Israel; Rosann Greenspan, Ph.D., is Research Director of the Police Foundation; Edwin E. Hamilton, M.A., is Senior Research Analyst at the Police Foundation; Hubert Williams, J.D., is President of the Police Foundation; and Kellie A. Bryant, M.S., formerly Research Associate at the Police Foundation, is a Deputy Marshal with the U.S. Marshals Service.
This study, conducted by the Police Foundation, was supported by Grant Number 97–CK–WX–0047, awarded on behalf of Community Oriented Policing Services, U.S. Department of Justice.

Findings and conclusions of the research reported here are those of the author(s) and do not necessarily reflect the official position or policies of the U.S. Department of Justice.

Values in Policing

By Robert Wasserman and Mark Moore

This paper explores the role that the explicit statement of police values can have on the pursuit of excellence within police departments. Values are the beliefs that guide an organization and the behavior of its employees. The most important beliefs are those that set forth the ultimate purposes of the organization. They provide the organization with its raison d'etre for outsiders and insiders alike and justify the continuing investment in the organization's enterprise.[1]

Often, however, the beliefs about purposes are hopelessly entangled with assumptions about the nature of the organization's environment, the principal means for achieving its purposes, and the sorts of relationships and expectations that exist within the organization. For example, in policing, the strong belief among many police officers that they stand as the front line of defense against community lawlessness—reflecting what is often a rather narrow definition of order—conditions the organizational environment within which the police operate. These beliefs can easily become the prevalent values of the force.

All organizations have values. One can see these values expressed through the actions of the organization—the things that are taken seriously and the things that are rejected as irrelevant, in appropriate, or dangerous. Jokes, solemn understandings, and internal explanations for actions also express values.

Police departments are powerfully influenced by their values. The problem is that police departments, like many organizations, are guided by implicit values that are often at odds are guided by implicit values that are often at odds cynicism rather than clarity, commitment, and high morale.

Almost as bad, the explicit values articulated by some police organizations are unsuited to the challenges confronting today's police departments. Finally, there is a reluctance on the part of some police executives to rely on explicit statements of values as an important management tool for enhancing the performance of their organizations. Still, some police executives are working towards superior police performance by articulating a new set of values, and by using these as a primary management tool.

"Value orientation" has been neither the driving force nor the basis of organizational life in American policing. Should the American police organization have a set of organizational values that are explicitly acknowledged and well known throughout the organization? Should police officers recognize that their survival in the police department rests on whether they embody these organizational values in their actions? This paper examines these questions.

How are values articulated or expressed? Some organizations state their values directly to clientele or employees. Even so, customers, clients, and

Robert Wasserman and Mark Moore, "Values in Policing," *Perspectives on Policing*, no. 8, pp. 1–7. Copyright in the Public Domain.

organizational authorizers (community residents, mayors, and city council members in the municipal setting, and bankers and institutional investors in the corporate sphere) become aware of an organization's values only through the actions of members of the organization or the work of public relations officials.

American corporations are far more sophisticated in communicating values than are government organizations. In industry, values often are expressed through corporate value statements, public advertising, and management pronouncements.[2] Yet, while public relations may create an illusion that a particular set of values is important to the corporation, actual consumer experience often determines eventually the true nature of the corporation's values.

There is often a disparity between the values explicitly established by an organization and those that are actually embraced and pursued. In such cases, corporate management focuses on one set of values while employees adopt an entirely different set. This occurs either because of the failure of management to communicate organizational values or because stated organizational values fail to take into account the reality of the workplace.

The disparity is particularly common in American policing. Mayors and city managers often give their police executives a dual set of objectives, such as "clean up the gangs in the park" and "don't break the law in doing it." Since cleaning up the park has primary importance, and the police are unsupported in developing tools and tactics necessary to solve the underlying problems creating the situation, the mayoral concern with "don't break the law" implicitly becomes "don't tell me about it if you must break the law."

Major corporations have had to deal with the same pressures and ambiguities. In the case of a large producer of orange juice, maintaining profitability was translated by midlevel managerial employees as being more important than product quality, thus making it acceptable to water down the juice as long as it went undiscovered.

In many organizations, values are taken for granted until a crisis centers public attention on the disparity between the organization's stated values and those actually pursued. High-performing commercial organizations consciously strive to ensure that values expressed by employee actions and comments match the values of the organization. Many other organizations, however, function with a dual standard of public relations pronouncements and actual workplace values.

Values as a management tool. The explicit statement and frequent pronouncement of organizational values becomes an important management tool in three circumstances: first, when management's explicit values are so well incorporated in the administrative systems and culture of an organization that they become workplace values; second, when management's values seem well suited to the challenges and tasks facing the organization, and their pursuit will lead to organizational success; and third, when the organization's operations are such that management through values is superior to any other kind of management control.

Values play this important role for several reasons. To the extent that the values actually influence substantive and administrative decisions facing the organization, they lend a coherence and predictability to top management's actions and the responses to the actions of employees. This helps employees make proper decisions and use their discretion with confidence that they are contributing to rather than detracting from organizational performance. That means that the necessity for strong control is lessened. Explicit values also lend significance and meaning to the activity of employers. They transform small transactions and events into expressions of personal commitment to particular values. Finally, explicit statements of values invite broad public support and facilitate accountability. To the extent that the values are attractive to shareholders, customers, and employees in the private sector, and to constituents, clients, and employees in the public sector, a flow of resources to the organization is initiated. To the extent that the values are actually expressed in organizational actions, accountability is preserved, and the flow of resources sustained.[3]

Note that management through values is a particularly important tool for organizations that find it difficult to codify procedures or measure their performance. This occurs in organizations where outputs are hard to define, adaptations of operations to individual cases are often necessary, and technical innovations are occurring. It also occurs in organizations where operations make close supervision impossible. The reason is that in such organizations, the principal alternative methods of control are obviously infeasible.

Values in policing. Policing styles reflect a department's values. A police agency that independently adopts an aggressive tactical orientation has a far different set of values than a police agency that carefully engages neighborhood residents in planning for crime control activities. The values inherent in policing before the reform efforts of the 1930's often reflected political and personal priorities of employees or special interest groups rather than a commitment to broad principles of professionalism.

Sometimes the values of police organizations have been publicly stated. O.W. Wilson, for example, published a set of values for the Wichita Police Department when he was that city's chief of police; he did the same for Chicago when he served as that city's police superintendent.[4] It is more usual, however, for the values that drive policing to be unstated. A number of police agencies, such as Los Angeles, have carefully incorporated values into their rules and procedural directives. Other police agencies, such as Madison (Wisconsin) and Houston, have articulated individual value statements reflecting organizational commitments.

Much of the current discussion about improving police performance is concerned about the values that should guide policing. To understand that discussion, it is useful to contrast the values of professional crime-fighting policing with the values of community problem-solving policing.

The values of professional crime-fighting policing.

Over the last four decades, as police departments have become increasingly professional, several key values have emerged to justify and guide the performance of police agencies. While often unstated, these values include the following:

- Police authority is based solely in the law. Professional police organizations are committed to enforcement of that law as their primary objective.
- Communities can provide police with assistance in enforcing the law. Helpful communities will provide police with information to assist them (the police) in carrying out their mission.
- Responding to citizen calls for service is the highest police priority. All calls must receive the fastest response possible.
- Social problems and other neighborhood issues are not the concern of the police unless they threaten the breakdown of public order.
- Police, being experts in crime control, are best suited to develop police priorities and strategies.

Other values reflect the common belief among police officers (and some chief police executives) that police departments exist to advance the profession of policing, not to serve as an important part of maintaining democratic values and improving the quality of life in urban communities. From these perspectives, there is little interest in, or respect for, the community basis for police authority.

The values of community policing.

In the ongoing dialog about community policing, there are two important new developments. A number of chiefs of police have defined a set of values reflecting internal (employee and administration) and external (community and government) consensus about the nature of the police function and operation of the police agency.

Second, from the discussion of values, these chiefs have discovered that communities are more thoughtful and receptive to discussion of police priorities and strategies if that discussion occurs within the context of mission and value considerations. No longer is the chief of police considered out of place when he suggests to his community that public consideration of policing values and standards is in order.

The experience of these chiefs has shown that the development of value statements can be illuminating to both the community and members of the police department.

In 1982, for example, Lee P. Brown, Houston's chief of police, made public a statement of the values of the Houston Police Department. This statement set forth the commitments of the police department in several critical areas such as policymaking, community access to decision making, standards of integrity, and field strategy development. As Chief Brown noted, the statement established the criteria for evaluating the performance of the department.

The value statement for the Houston Police Department includes the following:

- The Houston Police Department will involve the community in all policing activities which directly impact the quality of community life.
- The Houston Police Department believes that policing strategies must preserve and advance democratic values.
- The Houston Police Department believes that it must structure service delivery in a way that will reinforce the strengths of the city's neighborhoods.
- The Houston Police Department believes that the public should have input into the development of policies which directly impact the quality of neighborhood life.
- The Houston Police Department will seek the input of employees into matters which impact employee job satisfaction and effectiveness.

By publicly stating values, the beliefs underpinning organizational actions, Chief Brown wished to have both the community and the police department focus on important issues of police authority, standards, and operational limits. Indeed, he believed public acknowledgment of community-oriented values was an important step in his move to change the culture of the Houston Police Department from a defensive orientation designed to protect internal organizational patterns to an externally directed community-positive orientation.

The developing emphasis on community policing has generated a substantial amount of discussion about values because, by definition, community policing reflects a set of values, rather than a technical orientation toward the police function. It reflects a concern with the quality of police service delivery, the relationship between the police and the community, and the relationship within the police agency between management and employees. As opposed to the more traditional perspective of professional crime-fighting policing which emphasizes the maintenance of internal organizational controls, community policing emphasizes service output, the quality of results, and the impact of police service on the state of urban living.

There have been several examples of values that reflect this orientation. In Boston, Commissioner Francis M. Roache has set forth the following commitment for the police department:

- The department is committed to the positive evolution, growth, and livability of our city.

Sir Kenneth Newman, former Commissioner of the Metropolitan Police in London, England, set forth the following values for that department:

- In pursuing the aim and duty of maintaining a peaceful community, members of the Metropolitan Police view their role as one involving cooperation with others in the creation and maintenance of a way of life in communities which strikes the optimum balance between the collective interests of all citizens and the personal rights of all individuals.
- The aim of the Metropolitan Police will, therefore, be to work with other agencies to develop what is known as a "situational" or "problem-solving" approach to crime prevention.

Discussions of the Executive Session on Community Policing at Harvard University's John F. Kennedy School of Government have produced a set of values that represent the key characteristics of community policing. These characteristics are embodied in the following principles:

- Community policing is committed to a problem-solving partnership: dealing with crime, disorder, and the quality of life.

The value here is the orientation toward problem solving. In community policing, incidents (such as crime or 911 responses) are viewed from the perspective of community action which will seek to resolve the problem, not simply handle the incident.

- Under community policing, police service delivery is decentralized to the neighborhood level.

Community policing holds that policing a city's neighborhoods is best done at the individual neighborhood level, not by centralized command and control. Since the solutions to most neighborhood problems are through neighborhood action, the community policing effort concentrates on developing a cohesive neighborhood capability reflecting responsibility, self-help, and co-production of service with the police. The value of decentralization suggests that every police effort is pushed down toward the neighborhood level unless there is a specific reason for the effort to be centralized, such as a concern with a citywide problem or issue.

- The highest commitment of the community policing organization is respect for and sensitivity to all citizens and their problems. Community policing values the skills of positive social interaction, rather than simply technical application of procedures to situations, whether dealing with crime, disorder, or other problem solving.

As is the case with several notable private sector companies, community policing's officers have a service orientation. Citizens are supposed to be treated with respect, regardless of the involvement of the citizens in the incident to which the police are responding.

Police officers often find this value difficult to accept. There is a widespread tendency to think of, and describe, street criminals as maggots and other, even less endearing terms. With a service orientation, such characterizations are avoided, if for no other reason

than recognition that the initial police contact may erroneously describe the true nature of the individual.

- The community-oriented police department makes the highest commitment to collaborative problem solving, bringing the neighborhoods into substantive discussions with police personnel to identify ways of dealing with neighborhood problems.

The community-oriented police department recognizes that constructive action by police and community is always better than action by the police alone. Before any major action is undertaken, whether a shift in resources or implementation of a new problem-solving approach, the community-oriented police department discusses that change with the appropriate neighborhood. The willingness to discuss publicly priority setting or selection of problem-solving tactics reflects the high value the organization places on bringing the community into the business of policing. It is also recognition that the community is an important source of police authority.

- The community-oriented police department views both the community and the law as the source of the department's authority.

Since police action is not prescribed by the law, the community empowers the police agency to deal with difficult problems of importance to neighborhood residents and accepts the actions taken as long as the police are continually careful to engage the neighborhood in selecting tactics and priorities beyond those set forth under the law. When a police agency has lost its community authority, a range of responses always occurs, from widespread dissatisfaction with the department to substantial disorder when the police apply the law in the neighborhood.

- The community-oriented police agency is committed to furthering democratic values. Every action of the agency reflects the importance of protecting constitutional rights and ensuring basic personal freedoms of all citizens.

The commitment to democratic values is a corner-stone of community policing. Placement of a high value on the democratic process provides police agencies with the shield they need to ensure that actions proposed by communities do not infringe on others' rights. Embodiment of this value by the organization, and its use as a defense against inappropriate neighborhood initiatives, will succeed only if the police themselves strictly adhere to the law in all aspects of their work.

Implementing values. While a number of police agencies have set forth written statements of their values, few have carefully considered ways of implementing their values so that the actions of agency employees will match the value orientation of the organization.

Police departments that have adopted the community policing philosophy have found it helpful to develop concise value statements that reflect these principles and commitments. The philosophy then can be understood throughout both the department and the community, and serve as the basis for the application of discretion within the department.

Written value statements are useful if for no other reason than to force management to reach agreement on the organization's values. Experience in most police agencies indicates that this debate is not an easy task. But written value statements are not sufficient, since the values eventually must be reflected in all aspects of the organization, from training to field operations.

Presenting values through training must involve more than simply handing out value statements, as has occurred in some agencies. Carefully developed case materials, class discussion, tests, and field officer programs must all reflect the official values of the agency. Policy statements not only state the values explicitly but also provide explanations of the reasoning behind the derived policies.

When auditing field operations or investigative performance, the review must include careful consideration of the degree to which the actions follow stated department values. When riding in police cruisers, supervisors and managers must listen for the "talk of the department" to see if values expressed by police officers reflect those of the department.

Some police administrators will claim that officers will never match the values articulated in their street talk with those of the organization as it pursues excellence. That, of course, is the greatest challenge the police administrator faces; for only when the formal values of the organization match those acted out by the rank and file can the organization be considered "high performing." Community policing requires that match of values; it provides a structure and orientation that make such a match easier.

Summary. The values of community policing are different from those of previous eras in police history. Equally important, values are no longer hidden, but serve as the basis for citizen understanding of the police function, judgments of police success, and employee understanding of what the police agency seeks to achieve.

NOTES

1. In describing the characteristics of organizations, Peters and Waterman note that excellent companies "are fantastic centralists around the few core values they hold dear." Thomas J. Peters and Robert H. Waterman, Jr., *In Search of Excellence,* New York, Harper & Row, 1983: 15.

2. Thomas J. Watson, Jr., the founding father of IBM, authored an early work about how values must be articulated by the successful corporation. See Thomas J. Watson, Jr., A *Business and its Beliefs: The Ideas that Helped Build IBM,* New York, McGraw Hill, 1963.

3. See George L. Kelling, "Police and Communities: the Quiet Revolution," *Perspectives on Policing,* No. 1, Washington, D.C., National Institute of Justice and Haward University, June 1988; and George L. Kelling, Robert Wasserman, and Hubert Williams, "Police Accountability and Community Policing," *Perspectives on Policing* No. 7, Washington, D.C., National Institute of Justice and Harvard University, November 1988,

for a discussion of how management through values lessens the need for reliance on strong command and control systems.

4. Wilson published the values to provide both the police and the community with an understanding of why the police department undertook many of its actions. See Orlando W. Wilson, *On This We Stand,* Chicago Police Department, 1983.

CONCEPT #7: HIRE AND MANAGE YOUR PERSONNEL EFFECTIVELY

Start with good people, lay out the rules, communicate with your employees, motivate them and reward them. If you do all those things effectively, you can't miss.

—Lee Iacocca

In this chapter and in the following chapter, personnel issues are addressed. In this chapter some general issues are addressed and then, in the following chapter, specific legal issues relative to personnel are addressed. The topic of personnel is of prime importance for at least two major reasons. First, personnel costs most often make up over eighty percent of an agency's budget. Second, it is the personnel of the agency who get the get the gob done. Law enforcement is a service industry, it is the people who provide the service, not machines.

First, the state of police staffing is addressed in a reading on the topic of police recruitment. Recruitment is where it all begins as agencies must be able to hire the most qualified candidate for the job. And not only must the candidate be the most qualified, he or she must be the right fit for agency and jurisdiction served. This reading focuses on some of the many factors that hinder recruitment. Some of these factors include unfavorable social trends, intense competition for candidates and bureaucratic personnel regulations. Then, strategies to improve recruitment are addressed.

The second reading in this chapter is on the topic of civilianization in policing. Civilianization, or the use of non-sworn employees in policing is a trend that has gained attention in recent years. There are both substantial benefits and challenges to the use of civilians in policing and this reading presents information relative to both sides, so that you can assess the issues.

Next, are three readings that address employee problems and disciplinary issues. In the reading on the employee disciplinary matrix the issues of fairness in discipline are addressed. Fairness is accomplished through a mechanism called a disciplinary matrix. This is necessary as law enforcement has traditionally had a history of dispensing discipline without regard to fairness or effectiveness. In the reading on the early detection of the problem officer the focus is on the identification of the officer before he or she becomes too deeply involved in problems. Intervention is a strategy in dealing with these officers before the problems magnify. Then, in the reading on managing the problem employee, information is presented on types of problem employees and constructive steps for dealing with them.

In the sixth reading of this chapter, the topic of police turnover is addressed. The idea of turnover is often thought of in negative ways, but this reading presents some of the positive effects of turnover. In the seventh and final reading of this chapter, field training issues are addressed as they are specifically related to administrators. Program integrity, training, trust and the selection of field training officers are some of the many issues addressed in this reading.

Police Recruitment

Foundation Concepts

In the United States, each jurisdiction served by the nation's approximately 18,000 state and local law enforcement agencies determines how many sworn and nonsworn police employees it requires and can afford to hire, equip, train, and deploy. It falls to each agency to fill those positions with qualified employees.

Police executives generally agree that staffing their agencies is their most important administrative responsibility and perhaps the most difficult. Meeting the other operational challenges—terrorism, gang proliferation, a methamphetamine epidemic, offender reentry—depends on having enough officers and civilian employees on the job.

STATE OF POLICE STAFFING

Law enforcement agencies in the United States employ more than 1 million persons. The U.S. Bureau of Justice Statistics (BJS) says that state and local police agencies employ roughly 730,000 sworn officers and 345,000 civilian workers, and the nation's 65 federal law enforcement agencies outside the armed forces employ approximately 105,000 sworn officers.[1]

In recent years, several factors have created an unusually high number of vacancies in police departments, according to anecdotal evidence from the field. Police officers called to active duty with military reserve units and the National Guard left their posts to serve in Iraq and Afghanistan. Some veteran police officers, lured away by higher pay, separated from public service to pursue security work at big corporations or to take police trainer positions with contractors overseas. Officers from state and local agencies accepted positions with federal agencies that were ramping up to fight terrorism. Baby boomer officers who joined the police force in the 1960s and 1970s began retiring in high numbers. The general view among police leaders is that recruitment has not kept pace with the changes.

Stories of police agencies that are operating at less than full strength are easy to find. The Houston Police Department, which in 2006 had an authorized strength of 5,389 sworn officers, reports that its officer vacancies have risen sharply, from 51 unfilled positions in 2004 to 424 in 2005 and up to 605 in 2006. Its 2006 police academy class, its largest in at least 6 years, had just 236 members.[2] The New York City Police Department recently missed its recruitment goal by 2,000 officers, creating what Commissioner Ray Kelly has called a "crisis." News accounts put California's police staffing shortfall at 15,000 officers across 600 state and local agencies. In Macon, Georgia, a municipal police department authorized for roughly 300 sworn officers has 65 vacant officer positions.

These high-profile shortfalls notwithstanding, it is not clear how many police employment positions go unfilled nationwide in a given year. The most recent available data about police hiring suggest that state and local police departments, as a rule, are recruiting enough officers to offset losses caused by retirement, termination, or resignation, according to BJS statistician Matthew Hickman. "The total [state and local police] employment figure at June 30, 2003, includes 51,466 new hires including 7,669 lateral hires over the prior 12 months," Hickman wrote in a 2006 article. "There were 48,866 total separations from police employment. The balance of new hires and separations results in an overall net gain of 2,600 officers, or 0.4 percent during the 12-month period."[3]

In a recent survey of members of the International Association of Chiefs of Police (IACP), only a small percentage of respondents reported that their agencies are experiencing a severe staffing shortfall. When the data are weighted for agency size, the agencies of the survey respondents are operating with an average 93 percent of authorized sworn officer positions filled. Approximately 16 percent of agencies reported that the current number of sworn officers was less than or equal to 90 percent of authorized capacity, and about 3 percent of the agencies were under 80 percent authorized-capacity. (For a closer look at the method and results of the survey, see the Appendix.)

These figures suggest that police departments in the United States are in general doing an adequate job of recruiting new employees. But in recruitment, as in most other respects, the nation's police agencies vary widely. In other words, police recruitment is not a monolithic phenomenon. While some agencies recruit with seeming ease, others struggle to meet their goals, and some agencies experience unpredictable ups and downs in recruitment.

The findings of the IACP survey help clarify our understanding of the state of police recruitment. For instance, 70 percent of survey respondents believe that recruitment is more challenging than it was 5 years ago. Slightly more than half of the respondents report that their agencies receive fewer applications now than they did in years past, a trend police leaders have emphasized in recent years. In 2006, Mary Ann Viverette, retired chief of police in Gaithersburg, Maryland, and the 2005-2006 president of the IACP, told National Public Radio, "Most of us are seeing that our pools of [police officer] applicants have dwindled. Where we might have . . . gotten 300 applications for one position, now [we] may only get 50 to 75."[4] In Kentucky, the Lexington-Fayette Urban County Division of Police reports that applications for police officer positions with the department have declined steadily, from a recent high of 1,600 in 2002 to 756 in 2006. During that period, the department grew from 490 authorized sworn officers to 570 and had 20 unfilled positions at the end of 2006.[5]

CHANGES IN POLICE RECRUITMENT NEEDS

The goal of police recruitment is, and always has been, to hire not merely enough people but the right people. But police executives' notion of what constitutes the right people is changing. They now are more likely to seek to increase the diversity of their departments across the spectrum of race, ethnicity, gender, age, and sexual orientation.

For an earlier generation of law enforcement executives, hiring officers and civilian employees who reflect the community they serve simply meant recruiting more women, Blacks, or Hispanics. For today's executives, it may also mean recruiting employees who can speak Spanish, Hmong, Cape Verdean Creole, or a variety of other languages or dialects. Storm Lake, Iowa, is just one of the many small U.S. towns undergoing an immigration-driven transformation. The presence of good jobs and good schools has drawn newcomers from countries in Africa, Asia, and Central America. The chief of police in Storm Lake, Mark Prosser, wrote in the pages of *The Police Chief* that 63 percent of the children in the public elementary school were minorities, many of whom spoke little or no English at home. Public safety officials in Storm Lake now recruit aggressively among members of the many immigrant groups that are putting down roots in that city.

Going beyond racial, ethnic, and national diversity, police executives also seek employees who have expertise, such as computer skills, that police recruiters might not have looked for in a police officer a few years ago. A growing number of criminal cases, including felonies of all types, rely at least in part on digital evidence—e-mail messages and Internet browsing records, for instance—and officers and civilian employees who have an aptitude for computer investigations have immense value to police departments. Also on many agencies' wish lists are employees who can learn how to turn information into intelligence, conduct statistical analysis, make effective presentations to community groups, work with children, or manage volunteer programs.

FACTORS THAT HINDER POLICE RECRUITMENT

Just as the police recruitment experience varies from one jurisdiction to another, so do the causes of recruitment difficulties. The nature of the law enforcement officer's job—shift work, hazardous duty—understandably limits its appeal. Police work isn't for everyone. But other factors could discourage persons who might otherwise apply for police work, even as demographic trends appear to compound the problem by limiting the size of the pool from which law enforcement recruits its new members.

Unfavorable Demographic and Social Trends

Policing is vulnerable to demographic trends that affect the number of persons of eligible age for police service. America's population is aging, and declining birthrates have produced a series of smaller cohorts between ages of 21 and 35, the target age for new police officers. The average American family has fewer children today than it did a generation ago, creating a scarcity of children. Parents may be more reluctant than ever to encourage them to enter a line of work considered dangerous.

Police executives report that many traditional applicants fail to qualify because of drug use and ethics concerns that surface during background investigations, psychological assessment, or polygraph exams. U.S. Navy Vice Admiral John Cotton, commander of the Navy Reserve, recently told a gathering of senior military officers that "72 percent of American youth between 17 and 24 years of age are not eligible for military service [because of] fitness, academic and law enforcement deficiencies." He noted that some 30 percent of boys drop out of high school.[6] Because the military and the police draw recruits from the same labor pool, it is reasonable to believe that fitness-for-duty factors that exclude young men and women from military service may also exclude them from police employment. Nevertheless, there is little support among police chiefs for lowering standards.

Lack of Diversity in Some Police Departments

The underrepresentation of minorities and women police officers in some departments creates a shortage of role models for recruitment of these populations. Police chiefs must make agency diversification an organizational core value that is understood and embraced by all members if they are to find a force that accurately reflects the composition of the community.

Unattractiveness of Paramilitary Organizations

The nature of the U.S. system of policing causes confusion among those who may consider police service as a career option. The military appearance and structure of many police organizations is not always attractive to potential recruits who seek socially responsible work. To them, the police department may look more like a domestic army than a community service agency. The entertainment and news media portray police as primarily militaristic and combative, and police recruiters often reinforce this misperception by producing and distributing recruitment tools that focus exclusively on the tactical aspects of policing without regard to its service component. Such an image tends to attract applicants who expect a police career to consist primarily of thrill-filled days engaged in high-risk endeavors.

Recruitment efforts should focus on drawing people who are committed to serving in the spirit of service and possess the mental, intellectual, emotional, and physical attributes that will allow them to prevail when faced with a high-risk incident. The goal should be to select those committed to the role of policing in a free society and to exclude those motivated mainly by thrill seeking. Community policing helps create and maintain trust levels that serve the interests of the community and agency. This trust leads to relationships that are more likely to attract potential applicants to a career in police service.

Intense Competition for Candidates

Private security firms are also drawing employees from the same labor pool as police officers and they are recruiting them sooner. Because most private-sector security officers do not have the power of arrest or carry a firearm, firms can hire officers as young as age 18, years before they would be eligible for employment in public-sector policing. The private security industry is growing rapidly. At the same time, some jurisdictions are changing concealed-carry laws to allow private security to be armed, blurring the line between private security and public policing.

Police recruiters in some instances are competing head-to-head with military recruiters. Like private security firms, the military can offer entry into a career at age 18, whereas most police agencies require a new officer to be at least 21. In years past, the police industry benefited from a significant segment of the population that served, voluntarily or otherwise, in the U.S. military for a few years and returned to civilian life with an interest in continued service in something akin to the armed forces. This made police work an attractive employment option. Today, it is unclear how an all-volunteer military affects police recruitment.

Bureaucratic and Burdensome Personnel Regulations

Cumbersome civil service laws hamper modern human resource practices. Many agencies lack the flexibility to accelerate the testing cycle. Applicants are often subjected to repeated visits to participate in stages of the selection cycle. A superbly qualified candidate may be lost to another employer that is able to test and assess the candidate and make a firm job offer in less time. Of course, any change to civil service laws must be made with the knowledge that many of these laws are designed to protect applicants from abusive employment patterns and practices. But there is a need to streamline and improve the recruitment, selection, and employment process while preventing a return to practices that often gave preferential treatment for employment.

Many agencies are still bound by a legal requirement that applicants be citizens of the United States, some by a state residency requirement, and a lesser number by rules that mandate residency in the jurisdiction served by the agency. The citizenship requirement has limited the efforts by some agencies to employ individuals who have a mastery of languages other than English. Added language ability is essential to implement both intelligence-led policing and community oriented policing. A policy like that of the U.S. military, which does not require U.S. citizenship, could be of value in police recruitment. It could also improve police service to new immigrants who cannot speak, read, or write English, a disenfranchised group that is especially vulnerable to criminal victimization. Police executives should use their influence with elected officials to foster constructive change in this arena.

STRATEGIES TO IMPROVE RECRUITMENT

Many effective recruitment practices are described more fully elsewhere in the *IACP Recruitment Toolkit*, but the following list can serve as a starting point for agencies seeking both more and better applicants.

Collaborate with Other Police Agencies

Effective police recruitment exceeds the capacity of any one agency. Continuing the use of fragmented recruitment strategies and tactics is self-defeating for the police profession. Police leaders should seek ways to cooperate with each other to maximize their effectiveness. Consolidation of police services is not likely in most cases, but the door is open to interagency cooperation. Many agencies are in an all-out bidding war for police applicants and some recruitment teams are crisscrossing the country looking for applicants. Their effort may be admired, but the results are questionable, as applicants move from bidder to bidder. Police leaders must collaborate to protect the United States; they must do the same to staff America's police agencies.

Engage the Community

The city of Hartford, Connecticut, experimented with community engagement as a means to improve police recruitment of minority officers. Citizen focus groups helped police identify a primary barrier to recruitment, namely, the lengthy period between an applicant's expression of initial interest and the offer of a job.

In the mid-1990s, Lexington, Kentucky, lost some community support in the wake of an officer-involved shooting, two lethal-force incidents, and a charge of biased traffic enforcement. The chief of police supported a move to overhaul the police recruitment, selection, and training program and enlisted the help of a citizen minority recruitment committee.

The lesson learned in both Hartford and Lexington is that police leaders can benefit by making police recruitment a community concern. Community support can help lower the obstacles to progress, and shared responsibility can increase the likelihood of political support for needed changes. A police leader should increase community awareness of the recruitment problem and then include community representatives in defining and minimizing actions or steps that adversely affect this activity. The leader who engages the community as a full partner is likely to increase the opportunity to enrich the agency through broad diversification. Community representatives can provide a better understanding of cultural impediments to successful participation in the selection process. The community is more likely to encourage potential applicants to seek a police career if they know from hands-on experience that the recruitment and selection process is as open and fair as possible. Community representatives can also serve as knowledgeable mentors to help marshal applicants from the day they express a casual interest in policing to the day they became a newly sworn police officer.

Community engagement can be a slow process as awareness is created, volunteers come forward with a willingness to serve, and the grinding work is undertaken to reengineer a failed system or to upgrade an already workable system. Community representatives must believe that they are full partners in solving a local crisis. Citizens can provide an agency leader with informed counsel and the support to forge change.

Involving the community should include more than just developing the recruitment process and using citizens to lobby potential applicants to participate. Citizens should also have a voice at the selection step.

Improve Relations with External Human Resource Offices and Elected Officials

In some jurisdictions, the authority to recruit and select government employees is housed outside the police department. Many communities have centralized their human resources functions, while others use external bodies such as commissions and civil service boards to hire personnel. As such, a police leader may be an outsider to the very process that is highly critical to future performance of the agency. This can be a serious impediment to solving the recruitment problem.

External bodies and organizational units tasked to handle employee recruitment and selection may not be overly concerned about employing qualified personnel committed to the spirit of service. If such a situation exists, it is the police leader's responsibility to overcome it. The executive must understand both the legal foundation and the practices that govern the recruitment and selection of police officers. If the process is in need of improvement, it is the executive's task to forge partnerships committed to making system improvements.

The nature, scope, and intensity of police recruitment problems warrant total government commitment. Such a commitment begins with the highest-ranking elected official and administrator.

These positions may be one and the same, as in a strong mayor form of government, or separate, as in a city manager style. In either case, the obligation to engage government leadership rests with the police executive. He or she must provide compelling evidence for political commitment and involvement by the local governmental leadership and obtain a commitment from them to work toward a long-term, lasting solution.

Political involvement does not end with the government chief executive officer or chief administrative officer. It rightfully must include members of the legislative body. A police executive must take care to follow legal or accepted protocols that will allow direct contact with the legislative body. This certainly is the case in many city manager governments and also may be true in strong mayor forms. The legislative body needs to have full understanding of the nature and scope of the problem. Anything less may result in the denial of a budget request that is essential to support police recruitment.

Intragovernment communication, by law or practice, may flow from the police executive to the mayor or city manager to the governing body. Similar practices are frequently found at the county and state levels and are intended to aid in the separation of powers. The most notable exception is sheriff's offices that have direct access to the governing body. City councils or commissions frequently designate a member or subgroup to provide police oversight. In such systems, the police executive has an opportunity to launch awareness efforts and build consensus and momentum to move a decision to the legislative body for consideration and action. The same is true in communities that are served by an independent police commission or similar body.

Independent civil service commissions and merit boards in some communities are committed to the goals of agency diversity and quality staffing. In other communities they can form impediments to needed changes. Recall that the civil service and similarly named entities came about in large part in response to complaints about unfairness in the recruitment, selection, and retention of police and fire personnel in particular. Often these bodies have a limited number of professionals on staff and the sitting officials of the commission or board frequently serve pro bono. The police leader is obligated to work with these bodies in such a manner as to minimize resistance and political battles. Elected officials and appointed government leaders should be made fully aware of actions proposed by a police leader that require consideration by a civil service commission or merit board.

Streamline Your Recruitment and Selection Process

Police departments are often burdened with cumbersome recruitment and selection processes that can frustrate applicants and drive them to seek other employment. Common characteristics of weak recruitment processes included systems that were designed to select out (exclude) rather than select in (include) a candidate. In effect, the process is designed to find reasons not to offer an applicant a job rather than identify reasons to employ. The most effective recruitment and selection processes are those that are completed quickly and allow a candidate to move swiftly from application to employment decision points. Some agencies have reengineered police selection and recruitment as a one- or two-day event, commonly over a weekend, from first assessment to conditional offer of employment. At the other end of the spectrum, some systems can take a year or more to complete the process.

An understanding of recruitment and selection is essential if improvements are to be made. Monitoring every applicant at each step in the process is necessary. Applicant elimination points should be identified and meticulously scrutinized to ensure that exclusion decisions are based on failure to meet essential selection standards. The monitoring begins at the point of initial interest and continues until an applicant completes preservice and field officer training and satisfies requirements to be confirmed as a career status officer. This recognizes that recruitment and selection does not end until an officer has completed his or her probationary employment period satisfactorily.

Involve Everyone in the Department in Recruitment

A total-agency approach nearly always is the best course in problem solving. Law enforcement agencies are watched closely by the media and others, and reports of disagreement between police management and labor often create confusion in the community and can cause good programs to fail. Preliminary efforts to engage the entire agency in the task of developing recruitment strategies and tactics will increase the chances for success.

Put Someone in Charge of Recruiting

Commitment to meeting recruitment goals starts with the chief, but every agency, regardless of size, should have one person who has lead responsibility for police recruitment. In agencies with fewer resources, the recruitment task may be ad hoc.

Regardless of agency size, the person assigned to serve as a recruiter will require training. A recruiter needs to be conversant with applicable federal and state laws, maintain impeccable ethical standards, and stay focused on the mission of marketing the agency to the community while soliciting potential applicants. Favoritism or any other ethical breach has the potential of destroying community goodwill and exposing the recruiter and the agency to claims of wrongdoing. The selected recruiter needs intimate knowledge of the agency's personnel recruitment goals as well as deep commitment to the value of diversity. Even after the chief has given an employee direct responsibility for recruitment, all employees must still recognize their obligation to be recruitment ambassadors for the department.

Tell the Police Story

Perhaps the greatest task facing the police community is to tell the police story. Many Americans undervalue police service. "You can never find a cop when you need one," they say, usually when they mean "I don't want the police to be visible unless they serve my immediate purpose." Police leaders must develop and implement a plan to communicate an honest portrayal of police work directly with the American people. This is not going to be an easy task and the greatest challenge likely will be obtaining broad support, consensus, and cooperation from police executives.

Branding the police will require reaching agreement on the common purpose and responsibilities of the police. Are police officers crime fighters, service providers, homeland security agents, peacekeepers, mental health workers, or community problems solvers? In truth, police officers are all of these things and many more. Branding most professions is relatively simple, for comparatively speaking their scope of responsibility is narrow. But police officers handle problems that often have medical, legal, educational, and many other components; therefore, branding the police requires a collage of images and messages. Care must be taken to present a balanced picture of police work. Police leaders seek applicants who are honor-driven, are committed to community wellness, and possess the necessary attributes to deal with critical incidents and tragedies. When the situation arises, officers must have the wisdom to apply only that level of force that is reasonably necessary to stop a criminal act, a unique power afforded only to police officers in the civilian work environment.

Developing a marketing communication strategy that tells the true story of policing will offset media accounts of policing that are all too often negatively slanted or sensationalized. Telling factual stories of dedicated service by honorable police officers also values those who serve in the profession and increases the likelihood that potential applicants will be drawn to a career in police service.

Few law enforcement agencies have a coordinated marketing communication strategy. At best, some have developed limited efforts to portray police work. Some of these efforts are done exceptionally well, while others send confusing messages about policing as a career. Far too many of the promotional pieces focus excessively on the tactical aspects of police service.

While police agencies require a tactical component, this is certainly not where an officer spends most of his or her time. Police service is more about problem solving than crime fighting, and potential applicants must understand in practical terms the very special trust, responsibility, and obligation that society has placed in them.

With a lack of guidance, most agencies are left to their own devices. Police leaders need to explore the formation of collaborative efforts that maximize the value of marketing tools while minimizing the costs to individual agencies. This requires that agencies rethink how they approach the problem of police recruitment. The American police system does not intrinsically encourage cooperative ventures, but police recruitment demands a broad response that should begin with sharing resources toward the common good.

Forming a police recruitment consortium may provide business synergy that enables development of creative marketing tools that are easily adaptable by many police agencies. Such a practice provides an opportunity for cost containment. To accomplish this, it is important that graphics and message points are consistent across the array of marketing tools, such as the use of PowerPoint, CDs, pamphlets, posters, business cards, and the like. Public advertisement and web-based marketing should match hard-copy materials and electronic products. Marketing tools require close monitoring to ensure that message points are consistent and reflect current conditions.

At least one new nationwide marketing effort has been deployed: "Discover Policing" (www.discover-policing.org), a Bureau of Justice Assistance–funded IACP project designed to attract a qualified, diverse population of workers who possess the values and skills essential to law enforcement. The web site features descriptions of the personal and professional benefits of the law enforcement profession and serves as a conduit between prospective candidates and hiring agencies.

Discover Policing addresses a series of obstacles in police recruitment, including marketing. Today, agencies must create their own marketing campaigns to attract candidates, and few have the marketing resources to compete with better-funded employers in other fields. Discover Policing markets policing as an attractive and personally rewarding career choice for young applicants, persons seeking a career change, and others who may not have considered a career in law enforcement.

Beyond improving the image of policing, Discover Policing is also intended to broaden the field of potential candidates. Law enforcement competes with the military, the fire service, nursing, and teaching for a finite number of willing workers. Each of these fields attracts people who are answering the call of public service. A larger portion of these individuals can be recruited into policing with the right message, and DiscoverPolicing.org is designed to deliver that message.

Operational since November 2008, DiscoverPolicing.org aims to be the premier source of information on the Internet concerning policing as a professional option. Linked with this career information database is a full-featured career center, including current job openings and the capability for candidates to post their resumes and apply for jobs online.

Enhance Web Outreach

In general, police agencies have harnessed the power of web-based communications effectively. Home pages are well-done and attract visitors looking for quick information or desiring to learn more about crime in a particular community. Some police agencies have done an exceptional job of exploiting the power of the web while others have yet to fully use this new tool. Using the web for police recruitment can bring much of the global labor pool to an agency's electronic front door.

Sharing information over the web requires a high level of attention to detail. Information must be current, relevant, and consistent with the agency brand. The web allows an agency to easily accommodate a casual visitor interested in police service as well as the serious applicant seeking information, clear guidance, and a path to follow from initial interest to the application and through the selection process. Personnel needs and recruitment goals should be stated clearly, as should applicant standards. A user-friendly recruitment and selection process encourages participation. After visiting a web site, visitors, at a minimum, should know whether an agency is seeking applicants and should understand its recruitment goals, standards and candidate requirements, recruitment and selection processes, wage and benefits package, and basic job rules. They should also have had the opportunity to submit a statement of initial interest online or clearly understand how to make an application.

Enlist the Support of the Media

Much of the media are aware of police staffing problems, but generally do not understand their shared responsibility to solve the problem. Police executives should reach out to their media contacts to discuss the nature and scope of the challenges of recruiting police officers. Staffing shortfalls sometimes expose a police executive to media-driven criticism that officers are leaving because of poor pay and benefits, low morale, excessive overtime, or officers' safety concerns, or that the community is being endangered because of police personnel shortages. Proactive intervention with the media may rectify or blunt such criticism and serve to engage the media in finding workable and affordable solutions.

Media outreach should involve more than the news media. One should consider using public-access television channels, some of which have developed production capacities that equal those of commercial broadcast channels. They can provide an opportunity to go directly before a community to talk about issues requiring community action. A chief appearing as part of a diverse community panel discussing police recruitment goals can open the door for full or community engagement.

One should also consider using talk radio. The Nielsen Media Research web site can tell a police executive a great deal about media readership, viewers, and listeners. This information allows a police leader to direct his or her message to the entire community or drill down to a specific segment or niche of the population.

It is common for police executives to meet with reporters regularly. Such meetings provide another opportunity to increase awareness of the police recruitment problems and how they affect the agency and the community, and provide another means for soliciting assistance from the community to resolve the problem. In addition to the agency CEO, other police personnel who regularly meet with the media should be armed with the agency's talking points regarding police recruitment.

Reach Out to the Young

Children tend to think of police officers as friends and protectors, and many express a desire to be one someday. But, as they grow up, many lose interest in policing, and some even lose their faith in the police. It is in the best interests of the police and the community to change that trend. Agencies have built on children's positive view of police officers using a variety of tactics. They include participation in National Police Athletic Leagues/ Activities Leagues Inc., police cadet programs, and Law Enforcement Explorers, among others. At the least, police officers will help a future generation of citizens and taxpayers understand the importance of law enforcement. Better still would be to nurture a budding crop of future officers.

Hire Younger—and Older

Some agencies have modified their personnel employment rules to permit hiring applicants before they reach the minimum hiring age, which commonly is 21. Young hires are often enrolled in the police academy with a scheduled graduation date that coincides with their age requirement, allowing them to be commissioned as police officers. Other agencies find nonsworn support positions where a qualified applicant can work, earn, learn, and be readily available to continue in the selection process.

Laws and regulations in many jurisdictions bar agencies from hiring entry-level police officers beyond a specific age. Police executives in those jurisdictions should use their influence and collective voice to bring about a change in those laws if they exclude potential candidates for reasons that are not warranted.

Hire Transitional Workers

The police industry needs to take a hard look at hiring transitional workers. Many skilled professionals who have left careers in fields such as teaching, aviation, and medicine because of mandatory or preferred retirement dates still have a desire to serve. Others have grown stale in their current job and are seeking a new challenge. Empty nesters may be another group seeking a new opportunity as family financial obligations decrease. They have knowledge and skills that are desperately needed by the police industry. The police community would do well to welcome them to police work as long as they meet duty requirements.

Police leaders can be in a position to know when local employers are going to lay off workers in the wake of mergers, buyouts, and relocations. The police leader who has useful information about the labor market can move quickly to attract quality personnel.

Mentor Applicants Through the Process

In addition to streamlining its application process, a police agency needs to establish a personal relationship with applicants from the start. After all, these people will become coworkers and eventually leaders of the organization. A welcoming and supportive attitude will pay dividends in the long run. Supporting applicants includes accepting the fact that some may fall short at first, but they should be encouraged to continue involvement. A promising applicant need not always be excluded from employment because of a deficiency that could be overcome with additional preparation. An agency mentor working with such an individual should focus on building on the applicant's strong attributes and fortifying detected weaknesses.

NOTES

1. Bureau of Justice Assistance, *Police Census* 2004, press release, July 2007.
2. Unofficial figures supplied by Lieutenant Frank Rusinski of the Houston Police Department's Recruiting Unit.
3. Hickman, Matthew, "Impact of the Military Reserve Activation on Police Staffing," The Police Chief 73 (October 2006), August 12, 2007.
4. Siegel, Robert, "Big City Police Departments Face Recruit Shortage," National Public Radio, *All Things Considered*, aired March 21, 2006.
5. Unofficial figures supplied by Captain Michael Blanton of the Lexington-Fayette Urban County Division of Police.
6. Quoted in *Navy Times*, June 21, 2007.

Civilianization of Policing

A Review of the Literature and Best Practices

By Curt Griffiths, Adam Palmer, Larry Weeks, and Brian Polydore

Civilianization can be defined as the practice of assigning to non-sworn (civilian) employees police department work that does not require the authority, special training, or credibility of a police officer (Snow, 1989; City of Berkeley, 2002; City of San Francisco, 1998). Civilianization focuses on positions within a police department rather than on individual personnel who occupy positions.

CIVILIANIZATION AS A BEST PRACTICE

The involvement of civilians in policing has evolved from routine tasks such as providing clerical support to placing civilians in specialist staff positions (Guyot, 1979: 277). North American police departments have, to varying degrees, civilianized many positions that have traditionally been filled by sworn police officers.

Civilianization is a key feature of best practice police departments. The role of specially-trained civilians has increased significantly with the professionalization and specialization of police services. As Forst (2000:55) notes, "Police departments have become increasingly reliant on civilians to perform critical tasks as the needs of these departments have become increasingly diverse and specialized." There have also been pressures for fire departments to civilianize positions performed by uniformed personnel (Office of the Comptroller, City of New York, 2004).

This represents a significant departure for many police departments that had previously employed civilians primarily for clerical support and as volunteers. In a report on civilianization within the Kansas City Police Department (Funkhouser, 1998:17), the city auditor found in a survey of best-practices American police departments:

> … few have any sworn personnel in administrative activities such as budget and finance, human resources, and information technology. Several of the comparison departments have fully civilianized other support functions as well, such as maintaining records, handling of property and evidence, and conducting planning and research.

Among the more common sections in police departments that have been partially or fully civilianized are IT, Human Resources, Evidence, Forensic Identification, Research and Planning, Fleet and Facilities Management, Crime Analysis, Finance, and Media Relations.

A review of civilianization projects undertaken by police services across North America reveals the types of positions that have been re-classified as civilian and resulted in civilian personnel replacing sworn officers. These positions include:

- Liquor control enforcement
- Latent fingerprint examiners
- Ballistics examiners
- Document examiners
- Crime analysts
- Lawyers
- Planning and research specialists
- Budgeting and finance specialists
- Communication specialists
- Criminalists (crime scene technicians, forensic laboratory scientists)
- IT specialists
- Forensic accountants
- Forensic computer specialists

A review of six California police departments (Los Angeles, Riverside, Sacramento, San Diego, San Jose, and Santa Ana) conducted by the Office of the Budget Analyst in San Francisco (Rose, 1998:13) found that:

- Records, Identification, Communications, Property Control and Fiscal are almost fully civilianized in Los Angeles, San Jose, Sacramento and Santa Ana;
- Sacramento and Santa Ana have special civilian classifications to perform backgrounds investigations of applicants for sworn positions;
- Fleet Management is fully civilianized in Los Angeles;
- Los Angeles, Riverside, San Jose and Santa Ana use specialized civilian personnel for photographers and photography laboratory technicians;
- San Diego and Riverside use specialized civilian personnel for evidence collection and control;
- The Personnel, Payroll and Public Relations functions are also largely performed by civilian personnel in the other police departments surveyed; and,
- Other examples of the use of specialized civilian personnel for administrative or technical support functions include helicopter operation and repairs (Riverside), polygraph examinations (Los Angeles), psychiatric services (Los Angeles and Riverside), reproduction (Los Angeles), and station duty (Los Angeles).

This increasing civilianization is also reflected in recent changes in the Berkeley (CA) Police Department. A staffing audit (City of Berkeley, 2002) of the Department identified five management-level positions that could be civilianized, including: Support Services (Information Technology, Building Facility, and Records Bureau), Bureau of Inspection and Control (Budget), Communications Centre, the Crime Scene Unit, and the Jail.

Since July 2002, the Berkeley (CA) Police Department has completed the following conversions from sworn members to civilian personnel:

- A non-sworn Senior Budget Specialist was assigned to the Department, filling a vacant Senior Management Analyst position.
- The Lieutenant who managed the Department's computer systems in the Information Technology Department was replaced by a civilian.
- The Sergeant in charge of Crime Scene Unit has been replaced with a non-sworn Crime Scene Supervisor.

The audit also reviewed police departments in 16 cities and found that there were sworn Information Technology managers or staff in only three of them. The audit (City of Berkeley, 2005:32) noted: "The Chief of one of the three cities with sworn IT management said that he would probably civilianize the position when the incumbent retires '*because of the skills needed*'." (Emphasis in original). Only two of the jurisdictions surveyed had transferred control of police information technology to a citywide IT Department. As well, standard practice in the U.S. is for the Communication Center manager to be a civilian.

THE DRIVERS OF CIVILIANIZATION

Civilianization has generally occurred as part of the movement toward professionalism and has been a key component of community policing. It is widely acknowledged that having civilians in key positions in a police organization enhances the general organizational environment, brings specialized expertise, and produces numerous benefits for sworn police officers. As Forst (2000:24–25) notes, "[I]t has become increasingly clear that civilians tend to perform certain specialized roles more effectively than sworn officers, who are selected and trained as generalists and then rotated from one assignment to the next accordingly."

In a presentation to the 1999 annual general meeting and conference of the Canadian Association of Police Boards, Inspector Stuart Ruff of the Victoria (BC) Police Department stated that civilianization is a viable alternative that allows police administrators to maximize resources. This is particularly the case in an environment where there are increasing pressures to control spending while, at the same time, the demands on police services and the need for specialization in police organizations are both increasing. According to Inspector Ruff, the competencies that should be sought when a police department is seeking civilian members are "knowledge, transferable skills, communication and people skills, sensitivity to law enforcement issues, credibility, adaptability and shared vision."

In a comprehensive review of civilianization in policing, Parrett (1992:X) identified a number of change agents driving civilianization in policing. These include:

1. the increasing costs of police service delivery (sworn police officers are an expensive resource);
2. the general pressures to control expenditures on public services;
3. an emphasis on the requirement for effective and efficient management of resources;
4. pressure on police organizations to be sensitive to and responsive to community needs;
5. innovations in police technology;
6. increased functional specialization within the police organization;
7. development of an ethos directed towards examining alternative service delivery systems.

Civilianization within police organizations has been variously viewed as supporting the philosophy of community policing (Crank, 1989, Klockars, 1983, Oppal, 1994), realizing cost savings (City of New York, 2002; Loveday, 1989; Office of the Auditor General of Canada, 1992), improving the delivery of services (City of Berkeley, 2002; Frazier, 2003; Government of Hong Kong, 2004), and as a way to enhance organizational efficiency and effectiveness (Drake and Simper, 2001; Jones, et al., 1994).

Cost-Savings

In a report presenting the results of an in-depth study of the operations of the Dallas (Texas) Police Department, the researchers (Berkshire Advisors, Inc: 2003:X-1) stated that "The primary reason positions should be filled by civilians unless a sworn officer is needed to perform the job is that the cost of employing sworn officers is much higher than the cost of employing civilians."

Civilianization and Community Policing

Civilianization is, however, much more than simply an economic measure. Placing civilianization within the broader philosophy of community policing, Jones et al. (1994:166) have noted that "Civilianization means more than the simple transfer of police tasks to civilian staff, but more generally the increasing importance of the civilian element within the organization." Civilianization can thus be viewed as both a managerial practice and as a strategy to remove barriers between police and the communities they serve. In a presentation (1999) to the Canadian Association of Police Boards, Inspector Irena Lawrenson of the Ontario Provincial Police noted that police services are looking for innovative ways to improve service to the public while at the same time being cognizant that quality of service is equally as important as cost-savings. Civilianization, she noted, is one strategy for accomplishing this.

Strengthening the Police Organization

Re-examination of the role of police officers and civilians can lead to increased efficiency and effectiveness quite independent of any direct salary savings. Appropriate civilianization can have economic, organizational, and operational benefits (Addison, 1988:2). Sworn members have an opportunity to work closely with specially-trained civilians and, in so doing, improve their own skill sets.

A report (Institute for Law and Justice, 1999:19) prepared for the City of Portland and the Portland Police Bureau identified the benefits of increasing the number of civilians in the Department: "Increasing the number of qualified civilian positions will help the Portland Police Bureau develop more professionalism in key administrative and technical positions and will free up sworn members for community policing and problem solving. Bringing more civilians into the Bureau will also help meet the community's concern for more diversity in the organization."

The report (Institute for Law and Justice, 1999:19) noted that civilians had been hired in key administrative and technical positions, including the Planning and Support Division, with positive results:

> Civilianization brings more stability to the position and a greater knowledge of the specialty. The technology in these specialty areas changes rapidly ... It is hard to keep up with those changes unless one is dedicated to the specialty field ... This is not to say that the sworn members in those positions have not performed satisfactorily in the past. However, their expertise is in policing, not in research, data processing, communications, personnel, finance, or other administrative and technical positions.

The report (Institute for Law and Justice, 1999:19) recommended that the Portland Police Bureau "Review and audit all management, technical, and administrative positions to determine which ones could be filled by qualified civilian specialists". The key question to guide the position review was "Does this job require the authority of a sworn officer?"

Increasing "Blue on the Street"

Hiring civilians to perform many of the duties traditionally performed by sworn officers also has the potential to put more "blue on the street", that is making more police officers available to participate in front-line, high visibility duties that are more consistent with their training and experience (Heininger and Urbanek, 1983, Lee, 1994, Swanson et al, 2005, Wilkerson, 1994).

Police agencies in the U.K., the U.S. and Canada are increasing their efforts to employ more civilians so that savings and efficiencies can be realized as additional sworn officers are freed up for operational duties (Jones et al., 1994; Lee, 1994; Maguire et al, 2003). Wilkerson (1994) has noted that police departments are facing increasing demands for service and the need to increase the number of officers on the street, often within a context of fiscal restraint. One solution to this dilemma is to increase the number of civilian employees. As Wilkerson (1994) noted, "Civilianization enables more sworn police officers to answer service calls requiring full police powers, while still providing timely service for other types of calls."

Broadening the Talent Pool

Civilianization increases the number of potential applicants for positions in the police department and provides an opportunity to access specialized skills and expertise.

Increasing Opportunities for Civilian Members

An expansion in the number of civilian positions in a police department will provide more opportunity for civilian staff to be promoted to new positions or to transfer laterally to other civilian positions in the department. This will contribute to retaining civilian employees and ensuring that their expertise and skill sets will continue to be available. In addition, there would be more opportunities for lateral transfers for civilian members.

Having civilian positions throughout the police organization will provide civilian members with the incentive to remain with the department and to aspire to higher level civilian positions. There are currently positions in the department occupied by civilians who may have an interest to move laterally in the department or the skill sets and abilities to advance in the organization.

Increasing Diversity in the Police Department

Civilianization is also a mechanism whereby women and minority groups can be integrated into the organization and to further engage the community in policing (Bocklet, 1987, Crank, 1989, Snow, 1989, Wilkerson, 1995). In turn, some of these civilians may apply to become sworn officers, thus enhancing the agency's ability to reflect the community it serves.

Increasing Productivity

The City of San Francisco Office of the Budget Analyst (1998) has argued that "Hiring civilian employees with educational backgrounds, experience and expertise in functions currently being performed by sworn personnel, who do not typically have the same level of expertise in these areas, would improve productivity."

Increasing Continuity and Consistency

Many sworn police officers lack specialist training and credentials and are often transferred between sections every few years. To this end, civilianization is viewed as a strategy to improve police effectiveness, productivity, efficiency, and continuity of knowledge (Addison, 1998, City of Berkeley, 2002, Drake and Simper, 2001).

In the typical police department, sworn members are moved between positions on a frequent basis, either due to promotions or within the guidelines of departmental tenure policies. The

implementation of the "tenure" policy at the VPD in 2005 will likely improve the effectiveness and efficiency of police operations. The new policy will bring consistency and continuity by preventing officers from remaining in specialized positions (other than patrol and a few specialized units) for more than five years (see Appendix C for the VPD Tenure Policy). With the increasing specialization of certain police functions, it is likely that highly-trained civilians will have more appropriate skills, knowledge, and experience for certain positions in the department.

The Challenges to Civilianization

Despite the myriad of potential benefits, civilianization has been a contentious issue in policing and raises fundamental questions about the nature of policing and police work, the activities that are most appropriately carried out by sworn police officers, and the overall responsibilities of a police service (Her Majesty's Inspectorate of Constabulary, 2004). A report (PricewaterhouseCoopers, 2001:44) found that the proportion of sworn personnel as a percentage of total police employees in Canada has remained at approximately 74 per cent since 1986 as compared to 82 per cent in 1962. This suggests that there are challenges in increasing the civilian presence in police departments. These include organizational resistance to change and a perceived loss of control by the police. As Frazier (2003:12) notes:

> [T]he success of any initiative to increase the numbers and role of civilians in a police department is predicated upon an organizational philosophy which will not only accept and support the decision but, more importantly, a culture willing to relinquish managerial oversight of these positions to a non-sworn supervisory chain of command. It is generally the latter, transition to civilian management, to which many agencies are unwilling, or unable, to commit.

In her presentation to the Canadian Association of Police Boards (CAPB), Inspector Lawrenson (1999:1) noted that many challenges arose throughout the civilianization process in the Ontario Provincial Police (OPP), including pay issues, staff turnover, morale/career advancement, flexibility of resources/deployment and the bargaining unit. In particular, she noted that, although municipalities and police services may view civilianization as a means to control costs, civilians may, and often do, demand pay equal to that of sworn officers. In such a case, there is very little incentive to civilianize a position as a cost-cutting measure. Lawrenson also stated to the CAPB that the OPP has made an on-going commitment to review vacancies and new positions as they arise to determine whether positions should be classified as civilian.

A review of the published literature and the experiences of police departments in North American indicate that there have been challenges to increasing the civilian component of police departments beyond the traditional role of volunteers and clerical support. These include, but certainly are not limited to, the following:

Organizational Resistance

Inspector Stuart Ruff of the Victoria (BC) Police Department has pointed out that, in order for civilianization to be successful, there must be a commitment from the rank and file, senior management and the police board. In addition, the lines of responsibility and reporting between sworn and civilian members must be clear to everyone within the organization. As previously noted, the senior executive of the VPD is strongly committed to an active policy of civilianization in the Department.

A frequently-expressed concern among senior police executives is that civilianization will result in the loss of sworn positions. Among the general principles of civilianization is that an increase in the number of civilians should not, in itself, affect the determination of the authorized sworn strength of a police department.

Opposition from Police Unions and Associations

There is concern that any efforts to increase the numbers of civilians in a police department will meet with resistance from police unions and associations. This, however, has not generally been the experience of police departments in North America or in the United Kingdom (U.K.). With assurances that the staffing levels of sworn members are not directly tied to the number of civilian positions in a department, police unions and associations are likely to view the addition of specially-trained civilians as contributing to the overall quality of the police workplace and as a benefit to sworn members who have an opportunity to work with these civilians.

The Need for Police Officer Expertise and Experience

Critics of civilianization argue that the majority of inside positions within a police organization are best performed by persons with police experience and training (Crank, 1989). It is further argued that civilians lack sufficient training and expertise. However, it is often pointed out that this is not the case in other professions. As one police administrator (cited in Snow, 1989:60) stated, "You don't have to be a pilot to be an air-traffic controller." Another counter argument is that the extensive training undertaken by police officers equips them to work effectively on the frontline, not in "finance, general administration or human resource development or management" (PricewaterhouseCoopers, 2001:45).

The success of specially-trained civilians in police forces across North America and in the U.K. suggests that concerns that civilians are unable to fully comprehend the culture of policing and meet the unique demands that are made on police departments are largely unfounded. That said, it is important to carefully consider the professional and personal attributes of potential civilian employees to ensure that they have the requisite skills sets to work in highly demanding organizational and community environments.

Civilianization as a Threat to Officer Job Security and Promotion Opportunities

Some individuals and professional associations claim that civilianization is a threat to police job security. However, there is no research evidence to support the belief that civilianization leads to an erosion in police officer job security or a reduction in ranks (Crank, 1989; Heininger and Urbanek, 1983; Her Majesty's Inspectorate of Constabulary, 2004). Concerns about civilians negatively impacting the potential for career development have proven to be unfounded. Sworn officers are unlikely to have the requisite expertise to fill many of the positions that are occupied by specially-trained civilians. And, in many sections in police departments, there are mixed teams of sworn members and civilians, preserving opportunities for police officers to move laterally or vertically in the organization.

Civilianization as a Precursor to Privatization of Policing

Critics of civilianization have warned that it could "begin to take on the features of a Trojan horse by being, in effect, the first stage of a process in which the ultimate destination is privatization" (Loveday, 1989:94). Although there has been an exponential growth in private security forces in North America, these services focus primarily on property-related issues. Public police maintain a monopoly on public safety and security and there is nothing to suggest that this will change in the coming years.

Civilianization and Collective Bargaining Agreements

While an assessment of whether any one position in a police department should be identified as a sworn or civilian position can be based on established protocols,

there may be factors specific to each individual police department, e.g. collective agreements that prohibit certain positions from being subjected to civilianization. The experience in many police departments is that a creative approach to civilianization on the part of the police management and union provides opportunities to enhance the overall quality of the department and workplace.

Civilianization and Statutory Requirements

There are certain positions in a police department that require that the incumbent have the powers of a sworn police officer. The experience of police departments is that these issues can be addressed on a position-by-position basis. Where there are statutory requirements for the incumbent in the position to have the peace officer powers, this can be noted. In other instances, the job description may be altered.

The Need to Have Sufficient Numbers of Sworn Officers to Respond to Large-Scale Events

An additional concern that has been raised regarding civilianization is that the department retains a sufficient number of officers to respond to large scale events. While all police organizations must ensure that there are sufficient numbers of officers available to be deployed, there is no evidence from the police literature that civilianization has negatively affected the ability to deploy sworn officers. As the majority of personnel in the police department will always be sworn officers, effective deployment and adequate staffing, rather than civilianization, would seem to be the primary issue.

The Duty of the Department to Accommodate Officers

Discussions of civilianization often include the issue of "accommodation" – the requirement of a police department to provide positions for sworn police officers who, for whatever reason (e.g. medical) must be assigned to light duties. The Report of the Citizen's Budget Commission in New York (2002:vii) noted that: "Efforts at civilianization have often failed because police leaders want to keep a substantial number of assignments with limited risk available to officers as a type of reward or as a temporary assignment." The need for accommodation includes the requirement that the accommodation position be one of substance and not of the "make work" variety. There is the often-expressed concern that, as a result of civilianization, positions will no longer be available to accommodate light-duty officers.

Civilianization, however, is an assessment and classification of a position, not the staffing of it. In other words, while a position can be identified as one best filled by a civilian, a sworn officer on light duties can still fill the position on a temporary basis. All police agencies face the issue of accommodation, and this fact of organizational life has not prevented many departments from implementing a proactive civilianization policy.

The Need for Developmental Positions for Sworn Officers

Developmental positions are a key component of career planning and of leadership succession in police departments. There are concerns that civilianizing positions will reduce the number of developmental positions available for sworn members. However, in most instances, sections where there has been increasing civilianization have resulted in mixed teams of sworn officers and civilians. This is currently the situation in the VPD Planning and Research Section, where two Sergeants, who are in developmental positions, work with specially-trained civilians. These officers also bring skills and experience that is crucial to the work that is being done in the section. In some instances, it is unlikely that a sworn member would have the requisite skill set to meet the requirements of the position occupied by a specially-trained civilian. A beneficial attribute of a developmental position is

providing the sworn member with the opportunity to collaborate with highly-skilled civilians.

Recruiting and Retaining Civilian Staff

Concerns are often expressed that police departments will have difficulty recruiting, and retaining, highly-skilled civilians in specialized positions. There are a number of initiatives, however, that can be taken to increase the retention of civilian staff, including articulated career progression stages, access to in-service training opportunities, and opportunities for lateral or vertical movement within the department. Similarly, remuneration that is commensurate with specialized knowledge and skills will reduce staff turnover. Of equal importance is the development of an organizational culture within the police department in which civilian members are able to work seamlessly with sworn members and have their contributions recognized and valued by the organization.

Fiscal Savings

Generally speaking, police officers receive higher pay and benefits than civilian staff (Forst, 2000). Additionally, there are higher costs associated with training and equipping a police officer. Civilians tend to arrive in a specialist position with established skill sets. However, although a primary driving force in civilianization in policing is the effort to reduce policing costs, there is no certainty that civilianizing positions currently performed by sworn members will result in cost savings in every instance. As the authors (City of Berkeley, 2005:18) stated: "[R]eplacing sworn members with non-sworn members can free up substantial resources, since the cost of salaries and benefits for officers are substantially higher than the cost of other employees. However, for certain highly-specialized positions (e.g. crime analyst), the cost to recruit, and retain, such expertise may exceed that of a sworn member."

Much depends upon the specific position that is being re-classified from sworn police officer to civilian. For example, re-classifying the position of head of a planning and research unit will require the police department to compete on the open labour market for a person with specialized skills, expertise, and experience. To recruit and retain a person with these credentials may cost more initially, and going forward, than filling the position with a sworn member on a rotating basis. The same may hold true for a civilian doing motor vehicle accident investigations or reconstruction. Again though, that individual may be more capable in the position than a police officer who may transfer in two to three years.

The experience of police departments generally is that civilizing positions results in cost savings. On an annualized basis, civilizing 104 positions in the Toronto Police Service between 1994 and 2005 resulted in a $1.97 million dollar savings to the Service, or an average savings of $19,000 per position. Only four of the 104 positions resulted in a higher salary being paid to the civilian than the officer originally performing the same duty (City of Toronto, Budget Advisory Committee, 2005).

The majority (N=52) of the civilianized positions were in the Court Services and Traffic Services areas (N=21). Additional areas in which positions were civilized were Intelligence, Freedom of Information, Occupational Health and Safety, Human Resources, and Training and Education, among others (City of Toronto, Budget Advisory Committee, 2005).

Civilian Concerns

Civilians as well may be wary of increased civilianization in police departments. A recent Canadian report (Price water house Coopers, 2001:45) found that civilians expressed "concerns over perceived differences in pay, promotional opportunities and status between civilians and police officers. The absence of a defined career structure, official recognition, access to ongoing professional development opportunities, coupled with a perceived lack of respect from sworn officers, may result in civilians in police organizations viewing their position as "one of the major white-collar ghettos in the public sector" (Loveday, 1989, p. 88). However, this perceived lack of respect can be overcome as civilians assume more complex and demanding positions that are correspondingly associated with higher levels of prestige within the organization.

Employee Disciplinary Matrix

A Search for Fairness in the Disciplinary Process

Unfortunately, perceived unfairness is an all too common condition in law enforcement agencies. Employee discipline is never an easy matter to deal with in any employment environment, and law enforcement agencies are no exception. In the field of law enforcement there are additional forces that tend to complicate both the procedural and substantive aspects of employee discipline. In particular, because of the unique powers that police hold in a democratic society, there is greater demand for accountability among police departments and individual officers. Actions and behaviors of officers often have life altering consequences for the public and unauthorized behaviors or actions can have dire legal consequences for officers and their agencies. Consequently, ensuring that police officers act in accordance with law, departmental policy, rules, and training is an indispensable element of effective police management.

Traditionally, law enforcement has been long on discipline and short on remediation. In more recent times, police organizations have adopted disciplinary procedures that are designed not simply to impose negative sanctions but to provide employees with the opportunity to correct inappropriate behavior and learn from mistakes. Consistent with this more redemptive approach to personnel management has come the notion of progressive discipline—a key component, as shall be seen, in the construction and

use of a disciplinary matrix. Progressive discipline holds that, when punishment is warranted, it is most effective to mete it out in increasing levels of severity based on reoccurrences. Less serious forms of misconduct and those that are first offenses do not always deserve or require severe punitive actions. They can often be dealt with effectively by verbal reprimands or counseling, among other possible alternatives. In other words, the discipline must fit the misconduct, or be appropriate to the misdeed at hand. Progressive discipline, however, sometimes requires that employees receive different penalties for the same offense behavior because of different disciplinary histories.

In employment generally, and police work in particular, the notion of fairness in administration of discipline plays a key role. If employees believe that they are being dealt with fairly, they are more likely to be accepting of corrective actions and less likely to be alienated. In contrast, when discipline is viewed as unfair or unpredictable, employees often undermine the process and develop negative attitudes towards the organization. Unfair disciplinary processes (and those seen as unfair) support the development of a "code of silence" among employees and undermine the legitimacy of the disciplinary process.

The issue of fairness is comprised of at least two components of equal importance. The first of these is equality, which refers to consistency in the administration of discipline. Employees want to know that their punishment is no harsher than, and at least consistent with, the punishment of other employees who have committed the same type of misconduct. To be consistent, punishment for one person's act of misconduct must be the same or closely similar to the punishment given other persons who have committed the same or similar act. In other words, like penalties for like offenses in like circumstances. Equality also means that favoritism based on an employee's rank or position, race, gender, seniority or other characteristics does not play a part in determining appropriate discipline. Employee actions citing disparate treatment in disciplinary matters are often based on allegations that the police department's punishment was not in line with punishments given to other employees for the same or similar offense.

The second component of "fairness" is equity, meaning that underlying or contextual circumstances surrounding the misconduct or behavior need to be taken into account when deciding punishment. Mitigating circumstances may come into play. For example, in taking a prohibited action, the officer may have misunderstood the task or order that was given and acted inappropriately, the officer may have just learned of a death in the family and was not paying attention when engaged in the task at hand, or may have been confronted with highly unusual circumstances during the incident that warranted departure from established policy. On the other hand, determination of fair discipline must also take into account aggravating circumstances such as an officer's possible negative attitude toward the underlying incident, history of prior misconduct, prior attempts of the department to correct inappropriate behavior, or other factors.

Many if not most organizations generally, and police departments in particular, continue to find it difficult to successfully integrate the foregoing requirements into a cohesive disciplinary system. In larger departments in particular, it is difficult to achieve fairness of punishment when the authority for final disciplinary decisions is spread among a number of district, precinct, or division commanders who may not share the same views concerning appropriate punishment for the same offense. The perceived

fairness of disciplinary actions may be further eroded when supervisory or command level personnel are not held to the same standards as their line counterparts. Aggravating or mitigating information important to the fair determination of discipline may not be shared between departmental assignments or units, informal discipline and remedial actions of supervisors may not be fully documented, and problem employees often may be transferred rather than effectively dealt with by their superiors.

DISCIPLINARY MATRIX

The problem of developing a fair system of disciplinary sanctions in policing is similar to the problem of ensuring a fair system of criminal sentencing in the courts. At bottom the issue revolves around the existence of discretion in the disciplinary decision. While discretion is necessary for fairness since latitude allows penalties to be fine-tuned to match behaviors and circumstances, it also allows unfairness. The same system that allows a supervisor to grant leniency in cases involving well intentioned but inexperienced officers can also allow supervisors to grant or withhold leniency based on officer sex, race, age, or other characteristics.

There are three basic ways to control discretion. One way to control discretion is to eliminate it. Mandatory sentencing laws or mandatory penalty policies that require persons found in violation to receive a pre-set punishment act to eliminate discretion. The problem here is that while mandatory penalties can work to improve equality, they almost always undercut equity in the disciplinary process. A second way to control discretion is by developing a series of "checks" so that decisions are reviewed. Appellate review of criminal sentences provides a check on judicial decisions; an appeals process in the disciplinary procedures can do the same. Checks on discretion have a number of problems including the fact that they extend the length of the disciplinary process and thus add to officer and supervisory anxiety, undermine any deterrent effects, and add layers of decision making (and cost) to the process. Disciplinary decisions in most agencies are reviewable today (in addition to any departmental appeals there are often civil service reviews and, in the end, officers can seek court review of disciplinary decisions). Checking discretion may ultimately achieve more fairness, but given the current controversies, existing mechanisms do not seem to prevent disputes. A final way to limit discretion is through developing guidelines for decision makers. Guidelines inform the decision maker about the purpose of the decision, what factors should be considered (and how), and often, what has been the outcome in other similar cases.

In an effort to respond to charges of arbitrary and capricious disciplinary actions, police departments have sought several types of solutions, one of which is the development of a table of disciplinary actions often referred to as a disciplinary matrix. Such matrices attempt to answer the problem of fairness between individual disciplinary actions by the use of predetermined ranges of disciplinary alternatives. These disciplinary alternatives may be correlated to specific acts or various acts may be aggregated into a class of misconduct based on their perceived severity.

A disciplinary matrix provides the decision maker with a guideline for the disciplinary decision.

Disciplinary matrices are similar to matrix sentencing guidelines used in criminal courts around the country. The term "matrix" refers to a table that allows the decision maker to consider at least two things at the same time. Most criminal sentences are based on both the seriousness of the crime and the extent of the offender's prior record. Both more serious crimes and longer or more serious criminal histories lead to more severe penalties. The table plots offense seriousness against prior record and provides a suggested sentence or range of sentence for each combination of seriousness and prior record.

The matrix is like the mileage charts sometimes found on road maps that tell the reader how far it is between destinations. In these charts the same listing of destinations (usually cities) is printed across the top and down the side of the page. To find the distance between cities, the reader locates the first city on the vertical list (down the side) and then reads across the chart until reaching the second city on the horizontal list (across the top). At this point, where the two destinations intersect, the distance between the two places is printed. For discipline, the decision maker finds the seriousness of the behavior on one dimension and then reads across the chart to find a second dimension (such as prior disciplinary record). At the point where these two factors intersect, the matrix provides a range of appropriate sanctions or even a specific suggested sanction.

Progressive discipline is integral to disciplinary matrices or tables. Such tables are generally divided into several columns representing disciplinary history (a first, second, third, or even fourth repeat offense) and several rows representing seriousness of the misbehavior. Penalties increase as either seriousness or disciplinary history increase. For disciplinary history each repeated offense category carries a harsher form of punishment. Generally, repeated misconduct does not have to be of the same type or class in order to constitute repeated misconduct. The department establishes a period of time (typically between one and two years) wherein misconduct qualifies as a repeated offense.

Generally, disciplinary matrices are used for the imposition of punitive action for acts of misconduct rather than behavioral problems. Behavioral problems are often dealt with through counseling, remedial training, mentoring, increased supervision or related approaches. However, depending on the nature of the misbehavior and the frequency of its recurrence, it may be subject to sanctions within the disciplinary matrix.

The matrix is intended to provide officers with a general idea of the upper and lower limits of punishment for acts of misconduct. The matrix also provides guidance to supervisors and managers. In so doing, proponents hold, it takes some of the guesswork out of discipline, relieving officer apprehensions about potential penalties and reducing stress during the investigatory and deliberative stages of the disciplinary process. It is also purported to reduce individual concerns and potential grievances and appeals concerning disparate treatment. Strict adherence to a disciplinary matrix can limit the discretion of deciding officials and thereby level the playing field among supervisors who may have widely divergent ideas about discipline. Some also argue that a disciplinary matrix can enhance public information and police accountability in cases where a department's disciplinary table of penalties is made public.

While a disciplinary matrix may assist in bringing consistency to disciplinary decisions, some argue that it does not go far enough in many instances in ensuring the inclusion of mitigating or aggravating factors that could enhance or diminish the decision on severity of discipline. Still others argue that it removes important management discretion to impose punishment that is consistent with both mitigating and aggravating factors.

These are both legitimate concerns. A table of penalties, once accepted by management and line officers alike, could conceivably limit disciplinary discretion of supervisors and commanders. The question then becomes, by using a disciplinary matrix, would departments sacrifice a degree of equity for the sake of meeting demands for equality? The answer to this is both yes and no. Theoretically, to be fully consistent in all cases of punishment would exclude, in some cases, equity in discipline because it would have to overlook individual differences and circumstances in reliance on the formula of penalties. Theoretically, the specific act of misconduct would be the only issue at hand in making a disciplinary decision.

In reality, this is normally not the case for two reasons. First, equity and consistency do not have to be mutually exclusive, nor do they have to unacceptably compromise one another. Mitigating and aggravating factors can, and should, be incorporated into the disciplinary decision-making process when using a matrix. This has been done at the federal level, as we shall see, and to some degree in state and local disciplinary procedures. In fact, it would be problematic if provisions for considering extenuating circumstances were not included in a system that uses a disciplinary matrix given the fact that due process considerations allow employees to reply both orally and in writing to specific charges. Secondly, most tables of discipline do not identify discreet disciplinary penalties but rather a range of possible penalties, thus providing the deciding authority with necessary latitude in entertaining and incorporating extenuating circumstances into the

disciplinary decision. An example of one page of a disciplinary matrix is included in the appendix.

THE FEDERAL MODEL

Many elements of the federal government, as well as the Metropolitan Washington Police Department, rely on a disciplinary matrix to guide decision making on appropriate discipline.

The Office of the Secretary of Defense (OSD) for example, provides guidance on the use of the matrix and the incorporation of mitigating and aggravating factors in disciplinary decisions.[2] An overview of their system may provide a useful example for those departments considering the use of a disciplinary matrix.

In this case, supervisors are provided with the primary responsibility for initiating and recommending employee discipline, albeit with significant oversight by a senior commander and a personnel specialist from the Office of Labor Relations. In referencing the table of penalties, guidance provides that a particular penalty is not mandatory simply because it is listed in the table. In addition, the system provides that appropriate penalties for unlisted offenses may be derived by comparing the nature and seriousness of an offense to those listed in the table. Then, selection of an appropriate penalty should involve the balancing of the relevant factors in the individual case, consideration of the employee's previous disciplinary record, if any, and the recent offense giving rise to the disciplinary action.

The instructions further state:

> In selecting the appropriate penalty from the table, a prior offense of any type for which formal disciplinary action was taken forms the basis for proposing the next higher sanction. For example, a first offense of insubordination for which an official reprimand is in the employee's official personnel folder, followed by a charge of absence without leave (AWOL), triggers the second offense identified in the table, i.e., a proposed five-day suspension if the AWOL charge was for eight hours

or less or a proposed five-day suspension if the AWOL charge exceeded eight hours. Aggravating factors on which the supervisor intends to rely for imposition of a more stringent penalty, such as a history of discipline or the seriousness of the offense, should be addressed in the notice of proposed discipline, thereby giving the employee the opportunity to respond.

The federal system emphasizes that a matrix of penalties should not be employed in a mechanical fashion, but with practical realism. This approach was emphasized in the landmark case Douglas v. Veterans Administration,[3] in which the Federal Merit System Protection Board, a federal adjudicatory agency, outlined 12 factors that must be considered by supervisors when recommending or deciding employee disciplinary action. While not all are pertinent to every case, they provide a broad-brush approach of the types of mitigating (or aggravating) factors that can and should be considered when employing an agency table of penalties. Many, if not most, of these have application in the disciplinary decision -making environment of state and local law enforcement:

- The nature and seriousness of the offense, and its relation to the employee's duties, position, and responsibilities, including whether the offense was intentional or technical or inadvertent, or was committed maliciously or for gain, or was frequently repeated
- The employee's job level and type of employment, including supervisory or fiduciary role, contacts with the public, and prominence of the position
- The employee's disciplinary record
- The employee's work record, including length of service, performance on the job, ability to get along with fellow workers, and dependability
- The effect of the offense upon the employee's ability to perform at a satisfactory level and its effect upon supervisors' confidence in the employee's work ability to perform assigned duties

- Consistency of the penalty with those imposed upon other employees for the same or similar offenses
- Consistency of the penalty with any applicable agency table of penalties
- The notoriety of the offense or its impact upon the reputation of the agency
- The clarity with which the employee was on notice of any rules that were violated in committing the offense, or had been warned about the conduct in question
- The potential for the employee's rehabilitation
- Mitigating circumstances surrounding the offense such as unusual job tensions, personality problems, mental impairment, harassment, or bad faith, malice or provocation on the part of others involved in the matter
- The adequacy and effectiveness of alternative sanctions to deter such conduct in the future by the employee or others

IMPORTANCE OF DOCUMENTATION

It is essential for supervisors to document misconduct and both formal and informal discipline by using either a disciplinary matrix or other means to determine discipline. Without such documentation, it is not possible to ensure consistency between disciplinary decisions for the same employee or other employees who have been engaged in similar misconduct, nor is it possible to respond effectively to potential disciplinary appeals. Informal discipline such as verbal reprimands and counseling is no exception. These should be recorded in a supervisor's memorandum as a matter of record for performance review purposes and for future reference in cases of repeat misconduct. While informal discipline should not be placed in an employee's permanent personnel file and may not have an immediate impact on an officer's employment status or condition, repeated behavioral problems or an accumulation of minor infractions of policy or procedure should be taken into account when assessing an employee's performance or determining future penalties for misconduct. As such, this information must be available to other supervisors if necessary.

Such information is normally retained at the unit level for a limited period of time and is expunged after a set period of time if the officer does not engage in additional misconduct.

When conducting any type of informal discipline or corrective action, supervisors should fully document the details of the circumstances of the incident(s) on which the counseling or reprimand is based. The specifics of the counseling or reprimand should also be documented together with such information as the date it took place, persons present such as another supervisor as witness, name of the person conducting the counseling and any statements made by the subject officer that have bearing on the officer's performance or behavior. The officer should be notified that the counseling session or reprimand will be documented but will be used only for purposes of recording the incident unless misconduct or inappropriate behavior is repeated. In some cases, the supervisor and officer may decide to enter into an agreement involving informal remedial training, review of departmental policy and procedures, or related actions to help ensure that similar problems of conduct or misbehavior can be avoided. In such cases, the terms of such an agreement should be clearly defined in the memorandum.

The employee should be given the opportunity to read and discuss the contents of the memorandum once completed, asked to sign and date it to verify that the employee has read it, and given a copy if he or she requests one. Where differences of opinion concerning the contents of the memorandum exist, they should be discussed and documented in an attachment. If the employee refuses to acknowledge the memorandum by signature, this fact should be recorded on the document and witnessed by another supervisor.

The need for documentation is equally if not more important in instances of formal disciplinary actions that have direct impact on the terms and conditions of employment. These procedures and due process safeguards involving such matters as Garrity and Laudermill are generally well documented in departmental policy and need not be reexamined here.[4]

Comprehensive documentation in the realm of employee discipline may also serve the police department in other ways. When reports of misconduct are lodged in a central repository, they can provide the core data elements for an early warning system, both for individual employees and the organization as a whole. In all organizations, compilation of employee disciplinary offenses and subsequent penalties will prove invaluable for comparative purposes in determining the consistency of disciplinary actions between individuals and, in larger departments, between divisions, assignments, and varied departmental components. In addition, summary and comparative data on the overall nature of employee misconduct in the department can point to potential problems in departmental policy, training, or supervision as well as possible solutions. For example, public complaints that center on unacceptable delivery of services rather than officer conduct (such as response time) may also prove essential in making alterations in personnel allocation or other organizational change.

When systematically organized in this manner, whether manually or by computer programming, individual officer conduct that may point to more serious problems can be flagged and addressed on a preemptive basis. Repeated complaints regarding firearms discharges, excessive force, damage to motor vehicles, loss of departmental property, and related information can suggest underlying problems with an officer that deserve proactive attention. Finally, this information is vital to monitoring and assessing the operation of the disciplinary matrix. A consistent pattern of disciplinary decisions that fall outside the range suggested in the matrix may be evidence that the matrix should be revised, or that supervisors require additional training in the use of the matrix.

WHAT IS "REASONABLE" DISCIPLINE?

Possibly most problematic in development of a disciplinary matrix is the selection of appropriate or reasonable penalties for individual acts or classes of misconduct. As noted earlier, a basic criterion for discipline is that the punishment must be in reasonable proportion to the rule or policy violation or other prohibited conduct. Obviously, a penalty that may be reasonable to one person may not be to another. There is no nationally recognized table of disciplines that can be used commonly among disciplinary schedules across states and localities. Many would argue that such a model would be impractical in light of differences in community and individual agency value systems, goals, and priorities. This is not to say that examples from similarly situated police departments cannot be effectively and usefully employed. In fact, if disciplinary actions are challenged as unreasonable, the availability of comparative information from other law enforcement agencies could be useful. But the final decision for an individual department must be made by that police department.

In order for a disciplinary system of this type to function with reasonable effectiveness, there must be some degree of buy in by employees. Where labor unions represent the employment interests of workers, this will unavoidably require union involvement. Even where collective bargaining entities are not at issue, management and line employees will need to reach a degree of agreement on acceptable disciplinary penalties and sanctions. This does not mean that management must seek concurrence on all decisions of disciplinary action but that there needs to be some reasonable accommodation of interests in arriving at a final table of disciplinary penalties.

Such a process of give-and-take can take considerable time and will undoubtedly test the patience of all involved. But if it can be accomplished, the exercise alone can be valuable. For example, in some cases where departments have engaged in this undertaking, it has been reported that employees take a stricter view toward adherence to certain principles of conduct and advocate harsher penalties than management for certain employee transgressions; thus, such negotiation can assist the department in defining or refining its core values and goals. For example, on close examination, employees may determine that police work requires, among all else, reliance on the integrity and truthfulness of officers. As such, employee conduct that undermines these basic tenets must be dealt with decisively and harshly. By the same token, departmental management may endorse more stringent penalties for failure of officers to adhere to policy in critical enforcement areas. For example,

failure of officers to abide strictly to vehicular pursuit policy and procedures may be regarded as deserving strict enforcement and harsh penalties due to the department's involvement in a large number of crashes and injuries in such incidents. In this and related instances, a department can utilize the table of penalties to enforce and underline its commitment to specific priorities or goals.

Development of a table of penalties can be time consuming and laborious; however, the effort can be truncated somewhat by organizing acts of misconduct into conceptually similar classes with assigned sanctions on a collective basis. This approach has merit in that it is difficult to attempt to identify every discreet act of misconduct. And, failure to identify a specific act as impermissible could render any discipline in such a case as unreasonable based on the fact that employees were not informed in advance that it was prohibited. Identification of classes of prohibited actions combined with a defined list of mitigating and extenuating factors similar to those identified in Douglas under the federal model may be adequate to provide sufficient particularity to discipline based on the act of misconduct.

There is quite a bit of knowledge and experience with matrix sentencing guidelines that can ease the development of disciplinary matrices. It is not necessary to reinvent the wheel. Based on the experience with sentencing guidelines, there are two basic models for matrix development: descriptive or prescriptive. A descriptive matrix suggests sanctions based on what has typically been done in similar cases in the past. If disciplinary data are available, an analysis is done to identify the factors associated with different sanctions. Almost always this analysis will reveal that the severity of punishments is linked to the seriousness of the misbehavior and the prior history of the employee. Based on this analysis, a matrix can be derived that reflects these factors. In this way, the matrix actually describes current practice. In this case, the application of the matrix does little to change how discipline is decided but does increase consistency. Alternatively, a prescriptive matrix can be developed by first determining what factors should be important and how they should relate. Then this determination of how discipline should work forms the basis of a matrix that prescribes penalties for future violations. In this case, the matrix discipline system may bear no relation to existing practice. The choice of developmental method depends on several factors including the availability of data, the capacity to conduct the analyses, the levels of satisfaction with current discipline practices, and the like. If the primary complaint about the current disciplinary process is procedural (concerns equality) and not substantive (concerns equity), a descriptive model seems to be indicated.

If a disciplinary matrix is adopted, regardless of the developmental model it is important to institute a system of recording disciplinary actions that includes collecting information about the relevant factors (such as offense seriousness, prior history, and sanction) so that the workings of the matrix system can be documented and evaluated. Periodic reviews should be conducted to look for areas where the system might be improved.

No matter how sanctions are determined in an employee disciplinary system, it is important to realize that the penalties are only part of the process. A matrix system can improve fairness in disciplinary decisions but the integrity of the total disciplinary processes depends on fairness in detecting, reporting, investigating, and documenting infractions. A disciplinary matrix is part of a total employee discipline process.

NOTES

1. Investigation of Employee Misconduct: Concepts and Issues Paper, IACP National Law Enforcement Policy Center, International Association of Chiefs of Police, 515 North Washington Street, Alexandria, Virginia.

2. Department of Defense, Washington Headquarters Service, Memorandum for Supervisors and Managers: Disciplinary and Adverse Actions, March 1989.

3. Douglas v. Veterans Administration, 5 M.S.P.R. 280, 306 (1981).

4. See Investigation of Employee Misconduct, Model Policy and Concepts and Issues Paper, IACP National Law Enforcement Policy Center, International Association of Chiefs of Police, Alexandria, Virginia

Focus on Personnel

Early Detection of the Problem Officer

By Dino DeCrescenzo

Sadly, a disturbing trend has begun to emerge concerning the law enforcement profession. That is, allegations against those officers facing suspension or termination rarely seem to surprise members of their departments and, at times, many residents of their communities. Over the past several decades, investigative journalists have found that in some agencies, as few as 2 percent of officers held responsibility for 50 percent of citizen complaints.[1] In addition, numerous police chiefs reported that 10 percent of their sworn personnel caused 90 percent of the problems.[2] Also, studies on the issue repeatedly indicated that an extremely small and disproportionate number of officers incurred most of the accusations.[3]

In reality, the majority of law enforcement officers are supremely dedicated individuals severely offended by the behavior and acts committed by those few who have tarnished the image of their profession.[4] These officers and the citizens they serve have begun to demand reasons for why such employees have remained on the job, even though they have violated departmental and societal rules. The awareness of these problem officers has existed for some time. In 1981, the U.S. Commission on Civil Rights recommended that all police departments create an early warning system to identify problem employees who often receive the highest number of complaints or display patterns of inappropriate behavior.[5] In today's world

of terrorists and increasingly violent criminals, such efforts may prove more important than ever before.

INTERVENTION APPROACH

According to the U.S. Department of Justice, early warning systems take the form of databases that contain personnel information designed to identify problem behavior and allow early intervention to correct the misconduct. Generally nonpunitive, the systems include peer review, additional training, and counseling. They can provide supervisors and managers with information relating to potential patterns of at-risk conduct. Most systems require intervention after recording a certain number of complaints of a particular type within a specified time frame.[6] Although a few departments use only citizen complaints to select officers for intervention, most rely on a combination of behavior indicators.[7] Early warning systems should consider the totality of officer work histories, including accidents, pursuits, transfers, training, grievances, education, drug usage, civil suits, truthfulness, property damage, discourtesy, false arrest claims, and insubordination.[8] They should track all complaints, sick time used, resisting arrest incidents, assaults on officers, obstruction of officer arrests, and disorderly conduct arrests made by officers.[9] These last four behavior indicators appear to be significant measuring devices of potential problem employees. A higher

Dino DeCrescenzo, "Focus on Personnel: Early Detection of the Problem Officer," *FBI Law Enforcement Bulletin*, vol. 74, no. 7, pp. 14–17. Copyright in the Public Domain.

number of these types of arrests when compared with those of other officers may reveal personnel acting beyond their scope of authority.

The theory behind an early warning system is that such incidents *individually* may mean nothing, but the combined totality of behaviors may signal a developing problem that needs attention.[10] These indicators, compiled into a single place, can flag a potential pattern of problematic behavior and identify an officer at risk of engaging in misconduct.

The phenomenon of early detection or early warning systems within law enforcement agencies is a fairly new concept that has begun to spread more rapidly since Congress passed the Violent Crime Control and Law Enforcement Act, which empowered the federal government to investigate and bring suit against those officers who routinely abused their authority.[11] For the most part, when departments have suits brought against them, they enter into a consent decree with the government agency agreeing on the changes required and to being monitored until the judge lifts the decree.[12] More often than not, the recommendations stemming from such investigations include implementation of an early warning or detection system as a first step in the process of abolishing the pattern and practice of conduct by the officers.

RESEARCH FINDINGS

The first in-depth study of early warning systems found that 27 percent of the agencies surveyed in 1999 had such a mechanism in place while another 12 percent planned on implementing one.[13] The participating agencies were police departments employing a minimum of 80 officers and serving populations of at least 50,000. However, 87 percent of police departments in the United States have fewer than 25 sworn officers.[14] So, while less than 40 percent of the large agencies surveyed either had or planned to have an early warning system in 1999, the majority of police departments in the country most likely did not have nor plan on implementing such a system at the time.

If administered properly, an early warning and detection system should allow the department to quickly intervene and help modify the behavior of the officers identified. Moreover, a successful early detection system not only can identify negative behavior but also can recognize conduct worthy of commendation.[15] The study further indicated that early warning systems substantially reduced citizen complaints and other problematic behavior. For example, three large police departments with early warning systems in effect for at least 4 years had substantially fewer citizen complaints and use-of-force incidents after the intervention. A successful system can benefit the entire agency, the community, and the troubled or problem officer with prompt intervention administered properly. Experts stress that using an early warning system to punish officers will undermine its effectiveness, but applying the information learned from the data to counsel and train them will expand its value.[16]

Some departments have successfully employed early warning systems for over a decade with beneficial results.[17] However, these programs still may not accurately identify every specific pattern of behavior that may ultimately lead to misconduct. In addition, the study found that no standards had been established for identifying officers in the early warning systems examined. Instead, only a general agreement existed on some of the criteria that should influence their selection.[18] These issues demonstrate that agencies must carefully analyze the information compiled on their personnel and establish strict selection guidelines to ensure that they correctly determine those officers in need of intervention.

Finally, the study noted that the implementation of an early warning system can prove compatible with both problem-oriented and community policing. The law enforcement administrator can incorporate the warning system into the department's overall philosophy and goals, recognizing that the new system must involve counseling and training as the main objective in modifying the behaviors of the officers selected and flagged for intervention. The administrator, however, must remember that the police union and the officers may suspect a new warning system and possibly resist its implementation. One early warning discipline system stressed the police union's involvement in the process prior to implementation of a program that provided predictable sanctions agreed upon by management and the union.[19] Because most complaints by unions involve the unequal treatment of personnel and ambiguous, unknown, or unpredictable punishments, this system established a disciplinary matrix with minimum and maximum penalties and ensured that the administration and the collective bargaining unit agreed upon predictable, reliable, equitable, and valid sanctions. Such involvement by the union or collective bargaining unit can greatly increase the success of an early warning system.

POSITIVE CHANGE

Law enforcement agencies throughout this country generally have pursued a traditional approach when dealing with officer misconduct.[20] Most have dealt with this issue through reactive as opposed to proactive efforts, primarily using citizen and internal complaints to identify such behavior. In addition, most departments impose corrective action only after the misconduct has occurred.

To effect positive change in the behavior of the few officers that create the majority of problems, departments must begin to take sufficient action against those repeatedly accused of excessive force and continually look for patterns in officer conduct.[21] They also must seriously discipline such personnel, not merely reassign them to other duties. Finally, agencies must provide troubled officers with counseling and other services. As one official said, "We have a tendency to go from zero to 60, by focusing only on the egregious, but not having a system to correct or discipline the behavior that is nonegregious."[22]

Officers who have exhibited less than stellar behavior need help to return to their former standards of professionalism. Departments should endeavor to find out what these officers need to overcome their problems and, once again, become valuable, contributing members of their profession. To this end, an early warning system can offer an effective approach for agencies to use.

CONCLUSION

Today's law enforcement administrators must identify problem officers and intervene appropriately with counseling, training, and other methods in an attempt to modify and change their behavior. Managers will benefit their departments, communities, and problem officers with the implementation of a properly administered early warning system. Such an approach can help agencies combat the disturbing trend that seems to indicate that they disregard officer misconduct.

Early warning systems demonstrate that departments and administrators have developed a clear policy regarding misconduct, have put a program in place to correct negative behavior, and have made a good-faith effort to identify employees whose performance is less than satisfactory.[23] The majority of their officers who valiantly place themselves in harm's way every day to protect the citizens of their communities deserve no less.

NOTES

1. C.R. Swanson, L. Territo, and R.W. Taylor, *Police Administration: Structures, Processes, and Behavior*, 6th ed. (Upper Saddle River, NJ: Prentice Hall, 2004).

2. S. Walker, G.P. Alpert, and D.J. Kenney, "Early Warning Systems: Responding to the Problem Police Officer," *National Institute of Justice Journal* (July 2001); retrieved on January 28, 2005, from *http://www.ncjrs.org/pdffiles1/nij/188565.pdf*.

3. S. Slahor, "Earlier Is Better When Solving Problems," *Law and Order*, June 2004, 6.

4. J. Arnold, "Special Report II: Ethics—Early Misconduct Detection," *Law and Order*, August 2001, 8.

5. Supra note 2.

6. Supra note 4.

7. Supra note 2.

8. Supra note 3.

9. T.F. Kennedy, *Preventing, Detecting, and Investigating Employee Misconduct*, paper present-

ed at a Roger Williams University Conference, Bristol, RI, October 2003.

10. R.G. Dunlop and J. Adams, "System to Spot Troubled Officers Not Fully Used: Goal Is to Detect Small Problems, Prevent Big Ones," *Louisville Courier Journal*, April 2, 2000.

11. "Pittsburgh's Experience with Police Monitoring," *Vera Institute of Justice*, June 17, 2004; retrieved on January 28, 2005, from *http://www.vera.org/project/project1_1.asp?section_id=7&project_id=13*.

12. Ibid.

13. Supra note 2.

14. S.F. Kelly, "Internal Affairs: Issues for Small Police Departments," *FBI Law Enforcement Bulletin*, July 2003, 1–6.

15. Supra note 3.

16. "Best Early Warning Tool Is Informative," *Organized Crime Digest* 22, no. 13 (August 10, 2001).

17. Supra note 4.

18. Supra note 2.

19. R.W. Serpas, J.W. Olson, and B.D. Jones, "An Employee Disciplinary System That Makes Sense," *The Police Chief*, September 2003.

20. Supra note 4.

21. D. Washburn, D. Hasemyer, and M. Arner, "A Question of Force: Dealing with Multiple Shooters Has Been a 'Huge' Issue," *The San Diego Union-Tribune*, January 19, 2003; retrieved from *http://www.signonsandiego.com-news/reports/shootings/ 20030122-9999_mz1n-19questn.htm*.

22. Supra note 3.

23. Supra note 2.

Managing the Problem Employee

A Road Map for Success

By Thomas Q. Weitzel

Every department, at some time, faces the monumental task of managing problem employees. These workers possess varying degrees of competence and present problems for agencies in a number of ways, including abusing sick time, coming to work with their own agenda (i.e., conducting personal business at work), or having a "just-a-job" attitude, which breeds a selfish "What can the department do for me?" rather than a "What can I do for the community?" attitude. Such behaviors create a negative environment for coworkers, supervisors (who can feel inept at controlling the situation and may waste valuable time correcting the employees' mistakes and, possibly, defending their work habits), and the citizens the officers serve daily.

Law enforcement managers should strive to effectively deal with these workers to the satisfaction of the employee, as well as the employer. Considering the effects that these individuals can have on the department and the community, supervisors must intervene and systematically address such problems as quickly as possible before these situations escalate to enormous proportions. To this end, agencies must understand how to recognize problem employees and how to effectively handle them.

RECOGNIZING THE PROBLEM EMPLOYEE

Without a doubt, every organization has at least one problem employee. A challenge agencies face is identifying these individuals. Unfortunately, no formula for categorizing them exists. Variables, such as industry, level or status of job, race, sex, ethnicity, or any other category, prove meaningless.[1]

Problems with Supervisors

Sometimes, the problem in recognizing these workers may rest with the manager. For instance, supervisors may not want to admit they have a problem employee for fear that it will reflect poorly on their skill in managing people. In other cases, a worker may exhibit such extraordinary ability in certain areas that the supervisor is willing to overlook weaknesses in other endeavors. As another possible scenario, an employee may have a manager with relaxed standards. An uncomfortable situation also may exist when the supervisor and worker share a personal friendship or genuine fondness for each other. Or, managers may feel so overwhelmed with professional responsibilities or personal crises that they choose just to ignore the problem.

In other instances, a dilemma may exist as to whether a particular individual simply is called a problem employee or actually is one. The answer to this question could depend on the manager. Supervisors may be particularly harsh in their opinion and assessment of a worker. Or, the manager may not take into account that no two employees are alike, that each has a different personality and work ethic; perhaps, the supervisor's judgment of the individual is based on personal values or attitudes, which is subjective and unfair. Another unfortunate possibility is that the manager may not feel comfortable working with a person of a different age, race, sex, or ethnic origin. In still other cases, the supervisor's managerial style (which, perhaps, is problematic) may be the defining factor relating to the problem employee; the manager, in fact, simply may lack knowledge, understanding, and training in the art of supervising people.

Identification

To help determine whether or not an individual is a problem employee, law enforcement managers can evaluate a number of questions. These include, but are not limited to, the following examples:

- Do you receive negative feedback from citizens about the officer's demeanor or attitude?
- Do you receive complaints about how the employee treats coworkers?
- Do you need to regularly check the individual's work?
- Does the officer handle calls appropriately?
- Do scheduling problems arise because the employee fails to show up?
- Do you frequently spend time doing assignments that you should feel comfortable delegating to the individual?
- Does the officer rarely complete work on time?
- Does the employee frequently give reasons why assignments cannot be done?
- Do you receive reports that the individual complains about you to other people?
- Do you find it difficult to get your own work done because of the time you spend on the officer's problems and mistakes?
- Do you rarely give this person important assignments?

- Does the employee usually offer excuses or blame others for mistakes?
- Does the officer occasionally lie or stretch the truth?

A positive answer to any of these questions could indicate a problem employee, especially if it touches on an area of particular importance to the supervisor. An affirmative answer to two or more of these questions definitely identifies the individual as a problem employee.[2]

Issues with Employees

Problem employees do not necessarily lack competence. However, such workers present trouble for organizations when factors, such as a bad attitude, poor motivation, or an inability to get along with others, negatively influence the way they perform their jobs.[3] Many such individuals face trouble in their personal lives that adversely affects them at work. Examples include divorce, financial problems, death in the family, illnesses, or problems with their children. Other times, these employees are genuinely mismatched to the profession they have chosen; their personal characteristics do not fit the demands of the job.[4] In other cases, the particular department (these vary in managerial attitudes and climate) a prospective officer decides to join can impede performance.

Generally, problem employees fit into one of seven categories. These include hostile aggressives, who, when things do not go their way, bully and overwhelm others with snide comments or tantrums; complainers, who gripe incessantly, but never take action to improve the circumstances they are complaining about; silent and unresponsives, who respond to requests with a "yep," a "nope," or a grunt; super agreeables, who appear outgoing, personable, and supportive in the supervisor's presence, but then either do not produce what they promised or act contrary to expectations; negativists, who respond with a downtrodden spirit to the manager's every suggestion for improvement; know-it-all experts, who have a condescending and superior attitude and make the supervisor feel foolish; and indecisives, who have difficulty making decisions and cannot let go of anything until it is perfect (which means never).[5]

While supervisors in no way want to excuse the behavior of these workers, they can better understand them by looking at the big picture of what may cause such individuals to work and respond the way they do. In this regard, the five major internal sources of influence of an individual's behavior are motivation by needs, motivation by values, attitudes, norms, and self-esteem.[6]

To determine why problem employees behave negatively, supervisors first should consider what motivates them. Needs and values serve as the two types of motivation that drive everyone. Needs motivation refers to an individual's need for security, love, and growth; if these are not met, a person will react negatively. Values motivation denotes the way people are driven by the ethical standards by which they live their lives; when conflicts arise in the way an employee's values relate to the job, negative behavior likely will result.

The level of self-esteem of individuals also may show through their actions in the workplace. People with low self-esteem tend to have a distorted view of reality. They may have, for example, a "me-versus-the-supervisor" mentality, which certainly would interfere in the performance of their duties.

Employees' negative attitude also may affect them on the job. Such an attitude, of course, can result in negative actions, interfering with the way the officer responds to the public, as well as supervisors.

Norms refer to the guidelines by which a person gauges normal behavior. The way people were raised largely can shape their norms. For example, individuals that grew up among negative family members will tend to be negative.

MANAGING THE PROBLEM EMPLOYEE: WRONG APPROACHES

Once law enforcement managers determine that someone fits the description of a problem employee, they need to consider how not to deal with the individual. The four ineffective ways of handling such workers include avoiding, overreacting, complaining, and lecturing.[7]

Supervisors must recognize these negative tendencies; identify which, if any, they commonly use; and stop handling problem employees in these ways.

Managers may attempt to address these situations by avoiding them. For example, they may feel uncomfortable dealing with interpersonal conflict, so they try to avoid or suppress disagreements.[8] Supervisors may feel that a situation is beyond their control and an incredible amount of stress may arise if they confront the individual. The manager may fear that the employee will become defensive and retaliate or that performance may deteriorate. This fits the description of "catastrophic" thinking.[9] Managers also may have an attitude of "what good will it do anyway," especially if they already have met with the worker regarding poor performance. Perhaps, supervisors may feel that they lack the expertise to handle such situations, so, rather than risk making a mistake, they ignore the issue.

However, avoiding the problem does not eliminate it. In fact, avoidance most likely will make it worse. The manager is not the only one affected; other employees are as well. Not handling such dilemmas will become a mark against the supervisor's credibility as boss. If, in the end, the agency terminates this worker, the situation will become all the more difficult. In the process, managers, not wanting to face the inevitable confrontation, will lose their own self-respect.

Some managers may make the mistake of overreacting to the situation. This may entail acting in an abrupt, harsh, or explosive manner toward the individual, unloading frustration and disgust verbally or physically. Perhaps, this is the only way the supervisor knows how to react. It may be the only outlet for pent-up frustration over the problem employee. In fact, the manager may consider such behavior justified. Some supervisors even may feel that these actions are effective, giving them a sense of control over the situation, as well as the individual.

However, overreacting does not work. In fact, it has a negative effect, not only on the employee but the supervisor as well. It quite possibly could result in unhealthy physiological effects for managers that react this way. In particular, the body prepares itself for a fight. If this occurs often enough, side effects appear in the form of ulcers, high blood pressure, or other physical ailments related to this kind of emotional outlet.[10] Also, workers, in the end, lose respect for supervisors who respond in this manner.

Complaining about the problem employee is a vicious cycle. Instead of "taking the bull by its horns," supervisors may choose to discuss their frustrations with someone other than the individual. Everybody does this at one time or another. However, to fall into this cycle on a consistent basis serves no purpose other than to prolong addressing the real issue.

Also, the supervisor may superficially feel a sense of accomplishment by voicing all of these negative opinions. In reality, nothing is done and it is a waste of time.

Lecturing is yet another pitfall of managing problem employees. However right the manager may feel, this tends to fall on deaf ears. The worker oftentimes will completely tune out whatever the supervisor is saying, no matter how noteworthy it may be; thus, this approach tends to have the opposite of the desired effect.

Managers should carefully consider the relationship they have with problem employees to attempt to determine the root of the dilemma. Perhaps, the supervisor treats the worker with contempt or disdain, and the employee has no respect or affection for the boss. Rather than accepting responsibility for the issue, both parties will tend to blame the other person. It is in this situation that a problem relationship exists.[11]

Categories of Problem Employees

- Hostile aggressives
- Complainers
- Silent and unresponsives
- Super agreeables
- Negativists
- Know-it-all experts
- Indecisives

Constructive Steps

So, how can law enforcement supervisors effectively deal with problem employees? The manager first must formally analyze the worker's performance. This evaluation is followed by a performance-improvement interview. Then, follow-up with the employee can ensure that the worker is making appropriate progress.

The Analysis

In conducting the performance analysis, managers must be prepared to pinpoint the problem areas exactly. It is imperative that the supervisor document every incident of unsatisfactory performance for every employee. Managers need to remain fair in their documentation, including instances of both effective and detrimental behavior and stating facts, not opinions. All documentation should be consistent with oral comments and actions.[12] Supervisors tend to make four common mistakes in conducting the analysis. One, managers may not recognize a need to analyze an employee's performance; they may feel that it so obvious that a problem exists that there is no need to waste time doing an evaluation. This oversimplifies the problem, ignoring the importance of identifying the root causes.

Two, the supervisor may focus too much on the reasons behind the employee's poor performance and too little on the problem itself. This kind of speculation tends to draw the focus away from the worker's poor performance and, instead, leads the manager to make assumptions that may or may not explain the employee's behavior.

Three, the supervisor may generalize the employee's performance, instead of concentrating on specific areas that need improvement. If managers do not narrowly define the problem, they will find it difficult to convey to the individual the exact issues.

Four, supervisors may focus only on what the worker does wrong. Only discussing the negative aspects of the individual's performance can exacerbate the problem, alienating and discouraging the employee.

Legally, agencies should note that they must make the performance-improvement interview process as formalized, standardized, and objective as possible. They also must keep it as job related as possible, based on a formal job analysis for all employment positions, and ensure that the evaluations are uncontaminated and not deficient. They must see that employees are made aware of the performance standards to which they will be held accountable.[13] With this in mind, the analysis should include three main areas. First, it should contain a formulation of some positive goals describing ways in which employees can improve their performance. For example, instead of writing down that individuals never arrive on time for their shifts, supervisors should state that they need to be on time for roll call.

Second, the analysis should identify the behavior changes that the employee should make for each goal. The particular process for this involves stating the original problem, then the specified goal to improve performance, and then an answer to "What observable behavior can demonstrate to the supervisor that the goal has been achieved?"[14]

Third, managers should relate several areas where the employee performs effectively, with specific examples. This will end the evaluation on a positive note.

The Interview

After the manager completes the analysis, the next step is setting up an interview time with the employee. Supervisors should clearly explain to employees that the purpose of the meeting is to review their work performance. Managers should advise workers of the prepared documentation of their strong and weak areas. They also should encourage workers to prepare their own notes for the meeting.

The manager should conduct the interview in such a way that the employee knows what to expect. In the beginning, the supervisor should briefly describe the agenda. By doing so, the manager will set the structure and tone for the entire meeting, thus providing an opportunity for it to run smoothly.

Supervisors must listen to their employees. Their listening skills should be well polished for the interview if they expect to establish meaningful dialogue with the individual. Also, in this way, managers can minimize defensiveness.[15] Supervisors should find out from their employees how they generally feel the job is going, along with any problems they may be experiencing. Managers also should ask how they can make the employee's job less frustrating and more satisfying; here, the supervisor should be well versed in handling criticism. While such dialogue may make managers uneasy, feeling that they are "on the spot," this demonstrates to the employee that the supervisor genuinely cares and truly is interested in making the job more fulfilling. It opens up the lines of communication and gives the manager more credibility.

The next step in the interview process is having employees give a self-analysis of their work performance. This includes those areas where they consider themselves effective, as opposed to inadequate. At this point, supervisors can determine if the individual is aware of the problem areas or, perhaps, has no idea.

After the employee's analysis, supervisors present theirs. Managers should remain positive and rely on the prepared written evaluation. The more the supervisor and employee can agree on areas of effective performance and those needing improvement, the more the employee will be motivated to improve.[16] Managers also should listen to the worker's feedback during this section of the interview; this is a necessary step toward resolution of the problem or problems.

The next step is negotiating a promise of action from the employee. Appropriate results include the following:

- The employee volunteers to take action that will clear up the problem.
- The supervisor suggests steps to the worker that will resolve the issue.
- The manager asks the individual to take action to solve the problem.
- The supervisor tells the employee to take appropriate steps and explains what the manager will do if the employee fails to act.
- The supervisor spells out the consequences, in
- luding termination, if the worker does not take action.

The appropriate approach, of course, is determined by the severity of the situation.[17] The main objective is that at the conclusion of the interview, the employee will fully understand what the expectations are, as well as the consequences of not meeting those demands.

Wrong Approaches for Managers

- Avoiding
- Overreacting
- Complaining
- Lecturing

The Follow-up

After a stated period of time, managers should conduct a follow-up interview with the employee for performance reevaluation. This will enable supervisors to determine if workers have attempted to carry out appropriate actions as promised. More interviews should occur, if appropriate, to ensure that employees continue to make necessary progress.

If the worker fails to take action in the areas agreed upon, each particular department should follow an established sequence of events. Depending on the severity and type of the problem, the agency may deal with the employee in a variety of ways. Examples include oral or written reprimand; retraining; shadowing by another officer; a formal hearing in front of the police and fire board, which possibly can be followed by a suspension; or termination.

CONCLUSION

Identifying and managing problem employees can prove difficult. However, it is crucial that departments identify such individuals and handle them efficiently, objectively, and fairly. These workers can have a negative impact both inside and outside the department.

Supervisors may find situations involving problem employees intimidating. However, they can follow effective procedures to identify who these individuals are and to work with them to improve their performance or, if this is not possible, to take more drastic measures.

NOTES

1. Mardy Grothe and Peter Wylie, Problem Employees: How to Improve Their Performance (Dover, NH: Upstart Publishing Company, Inc., 1991), 5.
2. Supra note 1, 14. The author modified these questions to serve as examples for law enforcement agencies.
3. Supra note 1, 8.
4. Supra note 1, 7.
5. Robert M. Bramson, Coping With Difficult People (New York, NY: Anchor Press, 1981), 5.
6. Michael S. Kravitz, Managing Negative People (Menlo Park, CA: Crisp Publications, Inc., 1995), 11.
7. Supra note 1, 19.
8. Cynthia Berryman-Fink, The Manager's Desk Reference (New York, NY: Amacom, 1989), 45.
9. Supra note 1, 22.
10. Supra note 1, 25.
11. Supra note 1, 35–36.
12. Supra note 8, 224.
13. Supra note 8, 224.
14. Supra note 1, 53.
15. Deborah Bright, The Official Criticism Manual (New York, NY: Bright Enterprises, Inc., 1991), 18.
16. Supra note 1, 169.
17. Gareth Gardiner, Tough-Minded Management of Problem Employees (Springfield, IL: Smith Collins Company, 1989), 119.

Police Turnover

By W. Dwayne Orrick

Police departments across the country are reporting increased rates of staff turnover. Many agencies are spending enormous amounts of resources on recruiting, selecting, and training new employees. At the same time, they are unable to make progress because they are losing experienced officers to other employers.

Even though the problem of turnover is approaching critical levels for many law enforcement agencies, the issue has not received as much publicity as it has in other professions. For example, the turnover rate averages about 12 percent for nurses and 13 percent for teachers.[1] A recent study completed by the state of North Carolina revealed that police agencies across the state experienced an average turnover of 14 percent in patrol positions. The average tenure for a new officer is 33 months.[2]

Numerous factors have been cited as contributing to high turnover, including poor pay and tough competition in the labor market. Regardless of the cause, the increases have led some community leaders to be concerned with the financial costs of turnover. For police executives, high turnover rates have threatened agencies' ability to keep a sufficient number of well-trained, experienced officers on-duty.

POSITIVE SIDE OF TURNOVER

It should be pointed out, however, that having staff leave the department should not always be viewed as a bad thing. Staff turnover allows the department to spread the influence of its leadership, initiate greater change of the organization's culture, and replace ineffective and unethical staff. Despite these benefits, police organizations must continue to reassess fundamental philosophy of how their agencies operate and its impact on the selection and retention of officers.

When the department invests enormous resources to select and train staff, it is normal to view a good officer's departure as being a loss. However, if the officer performs well in his or her new position, the previous employer's reputation is enhanced as being a good department. Every department has its formal and informal communication networks. When leaders foster good relationships with their employees, staff transfers will allow both departments to have contacts in the other's organization. These relationships can be used as an extension of both the department's resources in other communities and the leader's influence.

No organizational success can be achieved without good followers. Although no one wants to admit it, the fact is that all departments have some amount of deadwood. By measuring employee's performance along two dimensions, critical thinking skills and activity, leaders can categorize followers. Critical thinkers are employees who can think for themselves and give constructive criticism; other employees have to be told what to do or don't think. Active employees take initiative and are self-starters, whereas passive employees are lazy, require constant supervision, and avoid responsibility.

Employees who score low on both dimensions are characterized as passive followers and make up 5 to 10 percent of the workforce. To improve their performance, the follower must improve his or her critical thinking skills and activity. When a follower is unwilling or unable to improve his or her behavior, the department and community are best served by inviting the employee to explore other career opportunities.[3]

A few years ago, most U.S. communities enjoyed a vibrant economy and agencies were faced with a condition known as negative employment. This situation occurs when there are more jobs available than qualified applicants. This leads to extreme competition between both public and private employers. Some departments were faced with the dilemma of not maintaining minimum staffing levels or lowering their hiring standards.

Unfortunately, some persons were employed as officers who should not have been and later became involved in improper or unethical conduct. The chief executive is considered the caretaker of the institution and cannot allow the integrity of the organization to be questioned. If an officer cannot be trusted, he or she cannot be allowed to remain in a position where their conduct will taint the reputation of the entire unit. According to the National Institute of Ethics, the average officer who was involved in improper behavior that resulted in their removal from duty had 7.3 years of service.[4] If this projection is accurate, police executives can expect to continue seeing a relatively high number of officers being involved in misconduct for several more years.

Turnover also allows the opportunity to change the organizational culture. The organizational culture is defined as "a shared basic assumption that the group has learned as it solved problems … that has worked well enough to be considered valid and is, therefore, to be taught to new members as the correct way to perceive, think, and feel in relation to those problems."[5]

Changing how an organization is perceived and how officers respond to problems is challenging for a chief in the best of circumstances. This is especially true when the department has a strong yet dysfunctional culture. With increased levels of turnover, leaders can better initiate the embedding and reinforcing factors necessary to effect positive change.

REASSESS THE FUNDAMENTALS

Even though there are some potential benefits when turnover occurs, the problem cannot continue without long-term effects on the department and how it interacts with the community. How does an agency best reduce the level of turnover? A number of practical solutions are available, but conceptual issues must also be evaluated.

As law enforcement leaders enter the 21st century they are faced with a rapidly changing environment and diverse workforce. To address the issues of turnover, leaders will be forced to reassess the fundamentals of their organization.

Develop Strong Organizational Values: Leadership researchers Kouzes and Posnar have found that the most motivated employees have values that align closely with the organization's values. Perhaps surprisingly, the second most motivated group of employees had a highly defined set of personal values even though their organizations did not have a highly defined set of values.[6] To foster this environment, leaders should seek to identify the core values of the department. Core values are the fundamental bedrock upon which the department operates. Unfortunately, for many agencies core values have not been identified or are lists copied from another department. For these values to have meaning, the staff must be involved in their developmental process. Second, values must be visibly reinforced through operational procedures. For example, if the department has a core value of honesty and officers routinely see staff lying or falsifying records without any consequences, the value has no meaning.

Move away from the Survival Mentality: Police work is a profession that provides officers with numerous opportunities to make a positive difference in the lives of others. But departments will never be able to retain and motivate staff until the survival mentality socialized into our new officers is addressed. As new officers are socialized into the police profession through the recruit academy, they are indoctrinated on the dangers inherent to law enforcement. This indoctrination focuses their attention on making it home at the end of the day without being complained about, disciplined, sued, injured, or killed.

In his needs hierarchy, Abraham Maslow proposed that individuals would not be able to move into or be motivated by higher-ordered needs of love and belongingness, self-esteem, or self-actualization until lower-ordered needs of physical needs and security are satisfied. "If the individual is in a survival mode, economic motives will dominate; if survival needs are met, social needs come to the fore; if social needs are met, self-actualization needs are released." [2]

Moving from the survival mentality is not to minimize the importance of teaching officers good tactical procedures or making them aware of the risks inherent in law enforcement. But service and problem solving, not combat, should be the focus of our academy instruction and socialization for new officers.

Change Compensation Systems: Employers demonstrate the worth of an employee to the organization every two weeks in the form of a paycheck. Unfortunately, many governing authorities view the police as a necessary evil and a dead-end cost because they do not realize the police department is critical to the community and its economic development. No one wants to move his or her family or business to a community with a high crime rate or a poor quality of life. As a result, some communities cling to parochial compensation systems, view trained police officers as little more than common laborers, and pay their staff as little as possible. Others are forced into adversarial roles with staff through collective bargaining agreements. This adversarial positioning permeates the entire department and how it interacts with the community they serve. To recruit and retain the caliber of officers needed for policing in the 21st century, agencies must pay a competitive salary. In addition, the system must reward officers with cost of living adjustments, longevity, and advanced certifications.

Establish Career Development Programs: As soon as a new employee is recruited, he or she is told of the opportunities to move out of patrol by way of promotions to supervisor; transfers to traffic, detectives, narcotics, or other elite units; or new job at larger agency. In reality, there are only a limited number of these opportunities available and employees who are anxious to move from the patrol function are often unwilling to wait for the few vacancies to occur. Rather than continue with this unrealistic expectation for moving out of patrol, a department can use job enhancement techniques and creative career development programs to provide individual patrol officers opportunities for growth and salary increases without making them supervisors or assigning them to special units. The department undertaking these steps will find that enhancing the patrol service provides for a stronger and better department that engages in problem solving and improving the quality of life for the community

Engage Officers' Minds: Generally, most police officers have a strong internal locus of control. That is, they feel they can make a difference in their environment. In fact, many officers join the police profession to make a difference in their communities. Yet most agencies continue to follow traditional incident-based policing techniques. This method of policing requires officers to repeatedly answer calls but take little corrective action. By training officers how to identify problems, develop solutions, and implement the strategy to correct the problem, police administrators can provide officers with a creative outlet that can improve their community. Officers who fix problems and do not merely treat the symptoms can make a bigger difference in their communities and have more rewarding careers.

Employ Mentoring: While still considered a revolutionary idea by some, mentoring programs have been around for thousands of years. Traditionally, apprentice programs have functioned as a conduit for passing along knowledge and experience. By implementing formal or informal mentoring programs, departments provide a wonderful opportunity to guide employees through a promising career. Mentoring programs have been shown to increase new officer success rates, build confidence, anchor officers to the department, and reduce turnover.[8]

Recruit Incumbents: In most agencies after the officer is hired and trained, they get into the routine of being on the job, and administrators get used to having them around and pay them little attention. But it is a basic human need to feel needed and important. Leaders too often focus their attention on the troubled employees and on new candidates. As a result, the good hardworking officers who make up most of our agencies are ignored and provided with little positive reinforcement. To avoid this, leaders must schedule time to celebrate, praise, and recognize employees who perform well.

Some employee turnover is unavoidable and normal, and there are some conditions in which employee turnover is beneficial to the department. At the same time, pronounced turnover can be detrimental to the department and prevent it from achieving its goals. Many of the problems contributing to unnecessary and unwanted turnover will continue to plague agencies until fundamental changes are made to the organizational culture. Failing to address these issues will make departments being unable to limit turnover for years to come.

NOTES

1. University of Washington Center for the Study of Teaching and Policy, Teacher Turnover, Teacher Shortage, and the Organization of Schools, by Richard B. Ingersoll (January 2001), 14.

2. North Carolina Criminal Justice Analysis Center, Recruitment and Retention Study Series Sworn Police Personnel, by Douglas L. Yearwood (April 2003), iv – v.

3. Howard Prince, John Halstead, and Larry Hesser, Leadership in Police Organizations, (McGraw-Hill, 2002), 153–156.

4. National Institute of Ethics, The National Law Enforcement Officer Disciplinary Research Project, by Neal Trautman (1997).

5. Edgar H. Schein, Organizational Culture and Leadership (San Francisco: Jossey-Bass, 1985), 9.

6. James E. Kouzes and Barry Z. Posner, The Leadership Challenge, 3rd ed. (San Francisco: Jossey-Bass, 2002), 49–50.

7. Schein, Organizational Culture and Leadership, 100.

8. International Association of Chief's of Police, Best Practices Guide for Institutionalizing Mentoring into Police Departments, by Harvey Sprafka and April Kranda (2002).

Field Training Issues for Administrators

By Richard Beaver

If everybody is thinking alike,
somebody isn't thinking.[1]
　　　　　—General George S. Patton

Field training administrators would do well to heed General Patton's advice. After all, they must fulfill many roles to ensure that the newly appointed recruits in their agencies receive the best coaching from the highest caliber law enforcement officers available. These administrators face a variety of challenges, including maintaining the integrity of the field training program, overseeing their trainers, and selecting the appropriate personnel to fill these positions. Such responsibilities require a great deal of thought, flexibility, and creativity for administrators to effectively lead such a crucial component of any law enforcement organization.

MAINTAINING PROGRAM INTEGRITY

Effective administrators have many issues to consider when implementing or revising a field training program. A strong, integral, and cohesive operation requires a solid foundation. When implementing a new program, it is worth the extra time and effort it takes to build a stable base. If an enterprise is put together too quickly, it may have too many holes that then will take a lot of time to fill. A strong foundation includes a well-designed field training manual,

written objectives, standardized evaluation guidelines, motivated field training officers, and leaders willing to keep the program up-to-date and to never compromise its integrity. Such administrators prove invaluable because the worst enemy of a strong field training program is complacency, a disease that will put every area of the venture at risk. It will eat away at the foundation, making even the strongest program too weak to be effective. If the administrators become infected, everyone down to the newest recruit also will succumb to the illness.

Most agencies have a training program in place, but it may need revising. This can pose a sometimes difficult, but not impossible, task. It may involve reassigning personnel, appointing line-level officers to a committee for brainstorming, or completely dissolving the present program, which may sound like a major undertaking but may prove the best option if existing problems continually reoccur. While dealing with current complications makes revising the program a bit more difficult, the extent of these obstacles should determine which option will best suit the needs of the organization. Whichever one an agency chooses should allow the administrator the greatest flexibility in eliminating past problems and addressing future ones before they arise.

Finally, to ensure the integrity of the program, administrators should periodically review their manuals regarding changes in law, procedures, and training

Richard Beaver, "Field Training Issues for Administrators," *FBI Law Enforcement Bulletin*, vol. 75, no. 9, pp. 11–17. Copyright in the Public Domain.

issues. A field training manual functions under the same principle as a standard operating procedure handbook: it needs constant updating and revising. The field manual is a working document that administrators cannot neglect if it is to remain an effective instrument. They should keep the words *update* and *eliminate* firmly in mind, updating new issues and revising those that need changing and eliminating outdated concerns or those no longer needed.

OVERSEEING FIELD TRAINING OFFICERS

Of all the roles field training administrators must fulfill, overseeing their field training officers (FTOs) ranks among the most important. Serving as an example of effective leadership and ensuring that recruits receive proper training can prove extremely challenging.

Train the Trainers

FTOs should attend an accredited field training officer course and first-line supervisor school as soon as possible. Such instruction will give them a foundation to begin building on and a working knowledge of *what* to apply. Administrators within their agencies will give FTOs direction on *how* to apply those acquired skills. This helps FTOs understand what is expected of them, which, in turn, helps them explain to recruits what they expect of these new officers. A program will not successfully function and thrive if FTOs are given a manual and told to "go to it." This leaves no room for growth and creates a breeding ground for negative issues to infect the initiative. Without proper directives and adequate knowledge of them, FTOs will not train recruits uniformly. While each FTO can develop an individual style of teaching, all must adhere to the program's guidelines, which will help eliminate variances in training.

Encourage Ideas

Administrators and FTOs need to operate from the same guidelines, but different ideas are part of what makes the infrastructure of the training program work. Administrators should solicit new ideas from FTOs. After all, they are in the field and administrators usually are not. FTOs have firsthand knowledge of issues and circumstances that arise in the field. Administrators should listen to new ideas and encourage FTOs to get involved in finding solutions. Such actions help boost morale by giving FTOs a sense of accomplishment and a feeling of making a difference. This, in turn, sets an example for them to follow for future leadership roles and opportunities. Moreover, it will make the program stronger, enhance its reliability and integrity, and foster a cooperative style of leadership.

Meet Regularly

Administrators should meet with their FTOs on a regular basis to discuss ideas, problems, and other issues appropriate for inclusion in an open environment. Open meetings provide an opportunity to identify trainers who sincerely want the operation to excel by the attitude they display toward the recruits and the program. But, these venues do not offer an appropriate environment to discuss personnel issues concerning individual trainees. Instead, administrators should address these concerns with FTOs privately to avoid the possibility of biasing other trainers' opinions of recruits before they have the opportunity to prove themselves or correct their performance.

Trust the FTOs

Some managers and line supervisors have a hard time delegating. Once they have given FTOs an assignment, administrators must allow them to do the job. Finding the correct way to operate can help avoid crossing the fine line between staying on top of issues and micromanaging. While several factors come into play, the most important is the style of leadership.

If administrators place too many constraints on them, FTOs never will learn to lead and develop managerial skills, thereby causing undue morale problems. Administrators should lead, guide, and direct FTOs but, at the same time, allow them to flourish in developing their own leadership styles. They should train FTOs to recognize a potential hurdle or problem, analyze why it is there, and find a solution by using their common sense, style, ingenuity, and skills. This can instill a sense of confidence and accomplishment when FTOs successfully handle a real-life situation by themselves. It also tells them that the administrator trusts their decisions.

Administrators should accompany FTOs in the field periodically to assist with training issues. This demonstrates that they have an active interest in the FTOs, the recruits, and the program. Participating in different types of training scenarios, including vehicle stops, building searches, and arrest procedures, gives administrators the chance to see firsthand how FTOs are developing as leaders and how the program is being taught and administered.

Enforce Accountability

To keep the integrity, reliability, and the foundation of a program strong, administrators must hold FTOs accountable for what and how they teach and for completing all necessary documentation. The training process involves a great deal of paperwork. When not properly completed, it can cause significant problems later. Administrators should ensure that FTOs properly document performance on all reports, evaluations, and written and oral tests, as well as completing the appropriate records relative to problem areas, strengths and weaknesses, and other training concerns. Administrators should not overload FTOs with paperwork but, rather, ensure that documentation and checklists exist for each area of training.

In addition, administrators should make sure that performance progress reviews are clearly written. While the FTO who compiled the notes may understand them, others who follow may not, which can lead to confusion. Moreover, if an officer becomes involved in a lawsuit a few years later, the court could subpoena the training records. If the administrator or FTO cannot discern what the reports say due to incomplete or poorly written notes, serious consequences could result. Complete, accurate, and proper records should remain a primary concern of

all administrators and FTOs because adhering to properly written guidelines on documentation, accountability, and promotional standards forms the support beams for the foundation and the walls of an effective field training program.

SELECTING APPROPRIATE PERSONNEL

Placing the right people in the right places will help preserve the integrity of the program. This sounds elementary but can prove invaluable. For example, appropriate personnel will greatly reduce the risk of liability issues in the areas of inadequate or improper training. Administrators should look for officers who have a genuine concern about these. Such employees try to stay abreast of training issues and legal decisions that will affect training. Administrators well versed in these areas are fully aware of the consequences that can arise.

Administrators should consider many qualities when choosing suitable training officers. Self-motivated, professional employees who have a positive attitude toward their agency usually make the best field trainers. To help other administrators select quality personnel, the author offers his PEARL model. This acronym stands for professionalism, ethics, adaptability, recruitment, and leadership. Agencies also can apply the method to other types of promotional processes.

Professionalism

Professionalism constitutes the first trait in the PEARL model. Applying it to law enforcement standards, professionalism can be summed up as consistency and proficiency in attitude, character, appearance, and actions. Officers live and work on different levels. Those who apply the higher standards and work ethics to their careers represent the ideal field trainers for a law enforcement agency.

Candidates should have a proven track record of proficiency in job performance. Operating with minimal supervision, making ethically sound decisions, keeping a positive attitude, and solving problems appropriately comprise the most outstanding traits of professionalism. In addition, when officers present themselves professionally, they create a credible image that people notice immediately. These officers know that they do not have a second chance to make a first impression. Officers possessing these characteristics give recruits solid role models to emulate. Other qualities that demonstrate professionalism include honesty, trustworthiness, creativity, and fairness.

Ethics

Ethics, the second attribute in the PEARL model, play a part in every aspect of law enforcement. Candidates' work, personal, and off-duty ethics should carry a lot of weight in the promotional process. Those who consistently make morally correct decisions in every area of their lives can become positive influences on their fellow officers and on those under their tutelage.

Adaptability

The third characteristic, the ability to adapt, can prove invaluable for an FTO. The ability to adapt to new people with different types of personalities and to new and diverse ideas while staying focused on the task at hand are crucial aspects to look for in choosing the right person.

Agencies spend a considerable amount of time training new recruits. Many officers do not like having an FTO in the patrol vehicle for hours at a time, especially when the trainer has to constantly watch, talk, train, and monitor what the recruit does at all times. So, FTOs must be able to reconcile potentially conflicting situations. They also must have the ability to adapt to continue the training started by another FTO because most programs run in phases. Moreover, an FTO able to adapt to new directives and orders and teach them to others with minimal coaching can prove priceless to a program administrator.

Recruitment

The fourth component in the PEARL model is recruitment. A promotional process for a new or an existing field training program makes the procedure fair and integral and ensures that the agency chooses the best of the best while following proper written guidelines. The choices can have no appearance of being prejudiced or biased in any way. There always will be some who are unhappy that they were not chosen. But, by following ethical and written guidelines in the promotional process, the agency can easily defend and justify its choices should the need arise.

For fairness and selection of the best candidate, administrators should use a standardized application process. When a position becomes available, it should be posted with a list of qualifications and a sign-up sheet for those interested. Candidates should submit a letter of interest to the administrator by a certain date. This will help preserve the integrity of the process by eliminating the "buddy system." After the posting, a background should be done on each candidate. Some major issues to consider include—

- past work history, performance, self-initiated activities, and education;
- the ability to associate and communicate well with others; and
- disciplinary actions within a specified time frame and the nature of each, as well as substantiated or exonerated citizen complaints.

Oral Interview Board

No magic number exists for how many people should sit on an oral interview board. The members can vary from line-level to command-staff personnel. Usually, officers above the rank of captain do not participate because, at most agencies, they make the final decision. Using personnel from within the organization, along with some from other departments, helps to preserve the integrity of the process. This gives an outside, unbiased opinion from those not readily familiar with the candidate.

Members of the board should have a standardized list of questions that they ask all of the applicants. This will help ensure the fairness of the oral interviews. Liability issues can arise when candidates do not receive the same questions and opportunities to answer. Videotaping the interviews for future reference can prove helpful, especially if the scoring is very close or the board needs to defend its choices.

The oral interview board will observe each candidate's appearance, command presence, verbal skills, personality traits, and nonverbal gestures, as well as acquire a general knowledge of the interests of the applicant. This gives the board an idea of the candidate's demeanor that will surface while training a new recruit. Board members should include ethically based questions. These portions of the videotaped interviews will show a candidate's nonverbal gestures and demeanor when making an "on-the-spot" decision based on morals.

Each member of the board should have an evaluation sheet, customized to fit the agency's needs, to grade the candidates. Departments can approach the grading in a number of ways. The best is to keep it as simple as possible, such as a number system that members can easily total. The evaluation sheet should include a comments section for members to record strengths and weaknesses, as well as likes and dislikes, about each candidate.

Written Test

The recruitment process should include a written, job-specific test tailored to the agency's individual needs and requirements. It should contain questions that relate to state law, search and seizure, elements of crimes, report writing, and liability issues, as well as ones that cover specific topics from its field training and standard operating procedures manuals.

After the written tests have been graded, the board should meet again to compile the scores and evaluations from the oral and written screening. Then, the board should choose the top few candidates and submit the results to the command staff or agency head for final approval.

Leadership

The final aspect of the PEARL model involves determining the leadership qualities that a candidate possesses. Administrators should ask themselves two questions.

1. Does this candidate have a vision for the future needs of the agency?
2. Will this candidate be instrumental in implementing the changes that will better the organization?

A true leader has a vision and the desire to try and implement new ideas that will help the training program grow and function efficiently. Administrators usually can separate employees who have self-centered motives. Most agencies have employees who tend to naturally attract others. These people seem to have an innate ability to inspire, an invaluable trait for an FTO. They can motivate others to see a vision and to assist in implementing it and the necessary changes for the betterment of the organization. This type of leader earns, not expects because of rank or position, the respect of others.

Multitasking and self-motivation represent two more important characteristics for FTOs to possess. Due to the amount of duties and the nature of their responsibilities, FTOs should be able to function while juggling several tasks without losing track of any. They never should have to be reminded of what to do or how to accomplish an assignment.

One last important issue concerning leadership involves the ability to effectively communicate. Because a comprehensive training manual covers a great deal of information, FTOs must communicate well to help recruits learn. Also, when FTOs need to conduct counseling sessions for poor performance, they must make recruits understand what they did wrong and offer them ways to improve. Furthermore, FTOs must effectively communicate ideas to the program administrator or command staff concerning training and personnel issues.

CONCLUSION

Field training administrators face many challenges in their capacity as leaders of an important component that supports the overall mission of their agencies. Maintaining the integrity of the training program, overseeing the officers who coach recruits, and choosing the best employees for that role can be a heavy burden but also a rewarding experience. Seeing recruits fresh from the academy gain real-life knowledge from highly motivated trainers can make these challenges worthwhile.

For help in selecting field training officers, administrators can use the PEARL model. While not a fail-safe method because of human behavioral factors that can arise for a variety of reasons, it can become a useful tool in implementing or revising a strong and integral field training program. Adhering to standards and guidelines, without compromising, can help agencies, administrators, and officers maintain the integrity of the law enforcement profession.

NOTES

1. *http://en.thinkexist.com/quotation/if_everybody-s_thinking_alike-somebody_ isn-t/12218.html*

CONCEPT #8: UNDERSTAND MAJOR PERSONNEL LEGAL ISSUES

All, too, will bear in mind this sacred principle, that though the will of the majority is in all cases to prevail, that will to be rightful must be reasonable; that the minority possess their equal rights, which equal law must protect, and to violate would be oppression.

—Thomas Jefferson

Your personnel can either help you achieve your goals, they can hinder you or they can cost you money, often in the form of lawsuit. For all of these reasons, specific legal issues are addressed in this chapter. The readings in this chapter are designed to help you identify some of the many legal issues that are relative to personnel. As with any legal issue, sound advice should always be obtained from your legal department and one should always realize that as issues are brought to the courts, they are sometimes interpreted differently and the rules change.

The first reading in this chapter discusses the Americans with Disabilities Act and its implications for law enforcement. Key issues such as interviews, medial examinations and reasonable accommodations are discussed. For those employees already on the job, the issues of reassignment and termination are also

addressed. Next, is a reading on the 1993 Family and Medical Leave Act (FMLA) and its impact on law enforcement. This reading answers questions related to who is eligible, what is a serious health condition that would be covered under this act, and how must FMLA leave be taken.

The third reading in this chapter moves away from medical issues to off duty conduct; specifically to the Constitutional authority to regulate off-duty relations. Numerous cases are discussed that address anti-nepotism rules, regulating off-duty sexual activity and the departmental prerogative to investigative. Another reading relative to Constitutional issues follows, now on the topic of speech and the public employee. The legal concepts of public concern and balancing of interests are addressed.

The fifth reading in this chapter deals with religion in the public workplace. This topic is approached from both the First Amendment, Freedom of Religion, and from Title VII of the Civil Rights Act of 1964. Issues of uniforms, grooming standards, job performance, assignments and scheduling are addressed. From this reading, administrators are able to identify which laws apply to the issues and more importantly they learn what they are.

The sixth reading in this chapter is on the on the Fair Labor Standards Act (FLSA) and police compensation. Issues of compensated activities, overtime considerations, overtime pay and compensatory time are addressed. The seventh and final reading for this chapter relates to statements compelled from law enforcement employees. The Supreme Court case, Garrity v. New Jersey, is discussed, along with the Fourteenth Amendment. Sanctions that trigger Garrity are discussed, along with overt versus implied threats of sanctions. Administrative remedies are explained for instances when employees refuse to provide voluntary statements.

The Americans with Disabilities Act

A Practical Guide for Police Departments

By Thomas Coldbridge

The Americans with Disabilities Act (ADA)[1] is a difficult statute to understand and implement in the workplace. The statutory definition of a disability is confusing and subject to infinite variations. Determining who is disabled, and therefore, protected by the act, is difficult at best. Defining what is or is not a reasonable accommodation for employees' disabilities is extremely difficult. To make matters worse, the Equal Employment Opportunities Commission (EEOC), the agency charged with enforcing the ADA, and the courts often disagree on the statute's meaning. This article will focus on providing practical advice to police administrators regarding the ADA's impact on departmental operations. It will discuss how the ADA impacts police hiring practices and day-to-day operations when departments are faced with disabled applicants and employees. Specifically, it will provide guidance regarding the questions that may be asked of applicants and employees, what tests may be administered at the various stages of the employment process, and what reasonable accommodations should be made for applicants' and employees' disabilities.

THE ADA PHILOSOPHY AND PRACTICAL REALITIES

The purpose of the ADA is to ensure that Americans with disabilities are given equal employment opportunities and equal access to all the benefits of the workplace. In short, the statute aims to ensure that employers judge the disabled on their abilities, rather than their disabilities. To accomplish that laudable goal, the ADA divides the employment process into three distinct stages: the application/interview stage; the post-conditional offer stage; and the working stage. At all of these stages, the statute attempts to strike a balance between the interest of the disabled in being judged fairly and the interest of employers in finding the most qualified workers and running an efficient enterprise. At the application/ interview stage, the interest of the disabled clearly wins, because employers are severely limited in their prerogatives. At the post-conditional offer stage, employers' interests are paramount, because there are few restrictions imposed by the statute on employers. During the working stage, a delicate balance is struck between the interests of disabled workers and the employers. Overlaying all of the employment stages is the employers' reasonable accommodation obligation.

The ADA has practical implications in three major areas. The first area is in the nature of "disability-related inquiries" employers may make at the different employment stages. The second area is what kind of "medical examinations" employers may conduct at the various stages. The last area is the kind of "reasonable accommodations" employers are required to make at all stages.

"Disability-related inquiry," "medical examination," and "reasonable accommodation" are terms of art under the ADA. Understanding how the ADA defines these terms is key to understanding what restrictions the ADA places on police managers.

Disability-related Inquiry

The EEOC defines a disability-related inquiry as a question or series of questions likely to elicit information about a disability.[2] A disability is any physical or mental impairment that substantially limits a major life activity, having a record of such an impairment, or being regarded as having such an impairment.[3] Disability-related inquiries include not only questions likely to elicit information regarding the existence of a disability, but also information regarding the nature of a disability and its severity. The definition includes employers' questions asked directly to applicants and employees, as well as inquiries directed to third parties and surreptitious searches for information.[4]

Medical Examinations

The EEOC defines medical examinations as procedures or tests that seek information about individuals' physical or mental impairments or health.[5] It is not always clear whether an examination or test is medical for purposes of the ADA. The EEOC suggests the following guidelines:[6]

- If the examination or test is administered or interpreted by health care professionals, it is likely to be considered medical in nature.

- If the examination or test is normally given in a medical setting or is administered using medical equipment, or is invasive, it is likely a medical examination.

- If the employer is trying to determine the nature or extent of applicants' or employees' disabilities, or the test or examination is designed to reveal impairments or disabilities, it is likely a medical test.

- If the examination or test measures individuals' responses to performing tasks, rather than simply their ability to perform tasks, it is likely to be considered medical.

Reasonable Accommodation

Reasonable accommodation is a change in the workplace environment or in the way of doing business that permits the disabled to enjoy equal employment opportunities and benefits.[7] The disabled have a fundamental statutory right to have their disabilities accommodated unless it would create an undue hardship on the employers or they pose a direct threat.[8] Employers' duty to accommodate the disabled extends to all facets of the employment relationship, from the hiring process to termination, and includes not only employment opportunities, but also access to job benefits.[9]

PRACTICAL CONSIDERATIONS FOR POLICE MANAGERS

The complexity of the ADA makes it a difficult statute for the police manager to apply to the workplace. However, the requirements of the ADA become less overwhelming when they are considered in terms of the stages of the employment relationship: the application/interview stage; the post-conditional offer stage; and the working stage. The following discussion will set out in broad terms ADA "dos and don'ts" for police managers during these three stages.[10] It will explore what inquires and examinations are permissible and what reasonable accommodations may be appropriate at each stage.

The Application/Interview Stage: Disability-related Inquiries

The impact of the ADA begins with employers' decisions to fill a vacancy. Congress found that many applicants with disabilities were being denied employment based upon "stereotypic assumptions not truly indicative of the individual ability" of disabled persons.[11] To avoid the danger of stereotypic thinking,

Congress, through the ADA, limits the application-interview process to exploration of only non-disability qualifications of applicants. The practical impact of this limitation has been great.

Employers must consider all potential applicants equally, including those with disabilities, and even those who have relationships with the disabled.[12] Nothing in job postings or vacancy notices should discourage the disabled from applying for open positions.

During the application/interview process, the ADA bars employers' disability-related inquiries (i.e., those that are likely to elicit information about disabilities.)[13] Consequently, applications and interviews should not include direct questions regarding the existence of disabilities, or their nature or extent. Employers may not ask if applicants will need reasonable accommodation to do the job for which they have applied, because the response is likely to reveal information regarding disabilities.[14] The ban includes asking questions concerning the applicants' workers compensation history, because any response is likely to include disability-related information.[15] Because employers are prohibited from directly asking applicants about disabilities at this stage, they may not solicit the same kind of information from third parties.[16]

The application/interview stage is entirely separate from the post-conditional offer and employment stages under the ADA. Therefore, while employers may not ask if applicants will need reasonable accommodation to do the job, they may ask if applicants will need reasonable accommodation to complete the application/interview process.[17] Employers should describe the process (written tests or job demonstrations), and ask if reasonable accommodation is needed. If it is, the employer may ask for documentation for the need if the disability is not obvious.[18]

Employers may ask applicants about nonmedical qualifications and skills required to perform the job: education, work experience, and mandated certifications and licenses.[19] Certain questions about attendance are permissible. For example, employers may state their attendance requirements and ask if the applicant can meet them. However, employers should avoid questions about the number of sick days the applicant has taken in the past, because the answer is likely to disclose disability-related information.[20] Applicants may also be asked to reveal their arrest or conviction records because the request is not likely to raise disability issues.[21]

While broad questions likely to reveal the existence of disabilities are prohibited during this stage, narrowly tailored questions concerning the performance of specific job functions are not.[22] For example, police recruiters may describe the functions of police officers and ask applicants if they can perform those functions, or to describe how they would do them, if all applicants are asked. In addition, applicants may be asked to demonstrate how they would perform these functions if all applicants are asked. If applicants reveal that they need reasonable accommodation for the demonstration, employers must provide the accommodation unless it would create an undue hardship.[23]

Questions concerning drug use are difficult. Addiction to drugs, both past and current, is a disability under the ADA,[24] so direct questions pertaining to addiction are prohibited. Therefore, questions such as "Are you addicted to drugs?" and "Have you ever been treated for drug addiction?" are impermissible. Current illegal drug[25] use, however, is not a disability under the ADA, even if the current use results from addiction.[26] Consequently, employers may ask applicants if they currently use illegal drugs. Past casual illegal drug use is not a disability, so questions regarding such use are permissible: "Have you ever used illegal drugs?;" "When was the last time you used illegal drugs?;" "Have you used illegal drugs in the last 6 months?"[27] It would violate the ADA, however, to ask applicants to list all medications they currently take because the question is likely to illicit information concerning disabilities. There is one exception to this prohibition against inquiring about current medication use. As noted below, employers are permitted to test applicants for current illegal drug use. If the drug test is positive, employers may validate the test by asking applicants about lawful drug use or other possible explanations.[28]

Like drug addiction, alcoholism is a disability under the ADA if it substantially limits a major life activity.[29] Consequently, employers are prohibited from asking applicants questions that are likely to elicit information about their addiction to alcohol.[30] However, employers may ask if applicants drink, as long as the questions are not aimed at discovering how much they drink.[31]

The Application/Interview Stage: Medical Examinations

Medical examinations are prohibited during the application/interview stage.[32] Tests for illegal drug use are not considered medical examinations under the ADA, so employers may test applicants for current illegal drug use.[33] However, the EEOC has ruled that tests for alcohol use are medical in nature, and violate the ADA at this stage of the employment process.[34]

Two other kinds of tests may also be given at this stage. Physical agility tests that demonstrate the ability to do actual or simulated job-related tasks, with or without reasonable accommodation, are permissible if given to all applicants.[35] Examples of such tests for police applicants are the trigger pull test, obstacle courses simulating police chases and vision tests designed to determine if applicants can distinguish objects or read license plates. Employers may also require that applicants take physical fitness tests that measure their ability to do physical tasks such as running and lifting, so long as all applicants must do so.[36] Neither test is considered a medical examination under the ADA unless applicants' physiological or psychological responses to the tests are measured.[37] It does not violate the ADA to require that applicants certify that they can safely perform these tests.[38] If such a certification is required, employers should describe the tests to the applicant, and simply have their physician state whether or not they can safely perform the tests. It is also important to understand that if either physical agility or fitness tests screen out or tend to screen out disabled applicants, employers must be prepared to defend the tests as both job-related and consistent with business necessity.[39]

Applicants may also be given psychological tests that are not aimed at uncovering recognized mental disorders.[40] Psychological tests that measure such things as honesty, tastes, or habits are not considered medical examinations under the ADA.[41]

Polygraph examinations of applicants at the application/interview stage do not violate the ADA if no disability-related questions are asked during the exam.[42] However, to ensure accurate results, examiners generally must ask examinees prior to the exam if they are taking any medications that might affect the results. Such a question could violate the ADA because the answer is likely to elicit information regarding disabilities. Consequently, it may be wise to postpone the polygraph examination to the post-conditional offer stage. Before administering any polygraph examinations, however, police administrators should consult with their legal advisors regarding their legality under state law and local labor contracts.[43]

The Application/Interview Stage: Reasonable Accommodation

The ADA's statutory obligation to reasonably accommodate disabilities applies to the interview/application stage.[44] Employers must accommodate all applicants' known disabilities unless it would create an undue hardship on them. Employers may become aware of applicants' disabilities because it is obvious, or because the applicants disclosed their disabilities in response to the employers' inquiry for the need to accommodate them during the application/interview process.

Once the need for accommodation is demonstrated, the parties should decide what accommodations are appropriate. Typical accommodations at this stage include changing testing dates to accommodate doctors' appointments, changing testing sites to those accessible by the disabled, and giving applicants with reading disabilities more time to complete written examinations. The forms of accommodation are as varied as the imaginations of employers and applicants.

As can be seen from this discussion, the ADA limits the application/interview stage to employer inquiries and examinations designed to judge all of the non-disability related qualifications of applicants. But what if employers know at this stage that applicants are disabled? Must they ignore the disabilities entirely, even if they reasonably believe the disabilities will impact the applicants' ability to do the job?

There are several ways employers could lawfully become aware of applicants' disabilities. The disability may be obvious, such as a lost limb, or the use of a wheelchair. The applicant may have voluntarily disclosed the disability through a request for reasonable accommodation during the application/interview stage, or in response to employers' inquiries about their ability to perform job functions.

The EEOC has stated that when employers reasonably believe that applicants will need reasonable accommodation to perform job functions, they may discuss with applicants if accommodation will be needed, and the form that accommodation may take.[45] After these discussions, employers may decide that they cannot accommodate the disability because the applicants cannot perform the essential functions of the job, or pose a direct threat, or because the accommodation needed is unduly burdensome.

If employers do not extend an offer to disabled applicants because of their disability, they must be prepared to defend their decisions against claims that they failed to hire the applicants because of the need to reasonably accommodate their disabilities.[46]

Once employers have judged applicants based upon their non-disability related qualifications during the application/interview stage, found them qualified, and made bona fide job offers to them, the ADA permits employers to face the issue of disabilities. Employers may now inquire about disabilities, require medical examinations, and condition their employment offers on the results of these medical examinations.

The EEOC considers job offers bona fide if they are made after employers have evaluated all of the relevant nonmedical information it reasonably could have gotten and analyzed before making the offer.[47] Conditional offers do not have to be limited to current vacancies. Conditional offers are still bona fide if they are made in reasonable anticipation of future vacancies. The number of offers may even exceed the number of current and anticipated vacancies if employers can demonstrate that a percentage of offerees will likely be disqualified or drop out of the pool.[48]

The Postconditional Offer Stage: Disability-related Inquiries

After making a conditional offer of employment, employers may ask applicants if they have disabilities and will need reasonable accommodation to perform the job.[49] There is no restriction on the nature of questions that may be asked. Consequently, employers may ask all of the questions prohibited during the application/ interview stage: questions regarding the existence of disabilities, workers' compensation histories, sick leave usage, drug and alcohol addiction, as well as questions regarding general physical and mental health. The only conditions imposed on employers by the ADA are that all offerees be asked these questions, and that information gathered in response to the questions be kept confidential.[50]

If inquiries uncover disabilities, employers are bound by the basic requirements of the ADA. They reasonably must accommodate the disabilities unless the accommodation would pose an undue hardship or the person poses a direct threat.[51] If the inquiries result in conditional offers being withdrawn because of the disabilities, employers must be prepared to show that the exclusionary criteria is not discriminatory based upon disability, or is job-related and consistent with business necessity,[52] or they could not reasonably accommodate the disability,[53] or because the offeree poses a direct threat to the health or safety of others.[54]

The Post-Conditional Offer Stage: Medical Examinations

The ADA permits employers to require medical examinations after bona fide job offers have been made to applicants. The only conditions on these examinations are that all applicants be subject to the examinations and the results be kept confidential.[55]

All of the medical examinations barred at the application/interview stage are now permitted. There are no restrictions on the nature of these examinations, not even a requirement that they be job-related or matters of business necessity.[56]

As with post conditional offer disability-related inquiries, if medical examinations given at this stage reveal a disability and result in the offer being withdrawn, employers must be prepared to defend their decision because it does not discriminate against the disabled, or the disability could not be accommodated, or because the criteria upon which the decision was based is job-related and a matter of business necessity, or because the offeree poses a direct threat to health or safety.

The Postconditional Offer Stage: Reasonable Accommodation

Because the ADA requires employers to reasonably accommodate disabilities at all stages of the employment process, accommodation must be made for the offerees' disabilities unless it creates an undue burden. It is impossible to specify all accommodation possibilities. Examples may include reformatting a written psychological tests for blind or dyslexic offerees, or rescheduling examination times to accommodate medical appointments.

Once the post-conditional offer stage is over, and offerees are officially employees, the ADA reimposes restrictions on employers' prerogatives. These restrictions apply to both disability-related inquiries and medical examinations. In addition, the full impact of the employers' reasonable accommodation obligation is felt at this stage.

The Working Stage: Disability-Related Inquiries

The ADA permits employers to make disability-related inquiries of employees only if the inquiries are job related and consistent with job necessity.[57] Consequently, employers are generally barred from asking employees about the existence of disabilities, or their nature and extent.[58] The prohibition includes questions concerning workers' compensation histories, questions about current or past prescriptions, and broad questions about impairments likely to elicit information about disabilities.[59] The statute does permit inquiries regarding employees' ability to perform job-related functions,[60] as well as current illegal drug use, because current illegal drug users are not protected by the ADA.[61] Information received from employees in response to these questions must be kept confidential.

Disability-related inquiries are job-related and consistent with business necessity when employers have a reasonable belief, based upon objective evidence, that employees' ability to do their jobs is impaired, or that employees pose a direct threat because of the condition.[62] That objective evidence generally comes in three forms: a deterioration in employees' work performance or attendance records; an employees' request for accommodation for a disability; or if employees are returning to work from medical or workers' compensation leave. In all three cases, employers may have legitimate concerns regarding the employees' abilities to perform the essential functions of their jobs, so inquiries are permissible if limited to issues of job performance, and responses are kept confidential.[63]

The EEOC recognizes that public safety employees are in a unique position. Because of that, police managers are sometimes given additional flexibility. For example, while asking employees about prescription medication use is generally prohibited, police officers taking certain medications may pose a direct threat to the public and other officers. Consequently, departments may require officers to report when they are taking certain medications that may impair their judgment or ability to use a firearm.[64]

Employers are also permitted to make disability-related inquiries of their employees if required to do so by federal law.[65] The EEOC cites federal safety regulations governing the transportation and airlines industries.

Another exception to the ban on posing disability-related questions to employees is when they are asked as part of a voluntary employee health program.[66] If the program is truly voluntary, such measures as blood pressure screening, weight control counseling, and cancer detection are permissible, if confidentiality is maintained.[67]

The Working Stage: Medical Examinations

As with disability-related inquiries, medical examinations of employees only may be required when the examination is job-related and a matter of business necessity,[68] meaning when employers reasonably believe employees cannot perform job-related functions.

Objective evidence of the employees' inability to perform is the same as discussed above: deterioration in employees' performance or attendance records, as part of a reasonable accommodation request, or upon employees' return to work after medical or workers' compensation leave. Employers also may require medical examinations to comply with federal regulatory requirements; or as part of a voluntary wellness program.

The EEOC and the courts have decided that periodic medical examinations of public safety personnel, even with no objective evidence of current job-related problems, are permissible under the ADA, because undetected medical problems of public safety personnel may pose a direct threat.[69] The EEOC has ruled that such examinations for public safety positions are permissible when tailored narrowly to address specific job-related concerns and are consistent with business necessity.[70] In *Watson v. City of Miami*,[71] a police officer challenged the city's required periodic testing of its police officers for tuberculosis. The federal Court of Appeals for the 11th Circuit decided that such testing was permissible under the ADA. If such tests reveal a disability, police managers reasonably must accommodate it. If the disability cannot be accommodated, they must be prepared to demonstrate that officers cannot perform their essential functions, or that they pose a direct threat.

The Working Stage: Reasonable Accommodation

The full impact of the ADA's reasonable accommodation obligation occurs when current employees become disabled. Failure to reasonably accommodate employees' disabilities is clearly discrimination under the ADA, unless employers can demonstrate an undue hard-ship,[72] or that disabled employees cannot perform essential functions,[73] or would pose a direct threat.[74]

It is impossible for police manager to identify all reasonable accommodations for employees' disabilities. However, it is possible to set out a general approach to the problem recognized by the courts and the EEOC.

Once employers become aware of employees' disabilities, they should begin to explore what, if any, reasonable accommodations are available. It is important to remember that only otherwise qualified employees who can perform the essential functions of the job sought or desired, with or without reasonable accommodation, are entitled to reasonable accommodation. Once it is decided that employees are entitled to ADA protection, certain logical steps should be followed.

Accommodation in Place

The first form of accommodation that should be considered is accommodation of employees in their current positions. The statute itself suggests certain kinds of appropriate accommodations: implementing part-time or modified work schedules; acquiring or modifying equipment or devices; restructuring jobs; and making existing facilities readily accessible to and usable by disabled employees.[75]

Modifying work schedules may be an easy solution to the problem. For example, ensuring that disabled employees get scheduled days off when they have doctors' appointments may be reasonable. Changing shifts or permitting employees to use sick or vacation time are other considerations. Employers are not required to consider these options, however, if they are unduly burdensome. For example, if employers can demonstrate these accommodations are too costly because of the need to hire temporary workers, or too disruptive because of the need to reassign the absent employees' work to others, the accommodation may be unreasonable and therefore not required.[76] Providing additional leave beyond that given to other employees is not required.[77]

Employers may also consider buying devises that will permit the disabled employee to perform the job.

It may be as simple as buying a different chair, or braille materials that can be read by blind employees. The accommodation may also include making the disabled workers' space accessible by adding a ramp or widening doors. As always, this form of accommodation is subject to undue hardship limitations of cost and disruption to the workplace.

Job restructuring means changing the job itself to accommodate the disability. This involves analyzing the various functions of the job, determining which functions disabled employees cannot do, and eliminating those functions if they are not essential to the job, or changing when or how a job function is done.[78] Both the courts and the EEOC have recognized that employers need not eliminate essential job functions as part of the reasonable accommodation process.[79] Job restructuring is also subject to the undue hardship limitation. If restructuring entails hiring additional workers to cover eliminated functions or unduly burdening other employees, it may be unreasonable.

Reassignment

If disabled employees cannot be accommodated in their current positions, employers should consider reassignment to jobs they can perform. They need only consider current vacancies or vacancies that will occur in the near future, and jobs for which the disabled worker is qualified.[80] Employers do not have to "bump" employees to make room for a disabled worker, nor are they required to promote a disabled worker in order to keep them in the company.[81] Employers should first attempt to reassign disabled workers to positions with equivalent pay and benefits. If it is not possible to do so, employers are not required to pay the disabled worker more than the position requires.[82]

Police departments often create "light duty" jobs for injured officers. While the practice is laudable, it is not required by the ADA.[83] The practice may have unintended consequences if employees stay in the position too long. For example, if disabled employees are transferred to newly created light duty positions with no understanding that they are temporary, courts may decide the disabled employees are entitled to ADA protection in the new positions.[84] To avoid this

situation, departments should create only light duty temporary positions to be filled by injured employees during their convalescence.[85]

It is currently unclear whether employers are required to reassign disabled workers to vacant positions when they have a more qualified applicant for the same position, or when the reassignment would violate a company policy. The EEOC takes the position that the disabled worker must be reassigned, not simply permitted to compete for the position.[86] The Commission also takes the position that a company policy to the contrary must be modified to allow the reassignment.[87] Some courts have agreed.[88] However, a recent court decision disagreed with that position, holding that disabled workers do not have to be given preference in reassignment to another position where employers had better non-disabled applicants, a policy of giving jobs to the best applicants, and the employees' disability played no role in the decision.[89] Most courts have found that employers need not assign disabled workers to vacant positions when the reassignment would violate seniority rights established under a collective bargaining agreement.[90]

Termination

If all forms of reasonable accommodation for employees' disabilities have been considered and proven ineffective or unduly burdensome, employers are under no legal obligation to continue employing disabled workers. The ADA does not prohibit termination of workers who cannot do the essential functions of the jobs they hold or seek, with or without reasonable accommodation.[91]

CONCLUSION

The ADA has a profound impact on the way police administrators manage their workplaces. To ensure that employers judge disabled applicants and workers fairly, the ADA strikes a balance between the interests of the parties. At the application/interview stage, employers are restricted to only asking questions and administering examinations aimed at exploring the nondisability-related qualifications of applicants.

Once applicants have been considered qualified, and the conditional offer of employment made to them, employers may fully examine the issue of offerees' disability. If disabilities are discovered, employers must accommodate them if it is reasonable to do so. If the disabilities cannot be reasonably accommodated, or the disabled applicant poses a health or safety risk, the offer may be withdrawn. If the offeree fails tests or examinations that are job-related and matters of business necessity, the offeree need not be hired.

Once offerees become employees, the ADA reimposes restrictions on employers. They are again limited regarding the kind of questions they may ask employees, and the kind of examinations they may require employees to take. If workers become disabled, employers are required to reasonably accommodate them unless it is unduly burdensome, or the employees pose a risk.

NOTES

1. 42 U.S.C. 12101, *et. seq.*
2. EEOC, ADA Enforcement Guidance: Preemployment Disability-Related Questions and Medical Examinations, 10/10/95.
3. 42 U.S.C. 12102(2).
4. *Supra* note 2; *Doe v. Kohn, Nast & Graf, P.C.,* 866 F.Supp. 190 (E.D. Pa. 1994).
5. *Supra* note 2.
6. *Supra* note 2.
7. 29 CFR Pt. 1630 App. 1630.2(o).
8. 42 U.S.C. 12112(b)(5)(A) and (B).
9. 42 U.S.C. 12112(a).
10. Police managers are urged to consult their legal advisors regarding specific ADA questions. Most states have enacted their own statutes regarding disability discrimination, which may differ from the provisions of the ADA.
11. 42 U.S.C. 12101(a)(7).
12. *See* 42 U.S.C. 12112(b)(1)-(7).
13. 42 U.S.C. 12112(d)(2).
14. *Supra* note 2.

15. *Supra* note 2.
16. *Supra* note 2.
17. *Supra* note 2.
18. *Supra* note 2.
19. *Supra* note 2. Employers should be aware that these types of qualification standards are also subject to the provisions of Title VII of the Civil Rights Act of 1964 (42 U.S.C. 2000e *et seq.*). Managers should consult their legal advisors regarding the possible impact of this antidiscrimination statute.
20. *Supra* note 2.
21. *Supra* note 2. Employers should consult their legal advisors regarding the impact of Title VII on this qualification standard.
22. *Supra* note 2.
23. *Supra* note 2.
24. *Supra* note 2.
25. Illegal drugs are those described in schedules I through V of the Controlled Substances Act, 21 U.S.C. 812; 29 CFR 1630.3(a)(1).
26. 42 U.S.C. 12114.
27. *Supra* note 2.
28. *Supra* note 2.
29. See 42 U.S.C. 12114(c)(4); *Bekker v. Humana Health Plan, Incorporated,* 2000 WL 1419610 (7th Cir. 2000); *Martin v. Barnesville Exempted Village School District Board of Education,* 209 F.3d 931 (6th Cir. 2000).
30. *Supra* note 2.
31. *Supra* note 2.
32. 42 U.S.C. 12112(d)(2)(A).
33. 42 U.S.C. 12114(d)(1).
34. *Supra* note 2.
35. *Supra* note 2; 29 CFR 1630.14(a); 29 CFR, App., Pt. 1630.14(a). Employers should also consult their legal advisors on the impact of Title VII of the Civil Rights Act of 1964, as amended, on the use of physical agility and physical fitness tests as selection criteria.
36. *Supra* note 2.
37. *Supra* note 2.
38. *Supra* note 2.
39. 42 U.S.C. 12112(b)(6). In addition, employers must be prepared to meet challenges to these tests

under Title VII of the Civil Rights Act of 1964, as well as other discrimination statutes.

40. Recognized mental disorders are listed in the American Psychiatric Associations' *Diagnostic and Statistical Manual of Mental Disorders* (DSM).

41. *Supra* note 2; *Barnes v. Cochran*, 944 F.Supp. 897 (S.D. Fla. 1996), affirmed 130 F.3d 443 (11th Cir. 1997).

42. *Supra* note 2.

43. In 1988, Congress passed the Employee Polygraph Protection Act (EPPA), 29 U.S.C. 2001 *et seq.* This law prohibits the use of polygraph screening by most private sector employers. It does not apply to federal, state, or local government employers. However, it does not preempt more restrictive state laws or collective bargaining agreements. Police administrators should consult their legal advisors concerning the use of the polygraph.

44. 42 U.S.C. 12112 (b)(5)(A).

45. *Supra* note 2.

46. 42 U.S.C. 12112(b)(5)(B).

47. *Supra* note 2.

48. *Supra* note 2.

49. *Supra* note 2; 29 CFR Pt. 1630, App. 1630.14(b).

50. *Supra* note 2.

51. 42 U.S.C. 12112(b)(5)(A).

52. 42 U.S.C. 12112(b)(6); 42 U.S.C. 12113(a).

53. 42 U.S.C. 12112(b)(5)(A).

54. 42 U.S.C. 12113(b).

55. 42 U.S.C. 12112(d)(3). The only exceptions to the confidentiality requirement are that supervisors may be informed about job necessary restrictions because of the medical condition, that safety personnel may be told if the condition may require emergency treatment, and that government compliance officials be given relevant information on request.

56. *Supra* note 2; 29 CFR Pt. 1630, App. 1630.14(b).

57. 42 U.S.C. 12112(d)(4)(A); 29 CFR 1630.14(c).

58. EEOC, Enforcement Guidance: Disability-Related Inquiries and Medical Examinations of Employees Under the Americans With Disabilities Act, Notice no. 915.002 (7/27/00).

59. *Id.*

60. 42 U.S.C. 12112(d)(4)(B).

61. 42 U.S.C. 12114(a); EEOC, Enforcement Guidance, *supra*, note 58.

62. EEOC, Enforcement Guidance, *supra*, note 58.

63. 29 CFR Pt. 1630, App., 1630.14(c); *Watson v. City of Miami*, 177 F.3d 932 (11th Cir. 1999).

64. EEOC, Enforcement Guidance, *supra*, note 58.

65. EEOC, Enforcement Guidance, *supra*, note 58. Employers should consult with their legal advisors regarding the impact of state laws on this exception.

66. 42 U.S.C. 12112(d)(4)(B).

67. 29 CFR Pt. 1630, App., 1630.14(d).

68. 42 U.S.C. 12112(d)(4)(A).

69. EEOC, Enforcement Guidance, *supra* note 58.

70. EEOC, Enforcement Guidance: Psychiatric Disabilities and the Americans With Disabilities Act (March 25, 1997). In addition, such tests are subject to challenges under Title VII of the Civil Rights Act of 1964, as amended. Departments should consult with their legal advisors to ensure that such periodic exams do not discriminate against protected Title VII classes.

71. *Supra* note 63.

72. 42 U.S.C. 12112(b)(5)(A).

73. *Id.*

74. 42 U.S.C. 12113(b).

75. 42 U.S.C. 12111(9).

76. 29 CFR Pt. 1630, App. 1630.15(d).

77. EEOC, Enforcement Guidance: Reasonable Accommodation and Undue Hardship Under the Americans With Disabilities Act (3/1/99). Employers also should consult their legal advisors regarding the impact of the Family and Medical Leave Act, 29 U.S.C. 2601 *et seq.*

78. *Id.*

79. *Benson v. Northwest Airlines, Inc.*, 62 F.3d 1108 (8th Cir. 1995), *supra* note 77.

80. *Cravens v. Blue Cross and Blue Shield of Kansas City*, 214 F.3d 1011 (8th Cir. 2000).

81. *Id.*

82. *Supra* note 77.

83. *Hoskins v. Oakland County Sheriff's Department*, 2000 WL 1043238 (6th Cir. 2000).

84. See *Haysman v. Food Lion, Inc.*, 893 F.Supp. 1092 (S.D. Ga. 1995).

85. See *Shiring v. Runyon*, 90 F. 3d 827 (3rd Cir. 1996).

86. *Supra* note 77.

87. *Supra* note 77.

88. *Smith v. Midland Brake, Inc.*, 180 F.3d 1154 (10th Cir. 1999).

89. *Equal Employment Opportunity Commission v. Humiston-Keeling, Inc.*, 2000 WL 1310519 (7th Cir. 2000).

90. See *Willis v. Pacific Maritime Association*, 162 F.3d 561 (9th Cir. 1998).

91. *Disanto v. McGraw-Hill, Incorporated/ Platts Division*, 220 F.3d 61 (2nd Cir. 2000); *Treanor v. MCI Telecommunications Corporation*, 200 F.3d 570 (8th Cir. 2000).

The Family and Medical Leave Act

Impact on the Law Enforcement Employer

By Richard Schott

I n 1993, Congress passed and President Bill Clinton signed into law the Family and Medical Leave Act (FMLA).[1] It was enacted to address the concern that people were sometimes losing their jobs when they missed work due to a serious illness or family crisis. The law is undoubtedly popular with the 50 million employees who have used its provisions during the past 12 years.[2] Conversely, some employers view the legislation as a strain on efficient day-to-day operations of the workplace, a burden on other workers who must compensate for absent coworkers, and a vehicle of abuse for some employees who manipulate it for personal time. There may be some reality in each of these conflicting perceptions of the FMLA. This article outlines the major provisions of the FMLA and illustrates how they impact the law enforcement employer.

The FMLA entitles eligible employees to a minimum of 12 weeks unpaid leave during any 12-month period because of their own serious health condition; to care for certain family members who have a serious health condition; or because of the birth of a child (and for the care of the child), or the placement of a child for adoption or foster care.[3] As self-explanatory as this language seems, disputes often arise over the meaning of certain terms used in the FMLA. For example, who are the eligible employees entitled to benefits? What is a serious health condition? For which family members can an employee take FMLA leave to provide care? How must FMLA leave be taken? The common theme that emerges when answering these questions is that when it passed the FMLA, Congress did not intend to cause a hardship on employers who could not afford to be without employees for up to 3 months during a 1-year period.

WHAT EMPLOYEES ARE ELIGIBLE?

To balance the interests of the employer in maintaining a set workforce and the personal situations of employees, there are limitations on the eligibility for FMLA leave. For employees to invoke protection under the FMLA, they must work for an employer to whom the provisions of the act apply. There usually is no guesswork involved in this determination for the law enforcement agency. While a private employer only is governed by the FMLA when it is "engaged in commerce [and] employs fifty or more employees for each working day during each of twenty or more calendar workweeks in the current or preceding calendar year,"[4] the FMLA applies to all public agencies. A public agency is defined as "the government of the United States; the government of the state or political subdivision of a state; or an agency of the United States, a state, or a political subdivision of a state, or any interstate governmental agency."[5] The only exclusion from the FMLA for a public agency is if the employee invoking the act is "employed at a

Richard Schott, "The Family and Medical Leave Act," *FBI Law Enforcement Bulletin*, vol. 75, no. 1, pp. 25–32.

worksite at which [the] employer employs less than fifty employees if the total number of employees employed by that employer within 75 miles of that worksite is less than fifty."[6] Because for this calculation a state or political subdivision of a state constitutes a single public agency, and, therefore, a single employer (for example, a state, a county, a city, or a town is a single employer), this calculation usually does not relieve even the smallest law enforcement agencies of compliance with the FMLA. As a result, the crucial factor determining whether a law enforcement agency employee is entitled to FMLA coverage is the status of the individual employee.

Eligible employees are individuals who have been employed for at least 1 year by the employer, and for at least 1,250 hours of service with such employer during the previous 12-month period.[7] In attempting "to balance the demands of the workplace with the needs of families,"[8] Congress stipulated that workers only become eligible for FMLA coverage after being employed for 1 year. Additionally, the 1,250 hours-of-service provision serves to exclude part-time and seasonal workers from FMLA coverage. It would seem that determining the number of hours worked by someone would simply be a matter of mathematics. However, calculating the number of service hours expended for an employer can be complicated.

Law enforcement employers must consider factors, such as time spent on leave, time spent on call, and time spent training when determining whether an employee has worked the requisite number of hours.

When Congress enacted the FMLA, it directed courts to use the "legal standards established under section 207 of this title"[9] to determine whether an employee had met the hours of service requirement.[10] The Supreme Court long ago pronounced that work for purposes of the Fair Labor Standards Act (FLSA) (and, by reference, hours of service for the FMLA)[11] means "physical or mental exertion (whether burdensome or not) controlled or required by the employer and pursued necessarily and primarily for the benefit of the employer. ..."[12] This definition should be considered when calculating whether leave, being on call, and training sessions constitute time spent working for a law enforcement employer.

Leave

Simply stated, neither paid nor unpaid leave is included in any calculation of hours of service under the FMLA. In *Plumley v. Southern Container, Inc,*[13] the U.S. Court of Appeals for the First Circuit was presented with an FMLA eligibility dispute. The legal issue resolved by the court was whether an employee had met the hours of service eligibility requirement contained in the FMLA. The court heeded the standard of *Tennessee Coal, Iron & R.R. Co.*[14] while delving further into whether leave time fit its criteria. The court relied on the Black's Law Dictionary definitions of *employment* and *work* in concluding that "only those hours that an employer suffers or permits an employee to do work (that is, to exert effort, either physically or mentally) for which that employee has been hired and is being paid by the employer can be included as hours of service within the meaning of the FMLA."[15] While employees are on leave, even if paid leave, they are not exerting physical or mental effort for their employer.[16]

On Call

The nature of law enforcement often requires those providing this essential public service to be considered on call. Agencies often have duty officers/agents who act as a first contact for periods of 12 hours, 24 hours, or even a week at a time. Unless called to respond to an actual incident, it is unlikely that time spent on call will be credited toward the 1,250 hours of service required for FMLA entitlement. The U.S. Supreme Court has held that whether an on-call employee is working during this time "depends on the degree to which the employee may use the time for personal activities."[17] In *Birdwell v. City of Gadsden,*[18] this Supreme Court principle was interpreted in the context of law enforcement employment. In *Birdwell*, a group of city police department detectives argued that they were entitled to compensation pursuant to the FLSA[19] for a week that they spent on call. The detectives were not required to remain at the police station, but they could not leave home unless they provided a forwarding number or owned a beeper. They testified that those who did not own beepers could not participate in outdoor activities, such as hunting or fishing; that none of them could leave town or go on vacation; that they could not go on family outings without taking two cars because of the possibility of being called to duty; and that they could not drink alcohol during the entire time period.[20] Despite the restrictions, the Eleventh Circuit Court of Appeals found that the detectives' on-call time was not work time.[21] The Eleventh Circuit panel reached this conclusion based on an extensive review of other circuit court decisions applying the Supreme Court test[22] to a myriad of circumstances.[23] It is obvious from this review that unless a department puts severe restrictions on officers substantially interfering with their personal lives, on call time simply will not be included in the computation of hours of service for FMLA eligibility.

Training

The law enforcement occupation also requires recurrent training for many of its personnel. For example, sworn officers must maintain proficiency with firearms during their careers and, thus, attend training to do so and also are expected to attend seminars and in-services to further hone their skills. Likewise, support personnel regularly attend conferences and training sessions to keep current in their areas of expertise.

Time spent by employees training to maintain their proficiency or to do their job better will count toward hours of service to their employers. The determination that time spent training should be credited to the employee's hours of service is based on the conclusion that the employer accrues the benefits of its employees' training.[24]

WHAT IS A SERIOUS HEALTH CONDITION?

Exactly what constitutes a serious health condition can be difficult to determine. While the FMLA provides seemingly clear standards,[25] "[t]he inquiry is necessarily extremely factually-intensive and often requires human resources personnel or individual supervisors with no medical training to make medical judgement calls about, for example, whether an employee is 'incapacitated' by an illness, or whether the employee is undergoing a 'regimen of continuing treatment.'"[26] For this reason, "the majority of FMLA cases turn on the issue of whether the employee or an immediate family member was suffering from a 'serious health condition.'"[27]

While the FMLA defines the term *serious health condition* as an illness, injury, impairment, or physical or mental condition that involves A) inpatient care in a hospital, hospice, or residential medical care facility, or B) continuing treatment by a health care provider, [28] relevant federal regulations provide much greater detail in explaining whether certain conditions satisfy the statute's definition. For example, the phrase *continuing treatment by a health care provider* is expounded upon in the regulations. It can include a period of incapacity (i.e., inability to work, attend school, or perform other regular daily activities due to the serious health condition, treatment therefor, or recovery therefrom) of more than 3 consecutive calendar days. Incapacity may be caused by a chronic serious health condition. One such chronic serious health condition is "one which may cause episodic rather than a continuing period of incapacity (examples include asthma, diabetes, and epilepsy)."[29] Employers should note that absences for such chronic conditions qualify for FMLA leave even though the employee does not receive treatment from a health care provider during the absence and even if the absence does not last more than 3 days. This would apply to asthmatics who may be unable to report to work because of the onset of an asthma attack or because their health care provider has advised them to stay home when the pollen count exceeds a certain level.[30]

Another serious health condition involving continuing treatment by a health care provider is described as a "period of incapacity which is permanent or long-term due to a condition for which treatment may not be effective."[31] The employee or family member must be under the continuing supervision of a health care provider but not necessarily be receiving active treatment. Examples provided for this type of condition include Alzheimer's, a severe stroke, and the terminal stages of a disease.[32]

Chemotherapy or radiation treatments for cancer, physical therapy to help with severe arthritis, and dialysis to treat kidney disease are considered continuing treatment by a health care provider because they constitute "multiple treatments ... for a condition that would likely result in a period of incapacity of more than three consecutive calendar days" if the treatments were not performed.[33] These types of treatments do not require an actual absence of 3 consecutive days, and, yet, they constitute the continuing treatment aspect of the definition for a serious health condition.

The regulations also provide guidance on conditions which ordinarily will not satisfy the FMLA definition of a serious health condition. Physical, eye, and dental examinations are not considered treatment for purposes of the act's second definition of a serious health condition.[34] Likewise, "[c]onditions for which cosmetic treatments are administered (such as most treatments for acne or plastic surgery) are not 'serious health conditions' unless inpatient hospital care is required or unless complications develop."[35] Finally, unless complications arise,[36] a common cold, the flu, earaches, an upset stomach, minor ulcers, headaches other than migraine, routine dental or orthodontia problems, and periodontal disease are additional examples of conditions that are not considered serious health conditions that qualify a person for FMLA leave.[37]

The regulations recognize that substance abuse may be a serious health condition, provided certain conditions are met. The guidance points out, however, that FMLA leave may only be taken for treatment for substance abuse by a health care provider or by a provider of health care services on referral by a health care provider. Absence from work because of employees' use of the substance, rather than for treatment, does not qualify for FMLA leave.[38]

Given the complicated nature of the definitions within the FMLA, it is incumbent upon law enforcement employers to consult medical professionals or legal counsel when confronting the issue of whether a certain condition meets the requirement of being a serious health condition for FMLA leave eligibility.

WHO IS A SPOUSE, PARENT, AND SON OR DAUGHTER?

The FMLA allows employees to take leave to care for certain family members with a serious health condition. Specifically, an employee is entitled to leave to care for "the spouse, or a son, daughter, or parent, of the employee" with such a condition.[39] As self-explanatory as these terms appear, the FMLA and related federal regulations provide guidance for applying the definitions in various contexts. The statute simply defines spouse as "a husband or wife, as the case may be."[40] The corresponding regulation goes further, finding the term to mean "a husband or wife as defined or recognized under state law for purposes of marriage in the State where the employee resides, including common law marriage in States where it is recognized."[41] Making the determination whether employees are entitled to leave to care for their spouses will require familiarity with the employer's respective state law regarding marriage.

The term *son or daughter* is defined in the FMLA as a biological, adopted, or foster child, a stepchild, a legal ward, or a child of a person standing in loco parentis, who is either under 18 years of age, or 18 years of age or older and incapable of self-care because of a mental or physical disability.[42] The corresponding regulation provides parameters to gauge whether the son or daughter is incapable of self-care because of a mental or physical disability.[43] The regulation further instructs that a biological or legal relationship is not required for someone to be considered an employee's son or daughter because "[p]ersons who are 'in loco parentis' include those with day-to-day responsibilities to care for and financially support a child."[44] This determination is necessarily governed by the factual circumstances in a given situation.

The term *parent* is set forth in the FMLA to mean "the biological parent of an employee or an individual who stood in loco parentis to an employee when the employee was a son or daughter."[45] As when the employee is the person who is in loco parentis for a child, there needs to be no biological or legal relationship between the employee and the person who was in loco parentis when the employee was a child for the employee to now use FMLA leave to care for this parent.[46] Conversely, the term *parent* does not include parental in-laws.[47]

HOW MUST FMLA LEAVE BE TAKEN?

Because eligible employees are entitled to up to 12 workweeks of leave in 1 year pursuant to the FMLA, agreement between the employer and employee over how best to take the leave may be challenging to reach. It is important for the employer to know exactly what the FMLA requires of the leave when dealing with the requesting employee. First, FMLA leave is not necessarily paid leave. When Congress drafted the FMLA, it was sensitive to the potential hardship its provisions would put on employers. Doing without an employee for upwards of 3 months creates a void that must be filled during the absence. The statute sets out to "balance the demands of the workplace with the needs of families,"[48] all the while doing it "in a manner that accommodates the legitimate interest of employers."[49] Toward that goal, the FMLA does not require employers to create additional paid leave for an employee taking leave pursuant to its provisions. The employee may elect or the employer may require that accrued paid vacation leave, personal leave, family leave, or medical or sick leave be substituted for any part of the 12 week period of leave guaranteed by the FMLA.[50] However, the employer is not required to provide paid sick leave or paid medical leave in any situation in which the employer does not normally provide such paid leave.[51] In other words, while the FMLA mandates time away from work for certain situations, it does not mandate that employers deviate from their leave-accrual or leave-usage policies.

Employers also should be aware that FMLA leave does not always have to be taken all at once. Rather, it may be taken intermittently or on a reduced leave schedule when certain circumstances exist. Intermittent leave is taken in separate blocks of time due to a single qualifying reason. A reduced leave schedule is when an employee's usual number of working hours in a workweek, or number of hours in a workday, are reduced.[52]

For FMLA leave to be taken on an intermittent or reduced leave schedule basis following the birth or placement of a child for adoption or foster care, the employer must agree. The employer's agreement is not required, however, when the mother has a serious health condition in connection with the birth of the child or when the newborn child has a serious health condition.[53]

Intermittent or reduced schedule leave is also available to care for certain health conditions. Because there must be a medical need to take leave in this fashion, agreement of the employer is not required.[54] Rather, the standard enabling its use is that the medical need "can best be accommodated through an intermittent or reduced leave schedule."[55] Furthermore, "[e]mployees needing intermittent FMLA leave or leave on a reduced schedule must attempt to schedule their leave so as not to disrupt the employer's operations."[56] This type of planning may be possible in some situations, such as when leave is to be taken several days at a time spread over 6 months for chemotherapy treatments; but not possible in others, such as when a pregnant employee takes intermittent leave for periods of severe morning sickness.[57]

CONCLUSION

For some employers, complying with the different requirements of the myriad of employment laws may seem as complicated as navigating a minefield. Unlike their private sector counterparts, public law enforcement employers must not only comply with both federal and state statutory guidelines but with Constitutional provisions as well. This article has addressed some of the more challenging aspects of the Family and Medical Leave Act. Reference to these provisions will help the employer recognize what the FMLA requires of it and, possibly more important, when providing a service linked directly to our nation's security, what the FMLA does not require of it. In determining this, it is worth noting that Congress attempted to craft the FMLA in a way that would be satisfactory to both employees and employers. While nothing in the FMLA prohibits employers from providing more benefits than is required, all employers to whom the FMLA applies must comply with its minimum mandates.

NOTES

1. 29 U.S.C. § 2601, *et seq.*
2. Cindy Skrzycki, "Lobbyists Play Tug of War Over Family Leave," *The Washington Post*, April 26, 2005, p. E1.
3. 29 U.S.C. § 2612.
4. 29 U.S.C. § 2611.
5. 29 U.S.C. § 203(x).
6. 29 U.S.C. § 2611.
7. *Id.*
8. 29 U.S.C. § 2601(b)(1)
9. 29 U.S.C. § 207 is part of the FLSA of 1938.
10. 29 U.S.C. § 2611(2)(C).
11. *Supra* note 9.
12. *Tennessee Coal, Iron & R.R. Co. v. Muscoda Local No. 123,* 321 U.S. 590, 598 (1944).
13. 303 F.3d 364 (1st Cir. 2002).
14. *Supra* note 12.
15. *Supra* note 13 at 370.
16. Military leave could be considered a caveat to the blanket exclusion of leave time being included in the computation of hours of service. The Uniformed Services Employment and Reemployment Rights Act (USERRA) of 1994 requires that people reemployed under its provisions be given credit for any months and hours of service they would have been employed but for the military service in determining eligibility for FMLA leave. For an in-depth discussion on the USERRA and its effect on law enforcement employers, see L. Baker, "Serving Their Country and Their Communities," *FBI Law Enforcement Bulletin,* July 2005, 25–32.
17. *Birdwell v. City of Gadsden,* 970 F.2d 802 (11th Cir. 1992), citing *Skidmore v. Swift & Co.,* 323 U.S. 134, 138 (1944).
18. *Id.*
19. *Supra* notes 9 and 11 (hours of service for the FMLA determined by FLSA's work hours standard).
20. *Supra* note 17 at 808.
21. *Id.* at 810.
22. *Skidmore v. Swift & Co.,* cited in note 17, *supra.*
23. For example, in *Bright v. Houston Northwest Medical Center Survivor, Inc.,* 934 F.2d 671 (5th Cir. 1991) (en banc), the plaintiff was on-call during all off-duty time, he could not become intoxicated, was required to be reachable by beeper, and was required to arrive at the hospital within approximately 20 minutes of being called. Bright was bound by these restrictions for 11 months, had no days off, and took no vacations. While acknowledging that these severe limitations made the plaintiff's job undesirable and perhaps oppressive, the en banc court ruled the on-call time was not working time under the FLSA.
24. See, e.g., *Rich v. Delta Air Lines, Inc.,* 921 F.Supp. 767 (N.D. Georgia 1996).
25. 29 U.S.C. § 2611 defines the term *serious health condition* as an illness, injury, impairment, or physical or mental condition that involves A) inpatient care in a hospital, hospice, or residential medical care facility, or B) continuing treatment by a health care provider.
26. Stephanie L. Schaeffer, *Causes of Action Under the Family and Medical Leave Act for Unlawful Termination,* 14 Causes of Action Second Series 85 (2004), at p. 34.
27. *Id.*
28. 29 U.S.C. § 2611.
29. 29 C.F.R. § 825.114(a)(2)(iii)(C).
30. 29 C.F.R. § 825.114(e).
31. 29 C.F.R. § 825.114(a)(2)(iv).
32. *Id.*
33. 29 C.F.R. § 825.114(a)(2)(v).
34. 29 C.F.R. § 825.114(b).
35. 29 C.F.R. § 825.114(c).
36. The U.S. Department of Labor issued an Opinion Letter in 1996 clarifying that the examples provided in 29 C.F.R. § 825.114(c) can constitute, under certain circumstances, a serious health condition. This followed federal court opinions holding that certain illnesses are not serious health conditions even when all criteria listed in the regulations are met because they were specifically excluded from coverage. See, e.g., *Brannon*

v. OshKosh B'Gosh, Inc., 897 F.Supp. 1028, 1036 (M.D. Tenn. 1995).

37. *Supra* note 35.

38. 29 C.F.R. § 825.114(d).

39. 29 U.S.C. § 2612(a)(1)(C).

40. 29 U.S.C. § 2611(13).

41. 29 C.F.R. § 825.113(a).

42. 29 U.S.C. § 2611(12).

43. 29 C.F.R. §§ 825.113(c)(1) and 825.113(c)(2)

44. 29 C.F.R. § 825.113(c)(3).

45. 29 U.S.C. § 2611(7).

46. 29 C.F.R. §§ 825.113(b) and 825.113(c)(3).

47. 29 C.F.R. § 825.113(b).

48. 29 U.S.C. § 2601(b)(1).

49. 29 U.S.C. § 2601(b)(3).

50. 29 U.S.C. § 2612(d)(2)(A) & (B).

51. 29 U.S.C. § 2612(d)(2)(B).

52. 29 C.F.R. § 825.203(a).

53. 29 C.F.R. § 825.203(b).

54. 29 C.F.R. § 825.203(c).

55. 29 C.F.R. § 825.117.

56. *Id.*

57. 29 C.F.R. § 825.203(c)(1).

Constitutional Authority to Regulate Off-Duty Relations

Recent Court Decisions

By Michael Bulzomi

I n recent years, a number of court cases have involved law enforcement employees who have faced departmental actions due to charges of nepotism or improper off-duty sexual activity. These employees have challenged departmental actions based on these charges on the grounds that the department is violating their First Amendment freedom of association. This article reviews two court decisions involving antinepotism rules and three cases involving the authority to regulate off-duty sexual activity. The article concludes with a discussion of departmental prerogatives to conduct internal investigations of alleged sexual misconduct.

GENERAL PRINCIPLES

The Supreme Court recognizes that an individual has a fundamental liberty interest in being free to enter into certain intimate or private relationships. First Amendment freedom of association "protects those relationships, including family relationships, that presuppose deep attachments and commitments to the necessarily few other individuals with whom one shares not only a special community of thoughts, experiences, and beliefs, but also distinctively personal aspects of one's life."[1] However, freedom of association is not an absolute right.

The government as a sovereign faces many hurdles in restricting an individual's freedom of association. In its capacity as an employer, however, the government has far broader powers. As an employer, the government's interest in "achieving its goals as effectively and efficiently as possible is elevated from a relatively subordinate interest ... to a significant one."[2] That is why it is not necessarily unconstitutional for the government to restrict an employee's First Amendment rights when it is acting as an employer.

When government actions are challenged by employees, the courts generally apply one of three standards of review. The most burdensome standard of review is called "strict scrutiny." This standard requires the government to prove that there are compelling reasons for the action taken. An intermediate standard of review is a balancing test where the interests of the individual are measured against the interests of the government. A third standard of review called the "rational basis" test is considerably more deferential to the governmental employer and merely requires the government to show that a legitimate rational objective existed for the action taken. The court determines which of these standards of review will apply based on the constitutional importance of the employee's rights implicated by the government action.

ANTINEPOTISM RULES

Public employers, concerned with public perception, may conclude that allowing two spouses to work

Michael Bulzomi, "Constitutional Authority to Regulate Off-Duty Relations," *FBI law Enforcement Bulletin*, vol. 68, no. 4, pp. 26–32. Copyright in the Public Domain.

together will give the appearance of favoritism or corruption and decide on the imposition of anti-nepotism rules. Two cases recently examined First Amendment challenges to antinepotism rules. The first case entails the demotion of an employee. The second case discusses the loss of employment by one spouse.

The case of *McCabe v. Sharrett*[3] involved the secretary to a police chief. Following her marriage to a police officer in the same department, she was transferred to a clerical position which involved less responsibility and more menial tasks. The chief explained that the transfer was prompted by a fear that the secretary's marriage "would undermine her loyalty to him and her ability to maintain the confidentiality of his office."[4] The secretary sued asserting a violation of her right to freedom of association guaranteed by the First Amendment.

In ruling in favor of the chief, the United States Court of Appeals for the Eleventh Circuit, began its analysis by setting forth a three-part test that requires the employee to demonstrate that 1) the asserted right is protected by the Constitution; 2) the employee suffered an adverse employment action because she or he exercised the asserted right; and 3) the adverse employment action was taken in such a way as to infringe the constitutionally protected right. The court applied this test and found that the plaintiff met the first two requirements—her right of intimate association was protected by the First Amendment, and she suffered an adverse employment action because of her marriage.

In regard to the application of the third prong of the test, the court failed to endorse a single analytic scheme and instead proposed three approaches for determining whether the secretary's transfer impermissibly infringed upon her fundamental right to marry. The first approach balanced the employee's interest, as a citizen, against the state's interest, as an employer, in promoting efficiency.

The court found that the employer's interest weighed more heavily when the challenged employment action closely served the interest of workplace efficiency. The court noted that the secretary had access to confidential material such as internal affairs files, and that spouses tend to possess a higher degree of loyalty to their marital partners than to their supervisors and often discuss workplace matters with each other. Based on these facts, the court decided that the police chief's concerns about confidentiality were objectively reasonable and that the secretary's transfer was necessary to preserve the confidentiality of the office.

The second approach focused on "a public employee's right to harbor certain political beliefs and on how exercising that right affects the performance of governmental functions by affecting employee loyalty."[5] Under this analysis, the court found that the secretary's intimate affiliation with a police officer employed by the same department categorically disqualified her from effective performance of her job in the same manner that a political affiliation might disqualify her. Even in applying a strict scrutiny analysis, the court found that transferring the secretary because of her marriage was "necessary to serve the compelling interest of preserving the effective functioning of the ... police chief's office."[6]

Because all three possibilities came to the same result, the court did not decide which one was most appropriate. It did, however, affirm summary judgment for the police chief, holding that any constitutional burden was justified by the government's interest in "promoting the efficiency of the public services it performs through its employees"[7] regardless of which analysis applied. The *McCabe* court has determined that intimate association, though protected, may be the basis for job demotion, transfer, or reassignment, if that relationship is deemed harmful to the inner workings of the department, in this case, the chief's office.

In *Parks v. City of Warner Robins*,[8] the U.S. Court of Appeals for the Eleventh Circuit applied the rational basis test in determining whether the city's antinepotism policy permissibly infringed upon an employee's First Amendment association rights. This case was brought by two officers who had joined the Warner Robins Police Department within two weeks of each other. One eventually became a sergeant in the special investigative unit, and the other a captain in the criminal investigative unit. Their subsequent engagement created a problem under the city's anti-nepotism ordinance, which prohibits municipal employees in supervisory positions from working in the same department. The couple was informed by their chief that if they got married, the less senior of the two would have to leave the force.

The wedding was postponed and the couple sued the city under 42 U.S.C. Section 1983 on grounds that the antinepotism policy denies the fundamental right to marry protected by the due process clause of the 14th Amendment, infringes upon the right of intimate association implicit in the First Amendment, and violates the equal protection clause of the 14th Amendment because it has a disparate impact on women.

The court reasoned that while there is a fundamental right to marry protected by the due process clause, the test for any regulation of that right depends on whether it significantly interferes with the decision to marry. The court found that the city's no-spouse policy did not substantially interfere with the right to marry because the terminated spouse could still work in another department or outside the municipal government. While the policy may place increased economic burdens on certain city employees who wish to marry one another, the policy does not forbid them from marrying. Since the policy does not directly and substantially interfere with the fundamental right to marry, it is subject to rational basis scrutiny rather than strict scrutiny. Therefore the policy did not violate the Due Process Clause since it is rationally related to a legitimate government interest[9].

The court cited a number of interests advanced by the city in support of the policy, including: 1) avoiding conflicts of interest between work-related and family-related obligations; 2) reducing favoritism or even the appearance of favoritism; and 3) preventing family conflicts from affecting the workplace.[10] The court found that alleviating supervisors from having to decide whether to exercise their discretionary power to hire, assign, promote, discipline, or fire their relatives is rationally related to the practical, utilitarian goals advanced by the city. Thus, the policy was valid under the due process clause. The court also found that the policy did not infringe upon the plaintiffs'

First Amendment right of intimate association since the policy neither ordered individuals to marry nor directly interfered with the right to marry.

Finally, the court rejected the equal protection claim that the antinepotism policy has a disparate impact on women. Pointing out that proof of discriminatory intent is necessary for an equal protection claim, the court observed that disparate impact "is insufficient to prove discriminatory intent,"[11] which was not shown to be the basis for the city's policy.

REGULATING OFF-DUTY SEXUAL ACTIVITY

In *Briggs v. North Muskegon Police Department*,[12] a federal district court held that the dismissal of a married police officer for living with another man's wife was a violation of the officer's privacy and associational rights. The court concluded that the police department did not have a legitimate interest in the sexual activities of its officers unless the activities affected job performance.

However, other courts have found that off-duty sexual activity can affect job performance. In *Oliverson v. West Valley City*,[13] a married city police officer allegedly had sexual relations with women other than his wife. The relations included sexual intercourse and sodomy. The officer alleged that the sexual acts were consensual, performed in private, nonprostitutional or commercial, and heterosexual. The female participants were unmarried adults and the conduct occurred during non-duty hours. The officer was suspended for 30 days without pay and the suspension was noted in his employment file for "violations of the law of the State of Utah" and "commission of any crime relating to public morals and decency or other laws involving moral turpitude." The officer sued the city for violating his First Amendment right of association and challenged the constitutionality of the Utah adultery statute.

The city contended that the officer's conduct, which became public, severely damaged public confidence in the police department. It should be noted that the females involved were all members of the West Valley City Police Explorer Post sponsored by the city to aid the development of young people.

The *Oliverson* court held that adultery was neither a fundamental right nor implicit in the concept of ordered liberty, and refused to strike down Utah's statute criminalizing adultery. The city's motion for summary judgment was granted. Thus a police officer's extramarital affair was not protected where the state had a law criminalizing adultery and the intimate relationship affected the public's perception of the department.

The public's perception of a police department is not the only factor in determining the ability of a department to regulate an officer's off-duty activities. The next case involves internal issues not known by the public and conduct that did not violate a state law.

In *Henery v. City of Sherman*,[14] a City of Sherman police officer became involved in an extramarital relationship with a city dispatcher. The dispatcher was the wife of a sergeant in the same department. The adulterous officer had recently ranked first on a city civil service list, making him eligible for promotion to a sergeant's position, which had come open. Shortly thereafter, a sign appeared on a department bulletin board and in the departmental mailboxes of most police officers that stated: "If you can't trust another officer with your wife, how can you trust him with your life?"[15] Before making the promotion decision, the chief ordered an investigation into the validity of rumors regarding the officer's relationship with the wife of another officer.

After confirming the existence of the affair, the chief decided to pass over the officer and award the promotion to an officer who had scored lower on the promotional exam. The chief cited the affair as the sole reason for passing over the officer, claiming that "the officer would not command respect and trust from rank-and-file officers," and that promoting him would "adversely affect the efficiency and morale of the department."[16] The officer appealed the decision to the Firemen and Police Officers' Civil Service Commission of the City of Sherman.

At the hearing, the chief admitted that the officer was very qualified for the sergeant's position. The chief acknowledged he had never before passed over a candidate for promotion based on infidelity, and that

there was no written rule in the department's manual or in state law authorizing him to deny the promotion due to the affair. The chief however, believed that the affair would have affected the officer's ability to lead in the department, and would have been disruptive. As evidence that the affair was disruptive, the chief pointed to the rumors and innuendo among officers, the sign posted on the bulletin board, and the emotional distress suffered by the husband of the woman involved. The chief also commented on the importance of trust that officers must have in each other in order to serve the public. He went on to say that this trust no longer existed between this officer and other officers of the department. The Commission upheld the denial of the promotion.

The officer then appealed the Commission's decision. The case eventually came before the Texas Supreme Court which held that the officer's private, adulterous sexual conduct, was not protected by the Federal or Texas Constitutions. The United States Supreme Court denied the appeal.[17]

DEPARTMENTAL PREROGATIVE TO INVESTIGATE

The cases discussed thus far have all involved intimate associations that actually existed. The next case examines the extent of potential liability if the alleged intimate association being investigated is found not to have occurred. In that regard, the U.S. Court of Appeals for the Sixth Circuit held that a clearly established constitutional right was not violated when a police department conducted an investigation into the marital sexual relations of a police officer accused of sexual harassment.

In *Hughes v. City of North Olmsted*,[18] a police officer and his wife brought a Section 1983 action against the City and various police officers alleging that an investigation violated their constitutional rights to privacy and freedom of association. The department had conducted an internal affairs investigation as a result of the following allegations: 1) that the officer had sexually harassed coworkers; 2) that he had dated a gang member's mother; and 3) that he had bragged to women while on duty that he maintained an open marriage and a "swinging" lifestyle. During the investigation the officer was interviewed and informed of his departmental rights. The officer denied all the allegations and gave permission for his spouse to be interviewed concerning the allegations.

Based on the investigation, the department concluded that the allegations of sexual harassment and improper conduct were unsubstantiated. Thus, the department's files concerning the investigation were destroyed. Defendants moved for summary judgment and the district court granted summary judgment to the City, but denied summary judgment to the individual defendants.

On appeal, the defendants argued that the district court erred in finding that they were not entitled to qualified immunity. They claimed that they were entitled to qualified immunity because they did not violate a clearly established constitutional right. The court advised that qualified immunity provides that "government officials performing discretionary functions, generally are shielded from liability for civil damages insofar as their conduct does not violate clearly established statutory or constitutional rights of which a reasonable person would have known."[19] "Whether an official may prevail in his qualified immunity defense, depends upon the objective reasonableness of [his] conduct as measured by reference to clearly established law."[20]

The court found that the individual defendants should have been granted qualified immunity because there was no evidence that the internal police investigation of the sexual harassment charges violated a clearly established constitutional right. The court noted that the Supreme Court has not definitively answered the question of whether the Constitution prohibits a state or its actors from regulating private consensual sexual behavior of adults, even though constitutionally guaranteed rights of free association and privacy have been found in several provisions of the Constitution.[21]

The court concluded that the police department did not have a legitimate interest in the sexual activities of its officers unless the activities affected job performance. However, due to the accusations against the officer, the department's investigation was reasonable.

The court noted that the department would have been derelict in its duties and possibly could have violated federal law had it ignored the claims of sexual misconduct against the officer.[22] Under the circumstances, the questions posed by the department in its investigation were justified because they concerned the sexual harassment allegations. Also, the conduct being investigated in this case had the potential to severely affect job performance. Additionally, the court advised that it did not condone the questioning of the officer's wife about the status of her marital relationship, but concluded that a reasonable person in the investigator's position would not have known that they were intruding on a privacy or associational right. Therefore, the Sixth Circuit reversed the district court's decision as to the individual defendants.

Police agencies are expected to investigate allegations of employee wrongdoing. In fact, in many instances they are required to do so. The First Amendment is not an impediment to conducting reasonable investigations into an officer's intimate affairs when managers reasonably believe the officer's relationship adversely affects departmental interests as discussed in the above case.

CONCLUSION

Law enforcement organizations may have the constitutional authority to regulate an employee's off-duty associational activities including off-duty sexual conduct when it involves a supervisory/subordinate relationship, and associations that impact adversely on employees' ability to do their job or otherwise materially impairs the effectiveness and efficiency of the police department. All personal decisions affecting associational freedom should be carefully tied to such demonstrably legitimate law enforcement interests. Other relevant factors in determining if a particular association can be constitutionally regulated are: 1) employee morale; 2) the need for personal loyalty between officers and/or supervisors; 3) officer integrity; 4) potential conflict of interest in operational matters; 5) the potential for favoritism in supervision and management; 6) the need to minimize corruptive influences; and 7) the need for public trust. In view of the complexities of First Amendment law, it is recommended that a departmental legal advisor be consulted before any actions are taken that may implicate an employee's First Amendment rights.

NOTES

1. See Board of Dirs. V. Rotary Club, 481 U.S. 537 (1987) at 545.
2. See Board of Comm'rs, Wabaunsee Cty. v. Umbehr, 116 S. Ct. at 2348 (citing Waters, 511 U.S. at 675).
3. 12 F.3d 1558 (11th Cir. 1994).
4. Id. at 1560.
5. Id. at 1567.
6. Id. at 1572.
7. Id.
8. 43 F.3d 609 (11th Cir. 1995).
9. Id. at 615.
10. Ibid.
11. Id. at 617.
12. 563 F.Supp. 585 (W.D. Mich. 1983), aff'd, 746 F.2d 1475 (6th Cir. 1984)
13. 875 F.Supp. 1465 (D. Utah 1995).
14. 928 S.W. 2d 464 (Sup. Ct. Texas), *cert denied*, 17 S. Ct. 1098 (1997).
15. Id. at 465.
16. Ibid.
17. Henery v. City of Sherman, 117 S. Ct. 1098 (1997).
18. 93 F.3d 238 (6th Cir. 1996).
19. Id. at 240.
20. Id. at 239.
21. Id. at 241–42.
22. Id. (citing Meritor Savings Bank v. Vinson, 477 U.S. 57, 72–73 (1986)).

Speech and the Public Employee

By Lisa Baker

The U.S. Supreme Court long has recognized that individuals do not relinquish their constitutional rights by entering into public service. However, the contours of these constitutional protections are interpreted in a manner to safeguard important governmental interests. Clearly, the government as employer has more authority than the government as sovereign. With regard to speech and expressive conduct engaged in by public employees, the proper formulation under the First Amendment historically has been to apply a balancing test: balancing the interests of a public employee as a citizen in commenting on matters of public concern against the interests of the government as an employer.

The analytical framework began to take shape in the late 1960s. In case law covering this time period, the Supreme Court established a four-part inquiry to determine whether a public employee's First Amendment rights were violated. The inquiry examines 1) whether the speech touched on a matter of public concern; 2) if so, whether the employee's interests in the speech outweigh the employer's interest in promoting efficient operations; 3) whether the speech played a substantial role in the adverse employment action; and 4) whether the government can show by a preponderance of the evidence that it would have taken the same employment action in the absence of the protected speech.[1] The first two parts of this inquiry are questions of law for the judiciary to consider when evaluating whether the speech is protected under the First Amendment.[2] The final two considerations are questions of fact "designed to determine whether a retaliatory motive was the cause of the challenged employment decision."[3]

The purpose of this article is to examine recent judicial activity interpreting and clarifying the first two prongs of the four-prong inquiry. The article discusses recent Supreme Court cases clarifying what constitutes public concern for purposes of assessing First Amendment protection, as well as the impact of speaking as an employee in the performance of official duties as opposed to speaking as a private citizen. In addition, the article explores the relative interests that are assessed when determining the scope of First Amendment protection.

FIRST PRONG: PUBLIC CONCERN

For speech by a government employee to possibly qualify for First Amendment protection, the Supreme Court in *Connick v. Myers*[4] set forth an initial threshold requirement that the speech must touch on a matter of public concern. Specific guidance on what amounted to public concern was not provided. However, the Supreme Court directed that the public concern analysis requires an examination of the content, form, and context of the speech, with content being the most important consideration.[5]

Lisa Baker, "Speech and the Public Employee," *FBI Law Enforcement Bulletin*, vol. 77, no. 8, pp. 23–32. Copyright in the Public Domain.

onnick involved an assistant district attorney who, unhappy with a decision by management to transfer her, prepared a questionnaire and circulated it within the office. The questionnaire solicited coworkers' views on office morale, work assignments, the need for a grievance committee, confidence in management, and whether employees felt pressured to work on political campaigns. The Supreme Court concluded that only one question possibly touched on a matter of public concern. The remaining questions related to internal workplace grievances, and, thus, the questionnaire was not protected by the First Amendment.[6] The Supreme Court commented that this threshold inquiry is critical given "government offices could not function if every employment decision became a constitutional matter."[7]

The Supreme Court later recognized that the boundaries of the public concern test were not well-defined and offered clarification in *City of San Diego v. Roe,*[8] in which a police officer with the San Diego Police Department (SDPD) was terminated after his employer discovered that he was selling homemade, sexually explicit videos and other police paraphernalia on an online Web site. The SDPD ordered the officer to "cease displaying, manufacturing, distributing or selling any sexually explicit materials or engaging in any similar behaviors, via the Internet, U.S. mail, commercial vendors or distributors, or any other medium available to the public."[9] The officer removed some of the items for sale from the Web site but retained his seller profile, which included information about the videos he posted for sale as well as their prices. Based on his refusal to remove the items from the Web site, the SDPD terminated the officer. The discharged officer brought suit in federal court pursuant to Title 42, U.S. Code, Section 1983, arguing that his termination violated his rights to free speech and expression as guaranteed by the First and Fourteenth Amendments to the Constitution. The district court ruled in favor of the city, concluding that the officer's conduct did not amount to speech on a matter of public concern. The officer appealed this ruling.[10]

The Ninth Circuit Court of Appeals agreed with the discharged officer, concluding that his conduct fell within the contours of speech on a matter of public concern and, given it was off duty and unrelated to employment, deserved First Amendment protection.[11] As stated by the court, "[the officer's] expressive activities—as crude as they may appear—were directed at a 'segment of the general public' and did not have 'any relevance to [his] employment.'"[12] Once it concluded that the officer's expressive activities touched on a matter of public concern, it remanded the case for further consideration under the *Pickering* balancing test, directing the lower court to weigh the interests of the department in restricting the expressive conduct at issue and the officer's interests in engaging in the expressive activities.[13] The city of San Diego appealed the ruling on the issue of public concern to the U.S. Supreme Court.

The Supreme Court acknowledged that while "the boundaries of the public concern test are not well-defined,"[14] *Connick* directs the Court to consider the "content, form, and context of a given statement" when assessing whether speech touches on a matter of public concern.[15] The Court further elaborated that public concern involves "something of legitimate news interest; that is, a subject of general interest and of value and concern to the public at the time of the publication."[16] Applying these principles to the expressive conduct engaged in by the officer in *Roe,* the Court stated, "there is no difficulty in concluding that [the officer's] expression does not qualify as a matter of public concern under any view of the public concern test."[17]

Starting with *Connick* and extending through *Roe,* the Supreme Court has narrowed the type of speech and expressive conduct requiring further judicial scrutiny under the First Amendment.[18] This interpretation of the contours of the First Amendment continued when the Court addressed the distinction of speech made pursuant to official duties as opposed to speaking out as a citizen.

FURTHER CLARIFICATION OF PUBLIC CONCERN: STATEMENTS MADE PURSUANT TO OFFICIAL DUTIES

The Supreme Court recently clarified that speech on a matter of public concern does not include speech made pursuant to the employee's official duties.

Prior to 2006, courts took differing views regarding the extent to which speech that was related to the employees' official duties could be protected under the First Amendment.[19] The Supreme Court provided clarification regarding this issue in the case of *Garcetti v. Ceballos*.[20] In *Garcetti*, Richard Ceballos, a supervising deputy district attorney assigned as a calendar attorney, drafted a memorandum regarding a pending criminal case in which he expressed concern that there were inaccuracies in an affidavit used to obtain a search warrant in the case. These allegations were conveyed to Ceballos by a defense attorney. Ceballos also expressed his concerns to his supervisors and prepared a memorandum recommending dismissal of the criminal case. The District Attorney's Office proceeded with the case. A hearing occurred before a judge to address the matter of the search warrant during which Ceballos testified for the defense. The trial court judge rejected the motion to dismiss the warrant.

Subsequently, Ceballos claimed that he was retaliated against when he was reassigned to another office as a trial attorney and denied a promotion in violation of his right to speech under the First Amendment. The District Attorney's Office denied any violation of the Constitution as Ceballos' memorandum setting forth his concerns was written pursuant to his official duties. The district court judge agreed and dismissed his lawsuit. The case was appealed to the Ninth Circuit Court of Appeals, which held that Ceballos' written memorandum was clearly speech on a matter of public concern.[21] On appeal, the Supreme Court rejected the Ninth Circuit's analysis and held

> [W]hen public employees make statements pursuant to their official duties, the employees are not speaking as citizens for First Amendment purposes, and the Constitution does not insulate their communications from employer discipline.[22]

In reaching this conclusion, the Supreme Court described the critical consideration as the fact that Ceballos' statements were made pursuant to his official duties and not that they were made within the context of his employment, rather than publically,

nor that they concerned that subject matter of his employment. The Supreme Court stated, "Ceballos did not act as a citizen when he went about conducting his daily professional activities, such as supervising attorneys, investigating charges, and preparing filings."[23] As stated by the Supreme Court

> Restricting speech that owes its existence to a public employee's professional responsibilities does not infringe on any liberties the employee might have enjoyed as a private citizen. It simply reflects the exercise of employer control over what the employer itself has commissioned.[24]

In post-*Garcetti* cases, courts have focused extensively on whether the employee was speaking pursuant to his official duties and have, in a majority of cases, concluded that the First Amendment does not offer protection for a large range of expressive activities related to one's employment. For example, in *Spiegla v. Hull*[25] a corrections officer alleged retaliation in violation of the First Amendment after she was reassigned following her reporting of suspicious conduct and a possible breach of prison security by other officers. Initially, and pre-*Garcetti*, the Court of Appeals for the Seventh Circuit held that her speech touched on a matter of public concern and remanded the case for trial.[26] A jury found in favor of the officer and awarded her several hundred thousand dollars. The defendants appealed. Following the appeal, *Garcetti* was decided. On appeal, the court applied *Garcetti* and held that the officer was not speaking as a citizen "but as a correctional officer charged with the duty to ensure the prison's safety. Accordingly, the First Amendment does not insulate her statements from employer discipline and the judgment in her favor must be vacated."[27]

Other courts interpreting *Garcetti* also have used a broad net to bring speech within an employee's duties. For example, in *Vose v. Klimment*,[28] Ronald Vose, a sergeant in charge of narcotics, resigned in the face of adverse action taken against him by his department when he voiced concerns to upper management about wrongdoing on the part of investigators assigned to a multiagency major case squad. He was concerned initially with how the activities of the major case squad might impact drug investigations under his supervision. Vose was told at some point to "get along" or transfer to the patrol unit.[29] He alleged that his subsequent resignation in the face of a demotion was in violation of his rights under the First Amendment. The court concluded that his speech fell within the scope of *Garcetti*, disagreeing with his argument that his role as a supervisor of a narcotics unit did not include investigating potential misconduct by officers in another unit and, thus, he argued, he spoke out as a citizen. As stated by the court

> Vose may have gone above and beyond his routine duties by investigating and reporting suspected misconduct in another police unit, but that does not mean that he spoke as a citizen and not as a public employee.[30]

Voses' speech, while going beyond his routine or daily job duties, was not beyond his official duties as a sergeant in charge of the narcotics unit to ensure the proper operation of the narcotics program. The court concluded by stating, "[W]e find that Vose's speech, albeit an honorable attempt to correct alleged wrongdoing, was not protected by the First Amendment."[31]

In another case, a jury had found in favor of a plaintiff–police officer and awarded him compensatory and punitive damages after it concluded that his employer, the Illinois State Police, retaliated against him in violation of his First Amendment rights. On appeal, the court overturned the jury verdict after it concluded that based on *Garcetti*, the officer's speech was made pursuant to his official duties and not as a citizen.[32] In this case, allegations that individuals convicted of a murder may have been wrongly convicted while the actual offender remained at large were investigated. The officer behind this investigation expressed concern that the coverup of this matter was politically motivated. He conveyed his concerns to his supervisors, who directed him to discontinue the murder investigation. The officer then complained to the Department of Internal Investigations, which,

after reviewing the matter, decided to take no action. As a result of the fallout from the officer's allegations, his agency decided to transfer him to another position, which he claimed was in retaliation for speaking out regarding the case and its handling. A jury found in his favor and awarded him over half a million dollars.[33] On appeal, the court agreed with the defendants that *Garcetti* was controlling and overturned the jury verdict. The court concluded that the officer was speaking pursuant to his official duties and not as a citizen and, thus, his speech fell outside the protections of the First Amendment.

In contrast is the speech in *Freitag v. California Department of Corrections*.[34] In this case, a female corrections officer sued her employer after she wrote a letter to the director of the California Department of Corrections and Rehabilitation complaining of a hostile work environment created by inmate sexual conduct directed at female corrections officers and subsequent retaliation against her after she spoke out regarding this conduct. A jury found in her favor regarding the sexual harassment claim, but the case was remanded in light of the Supreme Court's decision in *Garcetti*.[35] On remand, the Ninth Circuit concluded that her speech did not owe itself to her official duties, even though the letter may have had some official consequences and the conduct she complained of occurred at her workplace.[36]

The impact of *Garcetti* has been to enable employers to retain control over speech that "owes its existence to a public employee's professional responsibilities"[37] and to avoid "displacement of managerial discretion by judicial supervision."[38]

While rejecting the notion "that the First Amendment shields from discipline the expressions employees make pursuant to their official duties"[39] the Court in *Garcetti* was careful to note the important role of legislative enactments in the form of whistleblower statutes or labor code provisions to offer protection for employees who wish to expose governmental inefficiency and misconduct.[40]

If the employee is deemed to be speaking as a citizen on matters of public concern—in other words, the threshold tests established under *Connick, Roe, and Garcetti* are met—the second prong of the

Supreme Court's test requires a balancing of interests to determine whether the First Amendment shields the speech from retaliatory action.

SECOND PRONG: BALANCING OF INTERESTS

Recognizing that the effectiveness of government entities may be seriously undermined by unrestrained declarations on the part of employees, the Supreme Court held in *Pickering v. Board of Education*,[41] that the First Amendment requires a balancing of the interests of the government in promoting efficiency of operations with the interest of the employee as a citizen in commenting on matters of public concern. Relevant considerations often include whether the speech impairs close working relationships for which loyalty and confidentiality are important or whether it impedes the performance of duties or impairs discipline or harmony among coworkers.[42] When conducting this balancing test, the courts generally recognize the heightened interests of a law enforcement employer in maintaining discipline and harmony in the workplace and fostering a positive relationship with other agencies and the public.[43] Furthermore, in assessing the impact the speech may have on government operations, the employer does not have to wait to take action only upon a finding of actual harm but may act in the face of reasonable predictions of disruption.[44] As stated by the Supreme Court

> [W]e do not see the necessity for an employer to allow events to unfold to the extent that the disruption of the office and the destruction of working relationships is manifest before taking action.[45]

In *Locurto v. Giuliani*,[46] former New York City police officers and firefighters sued to get their jobs back after they were fired for participating in a Labor Day parade by riding on a float degrading of African-Americans. Officials in New York City, including the police commissioner, learned of the participation of these city employees in the parade after extensive media coverage of the event described the racially insensitive nature of the float and the role of police officers and firefighters in its creation and operation during the parade.[47] Shortly after the parade, Mayor Giuliani stated, "I've spoken to Commissioners Safir and Von Essen and we all agree that any police officer, firefighter or other city employee involved in this disgusting display of racism should be removed from positions of responsibility immediately. ... They will be fired."[48] The employees, including the officers, were subsequently terminated. The discharged employees sued, claiming their termination violated the First Amendment as they were engaged in off-duty, protected activity. The district court agreed with the officers, ruling that their expressive conduct touched on a matter of public concern given it was intended to send a message to the community about racial integration and the city failed to establish the potential disruption of their conduct to the agency's mission.[49] The court ordered the city to reinstate the officers and to provide back pay. The city appealed the district court's ruling.

On appeal, the Second Circuit Court of Appeals overturned the lower court's determination, holding that assuming the participation in the parade touched on a matter of public concern, the First Amendment offered no protection to the discharged employees as the interest of the city in restricting this type of expressive conduct outweighed the interests of the employees in its expression.[50] In reaching its decision, the court relied on *Pappas v. Giuliani*,[51] upholding the termination of a police officer after it was discovered that he was anonymously disseminating racially offensive and bigoted materials from his home in response to solicitations from charitable organizations. The court in *Pappas* did not address the issue of whether the officer's activities touched on a matter of public concern, choosing instead to focus on the potential disruption to departmental operations his activities presented.[52] The court concluded that the capacity for the officer's activities to severely damage the department was immense, stating

> The effectiveness of a city's police department depends importantly on the respect

and trust of the community and on the perception in the community that it enforces the law fairly, even-handedly, and without bias. ... If the police department treats a segment of the population of any race, religion, gender, national origin, or sexual preference, etc., with contempt, so that the particular minority comes to regard the police as oppressor rather than protector, respect for law enforcement is eroded and the ability of the police to do its work in that community is impaired. Members of the minority will be less likely to report crimes, to offer testimony as witnesses, and to rely on the police for their protection. When the police make arrests in that community, its members are likely to assume that the arrests are a product of bias, rather than well-founded, protective law enforcement. And the department's ability to recruit and train personnel from that community will be damaged.[53]

The court in *Locurto*, quoting the above passage, similarly concluded that the First Amendment did not require the city to subordinate its interests, concluding that "the defendant's interest in maintaining a relationship of trust between the police and the fire departments and the communities they serve outweighed the plaintiffs' expressive interests in this case."[54]

RECAP: APPLICATION OF PUBLIC CONCERN AND BALANCING OF INTERESTS

The case of *Nixon v. City of Houston*[55] illustrates the application of the initial threshold requirement of public concern and the *Garcetti* determination, as well as the balancing of interests that occurs once the initial public concern inquiry is satisfied in favor of the employee. In this case, Thomas Nixon, a former Houston police officer, sued the police department and the officials responsible for his suspension and termination, alleging he was retaliated against for making various statements during media interviews and publications he authored. For approximately 2 years, Nixon wrote columns for a local Houston periodical. In these articles, he identified himself as a police officer and often made caustic and derogatory comments about certain groups of citizens, including minorities, women, and the homeless. Following an investigation into the matter, he received a 15-day suspension without pay.[56] As a result of another incident in 2006, Nixon was fired. This incident involved a highly publicized police pursuit in which Nixon proceeded to the scene, even though he was ordered not to. Once at the scene, Nixon spoke to the media, criticizing the police department's decision to disengage the pursuit and stating that he was "embarrassed to be a police officer."[57] The next day, he continued his attack on the police department by calling into various radio talk shows and by giving a television interview. In response to his actions, the Houston Police Department terminated Nixon's employment.

Nixon sued, alleging his suspension and termination were in retaliation for protected First Amendment activities. Summary judgment was entered for the defendants, which Nixon appealed to the Fifth Circuit Court of Appeals. Applying *Garcetti*, the court stated that a "a formal job description is not dispositive ... nor is speaking on the subject matter of one's employment."[58] However, "[a]ctivities undertaken in the course of performing one's job are activities pursuant to official duties."[59] Based on this description, the court concluded that Nixon's statements to the media at the scene of the crash were made pursuant to his official duties and during the course of his employment. The court noted that Nixon spoke in uniform, while on duty, and made an effort to obtain approval to address the media. The court stated

> The fact that Nixon's statement was unauthorized by HPD and that speaking to the press was not part of his regular job duties is not dispositive. Nixon's statement was made while performing his job, and the fact that Nixon performed his job incorrectly, in an unauthorized manner, or in contravention to the wishes of his superiors

does not convert his statement at the accident scene into protected citizen speech.[60]

The court then considered the statements he made the next day to the media and concluded that while they may appear to be more like citizen speech given they were made off duty, they actually were an extension of the statements he made while performing official duties and, thus, not protected.[61] The court went on to add that even if these statements were not controlled by *Garcetti*, they would nonetheless be outside the scope of First Amendment protection. Speaking out to the media in this manner severely undermined the substantial interests of the government in providing efficient services and as stated by the court

> [I]t is entirely reasonable for HPD to predict that such insubordination and likely acts of future insubordination would harm HPD's ability to maintain discipline and order in the department, morale within the department, and close working relationships between Nixon, his fellow officers, and his supervisors.[62]

With respect to his authorship of the controversial articles, the court concluded that it did not have to resolve whether Nixon was commenting as a citizen or engaged in the performance of his official duties when he took part in these activities as the balancing of interests weighed heavily in favor of the HPD, and, thus, the articles were unprotected by the First Amendment.[63] The articles contained offensive and insensitive comments regarding various segments of the population, and it was reasonable for the HPD to conclude that such comments would harm relationships within and outside the department. To hold otherwise would be to undermine HPD's mission, and "HPD must be able to prohibit such speech if it is to perform its function and maintain its professionalism."[64]

CONCLUSION

The precise contours of the First Amendment relative to speech by public servants is not easily described. However, recent judicial guidance allows for some generalizations. For speech to garner First Amendment protection and, thus, be protected from retaliation, the speech must be made as a citizen, as opposed to owing itself to the performance of official duties, and must address a matter of public concern. If this foundation is set, the First Amendment will offer protection only if the interests of the employee in engaging in the expressive activity outweigh the substantial interests in maintaining efficiency of operations of a law enforcement employer.

NOTES

1. *Connick v. Myers,* 461 U.S. 138 (1983); *Pickering v. Board of Education,* 391 U.S. 563 (1968); *Mt. Healthy City School District v. Doyle,* 429 U.S. 274 (1977); *Rankin v. McPherson,* 483 U.S. 378 (1987); *Thomsen v. Romeis,* 198 F.3d 1022 (7th Cir. 2000) (officer demonstrated that his speech was protected but failed to show that the adverse action taken against him was motivated by his speech).

2. *See City Of San Diego v. Roe,* 125 S. Ct. 521 (2004) (per curiam); *Beckwith v. City of Daytona Beach Shores,* 58 F.3d 1554 (11th Cir. 1995).

3. *Battle v. Board of Regents,* 468 F.3d 755 (11th Cir. 2006).

4. 461 U.S. 138 (1983).

5. *Id.* at 146–147.

6. *Id.* at 141.

7. *Connick* at 143.

8. 125 S. Ct. 521 (2004).

9. *Id* at 523, *quoting Roe v. City of San Diego,* 356 F.3d 1108, 1111 (9th Cir. 2004).

10. 356 F3d 1108 (9th Cir. 2004).

11. *Id.*

12. *Id.* at 1113, *quoting U.S. v. National Treasury Employees Union,* 513 U.S. 454, 465 (1995).

13. *Id.* at 1122, *citing Pickering v. Board of Education of Township High School District 205,* 391 U.S. 563 (1968).

14. 125 S. Ct. at 525.

15. *Id.*

16. *Id.* The Court referred to its prior decisions involving a common law action alleging an invasion of privacy for guidance on what constitutes a matter of public concern. *See Cox Broadcasting Corp. v. Cohn,* 420 U.S. 469 (1975); *Time, Inc. v. Hill,* 385 U.S. 374 (1967).

17. *Id.* at 526.

18. *See Thaeter v. Palm Beach County Sheriff's Office,* 449 F.3d 1342 (11th Cir. 2006); *Tindle v. Caudell,* 56 F.3d 966 (8th Cir. 1995); *Murray v. Gardner,* 741 F.2d 434 (D.C. Cir. 1984) (FBI agent's criticism of furlough plan at an all-employee conference was "an example of the quintessential employee beef" that is not a matter of public concern); *Smith v. Fruinn,* 28 F.3d 646 (7th Cir. 1994); *Hasty v. Gladstone,* 247 F.3d 723 (8th Cir. 2001); *Hankard v. Town of Avon,* 126 F.3d 418 (2nd Cir. 1997).

19. *See Garcetti v. Ceballos,* 361 F.3d 1168 (9th Cir. 2006); *Urofsky v. Gilmore,* 216 F.3d 401 (4th Cir. 2000); *Buazard v. Meridith,* 172 F.3d 546 (8th Cir. 1999); *Bradshaw v. Pittsburgh Independent School District,* 207 F.3d 814 (5th Cir. 2000); *Cromer v. Brown,* 88 F.3d 1315 (4th Cir. 1996).

20. 126 S. Ct. 1951 (2006).

21. 361 F.3d 1168 (9th Cir. 2006).

22. *Id.* at 1960.

23. *Id.*

24. *Id.*

25. 481 F.3d 961 (7th Cir. 2007), *cert. denied,* 128 S. Ct 441 (2007).

26. *Spiegla v. Hull,* 371 F.3d 928 (7th Cir. 2004).

27. 481 F.3d at 962.

28. 506 F.3d 565 (7th Cir. 2007).

29. *Id.* at 569.

30. *Id.* at 570.

31. *Id.* at 572.

32. *Callahan v. Fermon,* 2008 WL 2096777,_ F.3d_ (7th Cir. 2008).

33. *Id.* at _ The jury awarded the officer $210,000 in compensatory damages and $276,700 in punitive damages with respect to one defendant and $195,600 with respect to the other. The district court judge accepted the verdict but reduced the punitive damages to $100,000 and $50,000, respectively.

34. *Slip op.* 2008 WL 1734181 (9th Cir. 2008). On remand from *Freitag v. Ayers,* 468 F.3d 528 (9th Cir. 2006).

35. 468 F.3d 528 (9th Cir. 2006).

36. 2008 WL 1734181 (9th Cir 2008).

37. *Garcetti* at 1960.

38. *Garcetti* at 1961. *See also Haynes v. City of Circleville,* 474 F.3d 357 (6th Cir. 2007), *cert. denied* _S. Ct._, 2007 WL 2692992 (officer who administered canine program was speaking pursuant to his official duties when he sent a letter to the chief criticizing cutbacks in canine training program); *Mills v. City of Evansville,* 452 F.3d 646 (7th Cir. 2006) (sergeant disciplined for speaking out against cutback to crime prevention program was not speaking as a citizen but was speaking pursuant to her official duties); *Morales v. Jones,* 494 F.3d 590 (7th Cir. 2007), *cert. denied* _ S. Ct. _, 2008 WL 59370; *Andrew v. Clark,* 472 F.Supp.2d 659 (D.Md. 2007) (commander's dissemination of written memorandum to the media initially prepared for his agency describing his concerns regarding the handling of a barricade situation did not change the fact that he was speaking pursuant to his official duties).

39. *Id.*

40. *Id.* at 1962. *See also, Sigsworth v. City of Aurora,* 487 F.3d 506, 511 (7th Cir. 2007) ("even employees who face retaliation for speech connected to a job duty may be entitled to protection under their state whistleblower statutes").

41. *Pickering v. Board of Education,* 391 U.S. 563 (1968).

42. *Rankin v. McPherson,* 483 U.S. 378 (1978).

43. *See generally Weicherding v. Riegel,* 160 F.3d 1139 (7th Cir. 1998); *Tindle v. Caudell,* 56 F.3d 966, 971 (8th Cir. 1995) ("Because police departments

function as paramilitary organizations charged with maintaining public safety and order, they are given more latitude in their decisions regarding discipline and personnel regulations than an ordinary government employer."); *Koch v. City of Hutchinson,* 847 F.2d 1436 (10th Cir. 1988); *Locurto v. Giuliani,* 447 F.3d 159 (2nd Cir. 2006); *Cromer v. Brown,* 88 F.3d 1315 (4th Cir. 1996).

44. *Nixon v. City of Houston,* 511 F.3d 494, FN 8 (5th Cir. 2007) ("a government employer need not produce evidence of actual harm or disruption of governmental operations"); *Weaver v. Chavez,* 458 F.3d 1096 (10th Cir. 2006); *Heil v. Santoro,* 147 F.3d 103 (2nd Cir. 1998).

45. *Connick* at 152.

46. 447 F.3d 159 (2nd Cir. 2006).

47. *Id.* at 164-165.

48. *Id.* at 165, *quoting* David W. Chen, "Officers and Firemen Wore Blackface on Float, Officials Say," *N.Y. Times,* Sept. 11, 1998.

49. *Locurto v. Giuliani,* 269 F.Supp. 368 (S.D.N.Y. 2003).

50. *Locurto v. Giuliani,* 447 F.3d 159 (2nd Cir. 2006).

51. 290 F.3d 143 (2nd Cir. 2002).

52. *Id.* at 146.

53. *Id.* at 146–147.

54. *Id.* at 178. *See also Eaton v. Harsha,* 505 F.Supp. 948 (D.Kan. 2007) (Police department's interest in maintaining efficient and effective operations outweighed the First Amendment interests of police officers in expressing their opinion that the city showed favortism to African-Americans. The statements could reasonably lead to disharmony in the workplace and a lack of trust on the part of the community and questioned the ability of management to effectively lead).

55. 511 F.3d 494 (5th Cir. 2007).

56. *Id.* at 496.

57. *Id.* at 497.

58. *Id.* at 497–498, *quoting Williams v. Dallas Independent School District,* 480 F.3d 689, 692 (5th Cir. 2007).

59. *Id., quoting Williams* at 692.

60. *Id.* at 498–499.

61. *Id.*

62. *Id.* at 499.

63. *Id.* at 500.

64. *Id.*

Religion in the Public Workplace

By Richard Schott

Law enforcement is a unique occupation in many ways. The majority of law enforcement officers wear a uniform while working; many have grooming standards and conduct regulations to which they must adhere; some have sworn to uphold laws with which they do not necessarily agree. For example, the federal Free Access to Clinic Entrance, or FACE, law criminalizes attempts to interfere with a woman's access to an abortion clinic. Enforcing the laws also is, by its very nature, a job requiring continuous staffing—24 hours a day, 7 days a week, 365 days a year. These unique aspects of the profession sometimes cause personal conflicts with individual employees' religious beliefs. For example, what happens when a uniformed patrol officer feels it is a religious duty to violate the department's ban on lapel pins by wearing a Christian cross lapel pin or when a group of Muslim male officers violate a department's "no facial hair" policy by growing beards as required by their religion? What about the captain who refuses to assign officers to maintain order at the sight of an abortion clinic protest because his Catholic faith frowns upon abortion? Finally, how should a department handle a potential scheduling nightmare when its officers raise objections to shift assignments conflicting with their Sabbaths or days of worship? This article addresses these issues and raises awareness of the myriad legal provisions that should

govern handling them. FIRST AMENDMENT: FREEDOM OF RELIGION

Because law enforcement entities necessarily are part of federal, state, or local governments, they must adhere to constitutional limits and mandates, as well as to relevant legislation relating to religion. In a recent First Amendment freedom of speech case involving an assistant district attorney, the U.S. Supreme Court pointed out that the First Amendment invests *public* employees with certain rights.[1] Therefore, law enforcement executives must be mindful of the First Amendment's freedom of religion[2] provision when dealing with employees of different faiths.

Uniforms/Grooming Standards

Uniforms are almost as much a part of the law enforcement culture as they are a part of the military culture. As such, policies and restrictions regarding the wearing of them are almost universally upheld. When a department has strict rules concerning the adornment of its uniform, an individual's ability to display a religious item on it may be curtailed. While the assertion of a First Amendment-protected religious right raises the legal bar for law enforcement departments in these cases,[3] courts typically find little sympathy for those individuals who find themselves in this predicament. In *Daniels v. City of Arlington, Texas,*[4] George Daniels, a 13-year veteran of the police department challenged his department's refusal to allow him to wear a small, gold cross pin on his uniform. Daniels wore the pin "as a symbol of his evangelical Christianity"[5] while working in a plainclothes position with the department, and he continued to wear it after reassignment to a uniformed position. The police department in Arlington, as part of its general orders, had a uniform policy that read "No button, badge, medal, or similar symbol or item not listed in this general order will be worn on the uniform shirt unless approved by the police chief in writing on an individual basis."[6] Daniels requested specific allowance, pursuant to this general order, to wear the cross pin on his uniform from the police chief at that time. The chief refused permission but offered several possible accommodations to resolve the situation, including 1) wearing a cross ring or bracelet instead of the pin; 2) wearing the pin under his uniform shirt or collar; or 3) transferring to a nonuniformed position where he would be allowed to wear the pin on his shirt.[7] Daniels declined all of the possible solutions and was fired for insubordination. In upholding his dismissal for violating the uniform policy, the Fifth Circuit Court of Appeals confirmed the district court's determination that "[a] police officer's uniform is not a forum for fostering public discourse or expressing one's personal beliefs."[8] Rather, the appellate court concluded that "[a] police department does not violate the First Amendment when it bars officers from adorning their uniforms with individual adornments, even when those decorations include symbols with religious significance."[9] In reaching this conclusion, the court pointed out that the "no-pins policy serve[d] a legitimate governmental purpose in the context of uniformed law enforcement personnel, and Daniels undoubtedly ha[d] myriad alternative ways to manifest this tenet of his religion."[10]

While law enforcement agencies may not receive the almost unbridled deference from courts that the military gets when restricting uniform adornments,[11] the Supreme Court typically has afforded a great deal of deference and latitude when it comes to the internal administration, including grooming policies, of law enforcement departments. In a 1976 case before the Supreme Court,[12] a law enforcement agency's regulation of hair styles worn by its male members

was at issue. Though not challenged on religious grounds, the Court's reasoning for upholding the restriction against the Fourteenth Amendment[13] liberty challenge often is cited in First Amendment cases.[14] Namely, the Court recognized that "[t]he promotion of safety of persons and property is unquestionably at the core of the state's police power, and virtually all state and local governments employ a uniform police force to aid in the accomplishment of that purpose. Choice of organization, dress, and equipment for law enforcement personnel is a decision entitled to the same sort of presumption of legislative validity as are state choices designed to promote other aims within the cognizance of the state's police power."[15] The Court went on to say that the choices regarding uniform issues, grooming standards, and equipment issuance "may be based on a desire to make police officers readily identifiable to the public, or a desire for the esprit de corps which such similarity is felt to inculcate within the police force itself,"[16] and that either of those justifications is sufficient to withstand Fourteenth Amendment scrutiny.

While recognizing that courts generally afford wide latitude to law enforcement executives in running their departments, there is no proverbial rubber stamp when it comes to internal policies. Several police departments have or have had policies restricting male officers from wearing facial hair of any kind. Because certain religious faiths expect or require males to grow beards, these restrictions have been challenged based on First Amendment grounds. Because of religious principles involved, restrictions must withstand exacting scrutiny.[17] Some policies have not stood up to the exacting scrutiny.

In *Fraternal Order of Police Newark Lodge No. 12 v. City of Newark*,[18] two devout Sunni Muslim police officers challenged the Newark, New Jersey, Police Department's requirement, in place since 1971, that male officers shave their beards. The officers challenged the restriction on a First Amendment basis because "[t]he refusal by a Sunni Muslim male who can grow a beard ... is a major sin."[19] In their challenge to the beard ban, the officers pointed out that the department made exemptions for medical reasons, typically because of a skin condition called folliculitis barbae, but refused to make exemptions based on religious beliefs.[20] The department attempted to withstand the challenge to its no-beard policy, even in light of the medical exemptions, by contending that it wanted to "convey the image of a 'monolithic, highly disciplined force' and that '[u]niformity [of appearance] not only benefit[ted] the men and women who risk their lives on a daily basis, but offer[ed] the public a sense of security in having readily identifiable and trusted public servants.'"[21] The department also asserted that "permitting officers to wear beards for religious reasons would undermine the force's morale and esprit de corps."[22] The Third Circuit Court of Appeals rejected the department's arguments and struck down the no-beards provision as applied to the Muslim officers. The Third Circuit determined that because the department granted exemptions for nonreligious reasons but would not grant an exemption based on religious grounds, heightened scrutiny of the denials was triggered. The court concluded that the policy simply could not withstand that scrutiny. It is worth noting that the court only applied the heightened scrutiny standard because the exemption had been made based on secular (medical) reasons. The department's stated reasons for denying the religious exemption request did not satisfy heightened scrutiny. It is arguable that safety concerns—for example, the need for achieving a snug fit when wearing a gas mask—would satisfy the heightened scrutiny applied in this situation. However, these same safety concerns may dictate against *any* exemptions being made to the facial hair restriction, and it was only because of the previous exemption that heightened scrutiny was applied to the denial of the subsequent, religion-based exemption request.

Job Performance/Assignments/Scheduling

Challenges to certain assignments based on those assignments conflicting with religious ideals rarely are successful. When a challenge does succeed, it is typically because of statutory provisions, such as those found in Title VII of the Civil Rights Act of 1964, and not because of any obligation imposed upon employers by the Constitution. When an FBI agent lost his job because of his refusal to fulfill an assignment that conflicted with his religious beliefs, the Seventh Circuit Court of Appeals pointed out that "[a]fter *Employment Division v. Smith*,[23] any argument that failure to accommodate [the agent's] religiously motivated acts violates the free exercise clause of the *First Amendment* is untenable."[24] The appellate court then went on to address the challenge from a statutory standpoint.

The Supreme Court's *Employment Division v. Smith*[25] decision concerned the denial of state unemployment benefits to individuals who lost their jobs because of their ingestion of peyote for sacramental purposes at a ceremony of their church.[26] The use of peyote was in violation of Oregon state law,[27] which led to job termination and the subsequent denial by the state of unemployment benefits. The affected church members argued that the denial was in violation of their First Amendment rights. In its holding against the challengers, the Supreme Court pointed out that the "free exercise of religion means, first and foremost, the right to believe and profess whatever religious doctrine one desires. Thus, the First Amendment obviously excludes all 'governmental regulation of religious *beliefs* as such.'"[28] However, the court went on to point out that its decisions "have consistently held that the right of free exercise does not relieve an individual of the obligation to comply with a 'valid and neutral law of general applicability on the ground that the law proscribes (or prescribes) conduct that his religion prescribes (or proscribes).'"[29] Likewise, the First Amendment will not allow a law enforcement officer to refuse a lawful order to carry out an assignment because it conflicts with his religion.[30]

Denials of employee requests to have certain days off or to work particular shifts based on religious faith also are frequently challenged. These requests do not have to be honored based on any constitutional obligation for the same reasons employers are not required to allow employees to refuse certain assignments. The employee may be more successful making this request based on certain statutory language contained in Title VII, rather than on any affirmative obligation imposed by the First Amendment.[31]

TITLE VII OF THE CIVIL RIGHTS ACT OF 1964

Title VII of the Civil Rights Act of 1964 makes it an unlawful employment practice for an employer to fail or refuse to hire or to discharge any individual or otherwise to discriminate against any individual with respect to compensation, terms, conditions, or privileges of employment because of such individual's religion.[32] This antidiscrimination statute also contains a reasonable accommodation provision, placing an affirmative duty on employers to reasonably accommodate an employee's or prospective employee's religious observance or practice as long as doing so does not create any undue hardship for the employer.[33] It is from this standpoint that many employment practices are challenged as unlawful discrimination.

Uniforms/Grooming Standards

In the *Daniels v. City of Arlington, Texas* case,[34] the uniform policy challenged by Daniels prohibited the adornment of the police uniform with any button, badge, medal, or similar symbol or item unless approved by the police chief in writing on an individual basis. It is easy to envision how this policy could be applied in a discriminatory manner. For example, if the chief allowed an officer of one religious sect to wear an emblem of his faith but flatly refused to allow an officer of another faith to display his faith's emblem, there would appear to be discrimination based on religion in violation of Title VII. In *Booth v. Maryland*,[35] for example, a facially neutral grooming policy was challenged under both the First Amendment and under federal statutes.[36] At issue in the case was the Maryland Department of Public Safety and Correctional Services' grooming policy and its application to certain correctional officers. The challenger was a uniformed correctional officer who wanted to wear his hair in dreadlocks, in violation of the challenged regulation, to conform with his Rastafarian religious beliefs.[37] After ruling out his First Amendment argument, the Fourth Circuit Court of Appeals addressed the statutory challenge to the regulation prohibiting the dreadlock hairstyle.

The appellate court remanded the case, acknowledging that if the department applied its facially neutral grooming policies in an uneven manner, a statutory violation may have occurred.[38]

Specifically, the plaintiff alleged that a Jewish employee and a Sikh employee both had been granted religious exemptions to the questioned grooming policy in the past but that his request for exemption had been denied because of his particular religion.[39] If, unlike the preceding situation, a department made no exception for any religious symbol, it would be difficult to attack the policy as being applied in a discriminatory manner; and, therefore, the same arguments used to support the policy from constitutional attack should withstand the discrimination attack under Title VII. For this reason, courts entertain more reasonable accommodation challenges to grooming and uniform standards than they do straightforward discrimination challenges. For example, the reasonable accommodation provision was used as one basis of challenge in *Daniels*.[40] The Fifth Circuit ruled against Daniels, finding that "Daniels failed to respond to the police chief's *reasonable* offers of accommodation"[41] and that the only accommodation proposed by Daniels was *unreasonable* and an undue hardship for the city.[42]

Job Performance/Assignments/Scheduling

Title VII, particularly its reasonable accommodation aspect, also has been used by law enforcement employees to argue that they are entitled to refuse certain assignments or to receive preference when scheduling issues arise. In *Endres v. Indiana State Police*,[43] Benjamin Endres, Jr., an Indiana State Police employee, refused to report for a new duty assignment at a gambling casino. The assignment occurred because the state police designated some of its officers as Indiana Gaming Commission agents. Those agents' duties included certifying gambling revenue, investigating complaints from the public about the gaming system, and conducting licensing investigations for the casinos and their employees.[44] Upon being assigned to a particular casino, Endres notified the state police that he was willing to enforce general vice laws at casinos but that providing the aforementioned specific duties required of the gaming commission agent position would violate his religious beliefs because he would be facilitating gambling itself.[45] As an accommodation to his religious beliefs, he asked for a different assignment and was denied. He was subsequently fired for insubordination when he failed to report for work. After first acknowledging that "assignment to this position *because of* (rather than in spite of or with indifference to) [Endres'] religious beliefs would violate the Constitution,"[46] the Seventh Circuit Court of Appeals addressed the reasonable accommodation aspect of Title VII.

In ruling that the state police was not required to afford its employee such an accommodation, the court went to great lengths in explaining its decision.

Endres contends that [title VII] gives law enforcement personnel a right to choose which laws they will enforce, and whom they will protect from crime. Many officers have religious scruples about particular activities: to give just a few examples, Baptists oppose liquor, as well as gambling; Roman Catholics oppose abortion; Jews and Muslims oppose the consumption of pork; and a few faiths (such as the one at issue in *Smith*) include hallucinogenic drugs in their worship and, thus, oppose legal prohibitions of those drugs. If Endres is right, all of these faiths, and more, must be accommodated by assigning believers to duties compatible with their principles. Does [Title VII] require the state police to assign Unitarians to guard the abortion clinic, Catholics to prevent thefts from liquor stores, and Baptists to investigate claims that supermarkets misweigh bacon and shellfish? Must prostitutes be left exposed to slavery or murder at the hands of pimps because protecting them from crime would encourage them to ply their trade and, thus, offend almost every religious faith?[47]

The court's answer, of course, was a resounding no for logical reasons. First, "[j]uggling assignments to make each compatible with the varying religious beliefs of a heterogenous police force would be daunting to managers and difficult for other officers who would be called on to fill in for the objectors."[48] Second, the court recognized that "[i]t is difficult for any organization to accommodate employees who are choosy about assignments; for a paramilitary organization

the tension is even greater."[49] Finally, "agencies such as police and fire departments, designed to protect the public from danger may insist that *all* of their personnel protect *all* members of the public—that they leave their religious (and other) views behind so that they may serve all without favor on religious grounds."[50] Based on these reasons, the Seventh Circuit concluded that "Endres ha[d] made a demand that it would be unreasonable to require any police or fire department to tolerate,"[51] and, thus, his firing was lawful.

When scheduling issues arise, what certain employees want (or think is required) is examined on a case-by-case basis. One instructive case for law enforcement agencies is *Beadle v. Hillsborough County Sheriff's Department.*[52] Aston Beadle was a member of the Seventh Day Adventist Church who became a member of the Hillsborough County, Florida, Sheriff's Detention Department after completing the required 11-week training period at the Corrections Recruit Academy. Beadle, as a Seventh Day Adventist, did not engage in secular labor during his Sabbath—a period lasting from sundown Friday to sundown Saturday.[53] Beadle did not notify his employer of this restriction until he had completed the academy and was scheduled to work during the time frame that conflicted with his religious beliefs. Responsible for securing the safety of the Hillsborough County prison, the Detention Department naturally operated 7 days a week, 24 hours a day, year round. To satisfy this staffing need, the department employed a "neutral, rotating shift system."[54] Beadle requested permanent days off in deviation of the department's scheduling system. The department rejected this request but did notify Beadle that he was free to arrange for voluntary shift swaps with other employees. To assist in this effort, the department provided Beadle with a roster sheet and allowed him to advertise his need for swaps during daily roll calls and on the department's bulletin board. Further, the department allowed Beadle to request the use of sick days, vacation time, and compensation time if he was not able to arrange for shift swaps.[55] On one occasion when Beadle was unable to swap shifts and his request for leave was denied,[56] he simply failed to report to work. On another occasion, "Beadle abandoned his post during the middle of his shift, leaving two other deputies alone to supervise an area of dangerous inmates."[57] Ultimately, Beadle was fired over this attendance/performance issue. When Beadle challenged his termination as a violation of Title VII, the Eleventh Circuit Court of Appeals had to decide whether the sheriff's department had satisfied its obligation to reasonably accommodate Beadle.

The appellate court first noted that the phrases *reasonably accommodate* and *undue hardship*[58] are not defined in the language of Title VII, and, "[t]hus, the precise reach of the employer's obligation to its employee is unclear under the statute and must be determined on a case-by-case basis."[59] Next, the court pointed out that the "Supreme Court has provided some guidance by generally defining 'undue hardship' as any act that would require an employer to bear greater than a 'de minimus cost' in accommodating an employee's religious beliefs."[60] Additionally, the Supreme Court has "stated that compliance with Title VII does not require an employer to give an employee a choice among several accommodations nor is the employer required to demonstrate that alternative accommodations proposed by the employee constitute undue hardship. Rather, the inquiry ends when an employer shows that a reasonable accommodation was afforded the employee, regardless of whether that accommodation is one that the employee suggested."[61] Applying these guidelines to the matter before it, the Eleventh Circuit found that the sheriff's department had done all it was required to do under Title VII.

As stated in the *Beadle* opinion, an employer's obligation to reasonably accommodate an employee must be determined on a case-by-case basis.[62] Various courts have analyzed different factors when determining whether certain accommodations are reasonable or, conversely, when they impose an undue hardship on the employer. Among those factors have been the length of time involved in the desired accommodation;[63] the availability of replacements, depending on the amount of advance notice given by the employee seeking the accommodation;[64] the cost of hiring additional employees;[65] the cost of paying premium wages for overtime;[66] the difficulty in securing qualified replacements for specialized skills;[67] the effect on workforce morale of anticipated or actual complaints of favoritism from other employees;[68] and the number of employees requiring religious accommodations at one time.[69] It is obvious from a review of the various factors that courts must look to the nature and size of individual employers (or departments) to determine whether a possible accommodation is reasonable or poses an undue hardship.

CONCLUSION

Often, people say that religion and politics are delicate subjects. The situation truly can become volatile when the workplace is added into the mix. The First Amendment gives people the freedom to engage in religious expression in this country. Title VII prohibits religious discrimination and requires employers to provide reasonable accommodations for religious reasons. Because governmental employers are required to abide by both the Constitution and the Civil Rights Act of 1964 (and, therefore, Title VII contained in that legislation), law enforcement agencies need to be familiar with the provisions of each. This article has illuminated some of the contentious issues disputed between employers and their individual employees, all in the name of religion.

NOTES

1. *Garcetti v. Ceballos*, 126 S. Ct. 1951, 1959 (2206) (emphasis added.)
2. U.S. Const. amend. I, in pertinent part, states "Congress shall make no law respecting an establishment of religion, or prohibiting the free exercise thereof."
3. For a broader discussion of uniform issues and the various legal challenges asserted and standards applied to tattoos, grooming standards, and other forms of body art (such as piercings), see L. Baker, "Regulating Matters of Appearance," *FBI Law Enforcement Bulletin*, February 2007, 25–32.
4. 246 F.3d 500 (5th Cir. 2001), *cert. denied*, 122 S. Ct. 347 (2001).
5. *Id*. at 501.

6. *Id.*

7. *Id.* at 501–502.

8. *Id.* at 502–503, quoting Judge Terry R. Means, U.S. District Court for the Northern District of Texas (unpublished opinion).

9. *Id.* at 507.

10. *Id.* at 505.

11. In *Goldman v. Weinberger,* 106 S. Ct. 1310 (1986), a commissioned officer in the U.S. Air Force who was an Orthodox Jew and ordained rabbi, contended that the Air Force's restriction on his wearing a yarmulke while in uniform violated his First Amendment right to religious expression. In upholding the Air Force's ban on the yarmulke, the Supreme Court acknowledged that its review of military regulations challenged on First Amendment grounds is far more deferential than constitutional review of similar laws or regulations designed for civilian society.

12. *Kelley v. Johnson,* 96 S. Ct. 1440 (1976).

13. U.S. Const. amend. XIV, § 1, in pertinent part, states "nor shall any State deprive any person of life, liberty, or property, without due process of law.

14. *See, e.g., Daniels v. City of Arlington, Texas, supra* note 4; *U.S. Department of Justice, I.N.S., Border Patrol, El Paso, Texas v. Federal Labor Relations Authority,* 955 F.2d 998 (5th Cir. 1992); *INS v. FLRA,* 855 F.2d 1454 (9th Cir. 1988).

15. *Supra* note 12, at 1445–1446.

16. *Id.* at 1446.

17. *Supra* note 3.

18. 170 F.3d 359 (3rd Cir. 1999), *cert. denied,* 120 S. Ct. 56 (1999).

19. *Id.* at 360.

20. *Id.*

21. *Id.* at 366 (quoting from appellant's brief).

22. *Id.* at 366.

23. 110 S. Ct. 1595 (1990).

24. *Ryan v. U.S. Department of Justice,* 950 F.2d 458, 461 (7th Cir. 1991) (emphasis added).

25. *Supra* note 23.

26. *Id.* at 1597.

27. *Id.,* referring to Ore.Rev.Stat. § 475.992(4) (1987).

28. *Id.* at 1599 (emphasis in original) (quoting *Sherbert v. Verner,* 83 S. Ct. 1790, 1793 (1963).

29. *Id.* at 1600 (quoting United States v. Lee, 102 S. Ct. 1051, 1058, n. 3 (1982) (J. Stevens, concurring in judgment).

30. *Ryan, supra,* note 24.

31. *See, e.g., Beadle v. Hillsborough County Sheriff's Department,* 29 F.3d 589 (11th Cir. 1994).

32. 42 U.S.C.A. § 2000e-2.

33. 42 U.S.C.A. § 2000e(j).

34. *Supra* note 4.

35. 327 F.3d 377 (4th Cir. 2003).

36. 42 U.S.C.A. §§ 1981 and 1983.

37. *Supra* note 35, at 379.

38. While the statutory challenge in Booth was not based on a Title VII violation, the appellate court allowed the case to continue while recognizing that the challenge could have been brought under Title VII.

39. *Supra* note 35, at 380–381.

40. *Supra* note 4, at 506.

41. *Id.* (emphasis added).

42. *Id.*

43. 349 F.3d 922 (7th Cir. 2003), *cert. denied,* 124 S. Ct. 2032 (2004).

44. *Id.* at 924.

45. *Id.*

46. *Id.* (citing *Personnel Administrator of Massachusetts v. Feeney,* 99 S. Ct. 2282 (1979)).

47. *Id.* at 925.

48. *Id.*

49. *Id.* at 926 (quoting *Ryan v. U.S. Department of Justice,* 950 F.2d 458, 462 (7th Cir. 1998)).

50. *Id.* (emphasis in original) (citing *Rodriguez v. Chicago,* 156 F.3d 771 (7th Cir. 1998) (C.J. Posner, concurring in judgment).

51. *Id.* at 927.

52. 29 F.3d 589 (11th Cir. 1994), *rehearing en banc denied,* 40 F.3d 391 (11th Cir. 1994), *cert. denied,* 115 S. Ct. 2001 (1995).

53. *Id.* at 590.

54. *Id.* at 591. The system, as explained in FN 2 of the opinion, assigned employees to work one

of three overlapping 9.6-hour shifts each day. The day shift was from 7:00 a.m. until 4:36 p.m.; the evening shift was from 3:00 p.m. until 12:36 a.m.; and the midnight shift was from 11:00 p.m. until 8:36 a.m. Each deputy received 2 consecutive days off during the week. Work assignments rotated forward (i.e., day to evening; evening to midnight) every 2 months, while days off rotated backward (i.e., Friday-Saturday to Thursday-Friday; Thursday-Friday to Wednesday-Thursday) every 28 days.

55. *Id.*

56. *Id.* The department acknowledged that it did not always approve Beadle's requests for use of leave because the jail was understaffed and the granting of some of these requests could have jeopardized jail security.

57. *Id.*

58. *Supra* note 33.

59. *Supra* note 52, at 592 (citing *United States v. City of Albuquerque*, 542 F.2d 110, 114 (10th Cir. 1976), *cert. denied*, 97 S. Ct. 2974 (1977)).

60. *Id.* (citing *Trans World Airlines, Inc. v. Hardison*, 97 S. Ct. 2264 (1977)).

61. *Id.* (citing *Ansonia Board of Education v. Philbrook*, 107 S. Ct. 367, 371 (1986).

62. *Supra* note 59.

63. *See, e.g., Padon v. White*, 465 F.Supp. 602 (S.D. Tex. 1979).

64. *See, e.g., Willey v. Maben Mfg., Inc.*, 479 F.Supp. 634 (N.D. Miss. 1979), *Wangsness v. Watertown School District No. 14–4 of Codington County, S.D.*, 541 F. Supp. 332 (D.S.D. 1982).

65. *See, e.g., Brener v. Diagnostic Center Hospital*, 671 F.2d 141 (5th Cir. 1982).

66. *See, e.g., Trans World Airlines, Inc. v. Hardison*, 97 S. Ct. 2264 (1977).

67. *See, e.g., Reid v. Memphis Pub. Co.*, 521 F.2d 512 (6th Cir. 1975).

68. *See, e.g., Draper v. U.S. Pipe & Foundry Co.*, 527 F.2d 515 (6th Cir. 1975), *Murphy v. Edge Memorial Hospital*, 550 F. Supp. 1185 (M.D. Ala. 1982).

69. *See, e.g., E.E.O.C. v. Blue Bell, Inc.*, 14 Fair Empl. Prac. Cas. (BNA) 1013, 1976 WL 13383 (W.D. Tex. 1976).

The Fair Labor Standards Act and Police Compensation

By Michael E. Brooks

Congress passed the Fair Labor Standards Act (FLSA)[1] during the economic depression in 1938 in an effort to expand the number of jobs available in the United States. They reasoned that if an employer was required to pay employees extra for working more than 40 hours a week, the employer, instead, would decide to hire new workers at the lower wage, thus creating more jobs. In 1974, Congress amended the FLSA, making it applicable to public sector employees. However, in National League of Cities v. Usery,[2] the U.S. Supreme Court held that the 1974 amendment of the FLSA was unconstitutional with respect to employees performing traditional government functions, such as law enforcement. In 1985, the Supreme Court reversed itself and ruled that Congress did have the power to apply the FLSA to state and local governments.[3]

It is essential that a law enforcement administrator charged with scheduling employees has an understanding of the applicability of the FLSA's compensation provisions to public sector employees. Failure could lead to significant financial liability for unpaid wages and overtime. For example, the failure to properly credit employees one-half hour per day for time spent performing a government function could mushroom into millions of dollars of liability when that one-half hour is multiplied by the number of employees performing the function and by the number of days the function was performed over a period of 2 to 3 years. This is especially true when considering that in some instances, such employees would be entitled to liquidated damages in an amount equal to the lost wages, as well as court costs and attorneys' fees.[4] To fairly compensate employees and avoid the consequences that may flow from miscalculation of wages, administrators must have a working knowledge of who is covered by the FLSA, what activities of covered workers must be compensated, what constitutes overtime under the FLSA, how much a covered employee must be paid for any overtime, and when a police agency can give a covered employee compensatory hours off in lieu of paying overtime wages. This article addresses these issues.

At the time that this article was written, the U.S. Department of Labor was proposing a number of changes to the definitions of exemptions from FLSA coverage. For example, under the proposed changes, most salaried managers and supervisors no longer will be entitled to overtime pay under the FLSA if their most significant responsibility involves the supervision of other employees. Currently, the law generally requires that such individuals spend a majority of their time engaged in the actual supervision of other employees to be exempt from these provisions.[5] Commentators have argued exactly how much impact these changes actually will have on law enforcement.[6] On April 19, 2004, Secretary of Labor Elaine Chao announced modifications to the proposed changes.

Michael E. Brooks, "The Fair Labor Standards Act and Police Compensation," *FBI Law Enforcement Bulletin*, vol. 73, no. 6. Copyright in the Public Domain.

Among these modifications is language that clearly states that police officers generally are covered by the FLSA.[7] The original proposed changes did not make this distinction. All of the proposed changes, which are scheduled to take effect in August 2004, are detailed at the Department of Labor Web site at www.dol.gov.

COVERAGE

The FLSA covers all public employees not specifically exempted by the law. However, there are a number of specific exemptions. First, elected officials and their appointed staffs specifically are exempted from coverage.[8] In a sheriff's department, that would include the sheriff and those policy-making officials directly appointed by the sheriff. One U.S. circuit court of appeals has expanded this exemption to sheriff's deputies.[9]

The most significant exemption to law enforcement agencies is the white-collar exemption. This provision exempts salaried executive, administrative, and professional personnel as long as the salary is greater than $8,060 per year.[10] Under this exemption, the salary may not fluctuate except for absences of more than 1 day.[11] In one case, the U.S. Supreme Court ruled that a salaried police sergeant still would fall within the white-collar exemption, even though the sergeant could be subject to discipline that could result in the loss of salary unless there was a "significant likelihood" such an event will occur.[12] Currently, the executive subgroup of the white-collar exemption encompasses the largest number of police personnel. As noted, under the current law, an executive or manager generally must spend a majority of work hours directly supervising the activities of other employees to qualify under this exemption. The Department of Labor's proposed change to the definition of an executive will exempt an individual who 1) is compensated on a salary basis in excess of $455 per week; 2) has the primary responsibility of managing the "enterprise" or managing a department or subdivision of the enterprise; 3) customarily or regularly directs the work of at least two or more full-time employees; and 4) has the authority to hire and fire or make suggestions and recommendations as to the hiring, firing, advancement, promotion, or any other change of status of other employees.[13] This change likely will result in a number of first-line police managers no longer being covered by the FLSA. For example, currently salaried sergeants who spend a majority of their time patrolling are covered by the FLSA. If the new executive definition takes effect, those same sergeants will not be covered by the FLSA if their most significant responsibility is the management of two or more employees and the sergeants evaluate those employees' job performance.

Currently, there is no maximum salary that exempts an employee from coverage under the FLSA. Instead, the responsibilities of a salaried employee determine whether that employee is exempt from coverage. Under the proposed Department of Labor changes to the definitions of exempt employees, most salaried employees who earn more than $100,000 per year in total compensation, not counting health and retirement benefits, will be exempt from coverage as a "highly compensated" white-collar worker as long as they have any duty identifiable as executive, administrative, or professional.[14] Most police officers have some duties that could qualify as administrative in nature under the new definitions. Therefore, a highly paid officer, even one who receives much compensation as a result of overtime, likely will be covered no longer by the FLSA once total compensation exceeds $100,000 per year. However, public employers who have a contractual or state statutory obligation to pay overtime will continue to be required to meet those contractual and statutory obligations.

One last issue in the area of covered employees is that of volunteers. There must be an employment relationship before the FLSA applies to an individual and an employer. A volunteer is not covered by the FLSA. Whether an individual is an employee or volunteer is a question of state law or contract. This does not allow a public employer to permit an employee to "volunteer" to perform the work of the employer during off-duty time. Such an employer would be required to compensate under the FLSA if that employer "allows" the employee to "volunteer" such work, even if the employer is not factually aware that the work is occurring.[15] However, one U.S. circuit court of appeals has ruled that under the FLSA, a police agency is not required to compensate an employee who volunteers to work at a rescue squad during off-duty hours, even though the rescue squad is directed by the same governmental agency that oversees the police department.[16]

COMPENSATED ACTIVITIES

Once an employee is determined to be covered under the FLSA, the next issue is what activities of the covered employee must be counted toward determining the number of hours that employee has worked and for which the employee must be compensated. In general, a covered employee must be compensated for performing the work of the employer. In law enforcement, the issues of the compensability of time on-call, in travel, in training, caring for equipment or animals, and during meal breaks are frequent problems for the law enforcement administrator.

Generally, time spent on-call is not compensable under the FLSA unless the employees are required to remain at the employer's premises or are so restricted that they cannot engage in personal activities.[17] In Ingram v. County of Bucks,[18] a group of county sheriff's deputies were subject to on-call shifts when they were not required to stay at work or wear their uniforms. They were required, however, to wear pagers, respond to a summons back to duty within a particular period of time; refrain from doing anything that would leave them incapable of returning to duty, such as consuming alcohol; and remain within a geographical boundary. The deputies sued, claiming that they should have been compensated under the terms of the FLSA for their time spent on-call. The Third Circuit U.S. Court of Appeals held in favor of the department. The court noted that the deputies could trade their on-call shifts and agreed with the Pennsylvania U.S. District Court, which concluded that the deputies were not limited significantly in their personal activities while on-call and that the on-call shifts were not so numerous as to be unduly burdensome.

Time spent commuting from home to work is not compensable under the FLSA. This is true even if the employee uses, or is required to use, a government vehicle in the commute.[19] In Imada v. City of Hercules, California,[20] a group of officers demanded compensation under the FLSA for time spent traveling directly from their home to training activities required for their law enforcement certification. They did not receive any such compensation unless such travel occurred during the normal work day. The officers noted that travel time from their station to the training site was compensated and that the training primarily benefitted the agency. The Ninth Circuit U.S. Court of Appeals upheld a lower federal court ruling that denied the compensation. The court noted that under the FLSA, employers are not required to compensate employees for "walking, riding, or traveling to and from the actual place of the performance of the principal activity or activities which such employee is required to perform."[21] The court also noted that training is a normal activity for a law enforcement officer and benefits both the officer and the agency. As such, travel time is not compensable under the FLSA. However, the statute only applies to the use of the employer's vehicle "within the normal commuting area for the employer's business or establishment." Therefore, an agency that requires an employee to use a government vehicle to travel to training outside the normal commuting area would have to compensate the employee driving the vehicle. However, the employer would not have to compensate other employees in the vehicle unless the travel occurs during the normal work day.[22] While time spent traveling to and from training generally is not compensable under the FLSA, time actually spent engaged in training, which primarily benefits the employer or is done at the employer's direction, is compensable.[23] The FLSA rules apply to law enforcement trainees, in a training academy, as long as they are factually employed by a law enforcement agency.[24] However, not all time at the academy is compensable. In Banks v. City of Springfield,[25] an Illinois U.S. District Court ruled that time spent at an academy not in class or involved in mandatory training is not compensable under the FLSA.

The FLSA does not require compensation for short periods of time spent caring for equipment. However, if the total period of time spent in such an activity is determined to be more than de minimis, then the employee must receive compensation. An employee who spends 30 minutes once a month cleaning a weapon need not be compensated for that activity. However, the same employee who spends 30 minutes every day caring for a dog that the employee uses as a canine officer must be compensated.[26] This is true regardless of who pays for the animal's food, equipment, and veterinary expenses.[27] Agencies may reach agreement with their employees on how they will be compensated for such activities. Any such agreement, however, must compensate the employee at least as generously as they would be compensated under the FLSA.[28]

The FLSA does not mandate the compensation of employees for time spent during meal breaks provided certain criteria are met. First, the break must be at least 30 minutes long.[29] Second, the employee must be relieved of work responsibilities during the break.[30] However, a law enforcement employee may be subject to recall during a break and may be required to receive permission before taking a break without requiring compensation under the FLSA.[31] If an employee is called back to duty during the first 30 minutes of the meal break, that employee must be compensated for all time actually spent on the break.

OVERTIME CONSIDERATIONS

For most employers, a covered employee must be paid overtime for all hours over 40 worked in a given week. This requires that an employer know how many hours an employee is working. This includes salaried employees who are not exempt from FLSA coverage. The FLSA does not permit most employers to "average" work hours (i.e., 60 hours one week and 20 the next) to avoid having hours count as overtime. However, there are special rules governing law enforcement employees that, in effect, permit a certain amount of averaging. For employees who perform law enforcement duties, as opposed to support positions, an agency may base compensation on a work schedule

that bases overtime entitlement on how many hours the employee works in a period of up to 28 days.[32] If the agency elects to use this so-called "7k method" of overtime, the agency does not have to start paying overtime, until after the employee works 171 hours during the 28-day period. As an example, Police Officer Smith works 50 hours a week for 4 consecutive weeks, or 28 days. She has worked a total of 200 hours and normally would have to be paid 10 hours of overtime each week for 40 hours total. Under Section 7k, she would not be paid any overtime until she has worked 171 hours (during the fourth week) and then will be entitled to only 29 hours of overtime pay. Agencies may use a shorter period and prorate the number of hours. For example, an agency which elects a 2-week, or 14-day, period would not have to begin paying overtime until the law enforcement employee has worked 85.5 hours.

This method allows the law enforcement administrator some flexibility when confronted with significant staffing requirements over a short period of time. More commonly, it allows agencies to use rotating shifts where employees routinely work one number of shifts one week and a different number of shifts the next. For example, an agency could work officers three 12-hour shifts the first week and four 12-hour shifts the second. Over a 28-day period, such a method would result in an officer working a total of 168 hours without any entitlement to overtime compensation under the FLSA. In the same situation, other non-law enforcement employers would be required to pay 8 hours of overtime for each of the 2 weeks the employee worked the four shifts.

OVERTIME PAY

The FLSA requires that covered employees be compensated for overtime at the rate of one and one-half times their regular hourly wage. For hourly wage employees, this is computable by simply multiplying the hourly wage times 1.5 and that result by the number of overtime hours. For nonexempt salaried personnel, there are several methods of computing the rate of overtime pay. The simplest is to figure the regular weekly wage (yearly salary divided by 52); divide that number by 40; multiply the result times 1.5; and then multiply that result times the number of hours worked over 40 in a given week.[33] If the Section 7k method is used for a 28-day period, the computation would be as follows: divide the yearly salary by 13 (the number of 28-day periods in a year); divide that number by 171 (the number of hours a law enforcement officer must work in a 28 day period before being entitled to overtime); multiply the result times 1.5; and then multiply that result times the number of hours worked over 171. The FLSA allows for another method of computing overtime for non-exempt salaried employees who work a fluctuating amount of overtime. Under this method, the employee must be paid a salary designed to compensate the employee for all hours worked, and the employee must work a fluctuating number of hours of overtime every week. The employer and employee must agree that this method of compensation will be used. This method requires a new computation every week based upon the number of hours actually worked. Payment under this method results in the employee generally receiving only one-half of their regular hourly wage for hours worked over 40. This method of compensation is rarely available to law enforcement in that such employees are typically scheduled for specific shifts, and, as such, the employer cannot argue that the employee works a "fluctuating" schedule depending upon the amount of work in a given week.[34]

COMPENSATORY TIME

The FLSA allows another method of overtime compensation for public employees—compensatory time. A public employee may be given one and one-half hours compensatory time off for every hour of overtime worked.[35] A public safety employee may only be allowed to accumulate 480 hours of compensatory time before that employee must be paid overtime.[36] When an agency has a collective bargaining agreement with employees, it is required to negotiate if and how the agency will use compensatory time in lieu of overtime pay. Any such agreement must be in conformity with the FLSA.[37]

The use of compensatory time creates a potential financial liability for an agency. Employees who leave an agency must be paid for accumulated compensatory time based upon their salary when they leave the agency or their average salary over the last 3 years, whichever is higher.[38] As such, an agency may wish to "force" employees to take compensatory time when it is advantageous to the department. In Christensen v. Harris County,[39] the U.S. Supreme Court ruled that the FLSA permits a public employer to order an employee to take compensatory time off whenever the employer chooses to do so. This raises another issue. Can an employee demand to be allowed to take compensatory time off whenever the employee wants to take the time off? The law on this issue is less clear. The FLSA provides that an employee who has earned compensatory time by working overtime must be allowed to take such time off within a reasonable time of the request unless doing so would cause an "undue disruption" to the agency's operations.[40] In 1994, the Department of Labor wrote an opinion letter on this issue wherein it stated that a police agency could not turn down a request to use compensatory time as an undue disruption because the agency would have to pay overtime to another employee.[41] Two U.S. circuit courts of appeals have interpreted the justification for denying compensatory time off less restrictively. In Houston Police Officer's Union v. City of Houston,[42] the Fifth Circuit U.S. Court of Appeals addressed a Houston Police Department policy that placed an inflexible cap prohibiting more than 10 percent of the force being scheduled off on a particular day for such things as annual leave and compensatory leave. Thus, an officer who requested to use compensatory time on a day when 10 percent already had scheduled off would have that request denied. The court found this policy in compliance with the FLSA, stating that the statute only requires that an agency permit an employee to take compensatory time within a "reasonable" period after the request. This court interpreted the Department of Labor's opinion letter as prohibiting the denial of compensatory time because of the requirement to pay another employee overtime when there was no period within a reasonable time after the request when the agency could avoid paying overtime and allow the employee to use compensatory time. In Aiken v. City of Memphis,[43] the Sixth Circuit U.S. Court of Appeals reviewed a challenge to a Memphis Police Department policy that required officers to sign a log book for the shift during which they wished to use compensatory time. Shift commanders decided how many time-off spaces were available in the log book for a given shift based upon anticipated staffing requirements. Once those spaces were filled, no other officer would be allowed to use compensatory time during the shift. The court ruled that this policy was in compliance with the FLSA as long as an officer would be permitted compensatory time off within a reasonable time of the request. However, in DeBraska v. City of Milwaukee,[45] a Wisconsin U.S. District Court ruled that a denial of compensatory time may not be based solely on the fact that another officer would have to be paid overtime even when the officer requesting compensatory time could be given another shift off within a reasonable time. The Debraska ruling is not binding on any other court, whereas the Aiken and Houston Police Officer's Union cases are binding in those circuits.

CONCLUSION

The rules contained in the FLSA are complex. The cost to a police department for failure to adhere to the rules can be astronomical. In addition, the police administrator involved in such scheduling and finance issues must understand and comply with contract terms and state statutes that deal with these same issues. Fortunately, there is a resource available. The Department of Labor will respond through its Web site, at http://www.dol.gov, to requests for interpretation of the FLSA. Good-faith reliance on such interpretations will allow a police department to avoid some of the damages caused by violation of the statute.45 In large departments, a professional support staff should be employed to conform to these requirements.

NOTES

1. Title 29 U.S.C. §§ 201 et seq.
2. 426 U.S. 833 (1976).
3. Garcia v. SAMTA, 469 U.S. 528 (1985).
4. Title 29 U.S.C. § 216(b). Unpaid employees are only denied such damages when the employer can establish that it acted in good faith upon a written opinion from the U.S. Department of Labor. See Title 29 U.S.C. § 259. An employer who can establish that it objectively acted in good faith and had no reason to know it was in nonconformity with the FLSA can avoid the liquidated damages. See Title 29 U.S.C. § 260. However, ignorance of the law is never good faith. See Thomas v. Howard University Hospital, 39 F.3d 370 (D.C. Cir., 1994).
5. Title 29 Code of Federal Regulations § 541.103. There are other methods by which an employee will be exempt as a manager/executive under the FLSA white-collar exemption without spending a majority of time managing other employees. These require that the exempt employee perform such tasks as hiring and firing. See Title 29 Code of Federal Regulations § 541.1.
6. The International Union of Police Associations, AFL-CIO, has claimed that the new rules would result in a minimum of 200,000 law enforcement officers becoming exempt from FLSA coverage. See Michael Leibig, "Report on Proposed DOL Rules Changes;" retrieved from http://www.iupa.org.newsroom/ DOLRulesChanges.html.
7. See http://www.dol.gov/esa/regs/compliance/whd/fairpay/fs17i_first_ responders.htm.
8. Title 29 U.S.C. § 203(e)(C)(ii).
9. Nichols v. Hurley, 921 F.2d 1101 (10th Cir., 1991).
10. Title 29 Code of Federal Regulations Section 541.1. Under the Department of Labor's proposed changes, this will increase to $23,600 per year.
11. Title 29 Code of Federal Regulations § 541.118.
12. Auer v. Robbins, 519 U.S. 452 (1995).
13. See http://www.dol.gov/esa/regs/ compliance/whd/fairpay/fs17b_ executive.htm.

14. See http://www.dol.gov/esa/regs/compliance/ whd/fairpay/fs17h_highly_comp.htm.
15. Title 29 U.S.C. § 203(e)(4)(A)(ii).
16. See Benshoff v. City of Virginia Beach, 180 F.3d 136 (4th Cir., 1999).
17. Armour and Co. v. Wantock, 323 U.S. 126 (1944). Title 29 Code of Federal Regulations § 785.17.
18. 144 F.3d 265 (3rd Cir., 1998).
19. Title 29 U.S.C. §§ 251–262.
20. 138 F.3d 1294 (9th Cir., 1998).
21. Title 29 U.S.C. § 254(a)(1).
22. Id.
23. Title 29 Code of Federal Regulations Sections 785.27–785.32. In Dade County v. Alvarez, 124 F.3d 1380 (11th Cir., 1997); cert. denied 523 U.S. 1122 (1998). Voluntary, off-duty training as part of a general physical fitness program was ruled not compensable under the FLSA.
24. Title 29 Code of Federal Regulations § 553.226(c).
25. 959 F.Supp. 972 (C.D. Ill., 1997).
26. See Reich v. New York City Transit, 45 F.3d 646 (2d Cir., 1995).
27. See Albanese v. Bergen County, 991 F.Supp. 410 (D.N.J., 1997).
28. See Leever v. Carson City,__F.3d__(9th Cir., 2004); 2004 WL 396269.
29. Title 29 Code of Federal Regulations, §§ 785.18– 785.19, 790.6(b).
30. Title 29 Code of Federal Regulations § 785.19.
31. See Henson v. Pulaski County Sheriff, 6 F.3d 531 (8th Cir., 1993).
32. Title 29 U.S.C. § 207(k).
33. Title 29 Code of Federal Regulations, § 778.113.
34. Title 29 Code of Federal Regulations, § 778.114.
35. Title 29 U.S.C. § 207(o).
36. Title 29 U.S.C. § 207(o)(3)(A).
37. Title 29 U.S.C. § 207(o)(2)(A)(i).
38. Title 29 U.S.C. § 207(o)(4).
39. 529 U.S. 576 (2000).
40. Title 29 U.S.C. § 207(o)(5).
41. 1994 WL 1004861.
42. 330 F.3d 298 (5th Cir., 2003).
43. 190 F.3d 753 (6th Cir., 1999).
44. 131 F.Supp.2d 1032 (E.D.Wis., 2000).
45. Title 29 U.S.C. § 259. See Supra note 4.

Statements Compelled from Law Enforcement Employees

By Michael E. Brooks

The self-incrimination clause of the Fifth Amendment to the U.S. Constitution prohibits forcing individuals to provide evidence against themselves in a criminal matter. The due process clause of the Fourteenth Amendment makes this requirement applicable to the states. However, individuals always can voluntarily decide to provide information to authorities that subsequently is admissible against them in a criminal proceeding.

The U.S. Supreme Court ruled in *Garrity v. New Jersey*[1] that a violation of the Fourteenth Amendment occurs when the government uses a police officer's statement in a criminal trial against that officer when the statement resulted from his being told that he might lose his job if he failed to answer the questions. In *Garrity*, local New Jersey police officers who were the subjects of a public corruption probe were interviewed by state investigators. The officers were told that they did not have to answer any questions, but, if they did, their answers could be used against them in criminal proceedings. The officers also were informed that New Jersey law provides that a failure to answer questions concerning their duties during a criminal probe, even when the answers might incriminate them, could result in their removal from office. Several officers answered questions put to them after receiving this warning and subsequently were tried in state criminal court where their answers were used against them. Upon conviction, these officers appealed to the

New Jersey Supreme Court that affirmed that the officers' statements were made voluntarily and, therefore, were admissible under both the New Jersey and the U.S. Constitutions.[2]

Justice Douglas wrote in *Garrity* that a person who chooses self-incrimination over job forfeiture is not waiving a constitutional right voluntarily. He rejected New Jersey's argument that because there is no constitutional right to be a police officer, the state should be allowed to obtain the cooperation of police officers by threatening job loss, even when that cooperation includes self-incrimination. He wrote, "We conclude that policemen, like teachers and lawyers, are not relegated to a watered-down version of constitutional rights." Therefore, public officials, including police officers, cannot be forced to make such a choice and answer questions and, then later, be found to have exercised their free will voluntarily, allowing their answers to be used against them in a criminal proceeding.[3]

The Supreme Court has subsequently held that a police officer can be threatened with job loss for failure to answer questions or otherwise cooperate with investigators. However, any answers given under such circumstances cannot be used against the officer in a criminal trial.[4] This ruling has led to the creation of the so-called "*Garrity* warning" used in internal investigations. This warning, in various forms, advises law enforcement employees that they must answer

Michael E. Brooks, "Statements Compelled from Law Enforcement Employees," *FBI Law Enforcement Bulletin*, vol. 71, no. 6, pp. 26–31. Copyright in the Public Domain.

questions posed by investigators or face the possibility of administrative sanction, including job loss. The warning also advises that answers provided by the employees cannot be used against them in a criminal proceeding. In cases where criminal prosecution against law enforcement employees is contemplated, the employees are advised that they do not have to answer questions but that any answers can be used against the employee in a criminal proceeding.[5]

This article addresses what triggers *Garrity* protection. It also discusses what administrative options a law enforcement manager has if an employee refuses to voluntarily answer questions during an internal investigation.[6]

SANCTIONS THAT TRIGGER GARRITY

All law enforcement officers regularly file reports of investigative activity. An officer who fails to do so in a particular case could be subject to administrative sanctions. An officer who never files reports eventually would be fired for non-performance. An officer who refuses a superior's order to file a report concerning a specific incident could be dismissed for insubordination. Does this mean that any investigative report is subject to *Garrity* protection because the officer filing the report is subject to administrative sanctions, which might include termination, for failure to file the report?

The case law since the *Garrity* decision clearly holds that only the threat of severe administrative sanctions will trigger the *Garrity* protection. For example, in *Chan v. Wodnicki*,[7] a Chicago police officer, Chan, sued a superior who had transferred him from a terrorist task force to uniformed duty after he had invoked his Fifth Amendment rights before a grand jury investigating corruption. In his task force assignment, Chan regularly received overtime pay and had the use of an official vehicle. After his transfer, he did not have either of these benefits, and he claimed that the transfer caused him a loss of prestige. He sued, arguing that the transfer was in retaliation for his refusal to testify before the grand jury.[8] The U. S. Circuit Court of Appeals, Seventh Circuit noted that the *Garrity* decision prohibits a government agency

from threatening job loss to obtain a statement from a public employee without first granting the employee immunity. However, in upholding a directed verdict for the officer's superior, the court held that, "... not every consequence of invoking the Fifth Amendment is considered sufficiently severe to amount to coercion to waive the right. Rather, the effect must be sufficiently severe to be 'capable of forcing the self-incrimination which the amendment forbids.'"[9] The court found that Chan's transfer did not result in any loss of base pay. It further noted that there were no reported cases where anything short of the threat of job loss or suspension constituted a severe enough threat to trigger *Garrity*.[10]

OVERT VERSUS IMPLIED THREATS OF SANCTIONS

What is not clear, however, is how overt the threat must be to trigger the *Garrity* protection. Is the implied threat of severe administrative sanction sufficient? In *United States v. Indorato*,[11] the U.S. Circuit Court of Appeals, First Circuit considered the appeal of a Massachusetts State Police officer who had been convicted of the theft of a trailer and its contents. Shortly after the theft, the officer was interviewed by his superiors and by FBI agents. Prior to one of the interviews, a superior began to read the officer his *Miranda* rights. The officer stopped his superior by saying that he already knew them. None of the other interviews were proceeded by warnings of any kind, and the officer was never in custody at the time of any of the interviews. The officer answered all of the questions put to him during the interviews, and some of his answers were used against him at trial. The officer, a lieutenant with over 20 years of experience, argued that he was aware that state police rules provided for the dismissal of an officer who refuses to follow the lawful order of a superior. In fact, the state police rules provided that officers must follow lawful orders promptly and that failure to do so could result in the convening of a trial board for failure to follow state police rules. Upon being found guilty by a trial board, an officer could be dismissed. Because of this, the officer claimed to reasonably believe at the time of the interviews that he was being ordered to provide information based on common practice. During one of the interviews, a superior overtly ordered the officer to divulge the name of an informant the officer claimed to have met at the scene of the theft. Therefore, in the officer's mind, his superiors were ordering him to provide information or face possible job loss. The officer argued that this belief was objectively reasonable.[12]

The First Circuit ruled that to trigger *Garrity*, a public employee must show that he was ordered to waive his Fifth Amendment right against self-incrimination *and* that a statute or municipal ordinance must mandate the dismissal of an employee who fails to do so. In this case, the court noted that neither criteria was present and, for that reason, held that the officer's statements were admissible. The court found that the officer was never told that refusal to answer would subject him to dismissal and that the state police rules did not specifically mandate that the officer answer questions or be dismissed. The court held that, "the subjective fears of [the] defendant as to what might happen if he refused to answer his superior officers [were not] sufficient to bring him within *Garrity's* cloak of protection."[13]

Other courts have not been as restrictive as the First Circuit was in *Indorato*. For example, in *United States v. Friedrick*,[14] the Circuit Court of Appeals for the District of Columbia ruled that where a suspect agent has an objectively reasonable belief that failure to answer questions will cause him to lose his job, his statement in response to the questions is "compelled" under *Garrity*. In *Friedrick*, an FBI agent, suspected of making false official statements, was summoned to Washington for interviews by U.S. Department of Justice attorneys.

These interviews continued over several days, and the agent was never told that his answers were "compelled." The District of Columbia Circuit Court ruled that such an overt warning was not required to make the agent's statements "compelled" under *Garrity* in light of the facts surrounding the interviews. Instead, the court ruled that the agent was objectively reasonable in believing that he would lose his job if he did not answer the attorneys' questions. This rendered his statements inadmissible against him in a criminal trial.[15]

ROUTINE INVESTIGATIVE REPORTS

Routine reports prepared by law enforcement employees will not be considered "compelled" under *Garrity* regardless of which of the two standards are applied to them. Even under the more liberal application of *Garrity* protection used by the District of Columbia Circuit Court of Appeals in *Friedrick*, it seems unlikely that an objectively reasonable officer could believe that failure to prepare a routine report concerning an incident would result in a severe administrative sanction.

Even if an officer specifically is ordered to prepare a particular report, the standard used by the First Circuit in *Indorato* would not provide *Garrity* immunity to the resulting statement absent an overt threat of severe administrative sanction coupled with a statute, ordinance, or regulation mandating the sanction. In the few cases that have addressed a specific order by a superior to provide a report using the *Friedrick* objectively reasonable standard, the courts have not found resulting statements to have been compelled under *Garrity*. For example, the Colorado Supreme Court addressed this issue in *People v. Sapp*.[16] Sapp and another officer were suspected of misconduct while handling a domestic dispute incident. They were called in by their superiors and both were told to prepare a written report concerning the incident. No warnings of any type were provided. Both complied and were subsequently charged criminally. They moved to suppress their statements pursuant to *Garrity* arguing that they believed they would have been fired had they not provided their reports. Their superiors testified that while they would have considered refusal to provide the reports as insubordination and would have punished the officers, they would not have fired the officers had they asserted their Fifth Amendment right and refused to provide a report. There was no regulation or statute that would have mandated a severe administrative punishment for a refusal to provide a report. The trial court suppressed the statement, and the Colorado Supreme Court reviewed.[17]

The Colorado Supreme Court adopted the standard detailed in *Friedrick* and held that as long as the officers had a subjective belief that they faced dismissal for a refusal to provide the report and that belief was objectively reasonable, *Garrity* would apply, and the report could not be used against them criminally. However, the court also noted that the objectively reasonable belief must be based upon an action of the state and cannot simply be the result of the general obligation to tell the truth in a report. The court reasoned here that although the officers held a subjective belief that they faced dismissal for refusal to provide a report, that belief was not objectively reasonable because their superiors had done nothing to give them their subjective belief other than directing them to provide the reports. As a result, *Garrity* did not apply, and the reports were admissible against the officers during their criminal trials.[18]

Legal commentators who have addressed this issue have been unanimous in arguing that the Supreme Court in *Garrity* required some kind of imminent severe administrative punishment for failure to provide information before the employee providing the information will be deemed to have acted under compulsion.[19] A review of case law fails to locate one decision where a court has extended any type of *Garrity* immunity to a routine investigative report. Instead, the courts have held that unless the employee has at least an objectively reasonable belief that failure to provide a specific report will lead to dismissal, there can be no finding of compulsion under *Garrity*.

ADMINISTRATIVE REMEDIES WHEN EMPLOYEES REFUSE TO PROVIDE VOLUNTARY STATEMENTS

In *Gardiner v. Broderick*,[20] the U.S. Supreme Court ruled that public employees may not be fired for invoking their Fifth Amendment rights against self-incrimination unless such employees have been given use immunity. In *Gardiner*, a police officer was fired because he refused to sign a waiver of his self-incrimination privilege. The Court ruled that

the firing was unconstitutional when it was based solely on the exercise of a constitutional right.[21] In light of *Gardiner*, what is the impact of a refusal to cooperate in an administrative investigation when the employee is not "compelled" to cooperate pursuant to *Garrity*?

The U.S. Supreme Court has ruled that a refusal to voluntarily waive the Fifth Amendment right against self-incrimination can be considered when determining an appropriate administrative punishment. In *Baxter v. Palmigiano*,[22] the Court held that telling a prisoner at a disciplinary hearing that he could remain silent but that his silence would be considered when imposing administrative punishment did not amount to compulsion triggering *Garrity* immunity protection. The Court held that while the exercise of a right to silence can never be considered by a criminal court, there is no such prohibition to its consideration during an administrative proceeding. The Court ruled that as long as the silence is not used, in and of itself, to justify an adverse finding, there is no violation of the Constitution when considering the exercise of the right against self-incrimination in a non-criminal proceeding.[23]

In *Harrison v. Wille*,[24] the U.S. Circuit Court of Appeals, Eleventh Circuit reviewed a case where a Florida deputy sheriff was fired after refusing to answer questions at an administrative hearing where he had been advised that he was not being compelled to answer any questions. The deputy, who was suspected of involvement in thefts from an evidence room, had previously answered investigators questions concerning the thefts after being told that his answers could not be used against him criminally. Upon learning at the administrative hearing that he was not being compelled, the deputy's attorney advised him not to answer any questions and assert his Fifth Amendment privilege against self-incrimination. The deputy followed this advise and was subsequently fired.[25] The Eleventh Circuit rejected the deputy's claim that his superiors could not consider his assertion of his Fifth Amendment right in deciding to fire him. The court ruled that all *Broderick* requires is that a termination cannot be based solely on the exercise of the constitutional right. There is nothing that prohibits an agency from drawing an adverse inference from the exercise of the right against self-incrimination and considering it along with other factors in deciding on an appropriate administrative action, which can include termination.[26]

OBLIGATION TO TELL THE TRUTH

It equally is clear that nothing in the U.S. Constitution prohibits taking severe administrative action, including employment termination, against individuals who lie during an administrative investigation. This is true regardless of whether subjects were told, or objectively believed, their statements were compelled. In *LaChance v. Erickson*,[27] a unanimous Supreme Court rejected a lower court ruling that there is a due process right to make false statements during an administrative inquiry. Federal employees who were suspected of misconduct were compelled upon threat of job loss to answer questions concerning the misconduct. The employees argued that being placed in the position of answering questions where truthful responses result in a severe administrative penalty violated the due process clause of the Fifth Amendment when they were disciplined for their false answers. The Supreme Court emphatically rejected this argument holding, "The core of due process is the right to notice and a meaningful opportunity to be heard (citations omitted). But we reject, on the basis of both precedent and principle, the view expressed by the Court of Appeals in this action that a 'meaningful opportunity to be heard' includes a right to make false statements with respect to the charged conduct."[28] This ruling is especially important to the law enforcement administrator who must ensure the integrity of the organization by taking swift and severe administrative action against any employee who engages in a lack of candor.

CONCLUSION

The *Garrity* ruling imposes significant restraints on law enforcement administrators investigating misconduct allegations within an agency. However, nothing in *Garrity* prohibits forcing cooperation by law enforcement employees with internal investigators. While those investigators must be careful to avoid "compelling" a subject to provide information when criminal prosecution is contemplated against that subject, they still have significant power to encourage cooperation by all law enforcement employees. More significant, the law enforcement administrators should not be concerned that routine investigative reports will be cloaked with any *Garrity* immunity.

NOTES

1. 385 U.S. 493 (1967).
2. Id. at 495.
3. Id. at 499–500.
4. See *Gardiner v. Broderick* 392 U.S. 273 (1968) and *Kastigar v. United States* 406 U.S. 441 (1972) where the Supreme Court ruled that governmental entities may compel a public employee to answer questions upon pain of job loss as long as the compelled statement cannot be used during criminal proceedings against the person who made it.
5. In the rare case where a law enforcement employee is in custody at the time of an interview, the warnings of rights provided in *Miranda v. Arizona* 384 U.S. 436 (1966) must also be given and a waiver of those rights must be obtained before any questioning. In addition, where a law enforcement employee has been indicted, that employee must be informed of the right to counsel provided in the Sixth Amendment regardless of whether the employee is in custody prior to questioning on the matter for which the employee has been indicted. *Massiah v. U.S.* 377 U.S. 201 (1964). Finally, under the Sixth Amendment, it is impermissible to approach a law enforcement employee who has appeared in court with counsel or who has requested counsel during a criminal court proceeding, without counsel being present, when the investigator desires to question the employee about the matter for which the employee has appeared in court. *Michigan v. Jackson* 475 U.S. 625 (1986).

6. For a more detailed discussion of *Garrity* and the types of immunity which a *Garrity* warning will convey, see Kimberly A. Crawford, "Compelling Interviews of Public Employees," FBI Law Enforcement Bulletin, (May 1993).

7. 123 F.3d 1005 (7th Cir., 1997) cert. denied 522 US 1117 (1998).

8. Id. at 1007.

9. Id. at 1009, quoting the U.S. Supreme Court decision in *Lefkowitz v. Cunningham* 431 U.S. 801 (1977).

10. Id. at 1010, citing *Fraternal Order of Police Lodge Number 5 v. City of Philadelphia* 859 F.2d 276 (3d Cir., 1988).

11. 628 F.2d 711 (1st Cir., 1980) cert. denied 499 U.S. 1016 (1980).

12. Id. at 715.

13. Id. at 716. The *Indorato* case was cited by a New York court in *People v. Marchetta* 676 N.Y.S.2d 791 (N.Y. City Crim. Ct., 1998) where an officer who had been accused of menacing motorists with a weapon was told prior to an interview with superiors, during which he was told to provide a written statement, that he "must" cooperate in the investigation upon pain of possible job loss but that he did not have to "provide evidence against himself." The New York court ruled that the officer's written statement could be used against him in a criminal trial because he was clearly told that he did not have to provide evidence. The officer, who was accompanied by a police union official at the time of his interview, also argued that the statement should be suppressed because it was taken in violation of his union's contract with the department. The court rejected this argument holding that employment contract violations do not make evidence inadmissible in a criminal trial. The following courts have also adopted the *Indorato* standard: *United States v. Johnson* 131 F.3d 132 (2d Cir., 1997) and *People v. Bynum* 512 N.E.2d 826 (Ill. App., 1987).

14. 842 F.2d 382 (D.C. Cir., 1988).

15. Id. at 397–400. This standard has been adopted by the following courts: *State v. Chavarria* 33 P.3d 922 (N.M. App., 2001); *State v. Lacaillade* 630 A.2d 328 (N.J. Super.A.D., 1993); *United States v. Comacho* 739 F.Supp. 1504 (S.D. Fla., 1990); and *State v. Connor* 861 P.2d 1212 (Idaho, 1993). In *People v. Coutu* 599 N.W.2d 556 (Mich. App., 1999) the court ruled that there must be an overt actual threat of dismissal before a statement will be deemed "compelled" under *Garrity.*

16. 934 P.2d 1367 (Colo., 1997).

17. Id. at 1370.

18. Id. at 1373.

19. See Robert M. Myers, *Police Shootings and the Right to Remain Silent*, 26 Golden Gate U. L. Rev. 497 (Spring 1996); and Steven D. Clymer, *Compelled Statements From Police Officers and Garrity Immunity*, 76 N.Y.U. L. Rev. 1309 (2001).

20. 392 U.S. 273 (1968).

21. Id. at 279.

22. 425 U.S. 308 (1976).

23. Id. at 317–18.

24. 132 F.3d 679 (11th Cir., 1998).

25. Id. at 681.

26. Id. at 683. See also *Buckner v. City of Highland Park* 901 F.2d 491 (6th Cir., 1990); *Benjamin v. City of Montgomery* 785 F.2d 959 (11th Cir., 1986); *Hoover v. Knight* 678 F.2d 578 (5th Cir., 1982); and *Uniformed Sanitation Men v. Sanitation Commissioner of New York* 392 U.S. 280 (1968).

27. 522 U.S. 262 (1998).

28. Id. at 266.

CONCEPT #9: KEEP YOUR ORGANIZATION HEALTHY

It's not the work which kills people, it's the worry. It's not the revolution that destroys machinery it's the friction.

—Henry Ward Beecher

The organization is comprised of people and as such you must develop methods to ensure that your employees remain healthy. Taking a holistic approach, healthy means more than the absence of disease. Healthy means that one is physically fit, emotionally stable and socially competent. Also, health may be viewed as a condition of the body or mind, with reference to soundness and vigor. With such variety, five readings are presented in this chapter.

First, is a reading on the importance of law enforcement fitness. Physical fitness is an important issue to be addressed, especially as law enforcement as an occupation already has high incidence of suicide, heart attack, divorce and alcoholism. Also, law enforcement is not immune from other health problems that currently plague our country, such as obesity and diabetes.

The second reading in this chapter focuses on reducing stress from an organizational perspective. It is seen that police officer stress is influenced by supervisory styles, field training programs, critical incident counseling, job assignments and shift schedules. Also, in this reading organizational benefits to stress reduction are discussed and these include financial savings to the agency, enhanced images and improved morale and efficiency.

Officers at all levels often work extended hours because of court commitments, shift shortages and a variety of other reasons. If kept up for long periods of time, this translates into police fatigue. The third reading in this chapter discusses fatigue and its negative consequences. Some of these consequences include accident risk, reduced social time and health consequences.

Praise and recognition is the topic of the fourth reading in this chapter. All too often in law enforcement there is a focus on discipline; however, it has been found that praise and recognition go a long way in the development of healthy individuals. This reading discusses morale, motivations, cynicism, emotional detachment and other key issues. Then, administering praise and methods of delivery are discussed.

Despite the best efforts of the agency, there may come a point when an employee must be examined to determine if he or she is fit for duty. The fifth and final reading of this chapter addresses psychological fitness-for-duty evaluations. These evaluations are conducted by trained professionals, but the administrator should have an understanding of how the process works and what is to be included in the report. This is especially important as the administrator may have to make employment decisions based on the report that is presented. This reading discusses the report structure and procedures to include: identifying data, reasons for the evaluation, background information, review of records, clinical interview, behavioral observations, collateral interviews, psychological test findings, and conclusions and discussion.

Physical Fitness

Tips for the Law Enforcement Executive

By Daniel E. Shell

Unique work demands and corresponding stress levels increasingly require that those in the law enforcement profession establish lifelong wellness habits. However, one 40-year longitudinal study from 1950 through 1990 found that, appallingly, the life expectancy of a retired male police officer in the United States was 66 years.[1]

Why do some officers succumb to life-threatening habits, such as the lack of physical activity and exercise, smoking and excessive drinking habits, and depression, that increase the risk of obesity? To counter the obesity epidemic and general lack of physical fitness, law enforcement professionals should spend as much time as necessary adequately establishing lifelong wellness routines.

EXAMINING THE RESEARCH

Using the body mass index (BMI)—a measurement tool to determine excess body weight in relation to height—obesity classifies as a range of 30 or higher and overweight between 25 to 29.9. The BMI has become a potential indicator of hypertension, certain cancers, and diabetes. Estimates place ranges of overweight and obesity between 60 and 65 percent in the general population with approximately onethird of the general population classified as obese.[2]

Many statistics and related information exist about the health status of the general population, and several concern the law enforcement profession. In October 2003, the author administered a questionnaire to 75 law enforcement executives and other professionals. Part of the questionnaire included a BMI exercise and nutritional assessment. Based on the BMI, 80 percent of the respondents classified as overweight with approximately one-third identified in the obese category.[3]

Additionally, research has identified 53 stressors associated with police work.[4] Officers suffer more often from heart disease, hypertension, and diabetes than the general public. They have an above average risk for heart attacks, obesity, arthritis, ulcers, and cancer while also prone to bouts of depression and suicide. Further, nearly 30 percent of police officers overindulge in alcohol compared with 10 percent of the general population.

The costs for illnesses and diseases are staggering. After adding expenses for injuries, the impact is beyond calculation. Many of the maladies to which countless law enforcement personnel succumb refer to "modifiable risk factors," which means that health conditions and related costs can be affected. For example, disease costs include heart diseases at $183 billion; cancer, $157 billion; diabetes, $100 billion; and arthritis, $65 billion.[5]

IDENTIFYING THE ISSUES

Most entry-level law enforcement training academies employ a significant amount of hours of physical training as a key component in their curricula, yet some may lack mandated guidance or standards relative to contemporary wellness or exercise science. Further, such training sometimes does not link physical fitness with the skills needed for the job. Exercises used in academy training should be performed correctly and be relative to the health requirements or job duties of veteran officers. Unfortunately, some departments have abandoned fitness standards after being sued by employees for failing to make these crucial connections. Further, disconnects in education and training can manifest unfavorably later in law enforcement officers' careers. Performing physical activity requires a sufficient knowledge base and a commensurate level of education and skill to avoid hazardous and even deadly lifestyles to an employee's health.

Furthermore, department leaders must believe and participate in lifelong wellness for their employees to embrace the concept. Some law enforcement organizations assign an individual to implement the standards without conducting the proper research regarding the needs of their particular agency; doing so may set up the department to fail. The standards implementation approach is effective but, generally, not the first step. Organizations must have adequate internal marketing and a genuine interest in employee health to respond to resistance from employee groups that might seek to thwart attempts to impose such mandates.

The law enforcement community should examine its physical fitness training and long-term health programs to ensure an efficient and competent force. The beginning point for establishing lifelong wellness habits starts with incorporating best practices (e.g., exercise science) in entry-level fitness programs. The physical training goal should match other mandated, physically demanding classes, such as arrest and control strategies and defensive tactics, that directly align with the actual skill needs of patrol officers. Contemporary exercise includes screening and testing fitness levels and designing individual exercise prescriptions linked to other physical demands of the law enforcement

profession. Departments can use professional resources to educate their law enforcement personnel to incorporate wellness habits at entry-level training that will last an entire career and, further, lifetime. For example, one research and education organization used law enforcement job task analysis data to develop corresponding fitness assessments, testing protocols, and related standards applicable to police and firefighter personnel.[6]

Arguments for not implementing fitness standards often center around the cost involved and, perhaps, a union's disapproval. Certainly, department heads should take cost-effectiveness into consideration when developing long-term health programs. And, they should examine other far more costly factors, such as police academy and related on-duty injuries, chronic use or abuse of sick leave, and early medical retirements. Organizations should implement plans to redirect this money to lifelong wellness initiatives. Every law enforcement agency should consider several factors as a worthwhile investment and savings, including corporate wellness programs; insurance companies that offer lower premiums to organizations demonstrating a commitment to lifelong wellness plans; and exercise and nutritional science education for employees.

SELECTING A PHYSICAL TRAINER

What does the law enforcement profession need to succeed in lifelong wellness initiatives? Mounting evidence points to the physical trainer as a critical link in the chain of physical fitness. The obesity epidemic and corresponding need to hire the most skilled physical trainers should particularly concern those in the law enforcement profession, their loved ones, and the communities they serve.

The goal of reengineering how and who should conduct the training can foster the momentum a department requires to educate, train, and sustain during the most stressful times, producing a workforce with a level of health and fitness commensurate with the job demands. Such a combination ensures that law enforcement leaders have personnel who embrace a quality of life, which increases dedication to the profession during their tenure of employment and beyond. Before hiring a physical trainer, managers should know the person's background, education, and certifications. Assigning unqualified trainers who place aggressive physical demands on personnel can prove harmful and even deadly. Departments should contact accredited professional organizations in the physical fitness industry, steering clear of vogue programs. Also, by teaming with the department's human resource manager, physician, cafeteria staff, union leaders, training academy director, certification personnel and professionals from accredited fitness organizations, agencies can begin holistically selecting a physical trainer. Once such a partnership is formed, organizations should ensure that trainers develop programs that match physical fitness demands with the body movements, joint actions, and biomechanics of an employee's particular job duties. For example, without properly training the shoulder and rotator cuff muscles (often neglected in shoulder training), the demands of defensive tactics training can end a career.

RECOMMENDATIONS FOR AGENCIES IN THE QUEST FOR LIFELONG WELLNESS

- Take time to properly plan an effective physical fitness program
- Hire qualified, professional trainers
- Develop fitness programs that match individual job duties
- Conduct internal marketing to educate employees and gain support
- Ensure consistent advocacy from agency leaders
- Discover the ongoing rewards

Departments should ensure that their physical trainers teach contemporary exercise science and use a functional fitness assessment, identifying the strengths and weaknesses in people seeking to be trained to a specific level of performance. Such an evaluation results in more individuals doing well, as opposed to a "one size fits all" approach in which only some survive.

Those who do not prevail often are viewed as unable to "cut it" when, in fact, they received poor training.

Further, positive reinforcement generates favorable results. The use of exercise as punishment for infractions (in the academy environment) does not reap rewards. In fact, it serves as a negative reinforcement, which will turn people away from embracing the important aspects of exercise.

CONCLUSION

The goal of lifelong wellness is not to produce a "super" law enforcement officer who can push cars; jump over buildings, walls, or other obstacles; and run all day. Law enforcement agencies should implement programs that prepare officers within their own genetical potential to perform their jobs in good health for the length of their careers. The physical trainer plays a critical role in producing this type of officer. By using existing exercise and nutritional science, technology, and the expertise of those most knowledgeable in the industry, agencies can complete this mission.

No matter the perspectives, operations, budgets, resource allocations, or human resources, the up-front preparation in ensuring wellness in law enforcement academies and beyond can prove far less costly than not doing so. Lifelong wellness and fitness proves an investment now and in the future of American public safety personnel. Thus, selecting the best physical trainers for them is paramount. Law enforcement leaders should thoroughly review varied aspects of the health and fitness arena *before* placing an individual in this essential position. Further, they should examine whether the person needs to be in a sworn position.

Leaders should prepare for a department of healthy and fit personnel by recruiting, hiring, training, and educating the workforce for the future. Physical activity, exercise, and nutritional lifestyle changes are not blocks of time in stand-alone presentations. Rather, they offer a lifetime of rewards if implemented and maintained correctly. Investing the time to properly plan a fitness program and select the most desirable physical trainer for the department will glean the most positive results; planning the program takes time and effort.

ENDNOTES

1. J.M. Violanti, J.E. Vena, and S. Petralia, "Mortality of a Police Cohort: 1950–1990, *American Journal of Industrial Medicine* 33, no. 4 (1997): 366–373.

2. U.S. Department of Health and Human Services, Centers for Disease Control and Prevention, National Center for Health Statistics, National Health and Nutrition Examination Survey, 1999–2000.

3. The Police Executive Leadership Program Class Exercise and Nutrition Questionnaire, administered by Daniel E. Shell, Division of Public Safety Leadership, Johns Hopkins University (Baltimore, MD, October 2003)

4. Information in this paragraph was derived from Scott Teeter, "Police Officers' Stress Can Be Managed," *The Oak Ridge Online-Community*, August 20, 1998; retrieved on November 16, 2004, from *http://www.oakridger.com/stories/082098/com_police.html*.

5. U.S. Department of Health and Human Services, National Institutes of Health, National Cost of Illness for Selected Diseases, 2000; *http:// www.nih.gov*.

6. For more information, visit the Cooper Institute at *http:// www.cooperinst.org*.

Reducing Stress

An Organization-Centered Approach

By Peter Finn

People in all walks of life experience, and must find ways to cope with, some degree of stress. However, in the past 25 years, researchers and criminal justice officials have identified stress factors unique to, or more pronounced among, law enforcement officers. Today, law enforcement is widely considered to be among the most stressful occupations, associated with high rates of divorce, alcoholism, suicide, and other emotional and health problems.[1]

Despite the growing understanding of stress factors within the law enforcement profession and enhanced treatment for stress-related problems, many officers feel that law enforcement is more stressful now than ever before. This sentiment can be traced to several factors, including the rise in violent crime during the 1980s and early 1990s; perceived increases in negative publicity, public scrutiny, and lawsuits; fiscal uncertainty; fear of airborne and blood-borne diseases, such as AIDS and tuberculosis; rising racial tensions; and the transition from reactive to problem-oriented policing.

Sources of stress for individual law enforcement officers can be placed into five general categories: issues in the officer's personal life, the pressures of law enforcement work, the attitude of the general public toward police work and officers, the operation of the criminal justice system, and the law enforcement organization itself. Many people perceive the danger and tension of law enforcement work–as dramatized in books, movies, and television shows–to be the most serious sources of stress for officers. In fact, the most common sources of police officer stress involve the policies and procedures of law enforcement agencies themselves.[2] This article examines the often-neglected effects that organizational stress has on agencies and officers. It then discusses why managers should change stress-inducing policies. Finally, it presents steps that several agencies have taken to reduce organizational stress and thus enhance the productivity and job satisfaction of officers.

TREATING THE SYMPTOM, NOT THE CAUSE

As part of a large-scale study conducted by the National Institute of Justice (NIJ) of programs devoted to reducing police officer stress, researchers interviewed nearly 100 stress-management program directors, law enforcement administrators, mental health providers, union and association officials, officers and their families, and civilians.[3] The respondents agreed that the negative effects of stress on individual officers typically harm agencies as well as officers. As observed by the respondents, the cumulative effects of stress among officers in a department can lead to:

- Impaired officer performance and reduced productivity
- Reduced morale
- Public relations problems
- Labor-management friction
- Civil suits stemming from stress-related shortcomings in personnel performance
- Tardiness and absenteeism
- Increased turnover due to leaves of absence and early retirements because of stress-related problems and disabilities, and
- The added expenses of training and hiring new recruits, as well as paying overtime, when the agency is left short-staffed as a result of turnover.

Most police stress programs and consulting mental health practitioners focus primarily, if not exclusively, on preventing and treating stress among individual officers. However, the "person-centered" approach currently employed by most departments fails to address the underlying organizational problems that form the basis of much of the stress experienced by officers.

It stands to reason, then, as one expert in the field suggested, that … "an organization-centered approach … identifying the problems the officers have with their work, supervisors, and pay, and making appropriate changes-may well have a greater influence on improving morale."[4]

According to the head of the Michigan State Police Behavioral Science Section, the emphasis placed by psychologists and police administrators on person-centered programs has overshadowed the importance of addressing organizational sources of stress.[5]

Unfortunately, stress program staffs and independent practitioners often lack the time to work with management to eliminate the sources of organizational stress. Moreover, few clinicians feel qualified to suggest organizational changes to law enforcement administrators.

At the same time, police administrators might not accept what they perceive to be the intrusion of a mental health professional into department operations. Administrators also may believe that they do not have the time or resources to make the desired changes, or they simply might not agree that organizational changes will reduce officer stress.

Yet, a growing number of agencies have found that even modest modifications in organizational structure can lead to enhanced morale and productivity among line officers. Although some administrators might institute organizational changes simply because they believe it is the right thing to do, there are a host of reasons that should compel reluctant administrators to consider such changes.

ORGANIZATIONAL CHANGE BENEFITS

Enhance the Department's Image

Bad press, public criticism, and legislative scrutiny can be sources of stress for both law enforcement administrators and line officers. Organizational changes that reduce officer stress can improve the department's image simultaneously. Negative publicity resulting from 8 officer suicides in 5 years–3 of them in 1994–prompted the Philadelphia, Pennsylvania, Police Department to create the agency's first stress manager position in 1995. Among other duties, the stress manager examines departmental policies and procedures and recommends ways to make them less stressful.[6]

A newly appointed police chief in a West Coast law enforcement agency decided to remedy years of bad press caused by what many community members considered to be the department's overly paramilitary image. The chief hired an organizational consultant and eventually won new community support by implementing several recommended changes designed to make the department less autocratic.

Save Money

Some departments have documented substantial cost savings resulting from organizational changes. The Mercedes, Texas, Police Department fields 25 sworn officers and serves a city of 14,000 residents. In 1986, the department reorganized to provide an employee development program that included establishing high professional standards, a reward system to promote superior performance, foot patrol assignments, and an increase in the annual in-service training requirement. In the 24 months following these changes, the department's turnover rate fell from 38 percent to 7 percent. Administrators estimate that the reduced turnover has saved the department at least $53,000.[7]

Police administrators understand all too well the costs associated with replacing officers who take early retirement or go on disability. The department not only must pay benefits to departing officers, but it also must pay to recruit, test, hire, train, and equip new officers. In smaller agencies, sudden turnover can result in serious staff shortages that require paying other officers overtime.

Improve Department Morale and Efficiency

Reducing organizational sources of stress should lead naturally to better morale, improved productivity, and, therefore, enhanced overall department efficiency. Even a well-publicized statement from the department's administration recognizing the stress officers experience and expressing support for measures to reduce sources of stress demonstrates management concern about officer well-being. Such pronouncements also help promote the good will necessary to implement change.

IMPLEMENTED CHANGES

Administrators in agencies across the country have implemented significant organizational changes as a way of reducing officer stress. The changes generally affect supervisory style, field training officer programs, critical incident counseling, command support after critical incidents, shift work, and job assignments.

Supervisory Style

One police department has undertaken a comprehensive effort to reduce organizationally generated stress among its 100 sworn officers.[8] A series of stress-related disability retirements prompted the Palo Alto, California, Police Department to commission a study in 1979 to identify sources of stress and suggest options for reducing or eliminating them. The report

concluded that the formal and informal organizational structures in the department inhibited effective communication and created strained relationships among ranks, divisions, and individuals. As a result, the department hired a management consultant and a mental health clinician to design and implement an 18-month trial program to alleviate organizational stress. Through team building and other methods, the consultant taught department members how to communicate, listen, and solve problems in an orderly, effective manner.

The program proved so successful that it has been continued ever since. It follows a 14-point written plan that serves as a basis for administrators to reduce organizational stress. First, administrators must identify sources of organizational stress and consult with work units and individual managers to resolve them. For example, the management consultant for the Palo Alto Police Department trained all sergeants in how to prepare for and conduct a performance appraisal and discussed the importance of providing employees with behavior-based feedback in a constructive manner.

In addition, administrators should monitor management decisions with regard to their stress impact, search for implementation methods that minimize the stressful impact, and advise management staff. For example, when the Palo Alto Police Department began to use computer-aided crime analysis to direct patrol and investigative resources toward apprehending career criminals, the consultant designed ways for the department's sworn and civilian personnel to influence and shape the change process.

It is also important to instruct field training officers, supervisors, and managers in communication, problem solving, conflict resolution, and supervisory skills that can minimize stress for employees. At the chief's request, the consultant hired by Palo Alto surveyed each manager on how the chief may have been creating undue stress for them, reported the results to the chief, and recommended changes based on the findings. Another important step in reducing organizational stress involves training individual managers on stress-inducing practices and events within their units. This training typically results from a manager's request for specific training in problem solving. On occasion, it can be delivered in response to a large number of complaints from line officers, which suggests a management problem.

FTO Programs

A number of departments in California have used a private counselor to train their field training officers (FTOs) in the most productive ways to interact with trainees. The counselor explains to the FTOs how people react when they are criticized and presents the best approaches for offering constructive criticism to recruits who perform poorly. The counselor also tests the FTOs on their supervisory style and presents them with the results so they can see which areas they need to improve. Field training officers who have received the instruction gain a new awareness of the tremendous impact that an FTO program has on the organizational health of a law enforcement agency.

The counselor also advises police executives that they can enhance their departments' FTO programs by designating only officers who volunteer for the program to become training officers. Officers selected to serve as FTOs who have no interest in the assignment often feel that they are being punished. By accepting only volunteers and providing them with supervisory training, departments recognize the tremendous role field training officers play in acculturating new officers. For better or worse, many rookies emulate their FTOs and later use the same helpful or harmful training techniques when they train new officers.

Critical Incident Counseling

The Michigan State Police Behavioral Science Section trains both experienced and new sergeants every year in techniques to manage critical incident stress among officers. The section director designed the training to help sergeants respond in a manner that avoids creating additional stress for officers and reduces the inevitable stress that officers experience from the actual incidents.

During the training, the section director brings in a trooper who has experienced a critical incident and has received counseling through the program.

The trooper gives a personal account of what first-line supervisors should—and should not—do when addressing the needs of troopers who require post-incident counseling. The sergeants learn what to expect from an officer who has experienced a critical incident, and the section director explains the warning signs that should alert sergeants that counseling is necessary.

The director of the Behavioral Science Section and another counselor also conduct 2-hour seminars for the agency's executive and command staffs. During this training, the counselors focus on helping managers recognize how their own work styles can impact subordinates. The counselors then suggest ways that managers can motivate their personnel to be more productive.

Command Support After Critical Incidents

The chief executive officer and other commanders of a law enforcement agency should make it a matter of policy to pay hospital visits to every officer shot or involved in a serious accident. This easily implemented policy can have a profound effect not only on the injured officers but also on the department as a whole. According to a veteran police counselor, "The impact of a shooting on the officers involved depends more on the attitude of the department toward the officers than on the incident itself."

The commissioner of the Buffalo, New York, Police Department, personally visits every police officer shot while on duty. If he cannot do so, he makes sure that his deputy or another command-level officer goes to provide support.

Command-level staff also can offer assurance and support to family members—including helping with paperwork, finding babysitters, providing telephone numbers for follow-up assistance, and simply spending time with them. Word of the command staff's concern typically spreads through the department grapevine to every officer on the force, instantly improving morale and alleviating stress.

Shift Schedules

Like many law enforcement agencies, the Michigan State Police used to rotate shifts every 7 days, causing considerable stress for many troopers and their families. As a result, the troopers association received a constant flow of grievances from members complaining of fatigue, eating disorders, and other problems. In an effort to encourage the department to change to a less stressful work schedule, the association asked the department's Behavioral Science Section for any available research that documented the harmful effects of rotating shifts on employee productivity.

The department allowed troopers to determine the frequency of their shift rotation and gave them the option of changing their rotation schedule at least annually. When additional research suggested that all rotating shift work might pose health and safety risks, the command staff included permanent shifts as an option. Today, staff members at each work site choose shifts by majority vote. Many have adopted fixed-shift schedules.

The troopers association succeeded in negotiating the changes, in part, due to the compelling evidence showing the negative effects of shift work on officer productivity. But the department's Behavioral Science Section also helped convince commanders by providing research findings. The president of the troopers association credits the successful resolution of this potentially divisive issue with the fact that the association did not enter into negotiations with the goal of simply winning concessions from the administration. Instead, the association demonstrated to commanders that the department would benefit from healthier, more productive employees. In other words, by changing the work schedule, the department, as well as the troopers, won.

Job Assignments

The psychologist for the San Antonio, California, Police Department worked with administrators to improve the agency's ability to match officers' capabilities to the needs of their jobs. In convincing administrators of the importance of such an effort, the psychologist argued that stress management should go beyond counseling, that careful selection of job candidates can reduce the stress that arises from a mismatch between the candidate and the job requirements.

The psychologist argued that by performing a "person–job fit analysis" before hiring and placing officers, the department could reduce the need for subsequent mental health treatment for officers ill-equipped to handle the job for which they were hired. Likewise, this preventive approach to mental health would help prospective officers avoid the deep feelings of frustration, disappointment, and self-blame that occurs when individuals attempt to perform a job for which they are unsuited.

To determine which skills are necessary for a patrol officer, the psychologist conducted a functional job analysis of the position. He asked a number of officers to identify the skills required to perform their jobs effectively. The department now uses the skills outlined in the job analysis to select officers for patrol.

The psychologist eventually conducted a functional job analysis of every position in the agency. The department now bases hiring and promotions not only on civil service exams but also on matching individuals' current skill levels with the job requirements for which they are applying. The psychologist also revised the training academy's curriculum to include more blocks on problem solving, critical thinking, and other skills related to preventing and managing stress. The changes in the curriculum involve identifying areas where recruits need expanded training to improve their future on-the-job performance and thereby reduce their levels of stress.

CONCLUSION

Everyone experiences stress. As any stress counselor would explain, a certain degree of stress is essential to a healthy, productive life. However, when stress impairs an individual's ability to function properly, the sources of that stress must be eliminated or reduced.

Likewise, organizations work with a certain degree of naturally occurring stress, generated by the pressures of performing the tasks for which the people in the organization are responsible. However, when an organization's policies and procedures themselves become overwhelming sources of stress, those policies and procedures should be reviewed and changed.

With pressures on law enforcement agencies to perform increasingly complex functions with minimized funding levels, police administrators must examine ways to enable officers to perform their responsibilities as efficiently as possible. The steps that a number of law enforcement agencies have taken to reduce organizational sources of stress illustrate that departments can change their policies and procedures in ways that enhance—and certainly do not compromise—their public safety missions. Given the pressures experienced by today's police officers, law enforcement administrators should address the problem of organizational stress by identifying recurring grievances among officers and working to change the policies that cause them.

NOTES

1. R.M. Ayres, Preventing Law Enforcement Stress: The Organization's Role (Washington, DC: Bureau of Justice Statistics, 1990), 1; C.A. Gruber, "The Relationship of Stress to the Practice of Police Work," The Police Chief, February 1980, 16–17; "A Comparative Look at Stress and Strain in Policemen," in Job Stress and the Police Officer, ed. W.H. Kroes and J.J. Hurrell (Washington, DC: U.S. Department of Health, Education, and Welfare, 1975), 60; C.D. Spielberger, The Police Stress Survey: Sources of Stress in Law Enforcement, Monograph Series Three (Tampa, Florida: Human Resources Institute, 1981), 43.

2. Ibid., Ayres; Ibid., W.H. Kroes and J.J. Hurrell; see also J.J. Hurrell, Jr., "Some Organizational Stressors in Police Work and Means for Their Amelioration," in Psychological Services for Law Enforcement, ed. J.T. Reese and H.A. Goldstein (Washington, DC: U.S. Department of Justice, Federal Bureau of Investigation, 1986).

3. The principal interviews took place in San Bernardino, California; Erie County, New York; Washington, DC; and throughout the state of Michigan (June–August 1995). Additional telephone interviews were conducted with similar individuals from San Antonio, Texas; Tulsa, Oklahoma; Metro-Dade, Florida; Rochester, New York; and Coventry, Rhode Island (June-August 1995). This research project was supported by the U.S. Department of Justice, National Institute of Justice, Contract OJP-94-C-007. See Peter Finn and Julie Esselman Tomz, Developing a Law Enforcement Stress Program for Officers and Their Families (Washington, DC: U.S. Government Printing Office, 1997).

4. Supra note 1, Ayres, 9.

5. G. Kaufman, "Law Enforcement Organizational Health Consultation," (paper presented at the Consultation with Police: Problems and Consideration Symposium, American Psychological Association 93rd Annual Convention, Los Angeles, California, August 23–27, 1985).

6. "Tired? Stressed? Burned Out? Panel Seeks Answers for Philadelphia Police Officers," Law Enforcement News 22, 1995, 1, 10.

7. J.L. Pape, "Employee Development Programs," FBI Law Enforcement Bulletin, September 1990, 20–25.

8. E.F. Kirschman, "Organizational Development," in Police Managerial Use of Psychology and Psychologists, ed. H.W. More and P.C. Unsinger (Springfield, Illinois: Charles C. Thomas, 1987), 85–106; S.E. Walima, "Organizational Health in Law Enforcement," in Psychological Services for Law Enforcement, ed. J.T. Reese and H.A. Goldstein, (Washington, DC: U.S. Department of Justice, Federal Bureau of Investigation, 1986), 205–214.

Police Fatigue

By Dennis Lindsey

The woods are lovely, dark and deep.
But I have promises to keep,
And miles to go before I sleep,
And miles to go before I sleep.

—Robert Frost

After working almost 35 hours straight on a case that involved high-stress surveillance, the controlled delivery of nearly 2 tons of marijuana, and the arrest of 5 suspects, a detective on a narcotics task force was driving over 350 miles back home. The judge in the case advised the prosecuting attorney that if the detective was not in court that day by 2 p.m., the case would be dismissed without prejudice. As the detective approached the midway point on his route home, his vehicle, according to witnesses, swerved left, traveled through the median strip, crossed the oncoming traffic lanes, flipped several times, and ultimately came to rest on the opposite side of the interstate. The detective was severely injured and out of work for over a year.

Accounts of tragedies associated with law enforcement fatigue are not new. In fact, such stories become more commonplace each year. Convincing federal, state, and local law enforcement organizations of the seriousness of fatigue as an occupational health, commercial, public safety, and legal issue ultimately will require law enforcement managers to have a paradigm shift to address this concern. Agencies must

acknowledge this problem to improve working conditions for their personnel and to protect them from the scientifically documented consequences that fatigue can cause. For example, researchers assessed neurobehavioral functions after 17 hours of wakefulness and reported performance impairment on a range of tasks.[1]

Impairments after 20 hours of wakefulness equaled that of an individual with a blood-alcohol concentration of 0.10, twice the presumptive level of intoxication in most states.[2] Further, the ability to maintain speed and road position on a driving simulator is significantly reduced when the awake period is prolonged by 3 hours.[3] The magnitudes of the decrements were similar to those found at and above the legal limits of alcohol consumption (0.05).[4] All of these studies indicated that moderate levels of sleepiness can substantially impair the ability to drive safely even before an individual actually falls asleep.

Exhaustion due to shift work, voluntary and mandatory overtime assignments, seemingly endless hours waiting to testify in court, physical and emotional demands of dealing with the public, and management expectations of doing more with less, combined with family responsibilities, puts the modern law enforcement professional at serious emotional and physical risk. Law enforcement fatigue and sleep deprivation also are becoming serious political and legal liabilities for police managers. What department can sustain multimillion dollar lawsuits or afford to lose a veteran officer for years?

The cumulative work hours for many professionals, such as pilots, locomotive engineers, ship captains, public transportation and commercial truck drivers, fire fighters, and emergency room doctors, are standardized and regulated through federal or state regulatory commissions (e.g., U.S. Department of Transportation or Federal Aviation Administration). Unfortunately, no such regulations exist for the majority of federal, state, and local law enforcement employees. "Police work is the one profession in which we would want all practitioners to have adequate and healthful sleep to perform their duties at peak levels. Not only is fatigue associated with individual misery, but it also can lead to counterproductive behavior. It is well-known that impulsiveness, aggression, irritability, and angry outbursts are associated with sleep deprivation. It is totally reprehensible that the cops we expect to protect us, come to our aid, and respond to our needs when victimized should be allowed to have the worst fatigue and sleep conditions of any profession in our society."[5]

Throughout the last century, the standard work week was 9 a.m. to 5 p.m., Monday through Friday, designed to not intrude on workers' premium social time, such as evenings and weekends. As such, the 8-hour workday evolved from the widely held belief that the 24-hour day should be split evenly between work, recreation/relaxation, and sleep. While many people take the 8-hour day for granted as a part of normal life, such working conditions are a relatively recent industrial development. Traditionally, law enforcement personnel work long hours for four main reasons. First, they seek monetary gain—the more they work, the more money they make. Traditionally, wages for law enforcement personnel have been low; therefore, the dependence on overtime, night-shift premiums, and moonlighting (working other jobs) has been necessary. Second, they encounter organizational or occupational expectations (we have to do more with less). "Many companies (law enforcement agencies) foster workaholism and actively seek out and reward workaholics."[6] Third, employees want personal satisfaction. The majority of law enforcement

professionals could make substantially more money doing something else, but the job is fun, stimulating, exciting, challenging, unpredictable, and dangerous. It attracts risk–aggressive individuals who have chosen not to passively sit behind a desk. Finally, they belong to an exclusive fraternity. Law enforcement gives a person a sense of self-identity, belonging, and self-worth.

Not surprisingly, as long hours, shift work, and irregular hours of work increase, the hours, quality, and quantity of sleep decrease, causing a sleep debt. Conversely, fatigue levels rise, leading to detrimental effects on both health and on-the job performance.

FATIGUE

What is fatigue? How does it relate to sleep? Although there is no universally accepted definition of fatigue, several exist. Fatigue is a "tiredness concerning the inability of disinclination to continue an activity, generally because the activity has been going on too long"[7] or "a feeling of weariness, tiredness, or lack of energy."[8]

People often use drowsiness and fatigue interchangeably, but they are not the same. Drowsiness is a feeling of the need to sleep or the state in which the body is ready to fall asleep. Fatigue is a lack of energy and motivation. Apathy, a feeling of indifference or not caring about what happens, and drowsiness can be symptoms of fatigue. It should be noted that fatigue can be a normal, healthy, and important response to physical exertion, emotional stress, boredom, or lack of sleep. However, it also can signify a more serious psychological or physical disorder. Because fatigue is such a common complaint, sometimes a potentially serious cause may be overlooked.

In the last 25 years, the job of enforcing the law has become increasingly complex from a cognitive perspective. Further, policing the community is creating tasks that require much higher levels of attentiveness than in the past. Long work hours are widely accepted as a major contributing factor to fatigue.[9] As hours of work increase, sleep is reduced with a concomitant elevation in fatigue and reduced levels of alertness.[10]

SLEEP

Humans typically have four to six sleep cycles that each last 70 to 90 minutes. At the end of each cycle, they are nearly awake. In light sleep, body movement decreases and spontaneous awakening may occur. People spend most of the night in intermediate sleep, which helps refresh the body. Deep sleep, the most restorative stage, lasts 30 to 40 minutes in the first few cycles and less in later ones. In this stage, people are the most difficult to arouse. Dreaming occurs in REM (rapid eye movement) and heart rate increases. This stage lasts about 10 minutes in the first cycle and 20 to 30 minutes in later ones. During a full night's sleep, these sleep cycles are repeated four to six times, moving from one stage of sleep to another.[11]

Several functions occur during sleep. These include—

- consolidation and optimization of memories;
- conservation of energy;
- promotion of physiological processes that rejuvenate the body and mind (some studies suggest that sleep restores neurons and increases the production of brain proteins and certain hormones);
- the process of unlearning that prevents the brain from becoming overloaded with knowledge; and
- avoidance of danger (prehistoric people adapted the pattern of sleeping in caves at night because it protected humans from species physiologically suited to function well in the dark, such as saber-toothed tigers).

Lack of sleep is considered one of the primary causes of fatigue. Humans need to sleep— it is not a matter of choice but essential and inevitable. The longer a person remains awake, the greater the need to sleep and the more difficult to resist falling asleep. Sleep will inevitably overpower the strongest intentions and efforts to stay awake.[12]

Little is known about the physiological role of sleep and ways in which it restores the brain to its full function, but the effects of fatigue on the brain can be measured. Studies have shown that after 24 hours of sustained wakefulness, the brain's metabolic activity can decrease by up to 65 percent in total and by up to 11 percent in specific areas of the brain, particularly those that play a role in judgment, attention, and visual functions. One study highlights nine dimensions of workplace performance susceptible to the effects of fatigue, including the inability to—

1. comprehend complex situations, such as processing substantial amounts of data within a short time frame, without distractions (the lack of focused attention associated with sleep deprivation is likely to reduce efficiency of such processing);
2. manage events and improve strategies;
3. perform risk assessment and accurately predict consequences;
4. think latterly and be innovative;
5. take personal interest in the outcome;
6. control mood and behavior;
7. monitor personal performance;
8. recollect timing of events; and
9. communicate effectively.[13]

People know when they feel tired—their eyes become a little glassy, they tend to have less eye movement, and yawning is more pronounced. As they try to fight through periods of fatigue, the human body, in an effort to rest, goes into microsleeps where a person literally falls asleep anywhere from 2 to 10 seconds at a time. It is difficult to predict when a person, once fatigued, might slip into a microsleep. Additionally, research has found that as little as 2 hours of sleep loss on one occasion can result in degraded reaction time, cognitive functioning, memory, mood, and alertness.

ACCIDENT RISK

Research suggests that fatigue-related errors are common well before the point at which an individual no longer can stay awake. Inattention may get much of the blame, but fatigue often is the culprit. Thus, fatigue studies likely are a conservative estimate of the overall incidence of reported fatigue-related accidents. "Human fatigue is now recognized around the world as being the main cause of accidents in the transportation industry."[14]

In addition to studying the direct link between accidents and fatigue, experts also have thoroughly researched the cognitive impairment thought to mediate the relationship. Major findings show that mood, attitude, and cognitive performance (judgment and competence) deteriorate with sleep deprivation.[15] Moreover, research shows that fatigue is four times more likely to cause workplace impairment than alcohol and other drugs.[16] Ironically, alcohol and drug abuse normally are addressed immediately by management. However, the lack of sleep, probably the most common condition adversely affecting personnel performance, often is ignored.

Fatigue in and of itself is not the key problem. Rather, the risks associated with fatigue impairment include poor judgment, accidents, and injuries. As such, fatigue is a context-dependent safety hazard, an important distinction because it can carry a significant risk in some situations and little or none in others. In some cases, fatigue-induced impairment and accidents may be inconsequential, creating only minor delays in completing a task, or may be detected by checks and balances (e.g., search warrants and fact patterns for probable cause court hearings are reviewed, checked, and proofread for accuracy before submission to judicial systems). In other situations, however, the risks of equipment damage, personal injury, and public safety can be far greater.

REDUCED SOCIAL TIME

The primary effect for law enforcement professionals working long hours is reduced social interactions and isolation from traditional community and social support systems, resulting in the "us against them" point of view. Furthermore, studies have shown that long work hours negatively impact an individual's family relations.[17]

HEALTH CONSEQUENCES

Fatigue is a symptom common to many diseases directly related to irregularity of daily life. Higher consumption of alcohol, caffeine, and tobacco; reduced physical exercise; stress; depression; social isolation; unbalanced diet and nutrition; and irregularity of daily meals all are hallmarks of law enforcement personnel around the world and can lead to an unhealthy increase in weight gain.[18] In fact, literature has indirectly linked long and irregular work hours with negative health issues to include disruptions of the body's biological rhythms, which may—

- change eating and sleeping habits;[19]
- raise blood pressure;[20]

Results of Lack of Sleep

1. Irritability with coworkers, family, or friends
2. Inability to remain alert to respond to the demands of work
3. Memory impairment
4. Lack of concentration
5. Lower frustration tolerance
6. Accidents on the job or in the home
7. Stress-related illness caused, in part, by a compromised immune system
8. Inattention
9. Obesity
10. Hypertension
11. Changes in metabolic functions
12. Alteration of hormonal functions in ways that mimic aging

---

- affect psychological well-being;[21]
- cause negative effects for pregnant women and fertility rates;[22] and
- result in gastrointestinal disorders,[23] stress-related disability claims, decreased productivity, and increased absenteeism.[24]

RECOMMENDATIONS

Law enforcement agencies should make a concerted effort to provide a strong and coherent research base for the development of sound policies. Equating fatigue-related impairment to blood-alcohol equivalent gives policy makers, employees, and community leaders a clear index of the extent of impairment associated with fatigue. Agencies should develop preventative strategies to implement within the diverse range of political, economic, and social environments in which the law enforcement community functions and ensure cooperation with federal, state, and local court systems.

Departments should establish strict policies and implement effective enforcement regarding employee moonlighting. Administrators should review the policies, procedures, and practices that affect shift scheduling, overtime, rotation, the number of work hours allowed, and the way the organization deals with overly tired employees. Administrators should review recruit, supervisor in-service, and roll-call training, as well as executive retreats, to determine if personnel receive adequate information about the importance of good sleep habits, the hazards associated with fatigue and shift work, and strategies for managing them. Are personnel taught to view fatigue as a safety issue? Agencies should consider either implementing and enforcing regulations regarding a strict time-based work/rest policy, placing responsibility on the organization, or an education-based policy that focuses responsibility on the individual.

Finally, agencies should consider several different work/rest rules. The most common policy is the 16/8 formula. For every 16 hours of work, departments must provide 8 hours of rest time. Work/rest policies are most appropriate for agencies that have suffcient manpower to work in shifts. If resources are limited, managers may have to choose between using volunteers/reserves, implementing mutual aid agreements, or declaring an emergency and breaking the work/rest policy; therefore, any policy must include flexibility. Also, offcers should not consider vacations just as missed days of work. They should turn off their cell phones and advise courts of scheduled leave. They always should take the time off that their departments provide and use it, remembering that no one is irreplaceable.

CONCLUSION

Modern law enforcement practices have developed well-entrenched unwritten rules that treat sleep in utmost disregard and disdain. Agencies often encourage and reward workaholics. A recent news report covering a large party proudly declared: "Four hours into his second 12-hour shift, [the officer] has been busy answering questions, giving directions, listening to drunken declarations of love, and drunken jokes amid the endless roar of the crowd."

When a person is deprived of sleep, actual changes occur in the brain that cannot be overcome with willpower, caffeine, or nicotine. The decline in vigilance, judgment, and safety in relation to the increase in hours on the job cannot be trivialized. Community perceptions of fatigue-related risk have changed and now are viewed as absolutely unacceptable, as well as preventable. As a consequence, law enforcement professionals face a greater reactive pressure both politically and legally to rethink and implement proactive strategies to reduce fatigue-related incidents.

Fatigue is a serious, challenging problem that requires informed, forward-thinking managers to take action sooner, rather than later. Police leaders and sleep research experts need to work in concert to assess each individual agency to minimize the threat that fatigue poses to the community and the individual law enforcement professional. Fatigue is not just an industrial issue to negotiate between employers, unions, and employees but an occupational health, commercial, and public safety concern. Local, state, and federal law enforcement organizations that fail to sensibly manage fatigue today certainly will face a broad range of damaging and enduring legal, ethical, physiological, and personal consequences in the future.

NOTES

1. N. Lamond and D. Dawson, "Quantifying the Performance Impairment Associated with Fatigue," *Journal of Sleep Research* 8 (1999): 255–262.

2. Ibid.

3. J. Arendt, G. Wilde, P. Munt, and A. McLean, "How Do Prolonged Wakefulness and Alcohol Compare in the Decrements They Produce on a Simulated Driving Task?" *Accident Analysis and Prevention* 33, no. 3 (2001): 337–344.

4. Similar levels of decrement in driving performance have been reported; see N. Powell, K. Schnecchtman, R. Riley, K. Li, R. Troell, and C. Guilleminault, "The Road to Danger: The Comparative Risks of Driving When Sleepy," *Laryngoscope* 111, no. 5 (2001): 887–893.

5. William C. Dement, M.D., Ph.D., in Brian Vila, *Tired Cops: The Importance of Managing Police Fatigue* (Washington, DC: Police Executive Research Forum, 2000): xiv.

6. Lawson Savery, "Long Hours at Work: Are They Dangerous and Do People Consent to Them?" (Curtin University, Australia).

7. European Transport Safety Council.

8. U.S. National Library of Medicine and the National Institutes of Health.

9. The author bases this conclusion on his extensive research on this topic.

10. J.C. Carey and J.I. Fishburne, "A Method to Limit Working Hours and Reduce Sleep Deprivation in an Obstetrics and Gynecology Residency Program," *Obstetrics and Gynecology* 74, no. 4 (1989): 668–672.

11. Information in this paragraph is derived from "Sleep: Your Body's Means of Rejuvenation"; retrieved on November 28, 2006, from *http://health. yahoo.com/topic/sleep/overview/article/mayoclinic/ F42249 5-751C-4684-A0A50B88AB19B576.*

12. Royal Society for the Prevention of Accidents, "Driver Fatigue and Road Accidents: A Literature Review and Position Paper," February 2001; retrieved on December 5, 2006, from *http://www. rospa.com/roadsafety/info/fatigue.pdf.*

13. Y. Harrison and J.A. Horne, "The Impact of Sleep Deprivation on Decision Making: A Review," *Journal of Experimental Psychology Applied* 6 (April 2000): 236–249.

14. *http://www.aph.gov.au/house/committee/cita/man-fatigue/mfcontents.htm*

15. A. Nocera and D.S. Khursandi, "Doctors' Working Hours: Can the Medical Profession Afford to Let the Courts Decide What Is Reasonable?" *Medical Journal of Australia* 168 (1998): 616–618.

16. T. Akerstedt, "Consensus Statement: Fatigue and Accidents in Transportation Operations," *Journal of Sleep Research* 9 (2000): 395.

17. D.L. Bosworth and P.J. Dawkins, "Private and Social Costs and Benefits of Shift and Nightwork," in *Night and Shiftwork Biological and Social Aspects: Advances in the Biosciences* 30, eds. A. Reinberg, N. Vieux, and P. Andlauer (Paris, France: Pergamon Press, 1980), 207–213.

18. M. Shields, "Long Working Hours and Health," *Health Rep* 11, no. 2 (1999): 33–48.

19. G. Costa, "The Impact of Shift and Night Work on Health," *Applied Ergonomics* 27, (1996): 9–16.

20. T. Uehata, "Long Work Hours and Occupational Stress-Related Cardiovascular Attacks Among Middle-Aged Workers in Japan," *J. Hum Ergol* 20, no. 2 (1991): 147–153.

21. S. Babbar and D. Aspelin, "The Overtime Rebellion: Symptom of a Bigger Problem? (Implications of Forced Overtime)," *The Academy of Management Executive* 12, (1998): 68–77.

22. C.W. Henderson, "Study Links Long Hours, Job Stress to Miscarriages," *Women's Health Weekly*, June 9-16, 1997, 9–10.

23. G. Costa, "Shift Work and Health," *Med Lav* 90, no. 6 (1997): 739–751.

24. C. Mulcany, "Workplace Stress Reaches Epidemic Proportion," *National Underwriter* 95, no. 4 (1991): 20–21.

Praise and Recognition

The Importance of Social Support in Law Enforcement

By Tracey G. Gove

Mark Twain once said, "I can live for 2 months on a good compliment." Wise managers in today's law enforcement agencies will adopt this adage as a means for leading employees. When used effectively, praise holds many benefits. Empirical research, social psychology, manager and employee surveys, and motivational experts repeatedly have proven this fact. A law enforcement agency that values and implements this ideology will create an environment that helps to alleviate employee stress, improve morale, increase productivity, and retain personnel.

STRESS IN POLICE WORK

Sources

People commonly consider violence and danger or the potential of such the leading antecedents to stress in police work. Other perceived main stressors include external, uncontrollable factors, such as protracted periods of low activity interspersed with brief periods of excitement. However, analyses of the officers themselves presented a different picture. One study revealed that they perceived most stress as originating within the workplace. Specifically cited were relationships with supervisors. One officer observed, "The most stressful call is the one that summons you to headquarters."[1]

When officers in both the United States and the United Kingdom listed significant causes of stress, they cited poor and insensitive supervision among the most primary sources.[2] Additional studies evidencing that management and organizational issues accounted for most workplace stress in the police service have supported these findings. This contradicts the long-held belief that factors external to the law enforcement organization primarily lead to stress.

Consequences

Stress represents a person's internal response to external stimuli. Typically, stress associated with the rigors of police work is defined as "distress," which occurs when a person faces challenges beyond regular coping abilities, resulting in taxed biological systems and, in turn, negative mental and physical effects. Some of the key consequences of police stress include—

- cynicism and suspiciousness;
- emotional detachment from various aspects of daily life;
- reduced efficiency;
- absenteeism and early retirement;
- excessive aggressiveness and a related increase in citizen complaints; and

- heart attacks, ulcers, weight gain, and other health problems.[3]

The police agency also will suffer because of the instances of lower morale, inefficiency, increased absenteeism, and friction with citizens due to rudeness or poor service that ultimately can hurt the department's public image.

Stress also exacts far-reaching burdens as it not only affects officers and agencies but also harms families of law enforcement personnel. This holds particularly true for their spouses, who often experience unusually high levels of stress due to the police occupation.[4]

PRAISE REAPPRAISED

Fortunately, unlike many of the external stressors of police work, managers can improve their supervisory skills, and organizations can provide a more supportive environment for their employees. In this regard, praise—although not a panacea for the mental and physical ailments common to police officers—has proven to have many benefits that should bear the attention of today's progressive police managers.

Societal changes have resulted in police agencies moving away from the paramilitary structure of years past. Today's more-educated officers hold degrees in a variety of areas. Gone are the days when a majority of police applicants held prior military experience, accustomed to taking orders without question. Agency leaders now utilize coaching and mentoring programs better served to influence desired behavior. This manner of leading requires praise to build self-esteem within the developing officer.

Mental and Physical Health

Ample proof exists that stress has debilitating effects on health and well-being. However, empirical studies also have shown that simply using forms of social support, such as praise, within the workplace can mitigate the effects of job stress on physical and mental health.[5] To this end, evidence uncovered a substantial buffering effect whereby social support

acts to cushion the blow and make the perception of stress less severe.

Additionally, studies have found that workers with lower levels of social support within the workplace suffered a higher prevalence of cardiovascular disease in strenuous jobs, such as police work, where high demands mix with low control.[6] The implications and benefits of social support are obvious as experts cite cardiovascular disease as the leading killer of Americans.[7]

Morale, Motivation, and Employee Retention

Praise not only promotes physical and mental well-being but also improves motivation. A recent survey found that "nearly 100 percent of respondents agree or strongly agree that giving recognition can make an impact on employee morale."[8] Additionally, empirical studies have shown that both American and English workers respond favorably to praise and that it does, in fact, influence job performance.[9]

Unfortunately, some managers fail to focus on employee motivation until morale sinks, motivation becomes lost, and, ultimately, employees quit.[10] A reactive response to morale issues, versus a more proactive approach, will make the task of improving employee attitudes more difficult than if supervisors nurture behavior and performance from the start.

The importance of employee retention represents another issue facing police managers. Limited job praise and recognition rank as primary reasons why employees leave.[11] Officers who receive ineffective or no praise more likely will believe that "the grass is greener" in another agency and will have no feelings of loyalty to their current employer. This can result in employee turnover, negatively affecting the department. Ultimately, it will cost the agency in new employment, training, and equipment.

Internal Versus External Awards

Some police officers will claim that in lieu of praise and recognition, they would rather receive rewards in their paychecks. Does this mean that money serves as a stronger motivator? Surveys do not bear this out.

In studies dating back to the 1940s, recognition and appreciation always have outranked salaries.[12] One recent study of 1,500 employees in various work settings revealed that personalized, instant recognition from managers served as the most powerful motivator of 65 potential incentives evaluated, followed by a letter of praise written by the manager.[13]

Of course, money would motivate if the employer did not pay a fair salary. However, once basic monetary needs are met, money becomes less important. Money is an *extrinsic* motivator—once it is given, it will become expected. Eventually, if money is withheld, employees will see this as a punishment and the reinforced behavior will stop. However, praise increases personal esteem that then becomes an *intrinsic* motivator— even if praise temporarily stops, the stock of personal pride developed will motivate and ensure productivity.

In this regard, Abraham Maslow, a humanistic psychologist, explained motivation as a series of needs. In his scheme, lower-order needs, such as physiological, safety, and love, first must be met. Once these become satisfied, they cease to motivate.[14] Fair compensation accords some of these lower-order needs. Higher-order needs, such as self-esteem and self-actualization, then motivate. Praise and recognition build esteem needs. Once satisfied, people seek a state of self-actualization where a desire exists to test their potential. Compensation alone will not build this motivation.

Frederick Herzberg, an organizational theorist, further supports the benefits of praise over money. He saw two variables functioning within the work setting. Salary represents a "hygiene," or "maintenance," factor, something that acts as an incentive only to do what is required. If agencies meet all hygiene factors, officers are not motivated—they simply are not dissatisfied.[15] Praise and recognition, however, are motivators that impel people to do their best work.[16]

PRAISE IN THE WORKPLACE

Breaking Down Barriers

In an ideal work setting, praise will come from the top and work down. However, if managers do not receive praise themselves, they may not know how to give it. Further, they may feel that because it does not represent part of their department's culture, it is not part of their job. Also, supervisors are even more prone to stress due to additional pressures required by their position. They confront the same work environment as officers, but with additional responsibilities, including facing the consequences for decisions they have made and being caught between the wants and needs of administrators and subordinates.

Additionally, administering praise properly requires supervisors to publicly talk about feelings. In doing so, they make themselves vulnerable to others, a condition some may find difficult and intimidating, particularly in an occupation where, for years, they have hidden emotion to be effective police officers.[17] Many will consider it necessary to learn and then practice giving praise.

All levels of leadership should educate, model, demonstrate, and reinforce recognition and feedback skills.[18] Additionally, not only should everyone from the chief down provide recognition but command-level staff should hold supervisors responsible for providing officer recognition. Praise opens lines of communication, which builds trust—leading to motivation. Employees are the product of their environment. Supervisors, especially first-line ones, have the opportunity to make an impact and to create a supportive workplace. Progressive leaders will initiate this environment even if it is not pervasive throughout the agency.

Administering Praise

To have maximum effect, supervisors must give praise correctly. To this end, they can gauge their efforts by six important characteristics.

1. Timely: Praise should immediately follow the laudable behavior and be specific. This will ensure that the individual will know and likely repeat the desired behavior.

2. Appropriate: Supervisors should not give an expression of praise without reason or base it solely on personality. Further, they must

consider their relationship with the officer (e.g., for a turbulent relationship, managers must give the praise carefully so that the employee will see it as sincere).

3. Given separately: Managers must not correct poor performance when giving praise. Of course, when disciplining an officer, kind words can help cushion the blow. However, supervisors must carefully separate these instances; if not, employees will accept future praise with caution as they steel themselves for the anticipated criticism to follow. They also may suspect insincerity.

4. Administered regularly: Supervisors should praise not only spectacular acts of courage but daily acts of solid police work on routine calls. A type of Pygmalion effect, or self-fulfilling prophecy, then will follow. As officers receive recognition more often for good work, it will build their confidence and help to increase performance.

5. Sincere: As trained observers keenly aware of human behavior, police officers can detect insincerity and will question the validity of contrived praise. Also, managers should not confuse praise with flattery— insincere praise used largely to win favor. Praise must be honest, straightforward, and spoken from the heart.

6. Public or private: Supervisors usually should give praise publicly. This can build esteem and encourage others to strive for similar recognition. However, managers must proceed with caution as some people truly dislike public attention and may prefer praise in private. The type of recognition must match the personality. For instance, if during public praise an individual appears uncomfortable, agitated, or defensive, a change to private recognition likely will elicit a different response.

Methods of Delivery

Face-to-face, spontaneous praise represents the easiest and, more important, the most desired form. Administering it in the presence of upper-level managers can help to bolster the purpose of recognizing

the behavior. Supervisors also can give written recognition. For an officer who may prefer private praise, department e-mail and voice mail systems offer less intrusive means of communication.

Supervisors also can consider less spontaneous, more formal ways to recognize officers using departmental resources. These include—

- an article in the department newsletter, be it official or unofficial;
- a posted message on an internal or external Web site;
- a letter written by the chief on the recommendation of a supervisor;
- a publicly exhibited "wall of fame" board displaying letters of commendation and citizens' letters of recognition; and
- roll-call praise, if all members of a shift performed well on a recent task.

CONCLUSION

Common sense should deem a quick pat on the back for a job well done not only deserved but necessary. Studies and surveys have proven the results of such reinforcing behavior stronger than once believed. Social support in the form of recognition and praise serves to increase morale, motivation, and productivity. Consequently, the physical and mental health of employees improve and organizations are better served and run more efficiently.

Police work represents a stressful, difficult, and, at most times, unforgiving occupation. Managers need to recognize officers for their commitment to service and show them their value to the agency. Praise delivers this message and costs nothing but compassion. Effective police leaders will value and demonstrate this ideology.

NOTES

1. Hans Toch, "Stress in Policing"; retrieved from *http://www.ncjrs.org/pdffiles1/nij/grants/198030. pdf.*

2. J. Brown and E. Campbell, "Sources of Occupational Stress in the Police," *Work and Stress* 4 (1990): 305–318.

3. U.S. Department of Justice, National Institute of Justice, "On-the-Job Stress in Policing-Reducing It, Preventing It," *National Institute of Justice Journal* (Washington, DC, January 2000).

4. Leanor Boulin-Johnson, "On the Front Lines: Police Stress and Family Well-Being," Select Committee on Children, Youth, and Families, U.S. House of Representatives, Washington, DC, May 20, 1991.

5. James LaRocco, James House, and John French, Jr., "Social Support, Occupational Stress, and Health," *Journal of Health and Social Behavior* 21 (September 1980): 202–218.

6. Jeffrey Johnson and Ellen Hall, "Job Strain, Workplace Social Support, and Cardiovascular Disease: A Cross-Sectional Study of a Random Sample of the Swedish Working Population," *American Journal of Public Health* 78, no. 10 (1988): 1336–1342.

7. American Heart Association, *Heart Disease and Stroke Statistics–2004 Update* (Dallas, TX: American Heart Association, 2003).

8. Roy Saunderson, "Survey Findings of the Effectiveness of Employee Recognition in the Public Sector," *Public Personnel Management* 33, no. 3 (2004): 255–275.

9. Christopher P. Earley, "Trust, Perceived Importance of Praise and Criticism, and Work Performance: An Examination of Feedback in the U.S. and England," *Journal of Management* 12, no. 4 (1986): 457–473.

10. Bob Nelson, "The Ten Ironies of Motivation," *Strategy and Leadership* 27 (January-February 1999): 26–31.

11. Bob Nelson, "Dump the Cash, Load On the Praise," *Personnel Journal* 75, no. 7 (1996): 65–70.

12. Ibid.

13. Ibid.

14. Charles Swanson, Leonard Territo, and Robert Taylor, *Police Administration: Structures, Processes, and Behavior* (Upper Saddle River, NJ: Prentice Hall, 2001).

15. Ibid.

16. Supra note 11.

17. Linda Davidson, "The Power of Personal Recognition," *Workforce* 78, no. 7 (1999): 44–49.

18. Supra note 9.

The Psychological Fitness for Duty Evaluation

By Laurence Miller

Physical problems, such as an injured knee or high blood pressure, sometimes arise that may affect officers' abilities to perform their duties effectively. Or, their performance may remain unchanged. However, if supervisors or commanding officers perceive that an individual's limp or frequent headaches impair job performance, they may recommend that the employee seek medical attention. If the problem persists, they may refer the officer for a medical evaluation, during which the examining doctor will declare the individual medically able to return to work, recommend a course of treatment to restore a proper level of health, or classify the officer as permanently unfit for duty.

Similarly, if supervisors suspect that personality disorders or stress reactions cause or contribute to problem behavior or substandard performance and the usual channels of review, coaching, counseling, and discipline have failed to effect a substantial change, they may order a formal psychological fitness-for-duty evaluation (FFDE).[1] Through such an exam, agencies hope to determine an officer's psychological capability of remaining on the job and to identify, if necessary, measures to help improve the employee's effectiveness or reasonable accommodations to allow the officer to work in spite of residual disabilities.[2]

The FFDE functions, in part, to provide a basis for recommendations concerning education, retraining, counseling, or treatment.[3] Ideally, agencies will use the evaluation to help find ways to rehabilitate officers. Humaneness aside, salvaging an established employee is more cost-effective than hiring, training, and supervising a new one; for obvious reasons, departments should resort to discipline and dismissal as a last resort. However, although it never should be used as a substitute for adequate supervision and discipline, a carefully conducted and documented FFDE can provide a psychologically justifiable and legally defensible rationale for terminating an officer who cannot or will not meet the standards of the employing agency.

THE PSYCHOLOGICAL FFDE

The Evaluation

Initial Considerations

The FFDE combines elements of risk management, mental health intervention, labor law, and departmental discipline.[4] According to current International Association of Chiefs of Police (IACP) guidelines, a licensed psychologist or board-certified psychiatrist with law enforcement experience must conduct the evaluation.[5] However, the guidelines do not specify how much experience is sufficient, and, as yet, no generally accepted formal credentialing exists for police psychologists as a distinct professional specialty. Thus,

Laurence Miller, "The Psychological Fitness-for-Duty Evaluation," *FBI Law Enforcement Bulletin*, vol. 76, no. 8, pp. 10–16. Copyright in the Public Domain.

the level of law enforcement training or experience of these clinicians may vary considerably by agency.

When referring an employee for an FFDE, supervisors should provide specific referral questions. For example, they should not simply note that "Officer Jones seems depressed, and this condition interferes with his work." Rather, the referring supervisor could state, "Officer Jones arrived late to shift five times this past month; on several occasions, has been visibly fatigued and in physical distress; has appeared absentminded and distracted; and has been the subject of three citizen complaints of abuse of force during the past evaluation period. These actions represent a clear deterioration from previous evaluation periods and reflect a pattern of substandard performance. Upon interview, Officer Jones denies any problem."

Recommendations for Officers

Understandably, officers probably will not look forward to an FFDE. However, they can take measures to help the process go smoothly and for the results to provide an accurate picture of their true psychological status.

First, officers should remain positive. They should recognize that the examiner's only job is to objectively evaluate the officer's mental status in view of the specific referral questions and to determine the employee's fitness for duty.

Officers also should know their rights and responsibilities and remain informed about the FFDE, either through their own research or in consultation with a legal representative. In this way, they can help protect themselves throughout the process.

Next, officers should come prepared, arriving on time and with all necessary records or other requested materials. Commonsense recommendations also include bringing reading glasses, if needed, and having an adequate lunch prior to an early afternoon exam. Accordingly, employees have the right to expect the examiner to come prepared and to begin on time.

Throughout the process, officers must ensure that they read everything they sign and clarify anything unclear or of concern. This includes questions asked and tests conducted by the psychologist. Officers should not feel intimidated about making reasonable inquiries

about the examination process and should expect straightforward answers. However, they must bear in mind that the psychologist may not be able to answer all of the questions (e.g., those relating to a particular test item or question) at the time of the evaluation.

Overall, officers must ensure that they remain honest and put forth their best effort. The entire validity of the FFDE hinges on the accuracy of the information they provide. Further, many interview protocols and psychological tests have controls for inconsistency and response manipulation. In other words, the examiner probably will detect any attempts at dishonesty and will then have no choice but to report that the officer lied. Officers must consider the consequences of such actions.

Finally, officers should both expect and give proper respect during the examination. Officers have the right to courteous and professional treatment, even as the examiner asks some troublesome, albeit necessary, questions. Psychologists should realize that if officers feel comfortable during the examination, their memories will serve them well and they will provide accurate information. Officers also should behave with respect and decorum. After all, both examiner and subject are professionals with a difficult, but important, job to do.

The Report

Ultimately, the examiner will prepare a report that, usually, first will go to the referring department. While there is no single universally accepted format, a useful and practical one exists for psychological FFDE reports.[6] The exact style and content may vary according to the needs and preferences of each psychologist and law enforcement agency, but it should contain several fundamental elements.

Identifying Data

The report will contain basic information about the officer and the evaluation. Examples of data include the officer's name and demographics, department identification, name of the evaluator, and dates of the evaluation.

Reason for the Evaluation

This section describes the main incidents, issues, and referral questions that have brought the officer to the examiner's office. Although a wide range of data may be relevant to the individual's overall psychological functioning, the focus of the evaluation itself should be relatively specific to the question at hand. In cases where officers are referred without clear reasons for an FFDE (e.g., that he has an "attitude problem"), the psychologist may have to help the referring agency refine its referral question (e.g., What problematic behaviors is this officer showing that reflect his bad attitude?). Also, a statement should be included that clarifies issues of informed consent and the potential uses of the evaluation findings.

Background Information

The information in this section can be narrow (e.g., what took place during or around the incidents in question) or broad (e.g., the officer's general experience within the department that may shed light on the specific referral questions). Relevance to the referral question defines the scope and range of such background data. For example, conflicts with previous employers may be relevant, but history of physical abuse as a child may not. Details of past dealings with drug suspects may be pertinent, while marital infidelities or off-duty barhopping may not if they have no impact on officer job performance.

Tips for Officers Referred for an FFDE

- Remain positive
- Know your rights and responsibilities
- Come prepared
- Read everything you sign
- Ask reasonable questions
- Be honest and do your best
- Expect and give courteous treatment

Review of Records

Depending on the case, the volume of pertinent records can range from a few sparse sheets to, literally, cartons of documents. Not all of these records may have direct relevance, but the examiner will not know that until after sorting through them. For most psychologists, distilling the raw data to a few paragraphs or pages that will summarize the main points and then integrating this with the information gained from the clinical interview and test findings can prove challenging and time-consuming. As Mark Twain wrote, "If I'd had more time, I would have written you a shorter letter." Further, psychologists should be clear about the sources of the records they cite. They may have to justify every statement they make at a subsequent deposition or trial.[7]

Clinical Interview and Behavioral Observations

During a face-to-face clinical interview, officers will provide much useful information by their speech content, voice tone, eye contact, body language, and general appearance. How they answer questions is just as important as what they say. Examiners will determine clinical status (e.g., anxious, depressed, delusional, evasive) most accurately through this one-on-one interaction. Psychologists develop rapport with officers to help ensure validity of responses and test results.

Collateral Interviews

Interviews—in person, by phone, through e-mail, or by written accounts—with other people who have information relevant to the case can contribute greatly to the evaluation. These individuals may include supervisors, employees, family members, citizens in the officer's patrol area, or others. Special sensitivity helps maintain the maximum degree of confidentiality possible for both the collateral sources and the subject of the FFDE.

Psychological Test Findings

No universally agreed upon psychological test battery for FFDEs exists, and examiners have their own preferences (some use no psychometric testing at all). But, certain standards cover what kinds of diagnostic issues these instruments should address. Some psychological tests are specifically designed for law enforcement assessment, while others that deal with general psychological functioning can be adapted to the law enforcement FFDE referral question. The basic areas that these measures should cover include general intelligence; cognitive functioning (attention, concentration, memory, and reasoning); personality; mood (e.g., anxiety or depression); and existence of psychotic symptoms (e.g., delusions or hallucinations). Some psychologists insert specific measures for malingering to gauge the subject's truthfulness in self-reports and test responses.

Psychologists should document both the actual test scores and their interpretations. For example, "A full-scale IQ score of 104 on the WAIS-III places this officer's overall intelligence in the average range.[8] A T-score of 86 on the Psychopathic Deviate scale of the MMPI-2 suggests high impulsivity and a characteristic disregard for rules and authority."[9]

Conclusions and Discussion

In the conclusion, the psychologist puts everything together. This section should consist of a succinct summary of the main points relevant to the FFDE questions with documentation of the examiner's reasoning on each point. For instance, the psychologist may summarize as depicted in the following example:

Psychological test findings are within normal limits, with the exception of a tendency to disregard rules and conventions and to respond impulsively under stress, as indicated by an elevated score on the Psychopathic Deviate scale of the MMPI-2. This is supported by the officer's statement that "If I know the SOP is wrong, I'll do what I think is right. If I try to go through channels and make recommendations to the brass, they just blow me off. That's why I went ballistic in the lieutenant's office when he told me I could be suspended." Records indicating three disciplinary actions in the officer's present department and at least one suspension in his previous job corroborate this. Overall findings are consistent with an officer of average intelligence, no major mental disorder, and a high level of skill in certain job-related areas (firearms and vehicles), but with a long-standing tendency to disobey authority and respond impulsively, albeit not violently, under conditions of stress.

Recommendations

Examiners should take special care with this section because here they distill their findings to specific recommendations that will affect the officer's life and career. Although no standard model for expressing this exists, one protocol of alternatives is both psychologically valid and practical.[10]

- Unfit for duty: The officer is unfit for duty and unlikely to become fit in the foreseeable future, with or without psychological treatment. Examples include officers with a traumatic brain injury, a longstanding severe personality disorder, or a substance abuse problem that continues to worsen.
- Unfit but treatable: The officer is currently unfit but appears amenable to treatment that will restore fitness in a reasonable amount of time. For example, a depressed, alcoholic officer agrees to enter a 12-step abstinence program, attend psychotherapy sessions, and take prescribed antidepressant medication as needed. Following the recommended course of treatment, the officer usually will be referred for a post treatment FFDE, the recommendations of which may include continued abstinence and periodic psychological follow-up for a specified length of time.
- No psychological diagnosis: The results of the psychological FFDE do not suggest that the officer's unfitness for duty is related to a mental disorder or mental heath diagnosis. In such cases, the officer usually will be referred for administrative coaching or counseling, further education and training, or disciplinary action. Psychologists

sometimes must conclude that people exhibit unprofessional behavior for self-serving reasons, without the presence of a particular psychological condition.

- Invalid evaluation: In this case, the officer has not cooperated with the evaluation, has not been truthful, or has shown malingering or other response manipulation on psychological tests. Perhaps, the officer has sat in silence with arms crossed, speaking only to voice a refusal to talk without a lawyer to the examiner. Maybe, the individual walked into the exam smiling, claimed that "I was framed," and worked a little too hard to impress the evaluator. Alternatively, a subject can behave appropriately, but the information presented does not agree with the records. Or, the test findings are inconsistent and invalid.

CONCLUSION

Used correctly, psychological fitness-for-duty evaluations serve as an essential component of law enforcement management. Of course, officers should not take these evaluations lightly because the results may enter into disciplinary or legal proceedings and, perhaps, impact an officer's entire career. However, officers also should realize that a properly conducted FFDE need not be unnecessarily stressful and will certainly not be demeaning. Law enforcement administrators and the mental health professionals they consult must ensure that FFDEs are carried out fairly and that the results are used properly.

NOTES

1. L. Miller, "Police Personalities: Understanding and Managing the Problem Officer," *The Police Chief*, May 2003, 53–60; "Good Cop-Bad Cop: Problem Officers, Law Enforcement Culture, and Strategies for Success," *Journal of Police and Criminal Psychology* 19 (2004): 3048; and *Practical Police Psychology: Stress Management*

and Crisis Intervention for Law Enforcement (Springfield, IL: Charles C. Thomas, 2006).

2. The psychological examination and report must meet the requirements of the Americans with Disabilities Act.

3. Supra note 1 *(Practical Police Psychology: Stress Management and Crisis Intervention for Law Enforcement)*.

4. A.V. Stone, "Law Enforcement Psychological Fitness for Duty: Clinical Issues," in *Police Psychology into the 21st Century*, eds. M.I. Kurke and E.M. Scrivner (Mahwah, NJ: Lawrence Erlbaum, 1995), 109–131; and A.V. Stone, *Fitness for Duty: Principles, Methods, and Legal Issues* (Boca Raton, FL: CRC Press, 2000).

5. International Association of Chiefs of Police, "Psychological Fitness for Duty Evaluation Guidelines," *The Police Chief*, September 2005, 70–74.

6. C.D. Rostow and R.D. Davis, "Psychological Fitness for Duty Evaluations in Law Enforcement," *The Police Chief*, September 2002, 58–66; *A Handbook for Psychological Fitness-for-Duty Evaluations in Law Enforcement* (New York, NY: Haworth, 2004); L. Miller, "Good Cop-Bad Cop: Problem Officers, Law Enforcement Culture, and Strategies for Success," *Journal of Police and Criminal Psychology* 19 (2004): 30–48; and *Practical Police Psychology: Stress Management and Crisis Intervention for Law Enforcement* (Springfield, IL: Charles C. Thomas, 2006).

7. L. Miller, "On the Spot: Testifying in Court for Law Enforcement Officers," *FBI Law Enforcement Bulletin*, October 2006, 1–7.

8. For additional information, see *http://en.wikipedia.org/wiki/Wechsler_Adult_Intelligence_Scale*.

9. For additional information, see *http://en.wikipedia.org/wiki/Mmpi-2*.

10. Supra note 6 (C.D. Rostow and R.D. Davis, *A Handbook for Psychological Fitness-for-Duty Evaluations in Law Enforcement*).

CONCEPT #10: PROTECT YOUR AGENCY FROM LIABILITY

A successful lawsuit is one worn by a policeman

Robert Frost

As most administrators are well aware, civil suits against the police are now commonplace. Tens of thousands of lawsuits are filed each year in the United States. These suits arise out of allegations of violations of constitutional, civil or statutory rights. Also, the numerous liability cases allege abuse of office, abuse of authority, misconduct, brutality or some act of negligence. This chapter presents six readings in an effort to help one fully understand the magnitude and diversity of liability.

First, is a reading that addresses Federal civil and criminal liability. The Federal civil cause of action that is most often used is Title 42 U.S.C. 1983 and the history and application of this statute is addressed. Federal criminal violations may come under Title 18 U.S.C. 242 and like the previous, the history and application of this statute is addressed. Also, you will see that there is no double jeopardy argument available as one statue provides for criminal penalties while the other provides for civil sanctions. Next, a reading on liability for failure to train is presented. In the reading concepts such as deliberate indifference are addressed and it is illustrated how failures in the department may result in Section 1983 liability.

The third reading of this chapter focuses on police pursuits and civil liability. Although numerous areas are of concern to administrators in recent years, the issue of police pursuits has gained momentum and widespread interest. About forty percent of all police pursuits end in collisions and hundreds of deaths are caused annually because of these pursuits, so there is interest in this police action. This reading provides a literature review to include a discussion of relevant court cases. Policy issues are discussed and recommendations for tighter controls on pursuits are made.

Minimizing risk by defining off-duty police misconduct is the topic of the fourth reading in this chapter. An agency may be liable for the off-duty conduct of its officers, so various elements are examined. Conduct unbecoming an officer, off-duty misconduct, unbecoming off-duty demeanor and off-duty deviant sexual behavior are all discussed. Model policies and mechanisms for accountability are presented, so that the administrator can effectively manage any potential liabilities.

The fifth reading in this chapter covers the topic of civil rights and law enforcement intelligence. As law enforcement intelligence operations are more and more commonly necessary, this reading is timely. A seven step process is presented by the author to help ensure that citizen's civil rights are protected. The sixth and final reading in this chapter addresses sexual harassment by supervisors. The legal basis for sexual harassment claims is first discussed. Then, legal concepts are discussed, such as quid pro quo, hostile work environment, vicarious liability, tangible employment and constructive discharge. The need for continuing training and policy is addressed.

Double Exposure

Civil Liability and Criminal Prosecution

By Richard Schott

The law enforcement profession comes with many risks, most of which are knowingly accepted by its members. As in many other occupations, lesser-known, more subtle risks also are inherent in law enforcement. When officers are involved in a physical struggle or violent confrontation, they run the risk of sustaining injury or even death to accomplish their law enforcement mission. They may be called upon to meet force with force, sometimes having to use deadly force. All uses of force by law enforcement are subject to review; none subject to more scrutiny than the use of deadly force. Officers can quickly become familiar with internal review boards, citizen review boards, presentations of cases to local grand juries to determine whether state criminal charges are appropriate,[1] and civil lawsuits brought in state courts by alleged victims against individual officers (or their employing agency) that allege wrongdoing on the part of the officer (or entity).[2] Under federal law, there are two additional and distinct causes of action that officers may find themselves encountering—a *civil* civil rights lawsuit[3] and a *criminal* civil rights prosecution.[4] Familiarity with these federal actions will help officers navigate the potential minefield of consequences that may result from one single action.

This article examines these distinct causes of action under federal law; how the two proceed independent from each other, as well as from state legal proceedings

or internal reviews; and why being the subject of both does not place the officer in double jeopardy.[5] It also traces the evolution of the relevant federal statutes and highlights certain nuances of the laws that sometimes leave officers defending themselves against unexpected and otherwise perplexing federal actions.

THE FEDERAL CIVIL CAUSE OF ACTION: TITLE 42 U.S.C. 1983

In 1871, the U.S. Congress passed the Ku Klux Klan Act (now know as the Civil Rights Act of 1871) in an attempt to discourage the corrupt influence of the Ku Klux Klan in state government.[6] The passage of the act meant that certain crimes, such as conspiracies to deprive citizens of the right to vote, hold office, serve on juries, and enjoy the equal protection of the laws, could be prosecuted at the federal level, rather than in state courts, which were often infected with or at least influenced by Klan members.[7] Additionally, those wronged by these actions also could bring an action at law (a civil lawsuit) against those responsible for the wrong if they were acting under color of state law. The efficacy of the statute in achieving its original goal can certainly be questioned. For various reasons, not the least of which was the extent of the Ku Klux Klan's strength in certain southern states, the "statute remained virtually dormant" for the first 90 years after its passage.[8] Beyond challenge, however, is the

Richard Schott, "Double Exposure Civil Liability and Criminal Prosecution," *FBI Law Enforcement Bulletin*, vol. 77, no. 5, pp. 23–32. Copyright in the Public Domain.

influence the statute has had on law enforcement officers in this country during the past half century.

In 1961, Title 42 U.S. Code Section 1983[9] (hereinafter § 1983) was recognized for the first time by the U.S. Supreme Court as the basis for a civil lawsuit against individual law enforcement officers. Based on the language of the statute, which at the time read "[e]very person who, under color of any statute, ordinance, regulation, custom or usage, of any State or Territory, subjects, or causes to be subjected, any citizen of the United States or other person within the territorial jurisdiction thereof to the deprivation of any rights, privileges, or immunities secured by the Constitution and laws, shall be liable to the party injured in an action at law, suit in equity, or other proper proceeding for redress,"[10] James Monroe sued several individual members of the Chicago Police Department, as well as the city of Chicago in its own capacity. In his federal civil lawsuit, Monroe alleged that 13 Chicago police officers broke into his family's apartment, woke him and his wife, and forced them to stand naked in the living room while they ransacked every room. They then took Monroe to the police station on open charges for 10 hours. Monroe was interrogated about a murder during his confinement but was ultimately released without ever being charged with a crime. The officers had neither a search warrant nor an arrest warrant at the time of the alleged behavior.[11] Monroe and other family members claimed that the officers and the city were liable for violating the Fourth Amendment to the Constitution, which prohibits unreasonable searches and seizures,[12] while acting under color of state law. The defendant officers and city sought dismissal of Monroe's lawsuit, in part based on the grounds that the actions alleged violated not only the U.S. Constitution but the constitution and laws of the state of Illinois also.[13] Both the federal district court and the appellate court entertaining the defense ruled that dismissal of the lawsuit was appropriate.[14] The Supreme Court reversed when it discounted the individual officers' position, recognizing that "[i]t was not the unavailability of state remedies but the failure of certain States to enforce the laws with an equal hand"[15] that led to the passage of the law in 1871.

The Court further noted that "[t]he federal remedy is supplementary to the state remedy, and the latter need not be first sought and refused before the federal one is invoked."[16] As a practical matter, to hold otherwise almost always would preclude a federal suit at the outset because nearly all law enforcement action violative of the U.S. Constitution (or federal laws) also is a violation of one or more state statutes.

While the primary focus of this article is exposure to individual liability facing law enforcement officers, it should be noted that the portion of Monroe's lawsuit against the city of Chicago was dismissed, as the Supreme Court ruled that the city was not subject to suit under the statute. Relying on the intent of Congress in passing the 1871 act, the Supreme Court ruled that it "did not intend to bring municipal corporations within the ambit of 1979."[17] This part of the ruling left individual officers as the only defendants liable to victims of their wrongdoing. In 1978, the Supreme Court reversed this portion of its *Monroe* decision.

In *Monell v. Department of Social Services*,[18] the Supreme Court changed course and found that an "analysis of the legislative history of the Civil Rights Act of 1871 compels the conclusion that Congress *did* intend municipalities and other local government units to be included among those persons to whom § 1983 applies."[19] While this decision would seem to have created a lucrative option for a plaintiff to sue the proverbial "deep pocket" defendant in lieu of the individuals who actually deprived the plaintiffs of their rights, individuals have remained the most likely liable defendants. Ironically, this is because of another aspect of the Supreme Court's pronouncement in *Monell*. While recognizing that nonstate government entities could be held liable for constitutional violations where "the action that is alleged to be unconstitutional implements or executes a policy statement, ordinance, regulation, or decision officially adopted and promulgated by that body's officers,"[20] the notion that the entity should be vicariously liable whenever one of its officers violates a person's constitutional rights was flatly rejected. Thus, for the government entity to be found liable, it must have somehow caused the constitutional violation to occur with an official policy or regulation, not simply because it employed the individual who violated someone's rights.

An example of this causation requirement is illustrated by the *Bryan County, Oklahoma v. Brown* decision.[21] In that case, Bryan County avoided liability even though the sheriff's decision to hire the reserve deputy who violated the plaintiff's Fourth Amendment right to be free from an unreasonable seizure was deemed a policy of the county.[22] The Supreme Court made clear that "it is not enough for a § 1983 plaintiff merely to identify conduct properly attributable to the municipality. The plaintiff must also demonstrate that, through its *deliberate* conduct, the municipality was the 'moving force' behind the injury alleged. That is, a plaintiff must show that the municipal action was taken with the requisite degree of culpability and must demonstrate a direct causal link between the municipal action and the deprivation of federal rights."[23]

Even though it has proven difficult for plaintiffs to reach the deep pockets of the employing entity defendant, § 1983 lawsuits still are often filed at the federal level, as opposed to filing a cause of action in state court, in part due to another feature of federal civil rights legislation. In 1976, Congress passed the Civil Rights Attorney's Fees Award Act, which allows the prevailing parties in § 1983 proceedings to receive a reasonable attorney's fee as part of their costs.[24] This recovery of attorney's fees is a lucrative aspect of federal suits not typically afforded litigants in state court.

THE BIVENS CAUSE OF ACTION

One hundred years after the Civil Rights Act of 1871 and 10 years after its *Monroe v. Pape* decision, the Supreme Court expanded the reach of civil liability for constitutional violations to those who were acting under federal authority when the violation occurred. In its *Bivens v. Six Unknown Named Agents of Federal Bureau of Narcotics* decision,[25] the Supreme Court created a cause of action that parallels § 1983. Like the plaintiff in *Monroe*, the plaintiff in *Bivens* claimed that he was subjected to both an unreasonable search and an unreasonable seizure. He sued the six unknown Federal Bureau of Narcotics agents who were

involved personally for $15,000 apiece.[26] His suit was filed in federal court. The district court dismissed for, among other reasons, failing to state a cause of action.[27] The federal court of appeals affirmed the dismissal.[28] The Supreme Court reversed and found that a federal cause of action against the federal agents did exist under the Fourth Amendment. While recognizing that "the Fourth Amendment does not in so many words provide for its enforcement by an award of money damages for the consequences of its violation,"[29] the Court pointed out "that it is ... well settled that where legal rights have been invaded, and a federal statute provides for a general right to sue for such invasion, federal courts may use any available remedy to make good the wrong done."[30] In creating this federal cause of action against federal officials, the Supreme Court rejected the notion raised by the defendants that because Congress had specifically created the § 1983 remedy against those acting under state authority, it did "not desire to permit such suits against federal officials."[31] As a result of the *Bivens* decision, any law enforcement officer, whether acting under color of local, state, or federal law, can be sued in federal court for violating someone's rights granted to them by virtue of federal law or the Constitution of the United States.

THE FEDERAL CRIMINAL VIOLATION: TITLE 18 U.S.C. 242

The criminal companion to Title 42 U.S. Code Section 1983 is Title 18 U.S. Code Section 242 (hereinafter "§ 242"). In wording extremely similar to that found in § 1983, § 242 establishes that

[w]hoever, under color of any law, statute, ordinance, regulation, or custom, willfully subjects any person in any State, Territory, Commonwealth, Possession, or District to the deprivation of any rights, privileges, or immunities secured or protected by the Constitution or laws of the United States ... shall be fined under this title or imprisoned not more than one year, or both; and if bodily injury results from the acts committed in violation of this section or if such acts include the use, attempted use, or threatened use of a dangerous weapon, explosive, or fire,

shall be fined under this title or imprisoned not more than ten years, or both; and if death results from the acts committed in violation of this section or if such acts include kidnapping or an attempt to kidnap, aggravated sexual abuse, or an attempt to commit aggravated sexual abuse, or an attempt to kill, shall be fined under this title, or imprisoned for any term of years or for life, or both, or may be sentenced to death.[32]

Like any other criminal statute, but unlike the remedy found in § 1983, the punishment imposed upon people who engage in a violation of § 242 includes monetary fines or, depending on the nature of the violation, a term of imprisonment up to life in prison or even a death sentence.

Noticeably absent from the plain language of § 242 is any reference to authority given by the state.[33] Clearly, Congress intended for all law enforcement officers (whether they be federal, state, or local) to be criminally culpable for willfully depriving people of constitutional rights. Furthermore, even private citizens are viable defendants in a § 242 prosecution if they act in concert with government officials acting under color of law.[34] A well-documented example of this theory involved a group of 18 defendants who were indicted following the disappearance of Michael Henry Schwerner, James Earl Chaney, and Andrew Goodman, three civil rights workers who disappeared in Philadelphia, Mississippi, on June 21, 1964. As alleged in the federal indictment, Deputy Sheriff Cecil Ray Price of the Neshoba County, Mississippi, Sheriff's Department detained the three victims in the Neshoba County jail in Philadelphia on June 21. He was then alleged to have released them, intercepted them later on Highway 19, and removed them from their vehicle and placed them in an official Neshoba County Sheriff's Office vehicle. At this point, he was alleged to have transported the three victims to a remote area where they were turned over to the 18 defendants, "including Deputy Sheriff Price, Sheriff Rainey and Patrolman Willis of the Philadelphia, Mississippi, Police Department."[35] The defendants then allegedly "'did willfully assault, shoot, and kill' each of the three."[36] The 3 law enforcement officials were indicted, along with 15 nonofficial individuals,

for conspiring together and also for committing substantive violations of § 242.[37] The U.S. District Court for the Southern District of Mississippi dismissed the substantive § 242 counts against the nonofficial defendants "because the counts d[id] not charge that the latter were officers in fact, or de facto in anything allegedly done by them under color of law."[38] The Supreme Court viewed the nonofficial individuals' conduct differently. The Court ruled that "[p]rivate persons, jointly engaged with state officials in the prohibited action, are acting under color of law for purposes of the statute,"[39] and, therefore, were criminally responsible under § 242.

Compounding the long reach of this criminal statute is the notion that the illegal conduct need not be authorized by governmental authority or occur while the violating officer is on duty. As early as 1879, the notion that the illegal act giving rise to the official's prosecution needed to be based on actual authority given him by the government was rejected by the Supreme Court.[40] If the criminal violation were to be interpreted otherwise—requiring the illegal action to be something authorized under government authority—the statute would be virtually useless. Consider, for example, the behavior that led to the prosecution of two law enforcement officials in *Catlette v. United States*.[41] The prosecution stemmed from the detention of a group of Jehovah's Witnesses by Nicholas County, West Virginia, Deputy Sheriff Martin Catlette and Richwood, West Virginia, Chief of Police Bert Stewart. On June 29, 1941, the group of Jehovah's Witnesses traveled to the Richwood Town Hall to request police protection while carrying out their work as Jehovah's Witnesses. Three individuals from the group were ushered into the mayor's office, which was also utilized by Deputy Sheriff Catlette, and were detained there. A short time into the detention, Deputy Sheriff Catlette removed his badge "and stated in substance and effect, 'What is done from here on will not be done in the name of the law.'"[42] The group was then subjected to blatantly illegal and unconstitutional treatment.[43] After being charged with violating Title 18 U.S. Code Section 52,[44] Catlette urged that the charge was "fatally defective in that it fails to charge the commission of a federal offense, because it does not state that the alleged acts were within the scope of Catlette's authority, …"[45] as evidence by the removal of his badge and accompanying statement before his illegal conduct. The U.S. Fourth Circuit Court of Appeals pointed out the fallacy in Catlette's argument in no uncertain terms. It countered that "it was certainly within the lawful authority of Catlette as a Deputy Sheriff to detain a person in his office."[46] In more harsh wording, the appellate panel concluded that "Catlette's argument is, therefore, reduced to nothing more than the notion that an officer can divorce himself from his official capacity merely by removing his badge of office before embarking on a course of illegal conduct, and thereby blithely absolve himself from any liability for his ensuing nefarious acts. We must condemn this insidious suggestion that an officer may thus lightly shuffle off his official role. To accept such a legalistic dualism would gut the constitutional safeguards and render law enforcement a shameful mockery."[47]

Another expansive view of the color of law notion was recognized by the U.S. Fifth Circuit Court of Appeals in 1991 and involved clearly off-duty conduct. In *United States v. Tarpley*,[48] William Tarpley, a deputy of the Collingsworth County, Texas, police force, learned of a past affair involving his wife and Kerry Vestal. Tarpley and his wife devised a plan to lure her former lover to their residence so that Tarpley could beat and threaten Vestal. When Vestal arrived at the house, "Tarpley immediately tackled Vestal and hit him repeatedly in the head. He also inserted his service pistol in Vestal's mouth. He told Vestal that he was a sergeant on the police department, that he would and should kill Vestal, and that he could get away with it because he was a cop."[49] The scheme also involved two other officers who, along with the Tarpleys, followed Vestal in their patrol cars until Vestal drove out of their town. Tarpley and one of the other officers were convicted of conspiring to and actually "subjecting Vestal to a deprivation of his constitutional rights, in violation of …§ 242,"[50] which, of course, requires the officers to have been acting under color of law. Tarpley appealed his conviction, arguing that he had not acted under color of law but, rather, that he had acted as a jealous husband.[51] The appellate court affirmed Tarpley's conviction, reasoning that a "rational juror could conclude that Tarpley was acting under color of law. Tarpley did more than simply use his service weapon and identify himself as a police officer. At several points during his assault of Vestal, he claimed to have special authority for his actions by virtue of his official status. He claimed that he could kill Vestal because he was an officer of the law. Significantly, Tarpley summoned another police officer from the sheriff's station and identified him as a fellow officer and ally. The men then proceeded to run Vestal out of town in their squad car. The presence of police and the air of official authority pervaded the entire incident."[52] Clearly, without these persuasive factors the outcome would have been different; however, it was no defense for Tarpley to simply argue that his actions were those of a jealous private citizen.

Historically, criminal prosecution for violating § 242 most often stems from arrest situations where an inappropriate amount of force is used, rather than from unique situations, such as those detailed above.[53] The constitutional deprivation occurring in the context of an arrest is the right to be free from an unreasonable seizure.[54] Probably the most well-known example of this type of prosecution came about as the result of the videotaped arrest and beating of Rodney King in 1991.[55] The individuals involved in the arrest of King who later faced federal prosecution for their actions during the arrest raised several defenses, two of which warrant discussion in the context of this article.

First, Sergeant Stacy Koon argued that he was not guilty of violating § 242 merely by being on the scene and not doing more to prevent the unnecessary use of force.[56] The district court judge considering Koon's argument disagreed. Relying on U.S. Ninth Circuit Court of Appeals precedent, the trial judge pointed out "that a police sergeant who stands by and watches while officers under his command use excessive force and refuses to order them to stop may, thereby, subject the victim to the loss of his or her right to be kept free from harm while in official custody or detention."[57] Similar to the absence of vicarious liability in its civil counterpart (§ 1983), to violate § 242, a supervisor's actions must be more than passive to satisfy the

Side-by-Side Comparison of the Federal Statutes	
Civil (§ 1983)	Criminal (§ 242)
Elements	
Who	Whoever
Color of Law	Color of Law
Deprives	Willfully Deprives
Constitutional Right	Constitutional Right
Remedy	
$$ Damages	Prison/Fine

willful component found in the criminal provision. Applying the proper legal analysis to Sergeant Koon's inaction in the King case, the district court did, in fact, find him guilty. The test was set forth as, "[t]he police sergeant must recognize that the force is excessive and that there are reasonable steps within his power that he could take to prevent the use of force" and "[f]inally, the police sergeant must *deliberately* or *willfully* refrain from preventing the excessive force."[58]

THE DOUBLE JEOPARDY ARGUMENT

The second defense raised in the federal prosecution of the officers involved in the Rodney King altercation that is relevant to the topic of this article was that, in light of the officers' acquittal in state court, the federal charges should have constituted double jeopardy. This was determined not to be the case. Four officers involved in the apprehension of King were "tried in state court on charges of assault with a deadly weapon and excessive use of force by a police officer. The officers were acquitted of all charges, with the exception of one assault charge … that resulted in a hung jury."[59] Only after the resulting widespread rioting left more than 40 people dead, more than 2,000 injured, and resulted in nearly $1 billion in property destruction did the United States seek and obtain indictments charging the same officers with violating § 242.[60] The officers argued that the federal prosecution constituted double jeopardy.[61] The Ninth Circuit Court of Appeals disagreed based on the doctrine of dual sovereignty, which, simply stated, excludes from the double jeopardy prohibition

prosecutions brought by separate sovereigns. Clearly, the state of California and the United States government constitute separate sovereigns.[62] The officers argued, however, that their prosecution satisfied a narrow exception to the dual sovereignty doctrine. According to the appellate panel considering their argument, the so-called *Bartkus*[63] exception is satisfied when "the second prosecution, otherwise permissible under the dual sovereignty rule, is not pursued to vindicate the separate interests of the second sovereign, but is merely pursued as a sham on behalf of the sovereign first to prosecute."[64] If that standard is proven, the second prosecution, although brought by the second sovereign, is barred based on double jeopardy. The officers in the instant case did not carry the burden. The fact that the state and federal investigators and prosecutors cooperated with each other did not turn the federal prosecution into a mere sham.[65]

For an even more obvious reason, there is no exposure to double jeopardy if an officer is sued civilly based on § 1983 and prosecuted under § 242 for the same action. Simply put, the Double Jeopardy Clause applies only to criminal cases.[66]

CONCLUSION

All actions carry certain consequences. Some are realized immediately, some may take years to materialize. The law enforcement profession is fraught with dangerous consequences. Awareness is always taught—awareness of surroundings and danger signs, for example. Awareness of the potential legal consequences of actions also is useful. This article has discussed federal civil actions against law enforcement officers and federal criminal prosecution of those same law enforcement officers. Having an awareness of the legal bases for these consequences can make being the subject of one, or both, much less stressful for the officers.

NOTES

1. For example, a Prince George's County, Maryland, police officer was indicted for two counts of vehicular manslaughter stemming from an accident he caused while engaged in a pursuit of a motorcyclist during rush-hour traffic. Megan Greenwell, "Md. Officer Indicted in Crash That Killed Two," *The Washington Post*, February 14, 2008, p. B1.

2. For example, in February 2008, a Prince George's County, Maryland, civil jury found a county police officer liable for assault and battery. The jury awarded the man the officer shot and wounded on January 1, 2006, a total of $2.4 million. This result followed an internal police investigation reviewed by the U.S. Department of Justice, which found the officer acted appropriately. Ruben Castaneda, "Man Who Was Shot by Officer Wins $2.4 Million Judgment," *The Washington Post*, March 1, 2008, p. B2.

3. 42 U.S.C. § 1983.

4. 18 U.S.C. § 242.

5. U.S. Const. Amend. V, in pertinent part, states "nor shall any person be subject for the same offence to be twice put in jeopardy of life or limb."

6. Randy Means, "The History and Dynamics of Section 1983," *The Police Chief*, May 2004.

7. Eric A. Harrington, "Judicial Misuse of History and § 1983: Toward a Purpose-Based Approach," *Texas Law Review*, March 2007.

8. *Supra* note 6.

9. The section of the original Ku Klux Klan Act that allowed for civil lawsuits to redress a constitutional violation later became, and remains, Title 42 U.S.C. § 1983.

10. *Monroe v. Pape*, 365 U.S. 167 (1961). It should be noted that the statute has remained virtually unchanged, with the notable exception that a person acting under authority derived from the District of Columbia is now included in its reach. The current version of Title 42 U.S. Code § 1983 reads, "Every person who, under color of any statute, ordinance, regulation, custom or usage, of any State or Territory *or the District of Columbia*, subjects, or causes to be subjected, any citizen of the United States or other person within the territorial jurisdiction thereof to the deprivation of any rights, privileges, or immunities secured by the Constitution and laws, shall be liable to the party injured in an action at law, suit in equity, or other proper proceeding for redress, *except that in any action brought against a judicial officer for an act or omission taken in such officer's judicial capacity, injunctive relief shall not be granted unless a declaratory decree was violated or declaratory relief was unavailable. For the purposes of this section, any Act of Congress applicable exclusively to the District of Columbia shall be considered to be a statute of the District of Columbia.*" Emphasis added to changes made after the *Monroe* decision.

11. *Id.* at 203 (Frankfurter, J., dissenting).

12. U.S. Const. Amend. IV reads, "The right of the people to be secure in their persons, houses, papers, and effects, against unreasonable searches and seizures, shall not be violated, and no Warrants shall issue, but upon probable cause, supported by Oath or affirmation, and particularly describing the place to be searched, and the persons or things to be seized."

13. *Supra* note 10, at 172. Illinois Const., Art. II, sect. 6 at the time was almost identical to U.S. Const. Amend. IV; the actions also constituted a violation of Ill. Rev. Stat., c. 38, sects. 252, 449.1, and Chicago, Illinois, Municipal Code, sect. 11–40.

14. 272 F.2d 365 (7th Cir. 1959).

15. *Supra* note 10, at 174.

16. *Id.* at 183.

17. *Id.* at 187.

18. 436 U.S. 658 (1978).

19. *Id.* at 690 (emphasis in original). In a footnote in its opinion, the Court made clear that, because of the plain language of the Eleventh Amendment, the *Monell* decision was "limited to local government units which are not considered part of the State." FN 54. U.S. Const. Amend. XI reads, "The Judicial power of the United States shall not be construed to extend to any suit in law or

equity, commenced or prosecuted against one of the United States by Citizens of another State, or by Citizens or subjects of any Foreign State."

20. 436 U.S. at 690.

21. 520 U.S. 397 (1997).

22. *Id.* at 404.

23. *Id.* (emphasis in original).

24. 42 U.S.C. § 1988 (b).

25. 403 U.S. 388 (1971).

26. *Id.* at 389.

27. 276 F.Supp. 12 (E.D.N.Y. 1967).

28. 409 F.2d 718 (2nd Cir. 1969).

29. *Supra* note 25, at 396.

30. *Id.*, quoting *Bell v. Hood*, 327 U.S. 678, 684 (1946) (footnote omitted).

31. *Bivens*, 403 U.S. at 429 (Appendix to opinion of Burger, C.J., dissenting).

32. 18 U.S.C. § 242.

33. Cf. 42 U.S.C. § 1983.

34. While this article examines the features of the Color of Law statute found at 18 U.S.C. § 242, it should be noted that there is a separate Conspiracy statute (18 U.S.C. § 241) that makes it a federal crime for two or more persons to conspire to injure, oppress, threaten, or intimidate any person in any state, territory, commonwealth, possession, or district in the free exercise or enjoyment of any right or privilege secured to him by the Constitution or laws of the United States or because of his having so exercised the same, which does not require the conspirators to have been acting under color of law.

35. *United States v. Price, et al.*, 383 U.S. 787, 790 (1966).

36. *Id.*

37. *Id.* at 792–794.

38. *Id.* at 793.

39. *Id.* at 794.

40. *Ex parte Commonwealth of Virginia*, 100 U.S. 339 (1879).

41. 132 F.2d 902 (4th Cir. 1943).

42. *Id.* at 904.

43. *Id.*, describing the actual treatment and unlawful acts.

44. The defendants were charged with violating Title 18 U.S.C. § 52, which later became § 242.

45. *Supra* note 41, at 905.

46. *Id.* at 906.

47. *Id.*

48. 945 F.2d 806, reh'g. denied (5th Cir. 1991), cert. denied, 504 U.S. 917 (1992).

49. *Id.* at 807.

50. *Id.* at 808.

51. *Id.* at 809.

52. *Id.*

53. The FBI's Web site points out that most color of law cases fall into five categories: excessive force, sexual assaults, false arrest and fabrication of evidence, deprivation of property, and failure to keep from harm; retrieved from *http://www. fbi.gov/ hg/cid/civilrights/color.htm*. From 2001 through 2007, the Criminal Section of the Department of Justice obtained convictions of 391 defendants in color of law cases; 256 defendants were convicted between 1994 through 2000. January 30, 2008 press release; retrieved from *http:// www.usdoj. gov*.

54. *Supra* note 12.

55. Because of the familiarity with the Rodney King incident that most law enforcement officers have, the facts giving rise to the subsequent court proceedings will not be recounted in this article. For a full discussion of the underlying events, see *United States v. Koon*, 833 F.Supp. 769 (C.D. Calif. 1993).

56. It should be noted that the court opinion referenced in *supra* note 55 recognizes that initially the conduct of the arresting officers and the amount of force used on King in effecting his arrest was reasonable and, therefore, not in violation of King's constitutional rights. The force became excessive at a certain point, and Sergeant Koon was present both before and after the point when it became excessive.

57. *United States v. Koon*, 833 F.Supp. 769, 779, (C.D. Calif. 1993), aff'd in part, vacated in part, 34 F.3d 1416 (9th Cir. 1994), aff'd in part, rev'd in part and remanded, 518 U.S. 81 (1996), quot-

ing *United States v. Reese*, 2 F.3d 870, 889 (9th Cir. 1993).

58. *Id*. at 779, quoting *Reese* at 890, (emphasis added).

59. *Koon v. United States*, 518 U.S. 81, 87 (1996).

60. *Id*. at 88.

61. *Supra* note 5.

62. *United States v. Koon*, 34 F.3d 1416 (9th Cir. 1994), aff'd in part, rev'd in part and remanded, 518 U.S. 81 (1996); *Heath v. Alabama*, 474 U.S 82, 93 (1985).

63. *Bartkus v. Illinois*, 359 U.S. 121 (1959).

64. *Supra* note 62, 1439.

65. *Id*. In footnote 19, the 9th Circuit panel pointed out that the *Bartkus* exception is narrow and seldom successfully pursued.

66. Kermit L. Hall, James W. Ely, Joel B. Grossman, and William M. Wiecek, eds., *The Oxford Companion to the Supreme Court of the United States* (New York, NY: Oxford University Press, Inc., 1992), 232.

Deliberate Indifference

Liability for Failure to Train

By Martin King

In virtually every instance where a person's constitutional rights were violated by a police officer, a plaintiff will be able to point to something the employing entity— ounty or municipality—could have done to prevent the unfortunate incident. Frequently, where the alleged violation of rights is caused by the use of force by a police officer, the injured party will attempt to hold the county or municipality responsible by asserting that the harm caused could have been avoided by a more adequate training program. This article addresses the issue of county or municipal liability under the federal statute Title 42, United States Code, Section 1983 (hereinafter Section 1983), which permits individuals to hold government employees and, in some cases, their employers accountable for violation of rights secured by the U.S. Constitution.[1] In particular, this article explores the contours of employer liability for claims that the constitutional violation was caused by a failure to adequately or properly train employees.

In resolving the issue of liability for failure to train, focus is placed on the adequacy of the training program in relation to the tasks particular officers must perform. However, it is not enough to merely show that a situation will arise and that an officer taking the wrong course of action in that instance will result in injuries to citizens. Even adequately trained officers occasionally make mistakes; the fact that they do says

little about the training program or the legal basis for holding a city or county liable for that mistake.

A city or county will not be liable simply because it employed the officer whose actions resulted in a deprivation of a citizen's constitutional rights. Rather, a plaintiff must establish that government policymakers either were or should have been aware that a training program was inadequate and did little or nothing about the problem. Which is to say, policymakers were deliberately indifferent to the harm that would likely result from the failure to train.[2]

"Deliberate indifference" is a standard of fault that requires a showing that government policy makers acted with conscious disregard for the obvious consequences of their actions.[3] A pattern of constitutional violations by officers may indicate that a lack of proper training, rather than a one-time negligent administration of the training program or factors peculiar to the officer involved in a single incident, is responsible for the plaintiff's injury.[4] If a training program does not prevent constitutional violations and a pattern of injuries develops, officials charged with the responsibility of formulating policy for the agency may be put on notice that a new program is needed and a failure to address the problem may constitute deliberate indifference.[5] In the absence of a pattern of violations, deliberate indifference may be inferred from the policy makers' continued adherence to a training program that they knew or should have

Martin King, "Deliberate Indifference: Liability for Failure to Train," *FBI Law Enforcement Bulletin*, vol. 74, no. 10, pp. 22–31. Copyright in the Public Domain.

known would fail to prevent violations in usual or recurring situations.[6] In such cases, the constitutional violation must be a highly predictable or plainly obvious consequence of the failure to train.

A training program must be quite deficient for the deliberate indifference standard to be met. To hold the city or county liable, a plaintiff must show that the level of training was so deficient that it fell below what is constitutionally acceptable. Liability does not attach where an otherwise adequate training program has occasionally been negligently administered. Neither will it suffice to prove that an injury or accident could have been avoided if an officer had received better or more training sufficient to equip the officer to avoid the particular injury-causing conduct.[7] The fact that training was imperfect or not in the precise form that a plaintiff would prefer is insufficient to make a showing of deliberate indifference.[8] Such second-guessing could be made about almost any encounter resulting in injury.

While a city or county may be exposed to liability only when it deliberately ignores the obvious consequences of the inadequacies of its training program, there is no neat set of rules that permits a city or county to determine with precision when a consequence will be deemed obvious. Predicting how a hypothetically well-trained officer would act under a specific set of circumstances is no easy task, particularly because matters of individual judgement may be involved. Nevertheless, one guiding principle is that by choosing the deliberate indifference standard of liability for Section 1983 claims, the U.S. Supreme Court has made it difficult for individuals to hold city and county governments liable for violations of rights secured by the U.S. Constitution based on an alleged failure to train.

EMPLOYER LIABILITY UNDER SECTION 1983

In *Monell v. Department of Social Services of City of New York*, the U.S. Supreme Court established the fundamental principle in the law of municipal liability under Section 1983 that local governments may be held liable only for their own conduct and not merely for the conduct of their employees.[9] That is, the government entity is not vicariously liable for the actions of its police officers simply because it employed the officer and the harm was caused while the officer was acting within the scope of his or her employment. Instead, liability only attaches to the county or city for injury caused by actions or omissions attributable to the government itself.[10] Government (as opposed to individual) liability under Section 1983 is restricted only to those cases in which "the action that is alleged to be unconstitutional implements or executes a policy statement, ordinance, regulation, or decision officially adopted or promulgated by that body's officers."[11] Government conduct by way of its policy, in addition to the individual employee's conduct that directly resulted in the harm, must be identified as causing a violation of a recognized constitutional right.[12]

A plaintiff seeking to find a city or county government liable under Section 1983 must establish a causal connection between the injury and a government policy or custom.[13]

Locating a policy ensures that liability attaches only for those deprivations of constitutional rights resulting from the decisions of its duly constituted legislative body or of those officials whose acts may fairly be said to be those of the government itself.[14] City or county government liability under Section 1983 attaches "where— and only where—a deliberate choice to follow a course of action is made from among various alternatives by the official or officials responsible for establishing final policy with respect to the subject matter in question."[15] The assessment of what official possesses final authority to establish policy is determined by state law. The discretionary decisions of lesser officials will not be imputed to the agency as actionable policy.[16]

IDENTIFICATION OF A "POLICY"

Generally, three possible avenues are open to plaintiffs to show the existence of a "policy" that allegedly caused a constitutional violation.

1. An express written policy or an actual directive from a policy-making official that, when enforced, causes a constitutional violation—in short, an unconstitutional policy. Where a plaintiff can demonstrate that an existing policy is itself unconstitutional when applied as intended or that a specific action taken or directed by the government itself violated a citizen's constitutional rights, resolving the issues of fault and causation is relatively straight forward. In these cases, there is clear governmental action that can be attributed as the cause, or moving force, behind the injury of which the plaintiff complains.[17] A policy also can be inferred even from a single decision made by the highest official responsible for setting policy within that area of a government's business.[18]

2. Widespread conduct that results in violations of constitutional rights, although not authorized by any written law or policy, that is so permanent and well-settled as to constitute a custom or practice with the force of law may serve as the functional equivalent of a written policy.[19] Essentially, a practice of condoning constitutional violations must be established. Because a custom or practice must be established, evidence of only a single alleged incident, particularly if it involved only actors below policy-making level, will typically not be sufficient.

3. An inadequate written policy or a practice that is not unconstitutional itself but which reflects deliberate indifference to persons' constitutional rights because the deficiency causes officers to violate constitutional rights.[20] This is often difficult for plaintiffs to establish because the deprivation of rights is allegedly caused not by affirmatively unconstitutional acts attributable to the government but by omissions or failure to take adequate steps to safeguard constitutional rights.[21] Most failure-to-train cases fall into this category. Few training programs are unconstitutional when applied as intended. For example, a county or municipality will rarely have an express written or oral policy permitting

the excessive use of force. Thus, for liability to attach, it is necessary to establish the existence of a custom or practice—a policy—that permitted excessive force to occur by demonstrating that the municipality deliberately failed to adequately train its police officers in a relevant respect.[22]

"DELIBERATE INDIFFERENCE" AS "POLICY"

In *City of Canton v. Harris*,[23] the U.S. Supreme Court established deliberate indifference as the standard required to show the existence of a policy or custom when a constitutional violation allegedly results from a failure to train. The Court described this standard as follows:

> Only where a failure to train reflects a "deliberate" or "conscious" choice by a municipality—a "policy" as defined by our prior cases— can a city be liable for such failure under Section 1983. *Monell's* rule that a city is not liable under Section 1983 unless a municipal policy causes a constitutional deprivation will not be satisfied by merely alleging that an existing training program for a class of employees, such as police officers, represents a policy for which the city is responsible. ... [I]t may happen that in light of the duties assigned to specific officers or employees, the need for more or different training is so obvious, and the inadequate training so likely to result in the violation of constitutional rights, that the policy makers of the city can reasonably be said to have been deliberately indifferent to the need. In that event, the failure to provide proper training may fairly be said to represent a policy for which the city is responsible, and for which the city may be held liable if it actually causes injury.[24]

Liability should attach only if the failure to train is a "deliberate choice to follow a course of action," and this failure to train must have led to—caused—the injury in question.[25] This standard ensures that isolated instances of misconduct are not attributable to a generally adequate policy or training program. The deliberate indifference standard requires a high degree of culpability on the part of the policy maker. A plaintiff must not only establish defects in training procedures but also that policy makers did nothing to cure those defects when they knew or should have known that violations of constitutional rights would be the obvious result. For example, where there has been a demonstrable effort to train officers to handle usual and recurring situations, evidence of a single alleged incident involving excessive use of force by an officer typically will not suffice to prove deliberate indifference that equates to a policy permitting the excessive use of force.

> After the 20-week basic-training course, the city required ... all officers to attend an annual 3-day training program that provided updated information on laws concerning arrest, detention, and search and seizure. [The plaintiff] has provided no evidence of defects in the city's training procedures. [The plaintiff] has shown neither that decision makers continued to adhere to a training program they know or should have known had failed to prevent officers' use of force, nor that a pattern of tortious conduct by inadequately trained officers indicated lack of proper training. At most, [the plaintiff] has shown a single violation of federal rights, which does not alone permit an inference of municipal culpability and causation. [The plaintiff] has shown that only [the officer] may have acted culpably, not the city.[26]

Taken together, the often intertwined considerations of fault in the form of deliberate indifference and causation amount to a requirement that liability be based on a finding that the policy makers have actual or constructive notice that a particular inadequacy in a training program is likely to result in a constitutional violation.[27] Therefore, in addition to establishing a constitutional violation, a plaintiff must make the following showings to proceed against a government employer under a failure-to-train theory.[28]

1. Inadequate training: Training must be shown to be deficient in a relevant respect given the injury sustained. The focus is on the deficiencies in the training program itself, not on whether the particular officer involved was adequately trained.
2. Causation: The failure of the program to provide training caused the injury. That is, the injury would have been avoided had the employee been trained under a program that was not deficient in the identified respect.
3. Deliberate indifference: The inadequate training program must be a "policy" of the municipality. This is demonstrated by circumstances that evidence that policy makers—individuals with final decision-making authority in the respective area of municipal responsibility—knew or should have known about the need for the identified training but remained deliberately indifferent to that need.

In *Canton,* the Court used training on deadly force to illustrate the standard of deliberate indifference. The Court noted that "city policy makers know to a moral certainty that their police officers will be required to arrest fleeing felons."[29] Moreover, "[t]he city has armed its officers with firearms, in part to accomplish this task."[30] In such a situation, "the need to train officers in the constitutional limitations on the use of deadly force ... can be said to be 'so obvious' that a failure to do so would properly be characterized as 'deliberate indifference' to constitutional rights."[31] Even where the need to train would not be obvious to a stranger to the situation, a particular context—such as a documented pattern of violations—might make the need for training or supervision so obvious to a policy maker that a failure to do so would constitute deliberate indifference. Thus, the Court suggested that "[i]t could also be that the police, in exercising their discretion, so often violate constitutional rights that the need for further training must have been plainly obvious to the city policy makers, who nevertheless, are 'deliberately indifferent' to the need."[32]

THE "DELIBERATE INDIFFERENCE" STANDARD

It is possible to discern three closely related requirements that must be met before a failure to train will constitute deliberate indifference to the constitutional rights of citizens.[33] First, the plaintiff must show that policy makers know to a moral certainty that their employees will confront a given situation as opposed to rare or unforeseen events. Second, the plaintiff must show that the situation either presents the employee with a difficult exercise of judgment that training will make less difficult, or that there is a history of employees mishandling the situation. There must be awareness of a problem that is susceptible to improvement through training. Third, the plaintiff must show that the wrong choice by the employee is likely to cause the deprivation of a citizen's constitutional rights. Training resources may appropriately be concentrated on those situations where an error in judgement by an officer is likely to result in a constitutional violation. Where a plaintiff can establish all three elements, then it can be said that the policy maker should have known that inadequate training was "so likely to result in the violation of constitutional rights, that the policy makers … can reasonably be said to have been deliberately indifferent to the need."[34]

In *Zuchel v. City and County of Denver, Colorado,*[35] the U.S. Court of Appeals for the Tenth Circuit found that a city police department was deliberately indifferent due to its inadequate training of police officers as to the practical aspects regarding use of deadly force. The court concluded that the circumstances giving rise to an unconstitutional shooting of a suspect by a police officer represented a usual and recurring situation with which city police officers were required to deal, so that the city could be liable under Section 1983 for the officer's actions. In reaching this conclusion, the court referred to a letter from the district attorney to the city police chief discussing six police officer-citizen encounters involving deadly force that had occurred in a 6-week period and recommending that periodic

shoot-don't-shoot live training should be made part of the training program to minimize unjustified shootings. In addition, testimony from the district attorney was provided at trial to the effect that it was foreseeable that officers would be placed in situations where they would have to make decisions on whether to shoot. An expert also testified that it was predicable in large cities that police officers would encounter situations in which they would have to make judgements as to whether to shoot.[36] Prior to the incident, the department's shoot-don't-shoot training consisted of a lecture and a movie presented to officers during basic training at the police academy. The inadequacies of that training program were identified by an expert witness as the cause of the shooting in question. The witness offered the opinion that strategic judgement cannot be taught in a classroom—particularly based only on the showing of a single film—and that the officer, due to lack of training, handled the situation with the suspect as a layperson, rather than a trained professional.[37]

The city argued that as a matter of law, it could not be found deliberately indifferent because it had some shoot-don't-shoot training and, thus, recognized the problem and was addressing it. The court rejected this argument, finding that the city did not properly apply the definition of deliberate indifference under *Canton.* In establishing deliberate indifference, focus must be placed on whether the need for more or different training is so obvious, and the inadequacy so likely to result in the deprivation of constitutional rights, that the policymakers can be said to have been deliberately indifferent to the need. "Thus, a city is deliberately indifferent if 1) its training program is inadequate and 2) the city deliberately or recklessly made the choice to ignore its deficiencies."[38] In this case, the court concluded that the testimony underscored the obviousness of the deficiency of the existing training program. The district attorney's letter expressly recommended that the police department institute expanded training in the areas of "strategic skills development; how to analyze situations, develop options, and select the option that minimizes the likelihood of a violent confrontation" and "periodic target course 'shoot-don't-shoot' live training under street conditions."[39] Because the police department presented no evidence of any attempt to address the deficiencies of its training program, the court found that the evidence was sufficient to permit a jury to reasonably infer that the city's failure to implement some form of periodic live training constituted deliberate indifference to the constitutional rights of the city's citizens.[40]

A finding of deliberate indifference requires that the government has disregarded a known or obvious risk of harm caused by its failure to develop an adequate training program. However, a showing of specific incidents that establish a pattern of constitutional violations is not necessary to put a municipality on notice that its training program is inadequate. A single violation of constitutional rights combined with a failure to train officers to handle that situation is sufficient to trigger municipal liability if the situation was likely to occur and presented an obvious potential for a constitutional violation.[41]

In *Young v. City of Providence*, the First Circuit Court of Appeals recently addressed the issue of municipal liability in a Section 1983 action in which there was no evidence of a prior similar constitutional violation.[42] *Young* involved a wrongful death action alleging excessive force after the victim, who was an off-duty officer responding to an incident under the city's always armed/always on-duty policy, was shot by two other officers who were responding to the same incident. The city had a use-of-force training program in place that included judgmental shooting. This training consisted of interactive video simulation and live range exercises that included don't-shoot scenarios. However, the city did not provide training that specifically addressed identification of officers responding under its' always armed/always on-duty policy and had no protocols in place governing off-duty officer response situations.[43]

Although there was no evidence of a past friendly fire shooting, the court concluded that a jury could find deliberate indifference because "the department knew that there was a high risk that absent particularized training on avoiding off-duty misidentifications, and given the department's always armed/always on-duty policy, friendly fire shootings were likely to occur."[44]

Young illustrates a number of factors that are considered when imputing government knowledge of an obvious risk of harm as required to show deliberate indifference. Even when there have been no prior violations, where a policy or practice of a police department creates an obvious risk of harm, where training would tend to reduce that specific type of harm, and where the wrong decision of an untrained officer will likely result in flagrant violations of constitutional rights, a municipality may be deemed deliberately indifferent if it does not afford some training that specifically addresses the particular potential for harm. In *Young*, there was evidence presented that the always armed/always on-duty policy was inherently dangerous because without specific training, it was likely that off-duty officers would intervene unwisely and that on-duty officers may mistake them for suspects. Indeed, the city also changed its always-armed/always on-duty policy after the friendly fire incident such that officers were not required to carry firearms while off duty and provided a specific protocol for any off-duty action that was taken.[45]

Although there had been no prior friendly fire incidents, there was evidence presented that the city was aware that such incidents were predicable based on numerous reports from police officers of past misidentifications of off-duty personnel that did not end with tragic results. The city was, therefore, deemed to be on notice that interactions between off-duty and on-duty officers were probable (a "usual and recurring situation with which its officers were required to deal").[46] Further, interactions between on-duty and off-duty officers are typically high stress situations. In such incidents, officers tend to fall back on training. That being the case, specific training would likely reduce the inherent dangerousness posed by intervening armed, off-duty officers. The severity of the consequences of a friendly fire incident were obvious and the need to train to avoid such an occurence was acknowledged by testimony of police personnel responsible for training.[47]

Deliberate indifference will not be imputed to a city or county government based on its failure to afford specific training to better handle unprecedented occurrences. An example is afforded by the Fifth Circuit case *Cozzo v. Tangipahoa Parish Council*,[48] which involved alleged violations of Fourth and Fourteenth Amendment rights stemming from a clearly unlawful eviction following a police captain's allegedly erroneous interpretation of the requirements of a temporary restraining order in a domestic case. Although the plaintiff was able to establish that there was a failure to set any specific rules or guidance regarding the actions allowed when enforcing restraining orders in domestic cases and that there was a direct causal connection between the lack of training and the alleged violation, the court found that there was no basis for municipal liability due to the unprecedented nature of the incident.[49] An unlawful eviction pursuant to a captain's interpretation of a restraining order had never before occurred in more than 20 years of documented sheriff's department history.[50] There was no deliberate indifference given the lack of prior similar constitutional violations and no evidence to support a finding that constitutional violations were a predictable consequence of a failure to afford specific training in the interpretation of temporary retraining orders.

CONCLUSION

Liability for failure to train will be imposed when it can be demonstrated that a municipal policymaker knew or should have known that inadequate training was so likely to result in the violation of constitutional rights that the policy maker can reasonably be said to have been deliberately indifferent to the need. The inadequacy of the training program must be obvious and likely to result in a constitutional violation.

Although deliberate indifference is most often found in cases that involve inaction in the face of a pattern of prior similar constitutional violations, a failure to act that results in a single unprecedented incident can support a finding of deliberate indifference where the constitutional violation was a highly predictable consequence of a failure to train.

NOTES

1. Title 42, U.S.C., § 1983 provides in pertinent part: "Every person who, under color of any statute, ordinance, regulation or custom or usage of any State … subjects or causes to be subjected, any citizen of the United States or other person … to the deprivation of any rights, privileges and immunities secured by the Constitution and laws shall be liable to the party injured in any action at law. …"

2. *City of Canton v. Harris*, 489 U.S. 378, 109 S. Ct. 1197, 103 L.Ed. 2d 412 (1989).

3. See Board of County Commission of Bryan County Oklahoma v. Brown, 520 U.S. 397, 117 S. Ct. 1382, 137 L.Ed. 2d 626 (1997).

4. *Id.* at 407–408

5. *Id.* at 409.

6. *Id.*

7. *See Palmquist v. Selvik*, 111 F.3d 1332,1345 (7th cir. 1997) (Where town gave police some training on handling suspects exhibiting abnormal behavior, argument that even more training should have been given failed.).

8. *See Canton* 489 U.S. at 391; *Young ex rel. Estate of Young v. City of Providence*, 404 F.3d 4, 27 (2005); *Grazier v. City of Philidelphia*, 328 F.3d 120, 125 (3rd Cir. 2003).

9. 436 U.S. 658, 690, 98 S. Ct. 2018, 2035–36, 56 L.Ed. 2d 611 (1978) (In *Monell,* the Supreme Court held that municipalities and other local governmental bodies are "persons" within the meaning of § 1983 and, therefore, are subject to liability based on their actions or policies that subjected a person to a deprivation of a constitutional right but that they are not liable merely because they employed the person who actually inflicted the deprivation.).

10. *Id.* at 689.

11. *Id.* at 691, 694.

12. *See Collins v. City of Harker Heights*, 503 U.S. 115, 120, 112 S. Ct. 1061, 117 L.Ed. 2d 261 (1992) (It should be stressed that a local government's failure to train that results in injury to a plaintiff is not actionable under § 1983 unless the failure

led to a violation of an established constitutional right that, in turn, caused the plaintiff's injuries.).

13. *Monell*, 436 U.S. at 693–94.

14. *Id.* at 694.

15. *Pembaur v. City of Cincinnati*, 475 U.S. 469, 483, 106 S. Ct. 1292, 1298 (1986).

16. *See City of St. Louis v. Praprotnik*, 485 U.S. 112, 108 S. Ct. 915, 99 L.Ed. 2d 107 (1988).

17. *See Brown*, 520 U.S. at 407–408.

18. *See Pembaur* at 475 U.S. 480 (In ordering deputy sheriffs to enter physician's clinic without a warrant to serve capiases on third parties in an investigation of alleged welfare fraud, county prosecutor was acting as final decision maker for county; therefore, county could be held liable under § 1983 for alleged violation of physician's Fourth Amendment Rights based on that single directive.).

19. *See Jett v. Dallas Independent School Dist.*, 491 U.S. 701. 109 S. Ct. 2702 (1989) (It is for a jury to determine whether policy making officials' decision have caused the deprivation of rights at issue 1) by policies that affirmatively command it to occur or 2) by acquiescence in a *longstanding practice or custom* that constitutes the standard operating procedure of the local governmental entity.); *ODonnell v. Brown*, 335 F.Supp 2d 787, 816 (W.D. Mich. 2004).

20. *See Canton*, 489 U.S. at 387 (*Canton* expressly rejected the argument that a city is liable only when the municipal policy is itself unconstitutional. Rather, "if a concededly valid policy is unconstitutionally applied by a municipal employee, the City is liable if the employee had not been adequately trained and the constitutional wrong has been caused by a failure to train."); *City of Oklahoma City v. Tuttle*, 471 U.S. 808, 822–823, 105 S. Ct. 2427 (1985).

21. *Brown*, 520 U.S. at 411 (Due to difficulty in establishing causation, inadequate screening of a reserve deputy applicant by county sheriff does not necessarily lead to liability on the part of the county for injury caused by that reserve deputy. For a finding of liability, the plaintiff must establish 1) a constitutional violation and 2) the specific injury that occurred was the *plainly obvious consequence* of the hiring decision.).

22. *Canton*, 489 U.S. at 388–89.

23. 489 U.S. 378.

24. *Id.* at 389–390.

25. *Pembaur*, 475 U.S. at 483–84.

26. *Ward v. City of DesMoines*, 184 F. Supp 2d 892, 898 (S.D. Iowa 2002).

27. *See, e.g., Cornfield By Lewis v. Consolidated High School Dist. No. 230*, 991 F.2d 1316 (7th Cir. 1993) (Student subjected to strip search failed to state a claim establishing deliberate indifference by school district so as to support imposition of liability on failure-to-train theory. Constitutional rights in this area not clearly established and the existence of only two prior incidents of strip searching fell short of a pattern of violations sufficient to put the school board on notice of potential harms to students.).

28. *See Palmquist*, 111 F.3d at 1345.

29. *Canton* 489 U.S. at 390, note 10.

30. *Id.*

31. *Id.*

32. *Id.*

33. This three-part test for deliberate indifference based on the language used in *Canton* was enunciated in *Walker v. City of New York*, 974 F.2d 293 (2nd Cir. 1992), *cert. denied*, 507 U.S. 961, 113 S. Ct. 1378, 122 L. Ed. 2d 762 (1993) (Various different tests for municipal liability based on a failure to train have been formulated in several federal circuits; all of these tests obviously contain a deliberate indifference component (*See, e.g., Fraire v. City of Arlington*, 957 F. 2d 1268 (5th Cir. 1992), *cert. denied* 506 U.S. 973, 113 S. Ct. 462, 121 L.Ed. 2d 371; *Allen v. Muskogee, Oklahoma*, 119 F.3d 837 (10th Cir. 1997), *cert. denied*, 522 U.S. 1148, 118 S. Ct. 1165, 140 L.Ed. 2d 176; *Young v. City of Augusta*, 59 F.3d 1160 (11th Cir. 1995); *Atchinson v. District of Columbia*, 73 F.3d 418 (D.C. Cir. 1996)).

34. *Canton* 489 U.S. at 388.

35. 997 F.2d 730 (10th Cir. 1993).

36. *Id.* at 740.

37. *Id.* at 739.

38. *Id.* at 740, note 5.

39. *Id.* at 747.

40. *Id.* at 741.

41. *Allen*, 119 F.3d at 849.

42. 404 F.3d 4 (1st Cir. 2005).

43. *Id.* at 8–10.

44. *Id.* at 18 (The court cited both the "highly predicable consequence language" of *Brown*, 520 U.S. at 409, and the "know to a moral certainty" language of *Canton*, 489 U.S. at 390 7n.10.).

45. *Id.* at 11.

46. *Id.* at 10.

47. *Id.*

48. 279 F.3d 273, 289–290 (5th Cir. 2002).

49. *Id.* (The claim with respect to the municipality failed because no municipal policy was shown. The sheriff had the authority as policy maker. There was no express policy that authorized the action taken by the police captain and there was no widespread practice or custom that fairly represented department policy. "Having failed to demonstrate the existence of a policy, the evidence simply did not substantiate a finding that sheriff … implemented a policy so deficient that it was a repudiation of … constitutional rights and was the moving force of the unconstitutional dispossession of property.").

50. *Id.* at 290.

Police Pursuits and Civil Liability

By Chris Pipes and Dominick Pape

As many as 40 percent of all motor vehicle police pursuits end in collisions[1] and some of these result in nearly 300 deaths each year of police officers, offenders, or innocent third party individuals.[2] Because many police pursuits result in accidents and injuries, agencies and officers become subjects of civil lawsuits. Initiated in state or federal courts, these law-suits have resulted cumulatively in case law that directs law enforcement agencies to develop pursuit policies. The U.S. Supreme Court recently issued a ruling that has changed the threshold of negligence before an agency or officer can be held liable, which will impact police agencies across the United States.[3]

Because of the critical nature of police pursuit situations, chief executive officers (CEOs) of law enforcement agencies must establish an appropriate policy governing the actions of their personnel during such incidents. In doing so, CEOs first must consider the constraints and allowances set forth by state and federal statutes and court decisions applicable within their jurisdiction. They must create a policy that balances the need to apprehend offenders in the interests of justice with the need to protect citizens from the risks associated with police pursuits. Additionally, the policy must protect the financial interests of the community based upon potential losses of taxpayer dollars following successful litigation against the agency as a result of law enforcement actions deemed inappropriate by the courts. Adopting a policy similar to that of another agency does not easily resolve the CEO's dilemma because a variety of philosophies exists among the pursuit policies of law enforcement agencies. U.S. federal courts have reviewed numerous police pursuit cases using different standards of conduct and the courts routinely have reviewed the agency's pursuit policy before rendering a decision. The policy, or lack of same, could impact the outcome of a civil action.

LITERATURE REVIEW

The published literature regarding police pursuit is voluminous, and individual studies focus on a variety of elements associated with the issue.[4] Some experts categorize pursuit policies as either restrictive or judgmental where, in the former case, the officer may only pursue given the existence of certain well-defined criteria, or, in the latter, where the officer may decide whether or not to pursue based upon certain factors.[5] Other experts prefer to label judgmental policies as discretionary, and further subdivide restrictive policies into two categories—restrictive and discouraging.[6] They define a restrictive policy as one that places only certain restrictions on the judgments of officers, and a discouraging policy as one that severely cautions against or prohibits pursuits except in extreme circumstances.[7]

Chris Pipes and Dominick Pape, "Police Pursuits and Civil Liabilty," *FBI Law Enforcement Bulletin*, vol. 70, no. 7, pp. 16–21. Copyright in the Public Domain.

One study discussed four factors that police officers and supervisors must consider when making the decision to pursue or to continue or terminate pursuit: the nature of the violation (e.g., traffic offense, felony); the characteristics of the area (e.g., freeway, commercial, residential); traffic conditions (e.g., congested or not congested); and weather conditions (e.g., wet or dry).[8] Among both officers and supervisors, the nature of the offense represented the most important variable involved in the decision to pursue, followed by the level of traffic congestion.[9] The study focused on the attitudes of the officers and supervisors independent of the actions that those individuals actually took in observance of policies in conflict with their personal beliefs.[10]

Other research describes the attitudes of the public with regard to police pursuit and some conclude that the public overwhelmingly supports pursuits for serious criminal offenses.[11] The data also suggest that public support for police diminishes proportionate to the seriousness of the offense, especially when the public is educated about the dangers of pursuit.[12]

Another study used data gleaned from interviews with prison inmates that attempted to describe attitudes toward police pursuit from the offenders' perspectives.[13] These findings concluded that the average individual who makes the decision to flee is a male in his mid-20s, and that few differences exist between the thoughts going through the minds of those offenders who eventually escaped and those who law enforcement captured.[14]

Lawsuits stemming from police pursuits allege civil rights violations pertaining to Title 18, Section 1983, U.S. Code. Traditionally, suits allege violations of the Fourth and Fourteenth Amendments. Police pursuits relate to the Fourth Amendment as to the citizens' rights against unreasonable seizures. The Fourteenth Amendment relates to citizens' right to treatment by governmental entities that is fundamentally fair.

DISCUSSION

Relevant Court Cases
Brower v. County of Inyo

The respondents in this case, which involved the use of police roadblocks to stop a fleeing vehicle, "allege the police acting under color of law, violated Brower's Fourth Amendment rights by effecting an unreasonable seizure using excessive force. Specifically, the complaint alleges that respondents placed an 18-wheel truck completely across the highway in the path of Brower's flight, behind a curve, with a police cruiser's headlights aimed in such fashion as to blind Brower on his approach."[15] The U.S. Supreme Court ruled in favor of Brower, which led many police agencies to restrict the use of roadblocks to stop fleeing vehicles. In its brief, the U.S. Supreme Court identified to the law enforcement community its interpretation of a seizure as it pertains to police pursuits. *Brower v. County of Inyo* states a seizure occurs "when there is a governmental termination of freedom of movement through means intentionally applied."[16]

Brower v. County of Inyo concerns an instance in which police activity brought about an intended result. The courts have rejected Fourth Amendment claims when action by the police during a pursuit brings about unintended results. Thus, third-party victims are not able to bring Fourth Amendment claims alleging unreasonable seizure arising from an action taken by police.

City of Canton, Ohio v. Harris

In its ruling in *City of Canton, Ohio v. Harris*, the U.S. Supreme Court dealt with another arena that directly affects law enforcement agencies and the duty to train employees.[17] Although this case did not involve a police pursuit, many subsequent cases involving pursuits mention it. The Court held that "the inadequacy of police training may serve as the basis for 1983 liability only where the failure to train amounts to deliberate indifference to the rights of persons with whom the police come into contact."[18]

Galas v. McKee

The U.S. Court of Appeals for the Sixth Circuit examined the issue of whether police agencies can use police pursuits to apprehend traffic violators. In *Galas v. McKee*, the court reviewed a case based in Nashville, Tennessee involving the police pursuit of a 13-year-old traffic violator.[19] On March 16, 1983, Officer McKee of the Metropolitan Nashville-Davidson County Police Department, observed a vehicle exceeding the speed limit. Officer McKee gave chase, which, at times, reached 100 miles per hour, on a police motorcycle. The pursuit culminated when the vehicle left the road and crashed. The driver sustained serious and life-long injuries. The district court ruled in favor of the police officer and the police department. The parents of the driver appealed the decision. The court of appeals held the following: "We conclude that the minimal intrusion on a traffic offender's Fourth Amendment right occasioned by the officers' participation in a high-speed pursuit does not out-weigh a longstanding police practice which we consider essential to a coherent scheme of police powers ... the use of high speed pursuits to apprehend traffic violators is not unreasonable and, thus, not violate of the Fourth Amendment."[20] Clearly, officers may engage in high-speed pursuits as an acceptable method to apprehend traffic violators. The court further reviewed the department's policy concerning traffic violators and police pursuits and held that, "The policy provides, at most, that officers may pursue, that is, follow, suspects. The policy of following traffic offenders who refuse to obey an officer's directive to pull to the side of the road does not infringe on the right to life."[21] This court affirmed the use of police pursuits to capture traffic violators.

Fagan v. City of Vineland

The U.S. Court of Appeals for the Third Circuit in *Fagan v. City of Vineland* reviewed a police pursuit, which resulted in the injury of several persons and the death of three others.[22] The court argued this case once, and then chose to reargue the case again to review the standard applied to police pursuits. On March 6, 1988, an officer with the City of Vineland, New Jersey, Police Department was on patrol when a vehicle with a t-top roof drove by. The car, which held several passengers, was not speeding, but a passenger in the vehicle was standing up through the roof. The officer intended to stop the vehicle to issue a warning concerning the person standing up and hanging out of the roof. At this point, no violation

or crime had occurred. When the officer activated his overhead lights to stop the vehicle, it began to pull away from the officer at speeds between 35 and 40 miles per hour. The vehicle failed to stop at several stop signs and began to increase in speed. A sergeant was notified and could have terminated the pursuit. In fact, the sergeant requested that the dispatch center contact the officer to find out why the officer was pursuing the vehicle. The officer never responded. The vehicle then increased its speed to between 70 and 80 miles per hour. Another officer attempted to block an intersection but the vehicle continued past the officer. The vehicle ran a red light and collided with a pickup truck resulting in a major crash. Two occupants in the pickup truck and one in the vehicle the officer had pursued were killed.

A federal civil lawsuit was initiated against the officers and the Vineland Police Department, including the chief of police. The plaintiffs argued that "the City and Police Chief violated section 1983 and the Fourteenth Amendment by following a policy of not properly training and supervising police officers in the conduct of high speed pursuits, and by following a policy of not enforcing the pursuit guidelines."[23] The lower court ruled in favor of the city and the police officers. The appeals court in *Fagan v. Vineland* reversed the judgment against the city stating, "A municipality can be liable under section 1983 and the Fourteenth Amendment for failure to train its police officers with respect to high speed automobile chases, even if no individual officer participating in the chase violated the Constitution."[24]

The complete Third Circuit re-argued the case under *Fagan v. Vineland* on only one issue.[25] The issue dealt with the legal standard to be applied to police pursuits. The majority ruled that the appropriate standard describes police behavior that "shocks the conscience." The dissenting opinion called for a lesser standard—"reckless or callous indifference." This latter standard, of course, represents a much lower threshold. The dissenting opinion was extensive in attempting to justify this lower standard in police pursuit cases. The majority, however, concluded that the police conduct in this case did not "shock the conscience" and ruled in favor of the police.

State courts have applied different standards in reviewing police pursuit cases. The Appellate Court of Illinois in *Nelson v. Thomas*[26] and *Urban v. Village of Lincolnshire*[27] referred to "wilful and wanton conduct." The Court of Appeals of Georgia in *Wilson v. City of Atlanta*[28] and *Thompson et al. v. Payne*[29] considered "whether, officer's act of pursuing suspect's vehicle was performed with requisite regard for safety of all persons." The District Court of Appeals of Florida in *Porter v. State Department of Agriculture* asked "if defendant's conduct creates foreseeable 'zone of risk' that poses general threat of harm to others and whether it was foreseeable that defendant's conduct would cause specific injury that actually occurred."[30] Clearly, prior to *Fagan*, federal courts had no clear direction from state courts in defining the standard by which to judge police behavior during pursuits.

County of Sacramento v. Lewis

In the U.S. Supreme Court decision in *County of Sacramento v. Lewis*,[31] the Court has clarified the federal standard that must be met by plaintiffs who allege police misconduct during vehicle pursuits. The Court held that "the issue in this case is whether a police officer violates the Fourteenth Amendment's guarantee of substantive due process by causing death through deliberate or reckless indifference to life in a high speed automobile chase aimed at apprehending a suspected offender. We answer no, and hold that in such circumstances only a purpose to cause harm unrelated to the legitimate object of arrest will satisfy the element of arbitrary conduct shocking to the conscience, necessary for a due process violation."[32]

On May 22, 1990, Sacramento County sheriff's deputies responded to a call regarding a fight. After handling the call, a motorcycle with a driver and a passenger approached the officers at a high rate of speed. The officers attempted to stop the motorcycle, but the driver chose to flee. A high-speed pursuit commenced with the vehicles reaching speeds of 100 miles per hour in a residential neighborhood. The pursuit ended when the motorcycle crashed. Unable to stop, the police vehicle ran over the passenger, who died at the scene. The district court ruled in favor of the police. The court of appeals reversed the decision based upon the standard of deliberate indifference. That court based its decision, in part, on the fact that the deputy violated his agency's general order concerning police pursuits. The Supreme Court held that the failure of the deputy to adhere to his agency's pursuit policy was irrelevant. This ruling, in effect, has given police agencies more protection from federal civil litigation generated by police pursuits.

Research and Review of Several Policies

Formal studies reflect that the general public believes police pursuits remain necessary for the apprehension of persons suspected of committing serious offenses, and that the need for pursuit to capture any offender should be balanced against the risk of danger to the innocent public.[33] These findings are consistent with the directives set forth in nine pursuit policies reviewed by the authors. Four of the agencies' policies and the IACP model policy can be characterized as judgmental, allowing pursuit for any offense as long as the danger to the officers and public created by the pursuit does not outweigh the necessity to capture the offender.[34] Three of the policies can be described as restrictive, based upon Alpert's definition[35] allowing pursuits only in the cases of felonies (one policy) or in the case of serious violent felonies (two policies).[36] One agency policy, of the West Midlands Police of Birmingham, England,[37] takes into account police driver proficiency as indicated by level of completion of a hierarchy of available driving courses. Depending upon current conditions and the seriousness of the offense, drivers who obtain advanced driving grades may pursue. All other drivers may pursue only in the event of serious, violent offenses.[38]

The Pennsylvania State Police, which has a "pursuit continuum" similar in many ways to the force continua that are components of many department use of force policies, characterizes another novel approach by an agency.[39] The Pennsylvania State Police Continuum provides clear direction for the consideration of supplementary tactics including the use of stop strips, roadblocks, induced stops, rolling roadblocks, ramming, and firearms.

Apparently few, if any, studies exist that attempt to determine if an offender, in deciding whether or not to flee, takes into account any chase prohibitions placed on officers by their agency's policy. Unfortunately, the often-heard argument against a restrictive policy states that once the members of a community learn that a local agency's policy prohibits pursuit except in the event of felonies, officers will suffer an increase in the number of offenders who choose to flee. While the empirical evidence in support of, or rebuttal against, this argument is insufficient, the anecdotal evidence suggests that such policies do not result in a change in the number of suspects who choose to flee.[40]

CONCLUSION

In *County of Sacramento v. Lewis*, the Supreme Court clearly defined the standard to be met when considering the liability of police agencies associated with vehicle pursuit. This standard is a much higher benchmark than previous rulings. However, this should not cause complacency.

Chief executive officers of every law enforcement agency must promulgate a written vehicle pursuit policy that provides clear guidance for that agency's officers. Such policy should include, at minimum, statements that officers will not continue pursuit once the risk of danger to the officer and public created by the pursuit exceeds the potential danger to the public should the suspect remain at large. Also, officers assessing the danger must consider the nature of the violation committed by the offender, as well as environmental conditions such as type of area, weather, and level of traffic congestion. Further, based upon the characteristics of the particular agency, the area it encompasses, and the people it serves, CEOs may desire to restrict pursuit to cases in which the offender has been involved in serious offenses. Additionally, CEOs also must heed state statutes and state-level court decisions applicable within their jurisdiction. Finally, although civil lawsuits likely will continue to be filed, CEOs can protect their agencies by proactively reassessing their agency's pursuit policy and providing adequate training regarding the policy and motor vehicle pursuit in general.

NOTES

1. R. G. Dunham, G. P. Alpert, D. J. Kenney, and P. Cromwell, "High-Speed Pursuit: The Offenders' Perspective," *Criminal Justice and Behavior*, (March 1998): 30–45; C. Eisenberg and C. Fitzpatrick, "An Alternative to Police Pursuits," *FBI Law Enforcement Bulletin*, August 1996, 16–19.

2. Supra note 1 (Eisenberg and Fitzpatrick).

3. *County of Sacramento v. Lewis* at 118 S. Ct. 1708 (1998).

4. The authors of this article reviewed pursuit policies of eight agencies, as well as the model policy of the International Association of Chiefs of Police (IACP). For an example of a model police pursuit policy, contact the IACP National Law Enforcement Policy Center, 515 North Washington Street, Alexandria, VA 22314-2357; telephone 800-THE-IACP; Web site: *http://www.theiacp.org/pubinfo/*.

5. G. P. Alpert, "A Factorial Analysis of Police Pursuit Driving Decisions: A Research Note," *Justice Quarterly*, June 1998, 348–359.

6. H. Nugent, E. F. Connors, J. T. McEwen, and L. Mayo, *Restrictive Policies for High-Speed Police Pursuits*, (Washington, DC: Institute of Law and Justice, Inc., 1988).

7. Ibid.

8. Supra note 5.

9. Supra note 5.

10. Supra note 4. All of the policies reviewed by the authors, as well as the model IACP policy, advised personnel of the environmental factors when making decisions related to pursuit.

11. J. M. MacDonald and G. P. Alpert, "Public Attitudes Toward Police Pursuit Driving," *Journal of Criminal Justice* 26 (1998), 185–194.

12. Ibid.

13. Supra note 1, (Dunham, Alpert, Kenney, and Cromwell).

14. Supra note 1, (Dunham, Alpert, Kenney, and Cromwell).

15. *Brower v. County of Inyo*, 109 S.Ct. 1378 (1989).

16. Ibid.

17. *City of Canton, Ohio v. Harris*, 109 S. Ct. 1197 (1989).

18. Ibid.

19. *Galas v. McKee*, 801 F.2d 200 (1986).

20. Ibid.

21. Ibid.

22. *Fagan v. City of Vineland*, 22 F.3d 1296 (C.A. 3 1994)(*en banc*).

23. *Fagan v. City of Vineland*, 22 F.3d 1283 (1994).

24. Ibid.

25. *Fagan v. City of Vineland*, 22 F.3d 1296 (1994).

26. *Nelson v. Thomas*, 668 N.E.2d 1109 (1996).

27. *Urban v. Lincolnshire*, 651 N.E.2d 683 (1995).

28. *Wilson v. City of Atlanta*, 476 S.E.2d 892 (1996).

29. *Thompson et al. v. Payne*, 453 S.E.2d 803 (1995).

30. *Porter v. State Department of Agriculture*, 689 So.2d 1152 (1997).

31. *County of Sacramento v. Lewis*, S.Ct. No. 96-1337 (1998); available from *http:// www.findlaw.com*; accessed on November 7, 2000.

32. Ibid.

33. Supra note 11.

34. "Operation of Sheriff's Office Vehicles," *Erie County Sheriff's Office General Orders Manual,* (unpublished, 1990), 1–6; "Emergency Vehicle Response/Pursuit," Marion County Sheriff's Office (unpublished, 1992), 1–10; "Police Pursuits, Legal Intervention, Road-blocks, Pennsylvania Police Pursuit Reporting System, and Pursuit Analysis," *Pennsylvania State Police Department Directives,* (unpublished 1996), 1–21; E. M. Sweeney, "Vehicular Pursuit: A Serious and Ongoing Problem," *Police Chief,* January 1997, 16–21; "Vehicular Pursuits," *Washington State Patrol Regulation Manual* (unpublished, 1999), 50–58.

35. Supra note 5.

36. "High Speed Pursuits," *City of Chesterfield Police Department General Orders Manual,* (unpublished, 1995), 1–5; "Vehicle Pursuit, Stop, Emergency Response, and Surveillance Driving," *Florida Department of Law Enforcement Policy Manual* (unpublished, 1999), 1–5; "Emergency Vehicle Operation/Vehicle Pursuit," *Odessa Police Department General Orders Manual* (unpublished, 2000), 1400–1406.

37. "Pursuit Policy," *West Midlands Police Departmental Directives* (unpublished, 1998), 1–12.

38. The number of the sample of agency policies revealed here is not large enough to be statistically valid as an indicator for which types of policies are most prevalent, nationally or internationally.

39. "Police Pursuits, Legal Intervention, Roadblocks, Pennsylvania Police Pursuit Reporting System, and Pursuit Analysis," *Pennsylvania State Police Department Directives* (unpublished, 1996), 1–21.

40. Supra note 11.

Minimizing Risk by Defining Off-Duty Police Misconduct

By Thomas Martinelli

When a professional sports team fails to make the playoffs year in and year out, sports pundits talk about their losing "locker room culture." Generally, in the sports environment this losing culture reflects a mindset of players in pursuit of individual statistics, a lack of coaching leadership, and an absence of organization-wide personal accountability requirements. A new coach must root out this culture in order to turn things around. But changing a culture that has been in place for years takes time and planning if subordinates are to buy into it. From a risk management perspective in police administration, a positive cultural change is worth the effort.

Instilling a culture of integrity in policing demands that an agency strive for a level of professionalism that demonstrates department-wide accountability through a written, comprehensive plan. This comprehensive plan must incorporate clearly written rules and regulations; a zealous implementation of these rules; and strict, swift, and uniform sanctions for any violations. At the very least, policy makers must draft a unique template of accountability for their own agencies, in order to avoid the costs of extended litigation, either from citizens or subordinates.

OFF-DUTY CONDUCT

Internal litigation and the costs associated with officer off-duty misconduct are not as easily manageable. For decades, police chiefs, arbitrators, and judges have had to wrestle with the disciplinary issues associated with off-duty misconduct. Generally, misconduct is considered to be an employee's noncompliance with the rules and regulations of the agency. Clearly, all off-duty *illegal* behavior committed by sworn personnel is unethical, but not all off-duty *unethical* behavior is illegal. An officer's termination for off-duty misconduct subjects an agency to the possibility of negative media coverage; long-term litigation costs; and allegations of corruption, mismanagement, agency cover-up, or administrative incompetence. A failure to educate subordinates regarding the agency's expectations of off-duty conduct could be defined as a neglect of duty on the part of the police administration.

Regulating off-duty officer behavior will always be a legal challenge, as there is a very fine line between balancing the organization's right not to employ an unethical officer versus the officer's right to off-duty privacy. The scales of justice dictate that courts weigh the differing interests of the parties before them and derive a fair and just resolution that benefits the majority's interests. Philosophically speaking, the majority's interest in policing must belong to the community the agency serves, not to the organization, individual officers, or the police union. A police agency that drafts and adheres to its own template of accountability demonstrates to its citizens, its employees, and the courts its commitment to provide professional police services by maintaining a level of integrity both professionally and personally.

Labor law, not unlike criminal law, seeks to define employee behavior that violates the rules and regulations of an organization. Mission statements, codes of ethics, and oaths of office provide all employees and policy makers with guidelines for an agency's expectations for both on- and off-duty behavior. Yet without clear and concise definitions of an agency's expectations, employees may never truly associate their own immoral off-duty behavior as noncompliant with an agency's expectations.

CONDUCT UNBECOMING AN OFFICER

Conduct unbecoming an officer is a charge used in policing to discipline officers for behavior that violates an agency's policies and expectations. The officer's perceived deviant behavior usually does not fit perfectly into an agency's rules and regulations, so administrators charge the offending officer with conduct unbecoming. It is used as a catch-all charge. Yet defining conduct unbecoming requires an approach similar to U.S. Supreme Court Justice Potter Stewart's attempt to define pornography in 1964—we'll know it when we see it.

One of the earliest Supreme Court cases that wrestled with this issue was *Parker, Warden, et al. v. Levy*.[1] In Parker, Dr. Levy was an Army captain who spoke out publicly against the Vietnam War. He urged African-American enlisted men to disobey orders to go to Vietnam and was successfully court-martialed on a variety of violations, the most serious charge being conduct unbecoming an officer and a gentleman.

The Supreme Court's majority opinion was that the military is a "specialized society separate from civilian society" with its own rules and a need for a higher standard of accountability. The Court quoted a previous case in saying, "… the rights of men in the armed forces must perforce be conditioned to meet certain overriding demands of discipline and duty

… ,"[2] suggesting that military personnel may have to sacrifice certain individual rights in order to accomplish the organization's mission. Soldiers should reasonably expect to be reprimanded or punished for engaging in unethical behavior while statutes, rules, and regulations are not only to punish, "but also to foster an orderly and dutiful fighting force."

The point is that soldiers, much like police officers, should know right from wrong and must live their lives, both professional and personal, in accordance with the higher standards and expectations of their agency. It is an honor and privilege to be employed as a soldier or police officer, and attached to that honor come certain unwritten expectations and a sacrifice of individual rights.

RISK MANAGEMENT AND OFF-DUTY MISCONDUCT

Managing risk in a police department includes minimizing officer misconduct that results in a loss of manpower hours, litigation costs, settlement payouts, and jury awards. For every police misconduct case found in written treatises, one can conclude that hours of internal investigations, paperwork, disciplinary hearings, and court appearances resulted in an appellate body reviewing that officer's alleged misconduct. It does not matter to this discussion whether the officer or the agency prevailed. The fact is that one off-duty misconduct case can cost taxpayers thousands of dollars that could have been better used. Proactive police supervision is managing risk.

The following examples of conduct unbecoming are not cited in order to imply they are the law of the land and must be followed; rather, they are cited as examples of what agencies have had to address regarding legal off-duty behavior by employees that was deemed unethical and resulted in litigation. The profile for off-duty conduct unbecoming cases is simple:

1. Alleged misconduct occurs while an officer is off duty.
2. The alleged misconduct is reported by a citizen, the media, or a fellow officer.

3. The allegation results in an internal investigation.
4. Charges are filed based on the chief's opinion that the behavior violated the organization's rules.
5. A disciplinary hearing results in the officer's discipline: days off without pay, reduction in rank, or termination.
6. A lawsuit is filed by the officer alleging a property loss resulting from the penalty for off-duty legal behavior.

Granted, not all officers terminated for off-duty misconduct file lawsuits. Of those that do file a suit and lose, not all appeal that ruling, and not all of these appeals make it to written treatises. But generally, the cases documented show that an agency can prevail if it can prove that there exists a nexus between legal off-duty misconduct and the officer's job performance and/or how it might affect the public's trust in the agency itself.

UNBECOMING OFF-DUTY DEMEANOR

Research of misconduct cases provides a seemingly endless list of scenarios that proved costly from a litigation standpoint, whether the department won or lost. For example, an appeals court upheld the suspension of an off-duty supervisor charged with conduct unbecoming an officer for using profanity and fighting with teenagers.[3] A state supreme court upheld the termination of an off-duty officer who verbally abused gays and created a disturbance.[4] A federal court upheld the 30-day suspension of an officer for his off-duty rude remarks to bank employees.[5] In these cases, the organization succeeded in demonstrating how employees' misconduct undermined the agency's mission statement.

In contrast, an appellate court overturned the termination of an assistant chief, charged with conduct unbecoming, for allegations that he associated with a known drug addict.[6] In another case, an arbitrator dismissed conduct unbecoming charges, ruling that in order for an employer to prevail in implementing an antifraternization policy, it must be in writing and disseminated throughout the agency.[7] A state supreme court ruled that an officer who exposed himself to other officers as part of fraternal banter was not guilty of unbecoming conduct within its definition.[8]

Without a written template of accountability, plaintiffs' attorneys can successfully persuade civil juries that chiefs abused their authority by acting in an arbitrary manner; such decisions result in costly judgments against departments. In labor law cases such as these, jurors must see a written plan, uniformly implemented, that demonstrates a chief's commitment to organizational accountability.

OFF-DUTY DEVIANT SEXUAL BEHAVIOR

The issue of sex and police has often resulted in internal litigation. Interestingly, police agencies often have a written policy that specifically prohibits officers from engaging in sex on duty—even though common sense would dictate that while on duty, police officers would restrain their sexual urges along with any other activities that waste taxpayer dollars. Sanctions for on-duty sex violations are generally a straightforward disciplinary matter, but disciplining officers for off-duty sexual behavior is a much grayer constitutional area.

Courts have struggled to balance an organization's public image and its need to foster an orderly and dutiful force with an officer's individual right to privacy while off duty. Over the years, costly litigation has still not provided clear-cut guidelines for agencies to follow.

For example, one court upheld an officer's three-day suspension for engaging in a "whipped cream race" with other officers while off duty, licking whipped cream off of a dancer's torso.[9] A federal court upheld the termination of an officer for an act of adultery in a public park while off duty, because such acts could jeopardize a department's effectiveness.[10] The U.S. Supreme Court declined to hear the appeal of an officer who was denied promotion because of his affair with the spouse of a fellow officer.[11]

Discipline was appropriate where there existed a nexus between the diminished effectiveness of an organization's service and an officer's videotaping his sexual activities with three women without their consent.[12] Appellate courts have sustained the termination of officers for off-duty "kinky sex" with prostitutes,[13] for consorting with prostitutes even though there was no payment of monies for sexual services,[14] and for being at an after-hours club, engaging in promiscuous relations with known prostitutes.[15] In these cases, the agencies successfully argued there was a rational basis between the proscribed conduct and the discipline meted out. As long as police have a valid "state objective" (i.e., the need to foster a professional force through accountability and maintenance of public image), reasonable disciplinary measures can be used to seek officer compliance in off-duty privacy situations.

AN EBAY CASE

Recently, the U.S. Supreme Court had to wrestle with the balance between discipline and off-duty privacy. An officer offered police equipment and uniforms for sale on the Internet auction site eBay, and in the adults-only section, he advertised a video of himself stripping off a nondescript police uniform and sexually stimulating himself.

An undercover internal-affairs investigator subsequently ordered one of the officer's custom videos. In the video, wearing a nondescript police uniform, the officer pretended to revoke a traffic ticket and stimulated himself. The department disciplined the officer for conduct unbecoming along with other charges and eventually terminated him after he continued to offer the adult tapes for sale when ordered not to do so.

The officer's lawyers sued his department alleging that his off-duty video sales were protected under his First Amendment right to free speech and was unrelated to his police work. The lower court upheld his termination. The Court of Appeals reversed it, however, ruling that the officer's off-duty speech was protected using a four-part test. The court decided that his off-duty behavior (1) had nothing to do with an internal workplace grievance, (2) took place while away from his employer's premises, (3) was unrelated to his employment, and (4) had no effect on the mission and purpose of the employer or had any adverse impact on the agency. The agency appealed.[16]

The Supreme Court reversed the Court of Appeals ruling, stating that the officer's speech did not fall under the protected category of being a matter of public concern. His production and sales activities did nothing to inform the public about the functioning, or dysfunction, of his agency. His expression was "widely broadcast, linked to his official status as a police officer, ... designed to exploit his employer's image[, and] ... detrimental to the mission and functions of the employer." His termination was upheld.[17]

Clearly this was a complex issue, or else the Supreme Court would have refused to hear the case. The facts of this case might lead reasonable police minds to agree that such off-duty officer behavior would warrant severe discipline, in some form. However, the purpose of this discussion is not to judge the officer's behavior or the agency's discipline; rather, the focus here is to emphasize the exorbitant litigation costs, manpower hours, and years spent proving that the agency was right. From such a perspective, the victory in this case appears empty: the agency won in court but at a high price to the taxpayers and the municipality.

RISK, RETALIATION, AND ABUSE OF AUTHORITY

A review of federal case law specifically addressing improprieties of chiefs and policy makers illustrates best that abuse of power can also prove costly, in terms of both finances and morale.

In one case, while a veteran officer's divorce was pending, an 18-year-old woman moved in with him, and he was terminated for conduct unbecoming an officer.[18] The officer successfully sued the department for violation of his First Amendment right to privacy and association. The court took exception to the fact that the investigation had no written guidelines and was not defined under any current policy. What the department defined as an "act of moral turpitude" was not in any written policy and in fact largely depended upon the personal standards of the particular police commissioner at the time.

The court wrestled with the First Amendment right to association and stressed that a department cannot violate an employee's zone of privacy in its attempt to regulate legal off-duty behavior of its employees in the furtherance of its own missions. The court acknowledged that some areas of personal sexual activity that may impact the officer's job performance could be considered, but a nexus between misconduct and job performance must be well documented and clearly evident.

A similar case dealt with a decorated veteran sergeant with an exemplary record. His divorce was pending, and his living arrangement with a single woman became the focus of an internal investigation after the chief reportedly received anonymous complaints from the community.[19] The investigation resulted in the sergeant's suspension, demotion, and eventual resignation.

In finding the chief, the city, and city board members liable for the deprivation of the sergeant's constitutionally protected rights to privacy and association, the court discussed the same zone of privacy and the need to establish a nexus between legal off-duty behavior and job performance. However, rather than basing its decision on the absence of standards of investigation or the lack of written policies, in this case the court found the chief's motivations to be purely malicious and vindictive.

Through discovery it was revealed that the chief held a personal grudge against the sergeant and was determined to destroy his career. Apparently the two men had had unresolved conflicts years earlier, and neither held the values of the other in high regard. In addition, the court learned that prior to the chief's appointment, the sergeant openly supported one of the other applicants for the open position.

To make matters worse, the court noted that one of the chief's lieutenants investigating the case was married but not yet divorced and was openly dating another woman. The lieutenant received only a written reprimand in his file for this infraction. Needless to say, the court ruled that the sergeant's attorney fees and costs of litigation were to be paid by the city and its taxpayers. The officer was reinstated to his sergeant's rank and was awarded full back pay, and the matter was expunged from his personnel file.

Defense allegations of administrative retaliation occasionally surface in police disciplinary matters, and when they are proven, the morale of a department's members suffers greatly. In a recent case, officers who unsuccessfully challenged their municipalities' residency requirement in court were terminated shortly thereafter.[20] They sued their department for retaliation. The appellate court noted that after investigating 25 city employees for violating the residency requirement, the city terminated only five officers— all of whom were parties to the residency lawsuit.

The court found that the city halfheartedly attempted to collect residency data from all city employees, and no employee was ever previously disciplined or terminated for violating the policy. Additional evidence suggested that other city employees who violated the policy, some of whom were police officers that did *not* partake in the prior lawsuit, were not disciplined. For these reasons, the court allowed the retaliation lawsuit to proceed to trial, and the community's taxpayers picked up the tab. This case illustrates that selective discipline, as well as policies that are poorly written or poorly executed, can result in costly internal litigation that can easily be avoided.

DRAFTING A TEMPLATE OF ACCOUNTABILITY

To reinforce an agency's culture of integrity and to provide for a long-term foundation of professionalism, a chief must first develop a written strategy to convince subordinates of the necessity of such a culture. When developing a template of accountability, police executives should be mindful that catchphrases can be unpopular with current employees. For example, employees most likely will resent a template title of "creating a culture of integrity" because it presupposes that one does not already exist, or never existed, in their agency. The objective in developing the template of accountability is getting all employees to buy into the strategy, not to offend current hardworking employees.

A critical element for the accountability template is appropriate training.[21] A specific training program on accountability, ethics, and integrity should be a part of every department's educational plan, and an ethics component should be a part of every training module. An ethics discussion can easily be integrated into training on topics such as evidence handling, interviewing, use of force, report writing, testifying, and a host of other subjects.

When designing specific ethics and integrity training programs, chiefs should remember that programs must incorporate both individual and team accountability concepts. Training using scenarios, case law, and arbitration awards can provide clear examples to employees and can illustrate the meaning of the IACP code of ethics and oath of honor as well as the agency's mission and value statements.[22] The ethics accountability training must be provided on an annual basis and must be updated regularly as policing continues to evolve. Case law examples and zone-of-privacy issues in the law will change just as the technology used by departments changes.

For years, police ethicists have espoused the need for ethical behavior to start at the top. Such a mandate dictates that a chief's actions minimize internal litigation, which is a cancer on an organization. As shown, retaliatory discipline, zone-of-privacy cases, and disciplinary sanctions for off-duty behavior with no nexus to job performance are costly, in terms of both finances and morale. Perceptions of favoritism, nepotism, or discipline with malice will only repel subordinates from any administrative attempts to instill accountability and will empower plaintiff attorneys to sue the department.

IACP MODEL POLICIES

There is no need to reinvent the wheel when researching and writing a template of accountability. IACP model policies regarding employee misconduct and a *Police Chief* article on shared responsibility are the best starting points.[23] Plaintiffs' attorneys will have no legal recourse when one cites these well-conceived authorities as a resource, during deposition or trial testimony.

The concept of shared responsibility dictates that each member of an agency has a duty to report and prevent colleague misconduct, including off-duty misconduct. Off-duty misbehavior reflects poorly on

the entire agency's public image when reported in the media and diminishes the public's trust in the agency. Drafting concise policies that address conduct unbecoming an officer and organizational expectations of off-duty behavior is the first step in the accountability template.

Educating officers on the content of department policies and the organization's expectations behind these policies is critical. Discussing the off-duty problems for which others have been disciplined can only benefit an agency and can supply a chief with an ample due-process defense in civil court. Failing to educate officers on the organization's definition of off-duty misconduct leaves the door open for juries to answer for themselves the meaning behind the policy and its implementation. When chiefs testify that their training methods highlight the department's own examples of off-duty violations and the resulting discipline, coupled with case law and arbitration examples, it demonstrates a written plan of commitment to agency-wide accountability. Professional police organizations must zealously police themselves, and a written philosophy of proactive prevention, ingrained in an agency's members, is a proactive defense.

PERCEPTIONS OF A CHIEF'S INTEGRITY

For subordinates to buy into a culture of ethics and integrity, employees and their unions must trust in the chief's own integrity as well as that of the agency's internal-affairs division. (The popular-entertainment media have often portrayed internal-affairs investigators as administrative dupes out to burn good cops. Citizens who serve on juries have been exposed to this backward mentality for years by watching movies and television shows.) Prepared with written guidelines for internal-affairs investigations, chiefs can successfully defend their disciplinary decisions and the agency itself if they have demanded consistently that internal investigations be conducted fairly, without personal bias, and with a sense of balance between individual privacy and organizational compliance. When officers perceive that they are treated fairly in disciplinary matters, internal distrust is minimized, and the organization benefits as a whole.

FOCUS ON THE TEAM

A chief must set team goals focused on reducing litigation costs by minimizing both employee and citizen lawsuits. If chiefs can demonstrate tangible savings to their city administration as part of their efforts to reduce litigation costs, those savings can be reallocated toward more critical agency needs. This is the core foundation for the employee "buy-in" strategy. By educating the rank and file of the organizational benefits of litigation reduction, police administrators can motivate and encourage officers to police each other on matters of ethics, both on and off duty. This requires not only the perception but the reality that the administration provides complete support to whistle-blowers.

Coaches are replaced for their failure to change a losing culture; similarly, chiefs have been replaced for their inability to achieve organizational accountability. In today's litigious society, a chief's job description also entails minimizing an agency's liability, internally as well as externally. By educating employees on the organizational expectations of their off-duty behavior, the chief can provide officers with a winning plan that benefits all interested parties.

NOTES

1. *Parker, Warden, et al. v. Levy*, 417 U.S. 731 (1974).
2. Ibid., quoting *Burns v. Wilson*, 346 U.S. 137, 140 (1953).
3. *Eilers v. Civil Service Commission*, 544 N.W. 2d 463 (Iowa App. 1995).
4. *Green v. City of Sioux Falls*, 607 N.W. 2d 43, S.D. Lexis 30 (2000).
5. *Harper v. Crockett*, 868 F. Supp. 1557 (E.D. Ark. 1994).
6. *Flosi v. Board of Fire and Police Commissioners of Rock Falls*, 582 N.E. 2d 185 (Ill. App. 1991).
7. *Monterey County and Individual Grievant*, CSMCS No. ARB-01-0050, 117 LA (BNA) 897 (2002).
8. *Pa. St. Police v. Pa. St. Troopers (Betancourt)* 656 A.2d 83, 540 Pa. 66 (1995).
9. *Shankle v. Bell*, U.S. District Court for the Western District of Penn., No. 2:04cv1885 (2006).
10. *Faust v. Police Civ. Serv. Commission*, 347 A.2d 765 (1983).
11. *Henry v. City of Sherman*, 117 S.Ct. 1098 (1997).
12. *Doe v. Department of Justice*, #CH-0752-04-0620-I-2, 2006 MSPB (2006).
13. *Freeman v. City of Mobile*, 590 So.2d 331 (Ala. Civ. App. 1991).
14. *Ruiz v. Brown*, 579 N.Y.S. 2d 47 (1992).
15. *Richter v. Civil Service Commission of Philadelphia*, 387 A.2d 131 (1978).
16. *Roe v. City of San Diego*, 356 F.3d 1108 (2004).
17. *City of San Diego v. John Roe*, 543 U.S. 77 (2004), no. 03-1669.
18. *Shuman v. City of Philadelphia*, 470 F. Supp. 449 (1979).
19. *Swope v. Bratton*, 541 F. Supp. 99 (1982).
20. *Phyllis Hill, et al. v. City of Scranton, et al.*, 2005 U.S. App. LEXIS 10709.
21. See Tag Gleason, "Ethics Training for Police," *The Police Chief* 73 (November 2006): 58–61.
22. See International Association of Chiefs of Police, "Achieving and Maintaining High Ethical Standards: IACP's Four Universal Ethics Documents," *The Police Chief* 69 (October 2002): 64–70.
23. See International Association of Chiefs of Police, *National Law Enforcement Policy Center Model Policy: Standards of Conduct*, October 1998, www.theiacp.org/profassist/ethics/model_policy.htm, April 18, 2007; and Patricia A. Robinson, "Shared Responsibility: The Next Step in Professional Ethics," *The Police Chief* 71 (August 2004): 76–81.

Civil Rights and Law Enforcement Intelligence

By David Carter and Thomas Martinelli

Since the terrorist attacks of September 11, 2001, many state, local, and tribal law enforcement agencies have reestablished and reengineered their intelligence capacity largely through guidance provided by the National Criminal Intelligence Sharing Plan, the Law Enforcement Intelligence Unit file guidelines, and various intelligence training programs developed under the sponsorship of the Bureau of Justice Assistance[1] and the Department of Homeland Security Office of Grants and Training.[2] While all of these intelligence programs include instruction on the constitutional guidelines regarding civil rights protections, new challenges are emerging that pose renewed concerns about past abuses.

In particular, there is increasing concern about the Information Sharing Environment,[3] the product of the Intelligence Reform and Terrorism Prevention Act of 2004 (IRTPA). Based largely on the recommendations of the 9/11 Commission Report,[4] this legislation is designed to maximize information sharing among all levels of government, including the sharing of terrorism information between the intelligence community and state, local, and tribal law enforcement agencies. The reason, of course, was to ensure that U.S. law enforcement agencies would have the information and the ability to detect an emerging terrorist threat in time to stop it. Although the goal of protecting the United States from terrorism is a noble one, critics of the legislation felt it went too far.

LEARNING FROM HISTORY

Some previous law enforcement intelligence activities have been criticized for trespassing on citizens' rights. Critics of law enforcement intelligence cite the history of police organizations collecting and retaining information on citizens based on their affiliations, beliefs, pronouncements, and other noncriminal attributes. As evidenced by a myriad of previous lawsuits, these abuses did occur in the past.[5] Unfortunately, today's critics do not recognize the many changes that have occurred in law enforcement practices or the professional nature of law enforcement intelligence. Higher educational standards, better training, adoption of ethical standards, and inculcation of law enforcement as a profession all indicate that the culture of law enforcement has changed, rejecting past practices that contributed to abuses of intelligence activities.

Beyond this history, it should be recognized that the public has a general misconception about the function of law enforcement intelligence; they envision it as involving spying, surreptitious activities, and acquisition of information by stealth. The public, including the media, needs to be reassured that law enforcement intelligence processes will strictly observe individual constitutional protections when collecting and retaining information. Moreover, the public should understand that intelligence analysis is simply the scientific approach to problem solving, similar to the way it has been effectively used in community policing. The difference, however, is that community policing focuses on crime and community disorder, whereas intelligence focuses on methods that may be used to prevent criminal threats from reaching fruition. Generally speaking, critics do not disapprove of using intelligence gathering and analysis to combat terrorism or solve crimes; rather, they demand simply that it be conducted in accordance with the constitutional parameters law enforcement officers are duty-bound to follow.

Commenting on the opening of the Massachusetts intelligence fusion center,[6] the American Civil Liberties Union (ACLU) of Massachusetts issued a press release with concerns that illustrate the need for public education on law enforcement intelligence gathering, expressing concern about the center's role and activities: "We need a lot more information about what precisely the fusion center will do, what information they will be collecting, who will have access to the information, and what safeguards will be put in place to prevent abuse."[7]

The concerns outlined by the Massachusetts ACLU are easily answerable. By simply providing this information to the community, through a public information document or in town hall presentations, a great deal of conflict, criticism, and cynicism can be avoided. Fear of the unknown generates citizen consternation, which translates into mistrust and allegations of abuse of authority. Clear, well-drafted civil rights protection policies pertaining to intelligence operations should be mandatory for agencies of any size that engage in intelligence gathering.

FOCAL POINTS OF CONCERN

In addressing these civil-rights issues, three primary areas of concern emerge:

- The information in a criminal-intelligence records system must be collected and retained in a proper manner, both legally and ethically.
- Individual privacy rights must be protected for all information that has been collected and retained.
- The integrity of data quality and data security must be ensured.

Although there are additional intelligence issues that have civil-rights implications, these three are among the most fundamental and challenging.[8]

Proper collection and retention of information in a criminal-intelligence records system: The authority of state, local, and tribal law enforcement agencies to participate in any type of intelligence operations lies in their statutory authority to enforce criminal law. As such, any information collected and retained in a criminal-intelligence records system must be based on a criminal predicate. That is, a relationship must be demonstrated between individuals identified in criminal intelligence records and criminal behavior. The level of that relationship is more than mere suspicion; reasonable grounds must be articulated to link suspected individuals to specific criminal behavior.

Protection of privacy for all collected and retained information: Ensuring that information about individuals is collected and retained with a proper legal basis constitutes one form of civil-rights protection. Formulating an explicit privacy policy helps to achieve this goal. A privacy policy is a published statement that articulates the policy position of an organization on how it handles the identifying personal information it gathers and uses in the normal course of business.[9] Law enforcement agencies must have mechanisms in place—including proper training, policies, procedures, supervision, and discipline—to make certain that identifying information is not disseminated to anyone who does not have the right or the need to access it. A privacy policy ensures the implementation of proper safeguards as long as the policy incorporates a clearly defined process of discipline, demonstrating strict, swift, and certain sanctions for any sworn department members who fail to strictly comply with the policy's provisions.

Ensuring the integrity of data quality and data security: Preserving the quality of data involves procedural mechanisms to ensure that raw information is collected and recorded in a valid, reliable, and objective manner. Ensuring data quality means maximizing the accuracy of raw information used in the intelligence records system. Preserving the security of data requires processes and mechanisms to ensure that individuals cannot access a given piece of information who do not have the lawful right and need to do so. Security measures reinforce the procedural processes of individual privacy protections without divulging the substance of the intelligence gathered. Giving procedure priority over substance is a broad policy philosophy that can be shared with the community to quell mistrust, without jeopardizing an agency's efforts to protect the quality of data retrieved.

STEPS TO ENSURE THE PROTECTION OF CITIZENS' CIVIL RIGHTS

Several mechanisms may be implemented to address the concerns of intelligence critics and ensure that civil-rights protections remain intact. By taking the following steps, an agency assures the public that it has made a reasonable effort to comply with the latest Supreme Court rulings pertaining to best police practices in accordance with the increased need for police vigilance in the post—September 11 era.

Step One—Policy: Every law enforcement agency should implement a privacy policy, a security policy, and an accepted-records management policy, such as those found in the Law Enforcement Intelligence Unit file guidelines.[10] Relying on policy models and policy development processes recommended by the Global Intelligence Working Group has a twofold advantage. First, it demonstrates to the community that the law enforcement agency has an intelligence policy foundation consistent with nationally recognized standards. Second, in the case of a lawsuit, following such recommendations can be used as an affirmative defense that the agency's policies are consistent with professionally recognized good practices.

Step Two—Training: Training has three fundamental levels. First, every agency should follow the recommendations of the National Criminal Intelligence Sharing Plan, which include an intelligence awareness training program for all officers.[11] Second, beyond these training standards, appropriate personnel within an agency should receive training on agency policy and fusion center policy related to all aspects of the intelligence function. Special attention should be devoted to collection, retention, and dissemination of intelligence as well as special issues such as suspicious-activity reports, intelligence related to juveniles, and other unique forms of information. Finally, sworn personnel must appreciate the gravity of constitutional-rights violations resulting from improper intelligence gathering. Not unlike other critical issues in policing, a "zero-tolerance policy" toward such infractions is mandatory. Such a policy demonstrates to law enforcement personnel as well as the community that an agency takes civil-rights violations very seriously and will take immediate disciplinary action against violators.

Step Three—Supervision: Good policy and training are only part of the equation—an agency must also ensure compliance with policies and procedures as intended. When systemic accountability and uniformity in meting out appropriate discipline are lacking, officers can misinterpret or otherwise fail to follow policy. Street-level supervisors must be vigilant in supporting their agency's commitment to constitutional policing and must hold their subordinates to the highest standards of the profession, especially when dealing with intelligence gathering. When investigators uncover patterns and practices of civil-rights violations over a period of time, plaintiffs' attorneys simply have to demonstrate to juries that street-level supervisors, as well as their supervisors, knew or should have known of these violations and deliberately chose not to take disciplinary action. Deliberate indifference has proven to be very costly for law enforcement agencies that have opted to look the other way when citizens, or officers, have reported possible civil-rights violations.[12]

Step Four—Public Education: A critical element of successful law enforcement intelligence is informing the public of law enforcement intelligence initiatives. There are two critical reasons for doing so. The first, as noted earlier regarding the ACLU's concerns, is simply to educate the public about the intelligence process. This helps to eliminate false assumptions and second-guessing. Much of the lay public assumes that law enforcement agencies perform some type of widespread clandestine information collection and operate in a manner similar to the national intelligence community. Correcting this misperception can go a long way toward developing positive support for the law enforcement intelligence process.

The second benefit to public education is to inform citizens of the signs and symbols of terrorism so that they can assist in the information collection process. For example, the Regional Community Policing Institute at Wichita State University, Wichita, Kansas, conducted a trial program in association with various Kansas police departments, providing community training on what to look for and how to report information regarding possible terrorist threats. Those attending the training were provided with a document called "Observe—Document—Report," describing how to recognize suspicious behavior, what to document, and how to report observations to law enforcement. This model also helps citizens feel that they can contribute to the security of their own community and helps minimize the level of distrust toward agencies' efforts to combat crime and terrorism.

Step Five—Transparent Processes: The processes of the intelligence function, like all other aspects of a U.S. law enforcement agency, should be clearly understood and transparent. Whereas certain information used for intelligence purposes must be secured, the process by which that information is used must be open. Critics of law enforcement intelligence argue that the intelligence process is too secretive and that agencies have committed widespread spying on citizens.[13] Agencies can counter this argument

successfully by being open and transparent about the inner workings of their intelligence processes, including their relationships with other organizations, such as fusion centers. Without divulging the substance of intelligence records, such efforts can help citizens to appreciate and support intelligence gathering.

Step Six—Accountability Audits: Periodic internal audits of intelligence processes should be mandatory within any agency. It is helpful to follow a two-step process. First, a supervisor or manager reviews and documents intelligence processes following a recognized checklist of variables and writes an inspection report.[14] After the completion of this report, an external auditor—a balanced, independent party such as a retired judge or other respected individual—reviews the report and asks challenging questions of both the author of the report and the agency's chief executive. It is important that the agency view the audit as a positive process designed to identify rectifiable weaknesses. An audit can proactively ensure that all aspects of the process are operating as constitutionally mandated. It can identify unforeseen problems and serve as affirmative evidence that the agency is operating in good faith and without malice.

Step Seven—Assistance of Legal Counsel: Case law, as it pertains to police misconduct, relies on police best-practice concepts such as good faith, reasonableness, and discretion without malice when judging an officer's conduct in hindsight. Juries typically prefer not to find officers guilty for their alleged misdeeds or policy violations and, more times than not, will give the officers the benefit of the doubt. But without clearly drafted policies, in-depth training scenarios, and evidence of an organization's strict compliance with constitutional law issues, an agency's legal counsel may find it difficult to defend against allegations of civil-rights violations in a court of law.

Competent legal counsel may be the best preventive measure agencies can take to avoid litigation involving allegations of civil-rights violations. Whether a sole practitioner or the department insurance carrier's legal counsel, an attorney well versed in municipal law, Section 1983 actions,[15] and police misconduct cases can assist with the drafting of the agency's privacy and security policies as well as the formulation of the processes for intelligence gathering and analysis.

THE FUTURE

In the evolving world of law enforcement intelligence, driven increasingly by fusion centers and the information sharing environment, law enforcement executives face new challenges in managing sensitive information and intelligence. As intelligence gathering becomes standard practice for agencies at all levels, the practice will draw greater scrutiny from civil-rights activists to ensure that information is collected, retained, and disseminated by law enforcement agencies in a lawful and ethical manner. Professional law enforcement has both the knowledge and the tools to accept the responsibility of preserving citizens' civil rights while protecting the community. Ensuring that law enforcement intelligence processes and tools are transparent and accounted for places them in the proper perspective for the future protection of civil rights.

David L. Carter, Ph.D., is a professor of criminal justice at Michigan State University (MSU) and the director of the MSU Intelligence Program. Dr. Carter manages several intelligence training grants from the Department of Homeland Security, is a member of the Department of Justice Intelligence Training Coordination Working Group, and is the author of the Community Oriented Policing Services (COPS)—funded book Law Enforcement Intelligence: A Guide for State, Local, and Tribal Law Enforcement Agencies.

Thomas J. Martinelli, J.D., M.S., is an adjunct professor at Wayne State University and an attorney who researches and writes about police misconduct issues. Mr. Martinelli trains police agencies in ethics and liability issues and is a member of the IACP's Police Image and Ethics Committee.

NOTES

1. Programs include the Criminal Intelligence for the Chief Executive (CICE) course, the State and Local Anti-Terrorism Training (SLATT) program, and the Criminal Intelligence Commanders course that is in preparation as of this writing. See the SLATT program Web site (slatt.org) for details.

2. Most notable among these programs is the Intelligence Toolbox Training Program. See the program's Web site (intellprogram.msu.edu) for details.

3. See "Program Manager, Information Sharing Environment," http://www.ise.gov .

4. National Commission on Terrorist Attacks upon the United States, *The 9/11 Commission Report: Final Report of the National Commission on Terrorist Attacks upon the United States* (New York: Norton, 2004).

5. See Frank J. Donner, *Protectors of Privilege: Red Squads and Police Repression in Urban America* (Berkeley and Los Angeles: University of California Press, 1990).

6. For more information on fusion centers, see Peter A. Modafferi and Kenneth A. Bouche, eds., "Efforts to Develop Fusion Center Intelligence Standards," *The Police Chief* 72 (February 2005): 47–53.

7. American Civil Liberties Union, "ACLU of Massachusetts Questions Scope of Fusion Center Activities," press release, Boston, Massachusetts, May 11, 2005, http://www.aclum.org/news/05.11.05.Fusion.pdf, April 26, 2007.

8. It should be noted that these issues concern only information and records that identify individuals. Aggregate information that describes trends, collective behaviors, philosophies, methodologies, or other information that is useful for the intelligence process but does not identify individuals is not afforded the same privacy protections. The Bill of Rights was added to the U.S. Constitution to protect individual citizens' rights, not intangible group rights such as methodologies or trends.

9. Global Justice Information Sharing Initiative, *Privacy Policy Development Guide and Information Templates* (Washington, D.C.: Office of Justice Programs, U.S. Department of Justice, n.d.), 4-1.

10. Law Enforcement Intelligence Unit, *Criminal Intelligence File Guidelines* (n.p., March 2002), http://it.ojp.gov/documents/LEIU_Crim_Intell_File_Guidelines.pdf, April 23, 2007.

11. Intelligence training resources can be found at the following Web sites: http://slatt.org, http://www.counterterrorismtraining.gov, and http://intellprogram.msu.edu.

12. Thomas J. Martinelli and Joycelyn M. Pollock, "Law Enforcement Ethics, Lawsuits, and Liability: Defusing Deliberate Indifference," The Police Chief 67 (October 2000): 52–57.

13. As an illustration, the reader is encouraged to conduct an Internet search of the phrase *spy files*; the results will provide insight on the breadth of concern about the intelligence process as well as the issues of concern for many citizens.

14. Two examples of intelligence audit checklists can be found in the appendices of David L. Carter, *Law Enforcement Intelligence*: A Guide for State, Local, and *Tribal Law Enforcement Agencies* (n.p.: U.S. Department of Justice, Office of Community Oriented Policing Services, November 2004), intellprogram.msu.edu/Carter_Intelligence_Guide.pdf, April 23, 2007, and Law Enforcement Intelligence Unit, *Audit Checklist for the Criminal Intelligence Function* (n.p., September 2004), http://it.ojp.gov/documents/LEIU_audit_checklist.pdf, April 23, 2007.

15. *Civil Rights Act* of 1871, 42 U.S.C. 1983 (1996).

Sexual Harassment by Supervisors

By Lisa Baker

Since 1976, Title VII of the Civil Rights Act[1] has been interpreted as supporting a cause of action on the part of employees against their employers for harm caused by unwelcomed conduct of a sexual nature.[2] This presents employers with a complex dynamic in which they must navigate with employees. On the one hand, efforts should be made to prevent improper sexual conduct and, if it occurs, to remedy the situation. On the other hand, Title VII does not mandate a workplace that is gender neutral. The U.S. Supreme Court itself has recognized that the antidiscrimination provisions within Title VII do not prohibit "genuine but innocuous differences in the ways men and women routinely act with members of the same sex and of the opposite sex … simple teasing, offhand comments, and isolated incidents (unless extremely serious) will not amount to [discrimination]."[3] Accordingly, the types of conduct that constitute actionable sexual harassment have been narrowly construed. As stated by the Supreme Court, "[w]e have made it clear that conduct must be extreme to amount to a change in the terms, conditions and privileges of employment."[4] However, recognizing the impact improper sexual conduct can have on the well-being of employees and work performance, the Court has taken a hard line when it comes to the accountability of the employer when supervisors engage in improper sexual conduct with respect to subordinate employees.

This article discusses the extent to which employers may be liable for the improper sexual conduct of supervisors. This includes how, in some cases, the employer may not even have the opportunity to offer a defense to liability.

WHAT IS SEXUAL HARASSMENT?

The conduct that falls within the ambit of Title VII of the Civil Rights Act must first of all be conduct that occurs because of one's sex. Conduct may be vulgar, hostile, and offensive, but unless the plaintiff is able to establish that it is conduct motivated because of the plaintiff's sex, it is not actionable under Title VII as "sexual harassment."[5] For example, in *Succar v. Dade County*,[6] a schoolteacher brought a sexual harassment claim against his school district alleging that it failed to eliminate a hostile environment caused by a co-worker with whom he had terminated a relationship. He claimed that she demeaned and ridiculed him and otherwise subjected him to a hostile environment. The circuit court agreed with the lower court's conclusion that the conduct was not because he was a male but, rather, a result of the acrimonious end to their relationship.[7]

Related to the requirement that the harassment be because of the gender of the person, as opposed to the sex being merely coincidental, is the Supreme Court's ruling in *Oncale v. Sundowner Offshore Services*.[8]

In this case, the Supreme Court held that same-sex harassment also is covered by Title VII when it is established that the offensive conduct was directed at the victim because of the person's sex.

Traditionally, once the conduct was determined to be based on gender, it then would be categorized as either quid pro quo sexual harassment or hostile work environment. While these terms are not found within Title VII of the Civil Rights Act, their role in determining whether an employer should be held liable became well established.[9]

Quid Pro Quo Sexual Harassment

Quid pro quo sexual harassment is predicated upon a showing by employees that their response to unwelcome sexual advances was subsequently used as the basis for a tangible employment action.[10] Establishing a link between the unwelcome, improper sexual conduct and the employer's action is crucial to proving quid pro quo sexual harassment.

Hostile Work Environment

The extent to which Title VII of the Civil Rights Act encompasses hostile conduct arising in the work environment has been well recognized since the U.S. Supreme Court's decision in *Meritor Savings Bank, FSB v. Vinson*.[11] In *Meritor*, the Supreme Court stated that the conduct, first of all, must be unwelcomed, and then emphasized that it must be so severe and pervasive as to "alter the conditions of [the victim's] employment and create an abusive working environment."[12]

An in-depth study of what specific behaviors and actions would create a hostile environment is not within the scope of this article. However, a few general principles have been offered to aid in assessing whether conduct has crossed the line. First, the Supreme Court has held that to be actionable under Title VII, a sexually objectionable environment must not be only objectionable in the eyes of a victim but a reasonable person of that gender also must conclude that it would be objectionable.[13] In addition, all of the circumstances surrounding the conduct should

be considered, including the frequency of the objectionable conduct, its severity, whether it is physically threatening or humiliating or simply utterances or gestures, and whether it interferes with the victim's ability to work.[14]

Employers have been held to a strict standard of liability, referred to as vicarious liability, for the sexually harassing conduct of supervisors, enabling employees alleging they were the victims of sexual harassment to hold employers liable without the need to establish knowledge or constructive knowledge of the offending conduct and failure to remedy it on the part of the employer. If the nature of the sexual harassment was quid pro quo, the employer had no defense to the claim. If it was hostile environment harassment, the employer still was vicariously liable but could assert a defense by proving it had preventive and corrective policies in place and establishing that the victim employee unreasonably failed to take advantage of the policies. While the terms *quid pro quo* and *hostile environment* still have significance when discussing sexual harassment, as a result of recent Supreme Court cases, their role in establishing employer liability for sexually harassing conduct engaged in by supervisors has diminished.

LIABILITY FOR HARASSMENT

In 1998, the U.S. Supreme Court handed out decisions in two sexual harassment cases, *Burlington Industries, Inc., v. Ellerth*[15] and *Faragher v. City of Boca Raton*,[16] retaining the vicarious liability standard for the harassing conduct engaged in by supervisory employees but bringing an end to consideration of the type of harassment as determining whether the employer may assert a defense to liability. As a result of these cases, employers are vicariously liable for the sexually harassing conduct of their supervisors vis-à-vis subordinate employees regardless of whether the employer knew of the conduct and regardless of what type of sexual harassment is involved. However, the Supreme Court ruled that in cases where the harassment culminates in a tangible employment action, the employer is vicariously liable regardless of whether the employer had preventive anti-harassment policies in place and regardless of whether the employer took remedial action once learning of the conduct.[17]

Rationale for Vicarious Liability

Given the significance of applying vicarious liability as the appropriate standard as opposed to negligence which would require a showing of knowledge on the part of the employer, it is important to understand which employees within the organization may subject their employer to this harsher standard and under what circumstances. The answer to this is not as easy as simply identifying who acts as the supervisor of the victim employee. In *Ellerth*, the Supreme Court provided guidance in determining who may subject the employer to vicarious liability for engaging in sexually offensive conduct by directing that the focus should be on whether the offending employee was aided in the misconduct because of his or her position with the employer. In other words, the victim is in a more vulnerable position because of the authority granted or delegated to the offender.[18]

In most civil actions involving claims against an employer for harm caused by employees, the employer is subject to liability for the harm caused by the employee provided the employee was acting within the scope of employment.[19] Thus, liability often is created by a combination of the employment relationship and the conduct causing the harm occurring within the scope of the employee's duties. In the context of sexual harassment, the Supreme Court rejected the notion that this analysis should dictate the outcome as sexual harassment by a supervisory employee if it is not generally within the scope of employment. Instead, the Supreme Court held that the appropriate analysis centers on whether the employees alleged to have engaged in the offensive conduct were aided due to their relationship to the employer or because of the delegation of authority through the employment relationship.[20] The Supreme Court further commented that in cases involving a tangible employment action, the agency relationship or delegation of authority is evident because of the existence of the employment action itself. In other words, it is attributable to an official action of the agency. As stated by the Supreme

Court, "[t]he supervisor has been empowered by the company as a distinct class of agent to make economic decisions affecting other employees under his or her control."[21]

When no tangible employment action results, the relationship between the offender and the employer is not so apparent. Therefore, the employer still is vicariously liable but is able to interpose a defense by showing it had antiharassment preventive and corrective policies in place that the victim employee unreasonably failed to take advantage of. As stated by the Supreme Court:

> [A] tangible employment action taken by the supervisor becomes for Title VII purposes the act of the employer. ... Whether the agency relation aids in the commission of supervisor harassment which does not culminate in a tangible employment action is less obvious. On the one hand, a supervisor's power and authority invests his or her harassing conduct with a particular threatening character, and in this sense, a supervisor always is aided by the agency relationship. ... On the other hand, there are acts of harassment a supervisor might commit which might be the same acts a coemployee would commit, and there may be some circumstances where the supervisor's status makes little difference.[22]

In other words, determining whether the employer can offer a defense to liability is appropriate may not necessarily hinge on the authority level of the offender. Instead, what also must be considered is whether an employment action impacting the employee relates back to the authority of the employer.

Tangible Employment Actions

In *Ellerth,* the plaintiff alleged that she was subjected to numerous and repeated offensive remarks and boorish behavior on the part of a supervisor in the company for which she worked. She claimed that the remarks could be taken as threatening in nature in that if she did not submit to his requests, he would retaliate. Thus, she framed her theory of harassment as quid pro quo harassment.

Burlington Industries countered, arguing that it was hostile environment harassment and asserted a defense to liability, arguing that the plaintiff never had complained of the offensive behavior and, therefore, it did not have knowledge nor could it have reasonably known of the conduct and, thus, should not be liable. The lower court decisions in this case reflect disagreement as to whether the conduct should be characterized as quid pro quo or hostile work environment harassment.[23] Resolution of this issue was critical to the lawsuit's outcome until the Supreme Court intervened and rejected the notion that the type of sexual harassment should dictate the outcome in cases involving supervisory level harassment, shifting the focus from the type of harassment to whether the employee was subjected to a tangible employment action.[24]

In *Ellerth*, the Court provided the following definition of tangible employment action:

> A tangible employment action constitutes a significant change in employment status, such as hiring, firing, failing to promote, reassignment with significantly different responsibilities, or a decision causing a significant change in benefits.[25]

Clearly, there will be many cases in which the existence of a tangible employment action will be indisputable. In *Ellerth*, the Supreme Court provided some examples that would constitute tangible employment actions, such as demotion with a decrease in salary, termination, less responsibilities, and loss of benefits.[26] A tangible employment action is not, however, always so easy to identify. To guide in determining whether a tangible employment action was taken, the Supreme Court described the types of actions that can result in liability as actions that often result in financial harm and require an official act of the employer often carried out by a supervisor who has been given the authority to act for the employer.[27]

With liability for supervisory-level sexual harassment often hinging on whether a tangible employment action was taken as opposed to the type of sexual harassment, any decisions affecting the employee will be closely scrutinized. For example, in *Dedner v. Oklahoma*,[28] the plaintiff, a correctional food service supervisor, alleged that her supervisor engaged in offensive and unwelcomed sexual conduct over a period of time. She complained to her employer, the State of Oklahoma Department of Corrections, about the offending conduct.

An internal investigation was initiated, and he was fired. The victim employee brought a Title VII action against her employer, alleging a tangible employment action was taken against her when her supervisor conditioned benefits in the form of what days off she would have on her willingness to engage in sex with him. The parties agreed that sexual harassment occurred. They disagreed as to whether the harassment resulted in a tangible employment action. The federal district court judge held that allowing an employee to take certain days off does not amount to a change in benefits or status as contemplated by the Court in *Ellerth,* and, thus, no tangible employment action was taken.[29]

Constructive Discharge as a Tangible Employment Action

While the typical case involves an employer-initiated employment action, the Supreme Court was presented with the issue of whether a decision by an employee to resign could be a tangible employment action giving rise to liability. In *Pennsylvania State Police v. Suders*,[30] a former employee sued her former employer, the Pennsylvania State Police (PSP), alleging that her decision to resign was in response to sexual harassment caused in part by her supervisor for which the PSP should be accountable.

The lower federal court dismissed the lawsuit holding that the employer took no adverse tangible employment action against her given that she resigned, enabling the PSP to defend itself under the *Ellerth-Faragher* affirmative defense.[31] The court then accepted the agency's effort to defend itself by demonstrating it had preventive and corrective policies in place of which she failed to take advantage. On appeal to the Federal Court of Appeals in the Third Circuit Court, the court disagreed with the lower court in a couple of significant ways. First, the circuit court concluded that there were critical issues still to be resolved with respect to the preventive and corrective polices the PSP had in place to address harassment. In addition, the circuit court concluded that material issues of fact remain with respect to whether the plaintiff had established that she was constructively discharged due to the hostile work environment and, perhaps, most important, if she was constructively discharged, whether that would amount to a tangible employment action, meaning no defense to liability could be offered.[32] The question of whether a constructive discharge would amount to a tangible employment action was appealed to the Supreme Court.

The Supreme Court agreed with the circuit court that a constructive discharge could be regarded as a tangible employment action on the part of the employer.[33] In deciding whether the decision to resign should be attributable to the employer in the form of a constructive discharge, the Court stated that the employee "must show working conditions so intolerable that a reasonable person would have felt compelled to resign."[34]

Once a case for constructive discharge is made by the plaintiff, it does not automatically preclude the possibility that the employer can raise the *Ellerth-Faragher* defense. The Supreme Court distinguished an actual termination of an employee with a constructive discharge, stating that "[u]nlike an actual termination, which is *always* effected through an official act of the company, a constructive discharge need not be."[35] Accordingly, if the employer can establish that the constructive discharge did not derive from an official act of the agency, then it may assert a defense to liability by showing what preventive and corrective antiharassment policies it had in place and that the employee unreasonably failed to take advantage of them (*Ellerth-Faragher* defense). If it is established that the constructive discharge derived from official acts of the employer, then no defense is available.

To illustrate the significance of the official act, the Supreme Court cited *Reed v. MBNA Marketing Systems, Inc.*,[36] a case involving a claim of constructive discharge based on the victim's assertion that her supervisor made repeated sexual comments and assaulted her. The Federal Court of Appeals for the First Circuit held that as the supervisor's actions involved no official act on the part of the employer and, in fact, is not at all authorized, the employer could raise the *Ellerth-Faragher* defense to vicarious liability. In contrast, the Court referred to *Robinson v. Sappington*[37] *to illustrate the role of official action in a* constructive discharge. In this case, the plaintiff complained that she was sexually harassed by the judge for whom she worked. The presiding judge told her he would reassign her to another judge, but he had a reputation for being very difficult, and that "it was in her best interest to resign."[38] The decision to resign was, therefore, at least in part, attributable to an official act of the employer.

The Continuing Need for Policy and Training

Despite the recent changes in the law relating to sexual harassment, one constant remains—employers should continue to demonstrate a strong commitment to the elimination of sexual harassment in the workplace. Employers should promulgate and post a policy statement on sexual harassment, including a clear description of the procedures to follow for reporting complaints. In addition, employers should assess their management training programs to determine whether they adequately address the issue of workplace harassment. Such training should include discussion of what constitues unlawful conduct, what managers must do when they become aware of such conduct, and the process established by the employer for reporting complaints.

CONCLUSION

As much as law enforcement professionals prefer clear and exact legal principles to guide them in their decision making in the workplace, the intricacies of the law makes this impossible. However, one constant in all employment settings is that they are made up of human beings with their own perceptions. The human factor is, perhaps, most evident when it comes to the interpretation of statutory provisions addressing conduct in the workplace occurring because of gender, in other words, sexual harassment. Recently, the Supreme Court provided guidance in assessing the liability of an employer for sexually offensive conduct engaged in by supervisors within the workplace. Central to this guidance is that liability no longer is based on the type of sexual harassment that occurred. Instead, the initial focus centers on whether there was a tangible employment action taken by or which can be attributed to the employer. Only in cases where no tangible action was taken will an employer be able to point to the preventive and corrective measures it has adopted to defend itself.

NOTES

1. 42 U.S.C. § 2000e-2(a) provides as follows: § 2000e-2. Unlawful employment practices a) Employer practices It shall be an unlawful employment practice for an employer— 1) to fail or refuse to hire or to discharge any individual, or otherwise to discriminate against any individual with respect to his compensation, terms, conditions, or privileges of employment, because of such individual's race, color, religion, sex, or national origin; or 2) to limit, segregate, or classify his employees or applicants for employment in any way which would deprive or tend to deprive any individual of employment opportunities or otherwise adversely affect his status as an employee, because of such individual's race, color, religion, sex, or national origin.

2. *Williams v. Saxbe*, 413 F.Supp. 654 (D.D.C. 1976) (sexual harassment actionable as discrimination on the basis of gender). In *Meritor Savings Bank v. Vinson*, 477 U.S. 57 (1986), the U.S. Supreme Court held that Title VII prohibits sexual harassment even in situations where an employee does not suffer economic loss and even if the conduct was consensual, as long as it was unwelcomed.

3. *Oncale v. Sundowner Offshore Services, Inc.*, 523 U.S. 75, 81–82 (1998). *See also Hartsell v. Duplex*, 123 F.3d 766 (4th Cir. 1997) (court refused to recognize demeaning remark as actionable under Title VII, stating that Title VII does not guarantee sophistication or proper behavior in the workplace; it only prohibits conduct that is so severe or pervasive as to create an objectionably reasonable hostile or abusive environment).

4. *Faragher v. City of Boca Raton*, 524 U.S. 775, 788 (1998).

5. *Ocheltree v. Scollon Productions, Inc.*, 335 F.3d 325 (4th Cir. 2003).

6. 229 F.3d 1343 (11th Cir. 2000).

7. *See also Holman v. State*, 211 F.3d 399 (7th Cir. 2000) (Lower court decision to dismiss complaint alleging sexual harassment upheld on appeal on the basis that victims, a husband and wife who worked for the same supervisor, could not be subjected to offensive conduct based on gender as the "equal opportunity" harasser offended both genders).

8. 523 U.S. 75 (1998).

9. *See Burlington Industries, Inc., v. Ellerth*, 524 U.S. 742, 753–754, *citing Davis v. Sioux City*, 115 F.3d 1365, 1367 (8th Cir. 1997); *Nichols v. Frank*, 42 F.3d 503, 513-514 (9th Cir. 1994).

10. *Robinson v. City of Pittsburgh*, 120 F.3d 1286 (3rd Cir. 1997); *Speaks v. City of Lakeland, Florida*, 315 F.Supp.2d 1217 (M.D. Fla. 2004).

11. 477 U.S. 57 (1986). See also Harris v. Forklift Systems, Inc., 510 U.S. 17 (1993); Faragher v. City of Boca Raton, 524 U.S. 775 (1998).

12. *Faragher* at 786, *quoting Meritor* at 67.

13. *Harris v. Forklift Systems, Inc.*, at 21–22.

14. *Id.* at 23. *See also Oncale v. Sundowner Offshore Services*, 523 U.S. 75 (1998).

15. 524 U.S. 742 (1998).

16. 524 U.S. 775 (1998).

17. *Id. See also, Leopald v. Baccarat*, 239 F.3d 243 (2d Cir. 2001).

18. *Ellerth* at 754–755.

19. *See* Restatement (Second) of Agency, § 219(1).

20. *Ellerth* at 760–762. *See also Faragher v. City of Boca Raton*, 524 U.S. 775, 784 (1998).

21. *Id.* at 762.

22. *Id.* at 762–763.

23. *Id.* at 749–750.

24. *Id.* at 754.

25. *Id.* at 761.

26. *Id.*

27. *Id.* at 762.

28. 42 F.Supp.2d 1254 (E.D.Oklahoma 1999).

29. *Id.* at 1258. As to the second basis for liability under *Ellerth-Faragher*, the Court held that the state took reasonable care to prevent and correct harassment and that she unreasonably failed to take advantage of the preventive or corrective policies of the state by waiting nearly 3 months to complain about the offending conduct, after the second incident already had occurred. *Id.* at 1260.

30. 542 U.S. 129 (2004).

31. *See* Brief for Appellant in No. 013512, p. 2

32. *Suders v. Easton*, 325 F.3d 432 (3rd Cir. 2003).

33. *Suders* at 141.

34. *Id.*

35. *Id. at 142* (emphasis supplied).

36. 333 F.3d 27 (1st Cir. 2003), *cited* in *Suders* at 140.

37. 351 F.3d 317 (7th Cir. 2003), *cited* in *Suders* at 140.

38. *Suders* at 140, *quoting Robinson v. Sappington*, 351 F.3d 317, 324 (7th Cir. 2003).

CPSIA information can be obtained at www.ICGtesting.com
Printed in the USA
LVOW03s2045170815

450493LV00012B/50/P

9 781621 315964